THE DRAMA 100

THE DRAMA 100

A Ranking of the Greatest Plays
of All Time

DANIEL S. BURT

Facts On File
An imprint of Infobase Publishing

The Drama 100: A Ranking of the Greatest Plays of All Time

Copyright © 2008 Daniel S. Burt

Facts On File, Inc.
An imprint of Infobase Publishing
132 West 31st Street
New York NY 10001

Library of Congress Cataloging-in-Publication Data

Burt, Daniel S.
   The drama 100 : a ranking of the greatest plays of all time / Daniel S. Burt.
     p. cm.
   Includes bibliographical references and index.
   ISBN 978-0-8160-6073-3 (hc : alk. paper) 1. Drama—History and criticism. I. Title.
   PN1721.B87 2007
   809.2—dc22 2007007019

Facts On File books are available at special discounts when purchased in bulk quantities for businesses, associations, institutions, or sales promotions. Please call our Special Sales Department in New York at (212) 967-8800 or (800) 322-8755.

You can find Facts On File on the World Wide Web at http://www.factsonfile.com

Text design by Joan M. McEvoy

Printed in the United States of America

MP ML 10 9 8 7 6 5 4 3 2 1

This book is printed on acid-free paper.

CONTENTS

INTRODUCTION

What follows is my ranking of the greatest dramas of all time. Here I would like to address the dual questions of why and how. Evaluating literary greatness in such a way is a perilous mission, fraught with challenges and difficulties. It can be argued that, like squaring a circle, such ranking of literature is really a futile exercise in quantifying the qualitative that is doomed from the start by bias and an all-too-limited perspective. Such a ranking, it can be claimed, is merely personal preference masquerading as objective truth. So, at the outset, I should probably plead guilty as charged and throw myself at the mercy of the court of critical opinion. By presenting my choices of the greatest plays of all time, I make no claims of possessing either an infallible scientific method for my ranking or an unassailable authority in making my choices. Although I have spent many years teaching these plays and writing about several of these playwrights, and in addition have relied on my scholarly colleagues' guidance to fill in gaps in my background and to challenge my perspective, this is without question one critic's attempt to collect and assess drama's greatest achievements. Reader's views and preferences will certainly collide with and diverge from mine. Disagreement is not only inevitable, it is encouraged and is in many ways the point of the exercise.

As the author of two other literary rankings—of the greatest literary artists and novels—I am no stranger to the contentiousness and objections such an effort can provoke. However, provocation can be a good thing when it leads to an engagement with questions of literary merit. Looking at writers and literary works comparatively, beyond narrow cultural and historical divisions, is a rejuvenating and liberating activity—for writer and reader alike. Too often critical debate on literary matters is the reserve of the specialist, with few willing to tangle with questions of merit that go beyond a particular writer or era. Even genre discussions, whether concerning poetry, fiction, or drama, seldom take a truly comprehensive or global perspective. That is what I have tried to offer here. There is, of course, much to learn from the big picture, the far-reaching perspective. It is exhilarating to get above the trees and take in the entire forest. By doing so, one can engage with crucial but often neglected critical questions, such as what makes a play and playwright great and how can that greatness be measured and compared. Often assumed by the classical status conferred on some texts or ignored in close critical readings, questions of literary greatness deserve a hearing. This ranking offers one way to frame and spark that debate. Students sometimes ask me as a teacher the absolutely right question: Why are we reading this poem, novel, or play? Why this text and not some other? We should ask this question often, because in formulating a response we become better readers and critics, better at understanding (and valuing), in Matthew Arnold's phrase, "the best that is known and thought in the world."

Although matters of literary greatness are contentious, the effort to reach some conclusions is as beneficial as any outcome. Debate over the best of anything is useful because it stimulates issues of values that can enhance enjoyment and judgment. Provoked by this listing, readers, it is hoped, will share in a collaborative exercise that should enrich an appreciation of both individual creative genius and the contributions these plays have made to the understanding of our world and ourselves.

To make any sense at all, such a listing requires a selection principle. To understand mine, consider a variation on the what-do-you-take-with-you-on-a-desert-island scenario as applied to drama. Which 100 plays would you take along? One option would be to gratify your taste, bringing with you for companionship plays that have been old valued friends. My listing here, however, needs to serve a different, less indulgent, imperative. Let me alter the scenario somewhat. Imagine that you have been given the responsibility of collecting for posterity the 100 plays that best represent the creative, intellectual, and cultural achievement of the form. Of all the plays that have ever been written, which best illustrate the capacity and expressive ability of drama? Which plays would you then choose? An initial temptation would be still to go with personal favorites, plays you have enjoyed and valued. But the responsible next response would be to subject your preferences to the tests of critical consensus and time. How do your choices stack up against the weight of posterity and critical judgment that have revered certain plays over countless others for their skill, enjoyment, ideas, and influence? The test of time is a particularly troublesome standard, however, since literary history is rife with examples of plays once valued and now forgotten or once obscure and now acclaimed. But posterity as well as current critical trends can serve the interest of identifying the best of the best.

My listing attempts to balance the personal, critical, and popular. I have tried to be guided by both the established and evolving critical canon. However, in making my selections I have resisted being either excessively subservient to posterity and critical consensus or overly trendy in disregarding established views in favor of contemporary fashion. I have also resisted the temptation of giving personal preference undue sway. Ultimately, the final list took shape in response to these core questions: Which plays have exerted the greatest impact, the greatest influence? Which plays are indispensable for our understanding and appreciation of drama as a unique artistic form? Which plays are the landmarks,the paradigm shifters, the plays that will still be performed, read, and enjoyed years from now, decades from now, centuries from now? Which plays define their age and alter our understanding? In answering these questions I have tried to do justice to the full range of dramatic history internationally, while ever mindful of the inevitable bias that my age, era, and background asserts in the proceedings.

Having made my selections, the next challenge was to rank them by considering each play's impact comparatively. In the profiles I have attempted to justify my selection by pointing out why each play is important in the context of the playwright's career and dramatic history. I have spent less time making the case why one play should be where it is, hoping that those decisions will be evident when the entire listing is considered. The ultimate justification of such a listing and ranking is what can be learned from the juxtaposition and counterpoint of so many playwrights and plays of such genius.

As the initial critic of my own ranking, and taking in the list in its entirety, let me conclude with a few observations regarding the commonality of the plays selected. The greatest plays reveal the greatest and most essential truths. Great dramas, like great poems and fiction, capture and highlight human experience and change the way we see ourselves and the world. The greatest plays continually force us to confront the most important human questions—of life's purpose, of the obligation of conscience and heart, of the values that sustain civilization and the threats that undermine it. I like Ezra Pound's succinct definition of literature: "News that stays news." Great dramas achieve that status of continual, compelling relevance. It is why Lear's rage, Oedipus's dilemma, and Hamlet's questions (and elements of the other 97 plays I have selected) still engage audiences and readers. In looking for the best, I wound up choosing not the plays that provided the best answers but posed the grandest and most essential questions. Anton Chekhov described the proper concern of a writer to be the "correct formulation of a problem," not its solution. "Not a single problem is resolved in *Anna Karenina* or *Onegin*," he wrote, "but they satisfy you completely only because all the problems in them are formulated correctly." Chekhov, as always, is right. The plays collected here are the ones that raise the most important questions.

The staging of existential questions is central both to the origin and nature of drama. Theater, it is believed, originated throughout the world from the communal ceremonies and rituals developed and performed to satisfy a community's spiritual, metaphysical, and emotional needs. Aristotle, in the *Poetics*, traces the origin of Greek tragedy to the spring rituals honoring Dionysus, the god of wine, fertility, and both the creative and irrational forces in humans. In Japan and China the earliest dramas similarly have their roots in religious rites associated with the planting and harvest seasons. Drama seems to have originated as a communal expression of fundamental relations between humans and powerful forces associated with the gods and with nature. At some point, stories narrated to explain and teach origins, destinies, and communal values became stories enacted, in which the storyteller imitated the character he had previously described in a story and was now performed. The result was a powerfully expressive art form in which human experience—our deepest fears, anxieties, hopes, and dreams—could come to life before our eyes.

In the West, the first great flowering of drama dealing with existential questions of human nature and experience occurred in Athens in the fifth century B.C. After the decline of the ancient world, a dramatic tradition would be revived in the West during the Middle Ages, again aligned to religious rituals, enacting the mysteries and miracles of Christianity. It would be the secularization of these themes, the shift of attention from the relationship between human and God to human social relationships and nature that would produce the next great flowering of drama in Europe in the 15th and 16th centuries. William Shakespeare, Molière, and others would create dramas to serve as mirrors reflecting actuality and psychological realities. Theater was restored as a challenging arena to test assumptions about human behavior and destiny. Drama would be refocused yet again in the modern period by playwrights such as Henrik Ibsen, Anton Chekhov, August Strindberg, and George Bernard Shaw as more and more aspects of human experience would be brought within view for reflection and debate. That tradition continues today. Drama, then, throughout its history, has served as a vehicle for expressing and enacting the core questions of human existence. The greatest plays must be those that ask the hardest questions, those that pose, as the first dramas did, the fundamental questions and dilemmas that define our lives and times.

I would like to thank the many individuals who have participated in discussions over the years regarding the merits of these plays and playwrights. I owe a great debt of gratitude to my faculty colleagues at Wesleyan University, who have always been generous in dealing with my queries. My students in Wesleyan's Graduate Liberal Studies Program over the years have forced me toward coherence that, I hope, is reflected in this book, and I am grateful to them all. My greatest debt, however, as always, goes to Debby Felder, my wife, whose support and assistance through the long climb to reach a hundred and beyond made this book possible.

KING LEAR

1

(c. 1605–06)   *by William Shakespeare*

There is perhaps no play which keeps the attention so strongly fixed; which so much agitates our passions and interests our curiosity. The artful involutions of distinct interests, the striking opposition of contrary characters, the sudden changes of fortune, and the quick succession of events, fill the mind with a perpetual tumult of indignation, pity, and hope. There is no scene which does not contribute to the aggravation of the distress or conduct of the action, and scarce a line which does not conduce to the progress of the scene. So powerful is the current of the poet's imagination, that the mind, which once ventures within it, is hurried irresistibly along.

      —Samuel Johnson, *The Plays of William Shakespeare*

For its unsurpassed combination of sheer terrifying force and its existential and cosmic reach, *King Lear* leads this ranking as drama's supreme achievement. The notion that *King Lear* is Shakespeare's (and by implication drama's) greatest play is certainly debatable, but consensus in its favor has gradually coalesced over the centuries since its first performance around 1606. During and immediately following William Shakespeare's lifetime, there is no evidence that *King Lear* was particularly valued over other of the playwright's dramas. It was later considered a play in need of an improving makeover. In 1681 poet and dramatist Nahum Tate, calling *King Lear* "a Heap of Jewels unstrung and unpolish'd," altered what many Restoration critics and audiences found unbecoming and unbearable in the drama. Tate eliminated the Fool, whose presence was considered too vulgar for a proper tragedy, and gave the play a happy ending, restoring Lear to his throne and arranging the marriage of Cordelia and Edgar, neatly tying together with poetic justice the double strands of Shakespeare's far bleaker drama. Tate's bowdlerization of *King Lear* continued to be presented throughout the 18th century, and the original play was not performed again until 1826. By then the Romantics had reclaimed Shakespeare's version, and an appreciation of the majesty and profundity of *King Lear* as Shakespeare's greatest achievement had begun. Samuel Taylor

Coleridge declared the play "the most tremendous effort of Shakespeare as a poet"; while Percy Bysshe Shelley considered it "the most perfect specimen of the dramatic art existing in the world." John Keats, who described the play as "the fierce dispute / Betwixt damnation and impassion'd clay," offered *King Lear* as the best example of the intensity, with its "close relationship with Beauty & Truth," that is the "Excellence of every Art." Dissenting voices, however, challenged the supremacy of *King Lear.* Essayist Charles Lamb judged the play to have "nothing in it but what is painful and disgusting" and deemed it "essentially impossible to be represented on a stage." The great Shakespearean scholar A. C. Bradley acknowledged *King Lear* as "Shakespeare's greatest achievement" but "not his best play." For Bradley, *King Lear,* with its immense scope and the variety and intensity of its scenes, is simply "too huge for the stage." Perhaps the most notorious dissenter against the greatness of *King Lear* was Leo Tolstoy, who found its fablelike unreality reprehensible and ruled it a "very bad, carelessly composed production" that "cannot evoke amongst us anything but aversion and weariness." Such qualifications and dismissals began to diminish in light of 20th-century history. The existential vision of *King Lear* has seemed even more pertinent and telling as a reflection of the human condition; while modern dramatic artistry with its contrapuntal structure and anti-realistic elements has caught up with Shakespeare's play. Today *King Lear* is commonly judged unsurpassed in its dramatization of so many painful but inescapable human and cosmic truths.

King Lear is based on a well-known story from ancient Celtic and British mythology, first given literary form by Geoffrey of Monmouth in his *History of the Kings of Britain* (c. 1137). Raphael Holinshed later repeated the story of Lear and his daughters in his *Chronicles* (1587), and Edmund Spenser, the first to name the youngest daughter, presents the story in book 2 of *The Faerie Queene* (1589). A dramatic version—*The True Chronicle History of King Leir and his three daughters, Gonerill, Ragan, and Cordella*—appeared around 1594. All these versions record Lear dividing his kingdom, disinheriting his youngest daughter, and being driven out by his two eldest daughters before reuniting with his youngest, who helps restore him to the throne and bring her wicked sisters to justice. Shakespeare is the first to give the story an unhappy ending, to turn it from a sentimental, essentially comic tale in which the good are eventually rewarded and the evil punished into a cosmic tragedy. Other plot elements—Lear's madness, Cordelia's hanging, Lear's death from a broken heart, as well as Kent's devotion and the role of the Fool—are also Shakespeare's inventions, as is the addition of the parallel plot of Gloucester and his sons, which Shakespeare adapted from a tale in Philip Sidney's *Arcadia.* The play's double plot in which the central situation of Lear's suffering and self-knowledge is paralleled and counterpointed in Gloucester's circumstances makes *King Lear* different from all the other great tragedies. The effect widens and deepens the play into a universal tragedy of symphonic proportions.

King Lear opens with the tragic turning point in its very first scene. Compared to the long delays in HAMLET and OTHELLO for the decisive tragic blow to fall, *King Lear*, like MACBETH, shifts its emphasis from cause to consequence. The play foregoes nearly all exposition or character development and immediately presents a show trial with devastating consequences. The aging Lear has decided to divest himself of kingly responsibilities by dividing his kingdom among his three daughters. Although the maps of the divisions are already drawn, Lear stages a contest for his daughters to claim their portion by a public profession of their love. "Tell me, my daughters," Lear commands, ". . . Which of you shall we say doth love us most." Lear's self-indulgence—bargaining power for love—is both a disruption of the political and natural order and an essential human violation in his demanding an accounting of love that defies the means of measuring it. Goneril and Regan, however, vie to outdo the other in fulsome pledges of their love, while Cordelia, the favorite, responds to Lear's question "what can you say to draw / A third more opulent than your sisters" with the devastatingly honest truth: "Nothing," a word that will reverberate through the entire play. Cordelia forcefully and simply explains that she loves Lear "According to my bond, no more nor less." Lear is too blind and too needy to appreciate her fidelity or yet understand the nature of love, or the ingenuous flattery of his older daughters. He responds to the hurt he feels by exiling the one who loves him most authentically and deeply. The rest of the play will school Lear in his mistake, teaching him the lesson of humanity that he violates in the play's opening scene.

The devastating consequences of his decision follow. Lear learns that he cannot give away power and still command allegiance from Goneril or Regan. Their avowals of love quickly turn into disrespect for a now useless and demanding parent. From the opening scene in which Lear appears in all his regal splendor, he will be successively stripped of all that invests a king in majesty and insulates a human being from firsthand knowledge of suffering and core existential truths. Urged to give up 50 of his attending knights by Goneril, Lear claims more gratitude from Regan, who joins her sister in further whittling down Lear's retinue from 100 knights to 50, to 25, 10, 5, to none, ironically in the language of calculation of the first scene. Lear explodes:

> O, reason not the need! Our basest beggars
> Are in the poorest thing superfluous.
> Allow not nature more than nature needs,
> Man's life is cheap as beast's.

Lear is now readied to face reality as a "poorest thing."

Lear's betrayal by his daughters is paralleled by the treachery of the earl of Gloucester's bastard son, Edmund, who plots to supplant the legitimate son, Edgar, and eventually claim supremacy over his father. Edmund, one of the most calculating and cold-blooded of Shakespeare's villains, rejects all the bonds of family and morality early on in the play by affirming: "Thou, Nature, art my goddess, to thy law / My services are bound." Refusing to accept the values of a society that rejects him as a bastard, Edmund will operate only by the laws of survival of the fittest in a relentless drive for dominance. He convinces Edgar that Gloucester means to kill him, forcing his brother into exile, disguised as Tom o' Bedlam, a mad beggar. In the play's overwhelming third act—perhaps the most overpowering in all of drama—Edgar encounters Lear, his Fool, and his lone retainer, the disguised Kent, whom Lear had banished in the first scene for challenging Lear's treatment of Cordelia. The scene is a deserted heath with a fierce storm raging, as Lear, maddened by the treatment of his daughters, rails at his fate in apocalyptic fury:

> Blow, winds, and crack your cheeks! Rage, blow
> You cataracts and hurricanoes, spout
> Till you have drenched our steeples, drowned the cocks!
> You sulphurous and thought-executing fires,
> Vaunt-couriers to oak-cleaving thunderbolts,
> Singe my white head; and thou all-shaking thunder,
> Strike flat the thick rotundity o' th' world,
> Crack nature's mould, all germens spill at once,
> That makes ingrateful man.

The storm is a brilliant expressionistic projection of Lear's inner fury, with his language universalizing his private experience in a combat with elemental forces. Beseeching divine justice, Lear is bereft and inconsolable, declaring "My wits begin to turn." His descent into madness is completed when he meets the disguised Edgar who serves as Lear's mirror and emblem of humanity as "unaccommodated man"—a "poor, bare, forked animal":

> Poor naked wretches, wheresoe'er you are,
> That bide the pelting of this pitiless storm,
> How shall your houseless heads and unfed sides,
> Your looped and windowed raggedness, defend you
> From seasons such as these? O, I have ta'en
> Too little care of this. Take physic, pomp,
> Expose thyself to feel what wretches feel,
> That thou mayst shake the superflux to them
> And show the heavens more just.

Lear's suffering has led him to compassion and an understanding of the human needs he had formerly ignored. It is one of the rare moments of regenerative hope before the play plunges into further chaos and violence.

Act 3 concludes with what has been called the most horrifying scene in dramatic literature. Gloucester is condemned as a traitor for colluding with Cordelia and the French invasion force. Cornwall, Regan's husband, orders Gloucester bound and rips out one of his eyes. Urged on by Regan ("One side will mock another; th' other too"), Cornwall completes Gloucester's blinding after a protesting servant stabs Cornwall and is slain by Regan. In agony, Gloucester calls out for Edmund as Regan supplies the crushing truth:

> Out, treacherous villain!
> Thou call'st on him that hates thee. It was he
> That made the overture of thy treasons to us,
> Who is too good to pity thee.

Oedipus-like, Gloucester, though blind, now sees the truth of Edmund's villainy and Edgar's innocence. Thrown out of the castle, he is ordered to "smell / His way to Dover."

Act 4 arranges reunions and the expectation that the suffering of both Lear and Gloucester will be compensated and villainy purged. Edgar, still posing as Poor Tom, meets his father and agrees to guide him to Dover where the despairing Gloucester intends to kill himself by jumping from its cliffs. On arriving, Edgar convinces his father that he has fallen and survived, and Gloucester accepts his preservation as an act of the gods and vows "Henceforth I'll bear / Affliction till it do cry out itself / 'Enough, enough,' and die." The act concludes with Lear's being reunited with Cordelia. Awaking in her tent, convinced that he has died, Lear gradually recognizes his daughter and begs her forgiveness as a "very foolish, fond old man."

The stage is now set in act 5 for a restoration of order and Lear, having achieved the requisite self-knowledge through suffering, but Shakespeare pushes the play beyond the reach of consolation. Although Edmund is bested in combat by his brother, and Regan is poisoned by Goneril before she kills herself, neither poetic nor divine justice prevails. Lear and Cordelia are taken prisoner, but their rescue comes too late. As Shakespeare's stage directions state, "Enter Lear with Cordelia in his arms," and the play concludes with one of the most heart-wrenching scenes and the most overpowering lines in all of drama. Lear, although desperate to believe that his beloved daughter is alive, gradually accepts the awful truth:

> Why should a dog, a horse, a rat, have life,
> And thou no breath at all. Thou'lt come no more,
> Never, never, never, never, never!

Lear dies with this realization of cosmic injustice and indifference, while holding onto the illusion that Cordelia might still survive ("Look on her, look, her lips / Look there, look there!"). The play ends not with the restoration of divine, political, or familial order but in a final nihilistic vision. Shakespeare pushes the usual tragic progression of action leading to suffering and then to self-knowledge to a view into the abyss of life's purposelessness and cruelty. The best Shakespeare manages to affirm in the face of intractable human evil and cosmic indifference is the heroism of endurance. Urging his despairing father on, Edgar states in the play's opposition to despair:

> . . . Men must endure
> Their going hence, even as their coming hither;
> Ripeness is all. Come on.

Ultimately, *King Lear*, more than any other drama, in my view, allows its audience to test the limits of endurance in the face of mortality and meaninglessness. It has been said that only the greatest art sustains without consoling. There is no better example of this than *King Lear*.

OEDIPUS THE KING

(c. 429 B.C.)

2

by Sophocles

The place of the Oedipus Tyrannus *in literature is something like that of the Mona Lisa in art. Everyone knows the story, the first detective story of Western literature; everyone who has read or seen it is drawn into its enigmas and moral dilemmas. It presents a kind of nightmare vision of a world suddenly turned upside down: a decent man discovers that he has unknowingly killed his father, married his mother, and sired children by her. It is a story that, as Aristotle says in the* Poetics, *makes one shudder with horror and feel pity just on hearing it. In Sophocles' hands, however, this ancient tale becomes a profound meditation on the questions of guilt and responsibility, the order (or disorder) of our world, and the nature of man. The play stands with the Book of Job,* Hamlet, *and* King Lear *as one of Western literature's most searching examinations of the problem of suffering.*

—Charles Segal, Oedipus Tyrannus: Tragic Heroism and the Limits of Knowledge

No other drama has exerted a longer or stronger hold on the imagination than Sophocles' *Oedipus the King* (also known as *Oedipus Tyrannus* or *Oedipus Rex*). Tragic drama that is centered on the dilemma of a single central character largely begins with Sophocles and is exemplified by his *Oedipus*, arguably the most influential play ever written. The most famous of all Greek dramas, Sophocles' play, supported by Aristotle in the *Poetics*, set the standard by which tragedy has been measured for nearly two-and-a-half millennia. For Aristotle, Sophocles' play featured the ideal tragic hero in Oedipus, a man of "great repute and good fortune," whose fall, coming from his horrifying discovery that he has killed his father and married his mother, is masterfully arranged to elicit tragedy's proper cathartic mixture of pity and terror. The play's relentless exploration of human nature, destiny, and suffering turns an ancient tale of a man's shocking history into one of the core human myths. Oedipus thereby joins a select group of fictional characters, including Odysseus, Faust, Don Juan, and Don Quixote, that have entered our collective consciousness as paradigms of humanity and the human condition. As classical scholar Bernard Knox has argued, "Sophocles' Oedipus is not only the greatest creation of a major poet and the classic representative figure of his age: he is also one of a long series of tragic protagonists who stand as symbols of human aspiration and despair before the characteristic dilemma of Western civilization—the problem of man's true stature, his proper place in the universe."

For nearly 2,500 years Sophocles' play has claimed consideration as drama's most perfect and most profound achievement. Julius Caesar wrote an adaptation; Nero allegedly acted the part of the blind Oedipus. First staged in a European theater in 1585, *Oedipus* has been continually performed ever since and reworked by such dramatists as Pierre Corneille, John Dryden, Voltaire, William Butler Yeats, André Gide, and Jean Cocteau. The French neoclassical tragedian Jean Racine asserted that *Oedipus* was the ideal tragedy, while D. H. Lawrence regarded it as "the finest drama of all time." Sigmund Freud discovered in the play the key to understanding man's deepest and most repressed sexual and aggressive impulses, and the so-called Oedipus complex became one of the founding myths of psychoanalysis. *Oedipus* has served as a crucial mirror by which each subsequent era has been able to see its own reflection and its understanding of the mystery of human existence.

If Aeschylus is most often seen as the great originator of ancient Greek tragedy and Euripides is viewed as the great outsider and iconoclast, it is Sophocles who occupies the central position as classical tragedy's technical master and the age's representative figure over a lifetime that coincided with the rise and fall of Athens's greatness as a political and cultural power in the fifth century B.C. Sophocles was born in 496 near Athens in Colonus, the legendary final resting place of the exiled Oedipus. At the age of 16, Sophocles, an accomplished dancer and lyre player, was selected to lead the celebration of the victory over the Persians at the battle of Salamis, the event that ushered in Athens's golden age. He died in 406, two years before Athens's fall to Sparta, which ended nearly a century of Athenian supremacy and cultural achievement. Very much at the center of Athenian public life, Sophocles served as a treasurer of state and a diplomat and was twice elected as a general. A lay priest in the cult of a local deity, Sophocles also founded a literary association and was an intimate of such prominent men of letters as Ion of Chios, Herodotus, and Archelaus. Urbane, garrulous, and witty, Sophocles was remembered fondly by his contemporaries as possessing all the admired qualities of balance and tranquillity. Nicknamed "the Bee" for his "honeyed" style of flowing eloquence—the highest compliment the Greeks could bestow on a poet or speaker—Sophocles was regarded as the tragic Homer.

In marked contrast to his secure and stable public role and private life, Sophocles' plays orchestrate a disturbing challenge to assurance and certainty by pitting vulnerable and fallible humanity against the inexorable forces of nature and destiny. Sophocles began his career as a playwright in 468 B.C. with a first-prize victory over Aeschylus in the Great, or City, Dionysia, the annual Athenian drama competition. Over the next 60 years he produced more than

120 plays (only seven have survived intact), winning first prize at the Dionysia 24 times and never earning less than second place, making him unquestionably the most successful and popular playwright of his time. It is Sophocles who introduced the third speaking actor to classical drama, creating the more complex dramatic situations and deepened psychological penetration through interpersonal relationships and dialogue. "Sophocles turned tragedy inward upon the principal actors," classicist Richard Lattimore has observed, "and drama becomes drama of character." Favoring dramatic action over narration, Sophocles brought offstage action onto the stage, emphasized dialogue rather than lengthy, undramatic monologues, and purportedly introduced painted scenery. Also of note, Sophocles replaced the connected trilogies of Aeschylus with self-contained plays on different subjects at the same contest, establishing the norm that has continued in Western drama with its emphasis on the intensity and unity of dramatic action. At their core, Sophocles' tragedies are essentially moral and religious dramas pitting the tragic hero against unalterable fate as defined by universal laws, particular circumstances, and individual temperament. By testing his characters so severely, Sophocles orchestrated adversity into revelations that continue to evoke an audience's capacity for wonder and compassion.

The story of Oedipus was part of a Theban cycle of legends that was second only to the stories surrounding the Trojan War as a popular subject for Greek literary treatment. Thirteen different Greek dramatists, including Aeschylus and Euripides, are known to have written plays on the subject of Oedipus and his progeny. Sophocles' great innovation was to turn Oedipus's horrifying circumstances into a drama of self-discovery that probes the mystery of selfhood and human destiny.

The play opens with Oedipus secure and respected as the capable ruler of Thebes having solved the riddle of the Sphinx and gained the throne and Thebes's widowed queen, Jocasta, as his reward. Plague now besets the city, and Oedipus comes to Thebes's rescue once again when, after learning from the oracle of Apollo that the plague is a punishment for the murder of his predecessor, Laius, he swears to discover and bring the murderer to justice. The play, therefore, begins as a detective story, with the key question "Who killed Laius?" as the initial mystery. Oedipus initiates the first in a seemingly inexhaustible series of dramatic ironies as the detective who turns out to be his own quarry. Oedipus's judgment of banishment for Laius's murderer seals his own fate. Pledged to restore Thebes to health, Oedipus is in fact the source of its affliction. Oedipus's success in discovering Laius's murderer will be his own undoing, and the seemingly percipient, riddle-solving Oedipus will only see the truth about himself when he is blind. To underscore this point, the blind seer Teiresias is summoned. He is reluctant to tell what he knows, but Oedipus is adamant: "No man, no place, nothing will escape my gaze. / I will not stop until I know it all." Finally goaded by Oedipus to reveal that Oedipus himself is "the killer you're searching for" and the plague that afflicts Thebes, Teiresias introduces the play's second mystery, "Who is Oedipus?"

> You have eyes to see with,
> But you do not see yourself, you do not see
> The horror shadowing every step of your life,
> . . . Who are your father and mother? Can you tell me?

Oedipus rejects Teiresias's horrifying answer to this question—that Oedipus has killed his own father and has become a "sower of seed where your father has sowed"—as part of a conspiracy with Jocasta's brother Creon against his rule. In his treatment of Teiresias and his subsequent condemning of Creon to death, Oedipus exposes his pride, wrath, and rush to judgment, character flaws that alloy his evident strengths of relentless determination to learn the truth and fortitude in bearing the consequences. Jocasta comes to her brother's defense, while arguing that not all oracles can be believed. By relating the circumstances of Laius's death, Jocasta attempts to demonstrate that Oedipus could not be the murderer while ironically providing Oedipus with the details that help to prove the case of his culpability. In what is a marvel of ironic plot construction, each step forward in answering the questions surrounding the murder and Oedipus's parentage takes Oedipus a step back in time toward full disclosure and self-discovery.

As Oedipus is made to shift from self-righteous authority to doubt, a messenger from Corinth arrives with news that Oedipus's supposed father, Polybus, is dead. This intelligence seems again to disprove the oracle that Oedipus is fated to kill his father. Oedipus, however, still is reluctant to return home for fear that he could still marry his mother. To relieve Oedipus's anxiety, the messenger reveals that he himself brought Oedipus as an infant to Polybus. Like Jocasta whose evidence in support of Oedipus's innocence turns into confirmation of his guilt, the messenger provides intelligence that will connect Oedipus to both Laius and Jocasta as their son and as his father's killer. The messenger's intelligence produces the crucial recognition for Jocasta, who urges Oedipus to cease any further inquiry. Oedipus, however, persists, summoning the herdsman who gave the infant to the messenger and was coincidentally the sole survivor of the attack on Laius. The herdsman's eventual confirmation of both the facts of Oedipus's birth and Laius's murder produces the play's staggering climax. Aristotle would cite Sophocles' simultaneous conjunction of Oedipus's recognition of his identity and guilt with his reversal of fortune—condemned by his own words to banishment and exile as Laius's murderer—as the ideal artful arrangement of a drama's plot to produce the desired cathartic pity and terror.

The play concludes with an emphasis on what Oedipus will now do after he knows the truth. No tragic hero has fallen further or faster than in the real time of Sophocles' drama in which the time elapsed in the play coincides with the performance time. Oedipus is stripped of every illusion of his authority, control, righteousness, and past wisdom and is forced to contend with a shame that is impossible to expiate—patricide and incestual relations with his mother—in a world lacking either justice or alleviation from suffering. Oedipus's heroic grandeur, however, grows in his diminishment. Fundamentally a victim of circumstances, innocent of intentional sin whose fate was preordained before his birth, Oedipus refuses the consolation of blamelessness that victimization confers, accepting in full his guilt and self-imposed sentence as an outcast, criminal, and sinner. He blinds himself to confirm the moral shame that his actions, unwittingly or not, have provoked. It is Oedipus's capacity to endure the revelation of his sin, his nature, and his fate that dominates the play's conclusion. Oedipus's greatest strengths—his determination to know the truth and to accept what he learns—sets him apart as one of the most pitiable and admired of tragic heroes. "The closing note of the tragedy," Knox argues, "is a renewed insistence on the heroic nature of Oedipus; the play ends as it began, with the greatness of the hero. But it is a different kind of greatness. It is now based on knowledge, not, as before on ignorance." The now-blinded Oedipus has been forced to see and experience the impermanence of good fortune, the reality of unimaginable moral shame, and a cosmic order that is either perverse in its calculated cruelty or chaotically random in its designs, in either case defeating any human need for justice and mercy.

The Chorus summarizes the harsh lesson of heroic defeat that the play so majestically dramatizes:

> Look and learn all citizens of Thebes. This is Oedipus.
> He, who read the famous riddle, and we hailed chief of men,
> All envied his power, glory, and good fortune.
> Now upon his head the sea of disaster crashes down.
> Mortality is man's burden. Keep your eyes fixed on your last day.
> Call no man happy until he reaches it, and finds rest from suffering.

Few plays have dealt so unflinchingly with existential truths or have as bravely defined human heroism in the capacity to see, suffer, and endure.

HAMLET

(c. 1600–01)   *by William Shakespeare*

With Shakespeare the dramatic resolution conveys us, beyond the man-made sphere of poetic justice, toward the ever-receding horizons of cosmic irony. This is peculiarly the case with Hamlet, *for the same reasons that it excites such intensive empathy from actors and readers, critics and writers alike. There may be other Shakespearean characters who are just as memorable, and other plots which are no less impressive; but nowhere else has the outlook of the individual in a dilemma been so profoundly realized; and a dilemma, by definition, is an all but unresolvable choice between evils. Rather than with calculation or casuistry, it should be met with virtue or readiness; sooner or later it will have to be grasped by one or the other of its horns. These, in their broadest terms, have been—for Hamlet, as we interpret him—the problem of what to believe and the problem of how to act.*
        —Harry Levin, *The Question of Hamlet*

Hamlet is almost certainly the world's most famous play, featuring drama's and literature's most fascinating and complex character. The many-sided Hamlet—son, lover, intellectual, prince, warrior, and avenger—is the consummate test for each generation's leading actors, and to be an era's defining Hamlet is perhaps the greatest accolade one can earn in the theater. The play is no less a proving ground for the critic and scholar, as successive generations have refashioned *Hamlet* in their own image, while finding in it new resonances and entry points to plumb its depths, perplexities, and possibilities. No other play has been analyzed so extensively, nor has any play had a comparable impact on our culture. The brooding young man in black, skull in hand, has moved out of the theater and into our collective consciousness and cultural myths, joining only a handful of comparable literary archetypes—Oedipus, Faust, and Don Quixote—who embody core aspects of human nature and experience. "It is *we*," the romantic critic William Hazlitt observed, "who are Hamlet."

    Hamlet also commands a crucial, central place in William Shakespeare's dramatic career. First performed around 1600, the play stands near the midpoint of the playwright's two-decade career as a culmination and new departure. As the first of his great tragedies, *Hamlet* signals a decisive shift from the comedies and history plays that launched Shakespeare's career to the tragedies of his maturity. Although unquestionably linked both to the plays that came before and followed, *Hamlet* is also markedly exceptional. At nearly 4,000 lines, almost twice the length of MACBETH, *Hamlet* is Shakespeare's longest and, arguably, his most ambitious play with an enormous range of characters— from royals to gravediggers—and incidents, including court, bedroom, and graveyard scenes and a play within a play. *Hamlet* also bristles with a seemingly inexhaustible array of ideas and themes, as well as a radically new strategy for presenting them, most notably, in transforming soliloquies from expositional and motivational asides to the audience into the verbalization of consciousness itself. As Shakespearean scholar Stephen Greenblatt has asserted, "In its moral complexity, psychological depth, and philosophical power, *Hamlet* seems to mark an epochal shift not only in Shakespeare's own career but in Western drama; it is as if the play were giving birth to a whole new kind of literary subjectivity." *Hamlet*, more than any other play that preceded it, turns its action inward to dramatize an isolated, conflicted psyche struggling to cope with a world that has lost all certainty and consolation. Struggling to reconcile two contradictory identities—the heroic man of action and duty and the Christian man of conscience—Prince Hamlet becomes the modern archetype of the self-divided, alienated individual, desperately searching for self-understanding and meaning. Hamlet must contend with crushing doubt without the support of traditional beliefs that dictate and justify his actions. In describing the arrival of the fragmentation and chaos of the modern world, Victorian poet and critic Matthew Arnold declared that "the calm, cheerfulness, the disinterested objectivity have disappeared, the dialogue of the mind with itself has commenced." *Hamlet* anticipates that dialogue by more than two centuries.

Like all of Shakespeare's plays, *Hamlet* makes strikingly original uses of borrowed material. The Scandinavian folk tale of Amleth, a prince called upon to avenge his father's murder by his uncle, was first given literary form by the Danish writer Saxo the Grammarian in his late-12th-century *Danish History* and later adapted in French in François de Belleforest's *Histoires tragiques* (1570). This early version of the Hamlet story provided Shakespeare with the basic characters and relationships but without the ghost or the revenger's uncertainty. In the story of Amleth there is neither doubt about the usurper's guilt nor any moral qualms in the fulfillment of the avenger's mission. In pre-Christian Denmark blood vengeance was a sanctioned filial obligation, not a potentially damnable moral or religious violation, and Amleth successfully accomplishes his duty by setting fire to the royal hall, killing his uncle, and proclaiming himself king of Denmark. Shakespeare's more immediate source may have been a now-lost English play (c. 1589) that scholars call the *Ur-Hamlet*. All that has survived concerning this play are a printed reference to a ghost who cried "Hamlet, revenge!" and criticism of the play's stale bombast. Scholars have attributed the *Ur-Hamlet* to playwright Thomas Kyd, whose greatest success was *The Spanish Tragedy* (1592), one of the earliest extant English tragedies. *The Spanish Tragedy* popularized the genre of the revenge tragedy, derived from Aeschylus's ORESTEIA and the Latin plays of Seneca, to which *Hamlet* belongs. Kyd's play also features elements that Shakespeare echoes in *Hamlet,* including a secret crime, an impatient ghost demanding revenge, a protagonist tormented by uncertainty who feigns madness, a woman who actually goes mad, a play within a play, and a final bloodbath that includes the death of the avenger himself. An even more immediate possible source for *Hamlet* is John Marston's *Antonio's Revenge* (1599), another story of vengeance on a usurper by a sensitive protagonist.

Whether comparing *Hamlet* to its earliest source or the handling of the revenge plot by Kyd, Marston, or other Elizabethan or Jacobean playwrights, what stands out is the originality and complexity of Shakespeare's treatment, in his making radically new and profound uses of established stage conventions. *Hamlet* converts its sensational material—a vengeful ghost, a murder mystery, madness, a heartbroken maiden, a fistfight at her burial, and a climactic duel that results in four deaths—into a daring exploration of mortality, morality, perception, and core existential truths. Shakespeare put mystery, intrigue, and sensation to the service of a complex, profound epistemological drama. The critic Maynard Mack in an influential essay, "The World of *Hamlet,*" has usefully identified the play's "interrogative mode." From the play's opening words—"Who's there?"—to "What is this quintessence of dust?" through drama's most famous soliloquy—"To be, or not to be, that is the question."— *Hamlet* "reverberates with questions, anguished, meditative, alarmed." The problematic nature of reality and the gap between truth and appearance stand behind the play's conflicts, complicating Hamlet's search for answers and his fulfillment of his role as avenger.

Hamlet opens with startling evidence that "something is rotten in the state of Denmark." The ghost of Hamlet's father, King Hamlet, has been seen in Elsinore, now ruled by his brother, Claudius, who has quickly married his widowed queen, Gertrude. When first seen, Hamlet is aloof and skeptical of Claudius's justifications for his actions on behalf of restoring order in the state. Hamlet is morbidly and suicidally disillusioned by the realization of mortality and the baseness of human nature prompted by the sudden death of his father and his mother's hasty, and in Hamlet's view, incestuous remarriage to her brother-in-law:

> O that this too too solid flesh would melt,
> Thaw, and resolve itself into a dew!
> Or that the Everlasting had not fix'd
> His canon 'gainst self-slaughter! O God! God!

How weary, stale, flat, and unprofitable
Seem to me all the uses of this world!
Fie on't! ah, fie! 'Tis an unweeded garden
That grows to seed; things rank and gross in nature
Possess it merely. That it should come to this!

A recent student at the University of Wittenberg, whose alumni included Martin Luther and the fictional Doctor Faustus, Hamlet is an intellectual of the Protestant Reformation, who, like Luther and Faustus, tests orthodoxy while struggling to formulate a core philosophy. Brought to encounter the apparent ghost of his father, Hamlet alone hears the ghost's words that he was murdered by Claudius and is compelled out of his suicidal despair by his pledge of revenge. However, despite the riveting presence of the ghost, Hamlet is tormented by doubts. Is the ghost truly his father's spirit or a devilish apparition tempting Hamlet to his damnation? Is Claudius truly his father's murderer? By taking revenge does Hamlet do right or wrong? Despite swearing vengeance, Hamlet delays for two months before taking any action, feigning madness better to learn for himself the truth about Claudius's guilt. Hamlet's strange behavior causes Claudius's counterinvestigation to assess Hamlet's mental state. School friends—Rosencrantz and Guildenstern—are summoned to learn what they can; Polonius, convinced that Hamlet's is a madness of love for his daughter Ophelia, stages an encounter between the lovers that can be observed by Claudius. The court world at Elsinore, is, therefore, ruled by trickery, deception, role playing, and disguise, and the so-called problem of Hamlet, of his delay in acting, is directly related to his uncertainty in knowing the truth. Moreover, the suspicion of his father's murder and his mother's sexual betrayal shatter Hamlet's conception of the world and his responsibility in it. Pushed back to the suicidal despair of the play's opening, Hamlet is paralyzed by indecision and ambiguity in which even death is problematic, as he explains in the famous "To be or not to be" soliloquy in the third act:

For who would bear the whips and scorns of time,
Th' oppressor's wrong, the proud man's contumely,
The pangs of despis'd love, the law's delay,
The insolence of office, and the spurns
That patient merit of th' unworthy takes,
When he himself might his quietus make
With a bare bodkin? Who would these fardels bear,
To grunt and sweat under a weary life,
But that the dread of something after death—
The undiscover'd country, from whose bourn
No traveller returns—puzzles the will,
And makes us rather bear those ills we have

Than fly to others that we know not of?
Thus conscience does make cowards of us all,
And thus the native hue of resolution
Is sicklied o'er with the pale cast of thought,
And enterprises of great pith and moment
With this regard their currents turn awry
And lose the name of action.

The arrival of a traveling theatrical group provides Hamlet with the empirical means to resolve his doubts about the authenticity of the ghost and Claudius's guilt. By having the troupe perform the *Mousetrap* play that duplicates Claudius's crime, Hamlet hopes "to catch the conscience of the King" by observing Claudius's reaction. The king's breakdown during the performance seems to confirm the ghost's accusation, but again Hamlet delays taking action when he accidentally comes upon the guilt-ridden Claudius alone at his prayers. Rationalizing that killing the apparently penitent Claudius will send him to heaven and not to hell, Hamlet decides to await an opportunity "That has no relish of salvation in't." He goes instead to his mother's room where Polonius is hidden in another attempt to learn Hamlet's mind and intentions. This scene between mother and son, one of the most powerful and intense in all of Shakespeare, has supported the Freudian interpretation of Hamlet's dilemma in which he is stricken not by moral qualms but by Oedipal guilt. Gertrude's cries of protest over her son's accusations cause Polonius to stir, and Hamlet finally, instinctively strikes the figure he assumes is Claudius. In killing the wrong man Hamlet sets in motion the play's catastrophes, including the madness and suicide of Ophelia, overwhelmed by the realization that her lover has killed her father, and the fatal encounter with Laertes who is now similarly driven to avenge a murdered father. Convinced of her son's madness, Gertrude informs Claudius of Polonius's murder, prompting Claudius to alter his order for Hamlet's exile to England to his execution there.

Hamlet's mental shift from reluctant to willing avenger takes place offstage during his voyage to England in which he accidentally discovers the execution order and then after a pirate attack on his ship makes his way back to Denmark. He returns to confront the inescapable human condition of mortality in the graveyard scene of act 5 in which he realizes that even Alexander the Great must return to earth that might be used to "stop a beer-barrel" and Julius Caesar's clay to "stop a hole to keep the wind away." This sobering realization that levels all earthly distinctions of nobility and acclaim is compounded by the shock of Ophelia's funeral procession. Hamlet sustains his balance and purpose by confessing to Horatio his acceptance of a providential will revealed to him in the series of accidents on his voyage to England: "There's a divinity that shapes our ends, / Rough-hew them how we will." Finally accepting his inability to control his life, Hamlet resigns himself to accept whatever comes.

Agreeing to a duel with Laertes that Claudius has devised to eliminate his nephew, Hamlet asserts that "There's a special providence in the fall of a sparrow. If it be now, 'tis not to come. If it be not to come, it will be now. If it be not now, yet it will come. The readiness is all."

In the carnage of the play's final scene, Hamlet ironically manages to achieve his revenge while still preserving his nobility and moral stature. It is the murderer Claudius who is directly or indirectly responsible for all the deaths. Armed with a poisoned-tip sword, Laertes strikes Hamlet who in turn manages to slay Laertes with the lethal weapon. Meanwhile, Gertrude drinks from the poisoned cup Claudius intended to insure Hamlet's death, and, after the remorseful Laertes blames Claudius for the plot, Hamlet, hesitating no longer, fatally stabs the king. Dying in the arms of Horatio, Hamlet orders his friend to "report me and my cause aright / To the unsatisfied" and transfers the reign of Denmark to the last royal left standing, the Norwegian prince Fortinbras. King Hamlet's death has been avenged but at a cost of eight lives: Polonius, Ophelia, Rosencranz, Guildenstern, Laertes, Gertrude, Claudius, and Prince Hamlet. Order is reestablished but only by Denmark's sworn enemy. Shakespeare's point seems unmistakable: Honor and duty that command revenge consume the guilty and the innocent alike. Heroism must face the reality of the graveyard.

Fortinbras closes the play by ordering that Hamlet be carried off "like a soldier" to be given a military funeral underscoring the point that Hamlet has fallen as a warrior on a battlefield of both the duplicitous court at Elsinore and his own mind. The greatness of *Hamlet* rests in the extraordinary perplexities Shakespeare has discovered both in his title character and in the events of the play. Few other dramas have posed so many or such knotty problems of human existence. Is there a special providence in the fall of a sparrow? What is this quintessence of dust? To be or not to be?

ORESTEIA

(458 B.C.)

Aeschylus

4

[The Oresteia is a] trilogy whose special greatness lies in the fact that it transcends the limitations of dramatic enactment on a scale never achieved before or since.
—Richard Lattimore, "Introduction to the *Oresteia*"
in *The Complete Greek Tragedies*

Called by Johann Wolfgang von Goethe "the masterpiece of masterpieces" and by Algernon Charles Swinburne "the greatest achievement of the human mind," Aeschylus's *Oresteia* is the monumental accomplishment of drama's greatest early visionary and progenitor. Considered by the Greeks the "father of tragedy," Aeschylus, "more than anyone," according to classical scholar C. M. Bowra, "laid the true foundations of tragedy and established the forms and spirit which marked it out from other kinds of poetry." The *Oresteia*, the only surviving Attic tragic trilogy, dramatizes the working out of the curse on the house of Atreus from Agamemnon's homecoming from Troy and his murder by his wife, Clytemnestra, through her subsequent death at the hands of her son, Orestes, and the consequences for human justice and cosmic order. Aeschylus presents the archetypal family tragedy, the influences of which can be felt in subsequent theatrical depictions of the houses of Oedipus, Tyrone, Loman, Corleone, and Soprano and other uses of the family as the locus for dramatic conflict. Aeschylus points the way by which a domestic tragedy can serve in the hand of a great poet and stage craftsman as a profound enactment of the human condition and human destiny on a truly colossal dramatic scale.

To understand Aeschylus's originality and achievement in the *Oresteia*, it is necessary to place the trilogy in the context of the origins and development of drama in ancient Greece. Western drama's beginnings are obscure, but most authorities have detected a connection with religious rituals that enact the central myths of a society's understanding of the powers that govern its well-being and its own interrelationships. Greek drama derived from the religious festivals that paid tribute to Dionysus, the Greek god of fertility, wine, revelry, and regeneration, who was celebrated and worshipped in choral song and dance. Aristotle, in the *Poetics* (c. 335–323 B.C.), the earliest extant account of how Greek drama originated, asserted that tragedy began with the speeches of "those who led the dithyramb," the choral lyric honoring Dionysus, and that comedy came from the "leaders of the phallic songs" performed by a group of singers and dancers representing satyrs—half men, half goats—who were the attendants of Dionysus. At some point during the sixth century B.C., the choral leader began to impersonate imaginary characters and to imitate, rather than narrate, the story of a deity or a mythical hero. Tradition credits Thespis (none of whose plays survive) with first combining the choral songs and dances with the speeches of a masked actor in an enacted story. As the first known actor, Thespis is memorialized in the term *thespian*, a synonym for actor. It is believed that Thespis first performed his plays at festivals throughout Greece before inaugurating, in 534 B.C., Athens's reorganized annual spring festival, the Great, or City, Dionysia, as a theatrical contest in which choruses competed for prizes in a festival that lasted for several days. During the City Dionysia, performed in an open-air theater that held audiences of 15,000 or more, businesses were suspended and prisoners were released on bail for the duration of the festival. The first day was devoted to traditional choral hymns, followed by the competition in which three dramatists each presented a tetralogy of three tragedies, as well as a comic satyr play.

   If Thespis is responsible for the initial shift from lyric to dramatic performance by introducing an actor, it is Aeschylus who, according to Aristotle, added the second actor to performances and thereby supplied the key ingredient for dialogue and dramatic conflict between characters on stage that defines drama. Aeschylus was born near Athens around 525 B.C. The known facts of his life are few. He fought during the wars against the Persians in the battle of Marathon in 490, and his eyewitness account of the battle of Salamis in his play *The Persians*, the only surviving Greek drama based on a contemporary historical event, suggests that he was also a participant in that battle. Although his role in Athenian politics and his political sympathies are subject to differing scholarly conjecture, it is incontestable that in his plays Aeschylus was one of the principal spokesmen for the central values of the Greeks during a remarkable period of political and cultural achievement that followed the defeat of the Persians and the emergence of Athens to supremacy in the Mediterranean world. Aeschylus wrote, acted in, and directed or produced between 80 and 90 plays, of which only seven—among the earliest documents in the history of the Western theater—survive. No other playwright can be credited with as many innovations as Aeschylus. Besides adding the second actor, Aeschylus also, according to Aristotle, reduced the number of the chorus from 50 to 12 and "gave the leading role to the spoken word." Aeschylus thereby centered the interest of his plays on the actors and their speeches and dialogue. He is also credited with perfecting the conventions of tragedy's grand poetic diction and introducing rich costuming and spectacular stage effects. Underlying his grandiloquence, Aeschylus produced some of the greatest poetry every created for the theater and used masterful representational stagecraft as a fundamental element in his plays, which helped turn the theater into an arena for exploring essential human questions. "In all probability," literary historian Philip Whaley Harsh has concluded, "Aeschylus is chiefly responsible for the essentially realistic nature of European drama—qualities which can be fully appreciated only by making a comparison between Greek tragedy and Sanskrit or Chinese drama. European drama, then, is perhaps more heavily indebted to Aeschylus than to any other individual."

Aeschylus won his first victory at the City Dionysia in 484 B.C. and followed it with 12 subsequent prizes, a clear indication of his great acclaim and preeminence as a dramatist. It is Aeschylus whom Dionysus recalls from the underworld as the greatest of all tragic poets in Aristophanes' *Frogs*. Aeschylus's plays include *The Persians, Seven against Thebes, The Suppliants*, and *Prometheus Bound*. Each is a third of a trilogy whose companion plays have been lost. With the *Oresteia*, however, we have the only intact tragic trilogy. If his fellow Greek tragedians, Sophocles and Euripides, concentrated on the individual play as their basic unit of composition, Aeschylus was the master of the linked dramas that explored the wider implications and consequences of a single mythic story, thus extending the range of tragedy to a truly epic scale. The three plays making up the *Oresteia—Agamemnon, The Libation Bearers*, and *The Eumenides*—can be seen as three acts of a massive epic drama that invites comparison in its range, grandeur, and spiritual and cultural significance to the heroic epics of Homer, Virgil's *Aeneid*, Dante's *Divine Comedy*, and John Milton's *Paradise Lost*.

Aeschylus reportedly stated that his plays were merely "slices of fish from Homer's great feasts." However, the *Oresteia*, combining themes from both the *Iliad* and the *Odyssey*, is in every sense a dramatic main course in which the playwright attempts nothing less than to explore with a truly Homeric amplitude the key conflicts in the human condition: between humans and the gods, male and female, parent and child, passion and reason, the individual and community, vengeance and justice. The background for his drama is the curse laid upon the ruling house of Argos when Atreus revenged himself on his brother Thyestes for having seduced his wife by serving Thyestes' children to him at a banquet. Cursing Atreus, Thyestes leaves Argos with his one remaining son, Aegisthus, vowing retribution. Thyestes' curse is visited on the next generation, on Atreus's sons, Menelaus and Agamemnon, through the seduction of Menelaus's wife, Helen, by the Trojan Paris, which provokes the Trojan War. The Greek force, led by Agamemnon, sets out to regain Helen and take revenge on the Trojans, but their fleet is initially beset by unfavorable winds. Agamemnon, choosing his duty as a commander over his responsibilities as a father, sacrifices his daughter Iphigenia as the price for reaching Troy and ultimate victory. The *Oresteia* considers the consequences of Agamemnon's act and the Greek's defeat of the Trojans at the decisive moment of his homecoming to Argos.

Agamemnon, the first play of the trilogy, which has been called by some the greatest of all Greek tragedies, works out the revenge of Agamemnon's wife, Clytemnestra, for their daughter's death. Having taken Thyestes' son, Aegisthus, as her lover, Clytemnestra both betrays her husband and plots to usurp his throne with his bitterest enemy. Agamemnon returns to a disordered homeland in which all is not as it appears. Clytemnestra's welcoming of her returned husband is shockingly revealed as a sinister pretense for his murder in what critic Shirley J. Stewart has called "a play of distortion." Agamemnon is shown arriving in his chariot, proud, self-willed, and oblivious to the insincerity of his wife or his own hypocrisy, riding alongside his prize from Troy, Cassandra, the embodiment of his excessive destruction of the Trojans and an insult to his wife. He is invited to walk on an outspread crimson carpet into his palace. The red carpet, one of drama's first great visual stage effects, becomes a striking symbol of Agamemnon's hubris, for such an honor is reserved for the gods, and Agamemnon figuratively trods a trail of blood to his own demise. "Let the red stream flow and bear him home," Clytemnestra states, "to the home he never hoped to see." After Cassandra's prediction of both Agamemnon's and her own death comes true, Clytemnestra returns to the stage, bloodspattered, revealing for the first time her savage hatred of Agamemnon and her bitter jealousy of Cassandra. Clytemnestra justifies her act as the avenger of the house of Atreus who has freed it from the chain of murder set in motion by Atreus's crime. Clytemnestra's murder of Agamemnon, however, only continues the series of retributive murders afflicting the house of Atreus, while demonstrating the seemingly unbreakable cycle that "Blood will have blood." The play ends with Clytemnestra and Aegisthus ruling Argos by force and intimidation with the renewal of the demands of blood vengeance suggested by the Chorus's reference to Agamemnon's son, Orestes, who must someday return to avenge his father's death.

In *The Libation Bearers* Orestes does arrive, echoing the homecoming of his father in the first play. Meeting his sister Electra before their father's grave, Orestes, Hamlet-like in his indecision, reveals his dilemma and the crux of the trilogy's moral, religious, and political conflict. Ordered by Apollo to avenge his father, by doing so, Orestes must kill his mother, thereby incurring the wrath of the Furies, primal avengers charged with protecting the sanctity of blood-kinship. By doing what is right—avenging his father—Orestes must do what is wrong—murdering his mother. His conflict is dramatized as a kind of cosmic schism between two divine imperatives and world orders, as a fundamental conflict between the forces of vengeance and justice. Orestes' seemingly insolvable quandary sets the tragic conflict of the entire trilogy that dramatizes the means by which the seemingly unbreakable cycle of violence begetting violence can come under the rule of law and the primal can give way to the civilized. If, as it has been argued, the essence of tragedy is the moment of concentrated awareness of irreversibility, then Orestes' decision to act, accepting the certain punishment of the Furies, is the decisive tragic moment of the trilogy. Entering the palace by a stratagem, Orestes kills Aegisthus but hesitates before killing Clytemnestra, who bears her breast before him to remind Orestes that she has given him life. Orestes, sustained by the command of Apollo, finally strikes, but he is shortly beset by a vision of the Furies, women, "shrouded in black, their heads wreathed, / swarming serpents!"

In *The Eumenides* Orestes is pursued by the Furies first to Delphi, where Apollo is unable to protect him for long, and then to Athens, where Athena, the patroness of the city, arranges Orestes' trial. In a trilogy that alternates its drama from the domestic conflict of Agamemnon and Clytemnestra to the internal conflict of Orestes, the third play widens its subject to the truly cosmic scale as Apollo, Hermes, the Furies, and Athena all take the stage, and the full moral, political, and spiritual implication of Orestes' crime is enacted. Aeschylus searches for nothing less than the meaning of human suffering itself and the ways by which evil in the world can be overruled by justice and chaos can be replaced by order.

Ancient critics indicated that Aeschylus's dramatic method was to aim at "astonishment," and all of the playwright's verbal and stage magic are fully deployed in *The Eumenides*. It is said that the first appearance of the Furies in *The Eumenides* caused members of the audience to faint and women to miscarry. In the trilogy's great reversal the competing gods' dilemma over what to do about Orestes' crime—matricide according to the Furies, justifiable manslaughter according to Apollo—is finally resolved by representatives of the play's first audience, Athenian citizens gathered by Athena into a jury. The Athenian legal system, not the gods, Aeschylus suggests, becomes the means for mercy and equity to enter the treatment of crime, breaking the seemingly hopeless cycle of blood requiring blood and ultimately lifting the curse on the house of Atreus. Orestes is acquitted, and the Furies are placated by being persuaded to become Athens's protectors. Old and new gods are reconciled, and a new cosmic order is asserted in which out of the chaos of sexual aggression and self-consuming rage, justice and civilization can flourish. The final triumphal exodus led by Athena of the jurors out of the theater into the city where the principles of justice and civilization are embodied must have been overwhelming in its civic, moral, and spiritual implications for its first spectators. For later audiences it is the force and intensity of Aeschylus's dramatic conception and his incomparable poetry that captivates. The *Oresteia* remains one of the most ambitious plays ever attempted, in which Aeschylus succeeds in uniting the widest possible exploration of universal human themes with an emotionally intense and riveting drama.

MACBETH

5

(c. 1606) *by William Shakespeare*

Macbeth . . . is done upon a stronger and more systematic principle of contrast than any other of Shakespear's plays. It moves upon the verge of an abyss, and is a constant struggle between life and death. The action is desperate and the reaction is dreadful. It is a huddling together of fierce extremes, a war of opposite natures which of them shall destroy the other. There is nothing but what has a violent end or violent beginnings. The lights and shades are laid on with a determined hand; the transitions from triumph to despair, from the height of terror to the repose of death, are sudden and startling; every passion brings in its fellow-contrary, and the thoughts pitch and jostle against each other as in the dark. The whole play is an unruly chaos of strange and forbidden things, where the ground rocks under our feet. Shakespear's genius here took its full swing, and trod upon the farthest bounds of nature and passion.

—William Hazlitt, *Characters of Shakespear's Plays*

Macbeth completes William Shakespeare's great tragic quartet while expanding, echoing, and altering key elements of HAMLET, OTHELLO, and KING LEAR into one of the most terrifying stage experiences. Like *Hamlet*, *Macbeth* treats the consequences of regicide, but from the perspective of the usurpers, not the dispossessed. Like *Othello*, *Macbeth* centers its intrigue on the intimate relations of husband and wife. Like *Lear*, *Macbeth* explores female villainy, creating in Lady Macbeth one of Shakespeare's most complex, powerful, and frightening woman characters. Different from *Hamlet* and *Othello*, in which the tragic action is reserved for their climaxes and an emphasis on cause over effect, *Macbeth*, like *Lear*, locates the tragic tipping point at the play's outset to concentrate on inexorable consequences. Like *Othello*, *Macbeth*, Shakespeare's shortest tragedy, achieves an almost unbearable intensity by eliminating subplots, inessential characters, and tonal shifts to focus almost exclusively on the crime's devastating impact on husband and wife.

What is singular about *Macbeth*, compared to the other three great Shakespearean tragedies, is its villain-hero. If Hamlet mainly executes rather than murders, if Othello is "more sinned against than sinning," and if Lear is "a very foolish fond old man" buffeted by surrounding evil, Macbeth knowingly chooses evil and becomes the bloodiest and most dehumanized of Shakespeare's tragic protagonists. *Macbeth* treats cold-blooded, premeditated murder from the killer's perspective, anticipating the psychological dissection and guilt-ridden expressionism that Feodor Dostoevsky will employ in *Crime and Punishment*. Critic Harold Bloom groups the protagonist as "the culminating figure in the sequence of what might be called Shakespeare's Grand Negations: Richard III, Iago, Edmund, Macbeth." With Macbeth, however, Shakespeare takes us further inside a villain's mind and imagination, while daringly engaging our sympathy and identification with a murderer. "The problem Shakespeare gave himself in *Macbeth* was a tremendous one," Critic Wayne C. Booth has stated.

> Take a good man, a noble man, a man admired by all who know him— and destroy him, not only physically and emotionally, as the Greeks destroyed their heroes, but also morally and intellectually. As if this were not difficult enough as a dramatic hurdle, while transforming him into one of the most despicable mortals conceivable, maintain him as a tragic hero—that is, keep him so sympathetic that, when he comes to his death, the audience will pity rather than detest him and will be relieved to see him out of his misery rather than pleased to see him destroyed.

Unlike Richard III, Iago, or Edmund, Macbeth is less a virtuoso of villainy or an amoral nihilist than a man with a conscience who succumbs to evil and obliterates the humanity that he is compelled to suppress. *Macbeth* is Shakespeare's greatest psychological portrait of self-destruction and the human capacity for evil seen from inside with an intimacy that horrifies because of our forced identification with Macbeth.

Although there is no certainty in dating the composition or the first performance of *Macbeth*, allusions in the play to contemporary events fix the likely date of both as 1606, shortly after the completion and debut of *King Lear*. Scholars have suggested that *Macbeth* was acted before James I at Hampton Court on August 7, 1606, during the royal visit of King Christian IV of Denmark and that it may have been especially written for a royal performance. Its subject, as well as its version of Scottish history, suggest an effort both to flatter and to avoid offending the Scottish king James. *Macbeth* is a chronicle play in which Shakespeare took his major plot elements from Raphael Holinshed's *Chronicles of England, Scotland and Ireland* (1587), but with significant modifications. The usurping Macbeth's decade-long (and largely successful) reign is abbreviated with an emphasis on the internal and external destruction caused by Macbeth's seizing the throne and trying to hold onto it. For the details of King Duncan's death, Shakespeare used

Holinshed's account of the murder of an earlier king Duff by Donwald, who cast suspicion on drunken servants and whose ambitious wife played a significant role in the crime. Shakespeare also eliminated Banquo as the historical Macbeth's co-conspirator in the murder to promote Banquo's innocence and nobility in originating a kingly line from which James traced his legitimacy. Additional prominence is also given to the Weird Sisters, whom Holinshed only mentions in their initial meeting of Macbeth on the heath. The prophetic warning "beware Macduff" is attributed to "certain wizards in whose words Macbeth put great confidence." The importance of the witches and the occult in *Macbeth* must have been meant to appeal to a king who produced a treatise, *Daemonologie* (1597), on witchcraft.

The uncanny sets the tone of moral ambiguity from the play's outset as the three witches gather to encounter Macbeth "When the battle's lost and won" in an inverted world in which "Fair is foul, and foul is fair." Nothing in the play will be what it seems, and the tragedy results from the confusion and conflict between the fair—honor, nobility, duty—and the foul—rank ambition and bloody murder. Throughout the play nature reflects the disorder and violence of the action. Opening with thunder and lightning, the drama is set in a Scotland contending with the rebellion of the thane (feudal lord) of Cawdor, whom the fearless and courageous Macbeth has vanquished on the battlefield. The play, therefore, initially establishes Macbeth as a dutiful and trusted vassal of the king, Duncan of Scotland, deserving to be rewarded with the rebel's title for restoring peace and order in the realm. "What he hath lost," Duncan declares, "noble Macbeth hath won." News of this honor reaches Macbeth through the witches, who greet him both as the thane of Cawdor and "king hereafter" and his comrade-in-arms Banquo as one who "shalt get kings, though thou be none." Like the ghost in *Hamlet*, the Weird Sisters are left purposefully ambiguous and problematic. Are they agents of fate that determine Macbeth's doom, predicting and even dictating the inevitable, or do they merely signal a latency in Macbeth's ambitious character?

When he is greeted by the king's emissaries as thane of Cawdor, Macbeth begins to wonder if the first predictions of the witches came true and what will come of the second of "king hereafter":

> This supernatural soliciting
> Cannot be ill, cannot be good. If ill,
> Why hath it given me earnest of success
> Commencing in a truth? I am Thane of Cawdor.
> If good, why do I yield to that suggestion
> Whose horrid image doth unfix my hair
> And make my seated heart knock at my ribs,
> Against the use of nature? Present fears

Are less than horrible imaginings:
My thought, whose murder yet is but fantastical,
Shakes so my single state of man that function
Is smother'd in surmise, and nothing is
But what is not.

Macbeth will be defined by his "horrible imaginings," by his considerable intellectual and imaginative capacity both to understand what he knows to be true and right and his opposed desires and their frightful consequences. Only Hamlet has as fully a developed interior life and dramatized mental processes as Macbeth in Shakespeare's plays. Macbeth's ambition is initially checked by his conscience and by his fear of the unforeseen consequence of violating moral laws. Shakespeare brilliantly dramatizes Macbeth's mental conflict in near stream-of-consciousness, associational fashion:

If it were done when 'tis done, then 'twere well
It were done quickly. If th'assassination
Could trammel up the consequence, and catch
With his surcease, success: that but this blow
Might be the be-all and the end-all, here,
But here, upon this bank and shoal of time,
We'd jump the life to come. But in these cases
We still have judgement here, that we but teach
Bloody instructions which, being taught, return
To plague th'inventor. This even-handed justice
Commends th'ingredients of our poison'd chalice
To our own lips. He's here in double trust:
First, as I am his kinsman and his subject,
Strong both against the deed; then, as his host,
Who should against his murderer shut the door,
Not bear the knife myself. Besides, this Duncan
Hath borne his faculties so meek, hath been
So clear in his great office, that his virtues
Will plead like angels trumpet-tongued against
The deep damnation of his taking-off,
And pity, like a naked new-born babe,
Striding the blast, or heaven's cherubin, horsed
Upon the sightless couriers of the air,
Shall blow the horrid deed in every eye
That tears shall drown the wind. I have no spur
To prick the sides of my intent, but only
Vaulting ambition which o'erleaps itself
And falls on the other.

Macbeth's "spur" comes in the form of Lady Macbeth, who plays on her husband's self-image of courage and virility to commit to the murder. She also reveals her own shocking cancellation of gender imperatives in shaming her husband into action, in one of the most shocking passages of the play:

> . . . I have given suck, and know
> How tender 'tis to love the babe that milks me.
> I would, while it was smiling in my face,
> Have plucked my nipple from his boneless gums
> And dashed the brains out, had I so sworn
> As you have done to this.

Horrified at his wife's resolve and cold-blooded calculation in devising the plot, Macbeth urges his wife to "Bring forth men-children only, / For thy undaunted mettle should compose / Nothing but males," but commits "Each corporal agent to this terrible feat."

With the decision to kill the king taken, the play accelerates unrelentingly through a succession of powerful scenes: Duncan's and Banquo's murders, the banquet scene in which Banquo's ghost appears, Lady Macbeth's sleepwalking, and Macbeth's final battle with Macduff, Thane of Fife. Duncan's offstage murder contrasts Macbeth's "horrible imaginings" concerning the implications and Lady Macbeth's chilling practicality. Macbeth's question, "Will all great Neptune's ocean wash this blood / Clean from my hand?" is answered by his wife: "A little water clears us of this deed; / How easy is it then!" The knocking at the door of the castle, ominously signaling the revelation of the crime, prompts the play's one comic respite in the Porter's drunken foolery that he is at the door of "Hell's Gate" controlling the entrance of the damned. With the flight of Duncan's sons, who fear for their lives, causing them to be suspected as murderers, Macbeth is named king, and the play's focus shifts to Macbeth's keeping and consolidating the power he has seized. Having gained what the witches prophesied, Macbeth next tries to prevent their prediction that Banquo's descendants will reign by setting assassins to kill Banquo and his son, Fleance. The plan goes awry, and Fleance escapes, leaving Macbeth again at the mercy of the witches' prophecy. His psychic breakdown is dramatized by his seeing Banquo's ghost occupying Macbeth's place at the banquet. Pushed to the edge of mental collapse, Macbeth steels himself to meet the witches again to learn what is in store for him: "I am in blood," he declares, "Stepp'd in so far that, should I wade no more, / Returning were as tedious as go o'er."

The witches reassure him that "none of woman born / Shall harm Macbeth" and that he will never be vanquished until "Great Birnam wood to high Dunsinane hill / Shall come against him." Confident that he is invulnerable, Macbeth responds to the rebellion mounted by Duncan's son Malcolm and Macduff, who has joined him in England, by ordering the slaughter of Lady

Macduff and her children. Macbeth has progressed from a murderer in fulfillment of the witches predictions to a murderer (of Banquo) in order to subvert
their predictions and then to pointless butchery that serves no other purpose
than as an exercise in willful destruction. Ironically, Macbeth, whom his wife
feared was "too full o' the milk of human kindness / To catch the nearest
way" to serve his ambition, displays the same cold calculation that frightened
him about his wife, while Lady Macbeth succumbs psychically to her own
"horrible imaginings." Lady Macbeth relives the murder as she sleepwalks,
Shakespeare's version of the workings of the unconscious. The blood in her
tormented conscience that formerly could be removed with a little water is
now a permanent noxious stain in which "All the perfumes of Arabia will not
sweeten." Women's cries announcing her offstage death are greeted by Macbeth with detached indifference:

> I have almost forgot the taste of fears:
> The time has been, my senses would have cool'd
> To hear a night-shriek, and my fell of hair
> Would at a dismal treatise rouse and stir
> As life were in't. I have supp'd full with horrors;
> Direness, familiar to my slaughterous thoughts,
> Cannot once start me.

Macbeth reveals himself here as an emotional and moral void. Confirmation
that "The Queen, my lord, is dead" prompts only the bitter comment, "She
should have died hereafter." For Macbeth, life has lost all meaning, reflected
in the bleakest lines Shakespeare ever composed:

> Tomorrow, and tomorrow, and tomorrow
> Creeps in this petty pace from day to day
> To the last syllable of recorded time;
> And all our yesterdays have lighted fools
> The way to dusty death. Out, out, brief candle!
> Life's but a walking shadow, a poor player
> That struts and frets his hour upon the stage
> And then is heard no more. It is a tale
> Told by an idiot, full of sound and fury,
> Signifying nothing.

Time and the world that Macbeth had sought to rule are revealed to him as
empty and futile, embodied in a metaphor from the theater with life as a his-
trionic, talentless actor in a tedious, pointless play.

Macbeth's final testing comes when Malcolm orders his troops to cam-
ouflage their movement by carrying boughs from Birnam Woods in their

march toward Dunsinane and from Macduff, whom he faces in combat and reveals that he was "from his mother's womb / Untimely ripp'd," that is, born by cesarean section and therefore not "of woman born." This revelation, the final fulfillment of the witches' prophecies, causes Macbeth to flee, but he is prompted by Macduff's taunt of cowardice and order to surrender to meet Macduff's challenge, despite knowing the deadly outcome:

> Yet I will try the last. Before my body
> I throw my warlike shield. Lay on, Macduff,
> And damn'd be him that first cries, "Hold, enough!"

Macbeth returns to the world of combat where his initial distinctions were honorably earned and tragically lost.

The play concludes with order restored to Scotland, as Macduff presents Macbeth's severed head to Malcolm, who is hailed as king. Malcolm may assert his control and diminish Macbeth and Lady Macbeth as "this dead butcher and his fiend-like queen," but the audience knows more than that. We know what Malcolm does not, that it will not be his royal line but Banquo's that will eventually rule Scotland, and inevitably another round of rebellion and murder is to come. We also know in horrifying human terms the making of a butcher and a fiend who refuse to be so easily dismissed as aberrations.

LONG DAY'S JOURNEY INTO NIGHT 6

(1956) *by Eugene O'Neill*

The simplicity of the play's dramatic form; the complexity of its four major characters and the progressive unfolding of their psychological richness; the directness of their presentation without gimmickry or sentimentality; the absorbing emotional rhythm of their interactions; the intensity of their quest for meaning; the natural yet expressive quality of their dialogue; their insights concerning guilt, vulnerability, and the need for family connection—these are among the qualities that have gained the play its status as a world classic. Long Day's Journey into Night *simultaneously marks the pinnacle of O'Neill's career and the coming of age of American drama.*

—Michael Hinden, *Long Day's Journey into Night: Native Eloquence*

Long Day's Journey into Night—the greatest American play by the United States's greatest playwright—is a harrowing work of personal memory universalized into the great American family tragedy. At the end of a remarkable career that produced more than 50 plays and after a seemingly inexhaustible series of theatrical experimentations that established the baseline and boundaries for a vital new American drama, Eugene O'Neill finally returned to simplicity itself: autobiography and a day-in-the-life repossession of his own family history as a summary statement of his long journey toward self-understanding and self-expression. The urgency and utility of O'Neill's dramatic version of *Remembrance of Things Past* (Marcel Proust's seven-volume epic autobiographical novel) is announced significantly and succinctly by Mary Tyrone, who early on in the play states: "The past is the present, isn't it? It's the future too." O'Neill's entire past is prelude and preparation for the tragic recognition that animates his masterpiece. Again, it is Mary Tyrone who summarizes the tragic sensibility that informs O'Neill's plays and finds its best expression in *Long Day's Journey*: "None of us can help the things life has done to us. They're done before you realize it, and once they're done they make you do other things until at last everything comes between you and what you'd like to be, and you've lost your true self forever."

Born in 1888 in a hotel room in the heart of New York's theatrical district, O'Neill was the son of matinee idol and onetime distinguished Shakespearean actor, James O'Neill, who made his reputation and fortune by continually touring in a melodrama based on Alexandre Dumas's *The Count of Monte Cristo*. The commercial theater of the day, in which his father squandered his considerable acting talent, consisted of gratifying public taste with the lowest popular denominator. Eugene O'Neill, his disappointed father, his drug-addicted mother, and his alcoholic elder brother were all in various ways products of the theater of the day. O'Neill's transient childhood was spent touring the United States with his parents and attending boarding schools. He was suspended from Princeton after a year for a college prank and introduced to the bohemian world by his actor-brother, James. O'Neill's aimless and dissipated youth is succinctly summarized by critic Jordan Y. Miller:

> At twenty, almost on a dare, he had married a girl he hardly knew, fathered a child he never saw until nearly twelve years later, went gold prospecting in Honduras, contracted malaria, and was divorced before he was twenty-two. He failed as a newspaper reporter, became intimate with all the more famous New York and Connecticut bordellos, to which he was guided by his brother James; evidence all of fast becoming a hopeless alcoholic; and, after attempting suicide, contracted a severe lung infection to place him in a Connecticut tuberculosis sanitarium at the age of twenty-four.

During his convalescence from 1912 to 1913, O'Neill read widely and decided to become a playwright. His first dramatic work was done for the Provincetown Players, of Cape Cod and in New York City's Greenwich Village, the most influential company in the "little theater" movement. His first stage production, *Bound East for Cardiff*, based on his experience as a seaman, was followed by *Beyond the Horizon* and *The Emperor Jones*, both in 1920, which established O'Neill as a powerful new force in the American theater. For the next 15 years, O'Neill would display an extraordinary range in his restless search for an expressive form that virtually catalogs the various methods of modern drama. As he stated in a 1923 interview, "I intend to use whatever I can make my own, to write about anything under the sun in any manner that fits the subject. And I shall never be influenced by any consideration but one: Is it the truth as I know it—or, better still, feel it?"

To arrive at truth in the face of a breakdown of traditional beliefs and its crippling effect on the psyche, O'Neill experimented with symbolism, masks, interior monologues, choruses, and realistic and expressionistic styles. His early plays were "slice of life" dramas, focusing on the delusions and obsessions of marginalized characters—seamen, laborers, roustabouts, prostitutes, and derelicts—who had never before been depicted on the American stage. Most are adrift and deeply divided from their identities and the traditional sources of sustaining values. Increasingly, his plays would dramatize a tragic vision in naturalistic plays such as *Anna Christie* (1921) and *Desire Under the Elms* (1924), and a series of expressionistic plays, including *The Emperor Jones*, *The Hairy Ape* (1920), and *The Great God Brown* (1926). In *Strange Interlude* (1928) O'Neill began dissecting character through interior monologue, never before attempted on stage on such a scale. His work in the 1930s included the monumental *Mourning Becomes Electra*, in which Aeschylus's drama of the house of Atreus is transferred to post–Civil War New England. His single comedy, *Ah, Wilderness!* (1933), is based on his happiest memories summering at his family's New London, Connecticut, home, the same setting he would use for his darkest tragic drama, *Long Day's Journey*. In 1934 the failure of his play *Days without End* began a 12-year period in which no new O'Neill plays were staged and initiated a final creative explosion prompted by O'Neill's commitment to write "plays primarily as literature to be read." In 1936 O'Neill became the second American (and to date the only American dramatist) to receive the Nobel Prize in literature. The first American Nobel laureate, Sinclair Lewis, praised the playwright as follows:

> Mr. Eugene O'Neill, who has done nothing much in American drama save to transform it utterly, in ten or twelve years, from a false world of neat and competent trickery to a world of splendor and fear and greatness . . . has seen life as not to be arranged in the study of a scholar but as a terrifying, magnificent, and often horrible thing akin to the tornado, the earthquake, the devastating fire.

The "horrible thing" that Lewis equates with a natural disaster continually threatens the Tyrone family in *Long Day's Journey*, just below the surface of their seemingly placid summer holiday routine in August 1912, at their Connecticut seaside home. O'Neill began work on *Long Day's Journey* in the summer of 1939 as war in Europe threatened and his own health was in significant decline from a debilitating nerve disorder. Feeling "fed up and stale" after nearly five years' work on an immense cycle of plays reflecting American history from the perspective of an Irish-American family, O'Neill decided to turn to private subjects, sketching the outline of two plays that "appeal most." One was based on his time spent in a bar on the Bowery in New York, which became THE ICEMAN COMETH; the other, a laceratingly honest portrait of his past, that he identified as the "N[ew]. L[ondon]. family" play, and later called "a play of old sorrow, written in tears and blood": *Long Day's Journey into Night*. Completing work on *Iceman* first, O'Neill spent most of 1940 on *Long Day's Journey*. His wife, Carlotta, recalled:

When he started *Long Day's Journey* it was a most strange experience to watch that man being tortured every day by his own writing. He would come out of his study at the end of the day gaunt and sometimes weeping. His eyes would be all red and he looked ten years older than when he went in in the morning. I think he felt freer when he got it out of his system. It was his way of making peace with his family—and himself.

Completing the second draft by his 52nd birthday, in October 1940, O'Neill made the final cuts to the typescript that Carlotta had prepared by the end of March 1941, recording in his diary: "Like this play better than any I have ever written—does the most with the least—a quiet play!—and a great one, I believe." Due to its autobiographical content, O'Neill stipulated that his play neither be published nor performed until at least 25 years after his death. However, after he died in 1953, Carlotta, claiming that her husband had orally withdrawn his prohibition shortly before his death, allowed the play to be staged by the Swedish Royal Dramatic Theatre in February 1956, to coincide with its American publication. The English-language premiere of the play occurred on Broadway in November 1956 to great acclaim. Reviewer John Chapman called it "O'Neill's most beautiful play . . . and . . . one of the great dramas of any time," while critic Brooks Atkinson declared that with *Long Day's Journey* "American theater acquires stature and size." The play has gone on to be recognized as O'Neill's greatest achievement and a triumph both for U.S. and world theater.

Its power derives from its relentless honesty linked to the simplicity of its dramatic form. The action is compressed to the events of a single day that progressively reveal the psychological complexity and tragic mutual dependency of the play's four major characters—James and Mary Tyrone and their sons Jamie and Edmund—along with the secrets that define and doom their family. It is Edmund's ill health, which his mother insists is only a summer cold but his doctor diagnoses as tuberculosis, that serves as a catalyst for the play's pounding series of revelations and recognitions. James, Jamie, and Edmund alternately accept and reject their suspicion that Mary has relapsed in her morphine addiction, while each family member is forced to face their guilt and responsibility for the past that haunts the family. Mary, who had abandoned her vocation to become a nun or a concert pianist to marry the handsome actor James Tyrone, ultimately blames her husband and sons for her addiction: specifically, Jamie for the accidental death of another son, significantly named Eugene; Edmund for his difficult birth that required medical care; and James for his stinginess that led to employing a second-rate doctor who started her on morphine. The others, in turn, confront their own complicity in the family's self-destruction, while each is given an aria of insight into the truth of their situation.

The patriarch, James Tyrone, reviews his acting career in which he exchanged seemingly unlimited artistic promise for financial security, fueled by his early lower-class Irish impoverishment. He confesses:

> That God-damned play I bought for a song, and made such a great success in—a great money success—it ruined me with its promise of an easy fortune. . . . It was a great romantic part I knew I could play better than anyone. But it was a great box office success from the start—and then life had me where it wanted me—at from thirty-five to forty thousand net profit a season! A fortune in those days—or even in these. What the hell was it I wanted to buy, I wonder, that was worth—Well, no matter. It's a late day for regrets.

Edmund, understanding for the first time the cost of his father's success and the origins of his miserliness, reciprocates his father's honesty with his own confession in one of the most moving and lyrical passages O'Neill ever wrote. Recalling his time at sea, Edmund admits to a moment of supreme transcendence:

> I lay on the bowsprit, facing astern, with the water foaming into spume under me, the masts with every sail white in the moonlight, towering high above me. I became drunk with the beauty and singing rhythm of it, and for a moment I lost myself—actually lost my life. I was set free! I dissolved in the sea, became moonlight and the ship and the high dim-starred sky! I belonged, without past or future, within peace and unity and a wild joy, within something greater than my own life, or the life of Man, to Life itself! To God, if you to put it that way. . . . For a second you see—and seeing the secret, are the secret. For a second there is meaning! Then the hands let the veil fall and you are alone, lost in the fog again, and you stumble on toward nowhere, for no good reason!

Edmund's ecstasy of affirmation gives way to a deeply tragic self- and existential awareness: "It was a great mistake, my being born a man. I would have been much more successful as a sea gull or a fish. As it is, I will always be a stranger who never feels at home, who does not really want and is not really wanted, who can never belong, who must always be a little in love with death!"

The play concludes with Jamie's confession of his resentment of his brother and his secret delight in his family's destruction that grants him the consoling role of damned and powerless victim: "The dead part of me hopes you won't get well. Maybe he's even glad the game has got Mama again! He wants company, he doesn't want to be the only corpse around the house!" Jamie's warning to his brother that he actually desires Edmund's and the family's destruction, that he secretly hates them all and himself, is ironically one of the great testaments of love and loyalty in the play. "Greater love hath no man than this," Jamie declares, "that he saveth his brother from himself."

These family revelations reach a crescendo with the appearance of Mary, carrying her wedding gown—in the bitter words of Jamie, "The Mad Scene. Enter Ophelia!" Completing the family tableau and individual monologues that probe the causes and costs of the family's dilemmas, Mary has retreated with the assistance of morphine into the fog that has threatened throughout the day. Escaping from reality, she has reverted to an earlier existence, before the consequences of marriage and motherhood, and ends the play heartbreakingly with her memories as a convent schoolgirl and her intention to become a nun:

> But Mother Elizabeth told me I must be more sure than that, even, that I must prove it wasn't simply my imagination. She said, if I was so sure, then I wouldn't mind putting myself to a test by going home after I graduated, and living as other girls lived, going out to parties and dances and enjoying myself; and then if after a year or two I still felt sure, I could come back to see her and we would talk it over again. . . . That was in the winter of senior year. Then in the spring something happened to me. Yes, I remember. I fell in love with James Tyrone and was so happy for a time.

Love here is balanced with loss, youthful hopes with crushing disappointment, completing the process by which each of the Tyrones is forced to come to terms with all that is intractable in one's self, one's family, one's existence. The play reaches a terminal point in which there seems no possibility of consolation or regeneration, signaled by O'Neill's final stage direction: "She stares before her in a sad dream. Tyrone stirs in his chair. Edmund and Jamie remain motionless."

The play's final tragic awareness is that we are who we are, condemned by family and history to forever seek transcendence and fail to find it. Yet the play's title metaphor of a journey toward closure, toward the dark recognition of frustration, disappointment, and mortality also implies a dawn of sorts, if only in the shattering illumination of naked truths.

OTHELLO

(1604) *by William Shakespeare*

Of all Shakespeare's tragedies . . . Othello *is the most painfully exciting and the most terrible. From the moment when the temptation of the hero begins, the reader's heart and mind are held in a vice, experiencing the extremes of pity and fear, sympathy and repulsion, sickening hope and dreadful expectation. Evil is displayed before him, not indeed with the profusion found in* King Lear, *but forming, as it were, the soul of a single character, and united with an intellectual superiority so great that he watches its advance fascinated and appalled. He sees it, in itself almost irresistible, aided at every step by fortunate accidents and the innocent mistakes of its victims. He seems to breathe an atmosphere as fateful as that of* King Lear, *but more confined and oppressive, the darkness not of night but of a close-shut murderous room. His imagination is excited to intense activity, but it is the activity of concentration rather than dilation.*

—A. C. Bradley, *Shakespearean Tragedy*

Between William Shakespeare's most expansive and philosophical tragedies— HAMLET and KING LEAR—is *Othello*, his most constricted and heartbreaking play. *Othello* is a train wreck that the audience horrifyingly witnesses, helpless to prevent or look away. If *Hamlet* is a tragedy about youth, and *Lear* concerns old age, *Othello* is a family or domestic tragedy of a middle-aged man in which the fate of kingdoms and the cosmos that hangs in the balance in *Hamlet* and *Lear* contracts to the private world of a marriage's destruction. Following his anatomizing of the painfully introspective intellectual Hamlet, Shakespeare, at the height of his ability to probe human nature and to dramatize it in action and language, treats Hamlet's temperamental opposite—the man of action. Othello is decisive, confident, and secure in his identity, duty, and place in the world. By the end of the play, he has brought down his world around him with the relentless force that made him a great general turned inward, destroying both what he loved best in another and in himself. That such a man should fall so far and so fast gives the play an almost unbearable momentum. That such a man should unravel so completely, ushered by jealousy and hatred into a bestial worldview that cancels any claims of human virtue and self-less devotion, shocks and horrifies. *Othello* is generally regarded as Shakespeare's greatest stage play, the closest he would ever come to conforming to the constrained rules of Aristotelian tragedy. The intensity and focus of *Othello* is unalleviated by subplots, comic relief, or any mitigation or consolation for the deterioration of the "noble Moor" and his collapse into murder and suicide. At the center of the play's intrigue is Shakespeare's most sinister and formidable conceptions of evil in Iago, whose motives and the wellspring of his villainy continue to haunt audiences and critics alike. Indeed, the psychological resonances of the drama, along with its provocative racial and gender themes, have caused *Othello*, perhaps more than any other of Shakespeare's plays, to reverberate the loudest with current audiences and commentators. As scholar Edward Pechter has argued, "During the past twenty-five years or so, *Othello* has become the Shakespearean tragedy of choice, replacing *King Lear* in the way *Lear* had earlier replaced *Hamlet* as the play that speaks most directly and powerfully to current interests."

Shakespeare derived his plot from Giraldi Cinthio's "Tale of the Moor," in the story collection *Hecatommithi* (1565), reshaping Cinthio's sensational tale of jealousy, intrigue, and murder in several key ways. In Cinthio's story, Alfiero, the scheming ensign, lusts after the Moor's wife, named Disdemona, and after she spurns his advances, Alfiero seeks vengeance by accusing her of adultery with Cassio, the Moor's lieutenant. Alfiero, like Iago, similarly arouses the Moor's suspicions by stealing Disdemona's handkerchief and planting it in Cassio's bedroom. However, the Moor and Alfiero join forces to kill Disdemona, beating her to death with a stocking filled with sand before pulling down the ceiling on her dead body to conceal the crime as an accident. The Moor is eventually captured, tortured, and slain by Disdemona's relatives, while the ensign dies during torture for another crime. What is striking about Shakespeare's alteration of Cinthio's grisly tale of murder and villainy is the shift of emphasis to the provocation for the murder, the ennobling of Othello as a figure of great stature and dignity to underscore his self-destruction, and the complication of motive for the ensign's actions. Cinthio's version of Iago is conventionally driven by jealousy of a superior and lust for his wife. Iago's motivation is anything but explainable in conventional terms. Dramatically, Shakespeare turns the focus of the play from the shocking crime to its causes and psychic significance, transforming Cinthio's intrigue story of vile murder into one of the greatest dramatic meditations on the nature of love and its destruction.

What makes *Othello* so unique structurally (and painful to witness) is that it is a tragedy built on a comic foundation. The first two acts of the play enact the standard pattern of Shakespeare's romantic comedies. The young Venetian noblewoman, Desdemona, has eloped with the middle-aged Othello, the military commander of the armed forces of Venice. Their union is opposed by Desdemona's father, Brabantio, and by a rival for Desdemona, Roderigo, who in the play's opening scenes are both provoked against

Othello by Iago. Desdemona and Othello, therefore, face the usual challenges of the lovers in a Shakespearean comedy who must contend with the forces of authority, custom, and circumstances allied against their union. The romantic climax comes in the trial scene of act 1, in which Othello successfully defends himself before the Venetian senate against Brabantio's charge that Othello has beguiled his daughter, "stol'n from me, and corrupted / By spells and medicines bought of mountebanks." Calmly and courteously Othello recounts how, despite the differences of age, race, and background, he won Desdemona's heart by recounting the stories of his exotic life and adventures: "She loved me for the dangers I had passed, / And I loved her that she did pity them." Wonder at Othello's heroic adventures and compassion for her sympathy have brought the two opposites together—the young, inexperienced Venetian woman and the brave, experienced outsider. Desdemona finally, dramatically appears before the senate to support Othello's account of their courtship and to balance her obligation to her father and now to her husband based on the claims of love:

> My noble father,
> I do perceive here a divided duty:
> To you I am bound for life and education;
> My life and education both do learn me
> How to respect you; you are the lord of duty;
> I am hitherto your daughter. But here's my husband;
> And so much duty as my mother show'd
> To you, preferring you before her father,
> So much I challenge that I may profess
> Due to the Moor, my lord.

Both Desdemona and Othello defy by their words and gestures the calumnies heaped upon them by Roderigo and Brabantio and vindicate the imperatives of the heart over parental authority and custom. As in a typical Shakespearean comedy, love, tested, triumphs over all opposition.

Vindicated by the duke of Venice and the senate, Othello, accompanied by Desdemona, takes up his military duties in the face of a threatened Turkish invasion, and the lovers are given a triumphal weddinglike procession and marriage ceremony when they disembark on Cyprus. The storm that divides the Venetian fleet also disperses the Turkish threat and clears the way for the lovers' happy reunion and peaceful enjoyment of their married state. First Cassio lands to deliver the news of Othello's marriage and, like the best man, supplies glowing praise for the groom and his bride; next Desdemona, accompanied by Iago and his wife, Emilia, enters but must await news of the fate of Othello's ship. Finally, Othello arrives giving him the opportunity to renew his marriage vows to Desdemona:

It gives me wonder great as my content
To see you here before me. O my soul's joy,
If after every tempest come such calms,
May the wind blow till they have wakened death,
And let the labouring barque climb hills of seas
Olympus-high, and duck again as low
As hell's from heaven. If it were now to die
'Twere now to be most happy, for I fear
My soul hath content so absolute
That not another comfort like to this
Succeeds in unknown fate.

The scene crowns love triumphant. The formerly self-sufficient Othello has now staked his life to his faith in Desdemona and their union, and she has done the same. The fulfillment of the wedding night that should come at the climax of the comedy is relocated to act 2, with the aftermath of the courtship and the wedding now taking center stage. Having triumphantly bested the social and natural forces aligned against them, having staked all to the devotion of the other, Desdemona and Othello will not be left to live happily ever after, and the tragedy will grow out of the conditions that made the comedy. *Othello*, unlike the other Shakespearean comedies, adds three more acts to the romantic drama, shifting from comic affirmation to tragic negation.

Iago reviews Othello's performance as a lover by stating, "O, you are well tuned now, / But I'll set down the pegs that make this music." Iago will now orchestrate discord and disharmony based on a life philosophy totally opposed to the ennobling and selfless concept of love demonstrated by the newlyweds. As Iago asserts to Roderigo, "Virtue? A fig!" Self-interest is all that matters, and love is "merely a lust of the blood and a permission of the will." Othello and Desdemona cannot possibly remain devoted to each other, and, as Iago concludes, "If sanctimony and a frail vow betwixt an erring barbarian and a super-subtle Venetian be not too hard for my wits, and all the tribe of hell, thou shalt enjoy her." The problem of Iago's motivation to destroy Othello and Desdemona is not that he has too few motives but too many. He offers throughout the play multiple justifications for his intrigue: He has been passed over in favor of Cassio; he suspects the Moor and Cassio with his wife, Emilia; he is envious of Cassio's open nature; and he is desirous of Desdemona himself. No single motive is relied on for long, and the gap between cause and effect, between the pettiness of Iago's grudges and the monstrousness of his behavior, prompted Samuel Taylor Coleridge in a memorable phrase to characterize Iago's "motiveless malignity." There is in Iago a zest for villainy and a delight in destruction, driven more by his hatred and contempt for any who oppose his conception of jungle law than by a conventional naturalistic explanation based on jealousy or envy. Moreover,

Shakespeare, by deliberately clouding the issue of Iago's motive, finds ever more sinister threats in such a character's apparently bottomless and unmerited hatred and capacity for evil.

Iago will direct the remainder of the play, constructing Othello's downfall out of the flimsiest evidence and playing on the strengths and weaknesses of Othello's nature and the doubts that erode Othello's faith in Desdemona. Act 3, one of the wonders of the stage, anatomizes Othello's psychic descent from perfect contentment in his new wife to complete loathing, from a worldview in which everything is as it appears to one in which nothing is as it seems. Iago leads Othello to suspect that love and devotion are shams disguising the basest of animalistic instincts. Misled by the handkerchief, his love token to Desdemona, that Iago has planted in Cassio's room and by a partially overheard conversation between Iago and Cassio, Othello, by the end of act 3, forsakes his wife and engages himself in a perverse version of the marriage ceremony of act 2 to Iago. As the pair kneels together, they exchange vows:

> IAGO   Witness you ever-burning lights above,
> You elements that clip us round about,
> Witness that here Iago doth give up
> The execution of his wit, hands, heart
> To wronged Othello's service. Let him command,
> And to obey shall be in me remorse,
> What bloody business ever.
>
> OTHELLO   I greet thy love,
> Not with vain thanks, but with acceptance bounteous,
> And will upon the instant put thee to't.
> Within these three days let me hear thee say
> That Cassio's not alive.
>
> IAGO   My friend is dead.
> 'Tis done at your request; but let her live.
>
> OTHELLO   Damn her, lewd minx! O, damn her, damn her!
> Come, go with me apart. I will withdraw
> To furnish me with some swift means of death
> For the fair devil. Now art thou my lieutenant.
>
> IAGO   I am your own for ever.

This scene has suggested to some critics that Iago's true motivation for destroying the marriage of Desdemona and Othello is a repressed homosexual love for Othello. An equal case can be made that Iago here completes his role as Vice, borrowed from the medieval morality plays, sealing the Faustian bargain for Othello's soul in this mock or black marriage scene.

The play moves relentlessly from here to catastrophe as Othello delivers justice to those he is convinced have wronged him. As he attempts to carry out his execution of Desdemona, she for the first time realizes his charges against her and his utter delusion. Ignoring her appeals for mercy and avowals of innocence, Othello smothers her moments before Emilia arrives with the proof of Desdemona's innocence and Iago's villainy. Othello must now face the realization of what he has done. He turns to Iago, who has been brought before him to know the reason for his actions. Iago replies: "Demand me nothing; what you know, you know: / From this time forth I never will speak word." By Iago's exiting the stage, closing access to his motives, the focus remains firmly on Othello, not as Iago's victim, but as his own. His final speech mixes together the acknowledgment of what he was and what he has become, who he is and how he would like to be remembered:

> I have done the state some service, and they know't.
> No more of that. I pray you, in your letters,
> When you shall these unlucky deeds relate,
> Speak of me as I am. Nothing extenuate,
> Nor set down aught in malice. Then must you speak
> Of one that loved not wisely but too well,
> Of one not easily jealous but, being wrought,
> Perplexed in the extreme; of one whose hand,
> Like the base Indian, threw a pearl away
> Richer than all his tribe.

Consistent with his role as guardian of order in the state, Othello carries out his own execution, by analogy judging his act as a violation reflected by Venice's savage enemy:

> And say besides, that in Aleppo once,
> Where a malignant and a turban'd Turk
> Beat a Venetian and tradu'd the state,
> I took by th' throat the circumcisèd dog,
> And smote him—thus.

Othello, likewise, has "tradu'd the state" and has changed from noble and valiant Othello to a beast, with the passion that ennobled him shown as corrosive and demeaning. He carries out his own execution for a violation that threatens social and psychic order. For the onlookers on stage, the final tableau of the dead Desdemona and Othello "poisons sight" and provokes the command to

"Let it be hid." The witnesses on stage cannot compute rationally what has occurred nor why, but the audience has been given a privileged view of the battle between good and evil worked out in the private recesses of a bedroom and a human soul.

WAITING FOR GODOT

8

(1953)   *by Samuel Beckett*

It is the peculiar richness of a play like Waiting for Godot *that it opens vistas on so many different perspectives. It is open to philosophical, religious, and psychological interpretations, yet above all it is a poem on time, evanescence, and the mysteriousness of existence, the paradox of change and stability, necessity and absurdity.*

—Martin Esslin, *The Theatre of the Absurd*

Two tramps in bowler hats, a desolate country road, a single bare tree—the iconic images of a radically new modern drama confronted the audience at the Théâtre de Babylone in Paris on January 5, 1953, at the premiere of *En attendant Godot* (*Waiting for Godot*). Written during the winter of 1948–49, it would take Samuel Beckett four years to get it produced. It is easy to see why. As the play's first director, Roger Blin, commented, "Imagine a play that contains no action, but characters that have nothing to say to each other." The main characters—Vladimir and Estragon, nicknamed Didi and Gogo—are awaiting the arrival of Godot, but we never learn why, nor who he is, because he never arrives. The tramps frequently say "Let's go," but they never move. We never learn where the road leads nor see the tramps taking it. The play gratifies no expectations and resolves nothing. Instead it detonates the accepted operating principles of drama that we expect to find in a play: a coherent sequence of actions, motives, and conflicts leading to a resolution. It substitutes the core dramatic element of suspense—waiting—and forces the audience to experience the same anticipation and uncertainty of Vladimir and Estragon, while raising fundamental issues about the nature and purpose of existence itself, our own elemental version of waiting. If modern drama originates in the 19th century with Henrik Ibsen and Anton Chekhov, Beckett, with *Waiting for Godot*, extends the implications of their innovations into a radical kind of theatrical experience and method. The theatrical and existential vision of *Waiting for Godot* makes it the watershed 20th-century drama—as explosive, groundbreaking, and influential a work as T. S. Eliot's *The Waste Land* is for modern poetry and James Joyce's *Ulysses* is for modern fiction. From its initial baffling premiere, *Waiting for Godot* would be seen, it is estimated, by more than a million people in the next five years and eventually became the most frequently produced modern drama worldwide, entering the collective consciousness with a "Beckett-like landscape" and establishing the illusive Godot as a shorthand image of modern futility and angst.

Like his fellow countryman and mentor Joyce, Beckett oriented himself in exile from his native Ireland, but unlike Joyce, who managed to remain relatively safe on the fringes of a modern world spinning out of control, Beckett was very much plunged into the maelstrom. He was born in Foxrock, a respectable suburb of Dublin, to Protestant Anglo-Irish parents. His education at Portora Royal School (where Oscar Wilde had been a student) and at Trinity College, Dublin, where he received his degree in French and Italian, pointed him toward a distinguished academic career. In 1928 Beckett won an exchange lectureship at L'École normale supérieure in Paris, where he met Joyce and assisted him in his labors on *Finnegans Wake*. Beckett returned to Trinity as a lecturer in French but found teaching "grim." He would state: "I could not bear the absurdity of teaching others what I did not know myself." In 1932 he left Ireland for good, except for short visits to his family. When World War II broke out Beckett ended a visit home and returned to Paris, later stating, "I preferred France in war to Ireland in peace." During the war Beckett joined the French resistance in Paris, and when his group was infiltrated by a double agent and betrayed to the Gestapo, he was forced to escape to unoccupied France in 1942, where he worked as a farm laborer until the war's end.

In 1946 Beckett struggled to restart his interrupted and stalled literary career that had produced a critical study of Marcel Proust, a collection of short stories (*More Pricks Than Kicks*), a volume of poems (*Echo's Bones*), and two novels (*Murphy* and *Watt*). The turning point came during a visit to his mother in Foxrock. He would later transfer the epiphany that gave him a new subject and method to the more dramatic setting of the pier in Dún Laoghaire on a stormy night in *Krapp's Last Tape*: "Spiritually a year of profound gloom and indigence until that memorable night in March, at the end of the jetty, in the howling wind, never to be forgotten, when suddenly I saw the whole thing. The vision at last. . . . What I suddenly saw then was this . . . that the dark I have always struggled to keep under is in reality my most." Krapp's revelation breaks off, but Beckett himself completed his sentence, saying "that the dark I have always struggled to keep under" was "my most precious ally." As Beckett biographer James Knowlson summarizes, Beckett's insight meant that he would "draw henceforward on his own inner world for his subjects; outside reality would be refracted through the filter of his own imagination; inner desires and needs would be allowed a much greater freedom of expression; rational contradictions would be allowed in; and the imagination would be allowed to create alternative worlds to those of conventional reality." Beckett would thereby find the way to bypass the particular to deal directly with the universal. His fiction and plays would not be social or psychological but ontological. To mine those inner recesses, Beckett would reverse the centrifugal direction of most writers to contain and comprehend the world for the centripetal, of reduction down to essentials. Beckett, who had assisted Joyce in the endlessly proliferating *Finnegans Wake*, would overturn the method of his mentor. "I realized that Joyce had gone as far as one could in the direction of knowing more, in control of one's material," Beckett would observe. "He was always adding to it; you only have to look at his proofs to see that. I realized that my own way was in impoverishment, in lack of knowledge and in taking away, in subtracting rather than in adding." This realization required a means of presentation that Beckett found in minimalism and composition in French, which he found "easier to write without style." Restricted to a voice and its consciousness, Beckett would eliminate the conventional narrative requirements of specificity of time and place and elaborate background for characters and a complex sequence of causes and effects to form his plots. In Beckett's work the atmosphere of futility and stagnation around which Chekhov devised his plays and stories has become pervasive. The world is drained of meaning; human relationships are reduced to tensions between hope and despair in which consciousness itself is problematic. Beckett's protagonists, who lack the possibility of significant action, are paralyzed or forced to repeat an unchanging condition. Beckett compresses his language and situations down to the level of elemental forces without the possibility of escaping from the predicament of the basic absurdity of existence.

Returning to Paris after his epiphany, Beckett began what he called "the siege in the room": his most sustained and prolific period of writing that in five years produced the plays *Eleutheria*, *Waiting for Godot*, and *ENDGAME*; the novel trilogy *Molloy*, *Malone Dies*, and *The Unnamable*; and the short stories published under the title *Stories and Texts for Nothing*. Beckett stated that *Waiting for Godot* began "as a relaxation, to get away from the awful prose I was writing at the time." It gave dramatic form to the intense interior explorations of his fiction. The play's setting is nonspecific but symbolically suggestive of the modern wasteland as the play's protagonists, Vladimir and Estragon, engage in chatter derived equally from metaphysics and the music hall while they await the arrival of Godot, who never comes. What Godot represents (Beckett remarked: "If I knew, I would have said so in the play," and "If by Godot I had meant God, I would have said God, not Godot.") is far less important than the defining condition of fruitless and pointless waiting that the play dramatizes. Beckett explores on stage the implications of a world in which nothing happens, in which a desired revelation and meaningful resolution are endlessly deferred. At art's core is a fundamental ordering of the world, but Beckett's art is based on the world's ultimate incomprehensibility. "I think anyone nowadays," Beckett once said, "who pays the slightest attention to his own experience finds it the experience of a non-knower, a non-can-er." By powerfully staging radical uncertainty and the absurdity of futile waiting, *Godot* epitomizes the operating assumptions of the theater of the absurd.

The most repeated critique of *Waiting for Godot* is voiced in Irish critic Vivian Mercier's succinct summary: "Nothing happens, twice." The play, subtitled *A Tragicomedy in Two Acts*, does not, in the words of Martin Esslin, "tell a story; it explores a static situation" that is encapsulated by the words of Estragon: "Nothing happens, nobody comes, nobody goes, it's awful." In act 1, Didi and Gogo await the anticipated arrival of Godot, to whom they have made "a kind of prayer," a "vague supplication" for something unspecified that Godot has agreed to consider. However, it is by no means certain whether this is the right place or day for the meeting. To pass the time they consider hanging themselves ("It'd give us an erection"), but the only available tree seems too frail to hold them, and they cannot agree who should go first. Another pair arrives: Lucky, with a rope around his neck, loaded down with a bag, picnic basket, stool, and great coat, being whipped on by the domineering Pozzo, who claims to be a landowner taking Lucky to a fair to sell him. They halt for Pozzo to eat, and he asks Gogo and Didi if they would like to be entertained by Lucky's "thinking," which turns out to be a long nonsensical monologue. After Pozzo and Lucky depart, a boy enters, addresses Vladimir as Mr. Albert, and delivers the message that Mr. Godot will not be coming this evening but will surely come tomorrow. After the boy exits, Vladimir and Estragon also decide to leave but make no move to do so.

Act 2 takes place apparently the next day at the same time and place, although the tree now has four or five leaves. Again Vladimir and Estragon begin their vigil, passing the time by exchanging questions, contradictions, insults, and hats, as well as pretending to be Pozzo and Lucky, until the originals arrive. However, Pozzo is now blind and bumps into Lucky, knocking them both down. After debating whether they should help them get up, Didi and Gogo also find themselves on the ground, unable to rise, with Vladimir announcing, "we've arrived . . . we are men." Eventually, they regain their footing, supporting Pozzo between them. Pozzo has no recollection of their previous encounter, and when asked what he and Lucky do when they fall and there is no one to help them, Pozzo says: "We wait till we can get up. Then we go on." When Didi asks if Lucky can "think" again for them before they leave, Pozzo reveals that Lucky is now "dumb"—"he can't even groan." Vladimir wonders about their transformation since yesterday, but Pozzo insists time is a meaningless concept:

> Have you not done tormenting me with your accursed time! It's abominable! When! When! One day, is that not enough for you, one day he went dumb, one day I went blind, one day we'll go deaf, one day we were

born, one day we shall die, the same day, the same second, is that not enough for you? They give birth astride of a grave, the light gleams an instant, then it's night once more.

After Pozzo and Lucky exit (with the sound of their falling again offstage), the boy arrives to announce that Godot will not be coming this evening but will be there without fail tomorrow. Although he appears to be the same boy as yesterday, he denies this and runs off when a frustrated Vladimir lunges at him. Estragon proposes going far away, but Vladimir reminds him that they must wait for Godot to come tomorrow. They return to the idea of hanging themselves, but when they try to use Estragon's belt cord, it breaks, and Estragon's pants fall down. They decide to bring a stronger rope the next day, and "We'll hang ourselves tomorrow. (*Pause.*) Unless Godot comes." The play concludes:

VLADIMIR   Well? Shall we go?

ESTRAGON   Yes, let's go.

They do not move.

Curtain.

Beckett generates meaning in *Waiting for Godot* through image, repetition, and counterpoint. In their bowler hats and pratfalls, Vladimir and Estragon are versions of Charlie Chaplin's tramp, tragic clowns poised between despair and hope. Act 2 repeats the sequence of action of act 1 but deepens the absurdity as well as the significance of their waiting for Godot. Unlike Pozzo and Lucky, whose relationship parodies the master-slave dynamic and a sadomasochistic conception of existence in which death is the only outcome of birth, Vladimir and Estragon complement each other and live in hope for Godot's arrival and the revelation and resolution it implies ("Tonight perhaps we shall sleep in his place, in the warmth, our bellies full, on the straw. It is worth waiting for that, is it not?"). The hope that Godot might come, that purpose is possible even in the face of almost certain disappointment, is their sustaining illusion and the play's ultimate comic affirmation. As Vladimir explains, "What are we doing here, *that* is the question. And we are blessed in this, that we happen to know the answer. Yes, in this immense confusion one thing alone is clear. We are waiting for Godot to come. . . . We have kept our appointment and that's an end to that. We are not saints, but we have kept our appointment. How many people can boast as much?" To which Estragon replies: "Billions." By the comic calculus of *Waiting for Godot* continuing to believe in the absence of the possibility of belief is true heroism and the closest we get to human fulfillment. Beckett's play makes clear that the illusions that prevent us from confronting the core truth of human existence must be stripped away, whether in the storm scene of act 3 of KING LEAR when bare unaccommodated man is revealed or here on a "Country road. A tree. Evening."

MEDEA 9

(431 B.C.) *by Euripides*

Medea, *with its conflict between the boundless egoism of the husband and the boundless passion of the wife, was a completely up-to-date play. Accordingly, the disputes, the abuse, and the logic used by all its characters are essentially bourgeois. Jason is stiff with clever- ness and magnanimity; while Medea philosophizes on the social position of women—the dishonourable necessity which makes a woman surrender herself in marriage to a strange man and pay a rich dowry for the privilege—and declares that bearing children is far more brave and dangerous than fighting in battle. It is impossible for us to admire the play wholeheartedly; yet it was a revolution in its time, and it shows the true fertility of the new art.*

—Werner Jaeger, *Paideia: The Ideals of Greek Culture*

When *Medea*, commonly regarded as Euripides' masterpiece, was first per- formed at Athens's Great Dionysia, Euripides was awarded the third (and last) prize, behind Sophocles and Euphorion. It is not difficult to understand why. Euripides violates its audience's most cherished gender and moral illusions, while shocking with the unimaginable. Arguably for the first time in Western drama a woman fully commanded the stage from beginning to end, orches- trating the play's terrifying actions. Defying accepted gender assumptions that prescribed passive and subordinate roles for women, Medea combines the steely determination and wrath of Achilles with the wiles of Odysseus. The first Athenian audience had never seen Medea's like before, at least not in the heroic terms Euripides treats her. After Jason has cast off Medea—his wife, the mother of his children, and the woman who helped him to secure the Golden Fleece and eliminate the usurper of Jason's throne at Iolcus—in order to marry the daughter of King Creon of Corinth, Medea responds to his betrayal by destroying all of Jason's prospects as a husband, father, and presumptive heir to a powerful throne. She causes a horrible death of Jason's intended, Glauce, and Creon, who tries in vain to save his daughter. Most shocking of all, and possibly Euripides' singular innovation to the legend, Medea murders her two sons, allowing her vengeful passion to trump and cancel her maternal affections. Clytemnestra in Aeschylus's ORESTEIA conspires to murder her husband as well, but she is in turn executed by her son, Orestes, whose punishment is divinely and civilly sanctioned by the trilogy's conclusion. Medea, by contrast, adds infanticide to her crimes but still escapes Jason's vengeance or Corinthian justice on a flying chariot sent by the god Helios to assist her. Medea, triumphant after the carnage she has perpetrated, seemingly evades the moral consequences of her actions and is shown by Euripides apotheosized as a divinely sanctioned, supreme force. The play simultaneously and paradoxically presents Medea's claim on the audience's sympathy as a woman betrayed, as a victim of male oppression and her own divided nature, and as a monster and a warning. Medea frightens as a female violator and overreacher who lets her passion overthrow her reason, whose love is so massive and all-consuming that it is transformed into self-destructive and boundless hatred. It is little wonder that Euripides' defiance of virtually every dramatic and gender assumption of his time caused his tragedy to fail with his first critics. The complexity and contradictions of Medea still resonate with audiences, while the play continues to unsettle and challenge. *Medea*, with literature's most titanic female protagonist, remains one of drama's most daring assaults on an audience's moral sensibility and conception of the world.

Euripides is ancient Greek drama's great iconoclast, the shatterer of consoling illusions. With Euripides, the youngest of the three great Athenian tragedians of the fifth century B.C., Attic drama takes on a disturbingly recognizable modern tone. Regarded by Aristotle as "the most tragic of the poets," Euripides provided deeply spiritual, moral, and psychological explorations of exceptional and domestic life at a time when Athenian confidence and certainty were moving toward breakup. Mirroring this gathering doubt and anxiety, Euripides reflects the various intellectual, cultural, and moral controversies of his day. It is not too far-fetched to suggest that the world after Athens's golden age in the fifth century became Euripidean, as did the drama that responded to it. In several senses, therefore, it is Euripides whom Western drama can claim as its central progenitor.

Euripides wrote 92 plays, of which 18 have survived, by far the largest number of works by the great Greek playwrights and a testimony both to the accidents of literary survival and of his high regard by following generations. An iconoclast in his life and his art, Euripides set the prototype for the modern alienated artist in opposition. By contrast to Aeschylus and Sophocles, Euripides played no public role in the life of his times. An intellectual and artist who wrote in isolation (tradition says in a cave in his native Salamis), his plays won the first prize at Athens's annual Great Dionysia only four times, and his critics, particularly Aristophanes, took on Euripides as a frequent target. Aristophanes charged him with persuading his countrymen that the gods did not exist, with debunking the heroic, and with teaching moral degeneration that transformed Athenians into "marketplace loungers, tricksters, and scoundrels." Euripides' immense reputation and influence came for the most part only after his death, when the themes and innovations he pioneered were better appreciated and his plays eclipsed in popularity those of all of the other great Athenian playwrights.

Critic Eric Havelock has summarized the Euripidean dramatic revolution as "putting on stage rooms never seen before." Instead of a palace's throne room, Euripides takes his audience into the living room and presents the conflicts and crises of characters who resemble not the heroic paragons of Aeschylus and Sophocles but the audience themselves—mixed, fallible, contradictory, and vulnerable. As Aristophanes accurately points out, Euripides brought to the stage "familiar affairs" and "household things." Euripides opened up drama for the exploration of central human and social questions embedded in ordinary life and human nature. The essential component of all Euripides' plays is a challenging reexamination of orthodoxy and conventional beliefs. If the ways of humans are hard to fathom in Aeschylus and Sophocles, at least the design and purpose of the cosmos are assured, if not always accepted. For Euripides, the ability of the gods and the cosmos to provide certainty and order is as doubtful as an individual's preference for the good. In Euripides' cosmogony, the gods resemble those of Homer's, full of pride, passion, vindictiveness, and irrational characteristics that pattern the world of humans. Divine will and order are most often in Euripides' dramas replaced by a random fate, and the tragic hero is offered little consolation as the victim of forces that are beyond his or her control. Justice is shown as either illusory or a delusion, and the myths are brought down to the level of the familiar and the recognizable. Euripides has been described as drama's first great realist, the playwright who relocated tragic action to everyday life and portrayed gods and heroes with recognizable human and psychological traits. Aristotle related in the *Poetics* that "Sophocles said he drew men as they ought to be, and Euripides as they were." Because Euripides' characters offer us so many contrary aspects and are driven by both the rational and the irrational, the playwright earns the distinction of being considered the first great psychological artist in the modern sense, due to his awareness of the complex motives and ambiguities that make up human identity and determine behavior.

Euripides is also one of the first playwrights to feature heroic women at the center of the action. Medea dominates the stage as no woman character had ever done before. The play opens with Medea's nurse confirming how much Medea is suffering from Jason's betrayal and the tutor of Medea's children revealing that Creon plans to banish Medea and her two sons from Corinth. Medea's first words are an offstage scream and curse as she hears the news of Creon's judgment. The Nurse's sympathetic reaction to Medea's misery sounds the play's dominant theme of the danger of passion overwhelming reason, judgment, and balance, particularly in a woman like Medea, unschooled in suffering and used to commanding rather than being commanded. Better, says the Nurse, to have no part of greatness or glory: "The middle way, neither high nor low is best. . . . Good never comes from overreaching." Medea then takes the stage to win the sympathy of the Chorus, made up of Corinthian women. Her opening speech has been described as one of literature's earliest feminist manifestos, in which she declares, "Of all creatures on earth, we women are the most wretched," and goes on to attack dowries that purchase husbands in exchange for giving men ownership of women's bodies and fate, arranged marriages, and the double standard:

> When a man grows tired of his wife and home,
> He is free to look about for someone new.
> We wives are forced to count on just one man.
> They say, we live safe at home while men go to battle.
> I'd rather stand three times in the front line than bear one child!

Medea wins the Chorus's complicit silence on her intended intrigue to avenge herself on Jason and their initial sympathy as an aggrieved woman. She next confronts Creon to persuade him to postpone his banishment order for one day so she can arrange a destination and some support for her children. Medea's servility and deference to Creon and the sentimental appeal she mounts on behalf of her children gain his concession. After he departs, Medea reveals her deception of and contempt for Creon, announcing that her vengeance plot now extends beyond Jason to include both Creon and his daughter.

There follows the first of three confrontational scenes between Medea and Jason, the dramatic core of the play. Euripides presents Jason as a self-satisfied rationalist, smoothly and complacently justifying the violations of his love and obligation to Medea as sensible, accepted expedience. Jason asserts that his self-interest and ambition for wealth and power are superior claims over his affection, loyalty, and duty to the woman who has betrayed her parents, murdered her brother, exiled herself from her home, and conspired for his sake. Medea rages ineffectually in response, while attempting unsuccessfully to reach Jason's heart and break through an egotism that shows him incapable of understanding or empathy. As critic G. Norwood has observed, "Jason is a superb study—a compound of brilliant manners, stupidity, and cynicism." In the drama's debate between Medea and Jason, the play brilliantly sets in conflict essential polarities in the human condition, between male/female, husband/wife, reason/passion, and head/heart.

Before the second round with Jason, Medea encounters Aegeus, king of Athens, who is in search of a cure for his childlessness. Medea agrees to use her powers as a sorceress to help him in exchange for refuge in Athens. Aristotle criticized this scene as extraneous, but a case can be made that Aegeus's despair over his lack of children gives Medea the idea that Jason's ultimate destruction would be to leave him similarly childless. The evolving scheme to eliminate Jason's intended bride and offspring sets the context for Medea's second meeting with Jason in which she feigns acquiescence to Jason's decision and proposes that he should keep their children with him. Jason agrees to seek Glauce's approval for Medea's apparent self-sacrificing generosity, and the children depart with him, carrying a poisoned wedding gift to Glauce.

First using her children as an instrument of her revenge, Medea will next manage to convince herself in the internal struggle that leads to the play's climax that her love for her children must give way to her vengeance, that maternal affection and reason are no match for her irrational hatred. After the Tutor returns with the children and a messenger reports the horrible deaths of Glauce and Creon, Medea resolves her conflict between her love for her children and her hatred for Jason in what scholar John Ferguson has called "possibly the finest speech in all Greek tragedy." Medea concludes her self-assessment by stating, "I know the evil that I do, but my fury is stronger than my will. Passion is the curse of man." It is the struggle within Medea's soul, which Euripides so powerfully dramatizes, between her all-consuming vengeance and her reason and better nature that gives her villainy such tragic status. Her children's offstage screams finally echo Medea's own opening agony. On stage the Chorus tries to comprehend such an unnatural crime as matricide through precedent and concludes: "What can be strange or terrible after this?" Jason arrives too late to rescue his children from the "vile murderess," only to find Medea beyond his reach in a chariot drawn by dragons with the lifeless bodies of his sons beside her. The roles of Jason and Medea from their first encounter are here dramatically reversed: Medea is now triumphant, refusing Jason any comfort or concession, and Jason ineffectually rages and curses the gods for his destruction, now feeling the pain of losing everything he most desired, as he had earlier inflicted on Medea. "Call me lioness or Scylla, as you will," Medea calls down to Jason, ". . . as long as I have reached your vitals."

Medea's titanic passions have made her simultaneously subhuman in her pitiless cruelty and superhuman in her willful, limitless strength and determination. The final scene of her escape in her god-sent flying chariot, perhaps the most famous and controversial use of the deus ex machina in drama, ultimately makes a grand theatrical, psychological, and shattering ideological point. Medea has destroyed all in her path, including her human self, to satisfy her passion, becoming at the play's end, neither a hero nor a villain but a fearsome force of nature: irrational, impersonal, destructive power that sweeps aside human aspirations, affections, and the consoling illusions of mercy and order in the universe.

TWELFTH NIGHT

10

(c. 1600–02)
by William Shakespeare

Twelfth Night is the climax of Shakespeare's early achievement in comedy. The effects and values of the earlier comedies are here subtly embodied in the most complex structure which Shakespeare had yet created. But the play also looks forward: the pressure to dissolve the comedy, to realize and finally abandon the burden of laughter, is an intrinsic part of its "perfection." Viola's clear-eyed and affirmative vision of her own and the world's rationality is a triumph and we desire it; yet we realize its vulnerability, and we come to realize that virtue in disguise is only totally triumphant when evil is not in disguise—is not truly present at all. Having solved magnificently the problems of this particular form of comedy, Shakespeare was evidently not tempted to repeat his triumph. After Twelfth Night *the so-called comedies required for their happy resolutions more radical characters and devices—omniscient and omnipresent Dukes, magic, and resurrection. More obvious miracles are needed for comedy to exist in a world in which evil also exists, not merely incipiently but with power.*

—Joseph H. Summers, "The Masks of *Twelfth Night*"

William Shakespeare was in his mid-30s and at the height of his dramatic powers when he wrote *Twelfth Night*, his culminating masterpiece of romantic comedy. There is perhaps no more rousing, amusing, or lyrical celebration of the transforming wonderment of love nor a more knowing depiction of its follies or the forces allied against it. *Twelfth Night* is the ninth in a series of comedies Shakespeare wrote during the 1590s that includes *The Comedy of Errors, The Taming of the Shrew, A MIDSUMMER NIGHT'S DREAM, The Merchant of Venice,* and *As You Like It* and is a masterful synthesis of them all, unsurpassed in the artistry of its execution. In recognizing the barriers to love it also anticipates some of the preoccupations of the three dark comedies that followed— *Troilus and Cressida, All's Well That Ends Well,* and *Measure for Measure*—the great tragedies that would dominate the next decade of Shakespeare's work, as well as the tragicomic romances—*Pericles, Cymbeline, The Winter's Tale,* and *THE TEMPEST*—that conclude Shakespeare's dramatic career. Given the arc of that career, *Twelfth Night* stands at the summit of his comic vision, the last and greatest of Shakespeare's pure romantic comedies, but with the clouds that would darken the subsequent plays already gathering. Shakespeare never again returned to the exultant, triumphant tone of sunny celebration that suffuses the play. Yet what makes *Twelfth Night* so satisfying and impressive, as well as entertaining, is its clear-eyed acknowledgment of the challenge to its merriment in the counterforces of grief, melancholy, and sterile self-enclosure that stand in the way of the play's joyous affirmation. The comedy of *Twelfth Night* is earned by demonstrating all that must be surmounted for desire to reach fulfillment.

Twelfth Night, or What You Will was written between 1600 and 1602. The earliest reference to a performance appears in the diary of barrister John Manningham who in February 1602 recorded that the play was acted in the Middle Temple "at our feast." He found it "much like the Commedy of Errores or Menechmi in Plautus, but most like an neere to that in Italian called *Inganni*." Manningham provides a useful summary of Shakespeare's sources and plot devices in which a story of identical twins and mistaken identities is derived both from his earlier comedy and its ancient Roman inspiration, Plautus's *The Twin Menaechmi*. This is joined with an intrigue plot of gender disguise borrowed from popular 16th-century Italian comedies, particularly *Gl'Ingannati* (*The Deceived Ones*), in which a disguised young woman serves as a page to the man she loves. Shakespeare also employs elements of the new comedy of humours, popularized by Ben Jonson's *Every Man in His Humour* in 1598, for his own invention of the duping of the choleric Malvolio. Mistaken identities, comic misadventures in love, and the overthrow of repression, pretense, and selfishness are all united under the festive tone of the play's title, which suggests the exuberant saturnalian celebration of the twelfth day after Christmas, the Feast of the Epiphany. For the Elizabethans, Twelfth Night was the culminating holiday of the traditional Christmas revels in which gifts were exchanged, rigid proprieties suspended, and good fellowship affirmed. Scholars have speculated that *Twelfth Night* may have been first acted at court on January 6, 1601, as part of the entertainment provided for a Tuscan duke, Don Virginio Orsino, Queen Elizabeth's guest of honor. Whether it was actually performed on Twelfth Night, the play is, like *A Midsummer Night's Dream*, a "festive comedy," in C. L. Barber's phrase, that captures the spirit of a holiday in which social rules and conventions are subverted for a liberating spell of topsy-turviness and revelry.

As in all of Shakespeare's comedies, *Twelfth Night* treats the obstacles faced by lovers in fulfilling their desires. In an influential essay, "The Two Worlds of Shakespearean Comedy," Sherman Hawkins has detected two basic structural patterns in Shakespeare's comedies. One is marked by escape, in which young lovers, facing opposition in the form of parental or civil authority, depart the jurisdiction of both into a green world where they are freed from external constraints and liberated to resolve all the impediments to their passions. This is the pattern of *Two Gentlemen of Verona*, *A Midsummer Night's Dream*, *The Merchant of Venice*, *The Winter's Tale*, and *Cymbeline*. The other dominant pattern in Shakespeare's comedies, as employed in *The Comedy of Errors*, *Love's Labour's Lost*, *Much Ado About Nothing*, and *Twelfth Night*, is not escape but invasion. In these plays the arrival of outsiders serves as a catalyst to upset stalemated relationships and to revivify a stagnating community. "The obstacles to love in comedies of this alternate pattern," Hawkins argues, "are not external—social convention, favored rivals, disapproving parents. Resistance comes from the lovers themselves." The intrusion of new characters and the new relationships they stimulate serve to break the emotional deadlock and allow true love to flourish.

As *Twelfth Night* opens, Orsino, the duke of Illyria, is stalled in his desire for the countess Olivia, who, in mourning for her brother, has "abjured the company and sight of men" to live like a "cloistress" for seven years to protract an excessive, melancholy love of grief. As Orsino makes clear in the play's famous opening speech, lacking a focus for his affection due to Olivia's resistance, he indulges in the torment of unrequited love:

> If music be the food of love, play on,
> Give me excess of it that, surfeiting,
> The appetite may sicken and so die.
> That strain again, it had a dying fall.
> O, it came o'er my ear like the sweet sound
> That breathes upon a bank of violets,
> Stealing and giving odour. Enough, no more,
> 'Tis not so sweet now as it was before.

Both have withdrawn into self-centered, sentimental melancholy, and the agents to break through the narcissistic impediments to true love and the stasis in Illyria are the shipwrecked twins Viola and Sebastian. Viola, believing her brother drowned, dresses as a man to seek protection as a page in the household of Orsino. As the young man Cesario, she is commissioned by Orsino, with whom she has fallen in love, as his envoy to Olivia. Viola, one of Shakespeare's greatest heroines in her wit, understanding, and resourcefulness, is, like Olivia, mourning a brother, but her grief neither isolates nor paralyzes her; neither is her love for Orsino an indulgence in an abstract, sentimental longing. It is precisely her superiority in affection and humanity that offers an implied lesson to both duke and countess in the proper working of the heart. Both Olivia and Orsino will be instructed through the agency of Viola's arrival that true love is not greedy and self-consuming but unselfish and generous. Initially Viola plays her part as persistent ambassador of love too well. In a scene that masterfully exploits Viola's gender-bending disguise (as performed in Shakespeare's time, a boy plays a young woman playing a boy) and her ambivalent mission to win a lady for the man she loves, Viola succeeds in penetrating Olivia's various physical and emotional defenses by her witty mockery of the established language and conventions of courtship. Accused of being "the cruell'st she alive / If you will lead these graces to the grave / And leave the world no copy," Olivia finally yields, but it is Cesario, not Orsino who captures her affection. In summarizing the romantic complications produced by her persuasiveness, Viola observes:

> . . . As I am man,
> My state is desperate for my master's love;
> As I am woman (now alas the day!),
> What thriftless sights shall poor Olivia breathe!
> O time, thou must untangle this, not I,
> It is too hard a knot for me t'untie.

Not too hard, however, for the playwright, as Shakespeare sets in motion some of his funniest and ingenious scenes leading up to the untangling.

The romantic comedy of Orsino, Olivia, and Viola/Cesario is balanced and contrasted by a second plot involving Olivia's carousing cousin, Sir Toby Belch; his gull, the fatuous Sir Andrew Aguecheek, whom Toby encourages in a hopeless courtship of Olivia for the sake of extracting his money; the maid Maria; Olivia's jester, Feste; and Olivia's steward, Malvolio. Maria describes the dutiful, restrained, judgmental Malvolio as "a kind of puritan," who condemns the late-night carousing of Sir Toby and his companions and urges his mistress to dismiss her jester. As the sour opponent of revelry, Malvolio prompts Sir Toby to utter one of the plays most famous lines: "Dost thou think because thou art virtuous there shall be no more cakes and ale?" Virtues, Toby suggests, must acknowledge and accommodate the human necessity for the pleasures of life. All need a holiday. Malvolio as the adversary of the forces of festival that the play celebrates will be exposed as, in Olivia's words, "sick of self-love" who tastes "with a distemper'd appetite." Malvolio is, therefore, linked with both Orsino and Olivia in their self-centeredness. By connecting Malvolio's particular brand of self-enclosure in opposition to the spirit of merriment represented by Sir Toby and his company of revelers, Shakespeare expands his critique of the impediments to love into a wider social context that recognizes the efficacy of misrule to break down the barriers isolating individuals. The carousers conspire to convince Malvolio that Olivia has fallen in love with him, revealing his ambition for power and dominance that stands behind his holier-than-thou veneer. Malvolio aspires to become Count Malvolio, gaining Olivia to command others and securing the deference his egotism considers his due. Convinced by a forged love letter from Olivia to be surly with the servants, to smile constantly in Olivia's presence, and to wear yellow stockings cross-gartered (all of which Olivia abhors), the capering Malvolio prompts Olivia to conclude that he has lost his wits and orders his confinement in a dark cell. Symbolically, Malvolio's punishment is fitted to his crime of self-obsession, of misappropriating love for self-gain.

With the play's killjoy bated, chastened, and contained, the magic of love and reconciliation flourishes, and *Twelfth Night* builds to its triumphant, astounding climax. First Sebastian surfaces in Illyria and, mistaken for Cesario, finds himself dueling with Sir Andrew and claimed by Olivia as her groom in a hastily arranged wedding. Next Viola, as Cesario, is mistaken for Sebastian by Antonio, her brother's rescuer, and is saluted by Olivia as her recently married husband, prompting Orsino's wrath at being betrayed by his envoy. Chaos and confusion give way to wonderment, reunion, and affection with the appearance of Sebastian on stage to the astonishment of Olivia and Orsino, who see Cesario's double, and to the joy of Viola who is reunited with her lost brother. Olivia's shock at having married a perfect stranger, that the man she had loved as Cesario is a woman, and Orsino's loss of Olivia are happily resolved in a crescendo of wish fulfillment and poetic justice. Olivia fell in love with a woman but gains her male replica; Orsino learns that the page he has grown so fond of was actually a woman. Viola gains the man she loves, and the formerly lovesick Orsino now has an object of his affection worthy of his passion.

The one discordant note in the festivities is Malvolio. He is released from his confinement, and Olivia learns of the "sportful malice" of his deception. Invited to share the joke and acknowledge its justification, Malvolio exits with a curse on the guilty and the innocent alike: "I'll be revenged on the whole pack of you." Shakespeare allows Malvolio's dissent to the comic climax of love and laughter to stand. Malvolio, as Olivia acknowledges, has "been most notoriously abused." Much of the laughter of *Twelfth Night* has come at his expense, and if the play breaks through the selfish privacy of Orsino and Olivia into love, companionship, and harmony, Malvolio remains implacable and unresolved. He is an embodiment of the dark counterforce of hatred and evil that will begin to dominate Shakespeare's imagination and claim mastery in the tragedies and the dark comedies. *Twelfth Night* ends in the joyful fulfillment of love's triumph, but the sense of this being the exception not the rule is sounded by Feste's concluding song in which rain, not sunshine, is the norm, and Twelfth Night comes only once a year:

> When that I was and a little tiny boy,
>   With hey, ho, the wind and the rain,
> A foolish thing was but a toy,
>   For the rain it raineth every day.
>
> But when I came to man's estate,
>   With hey, ho, the wind and the rain,

'Gainst knaves and thieves men shut their gate,
  For the rain it raineth every day.

But when I came, alas, to wive,
  With hey, ho, the wind and the rain,
By swaggering could I never thrive,
  For the rain it raineth every day.

But when I came unto my beds,
  With hey, ho, the wind and the rain,
With tosspots still had drunken heads,
  For the rain it raineth every day.

A great while ago the world begun,
  With hey, ho, the wind and the rain,
But that's all one, our play is done,
  And we'll strive to please you every day.

A DOLL'S HOUSE
11

(1879) *by Henrik Ibsen*

Whether one reads A Doll's House *as a technical revolution in modern theater, the modern tragedy, the first feminist play since the Greeks, a Hegelian allegory of the spirit's historical evolution, or a Kierkegaardian leap from aesthetic into ethical life, the deep structure of the play as a modern myth of self-transformation ensures it perennial importance as a work that honors the vitality of the human spirit in women and men.*
— Errol Durbach, *A Doll's House: Ibsen's Myth of Transformation*

More than one literary historian has identified the precise moment when modern drama began: December 4, 1879, with the publication of Ibsen's *Et dukkehjem* (*A Doll's House*), or, more dramatically at the explosive climax of the first performance in Copenhagen on December 21, 1879, with the slamming of the door as Nora Helmer shockingly leaves her comfortable home, respectable marriage, husband, and children for an uncertain future of self-discovery. Nora's shattering exit ushered in a new dramatic era, legitimizing the exploration of key social problems as a serious concern for the modern theater, while sounding the opening blast in the modern sexual revolution. As Henrik Ibsen's biographer Michael Meyer has observed, "No play had ever before contributed so momentously to the social debate, or been so widely and furiously discussed among people who were not normally interested in theatrical or even artistic matter." A contemporary reviewer of the play also declared: "When Nora slammed the door shut on her marriage, walls shook in a thousand homes."

Ibsen set in motion a transformation of drama as distinctive in the history of the theater as the one that occurred in fifth-century B.C. Athens or Elizabethan London. Like the great Athenian dramatists and William Shakespeare, Ibsen fundamentally redefined drama and set a standard that later playwrights have had to absorb or challenge. The stage that he inherited had largely ceased to function as a serious medium for the deepest consideration of human themes and values. After Ibsen drama was restored as an important truth-telling vehicle for a comprehensive criticism of life. *A Doll's House* anatomized on stage for the first time the social, psychological, emotional, and moral truths beneath the placid surface of a conventional, respectable marriage while creating a new, psychologically complex modern heroine, who still manages to shock and unsettle audiences more than a century later. *A Doll's House* is, therefore, one of the groundbreaking modern literary texts that established in fundamental ways the responsibility and cost of women's liberation and gender equality. According to critic Evert Sprinchorn, Nora is "the richest, most complex" female dramatic character since Shakespeare's heroines, and as feminist critic Kate Millett has argued in *Sexual Politics*, Ibsen was the first dramatist since the Greeks to challenge the myth of male dominance. "In Aeschylus' dramatization of the myth," Millett asserts, "one is permitted to see patriarchy confront matriarchy, confound it through the knowledge of paternity, and come off triumphant. Until Ibsen's Nora slammed the door announcing the sexual revolution, this triumph went nearly uncontested."

The momentum that propelled Ibsen's daring artistic and social revolt was sustained principally by his outsider status, as an exile both at home and abroad. His last deathbed word was *"Tvertimod!"* (On the contrary!), a fitting epitaph and description of his artistic and intellectual mindset. Born in Skien, Norway, a logging town southwest of Oslo, Ibsen endured a lonely and impoverished childhood, particularly after the bankruptcy of his businessman father when Ibsen was eight. At 15, he was sent to Grimstad as an apothecary's apprentice, where he lived for six years in an attic room on meager pay, sustained by reading romantic poetry, sagas, and folk ballads. He later recalled feeling "on a war footing with the little community where I felt I was being suppressed by my situation and by circumstances in general." His first play, *Cataline*, was a historical drama featuring a revolutionary hero who reflects Ibsen's own alienation. "*Cataline* was written," the playwright later recalled, "in a little provincial town, where it was impossible for me to give expression to all that fermented in me except by mad, riotous pranks, which brought down upon me the ill will of all the respectable citizens who could not enter into that world which I was wrestling with alone."

Largely self-educated, Ibsen failed the university entrance examination to pursue medical training and instead pursued a career in the theater. In 1851 he began a 13-year stage apprenticeship in Bergen and Oslo, doing everything from sweeping the stage to directing, stage managing, and writing mostly verse dramas based on Norwegian legends and historical subjects. The experience gave him a solid knowledge of the stage conventions of the day, particularly of the so-called well-made play of the popular French playwright Augustin Eugène Scribe and his many imitators, with its emphasis on a complicated, artificial plot based on secrets, suspense, and surprises. Ibsen would transform the conventions of the well-made play into the modern problem play, exploring controversial social and human questions that had never before been dramatized. Although his stage experience in Norway was marked chiefly by failure, Ibsen's apprenticeship was a crucial testing ground for perfecting his craft and providing him with the skills to mount the assault on theatrical conventions and moral complacency in his mature work.

In 1864 Ibsen began a self-imposed exile from Norway that would last 27 years. He traveled first to Italy, where he was joined by his wife, Susannah, whom he had married in 1858, and his son. The family divided its time between Italy and Germany. The experience was liberating for Ibsen; he felt that he had "escaped from darkness into light," releasing the productive energy with which he composed the succession of plays that brought him worldwide fame. His first important works, *Brand* (1866) and *Peer Gynt* (1867), were poetic dramas, very much in the romantic mode of the individual's conflict with experience and the gap between heroic assertion and accomplishment, between sobering reality and blind idealism. *Pillars of Society* (1877) shows him experimenting with ways of introducing these central themes into a play reflecting modern life, the first in a series of realistic dramas that redefined the conventions and subjects of the modern theater.

The first inklings of his next play, *A Doll's House*, are glimpsed in Ibsen's journal under the heading "Notes for a Modern Tragedy":

> There are two kinds of moral laws, two kinds of conscience, one for men and one, quite different, for women. They don't understand each other; but in practical life, woman is judged by masculine law, as though she weren't a woman but a man.
>
> The wife in the play ends by having no idea what is right and what is wrong; natural feelings on the one hand and belief in authority on the other lead her to utter distraction. . . .
>
> Moral conflict. Weighed down and confused by her trust in authority, she loses faith in her own morality, and in her fitness to bring up her children. Bitterness. A mother in modern society, like certain insects, retires and dies once she has done her duty by propagating the race. Love of life, of home, of husband and children and family. Now and then, as women do, she shrugs off her thoughts. Suddenly anguish and fear return. Everything must be borne alone. The catastrophe approaches, mercilessly, inevitably. Despair, conflict, and defeat.

To tell his modern tragedy based on gender relations, Ibsen takes his audience on an unprecedented, intimate tour of a contemporary, respectable marriage. Set during the Christmas holidays, *A Doll's House* begins with Nora Helmer completing the finishing touches on the family's celebrations. Her husband, Torvald, has recently been named a bank manager, promising an end to the family's former straitened financial circumstances, and Nora is determined to celebrate the holiday with her husband and three children in style. Despite

Torvald's disapproval of her indulgences, he relents, giving her the money she desires, softened by Nora's childish play-acting, which gratifies his sense of what is expected of his "lark" and "squirrel." Beneath the surface of this apparently charming domestic scene is a potentially damning and destructive secret. Seven years before Nora had saved the life of her critically ill husband by secretly borrowing the money needed for a rest cure in Italy. Knowing that Torvald would be too proud to borrow money himself, Nora forged her dying father's name on the loan she received from Krogstad, a banking associate of Torvald.

The crisis comes when Nora's old schoolfriend Christina Linde arrives in need of a job. At Nora's urging Torvald aids her friend by giving her Krogstad's position at the bank. Learning that he is to be dismissed, Krogstad threatens to expose Nora's forgery unless she is able to persuade Torvald to reinstate him. Nora fails to convince Torvald to relent, and after receiving his dismissal notice, Krogstad sends Torvald a letter disclosing the details of the forgery. The incriminating letter remains in the Helmers' mailbox like a ticking timebomb as Nora tries to distract Torvald from reading it and Christina attempts to convince Krogstad to withdraw his accusation. Torvald eventually reads the letter following the couple's return from a Christmas ball and explodes in recriminations against his wife, calling her a liar and a criminal, unfit to be his wife and his children's mother. "Now you've wrecked all my happiness—ruined my whole future," Torvald insists. "Oh, it's awful to think of. I'm in a cheap little grafter's hands; he can do anything he wants with me, ask me for anything, play with me like a puppet—and I can't breathe a word. I'll be swept down miserably into the depths on account of a featherbrained woman." Torvald's reaction reveals that his formerly expressed high moral rectitude is hypocritical and self-serving. He shows himself worried more about appearances than true morality, caring about his reputation rather than his wife. However, when Krogstad's second letter arrives in which he announces his intention of pursuing the matter no further, Torvald joyfully informs Nora that he is "saved" and that Nora should forget all that he has said, assuming that the normal relation between himself and his "frightened little songbird" can be resumed. Nora, however, shocks Torvald with her reaction.

Nora, profoundly disillusioned by Torvald's response to Krogstad's letter, a response bereft of the sympathy and heroic self-sacrifice she had hoped for, orders Torvald to sit down for a serious talk, the first in their married life, in which she reviews their relationship. "I've been your doll-wife here, just as at home I was Papa's doll-child," Nora explains. "And in turn the children have been my dolls. I thought it was fun when you played with me, just as they thought it fun when I played with them. That's been our marriage, Torvald." Nora has acted out the 19th-century ideal of the submissive, unthinking, dutiful daughter and wife, and it has taken Torvald's reaction to shatter the illusion and to force an illumination. Nora explains:

When the big fright was over—and it wasn't from any threat against me, only for what might damage you—when all the danger was past, for you it was just as if nothing had happened. I was exactly the same, your little lark, your doll, that you'd have to handle with double care now that I'd turned out so brittle and frail. Torvald—in that instant it dawned on me that I've been living here with a stranger.

Nora tells Torvald that she no longer loves him because he is not the man she thought he was, that he was incapable of heroic action on her behalf. When Torvald insists that "no man would sacrifice his honor for love," Nora replies: "Millions of women have done just that."

Nora finally resists the claims Torvald mounts in response that she must honor her duties as a wife and mother, stating,

> I don't believe in that anymore. I believe that, before all else, I'm a human being, no less than you—or anyway, I ought to try to become one. I know the majority thinks you're right, Torvald, and plenty of books agree with you, too. But I can't go on believing what the majority says, or what's written in books. I have to think over these things myself and try to understand them.

The finality of Nora's decision to forgo her assigned role as wife and mother for the authenticity of selfhood is marked by the sound of the door slamming and her exit into the wider world, leaving Torvald to survey the wreckage of their marriage.

Ibsen leaves his audience and readers to consider sobering truths: that married women are the decorative playthings and servants of their husbands who require their submissiveness, that a man's authority in the home should not go unchallenged, and that the prime duty of anyone is to arrive at an authentic human identity, not to accept the role determined by social conventions. That Nora would be willing to sacrifice everything, even her children, to become her own person proved to be, and remains, the controversial shock of *A Doll's House*, provoking continuing debate over Nora's motivations and justifications. The first edition of 8,000 copies of the play quickly sold out, and the play was so heatedly debated in Scandinavia in 1879 that, as critic Frances Lord observes, "many a social invitation in Stockholm during that winter bore the words, 'You are requested not to mention Ibsen's *Doll's House*!'" Ibsen was obliged to supply an alternative ending for the first German production when the famous leading lady Hedwig Niemann-Raabe refused to perform the role of Nora, stating that "I would never leave *my children*!" Ibsen provided what he would call a "barbaric outrage," an ending in which Nora's departure is halted at the doorway of her children's bedroom. The play served as a catalyst for an ongoing debate over feminism and women's rights. In 1898 Ibsen was honored by the Norwegian Society for Women's Rights and toasted as the "creator of Nora." Always the contrarian, Ibsen rejected the notion that *A Doll's House* champions the cause of women's rights:

> I have been more of a poet and less of a social philosopher than people generally tend to suppose. I thank you for your toast, but must disclaim the honor of having consciously worked for women's rights. I am not even quite sure what women's rights really are. To me it has been a question of human rights. And if you read my books carefully you will realize that. Of course it is incidentally desirable to solve the problem of women; but that has not been my whole object. My task has been the portrayal of human beings.

Despite Ibsen's disclaimer that *A Doll's House* should be appreciated as more than a piece of gender propaganda, that it deals with universal truths of human identity, it is nevertheless the case that Ibsen's drama is one of the milestones of the sexual revolution, sounding themes and advancing the cause of women's autonomy and liberation that echoes Mary Wollstonecraft's *A Vindication of the Rights of Woman* and anticipates subsequent works such as Kate Chopin's *The Awakening*, Virginia Woolf's *A Room of One's Own* and Betty Friedan's *The Feminine Mystique*. The impact of Nora's slamming the door of her doll's house is still being felt more than a century later.

THE CHERRY ORCHARD

(1903)

12

by Anton Chekhov

It is, as a rule, when a critic does not wish to commit himself or to trouble himself, that he refers to atmosphere. And, given time, something might be said in greater detail of the causes which produced this atmosphere—the strange dislocated sentences, each so erratic and yet cutting out the shape so firmly, of the realism, of the humor, of the artistic unity. But let the word atmosphere be taken literally to mean that Chekhov has contrived to shed over us a luminous vapor in which life appears as it is, without veils, transparent and visible to the depths. Long before the play was over, we seemed to have sunk below the surface of things and to be feeling our way among submerged but recognizable emotions. . . . In short, if it is permissible to use such vague language, I do not know how better to describe the sensation at the end of The Cherry Orchard, *than by saying that it sends one into the street feeling like a piano-played upon at last, not in the middle only but all over the keyboard and with the lid left open so that the sound goes on.*

—Virginia Woolf, "On *The Cherry Orchard*"

Modern drama has two indisputable founding fathers: Henrik Ibsen and Anton Chekhov. If Ibsen liberated drama's subject matter and restored the play as a serious criticism of life, Chekhov supplied the theater with a radically new method and dramatic form that altered all of the available conventions of dramatic production. In *The Seagull*, the first of his four major full-length plays, Chekhov has another playwright, Treplev, assert:

> I regard the stage of today as mere routine and prejudice. When the curtain goes up and the gifted beings, the high priests of the sacred art, appear by electric light, in a room with three sides to it, representing how people eat, drink, love, walk, and wear their jackets; when they strive to squeeze out a moral from the flat vulgar pictures and the flat vulgar phrases, a little tiny moral, easy to comprehend and handy for home consumption; when in a thousand variations they offer me always the same thing over and over again—then I take to my heels and run, as

Maupassant ran from the Eiffel Tower, which crushed his brain by its overwhelming vulgarity. . . . We must have new formulas. That's what we want. And if there are none, then it's better to have nothing at all.

Chekhov offered to drama the reformulation that Treplev calls for, a new formula that needed a new theory of acting and a radical reconception of drama itself to be understood and appreciated. No less a literary titan than Leo Tolstoy, who often disparaged Chekhov's plays in which "nothing happened," regarded Chekhov as his chief artistic rival. Chekhov, Tolstoy declared, "is an incomparable artist" who "created new forms of writing, completely new, in my opinion, to the entire world, the likes of which I have encountered nowhere." Of his drama, Tolstoy predicted "that in the future, perhaps a hundred years hence, people will be amazed at what they find in Chekhov about the inner workings of the human soul." Chekhov himself, with characteristic modesty, diminished his achievement, except as an innovator. "Everything I have written," he remarked, "will be forgotten in five or ten years; but the paths I have cut out will be safe and sound—my only service lies in this." No other dramatist in as few major works has asserted a comparable influence on the development of theater than has Chekhov. His two final plays are the culmination of his artistry as a playwright: If *THREE SISTERS* is Chekhov's most complex and ambitious drama, *The Cherry Orchard* is in many ways his most intriguing and emblematic play, the first of Chekhov's dramas to be translated into English and the first Russian play to command the world's stage. It continues to be his best-loved and most performed play, as well as one of the acknowledged foundation dramas upon which the modern theater has been built.

Remarkably, Chekhov fundamentally shaped two literary genres—modern drama and the modern short story—and it is a commonplace to view him as a fiction writer who turned to drama only in his final years. It is far more accurate to regard Chekhov as a lifelong dramatist who resorted to fiction by necessity to earn a living while the contemporary Russian theater caught up with his dramatic vision. In the words of Russian literature scholar David Magarshack, Chekhov

was a born dramatist whose first works of importance were three full-length plays, two written in his late teens and the third in his early twenties. He took up short-story writing for two reasons: first, because he had to support a large family which was entirely dependent on him, and the writing of short-stories was the quickest way of doing it; secondly, because the state of the Russian stage in the eighties and nineties of the last [19th] century was such that no serious playwright could hope to have his plays performed, let alone earn a decent living in the theatre.

Chekhov was born in 1860 in Taganrog on the Black Sea. His father was a former serf who rose to become a grocer but whose artistic interests as a choirmaster, violinist, and occasional painter took precedence over more practical considerations. Chekhov's interest in the theater was sparked by trips to the Taganrog Theatre and in home reenactments of such plays as Nikolai Gogol's *The Inspector General.* When Chekhov was 16, his father became bankrupt and relocated his family to a Moscow slum to avoid his creditors. Chekhov remained behind to finish his education at the local gymnasium, supporting himself by tutoring younger students. When he was 19, Chekhov joined his family in Moscow and assumed their financial support while enrolled in the medical program at Moscow University. He paid for his education and his family's upkeep by writing comic sketches and short stories for humorous magazines. When he became a doctor, in 1884, he continued writing stories and one-act satirical farces based on many of them, juggling a medical career ("my lawful spouse") and his writing ("my mistress"). Chekhov's career as a dramatist up to 1901 is treated in my consideration of *Three Sisters.* Here I will concentrate on Chekhov's final three years and the composition and staging of *The Cherry Orchard.*

By 1898, when Chekhov achieved his first great success with the Moscow Art Theater's landmark production of *The Seagull,* the tuberculosis that Chekhov had contracted during his student days had advanced beyond a cure. Chekhov settled in Yalta after suffering a pulmonary hemorrhage and did not see his plays staged by the Moscow Art Theater until their Crimean tour in 1900. At a rehearsal, however, he had met the actress Olga Knipper, who played Arkadina in *The Seagull,* and they were married in May 1901. If a biographically derived sense of provincial exile from Moscow stands behind the dramatic conflict of *Three Sisters,* Chekhov draws on other biographical circumstances in *The Cherry Orchard,* particularly his dispossession from Taganrog due to his father's bankruptcy. *The Cherry Orchard* was conceived and composed during the final stage of the illness that would take his life in 1904, yet Chekhov was adamant that what turned out to be his final work should be a comedy. Following the success of *Three Sisters* in 1901, Chekhov wrote to his wife, "I keep dreaming of writing a comic play, in which all hell will break loose. I don't know whether anything will come of it." Begun in 1902 and completed in September 1903, *The Cherry Orchard* "has turned out not a drama," Chekhov asserted, "but a comedy, in places even a farce." Konstantin Stanislavsky, who would produce and direct the play for the Moscow Art Theater, disagreed: "It isn't a comedy or a farce, as you claim—it's a tragedy." The dispute between playwright and director over *The Cherry Orchard*'s tone and intention that began with its first production has persisted in performances ever since. *The Cherry Orchard* is a play of such intriguing complexity and multiple (and at times contradictory) modes and methods that it can support either interpretation, while it ultimately is neither one nor the other—neither simply comedy nor tragedy—but something new altogether. In its challenge to the established dramatic genres, *The Cherry Orchard* helped establish the

tragicomic as the dominant modern dramatic mode, while its linkage of surface realism and the symbolic anticipated the techniques of the great literary
modernists of the 20th century, such as James Joyce and T. S. Eliot.

If *Three Sisters* is all about deferred and frustrated departures, *The Cherry
Orchard* by contrast commences with an arrival—the return to her heavily
mortgaged Russian estate of the widow Lyubov Andreevna Ranevskaya from
Paris where she had gone to forget the drowning death of her son five years
before. Like *Three Sisters*, in which the usual dramatic action is excluded, waiting establishes the central dramatic tension. Dominating the action is the
suspended question of what will become of the estate with its renowned cherry
orchard that must be sold unless a solution is found to recover the family's
fortune. Again, as in *Three Sisters*, Chekhov gathers together a large cast to
react collectively to the threat to the family while revealing its causes. They
include Madame Ranevskaya's indolent brother, Leonid Andreyevitch Gaev;
her daughter Anya and adopted daughter Varya; her son's former tutor, Trofimov; fellow landowner Pischchik; the bookkeeper, Yephikhov; and former
serf, now successful businessman Lopakhin. Included as well is a full compliment of servants—Charlotte, the governess; Yasha, the valet; Dunyasha, the
maid; and the ancient footman, Fiers. Act 1 of the play, subtitled "A Comedy
in Four Acts," appropriately is set in the nursery, where the family can evade
the present crisis by summoning up and recalling the past. As the Russian
critic A. R. Kugel has observed, "All the inhabitants of *The Cherry Orchard* are
children and their behavior is childish." To avoid the estate being auctioned,
Lopakhin offers the practical solution that the cherry orchard should be cut
down and the land divided into building lots for summer holiday makers. This
suggestion, which would pay off the family's debts and secure their future,
is greeted with shock and incredulity. "If there's anything of interest in the
entire district," Lyubov asserts, "even outstanding, it's none other than our
cherry orchard." For Gaev reference to the famous orchard in an encyclopedia
puts an end to such a suggestion. Both brother and sister reveal themselves
as incapable of decisive action or adult responsibility. Lyubov is a generous
but impractical sentimentalist; Gaev is more focused on his mental games of
billiards, his fruit candies, and considering hosting a jubilee celebration for
an old bookcase. His ideas to rescue the situation—Anya's marriage to a rich
man, Varya's marriage to Lopakhin, a gift from their rich great-aunt—are, in
his words, "several remedies, very many, and that really means I've none at
all." The often ridiculous, self-deluded behavior of all under the impending
threat of the family's dispossession sets the play's mixed tonality in which the
absurd collides with the portentous. The threat to the cherry orchard begins
to accumulate symbolic significance expressing the demise of an era in which
the Russian landed gentry and their entire leisured way of life are about to be
destroyed by the practicalities of a new materialistic order. Characteristically
Chekhov balances the accounts on both sides of the equation: Lyubov and

Gaev cherish the past and appreciate the beauty of the cherry orchard but are incapable of maintaining it; Lopakhin is so consumed by the practical that the orchard and house are nothing more than commodities. Lyubov and Gaev exist in the past; Lopakhin for the future, and the present is squandered in the often inconsequential and absurd behavior of all.

Act 2 shifts the scene outside near the orchard at sunset as each of the characters reacts to the impending now inevitable sale of the property, which begins to push them to a deeper understanding of themselves and their circumstances. Each member of the household is allowed a sympathetic moment. By revealing their suffering, loneliness, and isolation, Chekhov complicates and deepens his presentation of characters who are far too foolish to be taken as wholly tragic, but far too sensitive and recognizable in their suffering to be only laughed at. The breakup of the estate begins to put into perspective the characters' past, their natures, and a new set of future challenges. For Fiers, the coming dispossession means that the old order is passing. In the ancien régime, he says, "the peasants stood by the masters, the masters stood by the peasants, but now everything is all smashed up, you can't tell about anything." This tone of melancholy and nostalgic appraisal is countered by the young people, Anya, and Trofimov, whose idealism and commitment to a new future redeemed by work and selfless dedication cause Anya to ask, "What have you done to me, Petya, why don't I love the cherry orchard any longer the way I used to?"

The party scene of act 3—the ball following the auction—has been described by Chekhov scholar Laurence Senelick as "the supreme example of Chekhov's intermingling of subliminal symbol and surface reality." As desultory conversation takes place in the drawing room, against the forced gaiety of the dancing in the background, the characters await word about the result of the auction. The underlying tension surfaces in Madame Ranevskaya's argument with Trifimov about the value of her estate and her announcement of her intention to return to Paris and the lover who fleeced and deserted her. The tone of impending doom is broken by the comic elements of Charlotte's ventriloquism and magic tricks and Trofimov's tripping and falling down the stairs after delivering his moral judgments. The fateful news about the auction is delivered at the end of a farcical sequence in which Varya, squabbling with Yephikhov, strikes out at him with a pool cue only to hit the entering Lopakhin, who manages to announce that he has purchased the cherry orchard.

Symbolically act 4 returns to the nursery setting of act 1 but reverses its arrivals with departures. The dispossession and dispersal of the family is now complete as they all depart for an uncertain future, as an entire way of life is falling under the ax that can be heard outside. We are left suspended in uncertainty and a mixed mood. As the critic John Gassner observes, "Chekhov maintained a sensitive equilibrium between regret for the loss of old values and jubilation over the dawn of a new day. And it is the quality of detachment that also enabled him to equalize pathos and humor, and to render a probing account of the contradictions of human character."

Only Fiers remains as the curtain comes down:

> [*The stage is empty. The sound of keys being turned in the locks is heard, and then the noise of the carriages going away. It is quiet. Then the sound of an axe against the trees is heard in the silence sadly and by itself. Steps are heard.* FIERS *comes in from the door on the right. He is dressed as usual, in a short jacket and white waistcoat; slippers on his feet. He is ill. He goes to the door and tries the handle.*]

FIERS It's locked. They've gone away. [*Sits on a sofa*] They've forgotten about me. . . . Never mind, I'll sit here. . . . And Leonid Andreyevitch will have gone in a light overcoat instead of putting on his fur coat. . . . [*Sighs anxiously*] I didn't see. . . . Oh, these young people! [*Mumbles something that cannot be understood*] Life's gone on as if I'd never lived. [*Lying down*] I'll lie down. . . . You've no strength left in you, nothing left at all. . . . Oh, you . . . bungler! [*He lies immobile.*]

> [*The distant sound is heard, as if from the sky, of a breaking string, dying away sadly. Silence follows it, and only the sound is heard, some way away in the orchard, of the axe falling on the trees.*]

Curtain.

The conclusion here, despite a shared sonic effect, is contrary to that of Ibsen's *A DOLL'S HOUSE*. This is not the explosion of Nora's liberation and its blast to conventional orthodoxy; rather it is a slow and steady expiration, with the death of Fiers and the ceasing of his heartbeat echoed by the relentless sound of the ax falling on the trees. To the bang of Ibsen, Chekhov offers the whimper of a dying fall, frustrated wills and desires, a serious comedy of human errors and loss. Modern drama seems to gravitate between the poles of bang and whimper, between exploding the past certainties in decisive action and turning the focus of drama from action to inaction and paralysis. Chekhov is the master dramatist of inaction: He pioneered its stage representation by rejecting the long-functioning Aristotelian premises for a radically new dramatic method that replaced the reliance on a main plot and main characters with multiple plot lines, collective protagonists, and the fusion of all into a unified thematic whole. Chekhov's art, as expressed in *The Cherry Orchard* and his other works, features an essential humane truthfulness. "A play should be written," he argued, "in which people arrive, go away, have dinner, talk about the weather, and play cards. Life must be exactly as it is, and people as they are—not on stilts. . . . . Let everything on the stage be just as complicated, and at the same time just as simple as it is in life." Stripped of the usual dramatic action, Chekhov's plays locate their interest in the gradual revelation of character and circumstance "in all the grayness of their everyday life."

BACCHAE

13

(c. 406 B.C.)   *by Euripides*

In one key scene Dionysus asks the question which has perplexed theorists of tragedy: "would you really like to see what gives you pain?" Dionysus, ironic questioner and stage-manager of the action, is a double of the poet himself. The difference is that the god lacks the dramatist's compassion.
—John Davie, Preface to *Bacchae*, in *The Bacchae and Other Plays*

Euripides' *Bacchae* claims a preeminent place in both classical Greek drama and Euripides' career as his and his age's last great tragic drama. Written in Macedonia after the playwright's voluntary exile from Athens, the *Bacchae* was produced after Euripides' death around 406 B.C. A play of great poetry and suggestiveness, the *Bacchae* is in many ways Euripides' most provocative work. The only Greek drama to feature the god Dionysus as a central character, the *Bacchae* is a drama about belief and faith, expressed with Euripides' characteristic willingness to complicate easy answers. It has been interpreted as both Euripides' approval of Dionysian nature worship and his condemnation of its excesses. The violent natural forces Dionysus embodied are treated as both essential and terrifyingly destructive with Dionysus and his resister, Pentheus, presented in ways that raise as many questions as consolations. "*The Bacchae,*" poet and historian Thomas Macaulay wrote "is a glorious play. It is often very obscure; and I am not sure that I understand its general scope. But, as a piece of language, it is hardly equaled in the world. And, whether it was intended to encourage or to discourage fanaticism, the picture of fanatical excitement which it exhibits has never been rivaled." Critic J. Michael Walton has observed that "The sheer power and mystery of the *Bacchae* is so startling that it rightly belongs in the forefront of the greatest plays ever written." The *Bacchae* persists largely because of the play's astonishing capacity to harness psychological and emotional forces to form a central myth with far-reaching psychological, moral, and ontological implications.

As the Peloponnesian War (431–404 B.C.) ground on toward Athens's eventual defeat, Euripides completed a series of tragedies—*Electra* (413), *Phoenician Women* (409), and *Orestes* (408)—reflecting the playwright's bitterness and growing despair. In 408 Euripides left Athens at the invitation of the Macedonian king Archelaus, who hoped to establish a cultural center to rival Athens. Euripides' departure from Athens in his old age has been attributed to the playwright's disappointment with the hostility that greeted his works. Although invited to produce tetralogies for at least 22 of Athens's Dionysian festivals, Euripides won the competition only three times before his departure, compared to his contemporary Sophocles, who won 24 first prizes. Aristotle reported that, outraged by Euripides' disrespectful treatment of the immortals, the archon (chief magistrate) Kleon prosecuted him for blasphemy, but no record indicates the trial's outcome. Whatever the reason for his departure, Euripides spent his last 18 months enjoying royal patronage and support. Legends surrounding his death, no doubt influenced by the subject of his last completed play, suggest that Euripides was either killed accidentally or deliberately by the king's hunting dogs or torn apart by women outraged by the playwright's treatment of their sex. Found among his effects were three plays—the *Bacchae, Iphigenia at Aulis,* and the *Alcmaeon* (now lost)—produced as a trilogy in Athens in 407 under the direction of Euripides' son and securing posthumously the fourth first-place prize for the playwright whom Aristotle would call in the *Poetics* "the most tragic of dramatists."

What is initially striking about the *Bacchae* is its return to many of the themes treated in *Medea* and other plays written 20 or 25 years earlier, along with its being, for the iconoclastic and innovative Euripides, one of his most conventional dramatic structures. Summarizing Euripides' development, scholar H. D. F. Kitto has stated:

> Love and vengeance are the basis of the *Medea*; Aphrodite and Artemis in the *Hippolytus* are instinctive, non-moral forces, jealous of each other, beneficent to man only when each receives her due honour. The [Peloponnesian] war brought a new tragic theme to the fore, and the tragedy of rational man preyed on by irrational but necessary passions is pushed into the background. The war continued and the spirit of Athens flagged. Athens, and Euripides with her, turned from high tragic issues to a lighter or a more intellectual drama. At last Euripides escaped from the agony and weariness of Athens, and in Macedonia, where spirits were fresher and the tragic implications of political life were out of sight, he returned to his sources.

The *Bacchae* restages the primal battle between rationality and irrationality for a final summary statement on both divine and human natures.

The mythic backstory for the *Bacchae* is the relationship between Semele, the daughter of Cadmus, king of Thebes, and Zeus. Bearing a child by the god, Semele incurs the jealous wrath of Zeus's wife, Hera, who tricks her rival into demanding to see Zeus in all his godly splendor. Appearing to her in the form of bolt of lightning, Semele is immolated, but Zeus saves the unborn child, taking it into his thigh before delivering a son named Dionysus, an embodiment of the power of nature, revelry, wine, frenzy, and the irrational. Semele's sisters, however, refuse to believe that she could have given birth to a god, thinking that instead Zeus has killed her for blasphemously claiming an affair with him. It is the doubt about his divinity in Thebes that Dionysus intends to correct as the play opens, and the god himself, in human form, disguised as a priest in his cult, delivers the prologue. Standing beside his mother's tomb, where flames ignited at the time of her death still smolder, Dionysus announces his mission to call the Greeks to his worship, beginning in Thebes. To teach the nonbelievers a lesson Dionysus has driven the town's women into an ecstatic frenzy and away from their homes and responsibilities:

> up to the mountains where they wander, crazed of mind,
> and compelled to wear my orgies' livery.
> Every woman in Thebes—but the women only—
> I drove from home, mad. There they sit,
> rich and poor alike, even the daughters of Cadmus,
> beneath the silver firs on the roofless rocks.
> Like it or not, this city must learn its lesson:
> it lacks initiation in my mysteries;
> that I shall vindicate my mother Semele
> and stand revealed to mortal eyes as the god
> she bore to Zeus.

Dionysus is particularly incensed by the doubt and disrespect of Pentheus, Cadmus's grandson and Dionysus's cousin, who now rules Thebes and is to be tested. The prologue establishes the play's crushing central irony: The audience knows what the Thebans do not—the god's true identity and intention at the outset. Their doubt is therefore our certainty. Disbelieving the divinity of Dionysus, Pentheus considers what has happened to the Theban women to be perverse and abhorrent and the newly arrived foreign priest of a false god to be a charlatan who must be persecuted, thereby sealing his doom.

Following his monologue, Dionysus introduces the Chorus, women devotees who have followed him from the east and who sing an ode in Dionysus's honor and of the delight they feel in worshipping him. They, in turn, are followed on stage by the prophet Teiresias and Cadmus. Both old men are wearing the same garb as the Bacchants but offer different reason for their conversion. Cadmus embraces the worship of Dionysus out of family pride rather than from any genuine belief, while Teiresias rationalizes Dionysus's divinity, accepting the new god as a concept rather than a felt force. Pentheus enters, furious at both men for succumbing to the cult, and announces his determination to stamp it out by seizing the newly arrived priest. Certainly Pentheus's willful blindness merits Teiresias's condemnation: "Reckless fool, you do not know the consequences of your words. You talked madness before, but this is raving lunacy!" Yet Pentheus is responding to a crisis in which the women's departure has led to a breakdown of order in the city, threatening their survival. He has been called "prejudiced, rash, violent, deaf to advice" and a "Puritan with a prurient mind" in his obsession with what the women are up to in the mountains, yet Pentheus's skepticism and insistence on order are not unworthy attributes of a responsible leader. These virtues, when pursued exclusively and blindly, ignoring the unmistakable signs of Dionysus's godly powers, will produce his tragic fall. Euripides, however, complicates the audience's sympathy by not turning Pentheus into a simple tyrant who deserves his fate and by presenting Dionysus as brutally pursuing the vengeance aimed at destroying his entire human family.

Soldiers enter with the captured Dionysus. Pentheus taunts him; has some of his long hair cut; seizes his thyrsus, his staff tipped with a pinecone and twined with ivy; and interrogates him about the mysteries and rites of the new religion, though Dionysus warns him that it is forbidden to reveal anything to the uninitiated. Threatened with imprisonment, Dionysus insists that "The god himself will set me free whenever I wish," but Pentheus persists and orders him chained and locked in the palace stables, prompting a final set of warnings from Dionysus:

> You do not know
> the limits of your strength. You do not know
> what you do. You do not know who you are. . . .
>   I go,
> though not to suffer, since that cannot be.
> But Dionysus whom you outrage by your acts,
> who you deny is god, will call you to account.
> When you set chains on me, you manacle the god.

In all Greek tragedy there is no clearer or more effective dramatization of hubris than Pentheus's defiance of these warnings, made even more certain by the audience's knowledge that the speaker is divine. The Chorus calls upon the gods to punish Pentheus, and their pleas are answered at the end of their song as an earthquake shakes the palace and Dionysus emerges unbound. Pentheus follows, enraged at seeing his prisoner free, and receives a report about the Theban women, including Pentheus's mother, Agave, who are on a nearby mountain and whose nature worship includes the slaughtering of cattle and ravaging the countryside. Under Dionysus's spell Pentheus expresses a desire to see the women at their worship. Dressed as a woman to avoid detection, Pentheus, now feeling the effects of Dionysus's power, appears to be intoxicated, sees double, and foolishly and vainly fusses with his female attire. "The god is with us," says Dionysus sinisterly. "Now you are seeing what you ought to see." Here the absurdity of Pentheus's loss of control and rationality is mixed with the tragic suggestion offered by both Dionysus and the Chorus that Pentheus is going to his doom.

After Pentheus's departure the Chorus sings an ode calling for his destruction, followed by what is surely the most horrific messenger speech in Greek drama. Announcing Pentheus's death, the messenger reports that, led to the woods to spy on the women, Pentheus is seen, and thinking him a lion, the women, including his mother, Agave, tear him apart. Impaling his head on her thyrsus, Agave enters to display her prize:

> You citizens of this towered city,
> men of Thebes, behold the trophy of your women's
> hunting! *This* is the quarry of our chase, taken
> not with nets nor spears of bronze but by the white
> and delicate hands of women. What are they worth,
> your boastings now and all that uselessness
> your armor is, since we, with our bare hands,
> captured this quarry and tore its bleeding body
> limb from limb?

This extraordinary challenge to masculine power and gender conventions under the influence of Dionysian power is followed by one of the most excruciating moments in all of drama: Agave is slowly restored to her senses and made aware by Cadmus that she has murdered her son and his grandson. It is a scene of wrenching self-recognition and suffering as Agave realizes that her punishment for doubting the divinity of her sister's child is the death of her son by her own hands. "All our house," Cadmus exclaims, "the god has utterly destroyed." Cadmus draws the moral that "If there be any man who slights divinity, / let him look at Pentheus' death—and believe in gods."

Dionysus appears in all his glory atop the palace, and although lines from his speech are lost, it is clear from context and other sources that he proclaims his divinity and banishes Agave and Cadmus, who acknowledge their sins and beg for mercy but are refused. "Gods should not show anger like men," Cadmus asserts. Implacably, Dionysus responds "My father Zeus decreed this long ago." To which Agave says, "It is fated, Father. We must go." Euripides suggests that the powerful, instinctual, and irrational forces Dionysus embodies are repressed or ignored at our peril. Pentheus's rationality is no match for the power like a force of nature, that defies his understanding and owes nothing to human compassion or sympathy. Euripides' tragedy unleashes that force and shows how susceptible we are to it. Ultimately, the play is less about faith in the gods than an acknowledgment of the contradictory forces that rule the universe and human nature.

THE IMPORTANCE OF BEING EARNEST

14

(1895)   *by Oscar Wilde*

In The Importance of Being Earnest, *each person turns out to be his own secret opposite: Algy becomes Bunbury, Jack Earnest, as in Wilde's case the Irelander turned Englander. Whatever seems like an opposite in the play materializes as a double. For example, many critics have found in it a traditional contrast between the brilliant cynicism of the town-dwellers and the tedious rectitude of the rural people; but that is not how things work out. Characters like Canon Chasuble and Miss Prism are revealed to have contained the seeds of corruption and knowingness all along, while Cecily has her most interesting (i.e., evil) inspirations in a garden (rather reminiscent of her biblical predecessor). So every dichotomy dichotomizes. Wilde's is an art of inversion.*

—Declan Kiberd, *Inventing Ireland: The Literature of the Modern Nation*

There are several ways to consider Oscar Wilde. One is as the transplanted Irishman who left his native land for England and, as the Irish critic Declan Kiberd has observed, "proceeded to reconstruct his image through the art of the pose." That image has led Wilde to be seen by many as the premier late Victorian wit and fastidious bon vivant and by others as a ludicrous and pretentious aesthete, satirized by William S. Gilbert and Arthur S. Sullivan as Bunthorne, a "fleshly poet," in their operetta *Patience*, walking "down Piccadilly with a poppy or a lily" in his "mediaeval hand." Wilde, the aesthete, once remarked: "I treated Art as the supreme reality and life as a mere mode of fiction." Wilde can also be considered a heroic figure, whose open homosexuality ultimately doomed what had been a brilliant career and led to scandal, imprisonment, self-imposed exile, and an early death. He was a poet whose work was praised as clever and fluent yet often characterized as trivial; nonetheless, after suffering the indignity of a prison sentence, he brought forth a poignant final work, *The Ballad of Reading Gaol* (1898). He was a novelist who produced a novel of manners that is part tragedy and part horror story. He was also a playwright who revived the spirit of the comedies of manners of William Congreve and Richard Brinsley Sheridan.

Oscar Fingal O'Flahertie Wills Wilde was born in Dublin on October 16, 1854, the younger son of Sir William Wilde and Jane Francesca Elgee Wilde. His father was an eminent surgeon and a distinguished scholar, who wrote on Irish antiquities and folklore. His mother was an ardent feminist and Irish nationalist, who presided over literary salons and, under the pen name "Speranza," wrote patriotic verse and articles for nationalist journals, as well as collections of folklore. At 10 Wilde was sent to the Portora Royal School in Eniskillen. He was tall, awkward, and dreamy, disliked sports, and was a voracious reader. In 1871 he entered Trinity College, Dublin, where he studied Classics, and in 1874 went on to Magdelan College, Oxford.

After graduating in 1878 with honors, Wilde went to London, where he quickly established himself in the literary and artistic society of the capital. Influenced by his Oxford professors John Ruskin and Walter Pater, as well as the Pre-Raphaelites and the concept of *l'art pour l'art* (art for art's sake) espoused earlier in the century by the French novelist, poet, and critic Théophile Gautier, Wilde turned himself into the most noticeable public embodiment of the aesthetic movement. Eccentric in dress and behavior, with a penchant for bon mots, Wilde, tremendous talent aside, became, in today's parlance, famous for being famous. In 1882 he embarked upon his immensely successful lecture tour of the United States, arranged by impresario Richard D'Oyly Carte, who was taking Gilbert and Sullivan's *Patience* to America and hoped that Wilde's flamboyant presence would help to publicize the operetta. When the American customs official asked him if he had anything to declare, Wilde is famously said to have replied, "I have nothing to declare except my genius." In 1884 he married Constance Lloyd, the daughter of an Irish barrister, with whom he had two sons. By the age of 30, Wilde had produced one volume of poems and two unsuccessful plays. To earn an income he became a book reviewer and drama critic and the editor for the journal *Woman's World*, for which he wrote short stories. His most popular stories were published in an 1888 collection, *The Happy Prince and Other Tales*. In 1890 Wilde serialized the novel *The Picture of Dorian Gray*, which was published in book form the following year. He wrote critical essays and in 1892, with the production of *Lady Windermere's Fan*, began a series of four society comedies that would conclude with *The Importance of Being Earnest*. A poetic drama, *Salomé*, written in French and intended for Sarah Bernhardt, was banned on the stage in London but was published in 1894 with the sensual illustrations of Aubrey Beardsley.

The Importance of Being Earnest, Wilde's greatest play, represents the high-water mark of his career. It was originally written in four acts, but while it was in rehearsal, Wilde accepted the advice of actor-manager George Alexander and reduced it to three acts, which is now the standard version. The play begins in the luxurious London flat of Algernon Moncrieff, who is expecting his aunt, Lady Bracknell, and her daughter, Gwendolen Fairfax, for tea. He is surprised by the arrival of his wealthy friend

Ernest Worthing, who has come up to town to propose to Gwendolen. Algy is curious about his friend's cigarette case, left behind after his last visit, inscribed by "Cecily" to "her dear Uncle Jack." Algy discovers that his friend's name is really John (or Jack) Worthing. Algy refuses to believe Jack's assertion of his real name: "You have always told me it was Ernest. I have introduced you to every one as Ernest. You answer to the name of Ernest. You look as if your name was Ernest. You are the most earnest-looking person I ever saw in my life. It is perfectly absurd your saying your name isn't Ernest." Jack explains that he has invented a wild, irresponsible younger brother called Ernest in order to justify his frequent visits to London to escape the moral duties imposed upon him by his guardianship of his 18-year-old ward, Cecily Cardew. This inversely corresponds to what Algy calls his "Bunburying," named after his own "double," an imaginary invalid, whose poor health requires Algy's presence in the country whenever he needs an excuse to leave London.

Lady Bracknell and Gwendolen enter, and Algy takes his aunt into the music room so that Jack may proceed with his proposal. Jack haltingly declares his intentions to Gwendolen, who takes the initiative, proclaiming to him, "Even before I met you I was far from indifferent to you," and adding that her ideal "has always been to love some one of the name Ernest. There is something in that name that inspires absolute confidence." Since she refuses to consider "Jack" or "John" as acceptable alternatives, Jack is unable to tell her the truth. Lady Bracknell rejects Jack's suitability as a member of the family after she learns from him that he has "lost" his parents: "To lose one parent, Mr. Worthing, may be regarded as a misfortune; to lose both looks like carelessness." Jack explains that he has no known parents but was found as a baby, in a black leather handbag, in the cloakroom of Victoria Station, by Mr. Thomas Cardew, a wealthy and kindly old man who then adopted him and gave him the last name of "Worthing" because he had a first-class train ticket for Worthing. Lady Bracknell advises Jack to "try to acquire some relations as soon as possible" and sweeps out of the flat with her daughter. Frustrated by events, Jack decides to eliminate the ficticious "Ernest." Gwendolen escapes from her mother briefly to declare her lasting devotion to Jack and asks for his country address, which Algy, already interested in meeting Cecily, notes with delight.

The second act is set in the garden of the Manor House, Jack's country home. Cecily is being instructed by her governess, Miss Prism, a spinster who long ago once wrote a sentimental novel, the manuscript of which she mislaid, a fact that will figure later in the play. Dr. Chasuble, an unworldly cleric, lures Miss Prism away for a walk, leaving Cecily alone to greet a stranger who is announced as "Ernest Worthing." Cecily is already taken with the name and the reports of Ernest's wickedness: "I have never met any really wicked person before. I feel rather frightened. I am so afraid he will look just like every one else." Enter Algy masquerading as "Ernest," and the couple hit it off at once. After they go into the house, Miss Prism and Dr. Chasuble return in time to greet Jack, who is unaware of Algy's presence and is dressed in deep mourning: "Ernest," he claims, has died suddenly in Paris. He asks Chasuble to rechristen him Ernest. He is startled when Cecily reappears to inform him of "Ernest's" arrival and horrified to see Algy in the role. But Jack cannot unmask his friend without revealing his own deceit. Algy and Cecily declare mutual affection for each other, although he is disconcerted to discover that she finds him appealing in great part because of his name. He decides to become baptized as Ernest immediately. Gwendolen arrives unexpectedly, and the two women quarrel over which of them is actually engaged to "Ernest." The truth is revealed when the men enter, and the women unite in a sense of outrage. They withdraw while Jack and Algy trade recriminations, many of which reach the heights of triviality since they revolve around Algy's continual consumption of muffins, Jack's favorite teatime treat.

The third act, set in the morning room of Manor House, has the couples reconciled and a happy ending certain until the appearance of Lady Bracknell, who firmly forbids further communication between Jack and Gwendolen. She does, however, consent to the engagement of Algy and Cecily upon learning that Cecily has three addresses, a family firm of solicitors with "the highest position," and a large fortune. But Cecily must have her guardian's consent to the marriage until she legally comes of age at 35, and Jack refuses to give it unless Lady Bracknell will reconsider his engagement to Gwendolen. She refuses, prompting Jack to say, "Then a passionate celibacy is all that any of us can look forward to." Enter Miss Prism, who, it is revealed, was once employed by Lady Bracknell and 28 years earlier had mysteriously disappeared with the baby boy entrusted to her, leaving behind only the pram and the manuscript of her novel. She admits that she absentmindedly left her novel in the pram and deposited the baby, in her black leather handbag, at Victoria Station. Jack excitedly produces the handbag and embraces Miss Prism, crying, "Mother!" A shocked Miss Prism reiterates her status as a respectable spinster and repulses him. Lady Bracknell steps in to solve the mystery of Jack's parentage: He is the elder son of her late sister, Mrs. Moncrieff, and is Algernon's elder brother. To the ecstasy of Jack and Gwendolen, it is further revealed that Jack, as the elder son, was named after his father, General Ernest John Moncrieff. The couples, including Miss Prism and Canon Chasuble, embrace, and a final exchange between Jack and Lady Bracknell, brings the title pun home:

> LADY BRACKNELL   My nephew, you seem to be displaying signs of triviality.

> JACK   On the contrary, Aunt Augusta, I've now realized for the first time in my life the vital Importance of Being Earnest.

In his *Forewords and Afterwords* W. H. Auden, in writing on Wilde's plays, observes: "The solution that, deliberately or accidentally, he found was to subordinate every other dramatic element to dialogue for its own sake and create a verbal universe in which the characters are determined by the kinds of things they say, and the plot is nothing but a succession of opportunities to say them." Wilde's plays certainly contain gems of dialogue, such as "Experience is the name everyone gives to their mistakes" (*Lady Windermere's Fan*). But *The Importance of Being Earnest* is more than just a showcase for Wilde to display his genius for epigrammatic verbal gymnastics. The play's subtitle, "A Trivial Play for Serious People," suggests that satire disguised as farce is going to be presented. What follows is a wildly irreverent, topsy-turvy series of circumstances that lampoon Victorian melodrama with its twist on the theme of the foundling, found in Charles Dickens's novels, as well as in the operettas of Gilbert and Sullivan; a plot centered on the name Ernest that simultaneously mocks the Victorian concept of determinism exemplified in the word *earnest*; and the comedic situation taken one step further by having the male protagonists possess fictional doubles. The result is a faultlessly constructed comic masterpiece.

Defined by their social status and revealed through their manners, Wilde's characters—the witty men-about-town; the daunting, caustic dowager and her marriageable daughter; the precocious ingénue who is an heiress; the morally upright spinster governess; the imperturbable valet—would have been recognizable figures to the audiences of the 1890s. This was due to the influence of such actor-managers as Henry Irving, George Alexander, and Herbert Beerbohm Tree, who, by offering the domestic plays of such dramatists as Thomas Roberston, turned West End London theater away from crude farces, bawdy burlesques, and sensational melodramas. Opera was no longer the only respectable entertainment. Theaters, like those of the Restoration period, catered to a privileged leisure class that was either rich and aristocratic or fashionably bohemian. First nights were brilliant affairs, including that of *The Importance of Being Earnest*, which opened on Valentine's Day 1895 at the St. James's Theatre and was a tremendous popular and critical success.

Wilde's triumph was short lived. After unsuccessfully bringing a libel suit against the marquess of Queensbury, the father of his young lover Lord Alfred "Bosie" Douglas, who accused Wilde of corrupting his son, Wilde was arrested and stood trial for indecency and immorality. In May 1895 he was found guilty and sentenced to two years' imprisonment with hard labor. In Reading prison he wrote a long letter to Douglas, published in 1905 under the title *De Profundis*. Released from prison in 1897, Wilde immediately and permanently left England for France, where he died in Paris in 1900.

Wilde's plays were precursors to the drawing-room comedies of such playwrights as Noël Coward. Wilde's comedies continue to be performed and enjoyed by contemporary audiences, yet it is *The Importance of Being Earnest* that has, in particular, secured for Wilde a place in the history of the theater for having given the world one of the most singularly witty and clever comedies of all time, an achievement that is anything but trivial.

ANTIGONE

15

(441 B.C.)

by Sophocles

Within this single drama—in great part, a harsh critique of Athenian society and the Greek city-state in general—Sophocles tells of the eternal struggle between the state and the individual, human and natural law, and the enormous gulf between what we attempt here on earth and what fate has in store for us all. In this magnificent dramatic work, almost incidentally so, we find nearly every reason why we are now what we are.
—Victor D. Hanson and John Heath, *Who Killed Homer? The Demise of Classical Education and the Recovery of Greek Wisdom*

With *Antigone* Sophocles forcibly demonstrates that the power of tragedy derives not from the conflict between right and wrong but from the confrontation between right and right. As the play opens the succession battle between the sons of Oedipus—Polynices and Eteocles—over control of Thebes has resulted in both of their deaths. Their uncle Creon, who has now assumed the throne, asserts his authority to end a destructive civil war and decrees that only Eteocles, the city's defender, should receive honorable burial. Polynices, who has led a foreign army against Thebes, is branded a traitor. His corpse is to be left on the battlefield "to be chewed up by birds and dogs and violated," with death the penalty for anyone who attempts to bury him and supply the rites necessary for the dead to reach the underworld. Antigone, Polynices' sister, is determined to defy Creon's order, setting in motion a tragic collision between opposed laws and duties: between natural and divine commands that dictate the burial of the dead and the secular edicts of a ruler determined to restore civic order, between family allegiance and private conscience and public duty and the rule of law that restricts personal liberty for the common good. Like the proverbial immovable object meeting an irresistible force, *Antigone* arranges the impact of seemingly irreconcilable conceptions of rights and responsibilities, producing one of drama's enduring illuminations of human nature and the human condition.

Antigone is one of Sophocles' greatest achievements and one of the most influential dramas ever staged. "Between 1790 and 1905," critic George Steiner reports, "it was widely held by European poets, philosophers, [and] scholars that Sophocles' *Antigone* was not only the finest of Greek tragedies, but a work of art nearer to perfection than any other produced by the human spirit." Its theme of the opposition between the individual and authority has resonated through the centuries, with numerous playwrights, most notably Jean Anouilh, Bertolt Brecht, and Athol Fugard grafting contemporary concerns and values onto the moral and political dramatic framework that Sophocles established. The play has elicited paradoxical responses reflecting changing cultural and moral imperatives. Antigone, who has been described as "the first heroine of Western drama," has been interpreted both as a heroic martyr to conscience and as a willfully stubborn fanatic who causes her own death and that of two other innocent people, forsaking her duty to the living on behalf of the dead. Creon has similarly divided critics between censure and sympathy. Despite the play's title, some have suggested that the tragedy is Creon's, not Antigone's, and it is his abuse of authority and his violations of personal, family, and divine obligations that center the drama's tragedy. The brilliance of Sophocles' play rests in the complexity of motive and the competing absolute claims that the drama displays. As novelist George Eliot observed,

> It is a very superficial criticism which interprets the character of Creon as that of hypocritical tyrant, and regards Antigone as a blameless victim. Coarse contrasts like this are not the materials handled by great dramatists. The exquisite art of Sophocles is shown in the touches by which he makes us feel that Creon, as well as Antigone, is contending for what he believes to be the right, while both are also conscious that, in following out one principle, they are laying themselves open to just blame for transgressing another.

Eliot would call the play's focus the "antagonism of valid principles," demonstrating a point of universal significance that "Wherever the strength of a man's intellect, or moral sense, or affection brings him into opposition with the rules which society has sanctioned, *there* is renewed conflict between Antigone and Creon; such a man must not only dare to be right, he must also dare to be wrong—to shake faith, to wound friendship, perhaps, to hem in his own powers." Sophocles' *Antigone* is less a play about the pathetic end of a victim of tyranny or the corruption of authority than about the inevitable cost and consequence between competing imperatives that define the human condition. From opposite and opposed positions, both Antigone and Creon ultimately meet at the shared suffering each has caused. They have destroyed each other and themselves by who they are and what they believe. They are both right and wrong in a world that lacks moral certainty and simple choices. The Chorus summarizes what *Antigone* will vividly enact: "The powerful words of the proud are paid in full with mighty blows of fate, and at long last those blows will teach us wisdom."

As the play opens Antigone declares her intention to her sister Ismene to defy Creon's impious and inhumane order and enlists her sister's aid to bury their brother. Ismene responds that as women they must not oppose the will of men or the authority of the city and invite death. Ismene's timidity and deference underscores Antigone's courage and defiance. Antigone asserts a greater allegiance to blood kinship and divine law declaring that the burial is a "holy crime," justified even by death. Ismene responds by calling her sister "a lover of the impossible," an accurate description of the tragic hero, who, according to scholar Bernard Knox, is Sophocles' most important contribution to drama: "Sophocles presents us for the first time with what we recognize as a 'tragic hero': one who, unsupported by the gods and in the face of human opposition, makes a decision which springs from the deepest layer of his individual nature, his *physis*, and then blindly, ferociously, heroically maintains that decision even to the point of self-destruction." Antigone exactly conforms to Knox's description, choosing her conception of duty over sensible self-preservation and gender-prescribed submission to male authority, turning on her sister and all who oppose her. Certain in her decision and self-sufficient, Antigone rejects both her sister's practical advice and kinship. Ironically Antigone denies to her sister, when Ismene resists her will, the same blood kinship that claims Antigone's supreme allegiance in burying her brother. For Antigone the demands of the dead overpower duty to the living, and she does not hesitate in claiming both to know and act for the divine will. As critic Gilbert Norwood observes, "It is Antigone's splendid though perverse valor which creates the drama."

Before the apprehended Antigone, who has been taken in the act of scattering dust on her brother's corpse, lamenting, and pouring libations, is brought before Creon and the dramatic crux of the play, the Chorus of Theban elders delivers what has been called the finest song in all Greek tragedy, the so-called Ode to Man, that begins "Wonders are many, and none is more wonderful than man." This magnificent celebration of human power over nature and resourcefulness in reason and invention ends with a stark recognition of humanity's ultimate helplessness—"Only against Death shall he call for aid in vain." Death will test the resolve and principles of both Antigone and Creon, while, as critic Edouard Schuré asserts, "It brings before us the most extraordinary psychological evolution that has ever been represented on stage."

When Antigone is brought in judgment before Creon, obstinacy meets its match. Both stand on principle, but both reveal the human source of their actions. Creon betrays himself as a paranoid autocrat; Antigone as an individual whose powerful hatred outstrips her capacity for love. She defiantly and proudly admits that she is guilty of disobeying Creon's decree and that he has no power to override divine law. Nor does Antigone concede any mitigation of her personal obligation in the competing claims of a niece, a sister, or a citizen. Creon is maddened by what he perceives to be Antigone's insolence in justifying her crime by diminishing his authority, provoking him to ignore all moderating claims of family, natural, or divine extenuation. When Ismene is brought in as a co-conspirator, she accepts her share of guilt in solidarity with her sister, but again Antigone spurns her, calling her "a friend who loves in words," denying Ismene's selfless act of loyalty and sympathy with a cold dismissal and self-sufficiency, stating, "Never share my dying, / don't lay claim to what you never touched." However, Ismene raises the ante for both Antigone and Creon by asking her uncle whether by condemning Antigone he will kill his own son's betrothed. Creon remains adamant, and his judgment on Antigone and Ismene, along with his subsequent argument with his son, Haemon, reveals that Creon's principles are self-centered, contradictory, and compromised by his own pride, fears, and anxieties. Antigone's challenge to his authority, coming from a woman, is demeaning. If she goes free in defiance of his authority, Creon declares, "I am not the man, she is." To the urging of Haemon that Creon should show mercy, tempering his judgment to the will of Theban opinion that sympathizes with Antigone, Creon asserts that he cares nothing for the will of the town, whose welfare Creon's original edict against Polynices was meant to serve. Creon, moreover, resents being schooled in expediency by his son. Inflamed by his son's advocacy on behalf of Antigone, Creon brands Haemon a "woman's slave," and after vacillating between stoning Antigone and executing her and her sister in front of Haemon, Creon rules that Antigone alone is to perish by being buried alive. Having begun the drama with a decree that a dead man should remain unburied, Creon reverses himself, ironically, by ordering the premature burial of a living woman.

Antigone, being led to her entombment, is shown stripped of her former confidence and defiance, searching for the justification that can steel her acceptance of the fate that her actions have caused. Contemplating her living descent into the underworld and the death that awaits her, Antigone regrets dying without marriage and children. Gone is her reliance on divine and natural law to justify her act as she equivocates to find the emotional source to sustain her. A husband and children could be replaced, she rationalizes, but since her mother and father are dead, no brother can ever replace Polynices. Antigone's tortured logic here, so different from the former woman of principle, has been rejected by some editors as spurious. Others have judged this emotionally wrought speech essential for humanizing Antigone, revealing her capacity to suffer and her painful search for some consolation.

The drama concludes with the emphasis shifted back to Creon and the consequences of his judgment. The blind prophet Teiresias comes to warn Creon that Polynices' unburied body has offended the gods and that Creon is responsible for the sickness that has descended on Thebes. Creon has kept from Hades one who belongs there and is sending to Hades another who does not. The gods confirm the rightness of Antigone's action, but justice evades the working out of the drama's climax. The release of Antigone comes too late; she has hung herself. Haemon commits suicide, and Eurydice, Creon's wife, kills herself after cursing Creon for the death of their son. Having denied the obligation of family, Creon loses his own. Creon's rule, marked by ignoring or transgressing cosmic and family law, is shown as ultimately inadequate and destructive. Creon is made to realize that he has been rash and foolish, that "Whatever I have touched has come to nothing." Both Creon and Antigone have been pushed to terrifying ends in which what truly matters to both are made starkly clear. Antigone's moral imperatives have been affirmed but also their immense cost in suffering has been exposed. *Antigone* explores a fundamental rift between public and private worlds. The central opposition in the play between Antigone and Creon, between duty to self and duty to state, dramatizes critical antimonies in the human condition. Sophocles' genius is his resistance of easy and consoling simplifications to resolve the oppositions. Both sides are ultimately tested; both reveal the potential for greatness and destruction.

TARTUFFE

16

(1669)

by Molière

Whenever evoked in a modern or a postmodern cultural context, even outside France, Tartuffe still carries with it a considerable amount of polemical baggage. It may be argued that it delves far closer to the level of persistent cultural preoccupation than any of Shakespeare's plays, for instance, and that one must look to Don Quixote *or* War and Peace *to find a literary text so thoroughly joined to a particular concept of nationhood.*
— Ralph Albanese, Jr., *"Tartuffe* Goes to School"

On February 17, 1773, Molière coughed up blood while performing the title role in his final comedy, *Le Malade imaginaire* (*The Imaginary Invalid*). That the already desperately ill Molière should end his theatrical career pretending to be a hypochondriac is one of the theater's great dramatic ironies. He died a few hours after the performance at his home of a lung embolism. The priests at the parish of Saint-Eustache, where he had been baptized as Jean-Baptiste Poquelin, refused him last rites and the opportunity for the conventional deathbed renunciation of his profession that would have allowed the excommunicated actor to be buried in holy ground. France's greatest dramatist was finally buried, in the words of critic Nicholas Boileau, in a "piece of land obtained by supplication," through the intervention of Louis XIV on behalf of his friend. The king managed to persuade the archbishop of Paris to grant Molière a Christian burial, but only in the dead of night, without a public ceremony of mourning. The clergy refused to forgive Molière for his presumed impious and blasphemous attack on religion in *Tartuffe*, which had been first performed almost a decade before in 1664, and only reluctantly bowed to royal persuasion.

Tartuffe is one of the most contentious plays ever produced and the subject of the 17th-century's greatest censorship battle. Molière's shockingly delightful drama about religious belief radically redefined the targets and ends of comedy. That Molière would comically treat such a subject in a religiously sensitive age that still dealt with heresy at the stake was daring in the extreme, if not foolhardy. That his critics misperceived the play's exposure of false piety and religious hypocrisy as an attack on religion itself suggests that *Tartuffe* hit a sensitive nerve. It is easy to condemn the bias and blindness of Molière's clerical contemporaries at the time of his death, still smarting from the stings of *Tartuffe*. However, the play retains its ability to shock and touch audiences on sore spots, and the need to be able to distinguish true piety amidst sham is no less urgent today than it was in 17th-century France.

Controversy, such as that surrounding *Tartuffe* and Molière's passing, was a constant in the playwright's career, beginning with his return to Paris in 1658 after a 12-year provincial tour as actor, manager, and playwright with a struggling theatrical troupe. During this apprenticeship period, Molière perfected his craft as a comic farceur and playwright, converting elements from traditional French farce and the Italian commedia dell'arte into a radically new comic drama that challenged tragedy as a vehicle for delivering the most serious and profound truths. If 17th-century French tragedy had formulated a clear set of rules and conventions, as evidenced by the controversy surrounding Pierre Corneille's *LE CID* in the 1630s, French comedy was another matter when Molière took it up. The crude slapstick of French farce with its stock characters and exaggerated situations was enjoyed by the populace, while the sophisticated preferred the dignity, verisimilitude, and profundity of tragedy. Literary or high comedy needed to be similarly serious and refined. Molière, who developed his skills on the popular stage, would revolutionize French comedy by fusing the farcical with prescribed elements of neoclassical drama and the aspirations of serious drama. He showed that comedy, as well as tragedy, could reach psychological depths and essential human themes and that the caricatural distortions of farce aided rather than prevented the exploration of human nature and social experience. His was an innovative character comedy based on the lifelike portrayal of contemporary manners but with the theatrical inventiveness that provoked hearty laughter at human foibles and pretensions. Many were not amused.

In 1662 Molière presented *L'École des femmes* (*The School for Wives*), a play about a middle-aged man's scheme to prevent becoming a cuckold by raising his bride from girlhood isolated from the corruptions of society. Despite great commercial success, his satirical comedy that exposed the excesses and unflattering inclinations of the *beau monde* prompted charges of the playwright's immorality and defiance of dramatic decorum. The play touched off the so-called *guerre comique*, which became, after the controversy over Corneille's *Le Cid*, 17th-century France's second great debate over the ends and means of drama. To the charge that he had violated good taste by exposing the vices of the respectable and overturned the rules of dramatic decorum by provoking ridicule by his comic exaggeration of serious matters, Molière insisted that he had observed drama's fundamental rule by pleasing his audience. Preferring to treat men as they are rather than as they ought to be, the playwright insisted that comedy must represent "all the defects of men, and especially the men of our own time." Throughout the debate Molière insisted on a new realistic standard for drama that would extend the range of comedy with the goal of correcting men's vices by exposing them, by instructing the neoclassical ideals of reason and moderation, and by wittily showing their violations.

The ultimate test for Molière's conception of comedy would come with *Le Tartuffe*. A three-act version of the play was first performed for the king at Versailles during a lavish spring fete. It provoked shocked condemnation from the queen mother, from church officials, and from lay members of the Company of the Holy Sacrament, the era's spiritual thought police engaged in the protection of morality and orthodoxy. In the grip of the Counter-Reformation, the Catholic Church in France was divided into two dominant rival factions of the Jesuits and the puritanical Jansenists. Both sides saw themselves the target of Molière's satire, and less than a week after its first performance religious and moral pressure groups forced a royal ban. Molière was condemned as "a demon dressed in flesh and clothed as a man, and the most outrageously impious libertine who has ever appeared in centuries" by one cleric who called for the playwright to be burned at the stake. The ban led to Molière's five-year struggle to justify his play and his method and to get *Tartuffe* performed and published. He contended that his target was neither religion nor the truly pious but those who merely pretended to be and who used religion to conceal and justify their vices. Molière insisted that instead of belittling moral values his play was the most effective way to support morality by attacking "the vices of these times through ludicrous depictions." In 1667 a five-act version of the play—with a new title, *L'Imposteur,* and a renamed title character (Panulphe)— premiered in Paris. It likewise was immediately banned. Molière's theater was closed, and the archbishop of Paris decreed that anyone performing in, attending, or reading the play would be excommunicated. Molière appealed to the king, who was away from Paris with his army at the time, that the play was neither dangerous to religion nor the genuinely pious and threatened to stop writing comedy altogether if these "tartuffes" were unchallenged. Louis let the ban stand but agreed to reexamine the case upon his return to Paris. On February 5, 1669, the ultimate version of the play, entitled *Le Tartuffe, ou l'Imposteur,* finally opened to great acclaim and commercial success, as well as lingering clerical resentment.

Tartuffe has gone on to become Molière's most widely read and performed play. Its title character is among drama's greatest comic characters, and the story of his rise and fall as a devious usurper in the respectable bourgeois household of Orgon and his family is a masterpiece of characterization, social satire, and theatricality in its multiple discovery scenes and reversals. The basic elements of the comedy are inherited. The parasite, the tyrannical father, young put-upon lovers, and scheming servants recall the cast in Roman comedies. Tartuffe, the unctuous *faux dévot,* resembles the seductive Vice in the medieval morality plays. The uncovering of a fraud in which a cozener preys on the weaknesses of sinners and the gullible has its basis in the medieval and farce traditions, as well as such previous comedies as Ben Jonson's *VOLPONE* and *THE ALCHEMIST*. Molière's originality rests in the psychological and social uses he makes of these elements, working out believable motivations for his characters while embodying in their often ludicrous behavior serious social themes.

The most striking structural innovation in the play is keeping Tartuffe offstage until the second scene of the third act, the climax of most five-act dramas. His absence underscores Molière's focus in the play not on Tartuffe but on his gulls and the consequence of Tartuffe's deception. The opening scenes, recording the family's breakdown through the patriarch Orgon's falling for the lures of a religious hypocrite, was called by Goethe, "the greatest and best thing of the kind that exists." The household has been ruptured by Tartuffe's arrival into two warring factions: Orgon and his mother, Madame Pernelle, who have been taken in by Tartuffe's cant and pose of fervent religiousness, and the rest of the household, including Elmire, Orgon's wife; Cléante, his brother-in-law; Orgon's daughter and son, Mariane and Damis; and Mariane's maid, Dorine. Orgon's household, a microcosm of society, has been perverted and inverted by Tartuffe, who has made himself "master in the house." Orgon (originally played by Molière) is blinded by Tartuffe's promises of spiritual salvation and neglects and violates the temporal demands of love and responsibility he rightfully owes to his wife and children and is unable to see what is so evident to the others, that Tartuffe is a hypocrite and self-seeking manipulator. The family's patriarch prefers the illusions Tartuffe supplies to reality, and the opening scenes make clear the consequences of Orgon's self-delusion. Dorine summarizes the perverse overthrow of proper relations that afflicts Orgon: "He dotes on him, embraces him, and could not have, I believe, more tenderness for a woman he loves." Cléante, Molière's voice of reason and moderation, tries to get his brother-in-law to see clearly:

> There's a vast difference, so it seems to me,
> Between true piety and hypocrisy:
> How do you fail to see it, may I ask?
> Is not a face quite different from a mask?
> Cannot sincerity and cunning art,
> Reality and semblance, be told apart?
> Are scarecrows just like men, and do you hold
> That a false coin is just as good as gold?
> Ah, Brother, man's a strangely fashioned creature
> Who seldom is content to follow Nature,
> But recklessly pursues his inclination
> Beyond the narrow bounds of moderation,

And often, by transgressing Reason's laws,
Perverts a lofty aim or noble cause.

Orgon has transgressed "Reason's laws" and perverted religious faith by succumbing to its shows rather than its substance, while immoderately overthrowing judgment in his selfish pursuit of personal salvation. He thereby
becomes a petty tyrant in his home, willing to sacrifice all he is responsible
for—wife, son, daughter, and property—to his desires, while casting out all
who dissent as damned heretics. Orgon's violation of his parental responsibility is made clear when in act 2 he breaks Mariane's engagement to Valère and
orders her to marry Tartuffe, whom Mariane despises.

Having established a dysfunctional family as a result of Tartuffe's deceptive
manipulation, Molière finally brings the culprit on stage in act 3 with one of
the stage's greatest entrance lines: "Hang up my hair-shirt," Tartuffe instructs
his manservant, "put my scourge in place." His orders are clearly to impress
the encountered Dorine, whom he likewise orders to "Cover that bosom, girl.
The flesh is weak." The weaknesses of the flesh will become Tartuffe's undoing,
as he takes the stage at the height of his powers over Orgon and initiates his
own downfall. Molière addressed the late arrival of Tartuffe by stating, "I have
employed . . . two entire acts to prepare for the entrance of my scoundrel. He
does not fool the audience for a single moment; one knows from the first the
marks I have given him; and from one end to the other he says not a word and
performs not an action which does not paint for the spectator the character of an
evil man." The preparation establishes the play's delightful dramatic irony as the
audience is in no doubt, despite Orgon's blindness, of what lies behind Tartuffe's
every word, gesture, and action. Tartuffe's downfall will come, as it does in most
of Molière's plays, from immoderation and succumbing to the illusions of power
and control. So confident is Tartuffe in his power over Orgon that he risks
exposure by attempting to seduce Elmire. His initial lustful attack, overheard by
Damis, is reported to Orgon, and when confronted, Tartuffe blatantly confesses
the truth: "Yes, brother, I am an evil, guilty, wretched sinner filled with iniquity,
the greatest rascal ever." Tartuffe's confidence that he will not be believed is
confirmed when Orgon instead disinherits his son and hands over his patrimony
to his now-adopted son Tartuffe. Elmire realizes that Orgon, impervious to
argument, must see Tartuffe unmasked, and she stage-manages the play's comic
triumph. With Orgon concealed under a table, Tartuffe renews his pursuit of
Elmire; he reveals both his lusts and contempt for the morality he has espoused
by urging Elmire to ignore both "Heaven's wrath" and moral scruples:

No one shall know our joys, save us alone,
And there's no evil till the act is known;
It's scandal, Madam, which makes it an offense,
And it's no sin to sin in confidence.

Tartuffe, however, finds himself in Orgon, not Elmire's arms, and his unmasking is finally complete. Molière follows Orgon's discovery of Tartuffe's hypocrisy and the realization of his own gullibility, however, with a reversal. Orgon's breakthrough is too late. Tartuffe is now legally the master of all that Orgon owns and controls Orgon's destiny because he has been given a chest containing treasonable evidence against his patron. Villainy appears triumphant, and although Orgon is reunited with his family and chastened into the correct obligations toward them, the disorder and inversion that the hypocrite Tartuffe has unleashed appear complete with the family's eviction. Again, it is Tartuffe's immoderation and overconfidence in his ability to control all and complete his coup d'état that lead him to denounce Orgon as a traitor and thereby become known to the authorities as a wanted criminal. The king, able to see through Tartuffe's schemes, serves as the play's deus ex machina, and orders his arrest. It is the king, the wise and sensible patriarch of the French nation, who restores order in Orgon's household (as he does in his kingdom) and allows Orgon to benefit by the sobering lesson of his errors and delusions. A marriage between the reunited lovers, Mariane and Valère, closes the comedy.

Although *Tartuffe* invites the complaint that its ending is overly contrived—that events so thoroughly motivated by the characters themselves are now imposed on them to produce the desired poetic justice (as well as flattery of a royal patron)—in a thematic sense the play's ending is thoroughly satisfying. Orgon and the audience have been instructed in the difference between artifice and authenticity, appearance and reality, falsity and truth. The hypocritical religious zealot has been unmasked both by his own excesses and a monarch who possess both the ideals of reasonableness and moderation so needed by his subjects to insure that hypocrisy can be exposed and withstood and the good sense to allow Molière's comedy a hearing.

ANTONY AND CLEOPATRA

17

(c. 1607)

by William Shakespeare

Antony and Cleopatra *is the definitive tragedy of passion, and in it the ironic and heroic themes, the day world of history and the night world of passion, expand into natural forces of cosmological proportions.*
—Northrup Frye, "The Tailors of the Earth: The Tragedy of Passion," in *Fools of Time: Studies in Shakespearean Tragedy*

Among William Shakespeare's great tragedies, *Antony and Cleopatra* is the anomaly. Written around 1607, following the completion of the sequence of tragedies that began with HAMLET and concluded with MACBETH, *Antony and Cleopatra* stands in marked contrast from them in tone, theme, and structure. For his last great tragedy, Shakespeare returned to his first, ROMEO AND JULIET. Like it, *Antony and Cleopatra* is a love story that ends in a double suicide; however, the lovers here are not teenagers, but the middle-aged Antony and Cleopatra whose battle between private desires and public responsibilities is played out with world domination in the balance. Having raised adolescent love to the level of tragic seriousness in *Romeo and Juliet*, Shakespeare here dramatizes a love story on a massive, global scale. If *Hamlet*, OTHELLO, KING LEAR, and *Macbeth* conclude with the prescribed pity and terror, *Anthony and Cleopatra* ends very differently with pity and triumph, as the title lovers, who have lost the world, enact a kind of triumphant marriage in death. Losing everything, they manage to win much more by choosing love over worldly power. *Antony and Cleopatra* is the last in a series of plays, beginning with *Romeo and Juliet* and including *Troilus and Cressida* and *Othello*, that explores the connection between love and tragedy. It also can be seen as the first of the playwright's final series of romances, followed by *Cymbeline*, *The Winter's Tale*, and *The Tempest* in which love eventually triumphs over every obstacle. *Antony and Cleopatra* is therefore a peculiar tragedy of affirmation, setting the dominant tone of Shakespeare's final plays.

Structurally, as well, *Antony and Cleopatra* is exceptional. Ranging over the Mediterranean world from Egypt to Rome to Athens, Sicily, and Syria, the play has 44 scenes, more than twice the average number in Shakespeare's plays. The effect is a dizzying rush of events, approximating the method of montage in film. Shakespeare's previous tragedies were constructed around a few major scenes. Here there are so many entrances and exits, so many shifts of locations and incidents that Samuel Johnson condemned the play as a mere string of episodes "produced without any art of connection or care of disposition." Later critics have discovered the play's organizing principle in its thematic contrast between Rome and Egypt, supported by an elaborate pattern of images, contrasts, and juxtapositions. There is still, however, disagreement over issues of Shakespeare's methods and intentions in *Antony and Cleopatra*. Critic Howard Felperin has suggested that the play "creates an ambiguity of effect and response unprecedented even within Shakespeare's work." The critical debate turns on how to interpret Antony and Cleopatra, perhaps the most complex, contradictory, and fascinating characters Shakespeare ever created.

Antony and Cleopatra picks up where *Julius Caesar* left off. Four years after Caesar's murder, an alliance among Octavius, Julius Caesar's grandnephew; Mark Antony; and the patrician politician Lepidus has put down the conspiracy led by Brutus and Cassius and resulted in a division of the Roman world among them. Antony, given the eastern sphere of the empire to rule, is now in Alexandria, where he has fallen in love with the Egyptian queen Cleopatra. Enthralled, Antony has ignored repeated summonses to return to Rome to attend to his political responsibilities. By pursuing his desires instead, in the words of his men, Antony, "the triple pillar of the world," has been "transform'd into a strumpet's fool." The play immediately establishes a dominant thematic contrast between Rome and Egypt that represents two contrasting worldviews and value systems. Rome is duty, rationality, and the practical world of politics; Egypt, embodied by its queen, is private needs, sensual pleasure, and revelry. The play's tragedy stems from the irreconcilable division between the two, represented in the play's two major movements: Antony's abandoning Cleopatra and Egypt for Rome and his duties and his subsequent defection back to them. Antony's lieutenant Enobarbus functions in the play as Antony's conscience, whose sexual cynicism stands in contrast to the love-drenched Egyptian court.

Antony is forced to take action when he learns that his wife, Fulvia, who started a rebellion against Octavius, has died, and that Sextus Pompey, son of Pompey the Great, is claiming his right to power by harrying Octavius on the seas. His resolve to return to Rome to take up his duties there displeases Cleopatra, and they engage in a back-and-forth lover's exchange of insults, avowals of love, and jealous recriminations and, ultimately, a mutual awareness of Antony's dilemma in trying to reconcile his personal desires with his political responsibilities. Antony comforts Cleopatra by saying:

> Our separation so abides and flies,
> That thou residing here, goes yet with me;
> And I hence fleeting, here remain with thee.

The second act begins in the house of Sextus Pompey, who gauges the weakness of the three triumvirs, especially Antony, whom he hopes will continue to be distracted by Cleopatra: "Let witchcraft join with beauty, lust with both, / Tie up the libertine in a field of feasts." In the house of Lepidus, a quarrel between Antony and Octavius over Fulvia's rebellion and Antony's irresponsibility threatens to sever the bond between them. Agrippa, Octavius's general, suggests a marriage between Antony and Octavius's sister, Octavia. Antony agrees to the marriage as a political necessity, for the good of Rome and to patch up the quarrel. After Antony and Octavius leave to visit Octavia, Enobarbus tells Agrippa and Maecenas, another follower of Octavius, about the splendors of Egypt and Cleopatra's remarkable allure. Maecenas remarks sadly that, because of the marriage, "Now Antony / Must leave her utterly." Enobarbus, despite his cynicism, understands Cleopatra's powerful attractiveness and disagrees:

> Age cannot wither her, nor custom stale
> Her infinite variety. Other women cloy
> The appetites they feed, but she makes hungry
> Where most she satisfies.

Enobarbus's remarks make clear that the alliance between Antony and Octavius will be short lived, setting both on a collision course.

After his marriage Antony consults an Egyptian soothsayer, who predicts Octavius's rise and counsels Antony to return to Egypt:

> Nobel, courageous, high, unmatchable,
> Where Caesar's is not. But near him thy angel
> Becomes afeard, as being o'erpowered. Therefore
> Make space enough between you.

Angrily dismissing the soothsayer, Antony nevertheless agrees with his analysis, recognizing that "I'th' East my pleasure lies." Before Antony leaves for Egypt, however, the triumvirs and rebels meet on Pompey's galley for a night of drinking and feasting following negotiations. Antony's capacity for raucous merrymaking shows the self-indulgence that will lead to his downfall, while

Octavius's sobriety, if puritanical and passionless, nevertheless bespeaks an iron will and determination that eventually will insure his victory over his rivals.

As the third act begins, Ventidius, another of Antony's commanders, has conquered the Parthians, a victory for which he diplomatically plans to let Antony take credit. Antony, now in Athens with Octavia, learns that Octavius has slandered him and is warring against Pompey. The alliance between the two triumvirs, as well as Antony's control over his own forces, is further threatened when Antony discovers that Octavius has imprisoned Lepidus to solidify his position and that one of his officers has murdered Pompey. Octavia returns to Rome to try to repair the breach between husband and brother. There, Octavius tells her that Antony has returned to Egypt and convinces her that Antony is not only unfaithful but is preparing for war: "He hath given his empire / Up to a whore." Octavius responds by preparing to engage Antony in battle at Actium. In Egypt Enobarbus fails to convince Cleopatra not to take part in the battle, and the lovers also discount Enorbarbus's logical reasons for fighting Octavius on land rather than sea. This decision is partly due to Octavius's challenge: He dares Antony to meet him in a naval engagement. Cleopatra claims, "I have sixty sails. Octavius none better," and Antony is unable to resist either Octavius's challenge or Cleopatra's bravado. At Actium a sickened Enobarbus watches as Cleopatra's ships turn tail and flee, and a despairing, shame-filled Antony follows her "like a doting mallard" with his ships. Cleopatra apologizes to Antony for the retreat, and he forgives her, but when Antony sees Octavius's ambassador kissing Cleopatra's hand and her cordial behavior toward him, he becomes enraged, berating Cleopatra and ordering the messenger Thidias to be whipped. Again the couple are reconciled, and Antony decides to stake all on another battle. Enobarbus, however, has had enough of Antony's clouded judgment and makes plans to desert him and join Octavius.

In the fourth act Octavius scoffs at Antony's challenge to meet him in a duel and prepares for war with confidence, knowing that many of his rival's men have defected to him. When Antony learns of Enobarbus's desertion he forgives his friend and generously sends his treasure to him. Enobarbus reacts to Antony's magnanimity with remorse and dies desiring Antony's forgiveness. Antony scores an initial victory over Octavius, but in a later sea battle and on land in the Egyptian desert, Antony's army is routed. Enraged, Antony blames Cleopatra and accuses her of betraying him. Terrified by his anger, Cleopatra seeks refuge in her monument and plots to regain Antony's affection by sending word to him that she has slain herself. Her plan disastrously misfires when the news shames Antony into taking his own life:

> I will o'ertake thee, Cleopatra, and
> Weep for my pardon. So it must be, for now

All length is torture; since the torch is out,
Lie down and stray no farther.

He orders his servant Eros to stab him, but Eros takes his own life instead to prevent carrying out the order. Antony then falls upon his sword and when he is told that Cleopatra is still alive, asks to be taken to her in a final acknowledgment that his life and happiness are inextricably bound to her. Just before he dies Antony offers his own eulogy at the end of his long struggle between desire and duty:

The miserable change now at my end
Lament nor sorrow at; but please your thoughts
In feeding them with those my former fortunes
Wherein I liv'd the greatest prince o' th' world,
The noblest; and do now not basely die,
Not cowardly put off my helmet to
My countryman—a Roman by a Roman
Valiantly vanquish'd.

In the fifth act Octavius hears of Antony's death and mourns the passing of a great warrior before moving to procure his spoils: Cleopatra. He sends word that she has nothing to fear from him, but Cleopatra tries to stab herself to prevent the Roman soldiers from taking her prisoner and is stopped. When Dolabella, one of Octavius's lieutenants, attempts to placate her, she accuses him of lying, and he admits that Octavius plans to display her as his conquest in Rome. Octavius arrives, promising to treat her well if she complies with his wishes while ominously threatening her destruction if she follows "Antony's course." Pretending compliance, Cleopatra says of Octavius to her attendants when he departs: "He words me, girls, he words me, that I should not / Be noble to myself." Sending for a basket of figs containing poisonous snakes, Cleopatra prepares herself for death:

Give me my robe, put on my crown, I have
Immortal longings in me. Now no more
The juice of Egypt's grace shall moist this lip.

Stage-managing her own end, Cleopatra anticipates joining Antony as his worthy wife:

. . . Methinks I hear
Antony call. I see him rouse himself
To praise my noble act. I hear him mock
The luck of Caesar, which the gods give men

To excuse their after wrath. Husband, I come.
Now to that name my courage prove my title!

Placing one of the snakes at her breast, Cleopatra dies. When Octavius returns, he speaks admiringly of her:

> Bravest at the last,
> She levell'd at our purposes, and being royal,
> Took her own way.

Implying by his words an envy of Antony and Cleopatra's passion and eminence, Octavius commands:

> She shall be buried by her Antony;
> No grave upon the earth shall clip in it
> A pair so famous. High events as these
> Strike those that make them; and their story is
> No less in pity than his glory which
> Brought them to be lamented.

In the contest with Rome, Egypt must lose. Desire is no match against cold calculation for worldly power. Human frailty cannot survive an iron will, and yet the play makes its case that despite all the contradictions and clear character imperfections in Antony and Cleopatra, with all their willful self-indulgence, their love trumps all. By the manner of their going and the human values they ultimately assert, Antony and Cleopatra leave an immense emptiness by their death. Octavius wins, but the world loses by their passing. Shakespeare stages an argument on behalf of what makes us human, even at the cost of an empire. His lovers rise to the tragic occasion for a concluding triumph befitting a magnanimous warrior and a queen of "infinite variety."

MOTHER COURAGE AND HER CHILDREN

18

(1941)

by Bertolt Brecht

Mother Courage is a complex figure. Brecht correctly resisted anyone presenting her pri-marily as a mother who, "like Niobe," is unable "to protect her children from the vicis-situdes of war." For the playwright, Mother Courage is the "merchant-mother, a great living contradiction who is disfigured and deformed beyond recognition." In the scene on the battlefield she is "truly the hyena." In her "antitheses in all their abruptness and incompatibility" are united. The play does not intend to display "the indestructibility of a vital person afflicted by the iniquities of war" . . . but, on the contrary, the destructibility of even the most energetic human being. Therein lies her deeply moving tragedy for the audience.

—Franz Norbert Mennemeier, "Mother Courage and Her Children,"
in *Das deutsche Drama von Baroch bis zur Gegenwart*

Called by Tennessee Williams the greatest drama of the 20th century, Bertolt Brecht's *Mother Courage and Her Children* is both one of the most powerful antiwar dramas ever written and one of the masterworks of the playwright's conception of epic theater, Brecht's innovative and influential contribution to modern drama. Written on the eve of World War II in Scandinavia, where Brecht was living in exile from Nazi Germany, and first performed in Switzerland in 1941, *Mutter Courage und ihre Kinder* debuted in Germany in 1949 under Brecht's direction amidst the ruins of Berlin, a horrifyingly appropriate setting reflecting the consequences of ignor-ing Brecht's jeremiad on the all-consuming destructiveness of war. *Mother Courage* has become one of Brecht's most performed and admired plays, a classic of modern theater as well as a justification of and a challenge to Brecht's notions of drama. Set during the devastating 17th-century Thirty Years' War, the play chronicles the encounters of canteen woman Anna Fierling, nicknamed Mother Courage, as she tries to make her living selling her wares from her cart to the soldiers. As critic Victor Wittner wrote about the play's wartime premiere,

With all its cynicism, *Mutter Courage* is a compelling portrait, often with subtle humor, often with diabolical undercurrents of meaning, often with a certain fatalism, but also often with pure human simplicity and tenderness. And what moves us even more than that is the parallel with today's events, the actual recognition that one war is like another, one misery yields nothing to another in gruesomeness.

Mother Courage has gone on to reflect and respond to other wars and other atrocities, revealing powerful truths about the human condition.

At the play's center is one of drama's great paradoxical protagonists. Mother Courage defines the modern conception of the antihero as both an ultimate survivor of the worst humans can devise—a pathetic victim of war who loses her three children to it—and a collaborator in her own and her family's destruction. As critic Robert Brustein has argued,

> Like Falstaff (her Shakespearean prototype), she is an escaped character who baffles the author's original intentions. Salty, shrewd, hardbitten, and skeptical, Courage is a full-blooded personification of the anti-heroic view of life. At the end, childless and desolate, Courage straps herself to her battered wagon and continues to follow the soldiers, having learned nothing except that man's capacity for suffering is limitless. But this knowledge is the tragic perception; and Brecht, for all his ideologizing, has recreated a tragic universe in which the cruelty of men, the venality of society, and the indifference of the gods seem immutable conditions of life.

The brilliance of the play stems from the complex and ambiguous Mother Courage who both embodies Brecht's polemical lesson of the consequences of war and dehumanizing materialism and evades reductive ideological and moral categories.

Mother Courage is no less complex or paradoxical than her creator. Spanning and affected by the formative experiences of the 20th century, Brecht was born in 1898 in the Bavarian city of Augsburg into a respectable middle-class family. His father, the business director of a paper factory, was a Catholic; his mother, a Protestant. An indifferent and at times rebellious student, Brecht excelled at writing and published his first poems and reviews as a teenager in local newspapers. To evade the draft during World War I Brecht studied medicine at the University of Munich but was called up in 1918 to serve as a medical orderly in an Augsburg military hospital. There he witnessed firsthand the terrible cost of war that reinforced a lifelong pacifistic view. Following Germany's defeat Brecht responded to the postwar social chaos, including the turbulent formation of the Weimar Republic and the brutal suppression of the 1918–19 revolution, with his initial dramatic works and a commitment to socialism and the German Communist Party. His first play, *Baal*, written in 1918, concerns a poet who murders his best friend in a fit of jealousy. Composed of 22 loosely connected scenes, the play shows the combined influence of Georg Büchner's *WOYZECK* and the expressionists. His second play, *Trommeln in der Nacht* (*Drums in the Night*), a bitterly nihilistic drama about a war veteran who learns that his fiancée has been seduced by a war profiteer, was performed to acclaim in Munich in 1922. Praised for his stark and challenging assessment of postwar reality and innovative dramatic techniques, Brecht moved to Berlin in 1924 where he served as a play reader for the great German director Max Reinhardt, while continuing his theatrical experimentation in such plays as *Im Dickicht der Staedte* (*In the Jungle of the Cities*) and *Mann ist Mann* (*A Man's a Man*). He achieved his greatest popular success in 1928 with the musical *Die Dreigroschenoper* (*The Threepenny Opera*), an adaptation of John Gay's comedy, written in collaboration with composer Kurt Weill. A direct assault on the audience's expectations and complacency, *The Threepenny Opera* characteristically combines social and moral instruction with entertainment, employing the methods that Brecht would later codify in his conception of the *"episches Drama."*

Initially conceived in articles and notebooks during the 1920s and worked out in several essays in the early 1930s, Brecht's formulation of a new theory of drama is a crucial contribution to modern theater. "No other twentieth-century writer," drama historian Marvin Carlson has argued, "has influenced the theatre both as a dramatist and theorist as profoundly as Bertolt Brecht." Rejecting the assumptions of naturalism that had dominated the European theater after Henrik Ibsen, Brecht opposed the realistic "theater of illusion" that encouraged an audience's emotional involvement and complacency through verisimilitude with a different kind of drama designed to stimulate thought and action. Traditional Aristotelian or dramatic theater, in Brecht's view, was restrictive and falsifying. Brecht's alternative was a dramatic structure derived from the epic: an episodic narrative form in which each episode is significant not only for what it contributes to the whole but in itself. The epic further differs from drama in that it deals with past events rather than with the imaginary "present" of the drama, which unfolds before us as if it were happening for the first time. In his epic theater Brecht wanted the audience to see the action as something that has happened and is now being reenacted on a stage. The deliberate distancing of the audience from the onstage experience is encapsulated in the key Brechtian term *verfremdung*, "to make strange," or the so-called alienation principle. Contrary to the theater of verisimilitude that draws the audience into the illusion of life enacted on stage, Brecht endorsed techniques of dramatic structure, staging, and acting to maintain the audience's critical distance and judgment, to "make strange" habitual ways of seeing experience and thereby opening up new possibilities and perceptions.

Mother Courage and Her Children brilliantly illustrates both Brecht's dramatic method and its achievement. Composed of 12 scenes set in numerous locations in Sweden, Poland, and Germany between 1624 and 1636, the play dramatizes the central ironic contradiction between Mother Courage's struggles to provide for and protect her children and her business that insures their loss. Each scene is introduced by a summary of setting and situation, including outcomes that undermine dramatic suspense in favor of the audience's critique of characters and action. As the play opens Mother Courage and her wagon—the two constants in the succession of scenes—appear on stage being drawn by her two sons, Eilif and Swiss Cheese. Kattrin, her mute, traumatized daughter, rides in the wagon with her mother. Encountering Swedish recruiting soldiers, Anna tells how she got her nickname by intrepidly driving her cart through the bombardment of Riga to sell 50 loaves of bread that were going moldy and sings the first of several songs that ironically comment on the play's themes:

> Captains, how can you make them face it—
> Marching to death without a brew?
> Courage has rum with which to lace it
> And boil their souls and bodies through.
> Their musket primed, their stomach hollow—
> Captains, you men don't look so well.
> So feed them up and let them follow
> While you command them into hell.
> The new year's come. The watchmen shout.
> The thaw sets in. The dead remain.
> Whatever life has not died out
> It staggers to its feet again.

Mother Courage's clear-eyed awareness of the horrors and stupidity of war, sounded in the song, is also evident as she distracts efforts to recruit Eilif by fortune-telling in which the recruiting officers and all her children draw the black cross of death. However, while she is busy haggling with the sergeant over the sale of a belt, Eilif is led away to join the army. The scene closes as the sergeant sings in parting to Mother Courage and her remaining two children: "Like the war to nourish you? / Have to feed it something too."

Two years later while still following the Swedish army on their Polish campaign, the reduced family is briefly reunited as Eilif has achieved acclaim for having slaughtered peasants and stolen their oxen. Three years later Swiss Cheese has become paymaster of the Second Protestant Regiment, which is being overrun by Catholic forces. Mother Courage remains convinced of the superiority of the Protestant side, observing, "To go by what the big shots say, they're waging war for almighty God and in the name of everything that's good and lovely. But look closer, they ain't so silly, they're waging it for what they can get. Else little folk like me wouldn't be in it at all." The cost for the "little folk" is made clear when Mother Courage attempts to ransom her captured son. Willing to part with her wagon for 200 guilders, she reserves some of the money to live on, and the offered sum proves insufficient to save Swiss Cheese, who is executed. Mother Courage, therefore, loses a son a second time when her commercial practicality comes in conflict with her love and duty to her children. In one of the most intense moments of the play, the scene closes as Mother Courage is shown the dead body of her son but must show no recognition to save herself. "Know him?" the sergeant asks. "What, never seen him before he had that meal here? Pick him up. Chuck him in the pit. He's got nobody knows him."

In scene 5, two years have passed and the war has widened, taking Mother Courage and her wagon to Italy and Bavaria where she resists an appeal to convert the officer's shirts she is planning to sell into bandages for dying peasants unable to pay. By showing Mother Courage carrying on business as usual amid the carnage of the war, Brecht seeks to offset some of the sympathy the audience may feel for her as a war victim. War and capitalism are conjoined, each an aspect of the other, with greed and exploitation warping Mother Courage into a "hyena of the battlefield." This is made especially clear as peace momentarily breaks out in scene 8, and Mother Courage's first response is to lament the armistice's impact on her trade ("Peace'll wring my neck"). In her absence the condemned Eilif is led onto stage to be executed for continuing to kill and rob peasants during peacetime, the same actions that formerly brought him commendation. The scene closes with Mother Courage announcing that the war has resumed, and she encourages it and her trade in song:

> From Ulm to Metz, from Metz to Munich
> Courage will see the war gets fed.
> The war will show a well-filled tunic
> Given its daily shot of lead.
> But lead alone can hardly nourish
> It must have soldiers to subsist.
> It's you it needs to make it flourish.
> The war's still hungry. So enlist!

Now down to her final child Mother Courage in scene 11 is outside the Protestant village of Halle. Unprotected when Mother Courage goes for supplies to sell, Kattrin is captured along with several peasants who fear that the Catholic forces will strike the village without warning. In what has been called by critic Eric Bentley, "possibly the most powerful scene, emotionally, in twentieth century drama," Kattrin climbs onto a roof and sounds the alarm with a drum before she is shot. In the play's final scene Mother Courage sings a lullaby to her dead daughter, trying to convince herself that her child is only sleeping. Eventually realizing the truth, but still unaware that Eilif has been killed, Mother Courage, paying the peasants to bury Kattrin, follows the army, hitching herself to her wagon and closing the play with a final song:

> With all its luck and all its danger
> The war is dragging on a bit
> Another hundred years or longer
> The common man won't benefit.
> Filthy his food, no soap to shave him
> The regiment steals half his pay.
> But still a miracle may save him:
> Tomorrow is another day!
> The new year's come. The watchmen shout.
> The thaw sets in. The dead remain.
> Wherever life has not died out
> It staggers to its feet again.

Strategically, with its antirealist staging, its choral songs, soliloquies, and narrative structure that proceeds by repetition, contrast, and juxtaposition of scenes and images, *Mother Courage* reaches a level of mythic resonance that universalizes the human condition. Brecht's comments and revisions of the play make clear that he was concerned that audiences would overly sympathize with Mother Courage, that her losses, suffering, and indomitable spirit would obscure the play's thesis that war profits no one, least of all the "little folk," and that the pursuit of profit dehumanizes and destroys as inexorably as combat. Ultimately Brecht's efforts to overrule empathy in favor of criticism, reducing the vital complexity of the despicable and admirable Mother Courage down to a political and moral assertion, failed. In a sense audiences have continued to perceive an even greater play than the one Brecht intended by responding to its ambiguous protagonist who is heroic in her endurance and suffering but condemned by her foolish pursuit of profit from the war that has cost her so much. Brecht's stage innovations make clear both how the theater can dramatize the most profound and complex human and social questions but can never fully dispense with the power of felt experience to communicate, modify, and expand the message.

LYSISTRATA

19

(411 B.C.)   by *Aristophanes*

The Lysistrata *has behind it much suffering and a burning pity. Aristophanes had more than once risked his civic rights and even his life in his battle for peace, and is now making his last appeal. It is owing to this background of intense feeling that the* Lysistrata *becomes not exactly a great comedy, but a great play, making its appeal not to laughter alone but also to deeper things than laughter.*

—Gilbert Murray, *Aristophanes: A Study*

With its perennially relevant antiwar and gender themes, *Lysistrata* speaks to modern audiences more forcefully than any other of the playwright's remarkable comedies, making it one of the most frequently produced Greek dramas and the most famous of Aristophanes' plays. If Aristophanes cannot be credited with the actual invention of stage comedy, he is the earliest practitioner whose plays have survived intact. Aristophanes provides us with our only surviving examples of Greek Old Comedy, the raucous, profane, and intellectually daring dramatic form that, along with choral tragedy, was the great achievement of Attic drama during the fifth century B.C.

We know very little about Aristophanes' life and personality, but a great deal about his times as reflected in his plays (11 of his more than 40 works have survived). A native Athenian, Aristophanes was a political and intellectual gadfly whose dramas offer some of the best reflections of the period's controversies and preoccupations. It is said that when Dionysius, the tyrant of Syracuse, wanted to learn about the people and the institutions of Athens, Plato advised him to consult the comedies of Aristophanes. He was born around 450 B.C., in the years when Pericles was initiating the reforms that created the golden age of Athenian democracy and lived through the period of Athens's growth as an empire and as a center of extraordinary intellectual and cultural achievement. Nine of his surviving plays, however, reflect the tragic consequences of the punishing Peloponnesian War with Sparta, which was waged from 431 to 404 and culminated in Athens's defeat and rapid decline. When Aristophanes died in 385 B.C., the last surviving great fifth-century playwright, his passing ended a century of unparalleled dramatic accomplishment. His final years, however, were spent in a very different milieu from his heyday as a dramatist, one hostile to the freewheeling, nothing-is-sacred tolerance upon which his great comedies depended. The Old Comedy of Aristophanes would be replaced by the more sedate New Comedy of the fourth century, a more prosaic, less outrageous and fantastical comedy of manners. As written most notably by Menander, and adapted by the Roman dramatists Plautus and Terence, the New Comedy with its stock characters and situations formed the main tributary for Western comic drama. Aristophanes' comedy, however, should be regarded as more than a dead end and a cultural curiosity. His plays as a form established the bedrock of comedy's greatest resources by offering a serious reflection of the world while encouraging our ability to laugh at its absurdity, excesses, and pretensions. Aristophanes' dramas have remained a rich comic inspiration and influence, to be reworked and refashioned through the centuries. Echoes of his inventiveness and comic methods are readily found in the epic theater of Bertolt Brecht, the absurdist, existential dramas of Samuel Beckett, and the intellectual high jinks of Tom Stoppard. If later comic drama is less exuberant and more predictable than Aristophanes' plays, the essential elements in his works—irreverence, a mix of serious themes and low comic farce, a celebration of human nature's foibles and vitality, and an exhilarating liberation from repression and pretensions in their many guises—established comedy's core ethos and strategies.

The origins of Greek comedy are as obscure as those of tragedy. Both dramatic forms seem to have derived from the communal and ritual celebration of the god Dionysus. The Greek word *kômoidia*, from which the term *comedy* is derived, means the "song of a band of revelers"; the *komos* was a procession of revelers who sang and danced through towns or festivals, often dressed as and impersonating animals while celebrating the vital force of nature and fertility. Their raucous performances, filled with obscenity, scatology, and the direct taunts of the onlookers, were intended to disrupt routine and to provoke an emotional and sexual release. The *komos* formed the prototype for the comedy that Greek playwrights in the fifth century B.C. adapted into a chorus, with actors taking the parts of characters in a plot in which obstacles are surmounted, often in fantastical manner, to end in celebration and affirmation. Elements of these early comedies are found in the satyr plays that concluded tragic trilogies, and comedies were first included in Athens's annual drama festival, the City Dionysia, in 486 B.C., with a second festival, the Lenaea, featuring comedies, established in 442 B.C.

Aristotle, in the *Poetics*, established the accepted contrast between tragedy and comedy by the latter's depiction of less exalted characters and situations. The method and outcome of comedy are the opposite of tragedy in which pity and fear are evoked by a telling dramatization of a hero's exposed limitations.

In comedy laughter is the desired outcome, derived from the breaking of boundaries, from the shattering of illusions, and an emotionally satisfying transcendence over the ordinary or the preordained. Tragedy moves from order to disorder and death; comedy from disorder to a renewed stability, marked by obstacles overcome and a restored harmony in the repaired breach from the opposing forces that condemn the tragic hero. Different from tragedy's familiar mythological subjects involving heroes who are paragons, Attic comedy was original and invented, making use of both the fantastical and the details of ordinary life, with characters as flawed and as recognizable as anyone in the audience. If tragedy aspired to the timeless and universal, Greek Old Comedy exploited the local, reflecting specific controversies in the political, cultural, literary, and intellectual issues of the day. Aristophanes' comedies also make use of actual figures, such as Socrates, Euripides, Aeschylus, and the Athenian political leader Cleon. During a performance of the *Clouds*, it is said, Socrates stood up in the audience to show how well done his likeness was on the mask of the actor who played him. Aristophanes' targets include such revered institutions as Athenian democracy and the Athenian jury system that are exposed as falling comically short of the ideal. Euripides is ridiculed in several of Aristophanes' plays, making Aristophanes in a sense the original dramatic critic. Almost all of Aristophanes' surviving plays were produced during the Peloponnesian War, which the playwright daringly condemns as unjust and morally reprehensible. There is perhaps no better example of Aristophanes' topicality, as well as Athenian toleration of dissent and self-assessment, than Aristophanes' comic attack on war and its conduct as it is being waged. In the *Acharnians* (425), the earliest extant comedy, Dicaeopolis makes a separate peace with the Spartans and must get the better of a hard-line general whose patriotism is exposed as a destructive fraud. In *Peace* (421) the Goddess of Peace must be rescued from the pit in which she is imprisoned by Trygaeus, who ascends to heaven on a dung beetle. *Lysistrata* presents the provocative fantasy that war could be stopped by the women through denying sex to the combatants until peace is secured.

Aristophanes mounts his case in *Lysistrata* through paradox and inversion. It is the only extant ancient Greek comedy in which women take center stage and control the action. Lysistrata (whose name means "disbander of armies") conceives the so-called happy idea central to Old Comedy that women can end the madness of war and restore common sense and sanity, jeopardized by male dominance of public affairs, by witholding women's most powerful weapon: sexuality. As critic A. M. Bowie has observed, "*Lysistrata* portrays the temporary imposition of a gynaecocracy on the city of Athens." As the play opens Lysistrata summons females from across Greece to present her radical notion. Women simply convening an assembly before the sacred gates of the Acropolis would have struck Aristophanes' first audience as unthinkable and as an outrageous violation of accepted standards. Confined to domestic duties in their homes, Athenian women had no power and no place in the public sphere. Conspiring to take charge of the patriarchical Athenian society asserts the play's topsy-turviness that escalates into a series of comic reversals and witty ironies. To save the state its subservient dependents must take control of it. To make peace the women must go to war. Theirs will be a battle of the sexes in which their opponents are their own husbands. Women's sexual power is to be asserted by withholding sex; a normal, peaceful sexual life is to be reclaimed by foregoing it. To restore domestic tranquillity gender roles are reversed, with women becoming more masculine and men reduced to helpless dependence on their newly empowered mates. The men will be vanquished by their own virility to make peace and resume enjoying its blessings. Aristophanes' clever, dizzying inversions set in motion a delightful series of bawdy comic situations, an apparently inexhaustible stream of double entendres in which the erotic principle seems to infect every comment and aspect of Athenian life, outrageous sight gags of the males sporting near-crippling erections, as well as the playwright's many profound and serious points about the true cost of war and the true value of peace.

To start her rebellion Lysistrata must first get her sisters to assemble on time and then convince them to abstain from sex themselves. This proves to be no mean feat, and Aristophanes' play opens with confirmation of comic female stereotypes in the women's triviality, deceitfulness, drunkenness, and licentiousness. For Lysistrata's scheme (and Aristophanes' comedy) to work the physical realities of women and men's lives must be acknowledged. Sexual desire and the carnal must be shown as far stronger and far more important than political power or other abstract virtues. Erotic passion must trump the rational, and the life force must be shown superior to any death wish for conquest or vengeance in order to break war's hold on Greece that has subverted what is most central in human life. As Aristophanes makes clear, the women assembled are no more virtuous paragons of principles than their mates but are the first to recognize in their appetites and passions what truly matters. Wittily Aristophanes shows that women's gender liabilities—confinement to the domestic and their sexual preoccupations—are actually strengths and worth protecting, and Lysistrata manages to convince Athenian and Spartan women alike to just say no, as the play's rambunctious assault on dignity, propriety, and pretension commences.

Reflecting the gender discord that ensues, the play's chorus is divided into sparring, antiphonal contingents of old men and women who enact a version of the frustrated sexual act as the men try to storm the barred gates of the Acropolis held by the women with battering rams and flaming torches. The women, having taken control of the city's treasury as the younger women have kept their physical treasures from their husbands, extinguish the assault and cool the ardor of their attackers by throwing water on them. An Athenian magistrate arrives to reassert order, and his verbal combat with Lysistrata over the role and responsibilities of women to the state forms the core debate in the play. He asserts that state affairs and the conduct of war are no business of women, to which Lysistrata responds with an extended comparison between her plan for saving Greece and the domestic art of weaving. The Magistrate replies: "It takes a woman to reduce state questions to a matter of carding and weaving." Lysistrata powerfully responds to his charge of women's irrelevance by pointedly observing that women have the most to lose from a mismanaged state that leaves them widowed and unmarried. "Instead of the love that every women needs," Lysistrata states, "we have only our single bed, where we can dream of our husbands off with the army." For maidens there is an urgency that war disrupts. A bald and toothless man can still find a mate, but, as Lysistrata points out, "A woman's beauty is gone with the first gray hair," and an aging woman will wait in vain for a husband.

Having successfully turned away a physical and verbal male assault, Lysistrata and her rebellion must next deal with internal dissension as the women begin to waver, inventing elaborate ruses to return home for sex. Lysistrata is only able to steel the women's resolve by the promise of an oracle that Zeus will "set the lower higher." The strategy of delaying the gratification of the men is comically played out as the husband Cinesias, "simply bulging with love," tries to convince his wife Myrrhine to gratify the love that is "killing me." Myrrhine appears to comply but agonizingly delays in successive searches for a bed, mattress, pillow, coverlet, and perfume before leaving Cinesias cold after her failures to commit to the desired treaty. An embassy of erect Spartans arrive, and under the spell of an enormous statue of a naked woman representing reconciliation, they agree to peace terms with the Athenians. Lysistrata is allowed a final and moving speech on behalf of a common Greek heritage and past common cause that should cancel current differences before feasting and dancing conclude the play. The gender divide is repaired; the chorus joins in harmony, and the values of hearth and home and the life force have been reestablished as central under the temporary, comic management of the women. Aristophanes' dramatization of the principle "Make Love, Not War" pushes to a delightfully preposterous extreme certain absurdities in gender relationships and civic affairs to reach more basic truths in the power of life over death and love over hate.

DOCTOR FAUSTUS

20

(c. 1588–93) *by Christopher Marlowe*

More than any other play, Marlowe's Doctor Faustus *celebrates that God-like power of language, and shows us how words can soar, and tempts us to dizzying heights within our heads. But all the time, Marlowe is in control. He knows too much about the shaping power of words to be a Faustus. Marlowe is a magus too, all poets are, but one who tells us in this play to use that awesome power of words to fashion ourselves in God's image. Else, like his hero, we will be deformed by the servant we abuse.*

—A. Bartlett Giamatti, "Marlowe: The Arts of Illusion"

Christopher Marlowe in *Doctor Faustus,* one of the earliest and the most famous non-Shakespearean Elizabethan tragedies, manages not only to bridge the gap between the medieval morality plays and the secular, classically influenced dramas of the Renaissance but to produce one of the core myths of Western civilization. Like Oedipus, Faustus, who exchanges damnation for knowledge and power, has become a resonating tragic archetype, epitomizing the doomed but daring overreacher whose rebellion and defeat enact a struggle for transcendence against the gravitational pull of the human condition. Faustus's bargain with the devil, his ambitious rise and terrifying fall, encapsulate and typify the dilemma of the modem tragic hero. As critic T. McAlindon observes, 'What makes the play most remarkable is the fact that in composing it Marlowe so elicited the latent meanings of the devil compact—a type of story that had been familiar in the West for centuries—that he gave it the force and status of myth. Indeed, he shaped it into a myth that usurped the place in the Western imagination hitherto enjoyed by the myths of Lucifer and of Adam and Eve. The Faust figure has become the archetype of all human striving to reach beyond the human; more particularly, he has become the personification of that postmedieval phenomenon we call individualism." The descendants of Faustus include Byron's romantic outlaws, Shelley's Prometheus, Melville's Ahab, Brontë's Heathcliff, and Faulkner's Thomas Sutpen. Goethe, who marveled at Marlowe's dramatic construction—"How greatly it is all planned!"—would take up the story of Faustus for his own masterwork. Oswald Spengler in *The Decline of the West* saw in the drama a metaphor for Western technological hubris and cultural self-destruction that defined the modem world, which he called the "Faustian Age." The power of Faustus as a spiritual and cultural myth originates from Marlowe's remarkable dramatic conception and astonishing poetic skills that helped to transform Western drama. Synthesizing the conventions of the medieval morality play and the tradition of classical tragedy, Marlowe achieved both the overwhelming concentrated force of *Everyman* and the breathtakingly expansive, existential dramatic poetry of Aeschylus, Sophocles, and Euripides.

If *Doctor Faustus* continues to haunt our collective consciousness, its creator has proven to be no less fascinating. Christopher Marlowe was born in 1564 in Canterbury, two months before fellow playwright William Shakespeare. Both men came from the rising middle stratum of Elizabethan society, from the world of trade and the yeomanry. Like Shakespeare's father, who was a glover, Marlowe's father was a successful shoemaker, but Marlowe, unlike Shakespeare, gained a scholarship to attend Cambridge University to prepare for a clerical career. Marlowe received a bachelor's degree in 1584 and a master's in 1587, but only after Queen Elizabeth's Privy Council interceded on his behalf when university officials, suspecting Marlowe's Catholic sympathies, refused to grant his degree. Their suspicions were aroused by Marlowe's travels to Rheims a prominent center in France, for English Roman Catholic expatriates. The letter from the Privy Council on Marlowe's behalf asserted that "in all his accions he had behaved him selfe orderlie and discreetlie wherebie he had done her Majestic good service." What exactly the service was that Marlowe had provided is unknown, but his clandestine activities, possibly as a spy and informer, would continue to shadow Marlowe, as would his unorthodox, heretical ideas, as he rejected the approved point of his college education in holy orders and began to make his name as a poet and playwright in London.

As one of the so-called University Wits, a group that included such writers as John Lyly, Robert Greene, George Peele, and Thomas Nashe, Marlowe would bring his classical training and new secular humanistic ideas fostered at Cambridge to bear on English popular drama and would help to transform it into a sophisticated and expressive artistic form. Marlowe's six plays—*Dido, Queen of Carthage; Tamburlaine the Great; The Jew of Malta; The Massacre of Paris; Edward II;* and *Doctor Faustus*—were all written in a period of about six years, from 1587 to 1593. Marlowe's assault on the dramatic conventions of his day is clearly announced in the prologue of *Tamburlaine*, which first established his reputation as a dramatist, in which he contemptuously dismisses the prevailing "jygging vaines of riming mother wits" and the "conceits clownage keepes in pay." With the unprecedented power of what Ben Jonson described as his "mighty line" in some of the most eloquent poetry in English drama,

Marlowe puts at center stage the larger-than-life, cruel Mongolian tyrant who threatens "the world with high astounding terms." Marlowe thereby pioneered a new breed of hero for the Elizabethan stage: the master of his own destiny who succeeds by the strength of his will, claiming authority by his own human powers. Marlowe's dramatization of the cost of such powers would set a new focus and standard for drama that would dominate the Elizabethan period and tragedy ever since.

The violence and lawbreaking that Marlowe put on stage dogged the playwright's life as well. In 1589 Marlowe was arrested and jailed for a fortnight over his involvement in a fatal brawl. The homicide would be ruled "in self-defence" and "not by felony." For a time Marlowe shared quarters with playwright Thomas Kyd, and in 1593, when Kyd was arrested for sedition, the authorities discovered documents in his rooms containing "vile hereticall Conceiptes Denyinge the Deity of Jhesus Christ our Savior." Kyd insisted that the papers belonged to Marlowe, and the Privy Council issued an arrest warrant. Before it could be executed, however, Marlowe was killed in the house of Mrs. Eleanor Bull in Deptford, where the writer had spent the day with companions eating and drinking, in a scuffle ostensibly about who should pay the bill. An inquest ruled Marlowe's death accidental, but conspiracy theories have persisted that Marlowe was assassinated for political or religious reasons or in connection with his espionage activities. The manner of Marlowe's early death at age 29, as well as the details and rumors of a contentious and possibly shadowy secret life, have helped burnish the legend of a doomed literary artist of great genius who embodies baffling contradictions. Was Marlowe an Elizabethan apologist or an apostate? A scholar and intellectual, Marlowe was nevertheless a habitué of the seedy underworld of Elizabethan informers, spies, and tavern brawlers. He was the praised servant of the authoritarian, theocratic Elizabethan state but was also a radical freethinker and considered a dangerous religious skeptic. Marlowe's plays exalt daring rebels even as they work out their inevitable punishment for transgressions of accepted limits. At the core of Marlowe's life and works, therefore, are some of the fundamental contradictions of the Elizabethan (and the modern) age itself in its contention between the religious and the secular, the individual and the community, restraint versus liberation, power versus morality, ambition versus responsibility. These tensions are best expressed in the tragic moral fable of *Doctor Faustus.*

Like its author, *Doctor Faustus* has generated vexing unanswered questions and endless speculation. Scholars remain divided over whether the play was an early work composed shortly after Marlowe's popular success with *Tamburlaine* or whether it is one of his last plays. The earliest record of the play's production is in 1594, but most experts do not believe this reflects the play's first staging. The textual history of the play is no less cloudy and contentious as its compositional and performance history. *Doctor Faustus* was first published in a 1,485-line version in 1604, nearly a dozen years after Marlowe's death, and a longer 2,131-line version followed in 1616. The discrepancy between these texts and the degree to which other hands were responsible for many of the play's scenes have made *Doctor Faustus* one of the thorniest bibliographical puzzles in English literature. Although the origins and authorship of the pieces of the puzzle remain debatable, the impact and effectiveness of the whole trump academic conjecture. No one doubts that the overall conception of Faustus's rise and fall is Marlowe's alone, and in the power and forcefulness of its moral vision and stage spectacle, *Doctor Faustus*, in whatever version is preferred, is one of the wonders of English drama. It is a play that looks back for its effects to the allegorical, didactic roots of medieval drama while it anticipates in its psychological probing of human nature the fully developed tragedy of Shakespeare and the later Elizabethan dramatists.

The *Tragical History of the Life and Death of Doctor Faustus* makes clear its connections to the medieval morality play by enacting, like *Everyman*, the ultimate choice of a soul between salvation and damnation. The allegorical nature of Faustus's struggle is emphasized by the on-stage presence of devils, by the good and bad angels who externalize Faustus's inner conflicts, by the spectacular procession of the Deadly Sins that captivates him and seals his fate, and the final terrifying vision of hell of act 5. However, other elements help to pattern the drama of Faustus as a classical tragedy. Marlowe employs a chorus for exposition and commentary, and the particularity of Faustus as an exceptional hero, rather than a generic, representative Everyman, links his story with the Aristotelian tragic fall of a great man. Moreover, *Everyman* and the other morality plays end in a comic reconciliation between the wayward sinner and the sources of his salvation. *Doctor Faustus*, however, concludes with the protagonist's unconsoled damnation and hopeless extinction, caught between the irresistible drive of his nature and the immovable limitations of the human condition. Marlowe structures the play to emphasize the tragic pattern of a rise and fall, of choice and consequence.

In act 1 Faustus mounts his rebellion. "Glutted now with learning's golden gifts," but with his intellectual ambitions still unsatisfied, Faustus, a Wittenberg scholar, turns to magic and necromancy to "get a deity" and "reign sole king of all the Provinces." He conjures the devil, Mephistophilis, and makes a bargain with him: in exchange for 24 years of power and knowledge, Faustus agrees to forfeit his immortal soul. Refusing to believe "that after this life there is any pain," undeterred by his conscience, personified by the battling good and bad angel of his nature, and by Mephistophilis who frankly warns him about the torments of hell that he risks, Faustus seals his bargain in blood in act 2. Faustus reveals himself in the negotiation blinded by his desires, a megalomaniac who craves power and knowledge not to serve others but as ends in themselves, who denies the imperatives of anything but his own will. The wrong-headedness of Faustus's aspirations is emphasized in the comic scenes concluding both acts 1 and 2, in which Faustus's servant Wagner parodies his master's conjuring by trying to compel a servant of his own and in the attempt by Robin the ostler to use Faustus's magic to avoid work and satisfy his bodily appetites. In both cases, Faustus's daring and dignity are undercut by comic foolery that diminishes Faustus's overreaching while alerting the audience to his short-sighted self-indulgence. Critics and scholars remain divided on how to regard these comic scenes as well as the farcical episodes of acts 3 and 4 in which Faustus's gained supreme powers are translated into nothing more than conjuring tricks at the expense of the pope in Rome and to provide entertainment at the court of Charles V. Contrasting so markedly with the poetic intensity of acts 1 and 2, the prosy, episodic, so-called problematical middle of *Doctor Faustus* that so flagrantly violates the classical principle of tragic decorum has been apologized for by denying Marlowe's hand in its creation. These must be the scenes, the persistent argument runs, that hacks added to the more majestic and profound existential tragedy that Marlowe first devised. The play's descent into slapstick and somewhat tiresome farce has been interpreted as a remnant of the medieval religious drama that mixed the profane with the sacred, as well as evidence of pandering to the unrefined taste of the Elizabethan audiences who required comic diversion along with their profundity. A case can be made, however, that the ludicrousness of what Faustus makes of his damnable skills makes an effective thematic point underscoring Faustus's spiritual and aspirational decline after exchanging his soul. If the high drama of Faustus's quest is parodied by the low comedy characters in acts 1 and 2, Faustus joins in their horseplay in acts 3 and 4 with his acquired limitless power shown to be little more than silly trickery. The play makes clear that the cost far exceeds the worth of the prize, as the final reckoning that closes the drama powerfully demonstrates.

Faustus regains his dignity in Act 5 in the terrifying enactment of his final moments of life, and the play returns to the eloquent and intense poetry of the first two acts. Pity and terror are extracted in Faustus's climactic realization of the consequence of his bargain. Having first conjured the spirit of Helen of Troy for the delectation of his scholarly friends, Faustus recalls her for his own physical delight as his "paramour" with the most famous lines that Marlowe ever wrote:

> Was this the face that launched a thousand ships,
> And burnt the topless towers of Ilium?
> Sweet Helen, make me immortal with a kiss.
> Her lips suck forth my soul. See where it flies.

Ironically, Faustus's mating with the shadowy succubus Helen ("Was this the face" not "Is this the face") does ensure his immortality, but as one of the damned, as the righteous Old Man who makes a final appeal for Faustus to "leave this damnèd art" makes clear:

> Accursèd Faustus, miserable man,
> That from thy soul exclud'st the grace of heaven
> And fliest the throne of his tribunal seat!

The scene makes clear that even after signing his soul away, Faustus freely chooses his fate, that he is not simply a helpless victim of a poorly considered legal contract. Faustus thereby retains his status as a tragic hero. In his final soliloquy he counts down his last hour on earth, reversing the conclusions of his opening soliloquy. To escape from an eternity of damnation in a "vast perpetual torture-house," the existence of which he finally acknowledges, Faustus now craves extinction and denies the humanity that he had previously exalted: "O soul, be changed to little water-drops,/And fall into the ocean, ne'er be found!" His final words reach an intensity and sublimity equaled on the English stage only by Shakespeare, as Faustus mounts the ultimate existential battle to comprehend the limits and the nature of the human condition in the last grip of mortality and morality. The chorus, Marlowe's borrowing from classical drama that helps to frame the play's tragic dimension, is given the final word on Faustus's fall and its lesson:

> Cut is the branch that might have grown full straight,
> And burnèd is Apollo's laurel bough
> That sometime grew within this learnèd man.
> Faustus is gone. Regard his hellish fall,
> Whose fiendful fortune may exhort the wise
> Only to wonder at unlawful things,
> Whose deepness does entice such forward wits
> To practice more than heavenly power permits.

In language that combines both the Christian and classical cosmogony, Marlowe has synthesized the allegorical religious drama of salvation with the classical tragedy of the hubris of the exceptional hero who tests the limits of existence and humanity's deepest aspirations and darkest fears. *Doctor Faustus* is the only great religious drama of the Elizabethan period and anticipates the staging of the most profound human questions to follow by the only playwright who could rival the grandeur and terror of Marlowe's dramatic conceptions, William Shakespeare.

DEATH OF A SALESMAN

(1949) *by Arthur Miller*

21

Arthur Miller's Death of a Salesman is, perhaps, to this time, the most mature example of a myth of Contemporary life. The chief value of this drama is its attempt to reveal those ultimate meanings which are resident in modern experience. Perhaps the most significant comment on this play is not its literary achievement, as such, but is, rather, the impact which it has had on spectators, both in America and abroad. The influence of this drama, first performed in 1949, continues to grow in World Theatre. For it articulates, in language which can be appreciated by popular audiences, certain new dimensions of the human dilemma.

> —Esther Merle Jackson, *"Death of a Salesman:*
> Tragic Myth in the Modern Theatre"*

It can be argued that the Great American Novel—that always elusive imaginative summation of the American experience—became the Great American Drama in Arthur Miller's *Death of a Salesman.* Along with Eugene O'Neill's LONG DAY'S JOURNEY INTO NIGHT, Miller's masterpiece forms the defining myth of the American family and the American dream. F. Scott Fitzgerald's *The Great Gatsby* is the play's only rival in American literature in expressing the tragic side of the American myth of success and the ill-fated American dreamers. A landmark and cornerstone 20th-century drama, *Death of a Salesman* is crucial in the history of American theater in presenting on stage an archetypal family drama that is simultaneously intimate and representative, social and psychological, realistic and expressionistic. Critic Lois Gordon has called it "the major American drama of the 1940s" that "remains unequalled in its brilliant and original fusion of realistic and poetic techniques, its richness of visual and verbal texture, and its wide range of emotional impact." Miller's play, perhaps more than any other, established American drama as the decisive arena for addressing the key questions of American identity and social and moral values, while pioneering methods of expression that liberated American theater. The drama about the life and death of salesman Willy Loman is both thoroughly local in capturing a particular time and place and universal, one of the most popular and adapted American plays worldwide. Willy Loman has become the contemporary Everyman, prompting widespread identification and sympathy. By centering his tragedy on a lower middle-class protagonist—insisting, as he argued in "Tragedy and the Common Man," that "the common man is as apt a subject for tragedy in its highest sense as kings were"—Miller completed the democratization of drama that had begun in the 19th century while setting the terms for a key debate over dramatic genres that has persisted since *Death of a Salesman* opened in 1949.

Miller's subjects, themes, and dramatic mission reflect his life experiences, informed by the Great Depression, which he regarded as a "moral catastrophe," rivaled, in his view, only by the Civil War in its profound impact on American life. Miller was born in 1915, in New York City. His father, who had emigrated from Austria at the age of six, was a successful coat manufacturer, prosperous enough to afford a chauffeur and a large apartment overlooking Central Park. For Miller's family, an embodiment of the American dream that hard work and drive are rewarded, the stock market crash of 1929 changed everything. The business was lost, and the family was forced to move to considerably reduced circumstances in the Flatbush section of Brooklyn in a small frame house that served as the model for the Lomans' residence. Miller's father never fully recovered from his business failure, and his mother was often depressed and embittered by the family's poverty, though both continued to live in hope of an economic recovery to come. For Miller the depression exposed the hollowness and fragility of the American dream of material success and the social injustice inherent in an economic system that created so many blameless casualties. The paradoxes of American success—its stimulation of both dreams and guilt when lost or unrealized, as well as the conflict it created between self-interest and social responsibility—would become dominant themes in Miller's work. As a high school student Miller was more interested in sports than studies. "Until the age of seventeen I can safely say that I never read a book weightier than *Tom Swift*, and *Rover Boys*," Miller recalled, "and only verged on literature with some of Dickens. . . . I passed through the public school system unscathed." After graduating from high school in 1932 Miller went to work in an auto parts warehouse in Manhattan. It was during his subway commute to and from his job that Miller began reading, discovering both the power of serious literature to change the way one sees the world and his vocation: "A book that changed my life was *The Brothers Karamazov* which I picked up, I don't know how or why, and all at once believed I was born to be a writer."

In 1934 Miller was accepted as a journalism student at the University of Michigan. There he found a campus engaged by the social issues of the day: "The place was full of speeches, meetings and leaflets. It was jumping with Issues. . . . It was, in short, the testing ground for all my prejudices, my beliefs and my ignorance, and it helped to lay out the boundaries of my life." At Michigan Miller wrote his first play, despite having seen only two plays years before, to compete for prize money he needed for tuition. Failing in his first attempt he would eventually twice win the Avery Hopwood Award. Winning "made me confident I could go ahead from there. It left me with the belief that the ability to write plays is born into one, and that it is a kind of sport of the mind." Miller became convinced that "with the exception of a doctor saving a life, writing a worthy play was the most important thing a human could do." He would embrace the role of the playwright as social conscience and reformer who could help change America, by, as he put it "grabbing people and shaking them by the back of the neck." Two years after graduating in 1938, having moved back to Brooklyn and married his college sweetheart, Miller had completed six plays, all but one of them rejected by producers. *The Man Who Had All the Luck*, a play examining the ambiguities of success and the money ethic, managed a run of only four performances on Broadway in 1944. Miller went to work at the Brooklyn Navy Yard, tried his hand at radio scripts, and attempted one more play. "I laid myself a wager," he wrote in his autobiography. "I would hold back this play until I was as sure as I could be that every page was integral to the whole and would work; then, if my judgment of it proved wrong, I would leave the theater behind and write in other forms." The play was *All My Sons*, about a successful manufacturer who sells defective aircraft parts and is made to face the consequences of his crime and his responsibilities. It is Miller's version of a Henrik Ibsen problem play, linking a family drama to wider social issues. Named one of the top-10 plays of 1947, *All My Sons* won the Tony Award and the New York Drama Critics' Circle Award over Eugene O'Neill's *The Iceman Cometh*. The play's success allowed Miller to buy property in rural Connecticut where he built a small studio and began work on *Death of a Salesman*.

This play, subtitled "Certain Private Conversations in Two Acts and a Requiem," about the last 24 hours of an aging and failing traveling salesman misguided by the American dream, began, as the playwright recounts in his introduction to his *Collected Plays*, with an initial image

of an enormous face the height of the proscenium arch which would appear and then open up, and we would see the inside of a man's head. In fact, *The Inside of His Head* was the first title. . . . The image was in direct opposition to the method of *All My Sons*—a method one might call linear or eventual in that one fact or incident creates the necessity for the next. The *Salesman* image was from the beginning absorbed with the concept that nothing in life comes "next" but that everything exists together and at the same time within us; that there is no past to be "brought forward" in a human being, but that he is his past at every moment. . . . I wished to create a form which, in itself as a form, would literally be the process of Willy Loman's way of mind.

The play took shape by staging the past in the present, not through flashbacks of Willy's life but by what the playwright called "mobile concurrency of past and present." Miller recalled beginning

> with only one firm piece of knowledge and this was that Loman was to destroy himself. How it would wander before it got to that point I did not know and resolved not to care. I was convinced only that if I could make him remember enough he would kill himself, and the structure of the play was determined by what was needed to draw up his memories like a mass of tangled roots without ends or beginning.

At once realistic in its documentation of American family life and expressionistic in its embodiment of consciousness on stage, *Death of a Salesman* opens with the 63-year-old Willy Loman's return to his Brooklyn home, revealing to his worried wife, Linda, that he kept losing control of his car on a selling trip to Boston. Increasingly at the mercy of his memories Willy, in Miller's analysis, "is literally at that terrible moment when the voice of the past is no longer distant but quite as loud as the voice of the present." Reflecting its protagonist, "The way of telling the tale . . . is as mad as Willy and as abrupt and as suddenly lyrical." The family's present—Willy's increasing mental instability, his failure to earn the commissions he needs to survive, and his disappointment that his sons, Biff and Happy, have failed to live up to expectations—intersects with scenes from the past in which both their dreams and the basis for their disillusionment are exposed. In the present Biff, the onetime star high school athlete with seeming unlimited prospects in his doting father's estimation, is 34, having returned home from another failed job out west and harboring an unidentified resentment of his father. As Biff confesses, "everytime I come back here I know that all I've done is to waste my life." His brother, Happy, is a deceitful womanizer trapped in a dead-end job who confesses that despite having his own apartment, "a car, and plenty of women . . . still, goddammit, I'm lonely." The present frustrations of father and sons collide with Willy's memory when all was youthful promise and family harmony. In a scene in which Biff with the prospect of a college scholarship seems on the brink of attaining all Willy has expected of him, both boys hang on their father's every word as he exults in his triumphs as a successful salesman:

> America is full of beautiful towns and fine, upstanding people. And they know me, boys, they know me up and down New England. The finest people. And when I bring you fellas up, there'll be open sesame for all of

us, 'cause one thing, boys: I have friends. I can park my car in any street in New England, and the cops protect it like their own.

Triumphantly, Willy passes on his secret of success: "Be liked and you will never want." His advice exposes the fatal flaw in his life view that defines success by exterior rather than interior values, by appearance and possessions rather than core morals. Even in his confident memory, however, evidence of the undermining of his self-confidence and aspirations occurs as Biff plays with a football he has stolen and father and son ignore the warning of the grind Bernard (who "is liked, but he's not well liked") that Biff risks graduating by not studying. Willy's popularity and prowess as a salesman are undermined by Linda's calculation of her husband's declining commissions, prompting Willy to confess that "people don't seem to take to me." Invading Willy's memory is the realization that he is far from the respected and resourceful salesman he has boasted being to his sons as he struggles to meet the payments on the modern appliances that equip the American dream of success. Moreover, to boost his sagging spirits on the road he has been unfaithful to his loving and supportive wife. To protect himself from these hurtful memories Willy is plunged back into the present for a card game with Bernard's father, Charley. Again the past intrudes in the form of a memory of a rare visit by Willy's older brother, Ben, who has become rich and whose secrets for success elude Willy. Back in the present Willy is hopeful at Biff's plan to go see an old employer, Bill Oliver, for the money to start up a Loman Brothers sporting goods line. The act ends with Willy's memory of Biff's greatest moment—the high school football championship:

Like a young god. Hercules—something like that. And the sun, the sun all around him. Remember how he waved to me? Right up from the field, with the representatives of three colleges standing by? And the buyers I brought, and the cheers when he came out—Loman, Loman, Loman! God Almighty, he'll be great yet. A star like that, magnificent, can never really fade away!

The second act shatters all prospects, revealing the full truth that Willy has long evaded about himself and his family in a series of crushing blows. Expecting to trade on his 34 years of loyal service to his employer for a nontraveling, salaried position in New York, Willy is forced to beg for a smaller and smaller salary before he is fired outright, prompting one of the great lines of the play: "You can't eat the orange and throw the peel away—a man is not a piece of fruit." Rejecting out of pride a job offer from Charley, Willy meets his son for dinner where Biff reveals that his get-rich scheme has collapsed. Bill Oliver did not remember who he was, kept him waiting for hours, and resentfully Biff has stolen his fountain pen from his desk. Biff now insists that Willy face the truth—that Biff was only a shipping clerk and that Oliver owes him nothing—but Willy refuses to listen, with his need to believe in his son and the future forcing Biff to manufacture a happier version of his meeting and its outcome. Biff's anger and resentment over the old family lies about his prospects, however, cause Willy to relive the impetus of Biff's loss of faith in him in one of the tour de force scenes in modern drama. Biff and Happy's attempt to pick up two women at the restaurant interconnects with Willy's memory of Biff's arrival at Willy's Boston hotel unannounced. There he discovers a partially dressed woman in his father's room. Having failed his math class and jeopardized his scholarship, Biff has come to his father for help. Willy's betrayal of Linda, however, exposes the hollowness of Willy's moral authority and the disjunction between the dreams Willy sells and its reality:

> WILLY   She's nothing to me, Biff. I was lonely, I was terribly lonely.
>
> BIFF   You—you gave her Mama's stockings!
>
> WILLY   I gave you an order!
>
> BIFF   Don't touch me, you—liar!
>
> WILLY   Apologize for that!
>
> BIFF   You fake! You phony little fake! You fake!

Willy's guilt over the collapse of his son's belief in him leads him to a final redemptive dream. Returning home, symbolically outside planting seeds, he discusses with Ben his scheme to kill himself for the insurance money as a legacy to his family and a final proof of his worth as a provider of his sons' success. Before realizing this dream Willy must endure a final assault of truth from Biff who confesses to being nothing more than a thief and a bum, incapable of holding down a job—someone who is, like Willy, a "dime a dozen," no better than any other hopeless striver: "I am not a leader of men, Willy, and neither are you. You were never anything but a hard-working drummer who landed in the ash can like all the rest of them!" Biff's fury explodes into a tearful embrace of his father. After Biff departs upstairs the significance of his words and actions are both realized and lost by the chronic dreamer:

> WILLY, *after a long pause, astonished, elevated*   Isn't that—isn't that remarkable? Biff—he likes me!

LINDA   He loves you, Willy!

HAPPY, *deeply moved*   Always did, Pop.

WILLY   Oh. Biff! *Staring wildly*: He cried! Cried to me. *He is choking with his love, and now cries out his promise*: That boy—that boy is going to be magnificent!

Doggedly holding onto the dream of his son's prospects, sustained by his son's love, Willy finally sets out in his car to carry out his plan, while the scene shifts to his funeral in which Linda tries to understand her husband's death, and Charley provides the eulogy:

> Nobody dast blame this man. You don't understand: Willy was a sales-man. And for a salesman, there is no rock bottom to the life. He don't put a bolt to a nut, he don't tell you the law or give you medicine. He's a man way out there in the blue, riding on a smile and a shoeshine. And when they start not smiling back—that's an earthquake. And then you get a couple of spots on your hat, and you're finished. Nobody dast blame this man. A salesman is got to dream, boy. It comes with the territory.

Linda delivers the final, heartbreaking lines over her husband's grave: "Willy. I made the last payment on the house today. Today, dear. And there'll be nobody home. We're free and clear. We're free. We're free . . . We're free. . . ."

The power and persistence of *Death of a Salesman* derives from its remarkably intimate view of the dynamic of a family driven by their collective dreams. Critical debate over whether Willy lacks the stature or self-knowledge to qualify as a tragic hero seems beside the point in performance. Few other modern dramas have so powerfully elicited pity and terror in their audiences. Whether Willy is a tragic hero or *Death of a Salesman* is a modern tragedy in any Aristotelian sense, he and his story have become core American myths. Few critics worry over whether Jay Gatsby is a tragic hero, but Gatsby shares with Willy Loman the essential American capacity to dream and to be destroyed by what he dreams. The concluding lines of *The Great Gatsby* equally serve as a requiem for both men:

> Gatsby believed in the green light, the orgiastic future that year by year recedes before us. It eludes us then, but that's no matter—tomorrow we will run faster, stretch out our arms farther . . . And one fine morning—
>
> So we beat on, boats against the current, borne back ceaselessly into the past.

WOYZECK

(1836)

by Georg Büchner

The story of a simple soldier who murders his girl in a fit of jealous rage becomes the theme of a tragedy which Büchner wrote during the last months of his life. The play comes to us a fragment without a real ending. It nevertheless has become Büchner's most acclaimed and most frequently performed work. There is something almost uncanny about the spell it casts over audiences. Extraordinarily short, it vibrates with its compact intensity. A good performance need last no longer than forty minutes, although there are almost thirty scenes. The new dramatic structure, first attempted in Danton, *is here brought to perfection. The division into acts disappears and so does character development. Plot is kept to a minimum. Just a series of stark pictures, brief confrontations between a humble man and the various people who populate his narrow world. . . . It is especially the structure of the play which strikes us today as radical, but in 1837, when Büchner planned to publish it, the theme would have been just as startling. Here is a proletarian tragedy, some eight years before the modern bourgeois tragedy had been made respectable with the appearance of Friedrich Hebbel's* Maria Magdalene! *Even more shocking: kindly sympathy for a man who viciously murders a woman right on the stage! And it is not just any murderer, for Woyzeck is not the perverse invention of a writer, but an extraordinarily faithful portrait of one of the most publicized killers of the time.*

—Ronald Hauser, *Georg Büchner*

When tracing the development of the modern theater, Georg Büchner's *Woyzeck* is arguably the most significant European drama of the 19th century. Writing decades before the first appearance of the works of Henrik Ibsen, Anton Chekhov, or August Strindberg—the conventional founding fathers of modern drama—Büchner opened new doors and broke down previous barriers to dramatic expression. *Woyzeck* is one of the first plays in Europe about ordinary people. It radically alters the established Aristotelian dramatic formula by presenting "a poor good-for-nothing" as its tragic hero. A lower-class character, formerly marginalized and ignored in previous plays, suitable not for a revealed subjective or moral life but for comic relief, takes center stage for the first time. Büchner extends to his proletarian protagonist the same serious consideration formerly reserved for the heroes of high rank and stature of past tragedies. *Woyzeck*, however, does not just democratize drama by introducing a radically new dramatic subject. Concerned with the ways in which individuals are shaped by surroundings and social position, *Woyzeck* anticipates literary naturalism by almost a half-century. By its treatment of a notorious real-life murder case, *Woyzeck* is also one of the earliest examples of documentary theater and has been praised as the greatest social drama in German literature. Its open-ended, fragmented structure projecting internal, distorted states of mind anticipates expressionism, while its reduction of experience down to the incongruous and bizarre anticipates the theater of the absurd. For all of these reasons many critics have claimed Büchner as the first truly modern dramatist, and *Woyzeck* as the paradigm-shifting modern play. In 1941 critic Kurt List declared that *Woyzeck* "more and more has come to be the keynote of modern times," and critic George Steiner has argued that *Woyzeck* "poses in a new way the entire problem of modern tragedy." These are remarkable claims for the work of a playwright who died by the age of 23 and never saw a single one of his three plays performed. It would take nearly 50 years after his death for Büchner to be recognized in his native Germany as a distinctive and important literary figure and almost a century for international recognition of *Woyzeck* as one of the crucial works of world drama.

This early 19th-century writer who seems so uncannily to anticipate and predict our own time's literary methods and existential concerns was not an anomaly but fully a man of his time. Karl Georg Büchner was born in 1813 in the German village of Goddelau in Hesse, the eldest of six children. His father was a successful physician, an enthusiast of the French Revolution, and a fervent supporter of the social reforms instituted by Napoleon in Germany. While his father encouraged the young Büchner's interests in natural science and history, his mother, an ardent German nationalist who applauded Napoleon's downfall, fostered her son's reverence for nature and love of literature. Educated at the gymnasium in Darmstadt, where his family had moved when he was three, Büchner showed considerable intellectual promise and independence, including skepticism about received wisdom and rebelliousness against authority. His was the postromantic generation, contending with the collapse of the social idealism of the French Revolution and the repressive return to authoritarian dogmatism following Napoleon's defeat. The collapse of the democratic and romantic values stimulated by the French Revolution caused Büchner and other intellectuals of his time to search for a new belief system, a new realistic faith to oppose discredited romantic idealism and the despotism that followed. In 1831 Büchner studied medicine and natural science at the University of Strasbourg, which had become a haven and gathering place for Germans seeking intellectual freedom from the conservative and oppressive authorities across the border. There Büchner advocated democratic reforms in Germany and protested the increasing suppression of political opposition in France by the restored monarchy. Returning to Germany to continue his studies at the University of Giessen in 1833, Büchner founded the secret Society for Human Rights for students and laborers dedicated to radical social change. He also collaborated in 1834 on the political pamphlet *Der Hessische Landbote* (*The Hessian Messenger*) that promulgated his view that social reform in Germany would only come through the revolutionary awakening of the disenfranchised, oppressed, and impoverished German peasantry aligned with enlightened industrialists, politicians, and intellectuals. Under threat of arrest as a subversive Büchner returned home to Darmstadt. There, between October 1834 and January 1835, he composed his first play, one of the great imaginative works on the French Revolution, *Danton's Tod* (*Danton's Death*). Blending documentary and biographical materials into a series of scenes that echo William Shakespeare in its dazzling inventiveness and intellectual reach, Büchner presents the story of a dedicated social idealist who sees his dreams wrecked by the pettiness of others and by his own natural weaknesses. The play's passive hero whose progress rests in self-knowledge and increasing social awareness, as well as the play's episodic structure that proceeds by analogies, contrasts, and juxtapositions rather than through conventional continuities, would supply the model for *Woyzeck*. Before *Danton's Death* could be published in a German journal, however, Büchner fled the country, returning to Strasbourg after receiving a summons to appear in court. In Strasbourg he would complete a second play, the satirical comedy *Leonce und Lena* and the psychological novella *Lenz*. He also finished his research and dissertation on the nervous system of fish and received his doctorate from the University of Zurich, where he was offered a faculty position. While lecturing there in comparative anatomy during the autumn and winter of 1836–37, Büchner composed several draft versions of *Woyzeck*, which remained unfinished at his death from typhus in February 1837.

Woyzeck originated in Büchner's reworking the details of three case histories of soldiers who murdered their mistresses. These crimes formed the basis for the playwright's consideration of the conjunction between environment and psychology behind such violent acts. Of these the case of Johann Christian Woyzeck provided the play's essential details and title. In Leipzig in 1821 Woyzeck, a 41-year-old homeless ex-soldier and onetime barber, was apprehended for the stabbing death of a 46-year-old widow, his former mistress, whom Woyzeck killed in a jealous rage. Confessing fully to the police, Woyzeck was summarily tried and found guilty after evidence of insanity was discounted by the expert testimony of Dr. Johann Clarus, a clinical professor at the medical school of the University of Leipzig. After examining Woyzeck on several occasions, Clarus judged him free of any physical or mental impairment to justify the suspension of his legal responsibilities. "The only motive for the crime," Clarus concluded, "was the preponderance of passion over reason." Eventually, after three years of legal proceedings, Woyzeck was executed in 1824, the first public decapitation in

Leipzig in a generation. The notorious Woyzeck murder case, in which no mitigation in either the defendant's mental or social situation was allowed to compromise the pursuit of justice, provided the material for Büchner's reexamination of
the factors that could drive an ordinary man first to madness and then to murder.
As critic Ronald Hauser summarizes, Büchner "used the historical incident to
develop an answer to that question he had once posed in a letter and later put into
Danton's mouth: 'What is it in us that lies, whores, steals, and murders?'"

The dramatic response to this question takes the form of a series of nearly 30
disjointed vignettes showing Woyzeck's temperament and response to his environment that lead him to suspect the infidelity of his mistress, Marie, through his
murder of her and to its aftermath. In a sense Büchner rewrites William Shakespeare's *Othello*, with the heroic Venetian general replaced by an inconsequential
foot soldier and Iago by various representatives of the empowered in society
who are complicit in causing Woyzeck to run "through the world like an open
razor." To tell Woyzeck's story Büchner explodes the closed form of neoclassical
drama substituting an open, nonlinear form that more closely resembles a modern poetic sequence that moves not from crisis through rising action to climax
but by juxtaposing images that generate contrasts and deepen context. As the play
opens Franz Woyzeck, a lowly soldier who supports his mistress and child by
doing odd jobs such as gathering firewood, shaving the captain, and participating
in a doctor's medical experiments is already beset by the psychological disintegration that will result in his jealous rage and murder of Marie. Cutting branches in
an open field with his comrade Andres, Woyzeck observes:

> You know this place is cursed? Look at that light streak on the grass. Over
> there where the toadstools grow. That's where the head rolls every night.
> One time somebody picked it up. He thought it was a hedgehog. Three
> days and three nights, and he was in a box. Andres, it was the Freemasons,
> don't you see, it was the Freemasons!

The play opens then with Woyzeck's deranged revelation. His surrealistic
visualization that includes a hallucination of a fire breaking out in the nearby
town symbolizing the coming apocalypse establishes him as both a visionary
and psychotic. The next scene introduces Marie and establishes that their
domestic happiness has been undermined by Woyzeck's being haunted by
"Something that I can't put my hands on, or understand. Something that
drives us mad." The initial scenes, therefore, pose the question of what has
caused Woyzeck's decline and breakdown. A symbolic answer is indirectly suggested in the next scene set at a fair in which a barker pitches the extraordinary
ability of his performing horse:

> This is no dumb animal. This is a person! A human being! A human
> brute! But still an animal. A beast [*The horse conducts itself indecently*].

That's right, put society to shame. As you can see, this animal is still in a state of nature. Not ideal nature, of course! Take a lesson from him! . . . What we have been told by this is: Man must be natural! You are created of dust, sand and dung. Why must you be more than dust, sand and dung? Look there, at his reason. He can figure even if he can't count it off on his fingers. And why? Because he cannot express himself, can't explain. A metamorphosed human being.

If the horse on show here is a metamorphosed human being, Woyzeck is a metamorphosed animal, a lower-class trick pony to serve and entertain his betters but denied his humanity. Like the performing horse, Woyzeck is inarticulate because self-expression and communication have been overruled by his betters and repression has pushed him to a psychic break.

Subsequent scenes show this clearly. The Captain's condescending moral idealism inflates his own superiority by degrading Woyzeck. The Captain uses conventional morality, or at least moral jargon, to limit and control him. "Woyzeck, you have no morality!" says the Captain. "Morality, that's when you have morals, you understand. It's a good word. You have child without the blessings of the Church, just like our right reverend garrison chaplain says." Woyzeck's defense cites the words of Jesus to "Suffer the little children to come unto me" but draws only another outburst from the Captain: "Woyzeck, you have no virtue! You're not a virtuous human being!" Woyzeck responds: "You see, us common people, we haven't got virtue. That's the way it's got to be. But if I could be a gentleman, and if I could have a hat and a watch and a walking-stick, and if I could talk refined, I'd want to be virtuous all right."

Woyzeck's dilemma of being denied his humanity is underscored in his relationship with the Doctor. If the Captain represents inhumane morality, the Doctor symbolizes inhumane science. Put on a diet of peas for the Doctor to study the effect on his urine, Woyzeck is reprimanded by the Doctor for urinating without permission:

> I saw it all, Woyzeck. You pissed on the street! You were pissing on the wall like a dog! And here I'm giving you three groschen a day plus board! That's terrible, Woyzeck! The world's becoming a terrible place, a terrible place!

Woyzeck's defense is that he was only following Nature, prompting the Doctor's response:

> What has Nature to do with it? Did I or did I not prove to you that the musculus constrictor vesicae is controlled by your will? Nature! Woyzeck, man is free! In Mankind alone we see glorified the individual's will to freedom! And you couldn't hold your water!

When Woyzeck asserts his will and confesses his understanding of the world's "double nature" and the voices he hears, he gains only the Doctor's labeling jargon as a more interesting specimen: "Woyzeck, you have a most beautiful aberration mentalis parialis of a secondary order! And so wonderfully developed! Woyzeck, your salary is increased."

Woyzeck's dispossession and disorientation under the treatment of society's authority figures leads Marie to seek relief in an affair with a drum major, and her infidelity is the final impetus toward Woyzeck's psychic break. Taunted by the Captain and the Doctor that another man's beard hair is in his soup bowl, Woyzeck discovers Marie dancing in the arms of the Drum Major. The scene produces a new apocalyptic vision of venal carnality:

> WOYZECK (*choking*) Don't stop! Don't stop! (*beating his hands together*) Turn and roll and roll and turn! God! Blow out the sun so they can roll on each other in their lechery! Man and woman and man and beast! They'll do it in the light of the sun, they'll do it in the palm of your hand like flies!

Woyzeck's vision of the human beast leads him to kill Marie, who has become the incarnation of the evil that has tormented him. Ironically Woyzeck turns his existential fury on the one person he most loves, becoming the instrument of both of their deaths. Psychologically Woyzeck has internalized the regression to animality that society has defined for him and becomes its agent for self-destruction.

The play makes clear how wholly inadequate was the diagnosis of Dr. Clarus and the understanding of the murder of the actual Woyzeck. Büchner's drama widens sensibilities and sympathies so that Woyzeck becomes not an anomaly but representative, and his crime, a symptom of a far more complex and widespread social, moral, and psychological malaise. On one level the murderer is shown to be the ultimate victim of a society that has enshrined human reason and morality but denied its extension to the dispossessed, marginalized, and invisible among us. On another Büchner offers a radically altered sense of who the victim is in this existential tragedy. The true death-dealers here are the Captain, the Doctor, and the other respectable agents of civilization who cannot see with the clarity of the visionary Woyzeck and Büchner.

On multiple levels *Woyzeck* announces new possibilities for drama. It gives voice for the first time to individuals previously silenced in our literature. It points the way for a new kind of drama that is both intensely social and psychological. It puts in place a new operating system of dramatic construction that opens up the stage to the power of the psyche, dreams, and the associational logic of poetry.

VOLPONE, OR THE FOX

23

(1606)

by Ben Jonson

> Volpone *brilliantly exemplifies Jonson's unique jungle vision, with its self-contained world composed entirely of predators and prey. His contempt for mercenary motivation and capitalistic enterprise is blistering; the commanding indictment of the vicious habits of the new acquisitive society shows Jonson's forward leap in terms of intellectual and analytical maturity. The play demonstrates throughout Jonson's new-found ability to use the grim stuff of human wickedness and weakness, material not of a comic nature in itself, as the basis of satiric comedy. Obsessional greed, lust, the savage disregard of all other human beings and even eventually of personal survival—these are hardly funny, but Jonson makes them so. Yet never does he diminish the power of his portrayal of these ruthless materialists who embody "Appetite, the universal wolf."*
>
> —Rosalind Miles, *Ben Jonson: His Craft and Art*

With *Volpone*, William Shakespeare had, for the first time since the death of Christopher Marlowe, a serious dramatic rival, and Elizabethan drama had an important alternative method and material. The master of the urban satirical comedy of manners, Ben Jonson brought raw and unflattering contemporary life within dramatic range and harnessed disparate, rowdy Elizabethan life to the classically derived rules of dramatic construction that would shape neoclassical theatrical ideals for the next two centuries. Jonson has been fated to be forever overshadowed by Shakespeare's greater genius, to be, in John Dryden's estimation, compared to the Bard, admired rather than loved. But in the history of English drama only Shakespeare and George Bernard Shaw have contributed more plays to the permanent national repertory than Jonson did. It was Jonson who insisted that drama was a form of poetry, the noblest and profoundest human expression. It was Jonson, more than any other English dramatist, who helped to establish plays as literature, capable of the most serious inquiry into human nature and social life. Shakespeare is inimitable; however, it can be argued, more playwrights claim their descent as a "son of Ben."

A comparison between Jonson and Shakespeare, though irresistible and often misleading, is still instructive in underscoring their different relationships to the theater and dramatic practice. Born in 1572 or 1573, almost a decade after Shakespeare, Jonson was part of the next generation of Elizabethan and Jacobean dramatists who had Shakespeare's works and the drama that he pioneered to imitate, modify, and transform. Both Shakespeare and Jonson came from similar lower-middle-class backgrounds, but Shakespeare was a countryman, who drew extensively on his love and familiarity with rural life, while Jonson was a Londoner, whose arena and references were predominantly urban. Jonson was the son of a minister who died a month before his birth. His widowed mother married a bricklayer, and Jonson was raised near Westminster where he enrolled at the prestigious Westminster School located in the precinct of the abbey. He studied under the age's greatest classicist and antiquarian, William Camden, whom Jonson would later credit for "All that I am in arts, all that I know." Camden would spark Jonson's lifelong devotion to classical literature, his love of scholarship, and his self-consciously academic approach to his writing and aspirations. Jonson, in contrast to Shakespeare's purported "little Latin and less Greek," would proudly assert that "he was better Versed & knew more in Greek and Latin, than all the Poets in England." It was at Westminster that Jonson was introduced to drama in annual performances mounted by its scholars. When he left Westminster, he did not, as might have been expected, matriculate at Oxford or Cambridge. (He would later express his gratitude that *Volpone* was favorably regarded at "The Two Famous Universities" and dedicated the published play to them.) Instead he apprenticed as a bricklayer, becoming a journeyman by 1598. The premature end of Jonson's formal education and his working-class background no doubt made him excessively proud and protective of his scholarly attainments and anxious that his writing should be measured against the revered classical standards. Jonson married unhappily, losing both his children to early illness, fought as a volunteer foot soldier against the Spanish in the Netherlands, and began his career as a playwright, like Shakespeare, after first acting in one of London's professional theater companies. He would never, however, like Shakespeare, become a full partner of any playing company as a resident actor or writer. He took instead an independent line to protect his scholarly and poetic aspirations and to become more than a dramatic professional. Jonson would complain about "the lothed stage" that catered to popular tastes that were "not meant for thee, less, thou for them."

Jonson's debut as a playwright was inauspicious. In 1597 he completed a topical satire by Thomas Nashe, *The Isle of Dogs*, and was imprisoned for several weeks for sedition for acting in and having coauthored it. After his release Jonson continued to collaborate on a number of plays (now lost) and produced his first solo effort, *The Case Is Altered* (1598), a comedy derived from Plautus. It was followed by *Everyman in His Humour* (1598) and *Everyman out of His*

Humour (1599), performed by Shakespeare's company, the Lord Chamberlain's Men, which established Jonson as a coming playwright. Around the time of the debut of *Everyman in His Humour* Jonson killed a young actor in a duel and was again imprisoned, avoiding execution by pleading the ancient benefit of clergy because he could read. When James I came to the throne in 1603, Jonson won favor and patronage as the chief author of court masques and entertainments, despite being imprisoned for supposed slights to the king and the Scots in 1605 for the comedy *Eastward Ho!* Following Jonson's failure with the tragedy *Sejanus*, which was hissed off the Globe Theatre stage in 1603, Jonson returned to stage comedy with *Volpone*, his first undisputed masterpiece, which was performed to great acclaim at the Globe in 1606. *Volpone* signaled a new kind of moral comedy and demonstrated Jonson's mature style and construction that joined his admired classical models to the popular traditions of English drama. *Volpone* initiated a string of comic masterworks, including *Epicoene* (1609), THE ALCHEMIST (1610), *Bartholomew Fair* (1614), and *The Devil Is an Ass* (1616).

Jonson articulated his break with the theater of his day in his prologue to the revised version of *Everyman in His Humour,* declaring his allegiance as a comic writer to "deedes, and language, such as men doe use," and to the presentation of an "Image of the times," embodied in ordinary characters and everyday circumstances—"with humane follies, not with crimes." He criticized contemporary dramatists for "all license of offence to God and man" for their improbable plots that relied on accidents, coincidences, and the stale contrivances of mistaken and concealed identities, for their indecorous mixture of comedy, pathos, and tragedy and violations of the unities of time, place, and action in language inappropriate to the speaker and marred by artificial sentiment and bombast. *Volpone, or The Fox* clearly shows Jonson's response. Instead of the conventional romantic intrigue that Shakespeare had relied on in his comedies, Jonson submits to comic ridicule the "ragged follies of the time." Blending the fortune-hunting plot and character types of Roman comedies with native allegorical elements of the morality play and the beast fable, Jonson ingeniously arranges variations on the theme of human greed. At the center of the play is Volpone, the fox, a Renaissance Venetian schemer, and Mosca (the fly), his servant, who extort riches from those courting Volpone's favor as Volpone pretends to be a dying man in need of an heir. As the play opens Volpone delivers an invocation to gold that sets the play's theme of avarice:

> Good morning to the day; and next, my gold!
> Open the shrine, that I may see my saint.
> Hail the world's soul, and mine! More glad than is
> The teeming earth to see the longed-for sun
> . . . O thou son of Sol,

But brighter than thy father, let me kiss,
With adoration, thee, and every relic
Of sacred treasure in this blessed room . . .
Riches, the dumb god, that gives all men tongues,
That canst do nought, and yet mak'st men do all things;
The price of souls; even hell, with thee to boot,
Is made worth heaven. Thou art virtue, fame,
Honor and all things else. Who can get thee,
He shall be noble, valiant, honest, wise—

Volpone's morning devotional—his sacrilegious worshipping at a golden shrine from which all blessings are derived—sets the tone for the gulling of three birds of prey, snared by their own cupidity. The lawyer Voltore (vulture), the aging gentleman Corbaccio (crow), and the merchant Corvino (raven). The allegorical arrangement recalls the medieval beast fable in which a fox feigns death to catch and eat the carrion birds but with the appetite for food here replaced by a craving for gold. Each arrives with presents and is assured in turn that he is to be Volpone's choice to inherit his fortune if their gifts continue to find favor with him. Corbaccio is advised to disinherit his son and leave his fortune to Volpone; while Corvino, whose beautiful and virtuous young wife Volpone lusts after, is to deliver Celia to the supposed decrepit and impotent Volpone's bed for medicinal purposes. Compared to the slow-witted, unimaginative prey, Volpone and Mosca tower above them as ingenious, consummate actors, totally adaptable to their audience, totally consumed by their parts, with a zest for deception and intrigue that will be their eventual undoing. To relieve and expand the play's satirical attack on greed, Jonson introduces the foolish Sir Politic Would-Be and his wife, English travelers whose inflated self-regard shows how easily fools can be manipulated by self-centered delusions. What is striking about Jonson's arrangement here is his centering the play on a comic villain and his parasite. While Elizabethan tragedies featuring monstrous characters had been common since Marlowe's *Tamburlaine*, few Elizabethan comedies had ever dared such a complete capitulation to the villainous hero and his sidekick. *Volpone* presents a world inhabited exclusively by knaves, gulls, and the innocent victims of both. Jonson mounts his satiric argument here indirectly, not by opposing the vices and moral failings of his characters by the counter forces of good and virtue, but by multiplying and exaggerating through caricature greed, hypocrisy, and self-deception and thereby shaming his audience into rejecting these false values by ridicule. Central to Jonson's strategy is the notion that the characters' greed will ensure their own downfall. As Volpone observes, "What a rare punishment / Is avarice to itself."

The undoing begins as Volpone's scheming overreaches the deserved entrapment of Voltore, Corbaccio, and Corvino to severing the natural bonds between father and son and husband and wife to serve his ends. Bonario,

Corbaccio's disinherited son, is on hand to witness Volpone's reinvigoration as an ardent lover of Celia and prevents Volpone's rape. What should be the triumph of the innocents, however, quickly turns into an even more sinister victory of the rapacious self-servers. In the trial scene that follows, truth is suborned by lawyer Voltore who casts Celia and Bonario as foul schemers, lewd adulterers, and heartless victimizers of the innocent Volpone. The four Avocatori who judge the case are incapable of overcoming their own prejudices, self-satisfaction, and obsequiousness to wealth and rank. Justice is not just blind, it is insensible, and the witty inversion of all under the rubric of appetite appears complete and total.

Volpone celebrates his expected legal triumph by a final display of his power over the gulls who have perjured themselves on his behalf. He pretends to be dead and to have left his fortune to Mosca for the sheer enjoyment of seeing how his victims will respond when they learn that they have been deceived. It is finally not greed but pride that brings Volpone down, as Mosca, who shows himself loyal only to money, decides to retain the fortune. To recover it Volpone must reveal the plot and his own deceptions. Voltore withdraws his false testimony as the court reconvenes, and, as it appears he has been bested by Mosca, Volpone throws off his disguise and exposes all, including himself. Truth is finally revealed and order reasserted not by any powerful force of good but by the confession of the play's chief villain who sacrifices his safety for vengeance. The appropriate punishment is suited to the crimes of each, with the worst reserved for Mosca, who is condemned for life as a galley slave, and Volpone, who is to be imprisoned in chains until he becomes in fact the helpless invalid he pretended to be. One of the Avocatori sanctimoniously intones:

> Let all that see these vices thus rewarded,
> Take heart, and love study 'em! Mischiefs feed
> Like beasts, till they be fat, and then they bleed.

But there is precious little moral reassurance here in the wisdom of authority, in justice, or in the moral force of virtue over the appetites for self-supremacy. Jonson's bracing and daring comedy, grotesquely and ludicrously magnifying our worst capacities, is turned into a mirror by which we are forced to recognize unflattering and disturbing resemblances. By shifting the focus of comedy from dreamy and delightful wish fulfillment to actuality, Jonson helps establish drama as an instrument for both truth and moral instruction, even as he delights with the skill of his construction and the daringness of his conception.

HENRY IV

(c. 1596–97)   *by William Shakespeare*

None of Shakespeare's plays are more read than the first and second parts of Henry IV. *Perhaps no authour has ever in two plays afforded so much delight. The great events are interesting, for the fate of kingdoms depends upon them; the slighter occurrences are diverting, and, except one or two, sufficiently probable; the incidents are multiplied with wonderful fertility of invention, and the characters diversified with the utmost nicety of discernment, and the profoundest skill in the nature of man.*

—Samuel Johnson, *The Plays of William Shakespeare*

The two parts of *Henry IV* represent William Shakespeare's greatest achievement as a historical dramatist. Even though the enactment of history on stage is as old as Aeschylus's *The Persians,* Shakespeare made the dramatized historical chronicle one of his singular contributions to the stage and literature. Two centuries before Sir Walter Scott was credited with opening up the historical past as a subject for the novelist, Shakespeare had in his interweaving of historical fact and invention set the standard by which history could be animated into literature. Gaining his initial stage success with his *Henry VI* plays in the early 1590s, Shakespeare would eventually dramatize a turbulent century of English dynastic history from the fall of Richard II in 1399, through the War of the Roses it precipitated, to the death of Richard III in 1485 and the triumphant ascendancy of the Tudors. Coming between Shakespeare's poetic exploration of the private limitations and illusions of a weak king in *Richard II* and his grandest celebration of an English national hero's public triumph in *Henry V, Henry IV* draws on both the private and public aspects of kingship to present one of the most remarkable dramatizations of political power and the formation and consequence of leadership ever brought to the stage. The two plays are breathtaking in their abundance and panoramic in their sweep in capturing a wide range of English life during the so-called unquiet times of Henry IV. Shakespeare brilliantly modulates perspectives from the heroic to the comic and counterpoints multiple centers of interests:

the palace at Westminster where Henry IV struggles to hang onto his throne following his deposition of Richard II; the meeting places of members of the opposition, led by the chivalric Hotspur, who want to claim the crown for themselves; the tavern world of Eastcheap; and the country house of Justice Shallow in rural Gloucestershire. Linking all are the development stages and challenges faced by the heir apparent, Prince Hal, Shakespeare's portrait of a self-conscious youth caught in a web of circumstances that anticipates Prince Hamlet. Literally anchoring the plays is Sir John Falstaff, the greatest comic character Shakespeare ever devised, arguably his greatest invention, and one of drama and literature's incomparable creations. The plays, therefore, offer a seemingly inexhaustible supply of riches. They are vital chronicles of a crucial period of English history and a timeless and masterful exploration of human nature and the human condition, containing some of the funniest and most moving and profound scenes Shakespeare ever wrote.

Shakespeare created the *Henry IV* plays as he approached the midpoint of his career, between 1596 and 1597, when he had reached complete maturity as a dramatist, having learned how to embody in language and action an enormous range of characters and experience. Shakespeare's dramatic career had begun with his helping his audiences to participate in the imagined unfolding of past events and achievements that shaped present realities. Although the medieval England of Shakespeare's chronicle plays was as distant to his contemporaries as the Revolutionary War is to modern Americans, the issues of his historical plays were strikingly relevant. The toppling of a king and the chaos of civil war represented current anxiety and dangers for the Elizabethans. The deposition of the king was censored out of the first printed texts of *Richard II* as too explosive, while supporters of the ambitious Robert Devereux, earl of Essex, saw clear parallels in the drama with current circumstances. In fact, in 1601 they would arrange a special performance to rally followers to his cause before his failed coup d'état. Essex's rebellion underscored the possibilities of a bloody, uncertain future that would follow the death of the heirless Elizabeth. The impending succession battle presaged the return of a violent and destructive scramble for power and the social chaos that Shakespeare's plays brought to life on stage.

Shakespeare's eight-play cycle of English history begins with the fall of Richard II, a monarch who squandered and misused his power, bankrupted the kingdom, and allowed Henry Bolingbroke to maneuver him off the throne. Although Bolingbroke is shown to be the better man for the job—decisive, shrewd, and utterly committed to the responsibilities of ruling—Richard makes clear the potentially catastrophic step Bolingbroke is taking by circumventing the divine right of kingship:

> Not all the water in the rough, rude sea
> Can wash the balm from an anointed king.

> The breath of worldly men cannot depose
> The deputy elected by the Lord.

Deposing a rightful king overturns both the cosmic order as understood by the Elizabethans and the fundamental principles of English government and social order. It subverted essential concepts of inheritance and deference required in a hierarchical society and undermined fixed principle with the mutability of political fortune, the rule of law with expediency and brute force. Henry's act of rebellion unleashes the bloodletting and disorder that Richard forecasts.

Henry IV opens with Bolingbroke being forced to deal with the actualities of Richard's prophecy that "The blood of English shall manure the ground, / And future ages groan for this final act." His rebellion has not restored order to the kingdom but rather has emboldened England's border enemies and has legitimized the conviction of his ambitious subjects that they have as much right to raise their hands against him as he did against Richard, inspiring a seemingly endless cycle of revolt and disorder. *Henry IV* is Shakespeare's exploration of a world in which stability, law, and authority are under threat and radical new conceptions of political power and leadership fill the vacuum left by Bolingbroke's usurpation. As Henry IV he is a savvy politician who must cannily negotiate the shifting allegiances and loyalties of those he commands, not based on divine rights but on his practical skills and manipulation of popular support. Against a backdrop of warfare and rebellion the plays struggle with two central questions: How can the past sins of history be atoned? And What makes an effective leader in these fallen, imperfect times? To answer these questions Shakespeare centers the interest not on Henry IV but on his heir, Prince Hal, in his development as an effective leader, from prodigal son to great national hero who is able to heal the kingdom's wounds inflicted by his father. These are plays about the tests, temptations, and trials of leadership: its unavoidable burdens, the cruel necessities to which it is subject, the treachery by which it is surrounded, and, especially, the inevitable inadequacies of the men in high office who must be both human and exemplary, self-willed and selfless, able to subordinate the personal in pursuit of the greater good of the commonwealth.

Henry IV serves as a sequel to *Richard II* but with a markedly different, groundbreaking method. Deriving historical episodes from Raphael Holinshed's *Chronicles* and stories of Henry V's wastrel youth from various popular sources, Shakespeare divides his plays between the factual and the fictional, alternating between historically derived scenes at court and on the battlefield involving the nobles and invented comic scenes involving the unheroic world of ordinary citizens. None of Shakespeare's history plays before *Henry IV* had given such a prominent role to commoners and the details of ordinary life. The result is a wider sweep of English society, in which Shakespeare adapts and supplements historical fact with invention into a symphonic composition of contrasted but analogous movements. In *1 Henry IV* Hal is examined in relationship to three alternative settings and their corresponding values. The first is his father's palace at Westminster; the second is the camps of the rebels, led by Hotspur, whose historical age is adjusted to that of Hal's to underscore their comparison; the third is the tavern world ruled by Falstaff. All three are related in several ways, most notably by motive: Each is in someway defined by theft. Henry has stolen the throne; Hotspur wants to steal it; Falstaff finances his revels with thievery and involves Hal in an actual highway robbery. Each also is contrasted by their values. For Henry IV political survival at all cost determines every consideration. His world is defined by necessities and contingencies that must be continually calculated. For Hotspur circumstances are opportunities for personal glory and honor. For Falstaff neither political control nor personal ideals have any relevance. Responsibilities are to be avoided in favor of appetites indulged, and as he famously defines on the battlefield,

> What is honor? A word. What is in that word honor? What is that honor? Air. A trim reckoning! Who hath it? He that died o' Wednesday. Doth he feel it? No. Doth he hear it? No. 'Tis insensible, then? Yea, to the dead. But will it not live with the living? No. Why? Detraction will not suffer it. Therefore I'll none of it. Honor is a mere scutcheon. And so ends my catechism.

The political shrewdness of the king, the courageousness of Hotspur, and the common-sense materialism of Falstaff provide necessary ingredients in Hal's makeup. Forced to consider the claims of each, Hal eventually manages to achieve their proper balance, thereby defining the ideal qualities of a monarch who can restore order and legitimacy to the realm.

While the king is forced to deal with the threatened rebellion and disloyalty of the Percys and their Scottish and Welsh allies, Hal is diverting himself with the tavern company of Sir John Falstaff and his low-life associates, indulging in the revelry that Falstaff as a saturnalian lord of misrule represents. Like the figure of Vice in the morality plays, Falstaff is a tempter, delightful as a carousing companion, brilliant in his witty evasions of the truth and responsibility, but his philosophy of self-interest and the rejection of any claim beyond self-indulgence are disastrous to an heir to the throne. Hal reveals this in his initial soliloquy. As a self-aware prodigal he intends to confound expectations when his time comes to prove himself, comparing himself to the sun:

> Who doth permit the base contagious clouds
> To smother up his beauty from the world,
> That when he please again to be himself,
> Being wanted he may be more wondered at

By breaking through the foul and ugly mists
Of vapours that did seem to strangle him.

Hal reveals that his revelries are strategic and temporary:

If all the year were playing holidays,
To sport would be as tedious as to work;
But when they seldom come, they wished-for come,
And nothing pleaseth but rare accidents.
So when this loose behaviour I throw off
And pay the debt I never promisèd,
By how much better than my word I am,
By so much shall I falsify men's hope.

This soliloquy has long divided critics, directors, and actors in their interpretations of the play and its speaker. Some see Hal here as reassuringly self-aware, others as self-rationalizing, still others as Machiavellian, like his father, a calculating user of men for his own gain. Each position can be effectively argued, and all form at least a part of Shakespeare's complex portrait of an individual fashioning a strategy and identity to "pay the debt I never promisèd," that is, his reluctant but unavoidable royal inheritance that has come by accident through his father's usurpation. Whether by design or in self-deception, Hal is schooled by Falstaff to test his wits against a master and experience the world of contingencies outside the bounds of pomp and privilege that will ultimately help to fashion him into a superior monarch.

By act 5, at the battle of Shrewsbury, Hal has completed his practicum and must assume his role as heir apparent and protector of the realm, having correctly negotiated through the conflicting claims represented by his father, his rival Hotspur, and his surrogate father Falstaff. In his effective behavior on the battlefield Hal proves himself superior to the self-serving politics of his father through his treatment of the vanquished, superior to Hotspur's chivalric code of honor that is wasteful and destructive when not harnessed to a service greater than self-aggrandizement, and finally superior to Falstaff's survivalist pleasure principle that denies the validity of any end greater than self-fulfillment.

In 2 Henry IV factional warfare breaks out anew, and Hal must face additional challenges before succeeding to the throne. If 1 Henry IV shows the battle to save the kingdom from rebellion, 2 Henry IV shows how the kingdom, once secure, must be governed. Falstaff, as the medieval Vice figure, is here contrasted with the Lord Chief Justice, as Virtue, who both contend for Hal's ultimate allegiance. Ordered to recruit troops for the king, Falstaff uses his royal commission to avoid imprisonment from debt, while flagrantly accepting bribes and letting the able-bodied men buy their way out of service.

Meanwhile, the king's health is in decline, forcing Hal to pay the debt he never promised. The king's demands of his son and the heir's realization of the responsibilities of kingship are enacted in one of the greatest father-son scenes ever staged that includes one of the most succinctly profound statement ever uttered about the cost of command: "Uneasy lies the head that wears a crown."

As Henry IV fades, Falstaff grows in bulk and perfidy, threatening to expand his regime of misrule under the presumption of his close relationship with the future king. Falstaff's friendship with Hal, however, can exist only as long as Hal has no serious responsibilities. Falstaff fails to recognize the changes that come when Henry IV dies, and Hal is forced to choose between his friendship and his duty. His first challenge comes after his father's death, when Hal defends the conduct of the Lord Chief Justice (despite his having once jailed the prince during his wild youth) on behalf of "the majesty and power of law and justice" and pledges that the Chief Justice "shall be as a father to my youth." At the coronation Henry V confronts his former surrogate father, Falstaff himself. Hal must now choose between his past and his future. Falstaff should have known that Hal will not hesitate. To Falstaff's all-too-familiar greeting, "God save thy Grace, King Hal, my royal Hal! . . . God save thee, my sweet boy!" Henry V delivers the coup de grâce: "I know thee not old man. . . . Presume not that I am the thing I was." The new king orders his former companion to keep 10 miles away from him but with a promise of reinstatement if Falstaff reforms, and the fat knight exits convinced that the royal reprimand has all been for public show and that his old friend will certainly call for him privately.

The banishment of Falstaff is the climactic rhetorical confrontation of *2 Henry IV,* preceded by Hal's similarly decisive moments with his father and the Chief Justice. It is painful to watch a great favorite so treated, regrettable but inevitable, given the kingship theme that dominates the plays. Falstaff as a principle of misrule and selfish appetite must be banished as the new king assumes his responsibilities. The loss of Falstaff more than anything else makes us feel the grave consequence of Hal's accepting the crown and all that it entails. The power of both parts of *Henry IV,* and the genius of Shakespeare, is that there is a fair fight between rule and misrule, revelry and responsibility. Each has its claims and costs, and to recognize only one is to undervalue important aspects of human nature itself. A lesser playwright would have made Hal's decision easier. Hal as king must banish Falstaff, but the audience is allowed to retain him, encouraged to comprehend both sides in the debate and made aware not of the divinity that "doth hedge a king" but the humanity.

THE WAY OF THE WORLD

25

(1700)

by William Congreve

The one play that generations of readers, actors, audiences, and even critics have singled out as the triumphant quintessence of Restoration comedy is Congreve's The Way of the World. *Lytton Strachey is guilty of no exaggeration when he ranks it "among the most wonderful and glorious creations of the human mind." . . . What strikes us most is the language. If Shakespeare's diction, as one of Keats's sonnets suggest is "the voice of waters," then surely Congreve's is the sound of champagne, with all the virtues and limitations of that singular beverage.*

—Norman N. Holland, *The First Modern Comedies*

Secure today as his masterpiece and as one of drama's supreme comedies, William Congreve's *The Way of the World* was so slightingly received when it was first performed that its 30-year-old author resolved to write no more comedies. Congreve kept his word for nearly 30 years, to his death in 1729, offering for the stage only two opera libretti and a translation of a play by Molière. If Congreve's first audiences found *The Way of the World* plotless, labored, and opaque ("There is as much bullion in it," Alexander Pope observed, "as would serve to lace fifty modern comedies."), it has been subsequently acclaimed by later critics and audiences as the greatest of all Restoration comedies, and in the words of the poet Algernon Swinburne, as "the unequalled and unapproached masterpiece of English comedy." Voltaire, recognizing in the play the dazzling display of wit and ironic scrutiny of social manners and human nature that brought English drama to the level of Molière's achievement, asserted that "Congreve raised the glory of comedy to a greater height than any English writer before or since." For the essayist William Hazlitt, Congreve's greatness was his consummate artistry. "His style is inimitable, nay perfect," Hazlitt observed, and *The Way of the World* provides "the highest model of comic dialogue. Every sentence is replete with sense and satire, conveyed in the most brilliant and polished terms. . . . there is a peculiar flavour in the very words, which is to be found in hardly any other writer." Congreve, who has been called the English theater's wittiest playwright, unquestionably brought a new intellectual power and artistic polish to the English stage. With *The Way of the World* he produced one of the most challenging and intriguing of all English comedies.

Although born in England in 1670, Congreve was raised and educated in Ireland and can be grouped along with the other great Irish playwrights—to be followed by Oliver Goldsmith, Richard Sheridan, Oscar Wilde, George Bernard Shaw, and Samuel Beckett—who would significantly transform English drama. Congreve's father was a younger son of a Yorkshire gentry family, who, when Congreve was four years old, received an army commission and relocated his family to Ireland to serve in garrisons there. The young Congreve in 1681 entered Kilkenny College where he was briefly a classmate of Jonathan Swift. In 1686 Congreve followed Swift to Trinity College, Dublin, where they shared a common tutor. It is believed that Congreve saw his first plays in Dublin's Smock Alley Theatre. In 1688, in the wake of the violence in Ireland brought on by the clash between the Catholic forces loyal to James II and Protestant supporters of William of Orange, the family moved back to England, where Congreve enrolled in London's Middle Temple in 1691 to study law. However, as Congreve's early biographer Giles Jacob observed, "Mr. Congreve was too delicate a Taste, had Wit too fine a turn to be long pleas'd with a crabbed unpalatable Study. . . . his natural Inclination to Poetry, diverted him from the Bar to the declining Stage, which then stood in need of such a Support." Associating with the wits who met at Will's Coffee House, Congreve came to the attention of the age's greatest literary figure, John Dryden, who invited the younger man to collaborate with him in translating the Roman satirists. Congreve published translations of Juvenal and Horace as well as a novella, *Incognita*, which is noteworthy for its preface that distinguishes between the aims and methods of the earlier romances and the realism of the new novel and has been called the earliest important criticism of fiction.

Congreve's first play, *The Old Bachelor,* appeared in 1693 to great acclaim. The play borrowed heavily from earlier 17th-century playwrights, including Aphra Behn, William Wycherley, and George Etherege, presenting conventional Restoration comic situations and character types with a skillful freshness that established Congreve's literary reputation. Congreve followed it with four more plays between 1693 and 1700: *The Double Dealer* (1693), *Love for Love* (1695), *The Mourning Bride* (1697), and *The Way of the World* (1700). After the disappointing reception of *The Way of the World* Congreve remained involved with the stage as manager of the Lincoln Inn Fields Theatre and as a shareholder in the Haymarket Theatre. As a distinguished man of letters he was rewarded with government sinecures, given a post in 1714 in the Customs Office, and made secretary of Jamaica, which provided him with a comfortable living for the rest of his life. Congreve never married but had a close friendship with the actress Anne Bracegirdle, who played leading roles in all of his plays, including the part of Millamant in *The Way of the World*. He was also the lover of the second duchess of Marlborough and fathered her younger daughter who became duchess of Leeds. Congreve's final years were spent in retirement, enjoying the company of literary friends, such as Swift, Pope, and Richard Steele.

Congreve became the master of the Restoration comic conventions derived from the more realistic comedy of manners of Ben Jonson and influenced by the social satire of Molière. Confined to the milieu of the fashionable, Restoration comedy critiqued the affectations and contradictions of its age through a preoccupation with the battle between the sexes and the comic discrepancy between appearance and reality, principles and desires, virtues and appetites. Congreve's genius is expressed less in skillfully devising elaborate plots than in the witty repartee of his plays' dialogue. A delight in verbal pyrotechnics at the expense of accepted morality, as well as the often ribald sexual frankness of Restoration comedy, revived the attacks on drama that closed the theaters in 1642. The period's most famous attack on the theater came in 1698 from clergyman Jeremy Collier (1650–1726), whose pamphlet *Short View of Immorality and Profaneness of the English Stage*, took direct aim at the moral failings of Congreve's plays and the other Restoration comedies of the period. "The business of *Plays* is to recommend Virtue, and discountenance Vice," Collier asserted, "to shew the Uncertainty of Humane Greatness, the sudden Turns of Fate, and the Unhappy Conclusions of Violence and Injustice. 'Tis to expose the Singularities of Pride and Fancy, to make Folly and Falsehood contemptible, and to bring every Thing that is Ill under Infamy, and Neglect." Collier objected that too often in Restoration comedy vice is unchecked by sufficient reprimands, and the comic playwright is morally tarnished by his own brush. Congreve replied with *Amendments of Mr. Collier's False and Imperfect Citations* in which he defended drama's moral purpose and the playwright's service in depicting "vicious and foolish characters." The playwright should no more be held responsible for these characters' sentiments, Congreve argued, as "a Painter should be believ'd to resemble all the ugly Faces that he draws." "The business of Comedy is mainly to delight," Congreve asserted, "though it should instruct as well; And as vicious People are made asham'd of their follies or faults, but seeing them expos'd in a ridiculous manner, so are good People at once both warn'd and diverted at their Expense." Congreve insisted that the stage should reflect human nature as it is, with the failures to live up to how humans should be subject to the curative power of laughter. His most effective answer to Collier's attack, however, was reserved for *The Way of the World*, and its application of his conception of comedy in the service of truth.

As the play opens it is not hard to discover why Congreve's first audiences struggled mightily with their enjoyment or why the playwright wrote in a preface that success of the play on stage "was almost beyond my Expectation."

Beginning with a card game at a fashionable London chocolate house between two gentlemen of fashion—Mirabell and Fainall—the significance of what is said (and not said) only gradually emerges as the pair verbally fence with each other. The audience is thrust into the middle of a complex network of relations, innuendoes, and disguised motives. At the dramatic core of the play is a contest for the control of a family fortune in the hands of Lady Wishfort, Fainall's mother-in-law, and the guardian of her niece, Mrs. Millamant, whom Mirabell loves. It is only gradually revealed that Fainall and Mirabell are more than just competitors for Lady Wishfort's fortune, however. Mrs. Fainall has been Mirabell's mistress, and Fainall's current mistress, Mrs. Marwood, has betrayed Mirabell's motive of courting Lady Wishfort to conceal his true designs on Millamant out of jealousy. This dizzying web of intrigue, conflicting loyalties, and disguise establishes Congreve's central thematic point that nothing is as simple as it seems and that the polite mask of manners conceals a far different reality. As Mirabell and Fainall thrust and parry, Congreve proceeds by indirection, forcing the audience to detect his characters' motivations and the underlying currents of emotions as much by what they avoid saying as by explicit statement. Critic Maximillian E. Novak has observed: "The way Congreve moves the action forward while, at the same time, giving information about the characters and the situation is probably unmatched in English comedy."

In the second act the hints and innuendoes are clarified. The loveless marriage between Mr. and Mrs. Fainall and the divided motives of Mrs. Marwood as Fainall's mistress and Millamant's rival for Mirabell are made explicit. However, much still remains hidden, and first impressions are misleading. Millamant, in her first appearance, seems to be the archetypal, shallow young flirt, who takes the stage in "full Sail, with her Fan spread and Streamers out, and a Shoal of Fools for Tenders." The ensuing verbal sparring between Millamant and Mirabell, one of the high points of English drama, shows her to be far from the superficial ingénue of first impression and leaves Mirabell in a "whirlwind" trying to adjust conventional gender assumptions in Millamant's complex blend of the conventional and the iconoclastic:

> A fellow that lives in a windmill has not a more whimsical dwelling than the heart of a man that is lodged in a woman. There is no point of the compass to which they cannot turn, and by which they are not turned; and by one as well as another. For motion, not method, is their occupation. To know this, and yet continue to be in love, is to be made wise from the dictates of reason, and yet persevere to play the fool by the force of instinct.

Mirabell's scheme to overcome Lady Wishfort's objection to his pursuit of Millamant is to disguise his servant, Waitwell, as a nobleman to court and marry Lady Wishfort. Mirabell then intends to reveal the deception and threaten to expose her to public ridicule unless she withdraws her objections to his suit of her niece. The audience's expectations in watching this intrigue unfold are disappointed as the plot quickly fizzles when Mrs. Marwood in the third act discovers the scheme and warns Lady Wishfort. Mrs. Marwood also reveals to Fainall Mirabell's past affair with his wife, and Fainall uses this intelligence to threaten disclosure of her daughter's past unless Lady Wishfort signs over his wife's and Millamant's fortune to him. This counterplot, like Mirabell's, collapses as Mirabell produces a deed, made by Mrs. Fainall before her marriage, conveying all her estate to him as her trustee. Fainall is thereby rendered powerless, and all that has been hidden is now finally revealed. Lady Wishfort, enlightened by the truth of Fainall's villainy and the double-dealing of Mrs. Marwood, finally sets aside her objections and clears the way for Mirabell to marry Millamant.

Such a bald summary of the unwinding of Congreve's intrigue plot misses the point of the drama. Existing more as an ironic parody of the typical Restoration comic plot, the drama's tortuous and fortuitous turns of events serve mainly a thematic point about the complexity of relationships and the deceptiveness of taking character and relationships at face value. Moving from deception to truth, from disguise to revelation, *The Way of the World* suggests that the truth about individuals is complex and that authentic interactions are supremely difficult. These points are made explicit in the deepening relationship between Mirabell and Millamant whose process toward genuine love in a corrosive atmosphere of falsity and deception is one of the wonders of the stage. Finally shedding the elaborate social facade that has marked their sexual antagonism, Mirabell and Millamant negotiate the basis for a mutually satisfying relationship in one of the most brilliant exchanges in all Restoration comedies:

MILLAMANT   . . . And d'ye hear, I won't be call'd Names after I'm Marry'd; positively I won't be call'd Names.

MIRABELL   Names!

MILLAMANT   Ay, as Wife, Spouse, my Dear, Joy, Jewel, Love, Sweetheart, and the rest of that nauseous Cant, in which Men and their Wives are so fulsomely familiar,—I shall never bear that—Good *Mirabell* don't let us be familiar or fond, nor kiss before Folks, like my Lady *Fadler* and *Sir Francis*: Nor go to *Hide-Park* together the first *Sunday* in a new Chariot, to provoke Eyes and Whispers; And then never be seen there together again; as if we were proud of one another the first Week, and asham'd of one another ever after. Let us never Visit together, not go to a Play together, but let us be very strange and well bred: Let us be as strange as if we had been marry'd a great while; and as well bred as if we were not marry'd at all.

To Millamant's iconoclastic conditions, Mirabell adds some of his own:

MIRABELL   . . . That you continue to like your own Face, as long as I shall: And while it passes currant with me, that you endeavour not to new Coin it. To which end, together with all Vizards for the Day, I prohibit all Masks for the Night, made of Oil'd-skins, and I know not what—Hog's Bones, Hare's Gall, Pig Water, and the Marrow of a roasted Cat. In short I forbid all Commerce with the Gentlewoman in *what-d'ye-call-it* Court. . . . Lastly to the Dominion of the *Tea-Table* I submit—But with *proviso*, that you exceed not in your Province; but restrain yourself to native and simple *Tea-Table Drinks*, as *Tea*, *Chocolate*, and *Coffee*. As likewise to Genuine and Authoriz'd *Tea-Table Talk*—Such as mending of Fashions, spoiling of Reputations, railing at absent Friends, and so forth—But that on no Account you encroach upon the Mens Prerogative, and presume to drink Healths, or toast Fellows; for prevention of which I banish all *Foreign Forces*, all Auxilliaries to the *Tea-Table*, as *Orange-Brandy*, all *Anniseed, Cinamon, Citron* and *Barbado's-Waters*, together with *Ratafia*, and all *Dormitives*, those I allow.—These *Proviso's* admitted, in other things I may prove a tractable and complying Husband.

MILLAMANT   O horrid *Proviso's!* filthy Strong waters! I toast Fellows, Odious Men! I hate your odious *Proviso's!*

MIRABELL   Then we're agreed. Shall I kiss your Hand upon the Contract?

Millamant asserts her independence and refusal to be unduly dominated or possessed by her husband, while Mirabell rejects the vain fashions of the time. She finally agrees to "dwindle into a Wife," while he concedes to be "enlarg'd to a husband," but not before both have tested their hearts and wits against the ways of the world. The audience as well has been tested in being forced to enlarge a capacity to see that world in all its delightful and sobering contradictions and complexities.

A STREETCAR NAMED DESIRE   26

(1947)   *by Tennessee Williams*

I can recall where I was sitting at that first Streetcar *viewing. . . . It took only a few minutes to realize that the play and the production had thrown open doors to another theater world. This was not due to any invention in the play's structure, with its tangible, realistic story-telling line. Rather, it was the writing itself that left one excited and elevated. . . . In a word, this play made it seem possible for the stage to express any and all things and do so beautifully. What* Streetcar's *first production did was to plant the flag of beauty on the shores of commercial theater. The audience, I believe, somehow understood this and was moved by what, in effect, was a kind of tribute to its intelligence and spiritual vitality. For the play, more than any of Williams' other works before or afterward, approaches tragedy and its dark ending is unmitigated.*

> —Arthur Miller, Introduction to the New Directions edition
> of *A Streetcar Named Desire*, 2004

Few other single plays have asserted such a seismic shock that shifted the dramatic landscape or can comparably claim milestone status as Tennessee Williams's *A Streetcar Named Desire*. Indeed, American theater can be divided into before and after *Streetcar*. With it American drama in the post–World War II era gained a new subject, vocabulary, and grammar, as well as a new openness to deal with taboo subjects. Complex and hidden emotional and sexual drives that had never before been explored on an American stage were suddenly manifest with all their force and threat creating an electrifying experience for audiences. While opening up new fields for exploration Williams expanded the limits of existing theatrical practices by pioneering a new fusion of realistic, symbolic, and expressionistic techniques. He also added to the modern theatrical arsenal a lyricism that exploited the poetic and subjective possibilities of language, setting, and situation. Moving away from the drama of social protest that had dominated serious American drama in the 1930s, Williams rejected the role of sociologist, arguing that "What I am writing about is human nature." If his *THE GLASS MENAGERIE* (1944) signaled the arrival of a powerful, new force in American drama, *Streetcar*, which Williams considered his best play, represented the fulfillment of that promise. When it premiered, critic Joseph Wood Krutch wrote: "This may be the great American play." Critic Jordan Miller has called it "a work as important as any other written for the American stage" and "as close to genuine tragedy as any modern American drama." Testifying to the play's hold on the imagination and persistence as an influence, reviewer T. E. Kalem has observed: "The inevitability of a great work of art is that you cannot imagine the time when it didn't exist. You can't imagine a time when *Streetcar* didn't exist."

The play dramatizes passions and torments with the intimacy and familiarity of firsthand experience. "My work is *emotionally* autobiographical," Williams told an interviewer. "It has no relationship to the actual events of my life, but it reflects the emotional currents of my life." The actual events and the origins of those emotional currents are these: Born Thomas Lanier Williams, in 1911, in Columbus, Mississippi, Williams was the son of a traveling salesman from Tennessee and a Mississippi minister's daughter. With his father often on the road, Williams, his mother, and his older sister, Rose, lived in his grandfather's rectory. As a young child Williams survived a near-fatal bout of diphtheria that left him physically weakened and under the constant care of his overprotective mother. The boy's shyness, sensitivity, and dependence provoked the scorn of Williams's extroverted and robustly masculine father who nicknamed his son "Miss Nancy." When Williams was eight the family moved from rural Mississippi to St. Louis, Missouri, where his parents' marriage collapsed under the pressure of his father's increasing drinking and his mother's resentment about the move from her family, home, and her comfortable place in genteel southern society. Her son similarly felt displaced from a protective environment he described as "a dark, wide, open world that you can breathe in" to "a city I loathe." The imaginative opposition between city and country, North and South, romanticized past and dehumanizing and oppressive present would become central polarities in his writing. Often bullied by children in the neighborhood, Williams found his defense, and compensation, in reading and writing poems, plays, essays, and stories. His writing was "an escape from a world of reality in which I felt acutely uncomfortable. It immediately became my place of retreat, my cave, my refuge." Williams's sister, Rose, similarly retreated inwardly, becoming increasingly afflicted with the schizophrenia that would lead to her being institutionalized.

In 1929 Williams entered the University of Missouri, but, after failing his officer training course in his third year, his father withdrew his son from school to labor for three years in a shoe warehouse. The experience, which Williams called "a living death," led to a nervous breakdown in 1935, followed by a year convalescing in Memphis under the care of his grandparents. It was during his recovery that Williams had his first play produced, *Cairo, Shanghai, Bombay!*, a farce about two sailors on shore leave. Deciding on a writing career,

Williams returned to St. Louis to attend Washington University before finally transferring to the University of Iowa, where he studied playwriting, wrote two more long plays, and graduated in 1938. The next year he published a short story in *Story* magazine, his first work to appear under the name "Tennessee." Williams would claim that the name honored his father's family and their prominent role in the state's history. Others have suggested that it was a nickname he acquired in Iowa because of his southern accent that Williams had adopted as part of a new persona that emerged after college. Williams would spend the year following his graduation as a struggling, itinerant writer in Chicago, St. Louis, and most notably New Orleans, where he settled into the French Quarter as a "confirmed Bohemian." As Stella informs Blanche, "New Orleans isn't like other cities," and Williams himself wrote about the liberating impact of New Orleans: "I found the kind of freedom I had always needed. The shock of it against the Puritanism of my nature has given me a subject, a theme, which I have never ceased exploiting." New Orleans would feature prominently in his stories, in several one-act plays, and most notably in what is surely the greatest imaginative treatment of the city, *A Streetcar Named Desire*.

Reserving additional comments on Williams's apprenticeship and evolving dramatic method for the examination of *The Glass Menagerie* we pick up Williams's story following that play's Broadway opening and success in 1945. Acclaimed and honored as a new American dramatist of genius, Williams struggled with success as he had with previous failure. His growing feelings of isolation and depression would be chronicled in "On a Streetcar Named Success," an essay which served as the introduction to the printed version of *Streetcar*. Williams's stopgap Broadway follow-up to *The Glass Menagerie* was an earlier collaboration with his friend Donald Windham, *You Touched Me!*, an adaptation of a D. H. Lawrence short story. In 1946, to complete a new work called "The Poker Night," Williams left New York for Mexico. On the way he suffered a ruptured appendix. A confirmed hypochondriac, Williams was convinced that it was life-threatening and that his next play, which he struggled to complete recovering from the operation, would surely be his last. "The Poker Night," became *A Streetcar Named Desire*, which opened on Broadway, under the direction of Elia Kazan, on December 3, 1947.

Having elicited praise for his compassionate portrait of a frustrated family in *The Glass Menagerie*, in *Streetcar* Williams concentrates on the more elemental, starker passions of another family triangle. Williams would later warn that, having put "all the nice things I have to say about people" in *The Glass Menagerie*, his subsequent writing would deal with more challenging, harsher subjects. Like *The Glass Menagerie*, *Streetcar* is organized in a series of scenes but without the earlier play's narrator providing transitions and commentary. Blanche DuBois is a more conflicted and damaged version of Amanda Wingfield. Both are southern belles relying on memories of past triumphs to offset a shabbier present, but the conflict between appearance and reality confronting Amanda is played out within Blanche in the battle between aspects of herself as a genteel figure of culture and refinement and as an earthbound seductress. Underscoring the division of Blanche's nature, Williams brings her into collision with her polar opposite, Stanley Kowalski, the all-American brute, who will assault Blanche, literally and figuratively, prompting her psychic break. Set in postwar New Orleans, the play opens with Blanche's arrival at Elysian Fields, the rundown slum where her sister, Stella, is living with her husband Stanley. The play's title emphasizes the journey of the play's protagonist, while Blanche's route to her new home ("They told me to take a street-car named Desire, and then transfer to one called Cemeteries.") establishes the play's central conflict between desire and death, Eros and Thanatos. The play's naturalistic depiction of New Orleans's street life whose sights and sounds periodically invade the Kowalskis' apartment serves a symbolic and expressionistic function as objectifications of Blanche's mental disorientation and ultimate disintegration. Blanche has left the family mansion of Belle Reve after it and her job in Laurel, Mississippi, as a teacher have been lost. As Kazan records in his production "Notebook," the dispossessed and alienated Blanche has come to her sister searching for a place where she can "belong." Each of the play's 11 scenes represents, according to Kazan, a step in Blanche's "progression from arrival to expulsion," in what the playwright called a "tragedy of incomprehension."

In the initial scene Blanche, assuming the role of demure, prim southern lady, adjusts to the shock of Stanley, whom she will call a "survivor of the stone age," her sister and brother-in-law's apartment, and the neighborhood ("Only Poe! Only Mr. Edgar Allan Poe!—could do it justice! Out there I suppose is the ghoul-haunted woodland of Weir!"). The threat Blanche perceives outside the small apartment is more than matched by Stanley within, who early on perceives Blanche as a rival for Stella, is suspicious of Blanche's past, and responds to her genteel airs by bullying and taunting boorishness. In scene 3, "The Poker Night," Blanche flirts with Stanley's friend Mitch as the most sensitive of the card players, provoking a violent outburst by Stanley, who strikes the pregnant Stella. Seeking refuge in the upstairs apartment, the sisters are momentarily united before Stella returns to the supplicating Stanley. Williams's stage direction underscores the sexual shock of the play, intensified by a seething and iconic Marlon Brando in the debut production:

Stella slips down the rickety stairs in her robe. Her eyes are glistening with tears and her hair loose about her throat and shoulders. They stare at each other. Then they come together with low, animal moans. He falls to his knees on the steps and presses his face to her belly, curving a little with maternity. Her eyes go blind with tenderness as she catches his head and raises him level with her. He snatches the screen door open and lifts her off her feet and bears her into the dark flat.

Having lost the battle to separate Stella from Stanley, Blanche concentrates her efforts on winning Mitch, even as her carefully constructed facade as a prim and proper schoolteacher begins to crumble under Stanley's investigation of her past behavior. Blanche confesses to Mitch the central trauma of her life: the suicide death of her young husband when she had humiliated him after discovering him in bed with another man. Mitch reacts to Blanche's tragic tale with sympathy, embracing her and saying, "You need somebody. And I need somebody, too. Could it be—you and me, Blanche?" Blanche responds to his proposal and embrace by answering, "Sometimes—there's God—so quickly." Blanche's triumph with the truth and refuge with Mitch prove short lived, however. As Stella prepares Blanche's birthday dinner and her sister is heard singing merrily in the bathroom, Stanley arrives to tell his wife that the stories he has heard about Blanche are true, that she had been forced from a disreputable hotel in Laurel as a prostitute and had lost her high school teaching job after the discovery of her affair with a 17-year-old student. Mitch fails to arrive, and Stanley's birthday gift to his sister-in-law, after he has cleared the table by smashing the dinner dishes, is a one-way bus ticket home to Laurel. As the scene ends Stanley accompanies his wife, whose labor has begun, to the hospital. Blanche is left alone and isolated to endure the first of two violations as an angry Mitch finally appears. Declaring that he has never seen her in the light, Mitch tears the paper lantern off the bulb "So I can take a look at you good and plain!" Horrified, Blanche asked if he intends to be insulting. Mitch answers that he just wants to be realistic, to which she responds: "I don't want realism. I want magic! Yes, yes, magic! I try to give that to people. I misrepresent things to them. I don't tell the truth, I tell what *ought* to be truth." Blanche's admission leads to her recounting the sordid details of her promiscuity: "After the death of Allan—intimacies with strangers was all I seemed able to fill my empty heart with. . . . I think it was panic, just panic, that drove me from one to another, hunting for some protection—here and there, in the most—unlikely places—even, at last, in a seventeen-year-old boy." The urgency of Blanche's need is symbolically underscored when a blind Mexican woman appears outside the apartment selling flowers for the dead: the state she has resisted with desire. Death has been Blanche's principal legacy, caring for her dying family and the passing of their way of life. "Death," Blanche says, "was as close as you are. . . . The opposite is desire. So do you wonder?" Mitch responds not with understanding but by his own sexual desire, confirming Blanche's humiliation as sexual object. Rejecting her as a marriage partner Mitch declares: "You're not clean enough to bring in the house with my mother."

The consummation of Blanche's objectification occurs when Stanley returns from the hospital. Blanche has retreated into the fantasy of being rescued by a former beau, Shep Huntleigh. As a drunk outside struggles with a prostitute, inside Blanche futilely resists Stanley's advances with a broken bottle. Cornering her, Stanley declares before the rape: "We've had this date with each other from the beginning." Williams's stage directions indicate: "He picks up her inert figure and carries her to the bed. The hot trumpet and drums from the Four Deuces sound loudly." In the final scene Stella has returned home with her baby, and another poker game is in progress as Blanche is taken away to an asylum. Stella refuses to believe her sister's claim that Stanley has raped her, and Blanche's insanity is required for her to go on with her life with Stanley. To convince Blanche to leave quietly Stella tells her that Shep Huntleigh has come for her. When Blanche realizes the truth she is at first terrified but becomes compliant due to the respectful solicitude she receives from the doctor, as she delivers her memorable exit line: "Whoever you are—I have always depended on the kindness of strangers." The irony is multiple: Blanche has received precious little kindness from either family or friends, and the kindness she is now forced to depend on from strangers is more delusional than real. Blanche retreats, excluded from the world that has little time for or understanding of her strengths or failings, for her magic or truth as it ought to be. Blanche, however, claims a tragic dignity as a romantic dreamer driven by and ultimately destroyed by her and others' desires. At the end of the play Stanley "voluptuously, soothingly" comforts his sobbing wife, indicating that with Blanche's departure life for them will resume as before. The audience, however, is aware of the loss and human waste represented by Blanche's journey illuminated by a drama that is simultaneously psychologically astute, electrifying, and mythic in its capacity to represent the human condition.

THE TEMPEST

(1611) by *William Shakespeare*

Many commentators agree in the belief that The Tempest *is the last creation of Shakespeare. I will readily believe it. There is in* The Tempest *the solemn tone of a testament. It might be said that, before his death, the poet, in this epopee of the ideal, had designed a codicil for the Future. . . .* The Tempest *is the supreme denouement, dreamed by Shakespeare, for the bloody drama of Genesis. It is the expiation of the primordial crime. The region whither it transports us is the enchanted land where the sentence of damnation is absolved by clemency, and where reconciliation is ensured by amnesty to the fratricide. And, at the close of the piece, when the poet, touched by emotion, throws Antonio into the arms of Prospero, he has made Cain pardoned by Abel.*

—Victor Hugo, *Oeuvres complètes de Shakespeare*

It is inevitable, given the position of *The Tempest* as William Shakespeare's final solo dramatic work, to hear in Prospero's epilogue to the play, Shakespeare's farewell to his audience:

> Now my charms are all o'erthrown,
> And what strength I have's mine own,
> Which is most faint. . .
>   . . . Now I want
> Spirits to enforce, art to enchant;
> And my ending is despair
> Unless I be relieved by prayer,
> Which pierces so, that it assaults
> Mercy itself, and frees all faults.
> As you from crimes would pardoned be,
> Let your indulgence set me free.

Prospero bows out on a note of forgiveness, the tone that finally rules the play along with an affirmation in the essential goodness of humanity. It has been tempting, therefore, to view Prospero's sentiment and his play as Shakespeare's last word, his summation of a career and a philosophy, what critic Gary Taylor has called "the valedictory culmination of Shakespeare's life work." First performed at court on November 1, 1611, before the playwright's exit to Stratford, *The Tempest*, however, is technically neither Shakespeare's finale nor requiem. Two years later Shakespeare was back in London, collaborating with John Fletcher on *The Two Noble Kinsmen*, *Henry VIII*, and the lost play *Cardenio*. As intriguing as the biographical reading is, it is only one of *The Tempest's* multiple layers of meaning and significance. Called by critic T. M. Parrot, "perhaps the best loved of all Shakespeare's plays," and by William Hazlitt as among the "most original and perfect of Shakespeare's productions," *The Tempest* continues to be one of the most performed and interpreted plays in the canon, generating (and withstanding) autobiographical, allegorical, religious, metaphysical, and more recently postcolonial readings. The play's central figure has likewise shifted from Prospero, who fascinated the romantics, to Miranda, who has claimed the attention of feminists, to Caliban, who is exhibit A in the reading of the play as "a veritable document of early Anglo-American history," according to writer Sydney Lee, containing "the whole history of imperialist America," as stated by critic Leslie Fiedler. *The Tempest* has served as a poetic treasure trove and springboard for other writers, with allusions detectable in John Milton's *Comus*, T. S. Eliot's *The Waste Land*, W. H. Auden's *The Sea and the Mirror*, and countless other works. Based on its popularity, persistence, and universality, *The Tempest* remains one of the richest and most fascinating of Shakespeare's plays.

The Tempest is a composite work with elements derived from multiple sources. Montaigne's essay "On Cannibals," whose romantic primitivism is satirized in Gonzalo's plan for organizing society on Prospero's island in the second act, is a possible source. So, too, are a German play, *Comedy of the Beautiful Sidea*, by Jacob Ayrer, about a magician prince whose only daughter falls in love with the son of his enemy, and several Italian commedia dell'arte pastoral tragicomedies set on remote islands and featuring benevolent magicians. Accounts of the *Sea-Venture*, the ship sent to Virginia to bolster John Smith's colony that was wrecked on the coast of Bermuda in 1609, may have furnished Shakespeare with some of the details for the play's opening storm. However, the most substantial borrowing for the plot of *The Tempest* comes from Shakespeare's own previous plays, so much so, that scholar Stephen Greenblatt has described *The Tempest* as "a kind of echo chamber of Shakespearean motifs." The complications following a shipwreck revisits *Twelfth Night*; the relocation of court society to the wilderness is featured in *As You Like It* and *A Midsummer Night's Dream*, which also employs spirits and the supernatural to teach lessons and settle scores. The backstory of *The Tempest*—Prospero, the former duke of Milan, usurped by his brother—recalls *HAMLET* and *KING LEAR*. Miranda's being raised in ignorance of her past and status as well as the debate between nature and nurture echo *Pericles* and *The Winter's Tale*. Like both, *The Tempest* mixes light and dark, tragic and comic elements, yet compared to their baroque complexity, the shortest of Shakespeare's plays after *Macbeth* obeys the Aristotelian unities of place and time (the only other Shakespearean play to do so is *The Comedy of Errors*), with its action confined to Prospero's island, taking place over a period roughly corresponding to its performance time.

The *Tempest* begins with one of the most spectacular scenes in all of Shakespeare: the storm at sea that threatens the vessel whose passengers include King Alonso of Naples, his son Ferdinand, and Prospero's hated brother Antonio, the usurping duke of Milan. Their life-and-death struggle enacted on stage is subjected to a double focus as Prospero reassures his daughter, Miranda, distraught over the fate of the passengers and crew, that he controls the tempest and that their danger is an illusion. The disaster, which he calls a "spectacle," is artifice, and the play establishes an analogy between Prospero's magic and the theatrical sleight of hand that initially seemed so realistic and thrilling. Prospero stands in for the artist here: Both magician and playwrights are conjurors, able to manipulate nature and make others believe in a reality without substance. The contrast between illusion and reality will be sounded throughout the play, suggesting that *The Tempest* is a metadrama: a play about playwriting and the power and limitations of the imagination. Prospero finally tells his daughter how they arrived on the island; how his brother, Antonio, joined in a conspiracy with Alonso to usurp his place as duke of Milan; how 12 years before Prospero and Miranda were set adrift at sea, provisioned only by a compassionate Neapolitan, Gonzalo. Friend and foes, aboard the vessel Prospero has seemed to wreck, are now under his control on the island where Prospero intends to exact his vengeance. Prospero, therefore, will use his long-studied magical arts to stage a reckoning for past offenses. The play proceeds under Prospero's direction with a cast that either cooperates or complicates his intentions. Serving him are the ethereal Ariel, whom Prospero promises to free after completing his bidding, and the contrasting earthly and brutish Caliban, a witch's son, whom Prospero says he has "us'd thee / (Filth as thou art) with human care, and lodg'd thee / In mine own cell, till thou didst seek to violate / The honor of my child." Prospero, therefore, controls symbols of both sides of human nature: aspects of the imagination and fancy and baser instincts that come in conflict on the island as the play progresses.

As playwright Prospero must juggle three subplots: Miranda's relationship with Ferdinand, the son of Alonso, who mourns his loss at sea; the plotting of Prospero's brother, Antonio, and the king's brother, Sebastian, to murder Alonso and seize his throne; and Caliban's alliance with the jester Trinculo and butler Stefano to kill Prospero and reign in his stead. The first goes so well—Miranda and Ferdinand fall in love at first sight—that Prospero tests Ferdinand's fidelity by appearing to punish him by making him his servant. Ferdinand, however, proves his devotion by gladly accepting his humiliation to be near Miranda. Prospero ends Ferdinand's penance and testing in the first scene of act 4, declaring: "All thy vexations / Were but my trials of thy love, and thou / Hast strangely stood the test." To seal the nuptial vows a ritual masque is performed by various mythological goddesses and pastoral figures. In the midst of the dance Prospero stops the performance to deliver one of the most celebrated speeches in all of Shakespeare's plays:

> Our revels now are ended. These our actors,
> As I foretold you, were all spirits, and
> Are melted into air, into thin air;
> And, like the baseless fabric of this vision,
> The cloud-capp'd towers, the gorgeous palaces,
> The solemn temples, the great globe itself,
> Yea, all which it inherit, shall dissolve,
> And, like this insubstantial pageant faded,
> Leave not a rack behind. We are such stuff
> As dreams are made on; and our little life
> Is rounded with a sleep.

Jaques in *As You Like It* asserted "All the world's a stage," and Macbeth described life as "a poor player that struts and frets his hour upon the stage." Prospero's speech suggests the transience of both human life and art, with its reference to "the great globe," the name of Shakespeare's theater, that, along with towers, palaces, and temples, "shall dissolve . . . like this insubstantial pageant."

Made aware by Ariel of Caliban's conspiracy with Trinculo and Stefano, Prospero distracts them from their purpose of murder by rich attire, which Trinculo and Stefano put on before being set upon by spirits. Their comic rebellion is matched by the more serious plot of Antonio and Sebastian to kill Alonso. An assassination attempt is halted by the appearance of spirits providing a banquet for the hungry men. Just as they try to satisfy their hunger the food disappears, replaced by Ariel, "like a harpy," who accuses Alonso, Sebastian, and Antonio of their crimes against Prospero and delivers their sentences:

> . . . But remember,
> For that's my business to you, that you three
> From Milan did supplant good Prospero;
> Exposed unto the sea, which hath requit it,
> Him, and his innocent child; for which foul deed
> The powers, delaying not forgetting, have
> Incensed the seas and shores, yea, all the creatures,
> Against your peace. Thee of thy son, Alonso,

They have bereft; and do pronounce by me
Ling'ring perdition, worse than any death
Can be at once, shall step by step attend
You and your ways; whose wraths to guard you from—
Which here, in this most desolate isle, else falls
Upon your heads—is nothing but heart's sorrow,
And a clear life ensuing.

Prospero, approving of Ariel's performance, declares, "They now are in my pow'r," and the play turns on how he will decide to use that power.

At the start of the fifth act Prospero announces the climax of his plan: "Now does my project gather to a head," with his victims now imprisoned to confront their guilt and fate. It is Ariel who shifts Prospero from vengeance to forgiveness by saying, "Your charm so strongly works 'em / That if you now beheld them your affections / Would become tender." Ariel's suggestion of what should be the reaction to human suffering shames Prospero into compassion:

Hast thou, which art but air, a touch, a feeling
Of their afflictions, and shall not myself,
One of their kind, that relish all as sharply,
Passion as they, be kindlier moved than thou art?
Though with their high wrongs I am struck to th' quick,
Yet with my nobler reason 'gainst my fury
Do I take part. The rarer action is
In virtue than in vengeance. They being penitent,
The sole drift of my purpose doth extend
Not a frown further. Go release them, Ariel;
My charms I'll break, their senses I'll restore,
And they shall be themselves.

Prospero turns away from revenge and the pursuit of power that had formerly ruled the destinies of so many Shakespearean heroes, including Hamlet, Macbeth, and many more. Prospero changes the plot of his play at its climax and then turns away from his art to reenter the human community:

. . . But this rough magic
I here abjure. And, when I have required
Some heavenly music—which even now I do—
To work mine end upon their senses that
This airy charm is for, I'll break my staff,
Bury it certain fathoms in the earth,
And deeper than did ever plummet sound
I'll drown my book.

The end of Prospero's plot, his art, and the play conjoin. Ariel returns with the prisoners, and Prospero pardons all, including his brother, before reclaiming his dukedom and reuniting father and son. Miranda, overcome by so many nobles on their formerly deserted island, declares:

> O wonder!
> How many goodly creatures are there here!
> How beauteous mankind is! O brave new world
> That has such people in't!

Prospero, more soberly and less optimistically, responds to her words: "'Tis new to thee." Finally, Caliban, Stephano, and Trinculo are brought in. The lowly status and ridiculousness of the latter two are exposed, prompting Caliban to assert:

> I'll be wise hereafter,
> And seek for grace. What a thrice-double ass
> Was I to take this drunkard for a god,
> And worship this dull fool!

Having reestablished order and a harmonious future in the marriage of Miranda and Ferdinand, Prospero delivers on his promise to free Ariel before turning to the audience to ask for the same compassion and forgiveness he has shown. As Prospero has released the spirit Ariel, we are asked to do the same for Prospero. We now hold the power and the art to use it as we will:

> . . . Now 'tis true
> I must be here confined by you
> Or sent to Naples. Let me not,
> Since I have my dukedom got,
> And pardoned the deceiver, dwell
> In this bare island by your spell;
> But release me from my bands
> With the help of your good hands.

If the play is not Shakespeare's last will and testament, there scarcely can be a better: a play that affirms essential human goodness while acknowledging the presence of human evil, written in the full powers of the imagination, while conscious of its limitations and responsibilities.

MAJOR BARBARA

(1905)

by George Bernard Shaw

Recently I took my children to Major Barbara. *Twenty years had passed since I had seen it. They were the most terrific years the world has known. Almost every human institution had undergone decisive change. The landmarks of centuries had been swept away. Science has transformed the conditions of our lives and the aspect of town and country. Silent social evolution, violent political change, a vast broadening of the social foundations, in immeasurable release from convention and restraint, a profound reshaping of national and individual opinion, have followed the trampling march of this tremendous epoch. But in* Major Barbara *there was not a character requiring to be re-drawn, not a sentence nor a suggestion that this play, the very acme of modernity, was written more than five years before they were born.*

—Winston Churchill, *Great Contemporaries*

In contending with the dramatic achievement of George Bernard Shaw, it is tempting to resort to the critical stance taken by English writer G. K. Chesterton in assessing another inimitable writer, Charles Dickens. Chesterton asserted that there was in fact no single Dickens novel, but all are "simply lengths cut from the flowing and mixed substance called Dickens." Likewise, all of Shaw's plays collectively form a singular opus, and distinctions among them can seem beyond the point. Only William Shakespeare has contributed more to the repertory of established English classic plays. Moreover, Shaw can claim the unique distinction of being the greatest Victorian, Edwardian, Georgian, *and* modern English playwright, indeed the greatest English dramatist since Shakespeare who transformed existing dramatic conventions into an unprecedented criticism of life. Included here in this ranking are three of Shaw's works: MAN AND SUPERMAN and SAINT JOAN as his riskiest and most ambitious philosophical dramas and *Major Barbara* as his most representative play that turned the drawing room comedy of manners into an exhilarating, liberating, and unprecedented critique of human nature and the human condition. Shaw is principally responsible for giving the problem play that

Henrik Ibsen pioneered an English home, while establishing a modern drama of ideas that adapted comedy for a radical reassessment of accepted understandings. "All great truths," Shaw asserted, "begin as blasphemies." Bertolt Brecht observed: "It should be clear by now that Shaw is a terrorist. The Shavian terror is an unusual one, and he employs an unusual weapon—that of humor." *Major Barbara* is both one of Shaw's most witty plays and one of his most subversive. Both elements are best understood in the context of Shaw's background, development, and artistic intentions.

The most remarkable aspect of Shaw's life is surely its span. Born in 1856 into a gaslit Victorian world, Shaw survived the two world wars of the 20th century and the arrival of the atomic age, dying in 1950 after a seemingly inexhaustible creative life of nearly three-quarters of a century. Shaw came late to the theater by a circuitous and accidental route. Like the other great Irish-born comic dramatists and satirists—Jonathan Swift, Richard Brinsley Sheridan, and Oscar Wilde—Shaw would eventually establish his career as a contrarian, in opposition to the English status quo. He came from an impoverished Dublin Anglo-Protestant family. His father was a drunkard, and Shaw's mother moved to London to pursue a career as an opera singer and voice teacher. Her son remained behind until the age of 20. After schooling in Dublin, in which Shaw asserted he learned nothing except that schools are prisons, he worked for a time in an office. He would later recall:

> I made good in spite of myself, and found, to my dismay, that Business, instead of expelling me as the worthless impostor I was, was fastening upon me with no intention of letting me go. Behold me, therefore, in my twentieth year, with a business training, in an occupation which I detested as cordially as any sane person lets himself detest anything he cannot escape from. In March 1876 I broke loose.

Shaw left Dublin for London to write novels and music, art, and drama criticism. Setting himself the task of improving the popular tastes in the arts, Shaw became a champion of Wagner and Mozart in music and Ibsen in drama, while opposing the fashionable aesthetic movement's doctrine of "art for art's sake" on behalf of an artistic commitment to moral and social reform. Politically Shaw became active in the Fabian Society advocating its doctrine of gradual socialism. It is during this period that Shaw crafted his public persona, G.B.S., the jester, iconoclast, and shock therapist whose medium was the paradox. "I have never pretended that G.B.S. was real," he wrote. "The whole point of the creature is that he is unique, fantastic, unrepresentative, inimitable, impossible, undesirable on any large scale, utterly unlike anybody that ever existed before, hopelessly unnatural, and void of real passion." Shaw would transfer his role as eccentric provocateur eventually to the theater.

In 1885 Shaw and William Archer, a fellow drama critic and early advocate of Ibsen, collaborated on a play in which Archer contributed the plot and Shaw the dialogue. The result was *Widowers' Houses*, a play about wealthy slum landlords, in which Shaw's dramatic genius is first displayed. Shaw transformed the conventions of Eugène Scribe's well-made play in which plot is paramount into a vehicle to express his political theories of modern capitalism and to shock the cherished beliefs of his audience. "I avoid plots like the plague," Shaw would observe about his dramatic technique. "My procedure is to imagine characters and let them rip." He followed *Widowers' Houses* with a succession of plays, including *Mrs. Warren's Profession, Arms and the Man,* and *Candida* that presents in turn Shaw's daring rationale of prostitution in an exploitative society, his debunking of romanticized views of war and love, and his witty inversion of Ibsen's *A Doll's House* from the husband's viewpoint. None of his early plays was a theatrical success, but Shaw reached an audience by publishing his plays with detailed stage directions and witty, combative prefaces. In 1898, his first seven plays were published as *Plays Pleasant and Unpleasant*. In 1901, Shaw published *Plays for Puritans*, a collection that included *The Devil's Disciple* and *Caesar and Cleopatra*, plays that show him perfecting his trademark of employing an educator and a pupil, in which the prototypical Shavian realist offers instruction about the truth of the world to a student who starts by believing a set of traditional values and then undergoes a process of disillusionment and maturation. Strategically Shaw reverses the method of Molière, in which a deviant from the norm is exposed. Instead Shaw injects a provocateur into the center of conventional thought and behavior to expose their inconsistencies. For Shaw drama became the means to embody philosophy and a more enlightened and comprehensive view of life. "Though my trade is that of a playwright," he wrote, "my vocation is that of a prophet." All of Shaw's plays show his considerable wit and delight in confounding expectations and provoking new understanding, none more brilliantly than *Major Barbara* in which a passionate Salvation Army activist, Barbara, sets out to reform her capitalist arms manufacturer father, Andrew Undershaft, and is in turn made to reexamine her wrongheaded assumptions about wealth, poverty, economics, religion, and morality.

First performed in London in 1905, *Major Barbara* was published in 1907 along with Shaw's preface, or what he called "First Aid to Critics," informing them of what to say about it. Subtitled *A Discussion in Three Acts, Major Barbara*, like virtually all of Shaw's dramas, is constructed dialectically by opposing viewpoints. At its thematic core is a radical social analysis. "In the millionaire Undershaft," Shaw declared in his preface, "I have represented a man who has become intellectually and spiritually as well as practically conscious of the irresistible natural truth which we all abhor and repudiate: to wit, that the greatest of our evils, and the worst of our crimes is poverty, and that our first duty, to which every other consideration should be sacrificed, is not to be poor." For Shaw this economic imperative trumps all other orthodox moral and spiritual considerations, which he argues are complicit in maintaining inequality and perpetuating the abuses they allegedly oppose. The play works out the logic of this thesis in the conversion experience of Barbara, an idealist, which Shaw defines as someone who creates self-deceiving myths to make life less objectionable. Barbara's reeducation in the truth, as well as the audience's, begins in the fashionable suburban London home of her mother, Lady Britomart Undershaft. She has summoned her children—Stephen, Sarah, and Barbara—to contend with the family's financial constraints. Sarah is engaged to Charles Lomax, whose own inheritance is 10 years off; while Barbara, a major in the Salvation Army, is being courted by Adolphus Cusins, a poor classics professor. Lady Britomart has long been estranged from her husband, a wealthy munitions manufacturer, but he, too, is called on to assist, despite the disdain his children feel for the tainted Undershaft wealth and his wife's objections to Andrew's unconventional views that have led to his disinheriting Stephen in favor of turning over his business to another foundling like himself. Revealing the hypocrisy of the respectable that the entire opening act exposes, Lady Britomart explains that Andrew "didn't exactly do wrong things: he said them and thought them: that was what was so dreadful. He really had a sort of religion of wrongness just as one doesn't mind men practicing immorality so long as they own that they are in the wrong by preaching morality; so I couldn't forgive Andrew for preaching immorality while he practiced morality." For Barbara her father, an unapologetic "manufacturer of mutilation and murder," is a sinner ripe for conversion. Undershaft, however, proves a formidable challenge in his unrepentant defense of his trade and his challenge to conventional beliefs. "Your Christmas card moralities of peace on earth and goodwill among men are of no use to me," he asserts. "Your Christianity, which enjoins you to resist not evil, and to turn the other cheek, would make me a bankrupt. My morality—my religion—must have a place for cannons and torpedoes in it." The act ends with a conversion challenge: Undershaft agrees to inspect Barbara's good work done at the Salvation Army shelter in the London slums if she will visit his weapons factory in Middlesex.

Shifting from the Wildean drawing room to Dickens's underclass and George Gissing's Nether World, act 2 opens in the West Ham shelter as two of the destitute—Snobby Price and Rummy Mitchens—discuss how they routinely concoct their sinful ways to justify the interest of the Army to continue to receive free meals and shelter. They are joined by a truly desperate man, Peter Shirley, whose hunger overcomes his reluctance to accept charity. Another, the brutish Bill Walker, comes in to retrieve his girlfriend, whom the Army has rescued from his abuse. Walker shockingly strikes both Jenny Hill, a young Salvation Army worker, and Rummy before Barbara enters to take him on. In doing so Barbara shows both her courage and strength of character in the face of Walker's taunts and threats. What is striking is Shaw's refusal here to set up strawdogs for his philosophy to overwhelm with ease. The violence and abuse that Walker represents are graphically apparent, and the efforts of Barbara and the Salvation Army are shown as a needed lifeline to those like Shirley and Walker's girl who are otherwise abandoned to their dismal fate. The arrival of Undershaft raises the issue of what is the most beneficial response to poverty and its attendant vices. Undershaft offers not acceptance of sins and spiritual salvation but material improvement. It is the economic imperatives of the rich, the poor, *and* the righteous that Barbara faces as she attempts to balance her ideals with the practical necessities of raising sufficient funds to continue doing good works. She initially refuses her father's offer of a contribution considering its source. However, her superior officer, Mrs. Baines, jumps at the chance to have Undershaft match the contribution offered by the whiskey distiller Lord Saxmundham. As Walker taunts—"What price salvation, now?"—Barbara sadly takes off her Salvation Army badge and pins it on her father, who demonstrates that even the Army is for sale. "Drunkenness and Murder!" she cries in despair. "My God! why hast thou forsaken me?"

Act 3 opens with a return to Lady Britomart's library and Barbara, no longer in her uniform, preparing for her visit to her father's cannon foundry. Expecting an infernal place of exploited workers, Barbara is surprised to find a smoothly-running business set amid well-maintained churches, schools, libraries, and other services that make the town resemble "a heavenly city instead of a hellish one." The contrast between treating poverty with spiritual consolation and materially is unmistakable. All fall under the spell of this unexpected workers' paradise. Cusins reveals that because his parents' marriage was in violation of the Deceased Wife's Sister Act and unlawful, he is technically illegitimate and therefore eligible to succeed Undershaft in the business. While bargaining with Cusins over the position he offers him, Undershaft delivers his Armourer's creed:

> To give arms to all men who offer an honest price for them, without respect of persons or principles: to aristocrat and republican, to Nihilist and Tsar, to Capitalist and Socialist, to Protestant and Catholic, to burglar and policeman, to black man, white man and yellow man, to all sorts and conditions, all nationalities, all faiths, all follies, all causes and all crimes. The first Undershaft wrote up in his shop IF GOD GAVE THE HAND, LET NOT MAN WITHHOLD THE SWORD. The second wrote up ALL HAVE THE RIGHT TO FIGHT: NONE HAVE THE RIGHT TO JUDGE. The third wrote up TO MAN THE WEAPON: TO HEAVEN THE VICTORY. The fourth had no literary turn; so he did not write up anything; but he sold cannons to Napoleon under the nose of George the Third. The fifth wrote up PEACE SHALL NOT PREVAIL SAVE WITH A SWORD IN HER HAND. The sixth, my

master, was the best of all. He wrote up NOTHING IS EVER DONE
IN THIS WORLD UNTIL MEN ARE PREPARED TO KILL ONE
ANOTHER IF IT IS NOT DONE. After that, there was nothing left
for the seventh to say. So he wrote up, simply, UNASHAMED.

Challenged by Barbara to justify his considerable power and responsibility,
Undershaft retorts: "Cleanliness and respectability do not need justification,
Barbara: they justify themselves. I see no darkness here, no dreadfulness. In
your Salvation shelter I saw poverty, misery, cold and hunger. You gave them
bread and treacle and dreams of heaven. I give from thirty shillings a week
to twelve thousand a year. They find their own dreams; but I look after the
drainage."

The play closes with Cusins's decision to accept Undershaft's offer and
Barbara's agreement with it, completing her conversion from Salvation Army
officer to a different kind of martial crusader:

> BARBARA   I should have given you up and married the man who
> accepted it. After all, my dear old mother has more sense than any
> of you. I felt like her when I saw this place—felt that I must have
> it—that never, never, never could I let it go; only she thought it
> was the houses and the kitchen ranges and the linen and china,
> when it was really all the human souls to be saved: not weak souls
> in starved bodies, crying with gratitude or a scrap of bread and
> treacle, but fullfed, quarrelsome, snobbish, uppish creatures, all
> standing on their little rights and dignities, and thinking that my
> father ought to be greatly obliged to them for making so much
> money for him—and so he ought. That is where salvation is really
> wanted. My father shall never throw it in my teeth again that my
> converts were bribed with bread. [*She is transfigured*]. I have got
> rid of the bribe of bread. I have got rid of the bribe of heaven. Let
> God's work be done for its own sake: the work he had to create us
> to do because it cannot be done by living men and women. When
> I die, let him be in my debt, not I in his; and let me forgive him
> as becomes a woman of my rank.
>
> CUSINS   Then the way of life lies through the factory of death?
>
> BARBARA   Yes, through the raising of hell to heaven and of man
> to God, through the unveiling of an eternal light in the Valley
> of The Shadow. [*Seizing him with both hands*] Oh, did you think
> my courage would never come back? Did you believe that I was
> a deserter? that I, who have stood in the streets, and taken my
> people to my heart, and talked of the holiest and greatest things

with them, could ever turn back and chatter foolishly to fashionable people about nothing in a drawingroom? Never, never, never, never: Major Barbara will die with the colors. Oh! and I have my dear little Dolly boy still; and he has found me my place and my work. Glory Hallelujah!

Barbara's final capitulation has been criticized as unearned, more in keeping with the Utopianism that resolves all in wish fulfillment and reduces a lively and believable protagonist to a mouthpiece for Shaw's philosophy. Shaw himself was troubled by his conclusion, complaining early on, "I don't know how to end the thing." He was still rethinking the ending 35 years later when *Major Barbara* was filmed, suggesting in his revision not Barbara's capitulation but a completion in which Undershaft's power is joined to Cusins's classical intelligence and Barbara's spirituality. Ultimately the strengths of the play overpower any intellectual reformulation. In *Major Barbara* Shaw has submitted our most cherished notions to a witty and profound reassessment meant to provoke and challenge understanding long after the final curtain.

ENDGAME

29

(1957)

by Samuel Beckett

Nothing happens in Endgame *and that nothing is what matters. The author's feeling about nothing also matters, not because it is true or right but because it is a strongly formed attitude, a felt and expressed viewpoint. . . . The yardsticks of dialectical materialism and moralism are equally out in appraising the play. Dialectical materialism could only say that* Endgame *is decadent. Moralism and theology would say that the play is sinful, since nothing damns the soul so much as despair of salvation. Neither yardstick could tell us that this hauntingly powerful work of the imagination is art.*
                                                              —John Gassner, *Theater at the Crossroads*

Endgame is Samuel Beckett's terminal work. If WAITING FOR GODOT presents a repeating sequence of frustrated anticipation, *Endgame* imagines the moment before extinction, before the lights go out and a final realization, encapsulated in the play's opening line: "Finished, it's finished, nearly finished, it must be nearly finished." As its chess title suggests, the play stages the final moves in a game ending either in checkmate or stalemate. Contracted down from the two acts of *Godot* and its blank open road to a single act in a claustrophobic bare room, *Endgame* enacts the apocalyptic moment that Gogo and Didi anticipate, but it is far from the relief they imagined. If *Waiting for Godot* is Beckett's existential comedy of affirming persistence, *Endgame* is his existential tragedy of willed cessation. Harold Hobson, writing about *Endgame* in 1973, commented: "In recent years there has been some danger of Mr. Beckett being sentimentalized. Self-defensively we are driven to persuade ourselves that his plays are not really filled with terror and horror, but are, at bottom, jolly good fun. Well, they are not jolly good fun. They are amongst the most frightening prophecies of, and longing for, doom ever written." In *Endgame*, critic Ruby Cohn has suggested, Beckett presents "the death of the stock props of Western civilization—family, cohesion, filial, parental, and connubial love, faith in God, artistic appreciation and creation." A work of astonishing economy and suggestive power, *Endgame* is a last will and testament of a desperate consciousness seeking relief from the pain of itself.

Endgame emerged out of one of the most tormenting periods of Beckett's life. Following the remarkable creative burst that produced his three great novels—*Malloy, Malone Dies,* and *The Unnamable*—and the groundbreaking *Waiting for Godot,* Beckett struggled through several years of "inertia," in which he confessed not having "the least desire to put pen to paper." Having completed *Waiting for Godot* in 1949, his second full-length play, *Endgame,* would not appear until 1956. In the intervening years Beckett spent time in Ireland attending to both his mother and brother during their final illnesses. It was his daily, three-month-long vigil at his brother Frank's bedside before he succumbed to lung cancer, in particular, that stimulated the writing of *Endgame.* Watching his brother's slow decline, Beckett wrote in letters, "things drag on, a little more awful every day, and with so many days yet probably to run what awfulness to look forward to" and "Waiting [is] not so bad if you can fidget about. This is like waiting tied to a chair." *Endgame* would be built on "waiting tied to a chair." After his brother's death, in September 1954, Beckett returned to France and gradually began work on the first version of what would become *Fin de partie (Endgame).* As Beckett's biographer James Knowlson states, "it followed hard on the heels of Beckett's experience of the sickroom and of waiting for someone to die, and is not only preoccupied with the slowness of an approaching end but haunted by the tiny, practical details of caring for a dying patient." His initial draft was a two-person, two-act play involving a patient and his attendant, designated A and B. In a letter Beckett wrote: "I have A out of his armchair flat on his face on the stage at the moment and B trying in vain to get him back. I know at least I'll go on to the end before using the waste-paper basket." A month later he announced: "Yes, I finished the play, but it's no good and I have to begin all over again." A final version, now with four characters, in a single act to be "played without a break," was ready by 1956. However, despite Beckett's notoriety and success with *Waiting for Godot,* no Paris theater could be found for the premiere of *Fin de partie.* George Devine, the director of the English Stage Company in London, had contracted to produce Beckett's English translation of the play when it was finished; however, when he learned of Beckett's difficulty in opening the play in Paris, Devine decided not to wait for the translation, and *Fin de partie* had its world premiere at London's Royal Court Theatre in April 1957. In May the French text was published, and the play finally opened in Paris. In 1958 the English-language version opened in London on a double bill with Beckett's *Krapp's Last Tape.* Beckett admitted that *Endgame* was "rather difficult and elliptic" and "more inhuman than *Godot,*" which helps to explain its initial reception. Beckett described the premiere as "rather grim, like playing to mahogany, or rather teak." The woodenness of the audience was matched by the hostility of reviewers who were baffled or annoyed by the play. Kenneth Tynan observed that Beckett's new play made it "clear that his purpose is neither to move nor to help us. For him, man is a pygmy who connives at his own inevitable degradation." Comparing it to his first play, reviewer T. C. Worsley said that in *Waiting for Godot*, "Mr. Beckett's neurosis and mine were for quite long stretches on the same theme; in *Endgame* they never tangled. He has, in *Endgame* . . . expanded not the public but the private images. He has concentrated not on what is common between his audiences and him but on what is private in himself." Beckett would long insist that *Endgame* was one of his two favorite works (*Malone Dies* being the other). It would not be until several successful revivals in the 1960s that *Endgame* would be increasingly recognized as a masterpiece and one of the most suggestive and profound modern dramas.

The play opens with Clov stiffly and staggeringly entering a "bare interior," drawing the curtains from the room's two high windows and removing old sheets covering three forms: two trash cans and the blind Hamm, confined to an armchair on castors in the center of the room. Roused, Hamm begins to issue commands and insults to his truculent attendant. Clov, the only one of the play's characters who can move, resembles the chessboard's knight; while Beckett described Hamm as "a king in this chess game lost from the start. From the start he knows he is making loud senseless moves. . . . He is only trying to delay the inevitable end." As in *Waiting for Godot*, *Endgame* focuses on the interdependence of linked pairs, but the patient-attendant roles assumed by Hamm and Clov suggest not the more affable and collegial Didi and Gogo, but master and slave Pozzo and Lucky. Asked by Hamm, "Why do you stay with me?" Clov replies: "Why do you keep me?" Hamm responds, "There's no one else," and Clov counters, "There's nowhere else." In the details that emerge from their dialogue, there is the suggestion that the occupants of this room, with one window looking out onto the sea and the other toward land, are the sole survivors of some devastating apocalyptic event. "Outside of here it's death," Hamm remarks. Inside, the provisions that Hamm controls in a cupboard with a combination lock are running out along with other essentials. Clov reports there are no more bicycle wheels for Hamm's chair, no more of the painkiller Hamm demands, nor the "pap" to feed Hamm's legless parents—Nagg and Nell—whose heads pop out of the two trash cans. To the master-servant relationship of Hamm and Clov Beckett adds a generational conflict involving Hamm and his parents and Clov as Hamm's actual or adopted son ("It was I was a father to you," Hamm tells Clov). Hamm treats his parents with the same insults and recriminations he directs at Clov. Ordered to be quiet, Nagg regales Nell with a joke that made her laugh years earlier when they were young, healthy, and in love at Lake Como. It concerns a tailor who takes more than three months to make a pair of trousers, provoking his exasperated customer to complain that God made the entire world in six days. "But my dear Sir," says the tailor, ". . . look—at the world—and look—at my TROUSERS!" Hamm furiously interrupts the couple's recollections, declaring, "Have you not finished? Will you never finish? Will this never finish?" and orders Clov to "screw down the lids."

Reclaiming his preeminence as the center of attention, Hamm orders Clov to take him on a turn around the room—"Right round the world!"—before being returned, precisely, to his place in the center. Asked for a weather report and a survey of what can be seen outside the windows, Clov reports that all is "As usual": "Light black. From pole to pole." Characterizing the world outside in a single word, Clov offers "Corpsed." After Clov observes that "Something is taking its course," Hamm responds by asking: "We're not beginning to . . . to . . . mean something?" Speculation is broken off when Clov feels a flea biting him, and Hamm anxiously urges its extinction, lest "humanity might start from there all over again." Calling for his makeshift, three-legged toy dog, Hamm puts it through its paces before asking Clov if "this thing has gone on long enough?" Clov agrees, and while Hamm cannot leave, he can, prompting Hamm to ask how he will know whether or not Clov has left or died, since the stench of rotting corpses is pervasive. Clov's solution is to set an alarm clock: If it rings, he has gone; if it does not, he is dead. Testing the clock to see that it still rings, Clov observes "The end is terrific!" Hamm replies: "I prefer the middle."

Announcing that it is time for "my story," Hamm orders Clov, who refuses to listen, to rouse Nagg to serve as his audience. Hamm recollects a past Christmas Eve when he was visited by a poor man begging food for his infant son. Agreeing to take the man in as a gardener and care for his son (who may have been Clov), Hamm is interrupted in this pleasing memory of his own beneficence by Nagg demanding a sugarplum, his reward for listening to the story. When Clov informs them that there are no more sugarplums, Nagg curses his son, saying, "I hope the day will come when you'll really need to have me listen to you, and need to hear my voice any voice. Yes, I hope I'll live till then, to hear you calling me like when you were a tiny boy, and were frightened, in the dark, and I was your only hope." Knocking on the lid of Nell's bin, Nagg gets no response and sinks back into his bin, prompting Hamm to repeat Prospero's line from *The Tempest*: "Our revels now are ended." Ordered to investigate the bins, Clov reports that Nell appears to be dead, and Nagg is crying. "Then he's living," Hamm concludes. Asking Clov for another report on what he sees from the windows, Hamm is surprised when Clov sees through his telescope a small boy. This sign of continuing life or, as Clov speculates, "a potential procreator," causes Hamm to declare: "It's the end, Clov, we've come to the end. I don't need you any more." Clov responds with his intention to leave, imagining his departure: "I open the door of the cell and go. I am so bowed I only see my feet, if I open my eyes, and between my legs a little trail of black dust. I say to myself that the earth is extinguished, though I never saw it lit. It's easy going. When I fall I'll weep for happiness. . . . That is what we call making an exit." Returning from the kitchen dressed for departure with a panama hat, tweed coat, raincoat over his arm, umbrella, and bag, Clov halts before the door and turns to watch Hamm deliver the monologue that closes the play. "Me to play," Hamm says wearily. "Old endgame lost of old, play and lose and have done with losing." As he makes his preparations for the end, fragments of his earlier story emerge that seem to address the child he took in. After calling twice for his father and once for Clov, he unfolds his bloody handkerchief ("Old stancher!"), placing it over his face while saying, "Since that's the way we're playing it . . . let's play it that way . . . speak no more. Old stancher! You . . . remain." Clov stands motionless.

Endgame supports, and demands, multiple interpretations. On one level the play seems to enact a kind of morality drama in which the imperious and selfish Hamm must meet his end, forecasted in his own threat to Clov: "Infinite emptiness will be all around you, all the resurrected dead of all the ages wouldn't fill it, and there you'll be like a little bit of grit in the middle of the steppe. Yes, one day you'll know what it is, you'll be like me, except that you won't have anyone with you, because you won't have had pity on anyone and because there won't be anyone left to have pity on." On a symbolic level the enthroned and commanding Hamm is the king in this endgame with Clov, unable to sit, the knight in service to the king, forever mounted on his horse, and Nagg and Nell, ineffectual pawns in a fated and futile game, encapsulated by Hamm's realization that "The end is in the beginning and yet you go on." On a psychological level the play, with its brain-gray interior and its two windows, suggests the inside of a skull with its four characters as conflicting aspects of a single personality or consciousness. An inner, subjective world is suggested by Hamm's story of a madman he once visited in his asylum: "I'd take him by the hand and drag him to the window. Look! There! All that rising corn! And there! Look! The sails of the herring fleet! All that loveliness! He'd snatch away his hand and go back into his corner. Appalled. All he had seen was ashes." From inside the play's consciousness all is ashes, as the constituent parts of the integrated identity war with each other. In such a reading the blind self-centered Hamm represents the id; Clov, the rational caregiver and stickler for order, suggests the ego; and Nagg and Nell, the internalized voice of parental authority and conscience, resemble the superego. On the point of extinction, these forces enact a final death struggle as consciousness itself aspires to the terminal condition conjured by Clov: "A world where all would be silent and still and each thing in its last place, under the last dust."

Few plays have ever reached the existential core as Endgame does. Replacing conventional characterization and incident with basic and resonating patterns of meanings and suggestive images, Beckett manages to find a dramatic equivalent for the instant between being and nothingness.

ŚAKUNTALĀ 30

(c. fifth century) *by Kālidāsa*

Poetical fluency is not rare; intellectual grasp is not very uncommon: but the combination has not been found perhaps more than a dozen times since the world began. Because he possessed this harmonious combination, Kālidāsa ranks not with Anacreon and Horace and Shelley, but with Sophocles, Vergil, Milton.
—Arthur W. Ryder, Introduction to *Shakuntala and Other Writings*

Kālidāsa's *Śakuntalā* is the masterpiece of Indian classical drama, the greatest of all Sanskrit plays. For more than 1,500 years the work and its creator have been accorded an unrivaled preeminence in Indian literature, inspiring imitation but never surpassed. Regarded as one of the supreme poets of nature and love, Kālidāsa prompted the seventh-century writer Bana to ask:

> Where find a soul that does not thrill
> In Kalidasa's verse to meet
> The smooth, inevitable lines
> Like blossom-clusters, honey-sweet?

In 1789 *Śakuntalā* became the first work in Sanskrit to be translated into a modern European language. Goethe praised it as a masterpiece, and Kālidāsa was proclaimed by his translator, William Jones, to be "the Shakespeare of India." One of the greatest dramatic works of world literature and the finest expression of classical Indian dramaturgy, *Śakuntalā* provides the best possible introduction to Kālidāsa's genius and to the conventions and traditions of Indian drama.

Virtually nothing is known for sure about Kālidāsa. His name translates as "servant of Kali," suggesting that he was a follower of the destroyer god Shiva, the patron of literature, whose consort was Kali. It has been speculated that he was a high-caste Brahman, both highly learned and widely traveled in India. We know from his writings that he spent at least a part of his life in the city of Ujjain, in west-central India. Some scholars have included Kālidāsa as one of the "nine gems"—poets, scientists, and artisans—of the court King Vikramāditya of Ujjain, the great patron of learning whose reign (c. 380–415) marked one of the great flowerings of Indian culture. Kālidāsa's works, according to K. Krishnamoorthy, indicate that he "lived in times of peace, when the leisured class would pursue the fine arts, free from threats of invasion from without or from conflicts within." This suggests that Kālidāsa lived and worked sometime between the fourth and fifth centuries. Seven of his works have survived: two epics, *Raghuvamśa* (*Dynasty of Raghu*) and *Kumārasambhava* (*Birth of the War God*); an elegy, *Meghadūta* (*The Cloud Messenger*); a descriptive poem, *Ritusamhara* (*The Cycle of the Seasons*); and three dramas. *Mālavikāgnimitra* (*Mālavikā and Agnimitra*) is believed to be his earliest play, a conventionally comic harem intrigue. *Vikramorvaśī* (*Urvaśī Won by Valor*), about a mortal's love for a divine maiden, may be his last based on some evidence of artistic decline. *Śakuntalā* is therefore his most accomplished drama, written at the height of his poetic skill and in full mastery of the procedures and aesthetic potentialities of Sanskrit drama.

The classical drama of India grew out of both Hindu religious temple ceremonies and popular folk entertainment combining dance, acrobatics, mime, and singing. The chief treatise on Indian drama and the most important source for establishing the character of the Sanskrit theater tradition is the *Nātyaśāstra* (The science of dramaturgy) attributed to the sage Bharata, written c. 200 B.C.–A.D. 200. According to it, drama originated when Indra, king of the gods, asked Brahma, the creator of the universe, to devise an art form to be seen, heard, and understood by all men. Brahma considered the four Vedas, the sacred books of Indian wisdom, and selected one component from each—the spoken word from the *Rig-Veda*, song from the *Sama-Veda*, mime from the *Yajur-Veda*, and emotion from the *Atharva-Veda*—and combined them to form drama. Brahma requested that Indra compose plays based on the fifth, *Natya-Veda*, and have the gods enact them, but as Indra did not consider it appropriate for gods to act, priests were selected to serve, and Bharata was summoned to be instructed in the art of the drama from Brahma himself. Bharata then recorded the divine rules of dancing, acting, and stage production that define Sanskrit drama in the *Nātyaśāstra*, the most complete book of ancient dramaturgy in the world, covering acting, theater architecture, costuming, makeup, dance, music, play construction, the organization of theater companies, and many more topics.

Fragments of the earliest known Sanskrit plays date from the first century A.D., but the sophistication of their style suggests that a fully evolved theater tradition must have existed at a much earlier date. There are references to theatrical performance in the two great Indian epics, the *Mahabharata* and the *Ramayana*, written sometime between 1000 and 100 B.C., which served as the primary source material for dramatic stories. Twenty-five Sanskrit plays, written between A.D. 320 and the 12th century, have survived. Unlike Western drama, Sanskrit dramas are not classified into categories of comedy, tragedy, and tragicomedy, and neither action nor character or thematic development is as important as achieving an appropriate *rasa*, variously translated as "mood," "sentiment," or "aesthetic delight." As the *Nātyaśāstra* states, "Nothing has meaning in the drama except through *rasa.*" Human experience, according to Indian dramaturgy, is divided into eight basic sentiments or *rasas*: the erotic, the comic, pathos, rage, heroism, terror, odiousness, and the marvelous. These sentiments are aroused in the audience by actors' representation of the corresponding eight states of emotions or feelings. Every play has a predominant emotion, producing a corresponding *rasa* through the artful combination of words, action, movement, costume, make-up, music, etc. Since the goal of all Hindu plays is to provide a sense of harmony and serenity, all must end happily, with death and violence occurring offstage, and right and wrong clearly differentiated. However, in replicating the unity among all things, plays could intermingle the exalted and the commonplace, poetry and prose, the learned language of Sanskrit (spoken by gods, kings, and sages) and the everyday speech, called Pakrit (spoken by peasants, soldiers, servants, women, and children). Of the prescribed 10 categories of plays, the most important were the *nataka*, based on mythology or history and involving an exemplary hero, such as a king and royal sage, dealing with the sentiments of love and heroism, and the *prakarana* in which its plots and characters are entirely imaginary. A Brahman, merchant, or minister could serve as the hero, a courtesan, as the heroine, and love was its dominant sentiment. Plays of between one and 10 acts would be mounted on specially built stages for each performance before a largely aristocratic audience. No scenery was used, but place and situation would be established by narration or pantomime. Both men and women acted with costume, makeup, gesture, and movement strictly refined and stylized. Characters of many social ranks and types could appear, but the hero was almost always a ruler or an aristocrat, often paired with a clown who served as comic relief. The basic human emotions (*bhavas*) that could be portrayed on stage were identified and represented by a set number of approved movements, hand gestures, and facial expressions. A Sanskrit drama was, therefore, an elaborate blend of rigidly codified emotions, character types, costumes, makeup, gesture, movement, situations, and music, all orchestrated to arouse the appropriate audience response. The goal of Sanskrit drama, a theater of elevated principles, was to edify and inspire through the idealization of the characters, their values, and the actions represented.

The great achievement of *Śakuntalā* is Kālidāsa's remarkable ability to achieve an expressive lyric power of great subtlety within the drama's tightly prescribed conventions. Based on an ancient Hindu legend recounted in book 1 of the *Mahabharata* about a charm that causes a lover to forget his beloved, *Śakuntalā* artfully reworks the familiar much as the ancient Greek drama based on well-known myths did. Its story becomes the vehicle for Kālidāsa to explore love in multiple aspects and under the most testing circumstances. In the first of the play's seven acts, King Dusyanta is on a hunt and enters a forest that is the residence of the sage Kanva and his stepdaughter, Śakuntalā. In the *Mahabharata* Śakuntalā is identified as the daughter born of a union between a heavenly nymph and a royal sage. Abandoned at birth by her mother, she is found by Kanva and brought to live in his forest hermitage. When first seen by the king, Śakuntalā is an unspoiled beauty on the verge of womanhood, as she and her friends are watering the trees in the sacred grove. When Śakuntalā is attacked by a bee, Dusyanta comes out of his hiding place as her protector, and passion stirs in both of them. In the second act, Mathavya, the king's jester, complains that they have spent long enough hunting. To placate him, but actually to remain closer to Śakuntalā, Dusyanta calls off the hunt and orders his retinue to camp near the sacred grove where Śakuntalā lives. Summoned home by his mother, the king instead sends his retainers back to court while he remains in the hope of seeing Śakuntalā again. In the third act, Dusyanta eavesdrops on Śakuntalā and hears her profession of love for him. It is sufficient for Dusyanta to propose marriage. Śakuntalā eventually agrees to a secret marriage by mutual consent but decides when the king departs to remain at the grove until the return of Kanva. Before leaving Dusyanta gives her a ring as a token of their union. Distracted by her lover's parting and neglecting her duties in the hermitage, Śakuntalā ignores the arrival of the ill-tempered, self-important sage Durvāsas. Feeling slighted by Śakuntalā for not performing the expected rites of hospitality to suit him, Durvāsas places a curse on Śakuntalā making the king forget her until he sees the ring again.

When Kanva returns he learns that Śakuntalā is pregnant, but after hearing a supernatural voice prophesying that Śakuntalā's son is destined to rule the world, he is reconciled to the marriage. Insisting that the child should be born in his father's palace, however, he sends her off to join her husband. Śakuntalā's departure from the sacred grove and her father's sadness at losing his daughter provide the occasion for some of the most beautiful lyrics in all of Sanskrit literature. While worshipping at a river shrine during the journey, Śakuntalā loses the ring, and when she presents herself before Dusyanta at court he has no memory of her, in fulfillment of the curse, and dismisses her from his presence. Devastated and angered by the king's rejection, Śakuntalā prays for the earth to open and receive her. In response a light in the shape of a woman carries her off into heaven. The ring is eventually discovered in the possession of a poor fisherman, who found it in the belly of a fish. When Dusyanta sees it, the curse is lifted, his memory returns, and he is stricken with remorse. His contrition causes the nymph who had taken Śakuntalā to pity him, and she sends the chariot of the god Indra down to earth to convey the king to heaven to be reunited with Śakuntalā. In heaven Dusyanta encounters a young boy who is revealed to be his son, Bharata (considered the forefather of the Indian nation). Dusyanta is finally reunited with Śakuntalā who, having learned of the curse, readily forgives her lover. The gods send husband, wife, and son back to earth and a life of happiness together.

In keeping with the fundamental principle of Sanskrit drama that subordinates plot and characterization to produce a dominant emotion or sympathy, Śakuntalā displays the full gamut of human love with each act offering a variant and the obstacles faced by the lovers testing the intensity, depth, and breadth of their love. Beginning with infatuation, the love between Śakuntalā and Dusyanta is inflamed into an intense physical passion that then must be tested and refined by the effects of the curse. The lovers are separated, and when she is unrecognized by her lover, Śakuntalā experiences betrayal and is desolated by love's denial. Recovering his memory Dusyanta experiences guilt, remorse, and despair over his lost love, yet his devotion sustains him to face the supernatural challenge in heaven. Proving his kingly courage and his duty as hero and lover, Dusyanta is made worthy of his reward in recovering son and wife, as love culminates in the bliss of marriage and family. In this way, *Śakuntalā* demonstrates not just passion achieved and denied, love's raptures and torments, but centrally important values of duty, spiritual reverence, and the ennobling power of love. *Śakuntalā* joins with *Romeo and Juliet* and THE PEONY PAVILION as the preeminent dramas of love in world literature. Let Goethe offer the final accolade:

> Wouldst thou the young year's blossoms and the fruits of its decline,
> And all by which the soul is charmed, enraptured, feasted, fed?
> Wouldst thou the earth and heaven itself in one sole name combine?
> I name thee, O Sakuntala, and all at once is said.

MISS JULIE

(1888)

31

by August Strindberg

[Henrik Ibsen had] revolutionized drama by writing tragedies about ordinary middle-class people in everyday prose, instead of poetic dramas about kings and queens. . . . Where Strindberg broke new ground in Miss Julie was, firstly, in the "irregularity" of his dialogue; secondly, in dramatic concentration; and thirdly . . . in his boldly realistic treatment of sex. Ibsen's characters think and speak logically and consecutively; Strindberg's dart backwards and forwards. . . . Strindberg achieved an economy beyond Ibsen's. . . . Take a lamb cutlet, he said; it looks large, but three-quarters of it is bone and fat, containing a kernel of meat. I strip off the bone and fat and, like the Greeks, give you the kernel. As regards sexual realism, Strindberg, unlike any dramatist before him, showed that men and women can hate each other yet be sexually welded. . . . Before Strindberg, sex in drama is something in which only married people or wicked people indulge.

—Michael Meyer, *Strindberg*

Of the accepted triumvirate as the principal shapers of modern drama—Henrik Ibsen, Anton Chekhov, and August Strindberg—the last is by far the most perplexing and contentious. Strindberg is also perhaps the more boldly original, as well as the one who is most aggressively our contemporary. No other modern writer, with the possible exception of Franz Kafka, has so embodied the conception of art as the product of torment and neurosis as has Strindberg. The darker counterpart to his fellow Scandinavian and nemesis Ibsen, Strindberg exerted a comparable influence on the history of drama. In an immense body of work that includes more than 50 plays, 15 novels, more than 100 short stories, and three volumes of poetry, as well as historical works, scientific treatises, and essays on chemistry, botany, politics, economics, philosophy, and religion, Strindberg's writing relentlessly chases his personal demons in a search for understanding that covers virtually every ideological option available—from spiritualism and the occult to Darwinian determinism and faith in the individual will and the life force. "I find the joy of life," he wrote in the preface to *Miss Julie*, "in the strong, cruel struggles of life." A massive contradiction, Strindberg was a virulent misogynist and admirer of authoritarianism, as well as an unsurpassed creator of psychologically compelling and complex male and female characters whose sheer vitality and inconsistencies annihilate any scientific or social theory to define them. As a playwright Strindberg is no less contradictory than his characters. He would achieve artistic greatness in plays of both groundbreaking realism and antirealism, producing some of the finest examples of dramatic naturalism and expressionism.

Of his plays written at least in part in response to Ibsen's new realistic dramas and reflecting Émile Zola's theory of literary naturalism that advocated an objective depiction of the workings of heredity and the environment on human behavior, *Fröken Julie* (*Miss Julie*) is his masterpiece. With it Strindberg set out to revolutionize the theater. "This play," he proclaimed, "will be a milestone in history." Written for the Théâtre Libre in Paris, a private subscription theater where the contentious and often banned works of the new realist and the naturalist playwrights could be performed beyond the reach of the censor, Strindberg's play about a young Swedish noblewoman's sexual affair with her father's valet proved too incendiary even for the Théâtre Libre. Privately produced in Copenhagen in 1889, *Miss Julie* would be subsequently banned throughout Europe and would not be performed in Strindberg's native Sweden until 1906; its prohibition in Britain would not be lifted until 1939. The first play to depict sex separated from love and the power of sexual desire that obliterated gender and class conventions, *Miss Julie* provoked howls of outrage. It was called "a filthy bundle of rags which one hardly wishes to touch even with tongs" and "a heap of ordure" with "language that is scarcely used except in nests of vice and debauchery." *Miss Julie* has gone on to become the most frequently performed of Strindberg's plays and one of the recognized classics of modern drama and Strindberg's unique refinement and expansion of dramatic naturalism. The play is Strindberg's contribution to the articulation of a new dramatic form to embody new conceptions of human nature and the human condition. "The French today," Strindberg insisted, "are looking for the formula, but I have found it."

Strindberg's revolt from orthodox solutions and his restless exploration for a sustaining formula of human understanding and literary expression began in Stockholm, Sweden, in 1849. He was one of 12 children, the son of the mistress whom his father later married. His father, a shipping clerk, became bankrupt, and Strindberg grew up in grinding poverty, neglect, and torment at the hands of the family's housekeeper whom his father married after Strindberg's mother died when he was 13. His opposition to authority was established early on. After completing secondary school he attended the University of Uppsala but despised formal studies and quarreled with his professors. He worked for a time as an elementary school teacher, a journalist, and a librarian. He tried to become an actor and failed, but his stage experience convinced him to pursue a career as a playwright. His earliest plays dramatize the opposition between the individual will and social conventions in plots derived mainly from Swedish history. Strindberg's love affair and subsequent troubled domestic life with a married woman, Siri von Essen, whom he later married in 1877, proved to be a major source for his early writing, which included the collection of stories *Giftas* (1884–85; *Married*), whose frank sexuality and critique of respectable society was deemed immoral and resulted in Strindberg's being prosecuted for blasphemy, and the groundbreaking drama *Fadren* (1887; *The Father*). A modernized version of the Agamemnon story, *The Father* is a full-frontal assault on patriarchy produced by the clash between a husband and wife over control of their child. Laura drives her husband, Captain Adolf, to psychic destruction by undermining his confidence that he is in fact the father of his daughter and causing him to realize that the secure principle of fatherhood itself, the foundation for the patriarchal paradigm of society, is a legal fiction and a delusion. By the play's conclusion the formerly secure Captain has regressed to the level of a child himself as the cherished assumptions about gender, sexuality, and class in the 19th century have been radically and powerfully reevaluated.

Strindberg continued his treatment of the battle between the sexes with *Miss Julie*, written as his own marriage to Siri von Essen was collapsing. The play considers the motives and makeup of a young aristocratic woman who violates class boundaries and gender assumptions and yields to the sexual compulsion that destroys her. With its single-act structure and reduction down to only the essential characters and their central conflict, *Miss Julie* became the occasion for Strindberg's announcing his break from established dramatic conventions in the play's preface, which has become one of the seminal texts in the theory of modern drama. In it Strindberg opposes efforts "to create a new drama by using the old forms with up-to-date contents." In *Miss Julie* Strindberg insists "I have not tried to do anything new, for this cannot be done, but only to modernize the form in accordance with what I imagined would be required of this art today." The preface articulates Strindberg's refinement and expansion of the conception of naturalism, which he insisted "is not a dramatic method like . . . a simple photography in which includes everything." The latter, Strindberg argued, "is realism; a method, lately exalted to art, a tiny art which cannot see the wood for the trees. That is the false naturalism, which believes that art consists simply of sketching a piece of nature in a natural manner; but it is not the true naturalism, which seeks out those points of life where the great conflicts occur, which rejoices in seeing what cannot be seen every day." For Strindberg naturalism should not be a passive reproduction of ordinary experience but life captured at a critical moment when essential truths are strikingly and uniquely revealed. Like Zola, Strindberg is concerned with the various psychological, physiological, social, and environmental forces impacting behavior, but he advocates on behalf of new theatrical methods to capture the complexity of these forces and to bring to the surface the inner contradictions and compulsions of the individual, closed by a narrow fidelity

to ordinary experience. Although Strindberg argues on behalf of stage realism, it should be the foundation for the exploration of universal truth. A play's
setting, Strindberg asserts, should be a realistic interior unadorned by the
unnatural illumination of the footlights; the actors, whose makeup should be
minimal, should ignore the audience and play to each other, while the dialogue
should avoid the "symmetrical, mathematical construction" of the well-made
play and let "people's minds work irregularly, as they do in real life." Most
important, the preface defines Strindberg's conception of the "characterless
character," which rejects simplified character types in favor of ambiguity and
complexity:

> I do not believe in simple characters on the stage. And the summary judg-
> ments of authors—this man is stupid, that one brutal, this one jealous,
> that stingy, and so on—should be challenged by naturalists, who know
> the richness of the soul-complex and realize that vice has a reverse side
> very much like virtue. . . . My souls are conglomerations from past and
> present stages of civilization; they are excerpts from books and newspa-
> pers, scraps of humanity, pieces torn from festive garments which have
> become rags—just as the soul itself is a piece of patchwork.

Miss Julie shows Strindberg's attempt to apply these principles of dramatic
construction and a widened conception of psychology onstage. The core situation is the unmarried Swedish noblewoman Julie's sexual involvement with
Jean, her absent father's servant. Set during the festivities of Midsummer Eve,
which serves, as in Shakespeare's comedy, as a disruption of social distinctions
that allows Julie's seeking out Jean as her dance partner, the play releases
instinctual forces and desires repressed under social and psychological constraints. Freed from her father's supervision and class strictures, Julie reverts
to the instinctual and gratifies her sexual desires. Conditioned by her mother
as a man-hater and an imperious emancipated woman and by her father to live
up to the aristocratic code of honor and duty, Julie reveals herself incapable of
integrating either set of values with her sexual needs. Subtitled *A Naturalistic
Tragedy*, *Miss Julie* traces the disintegration of its title character, who Strindberg calls a "man-hating half-woman," crippled by the contradictions of her
gender and class identity. In contrast to Julie's emotional and psychological
limitations Jean, despite his lowly birth and subservient station, emerges as
superior to Julie in his demonstrated self-mastery and domination over his
circumstance. To illustrate their core identities and the cause and effect of
the seduction Strindberg brings them together in a single one-act format,
eliminating all intermission to sustain the play's illusion and intensity. The
play opens with Jean and Kristine, the cook, in the kitchen of the count, their
master, discussing Miss Julie's indiscretion of dancing with the servants at the
Midsummer's Eve celebration. After persuading Jean to dance with her, Julie

converses with him, while Kristine sleeps at the kitchen table. Julie alternately urges him to treat her as an equal and demands his subservience, while ignoring Jean's warning that it is dangerous to flirt with a man such as him, risking her reputation in associating with a servant.

Interrupted by the sounds of other servants about to enter the kitchen, Jean and Miss Julie seek refuge and protection for Julie's reputation in Jean's room. Prevented from depicting sexual intercourse on stage, Strindberg suggests the offstage seduction in the dancing and singing of the servants, whose performance both replaces the standard interval in a play and divides *Miss Julie* between the cause and effect of Julie's sexual transgression. When they return to the kitchen Jean and Julie confront what they have done. While Jean suggests that they escape together, Julie attempts to redeem their purely carnal encounter with romantic affection that Jean rejects as only possible when he can realize his ambitions and they can become social equals. Julie alternates between her need for Jean's affection and her hatred of him for forcing this dependence on her in shockingly graphic dialogue that underscores the contradictions and role reversal that the drama has arranged:

> JULIE   Menial! Lackey! Stand up when I speak to you.
>
> JEAN   Menial's whore, lackey's harlot, shut your mouth and get out of here!! Are you the one to lecture me for being coarse? Nobody of my kind would ever be as coarse as you were tonight. Do you think any servant girl would throw herself at a man that way? Have you ever seen a girl of my class asking for it like that? I haven't. Only animals and prostitutes.
>
> JULIE   Go on. Hit me, trample on me—it's all I deserve. I'm rotten. But help me! If there's any way out at all, help me.

Unable to find a way out of her dilemma, Julie gives over command to Jean and awaits his orders. He sends her to dress for their departure. When she returns with her caged bird Jean refuses to allow the pet finch to accompany them, and after Julie allows Jean to decapitate it she reverts to her vehement hatred of Jean:

> Kill me too! Kill me! You who can butcher an innocent creature without a quiver. Oh, how I hate you, how I loathe you! There is blood between us now. I curse the hour I first saw you. I curse the hour I was conceived in my mother's womb.

The bell sounds the count's return, and Jean reverts to his servile position in the household, handing his razor to Julie and delivering the play's final words:

"It's horrible. But there's no other way to end it . . . Go!" Julie walks offstage carrying the razor.

If Nora Helmer's slammed-door exit is shocking in Ibsen's *A DOLL'S HOUSE*, Julie's exit to suicide is devastating. To Ibsen's liberation Strindberg adds the caution that repression is not so easily left behind, and autonomy cannot be claimed without consequence. Before *Miss Julie* drama had rarely as brutally or as frankly dealt with the power of sexual desire or with the psychic disintegration brought on by gender, class, and sexual conflict. By holding to the real, to heredity, and environment forces, Strindberg identifies a new basis for tragedy; by pushing his characters to extremes he also reveals the ways in which dramatic naturalism can reveal both the particular and the universal, while opening up the hidden recesses of consciousness itself.

THE PEONY PAVILION

(1598)

by Tang Xianzu

Has the world ever seen a woman's love to rival that of Du Liniang? Dreaming of a lover she fell sick; once sick she became ever worse; and finally, after painting her own portrait as a legacy to the world, she died. Dead for three years, still she was able to live again when in the dark underworld her quest for the object of her dream was fulfilled. To be as Du Liniang is truly to have known love.

—Tang Xianzu, Preface to *The Peony Pavilion*

In world drama there is no more extensive or beautiful exploration of love than Tang Xianzu's *Mudan ting* (*The Peony Pavilion*). In 55 scenes and a performance time of more than 18 hours, *The Peony Pavilion* merits the designation of epic. Its central character, the young woman Du Liniang, embarks on a journey of discovery to reach her heart's desire, facing down life-and-death obstacles in this world and the next. Along the way an entire culture's values and traditions are displayed. In a Western context *The Peony Pavilion* combines elements of Homer's *Odyssey*, Virgil's *Aeneid*, Dante's *Divine Comedy*, and John Milton's *Paradise Lost*. Moreover, it is arguably the first great epic with a complex, believable woman protagonist. Despite its vast scope, *The Peony Pavilion* is anchored by a remarkable psychological depth and earthy realism. In turns lyrical, philosophical, satirical, fantastical, and bawdy, interweaving sentiment and humor, *The Peony Pavilion* provides one of the great entry points for an understanding of Chinese culture and Chinese classical dramatic traditions.

As in the West, the origins of Chinese drama are rooted in religious ritual. Records of performances combining dance, music, and mime date back to around 1500 B.C. During the Han dynasty (208 B.C.–A.D. 221) popular entertainments including acrobatic displays, conjuring, juggling, music, dance, and mime were performed at fairs and markets around the country, as well as at court. During the Tang dynasty (618–906), the emperor Xuanzong created a school, the Pear Garden, to train singers, dancers, and other court performers. Actors today trace their technical descent from this school. In the Song dynasty (960–1279) a narrative tradition flourished, and a great variety of Chinese tales were narrated by professional storytellers at teahouses and dramatized for puppet and shadow-play theaters. A fully developed drama form combining verse, dance, and pantomime began to emerge during this period, producing the oldest extant Chinese drama, Zhang Xie's *The Doctor of Letters*, in which its story is told through dialogue and song. Talented performers were recruited for elaborate court entertainments; others banded together into troupes playing in teahouses and improvised theaters. In cities playhouses were located in special areas called "tile districts" and consisted of fenced enclosures with a roofed platform, open on three sides and, like Elizabethan theaters, with a standing area at ground level surrounded by raised stands and balconies.

The classical Chinese theater took shape, ironically, with the Mongols' conquest of China in the 13th century. During the Yuan dynasty (1279–1368), under Mongol control, Chinese intellectuals were excluded from holding government positions. Many, therefore, turned their attention to practicing and perfecting native Chinese arts, including drama. An explosion of dramatic works of increased literary accomplishment resulted. Drawing their stories from history, legend, novels, epics, and contemporary events, Yuan dramatists produced a wide array of dramatic works that evolved into two distinct styles. The dramatic form popularized in northern China consisted of four acts with 10 to 20 songs, or arias, performed by the protagonist. The best known "northern" style plays are Guan Hanqin's *The Injustice Done to Tou Ngo*, about a widow wrongfully accused of murder by a rejected suitor, and Wang Shifu's *Romance of the Western Chamber*, concerning the trials and tribulations of two lovers. In the 14th century a "southern" style of drama began to emerge in the area around Hangzhou. In contrast to the northern dramas a southern play could have 50 or more acts with multiple subplots, all happily resolved by the final scene. All the characters, not just the protagonist, could sing, and there are solos, duets, and choruses. The result is both an increase in breadth, as plays expanded to consider more varied characters and situations, and in lyrical depth, as the role of verse and singing increased.

The greatest of the dramatists in the southern style during the Ming dynasty (1368–1644) was Tang Xianzu. Born in 1550, Tang came from a distinguished gentry family of scholars in Linchuan, Jiangxi Province. Early on he displayed considerable intellectual and artistic talents. An accomplished student and a poet, Tang succeeded in the provincial examinations at the age of 21, and by the age of 33 had passed the Advanced Scholar examination, qualifying for the highest-level appointments in the imperial bureaucracy. While serving as an official in Nanjing Tang complained to the emperor that the grand secretary was preventing the counsel of honest advisers from being heard, and his criticism was taken as a royal insult. Tang was demoted to service as a jail warden in a remote part of Guangdong. Subsequently, he never reached a higher rank than a district magistrate, and in 1598, at the age of 48, Tang retired from government service to his family home to devote himself to writing. He produced four major dramatic legends, or dream plays, that are collectively known as *The Four Dreams of Linchuan*. *The Peony Pavilion*, the second of these and his masterpiece, is based on a Song dynasty short story about a young woman who dreams of a lover, pines for him, and dies but is permitted to return from the underworld. Tang elaborated his source material into his longest and most profound meditation on the nature of love and life. Tang's plays were intended for private performance before a select audience, usually in a home, performed by a well-to-do family's private troupe of actors or servants without stage scenery. *The Peony Pavilion* was first performed over several days in Tang's home, under his direction. Copies of Tang's play subsequently circulated to great acclaim. After Tang's death, in 1616, adaptations in the opera style known as *kunqu* (for its place of origin in the town of Kunshan, near modern Suzhou) were created, and *The Peony Pavilion* entered the Kun opera repertoire as one of its preeminent works. As Beijing opera supplanted Kun in the 19th century *The Peony Pavilion* ceased to be regularly performed in its entirety, and the play became more of an antiquarian literary work. However, to commemorate the 400th anniversary of its first performance, in 1999, three new productions of *The Peony Pavilion* were mounted: an innovative abridged version by American director Peter Sellars; Chen Shi-zheng's 18-hour version, and a rival "authorized" production in Beijing as part of the festivities marking the 50th anniversary of the founding of the People's Republic of China. Of these Chen's adaptation, performed by actors and musicians of the Shanghai Kunju Company, created an international incident when Chinese authorities declared that the production contained "feudalistic, superstitious, and pornographic" elements and stopped the production from leaving the country for a scheduled run at New York City's Lincoln Center. The controversy, these productions, and a recent full translation of the play for the first time in English by Cyril Birch have stimulated increased awareness of *The Peony Pavilion* and its recognition as one of the masterworks of world drama.

The *Peony Pavilion* opens with introductions of Du Bao, prefect of Nan'an; Madam Du; their daughter, Du Liniang; and the young, struggling student Liu Mengmei. Concerned that the cloistered Liniang should be educated sufficiently to attract a learned husband, Du Bao engages Tutor Chen, whose pompous pedantry contrasts with the earthy sassiness of Liniang's maid Spring Fragrance. Taking refuge from her studies in the garden on a beautiful spring day, Liniang, enchanted by the place, falls asleep and dreams of a young student carrying a willow branch in his hand beside the peony pavilion. Asked his intentions, the student replies that he desires to

Open the fastening of your neck
Loose the girdle at your waist
While you
Screening your eyes with your sleeve,
White teeth clenched on the fabric as if against pain,
Bear with me patiently a while
Then drift into gentle slumber.

Blushing at first and resisting, Liniang yields to him before waking to find that he has departed. Pining for her dream lover, Liniang's health fails. Recognizing that her decline will be fatal, she paints her portrait, writes a poem, and asks Spring Fragrance to conceal them in the garden as a memorial to her love. Liniang dies and is also buried in the garden. The pathos of a young girl dying from love is balanced by Tang's believable characterization in which Liniang is presented as forthright and perceptive rather than as a delicate and wilting flower of girlhood. She is also surrounded by convincingly human portraits of her well-intentioned, practical parents. Sentiment alternates with comedy in the earthy realism of Spring Fragrance, Tutor Chen, and the marvelously oversized and earthbound sorceress Sister Stone, who tries in vain to cure Liniang.

Three years pass as Prefect Du Bao is charged with protecting the district from rampaging bandits, Madame Du Bao contends with her grief, and Liu Mengmei readies himself for the examinations that will determine his future. In the underworld Liniang is brought before the Judge of the Infernal Court to investigate the nature of her death and to determine her punishment or reward. "When in the world did anyone die of a dream?" the incredulous Judge asks when he learns of the cause of Liniang's death. The Flower Spirit from the garden corroborates Liniang's story, and the Judge consults the Register of Heartbreaks that records that Liniang was intended to wed Mengmei, "Prize Candidate in the next examinations." The Judge, equally impressed by the sentiment of Liniang's story and her family connections, releases her from the "City of the Wrongfully Dead" back to life to search for Mengmei.

Among the living Mengmei finds his way to the garden where he recovers Liniang's portrait and poem, falling deeply in love: "Ah, my young lady, image without form, your gaze destroys me!" Falling asleep, Mengmei dreams of Liniang and is united with her spirit in the emotional core of the play as they express and celebrate their love for each other. Liniang's spirit, however, sets Mengmei a decisive test: He must exhume Liniang's remains for her to be resurrected. Having discovered that his beloved is a ghost, he must now overcome his revulsion at what the grave might reveal. This highly charged and macabre situation is tonally undercut by employing the comic figure Scabby Turtle to assist in the disinterment. He first appears singing:

Balls big as gourds, like warts on a hog:
No pants.
Dig the soil and it comes apart:
No chance.
Live bride not good enough, he's after a ghost:
No sense.
Caught robbing graves, get buried alive:
No thanks!

Opening her coffin, Mengmei revives Liniang. Having overcome the challenges of the dream world and the underworld, the final test for the lovers comes from the formidable paterfamilias, Prefect Du Bao. Before taking on that final obstacle the couple departs for Mengmei to take his examination. After he passes he goes to visit Liniang's father, who has been contending with the siege of Huaian. Although bearing Liniang's portrait Mengmei is accused by Du Bao of being merely a grave robber and has him jailed. Even when his daughter arrives the ever practical Du Bao refuses to believe Liniang has come back to life. Finally it is by the emperor's decree that the lovers are allowed to marry in the play's final celebratory scene at court. "Henceforth," Mengmei asserts, "together we shall trace our peony-pavilion dream." To which Lingiang responds triumphantly,

My bridegroom, sun-warmed "southern branch"
Wheron I, northern bloom, may rest—
Did ever ghost in all the world
Know such a love as mine?

The play concludes with a rousing affirmation on behalf of love's power to overcome the greatest obstacles. To make his case Tang Xianzu shows himself to be a master of expressing the emotions of love, the nature of lovers, and the real and imagined world that they, and all, inhabit.

THE MISANTHROPE

33

(1666)

by Molière

I think the Misanthrope *the finest, most complete production of its kind in the world.*
—George Eliot, Letter to Mme. Eugène Bodichon, December 5, 1859

Le Misanthrope, ou l'Atrabilaire amoureux (*The Misanthrope*) is deservedly regarded as Molière's masterpiece and perhaps the greatest comedy of manners ever written. It is both a brilliant social satire in its deft dissection of the customs and pretenses of fashionable 17th-century French society and a skilled psychological study. Alceste, its self-righteous title character, who both stubbornly speaks his mind and tells people what he really thinks of them and misperceives central truths about himself and his society, is one of the most complicated and intriguing characters Molière ever created. *The Misanthrope,* perhaps more than any other of Molière's works, displays the playwright's remarkable verbal and technical artistry that reshapes the manners and values of a particular time and place into universal representations of human nature and the human condition. *The Misanthrope* can be described as *the* drama of human social behavior, of the roles we play and the illusions that flatter our sense of honesty and integrity and conceal our foibles, limitations, and ignoble human needs. Few comedies have combined such an entertaining and profound mix of incisive social satire and essential truths about humanity. As critic George Brandes observed, "By most French critics this play is held to be the loftiest achievement of French comedy, the unapproachable masterpiece of the foremost of comic dramatists."

Born Jean-Baptiste Poquelin, Molière was the son of a prosperous Paris upholsterer, and it was expected that he would continue in the family business. In 1643, after a conventional education and a brief turn at legal studies, to the horror of his family Molière gave up his business prospects for a far-from-respectable career in the theater, adopting the stage name of Molière to avoid family embarrassment. He formed L'Illustre Théâtre company with his mistress, Madeleine Béjart, an experienced actress six years his senior.

The company performed sporadically and incurred crippling debts for which Molière was imprisoned and rescued by his father. In 1646 Molière's acting company left Paris for a 12-year tour of the provinces, during which time he began to write plays to exploit his comic skills. As an actor Molière lacked the prescribed abilities to succeed in tragic roles. He had, in the words of a contemporary, "a muffled voice, harsh inflections, and hurried speech which made him declaim too quickly." His vocal and stage gifts, however, were ideal for comedy, and Molière would eventually earn the accolade, *"le premier farceur de France."* Molière's theatrical skills as an actor, director, and manager were augmented by his unique genius for adapting conventional comic forms to new and provocative uses. The popular comedy of Molière's day derived from the French medieval farcical tradition: brief sketch comedies with simple plots and satirical portraits of easily recognizable social types, such as the lecherous monk, henpecked husband, and domineering wife. By the 17th century French farce was influenced by the more inventive techniques of the Italian commedia dell'arte, to which Molière was exposed on his troupe's tour of the southern provinces. Based on set comic routines, the commedia depended on stock roles familiar to the audience and witty improvisations by the actors, which included topical references. In the long apprenticeship of the provincial tour Molière mastered these farcical bases upon which he began to build a new kind of character and theme-driven comedy of manners. If French popular comedy before Molière was exclusively a rough-and-tumble entertainment of low humor with only the aspiration to generate belly laughs, Molière would transform it into a refined and challenging critique of life, establishing a literary and artistic dramatic form to rival tragedy as a serious instrument of truth telling.

In 1658, Molière's company returned to Paris and performed for Louis XIV a Pierre Corneille tragedy and an afterpiece, Molière's own farce *Le docteur amoureux* (The doctor in love), now lost. The king was so amused by the farce that he allowed Molière's company to remain in Paris and join the other three professional companies in the city. This was the beginning of Louis XIV's important patronage that eventually led to friendship with the playwright and his designating Molière's company as "the troupe of the king." For the remaining 15 years of his life Molière wrote, produced, and acted in an extraordinary series of groundbreaking plays that included *L'École des femmes* (1662, *The School for Wives,*) TARTUFFE (1664), *Dom Juan* (1665), *The Misanthrope* (1666), *L'Avare* (1668; *The Miser*) and *Le Malade imaginaire* (1673; *The Imaginary Invalid*). Controversy and personal attack greeted most of these works as his comedies challenged both literary conventions and orthodox values. *The School for Wives* sparked a contentious debate on the proper subject and manner for comedy. *Tartuffe*, Molière's play about a religious hypocrite, was banned by irate church officials for five years. His next major play, *Dom Juan*, about an irreligious, blasphemous libertine, was forced to be withdrawn from performance. To fill the gap in his company's offerings Molière brought to the stage *The Misanthrope*, a play whose darkly ironic comedy reflects the playwright's professional and personal setbacks. If Molière's professional life was marked by contentiousness with his critics and the censors, the playwright's personal life was complicated by his unhappy marriage to actress Armande Béjart, the younger sister, or possibly the daughter, of his former lover and theatrical partner, Madeleine. Molière would be the first Alceste in *The Misanthrope*, opposite his wife as the coquettish heartbreaker Célimène, adding a significant, private resonance to the skirmishing of the play's leads.

Like *Tartuffe* and *Dom Juan*, *The Misanthrope* explores the abuses of power (or at least the illusion of power) of the individual over the social order. The play takes up the serious, essential question of Molière's neoclassical age of the rights and responsibilities of the individual to society and the concessions that civilized human relationships require. Alceste, the play's self-styled opponent of human corruption and pretensions, rails against genteel society's inauthenticity and hypocrisy, allowing Molière's witty display of the pros and cons of Alceste's moral opposition to the ways of the world. Molière complicates the truism that honesty is the best policy, while exploring the crucial difference between being honest to one's neighbor and with one's self.

Act 1 begins with Alceste quarreling with his friend Philinte over the latter's flattery of someone that Philinte hardly knows. Alceste demands that everyone should "be sincere and say only what is in the heart, like an honorable man." Philinte counters that "when one moves in society, one must pay back people with the customary civil compliments." Simple politeness requires a certain degree of insincerity, according to Philinte, but Alceste categorically denies such a justification for violating the moral absolutes of truth and honesty. If he had acted as Philinte had done, Alceste asserts, "I would go out and hang myself in remorse." Philinte blithely responds: "Well, personally, I don't see that it's a hanging matter." Philinte emerges in the play's opening skirmish as a realist, a rationalist, and a moderate who correctly balances the personal and the social while acknowledging the price that must be paid for social cohesion. In contrast Alceste reveals himself as an inflexible extremist and absolutist whose high moral tone masks an out-of-control ego in his opposition to "all the human race" and his intention to "flee in a wilderness any human contact." Beneath the surface of Alceste's pose as the destroyer of social illusions can be glimpsed a man equally driven by social approval who is as busily involved in the social game playing Philinte acknowledges.

The comedy of *The Misanthrope* comes from two directions: from Alceste's outlandish self-rectitude and opposition to the social norms and from his blindness to his own subservience to those same disdainful norms. The first practical test of Alceste's philosophy of honesty at all cost comes when he is asked to evaluate the merits of a poem by the courtier Oronte. Despite at first hesitating to be rude, in defiance of his earlier position with Philinte, Alceste eventually unmercifully criticizes the mediocre poem. He destroys the illusion of Oronte's poetical talents, while still sustaining his own illusions of complete honesty yet disguising an inescapable motive behind his critique: The love poem is addressed to Célimène, whom Alceste loves. Oronte is therefore a rival, and Alceste's truthfulness about his qualities as a love poet is self-serving, emotionally based, and biased.

The contradictions between Alceste's professed selfless principles of honesty and selfish motives are further displayed in act 2 as Alceste calls on Célimène to criticize her duplicitous and hypocritical conduct of flattering all in attendance on her while acidly slandering and ridiculing them behind their backs. With the arrival of several callers and a round of gossipy conversation at the expense of others, Alceste's charges are confirmed. However, beneath Alceste's desire for Célimène to be truthful is the hope that she will be true to only him, that she will reject her various suitors for his exclusive love. Alceste shows that he craves the flattery that he ostensibly abhors. While he prides himself on offering clear-eyed criticism, emotions, not reason, form the basis for his actions. Célimène, who seems Alceste's opposite by her hypocrisy and evident delight in social performance, actually has much in common with Alceste. She relishes the admiration of her many suitors in the same way that Alceste glories in his role as the great contrarian. Both need others to validate their identities, and both are extremists—Alceste in his moral rigidity and Célimène in her moral relativity. Both are also masters of evasion—Célimène in refusing to commit or to treat love as more than a game of one-upmanship and Alceste in his blindness to the contradiction between his principles and the facts of his evident contradictory needs and desires. Both crave the illusion of power and control and must contend with the reality of their losing both. The act ends with Alceste's summons before a tribunal to prevent a possible duel with Oronte.

In the third act the self-righteous Arsinoé, a woman motivated by her own love for Alceste, warns Célimène that her flirtatious conduct is becoming scandalous. The younger woman rejects Arsinoé's warnings as jealousy and prudery masquerading as morality. Angered, Arsinoé responds by trying to dissuade Alceste from trusting Célimène. Alceste requires proof of his lover's duplicity, which he gains in the form of an unsigned letter purportedly written by Célimène, which describes him in malicious terms and reveals her unfaithfulness. In the fourth act the outraged Alceste confronts Célimène with the evidence, which she expertly and ingeniously turns to her own advantage in further inflaming Alceste's passion for her. Alceste's desperate desire to believe Célimène true to him causes him to ignore the facts, and he succumbs to the more pleasing, flattering illusions that he has condemned in others. The scene closes with the revelation that he has lost his suit in the quarrel with Oronte.

In the final act Alceste and Philinte repeat their quarreling in act 1, with Philinte urging Alceste to appeal the court's decision and make the necessary concessions, but Alceste prefers the role of martyr to injustice. The case provides him with the proof of social and human corruption, and he is now prepared to follow through on his previous threat to "flee in a wilderness any human contact." Philinte concedes that "This is a low, conniving age" and that "Nothing but trickery prospers nowadays":

> Yes, man's a beastly creature; but must we then
> Abandon the society of men?
> Here in the world, each human frailty
> Provides occasion for philosophy,
> And that is virtue's noblest exercise;
> If honesty shone forth from all men's eyes,
> If every heart were frank and kind and just,
> What could our virtues do but gather dust.

Moderation, again, is Philinte's advice and engagement with, not isolation from, society as the proper testing ground for virtues. Alceste remains adamant and intends to convince Célimène to join him in the wilderness. Before he can do so Célimène's several suitors confront her with additional evidence that she despises them all equally. All depart vowing revenge, save Alceste. Now the audience is ready for the expected comic resolution in Célimène's repentance and capitulation to Alceste's redeeming love. He plays his part by urging her to come away from Paris and its vices to live with him happily ever after in exile:

> Woman, I'm willing to forget your shame,
> And clothe your treacheries in a sweeter name;
> I'll call them youthful errors, instead of crimes,
> And lay the blame on these corrupting times.
> My one condition is that you agree
> To share my chosen fate, and fly with me
> To that wild, trackless, solitary place
> In which I shall forget the human race.

Célimène, however, delivers Molière's final shock. To Alceste's offer she responds: "What! *I* renounce the world at my young age, / And die of boredom in some hermitage?" Alceste's principal rival all along has not been the various suitors, but Society, the fashionable arena for the role-playing and manipulation that Célimène prizes above love. Alceste exits alone. The marital union that should close a comedy is reserved for the sensible, secondary characters, Philinte and his cousin Éliante, but the main antagonists—Alceste, Célimène, and Society—remain implacable and unreformed. Alceste heads off to an uncertain fate as an outsider and exile, nursing his sense of moral superiority and missing the contradictions that connect him with Célimène as socially dependent, if only to provide him with the opportunity to cast himself as the tragic hero in his own drama. Célimène will presumably return to the game of human relationships, played with no other end but for the illusion of power and mastery it gratifies. Finally, Society continues on: a corrupt but inescapable arena for the display of virtue and villainy.

The Misanthrope restores order, as a comedy must, neither in the maturation of the lovers, nor in the triumph of love in opposition to the falsity and unnatural constraints of society, but in the audience's bracing exposure to the illusions of egoism and the social stage that define our lives. Louis XIV famously declared, "I am the State," and Molière demonstrates how true that is for each of us: We are all, like Alceste and Célimène, autocratic egoists and shaped and defined by the society that surrounds us.

THREE SISTERS 34

(1901) — *by Anton Chekhov*

Like steam, life can be compressed into a narrow little container, but, also like steam, it will endure pressure only to a certain point. And in Three Sisters, *this pressure is brought to the limit, beyond which it will explode—and don't you actually hear how life is seething, doesn't its angrily protesting voice reach your ears?*
    —Leonid Andreev, *"Three Sisters," in* The Complete Collected Works

Regarded by many as the playwright's masterwork, *Three Sisters*—the third of Anton Chekhov's four major full-length dramas—is his longest and most complex play. Chekhov's contemporary Maxim Gorky memorably praised its initial production in 1901 as "music, not acting," and considered *Three Sisters* the most profound and effective of Chekhov's plays. It is in many ways the archetypal modern drama that pioneered a new dramatic vision and method for the stage. Contemporary audiences and readers now familiar with the dramatic lessons of futility and frustrated expectations by such playwrights as Samuel Beckett and Harold Pinter may overlook just how radical and trailblazing *Three Sisters* was. Half a century before *WAITING FOR GODOT*, Chekhov based his play on waiting for something that never happens, in which decisive actions and resolvable conflicts—essential ingredients of conventional drama—are replaced by paralysis, ennui, and the inconsequential. Almost a century before Jerry Seinfeld promoted a situation comedy in which "nothing happens," Chekhov offered a tragicomedy on the same terms: keeping the expected dramatic climaxes offstage, concentrating instead on the interior drama just below the surface of the routine and ordinary. By doing so *Three Sisters* fundamentally challenged the accepted stage assumptions of its day, while establishing a new dramatic logic and procedure that have influenced and shaped the drama that followed it.

   The Russian stage that Chekhov would transform was derivative, stultifying, and moribund in the 1880s and 1890s when he began as a dramatist. Censorship was more severe for the stage than for print, and consequently the Russian theater was dominated by the innocuous, by irreproachable patriotic spectacles, by well-worn melodramas, diverting musical plays, and safe imports. Moreover, the playwright's financial reward for a successful play was much less than for fiction. This was a key factor why Chekhov, who had a lifelong interest in the theater, supported his family in Moscow in the 1880s as he studied medicine mainly by writing short stories and comic sketches. The Russian stage could neither sustain nor accommodate serious writers, and Russian drama fell far short of the achievement of Russian poetry and fiction during the 19th century. Feodor Dostoevsky, that most dramatic of all novelists, did not compose a single play, while Ivan Turgenev, whose atmospheric and nuanced slice-of-life dramas, particularly *A Month in the Country* (1850), anticipated Chekhov's works, abandoned the theater early in his career. The gradual movement toward an indigenous drama and stage realism in Russia, initiated by Nikolai Gogol in *The Inspector General*, was sustained by the era's most popular dramatist, Aleksandr Ostrovsky (1823–86), the first Russian writer to devote himself exclusively to the theater. Ostrovsky helped popularize the appearance of ordinary Russian characters and recognizable situations on stage in his nearly 50 plays that depicted scenes from Moscow life. Chekhov, who would build on the foundations that Gogol and Ostrovsky had laid, began his dramatic career composing vaudeville sketches and short comic curtain-raisers, many adapted from his short fiction and sketches. His first full-length play, *Ivanov* (1887), is mainly conventional in its dramatic structure but contains traces of the innovations of psychological realism, atmosphere, and indirect action that would define the masterpieces to come. "I wanted to create something original," Chekhov commented. "I did not portray a single villain or angel . . . did not indict anyone or acquit anyone. . . . Whether I succeeded in this, I do not know." His second full-length play, *The Wood Goblin*, appeared in 1889 to poor reviews in which the playwright was taken to task for "blindly copying everyday life and paying no attention to the requirements of the stage." Despite such censure Chekhov stood firm on the side of innovation, advising his brother in his own theatrical aspirations to "try to be original and as intelligent as possible, but don't be afraid to look like a fool. . . . Don't lick everything clean, don't polish it up, but be clumsy and audacious. . . . Remember, by the way, that love scenes, wives and husbands cheating on one another, widows, orphans, and all the rest of the tear jerking have long since been described. The topic has to be a new one, but a plot is not necessary."

It would finally take the conjunction of a unique play, a playwright of genius, and an independent and innovative theatrical company to bring Chekhov's dramatic vision to fruition and public acceptance. The end of the monopoly of the imperial theaters in St. Petersburg and Moscow in the 1880s that had contributed to a conservative and staid Russian dramatic tradition provided an opening for inventive and original private theaters. The most famous of these was the Moscow Art Theater, founded by Konstantin Stanislavsky (1863–1938) and Vladimir Nemirovich-Danchenko (1858–1943). Their company would emphasize ensemble acting and a scrupulous attention to stagecraft in which every aspect of a production—music, scenery, costumes, lighting, and especially acting styles—was joined into a unified dramatic whole. Stanislavsky, who would become one of the most important modern stage theorists, encouraged his acting troupe to replace the fashionable declamatory acting style with a psychological and emotional authenticity. These innovations perfectly suited Chekhov's drama of subtext and atmosphere. The Moscow Art Theater's second production was a revival of Chekhov's *The Seagull*, his most innovative drama yet, written in Chekhov's words, "contrary to all the rules of dramatic art." Initially performed in St. Petersburg in 1896, its premiere was a disaster with actors who neither understood their roles nor their lines. Chekhov fled the theater during the second act, and critics blasted the play as inept and ridiculous. Nemirovich-Danchenko, however, was in attendance and convinced his partner, Stanislavsky, that the play had great potential. They managed to persuade Chekhov to let them take it on, and the Moscow Art Theater mounted it to great acclaim in 1898. The seagull would become the identifying logo of the Moscow Art Theater, which would go on to premiere Chekhov's subsequent dramas and came to be called "the house of Chekhov." *The Seagull* is a nuanced study of the nature of art and love in which conventional stage action takes place offstage. Traditional dramatic conflict between characters is replaced by inner conflict within characters. Meaning is generated by counterpoint and juxtaposition of ideas and images, a dramatic method perfectly suited to the rich interplay of text, subtle stagecraft, and the psychological penetration pioneered by Stanislavsky and his company. Chekhov's next play, *Uncle Vanya* (1899), a reworking of *The Wood Goblin*, continued the innovations of *The Seagull*; external action is minimal, dramatic interest is extended to several characters who refuse to conform to conventional categories of heroes and villains, and the overall force of the play depends on the unspoken and on its atmosphere and mood, as in a lyrical poem.

Three Sisters, which followed next, was the first of Chekhov's plays to be written specifically for the Moscow Art Theater, drawing intentionally on the company's strengths and production possibilities. At the outset Chekhov realized that his conception would prove "more difficult than the earlier plays." As he observed, "I am writing not a play but some kind of maze. Lots of characters—it may be that I lose my way and give up writing." Begun around November 1899, *Three Sisters* would not be completed until January 1901. Interweaving the complex relationships of multiple characters over a number of years, the play is possibly the closest Chekhov ever came to writing with the scope and texture of a novel. *Three Sisters* is Chekhov's version of the fall of the house of Atreus in which a family implodes, not as in Aeschylus's tragedy from overt crimes and betrayals, but from the covert, from the subtle collusion of time, place, and human nature. Set in a provincial backwater, the play focuses on the Prozorov family—sisters Olga, Masha, and Irina and their brother, Andrei—who have settled there from Moscow when their widowed father, a Russian general, was put in charge of the local regiment 11 years before. In act 1 it is the name day of the youngest of the three, 20-year-old Irina, as well as the first anniversary of their father's death. A trivial series of external activities— the arrival of celebrating guests, small talk, a family dinner—eventually expose a complex inner conflict in which oppressiveness and aimlessness overwhelm the family. Beneath the placid surface of respectability and cultured chatter the Prozorovs and their guests feel stifled "as weeds do grass," with signs of decay everywhere around them. Andrei, the family's great hope to become a professor in Moscow and rescue them all from the provinces, has grown fat and lazy in the year since his father's death; Olga, bitterly unmarried and long- ing for domestic tranquillity, suffers from headaches and continual exhaustion as a schoolteacher, while Masha, miserable in her marriage to a pompous schoolmaster, indulges in poetic melancholy. Only Irina remains hopeful and committed to achieving a new purposeful life while holding true to the dream that has sustained them all for more than a decade: getting back to Moscow. The act reveals, indirectly by innuendo and symbol (such as constant reference to time), a spent family group in which the old values and prospects no longer sustain them. The sisters and their brother have been raised to a level of cul- tural refinement that their tawdry provincial environment neither values nor shares. The Prozorovs are shown to be incapable of adapting to their altered circumstances. The new order that will vanquish the old is represented by a local girl—Natasha—who, despite her vulgarity and awkwardness among the sisters and their circle of fashionable officers, succeeds in captivating Andrei, and the act ends with his marriage proposal.

Act 2 takes place at least a year later in the same setting, but with the focus on the changes that have occurred: Andrei has lost all ambitions to become a Moscow professor and spends much of his time gambling and trying to forget how ill bred and selfish the woman he has married is; Olga is exhausted by her teaching and has largely given over the running of their house to Natasha, who demands more and more deference from the sisters. Irina has taken a job she despises in the telegraph office, while Masha is the object of affection of Vershinin, the battery commander, who is seeking relief from his neurotic, suicidal wife. Such exposition, as well as evidence of the further erosion of the family, emerge only gradually from snatches of dialogue and details that break through from another sequence of ostensibly trivial external activities. Natasha overrules the family tradition of entertaining the Carnival mummers on behalf of her baby son, who "is not at all well," and later quietly intimi- dates Irina to give up her room: "My dear, my own, move in with Olga for a while! . . . You and Olga will be in one room, for this little while, and your room will be for Bobik." Breaking through the placid domestic routine is the unmistakable signs of the dispossession of the Prozorovs by Natasha and the new order that she represents. Using her son as a weapon against the sisters, Natasha dominates the sisters and their brother, and the Prozorovs have neither the spirit nor the will to resist this ambitious arriviste.

In act 3, a few more years have passed. The action takes place in Olga and Irina's cramped upstairs bedroom as a fire rages in the town. As he had done in *The Seagull* and would repeat in THE CHERRY ORCHARD, Chekhov irradiates his naturalistic details with symbols that comment on and clarify the dramatic action. Here the fire serves to underline the crisis that threatens to destroy the Prozorovs as their collective and individual dreams are consumed and extinguished. Natasha has grown mercilessly and rudely imperious; Masha seeks relief in a doomed affair with Vershinin, while Irina reluctantly agrees to marry her persistent suitor, Baron Tusenbach, whom she does not love, resigned to her fate that she will never get back to Moscow and that she is drying up into "nothing—no satisfaction of any kind." For the sisters all their dreams of a useful and emotionally satisfying life in Moscow are abandoned, leaving them, like the town around them, in ruin.

The play that had begun in the spring with the exuberant dreams of youth at Irina's name day concludes symbolically in autumn with the news that the last bulwark for the Prozorovs to support their claim to culture and distinction and ward off terminal boredom—their relationship with the officers of their father's former regiment—is ending with the unit's transfer to Poland. Set in the barren garden of the Prozorovs' home, the act is a series of crushing leave-takings and reassessments, each more painful than the last, underscoring the completion of the Prozorovs' dispossession. Olga, now schoolmistress, is departing to live in meager quarters in the school. Irina and Tusenbach are to be married the next day, and then they will leave for a proposed new, active life. The Baron is to manage a brickyard, while Irina will teach school. However, the Baron's rival for Irina, the bully Solyony, has picked a fight and challenged Tusenbach to a duel. As the marching music of the departing regiment is heard, the news arrives that the Baron has been killed. The play closes with the three sisters supporting one another, sustained by an uncertain future consolation, much as they had been by their dream of returning to Moscow. Olga remarks:

> The music is playing so gaily, cheerfully, and I feel like living! Oh, dear Lord! Time will pass, and we'll be gone forever, people will forget us, they'll forget our faces, voices, and how many of us there were, but our suffering will turn to joy for those who live after us, happiness and peace will come into being on this earth, and those who live now will be remembered with a kind word and a blessing. Oh, dear sisters, this life of ours is not over yet. Let's go on living! The music plays so gaily, so cheerfully, and it looks like just a little while longer and we shall learn why we're alive, why we suffer . . . If only we knew, if only we knew!

Facing the reality of their suffering and its causes while persisting in the business of living are the best that Olga can offer her family and what Chekhov offers his audience. In *Three Sisters* Chekhov, through his group protagonist and integration of surface detail and symbol, has discovered a powerful means of dramatizing the often unconscious and mainly hidden sources of human passion, dreams, and delusions. By restricting the conventional dramatic conflicts and climaxes offstage, Chekhov brings to center stage a drama of everyday life that is simultaneously utterly convincing in its specificity and profound in its universal significance.

LIFE IS A DREAM

35

(1635)

by Pedro Calderón de la Barca

The mannered ornamental style of a Calderon was understood and enjoyed by the Madrid public, always eager for a good show. His recondite images and comparisons were borne on the stream of a ringing rhetoric which delighted the ears even of the common man. To the conceptos, with their plays on words and ideas, the common man was receptive too. The imagery of writing and the book was for the most part, as we have seen, a private domain for educated, if not for erudite, circles. Calderon makes it popular once again; at the same time he represents its final apogee in Western poetry.
—Ernst Robert Curtius, *European Literature and the Latin Middle Ages*

La vida es sueño (*Life Is a Dream*), Pedro Calderón de la Barca's masterpiece, is considered by many the greatest of all Spanish dramas. Along with Félix Lope de Vega, Calderón defined the Golden Age of Spanish drama, which has characteristically been viewed as beginning with Félix Lope de Vega's rise to prominence in the 1580s and Calderón's death in 1681. If Lope de Vega established a national drama and formulated the rules and the literary and dramatic possibilities of the Spanish *comedia*, a three-act secular verse drama, Calderón brought it to its highest level of artistic and intellectual expression. Calderón has been described as the finest of all poetic dramatists, who secured for the stage the expressive language of Renaissance lyric poetry and refined and elevated Spanish dramaturgy, which became a significant legacy to the European stage. He is also considered the greatest intellectual among Spanish dramatists who incorporated into drama an unprecedented philosophical reach. The Spanish critic Marcelino Menéndez y Pelayo rated Calderón as a less spontaneous and inventive dramatist than Lope de Vega and inferior in characterization to Tirso de Molina, but superior to both, and all other Spanish (and most world) dramatists, in profundity and poetry, calling Calderón history's greatest playwright after Sophocles and William Shakespeare. Calderón's international reputation has largely been secured by *Life Is a Dream*, which many regard as the most important play of the Spanish theater and an undeniable masterwork of world drama. Few other plays are as breathtaking in the grandeur of its verse or as ambitious in the essential human and moral questions it raises. A metaphysical drama that shifts and expands under repeated reading and viewing, *Life Is a Dream* has been variously interpreted as a Christian, romantic, existential, and absurdist drama, in which multiple and contrary lessons can be drawn from the conflicts it arranges, from the paradoxes of its imagery, and from the implication of its multiple themes.

Like other inevitable literary pairings—Charles Dickens and William Thackeray, Leo Tolstoy and Feodor Dostoevsky, Ernest Hemingway and F. Scott Fitzgerald—Calderón invites comparison with his predecessor, Lope de Vega. Both were Madrid natives; both were educated by the Jesuits and served in the military; both wrote their first plays as boys; and both eventually entered the priesthood. However, except for a period of youthful wildness that included duels and romantic adventures de rigueur for the aspiring Spanish courtier and imitative of Lope's tempestuous and philandering lifestyle, Calderón is both temperamentally and artistically Lope's opposite. Born in 1600 into an aristocratic family with connections to the royal court, Calderón was educated at the Colegio Imperial, a Jesuit school, and later attended the universities at Alcalá de Henares and Salamanca, where he studied theology and canon law. His professional literary career began after he entered a poetry contest to celebrate the beatification of Saint Isidore, patron saint of Madrid. His submission drew praise from one of the judges, Lope de Vega, the preeminent dramatist at the time. Calderón's first play, *Amor, honor y poder* (Love, honor, and power) was performed in 1623. For the next two decades, Calderón composed 66 plays that established his reputation as one of Spain's leading dramatists. A favorite of King Philip IV, Calderón replaced Lope de Vega as the principal court dramatist when Lope died in 1635, the same year that *Life Is a Dream* premiered. The king subsequently made Calderón a Knight of Santiago in 1637. He saw military service during the Catalan Revolt in 1640 but retired from active duty when he was injured and reurned to Madrid where he wrote *El alcalde de Zalamea* (*The Mayor of Zalamea*), after *Life Is a Dream*, Calderón's most popular play, concerning the mistreatment of peasants by the Spanish military. Calderón was ordained a priest in 1651 and for the next 30 years largely withdrew from the world for a contemplative life. He continued to write one or two *autos sacramentales*, one-act verse religious allegories, each year and mythological *comedias* for court performance. He served as a chaplain in Toledo until the king recalled him to his former post at court in 1663. There he remained until his death in 1681.

If Lope catered to the largely unsophisticated and undeveloped taste of his popular audience in the *corrales*, the open-air, Elizabethan-like public theaters of the time, Calderón essentially served a more educated, discriminating court audience that could appreciate both the quality of his dramatic verses and the sophistication of the ideas his plays expressed. If Lope was Spanish drama's great, inexhaustible inventor and improviser, Calderón was the more careful dramatic craftsman who delicately constructed his urbane, intricate dramas and polished verse forms out of the models Lope had pioneered. Calderón reshaped the *comedia* by tightening previously disjointed and unconnected plot elements and eliminating redundancies and irrelevancies. If Lope was the great genius of unfolding action and suspense, Calderón subordinated his plots to serve his themes. If Lope was the supreme stage entertainer who gratified his audience's tastes, Calderón strove to challenge and instruct. Calderón wrote far less than Lope, producing some 120 *comedias* and 80 *autos*, works roughly divided into three groups: secular, religious, and philosophical. *Life Is a Dream* combines themes from all three.

Life Is a Dream is a complex play that weaves together plot and subplot to consider such grand themes as the conflicts between appearance and reality, free will versus determinism, the individual versus society, freedom versus constraint, and passion versus reason. The play opens in the wild, mountainous country between Poland and Russia as Rosaura, a Russian noblewoman, journeys to the Polish royal court. Having been seduced and abandoned by the nobleman Astolfo, Rosaura dons male garb to search for her faithless lover and reclaim her honor. She comes upon an isolated fortress where Segismundo, the son of the Polish king Basilio, is being held. Basilio, who regulates his life by astrology, hopes by imprisoning his son to forestall the prophecy made at the prince's birth that Segismundo would usurp the throne and become a murderous tyrant. At the play's outset, therefore, the drama's two unfortunate victims of circumstances—Rosaura, abandoned by her lover, and Segismundo, who knows neither who he is nor why he is a captive—meet. Rosaura's story is the familiar honor plot of Spanish drama, while Segismundo's circumstances set in motion the main philosophical themes of the play surrounding the issues of free will and destiny, human liberty and justice, truth and illusion. In the first of Segismundo's major soliloquies, he struggles to comprehend the cause of his imprisonment and its justification. "I long to know," Segismundo declares, "What greater crime, apart from being born,/Can thus have earned my greater chastisement./Aren't others born like me? And yet they seem/To boast a freedom that I've never known." Calderón builds from the conventional contrivance of the *comedia*—concealed identity and court intrigue—an existential drama that considers life as a prison in which fate dictates punishment without cause.

Clotaldo, Segismundo's warden and tutor, seizes Rosaura for trespassing and, recognizing the sword she carries, realizes that she must be his own child, implicating him in the issue of Rosaura's dishonor. Meanwhile, the king, determined to resolve the issue of succession and to ease his conscience over his treatment of his son, decides to test the veracity of the prophecy. The stars, he argues, "can but influence, not force,/The free will which man holds direct from God." Drugged into a deep sleep, Segismundo is transported to the palace. On waking, if he proves himself to be restrained and sensible, he will be permitted to remain and rule. If he shows himself to be the dangerous monster of the prophecy, however, he will be returned to prison and told that all he experienced at court was just a dream. The experiment fails, and Segismundo is unable to control his passions or newfound power in his unexpected liberation. Told by Clotaldo that he is the heir to the throne, imprisoned for a prophecy, Segismundo is enraged, threatens vengeance, throws a servant out a window, tries to assault the noblewoman Estrella, and fights with his cousin, Astolfo, who hopes to marry her. Seeing his son behaving like a wild animal, Basilio is now convinced that the forecast about the prince is true, and Segismundo is again put to sleep and returned to his prison. On awakening, he is assured by Clotaldo that all had been a dream. The experience begins the process of Segismundo's enlightenment and redemption as he becomes aware of the conflict between truth and illusion and explores the basis for moral action amidst the illusory. As Clotaldo draws the important lesson that "even in dreams . . . nothing is lost by trying to do good," Segismundo in a famous soliloquy at the end of act 2 underscores the point that life is a dream:

> And now experience shows me that each man
> Dreams what he is until he is awakened.
> The king dreams he's a king and in his fiction
> Lives, rules, administers with royal pomp.
> Yet all the borrowed praises that he earns
> Are written in the wind, and he is changed
> (How sad a fate!) by death to dust and ashes.
> What man is there alive who'd seek to reign
> Since he must wake into the dream that's death.
> The rich man dreams his wealth which is his care
> And woe. The poor man dreams his sufferings.
> He dreams who thrives and prospers in this life.
> He dreams who toils and strives. He dreams who injures,
> Offends, and insults. So that in this world
> Everyone dreams the thing he is, though no one
> Can understand it. I dream I am here,
> Chained in these fetters. Yet I dreamed just now
> I was in a more flattering, lofty station.
> What is this life? A frenzy, an illusion,
> A shadow, a delirium, a fiction.
> The greatest good's but little, and this life
> Is but a dream, and dreams are only dreams.

Resigned that he cannot resolve the discrepancy between dream and reality, Segismundo nevertheless accepts his fate and resolves to master his passions by reason as instructed by the experience of his dream that illustrated the opposite lesson.

The second of Segismundo's tests takes place when insurgents who object to the king's selection of the foreign prince Astolfo to succeed him, liberate the prince and claim him as the rightful heir. Segismundo now finds himself in fulfillment of the prophecy as a usurper and potential agent of his father's destruction. Although he suspects that he may be dreaming yet again, based on his insights that although life is as incomprehensible and apparently purposeless as a dream, it still demands honorable action and responsibility, Segismundo forgives his father and restores peace and harmony to the kingdom. Learning discretion and prudence from his son, Basilio surrenders his crown to him, and Segismundo orders the marriage of Astolfo to Rosaura, restoring her honor, while he claims Estrella as his queen. Questioned about his wonderful transformation to model ruler, Segismundo concludes the play with the following explanation:

> Why do you marvel, since
> It was a dream that taught me and I still
> Fear to wake up once more in my close dungeon?
> Though that may never happen, it's enough
> To dream it might, for thus I came to learn
> That all our human happiness must pass
> Away like any dream, and I would here
> Enjoy it fully ere it glide away,
> Asking (for noble hearts are prone to pardon)
> Pardon for faults in the actors or the play.

As the illusion of the play ends, dream and reality touch in Segismundo's direct appeal to the audience for their understanding and sympathy. Three centuries before writers such as Jean-Paul Sartre and Albert Camus explored the implication of moral relativity and the chimera of absolutes, Calderón did just that. Calderón's dramatic achievement was to expand the philosophical and poetic possibilities for the stage, embodying in plot and verse some of the knottiest paradoxes of human existence.

HEDDA GABLER

36

(1891)   *by Henrik Ibsen*

Ibsen was in fact, in Hedda Gabler, *consolidating the features of much of his early work—work of which the younger Strindberg was well aware.* Hedda Gabler, *too, is thematically centred in Ibsen's major work, for, like so many others, Hedda is destroyed by her inherited debt. But there is no mercy; "merciless" indeed is the predominant mood.*
—Raymond Williams, *Drama from Ibsen to Brecht*

Called by playwright and critic William Archer "surely one of the most poignant character-tragedies in literature," *Hedda Gabler* is now, along with *A Doll's House*, the most consistently produced and critically debated of Henrik Ibsen's plays. It is without doubt his most skillfully constructed drama, whose title character is one of the greatest roles in the modern theater. Hedda Gabler, a frustrated aristocratic woman who vengefully destroys herself and those around her, can claim kinship with a handful of drama's other titanic, complex, and contradictory women—Medea, Clytemnestra, Lady Macbeth, and Phèdre. An ominous and disturbing alternative to the liberation experience of Nora Helmer in *A Doll's House*, *Hedda Gabler* is a searing psychological study of the self-possessed and independent "new" woman Nora wished to become, whose aspirations, limitations, and dissatisfactions annihilate her. When it was first performed in 1891 *Hedda Gabler* was savaged by the public and the press. Critics derided the play as "a base escape of moral sewage gas" and held that its title character was "acrawl with the foulest passions of humanity." Play and protagonist have continued to provoke and challenge interpretation ever since. Is Hedda a victim or victimizer? Is she heroic in her self-sacrifice or a monstrous femme fatale, damnable in her wanton destruction? Of equal contention are questions of Ibsen's intent and the play's ultimate meaning. To what degree does *Hedda Gabler* fit with the realistic social problem play and its reforming zeal that Ibsen pioneered? How does this often contradictory drama elucidate Ibsen's career and beliefs? Whether from the perspective of theatrical history, biography, psychology, or social criticism,

Hedda Gabler remains one of the stage's most intriguing dramas with a still-powerful modern relevance.

Hedda Gabler stands in Ibsen's body of work as both culmination and new departure. It brings to a close his remarkable series of realistic social problem, or thesis, plays begun in 1877 with *A Pillar of Society* through *A Doll's House* (1879), *Ghosts* (1881), *An Enemy of the People* (1882), and *The Wild Duck* (1884), plays that revitalized the theater by anatomizing contemporary life with recognizable realistic characters and settings. The two plays that preceded *Hedda Gabler*, however, *Rosmersholm* (1886) and *The Lady from the Sea* (1888), recall Ibsen's earlier works, such as *Brand* (1866) and *Peer Gynt* (1867), in their use of symbolism and antirealistic elements. *Hedda Gabler*, in treating the struggles of the individual against social conventions shares a central theme of Ibsen's previous social problem plays as well as his increasing interest in the psychological dilemmas of the isolated individual. In method it marks a final return to the technique of the well-made play of his realistic dramas, while it incorporates a symbolic and mythic subtext that would begin to dominate Ibsen's concluding dramas, from *The Master Builder* (1892), *Little Eyolf* (1894), and *John Gabriel Borkman* (1896) to *When We Dead Awaken* (1899).

When Ibsen wrote *Hedda Gabler* in 1890, he was 62 and an established though highly controversial dramatist, whose works generated considerable appreciation and respect in his native Scandinavia and Germany but were either unperformed or disputed elsewhere. Although the publication of *A Doll's House* in 1879 brought Ibsen international notoriety, it was *Hedda Gabler* that finally established Ibsen's reputation as the master dramatist of Europe and one of the greatest playwrights of all time. Before 1890 Ibsen's work had not been presented in France. In England Ibsen's supporters still contended with a dominant view that Ibsen was a gutter sensationalist dealing in unmentionables. Henry James complained that he found Ibsen's plays "dreary" and not "dramatic, or dramas at all," yet his favorable 1891 review of the first English production, "On the Occasion of *Hedda Gabler*," was symptomatic of a general shift in views. James saw in the play "the picture not of an action but a condition," which fascinated him. The same year George Bernard Shaw published *The Quintessence of Ibsenism*, his ringing endorsement of Ibsen's greatness as a playwright, rivaling and even surpassing William Shakespeare, which vanquished whatever remained of significant critical opposition.

More preliminary notes survive for *Hedda Gabler* than for any other of Ibsen's plays, affording a rare opportunity to trace the development of Ibsen's masterpiece. As early as 1889 Ibsen conceived the idea for a new play about a woman's jealousy of a man with a mission, with the action turning on a misplaced manuscript that represented that mission. Ibsen's notes show him refining his ideas and shaping the play's evolving characters, plot, and motives in fragments of dialogue and clarifying statements. One of the most revealing is the following:

Main Points: 1. They are not all made to be mothers. 2. They are passionate but they are afraid of scandal. 3. They perceive that the times are full of missions worth devoting one's life to, but they cannot discover them.

Ibsen's list captures the core contradictions that the play will explore in a woman who is caught between passionate intensity to transcend the stifling conventions that surround her and a fear of sexuality and love that prevents any meaningful, fulfilling relationship with another and a channel for her passion. Ibsen's fascination with Hedda's psychic and emotional contradictions structures the drama. "It was not my desire to deal in this play with so-called problems," he wrote. "What I principally wanted to do was to depict human beings, human emotions, and human destinies, upon a ground work of certain of the social conditions and principles of the present day."

Hedda Gabler is one of the most compressed and tightly constructed of Ibsen's dramas. Restricted to a single setting—the drawing room of a fashionable Norwegian villa, which Hedda and George Tessman have moved into the night before, following their six-month wedding tour—and to a 36-hour period, the play builds toward its catastrophe with a relentless focus and momentum. The opening scene of act 1—the conversation between George's doting aunt Juliana and Bertha, the maid—supplies the necessary exposition to prepare for Hedda's entrance. The daughter of a deceased general, whose portrait dominates the drawing room, the beautiful and privileged Miss Gabler, at age 29, has surprised everyone by marrying the amiable but somewhat plodding and ineffectual George Tessman on the basis of his prospects as a scholar. Ibsen observed about Hedda and the title of his play that "I intended to indicate thereby that as a personality she is to be regarded rather as her father's daughter than as her husband's wife." When she enters, she shows herself to be the opposite of a happily married newlywed. She is exasperated with her husband and ill mannered, cruelly deflecting the older woman's familiarity and putting Juliana in her place by threatening to have Bertha discharged for leaving her old bonnet on a chair. It is actually Juliana's new hat, which Hedda knows full well, as she confesses in the second act. Hedda is condescending and caustic in dealing with the solicitous attention from George and his aunt, as well as dismissive, particularly of allusions to her possible pregnancy. She manages, however, to summon up considerable interest and ostensible sympathy when an old school rival, Mrs. Thea Elvsted, calls. Thea tells Hedda about her unhappy marriage and her relationship with her stepchildren's tutor, the writer Eilert Lovborg. Thea's devotion has inspired and reformed his erratic genius. However, Thea is convinced that Lovborg may backslide to his previous debauched lifestyle and renew his relationship to an unknown woman who once threatened him with a pistol. Hedda agrees to assist by convincing George to invite Lovborg to visit. The family friend Judge Brack next arrives with the news that George's anticipated professorial appointment may now depend on a competition with Lovborg, whose new book has garnered acclaim. Hedda does not share George's new worries about their financial prospects and is detached enough to state that she is "most eager to see who wins." As the act ends Hedda retires to play with her pistols, her legacy from General Gabler.

Act 2 shows Hedda confiding to Judge Brack about the boredom of her honeymoon and her indifference to her husband, whom she confesses to have married because "her day was done." Disgusted with the concept of love and the knowledge of her own pregnancy, pressed by Judge Brack for a more intimate "triangular" friendship, Hedda reveals herself to be emotionally incapable of committing to another or overcoming her psychological detachment and isolation. Aspiring to magnificence, she admits her one talent is "Boring myself to death." When Lovborg arrives he reveals that he has written a second book even more important than the first and has brought the manuscript with him to read it to George. Instead he is invited to Judge Brack's bachelor party, which he initially refuses. Hedda and Lovborg are left alone to revisit their former relationship; it is made clear that Hedda was Lovborg's former attachment, who once threatened to shoot him. She confesses that his appeal was mainly the thrill of their secret intimacy and that she broke it off when he threatened to become serious. Brought to the brink of confessing a regret for cowardly backing down from their relationship, Hedda is interrupted by Thea's arrival. Lovborg's evident devotion to her and their happy, supportive relationship cause Hedda to urge Lovborg to take a drink and to reconsider attending the Judge's party. Lovborg is, by Hedda's plan, to return later "with vine leaves in his hair." Asked by Thea why she has goaded Lovborg into a probable relapse to his former alcoholic and disorderly state, Hedda confesses: "I want for once in my life to have power to mould a human destiny." On one level Hedda's behavior stems from her jealousy of Thea and resentment of what she has gained and Hedda has lost with Lovborg. On a deeper level her motives are connected with her irresistible urges, as in the bonnet incident, to inflict injury rather than express empathy and love, which frighten and disgust her. In sending Lovborg off to his fate Hedda stage-manages a break from the social proprieties that stifle her, with Lovborg recast as Dionysius, whose passionate free spirit she can release and revel in at a safe unassailable distance.

In act 3 the reversals begin that destroy both Hedda's plans and herself. Waiting all night for the return of George and Lovborg, Hedda learns that Lovborg has drunkenly lost his manuscript, which George has found and brought back for safekeeping. Judge Brack arrives to tell Hedda that Lovborg, far from becoming the free spirit with "vine leaves in his hair," was just an indiscreet drunk enjoying the company of a red-haired singer whom he accused of stealing his manuscript. A despairing Lovborg, who now believes that he has no strength to live the kind of life Thea has helped him achieve, tells Thea that he has destroyed his manuscript, which is equated to "child-murder." To Hedda, however, he admits to have merely lost his manuscript, which he regards as even worse than consciously destroying it. When Lovborg declares his intention to kill himself Hedda urges him to do it "beautifully" and gives him one of her pistols. After he leaves Hedda throws the manuscript in the fire, whispering to herself, "Now I am burning your child, Thea!— Burning it, curly-locks! Your child and Eilert Lovborg's. I am burning—I am burning your child." Having failed to create a proxy Dionysius in life, Hedda now arranges Lovborg's heroic, courageous death, while again betraying her jealousy of Eilert and Thea's literary procreation, which she aborts.

In act 4 Hedda is disappointed a second time. When the news arrives that Lovborg has shot himself Hedda persists in calling his act noble and beautiful: "Eilert Lovborg has himself made up his account with life. He has had the courage to do—the one right thing." Her view changes when Judge Brack reveals the truth—shot, most likely accidentally, while in the red-haired singer's bedroom—to which Hedda asks what curse makes everything she touches "turn ludicrous and mean." It shortly turns even more ludicrous and mean as Judge Brack reveals that he has recognized the pistol Lovborg has used and threatens exposure and scandal unless Hedda submits to him:

> BRACK   Well, fortunately, there is no danger, so long as I say nothing.
>
> HEDDA   [*Looks up at him.*] So I am in your power, Judge Brack. You have me at your beck and call, from this time forward.
>
> BRACK   [*Whispers softly.*] Dearest Hedda—believe me—I shall not abuse my advantage.
>
> HEDDA   I am in your power none the less. Subject to your will and your demands. A slave, a slave then! [*Rises impetuously.*] No, I cannot endure the thought of that! Never!
>
> BRACK   [*Looks half-mockingly at her.*] People generally get used to the inevitable.
>
> HEDDA   [*Returns his look.*] Yes, perhaps.

Faced with a loss of freedom and independence by submitting to the sexual dictates of Brack, Hedda retreats to an inner room where she uses the remaining pistol as she had intended Lovborg to use it: "beautifully," with a shot to the temple. The curtain comes down with Judge Brack's statement: "Good God! People don't do such things."

The play concludes with the core ambiguity of Hedda's act. Is it a cowardly way out of the entrapment she has brought on herself or a courageous act she said she was incapable of to achieve the only freedom that is open to her? Ibsen does not take sides here but offers evidence to support either view, while creating one of the most fascinating of stage heroines who is simultaneously craven in her cruelty and captivating as an irresistible force meeting the immovable objects of time, place, and human nature.

THE SCHOOL FOR SCANDAL   37

(1777)   *by Richard Brinsley Sheridan*

I am prepared to swear that whatever mortifying circumstances attend the life of the Theatre throughout the world, this play will never grow old.
    —Laurence Olivier, in the Folio Society edition of *The School for Scandal*

Echoing Laurence Olivier's assertion of the perpetual freshness and vitality of Richard Brinsley Sheridan's *The School for Scandal* is a review of an 1815 production of the play in the *London Examiner* that plaintively asked, "Why can we not always be young, and seeing *The School for Scandal?*" Romantic essayist Charles Lamb seconds this sentiment in declaring the comedy a delightful respite from the everyday—"two or three hours, well won from the world"—but with a more lasting benefit: "Amidst the mortifying circumstances attendant upon growing old, it is something to have seen *The School for Scandal* in its glory." Sheridan's masterpiece has been called by the essayist William Hazlitt, "the most finished and faultless comedy we have," while Henry James acknowledged, somewhat more reluctantly due to its "coarseness and harshness," that "for real intellectual effort, the literary atmosphere and the tone of society, there has long been nothing like *The School for Scandal.*" The play has, along with Oliver Goldsmith's *She Stoops to Conquer* and Sheridan's earlier *The Rivals*, entered the established English dramatic repertory, one of the few 18th-century English dramas that still command both critical attention and audience delight. Regarded by many as the greatest English playwright between William Shakespeare and George Bernard Shaw, Sheridan has been critically linked with his contemporary Goldsmith through their mutual and roughly simultaneous attempts to revitalize and reanimate the comic drama of their day in the face of a contemporary taste for sentimental, or as Goldsmith called it, "Weeping Comedy." By the 1770s a vogue of sentimentality and genteel decorousness had largely driven low characters, coarse language, and broad comedy from the stage—and laughter with them. Anything beyond the stylized declamation of emotional platitudes and tugs on the heartstrings was regarded as vulgar, crude, and offensive. The sexual frankness and unflattering comic realism of William Congreve and the Restoration dramatists were dismissed as morally debauched and underbred. Pathos and tears were the rewards of the drama of the day, with laughter in public regarded as unseemly and improper. If Goldsmith set out in *She Stoops to Conquer* (1773) to restore the subjects and methods of "Laughing Comedy" by reestablishing the humor of believable human high-born *and* low-born characters in laughable situations outside the dignified drawing room, Sheridan four years later, attempted to restore the satiric wit of the Restoration dramatists, resuscitating the drawing room comedy into a potent source of entertainment and truth telling. *The School for Scandal*, the most popular comedy of manners in English, helped to reinstate brilliant and insightful social drama, aligned with Sheridan's skill in creating original characters, dazzling theatrical scenes, and brilliant dialogue, as the mainline of English comedy. With *The School for Scandal* Sheridan bridged the comic tradition of Shakespeare and Ben Jonson with the later comedies of Oscar Wilde, Shaw, and others.

The author of *The School for Scandal* is one of the most fascinating characters in English literary history. As Lord Eldon deftly summarized, "Every man has his element; Sheridan's is hot water." Scandal, a central topic of *The School for Scandal*, was something its creator knew intimately. Like Goldsmith, and Wilde and Shaw after him, Sheridan was an Irishman who came to London to make his fortune on the stage. Born in Dublin in 1751, Sheridan came from a literary and theatrical family. His grandfather was an intimate of Jonathan Swift; his father was an actor and for a time managed Dublin's Smock Alley Theatre; his mother was a playwright and novelist. Sheridan was educated at Harrow in England, but his family's precarious finances prevented him from going on to university. Instead, after his family had left Dublin to avoid creditors, he joined them in Bath in 1770. There, he wrote his first play, *Ixion*, a burlesque in the form of a play rehearsal, which was never staged but anticipates his last comedy, *The Critic* (1779). He also met the 16-year-old singer Elizabeth Linley, the so-called siren of Bath, who precipitated Sheridan's first exposure to scandal. To help Elizabeth escape the unwanted attention of a married man, Captain Thomas Mathews, Sheridan escorted her to France to deliver her to a convent. Instead they were married illegally, since they were both minors and required parental consent. When they returned to Bath two months later Sheridan engaged in two duels with Mathews, who had insulted the couple publicly. Having bested Mathews in his first duel and forced him to apologize, Sheridan was seriously wounded in the second. The scandal and rumors stirred by the incident reached print, and Sheridan observed that during his recovery he consulted the newspaper to find out whether he was alive or dead. Parental resistance to the match eventually gave way, and the couple was married legitimately in 1773, settling in London.

Refusing to let his wife perform professionally, Sheridan scrambled to support a family, giving up an intended legal career for the more rapid and lucrative prospects of the theater. His first play, *The Rivals*, opened at Covent Garden in 1775 to general disapprobation. Sheridan, however, revised the play, recast it, and offered it again to great success. His second work, a farce, *St. Patrick's Day*, opened a few months later, followed by a hugely popular operatic play, *The Duenna*, cowritten with his father-in-law. At the age of 24, in a single year, Sheridan had written and produced three successful plays, and in 1776 succeeded the great David Garrick as a coowner and the manager of London's other great theater, the Drury Lane, a position he would hold for the next 33 years through ever rising debt and disasters. Sheridan's first work in his new position was an adaptation of Sir John Vanbrugh's Restoration comedy *The Relapse* (1697), called *A Trip to Scarborough* (1777). He followed it with revivals of Congreve's comedies before presenting his own brilliant social comedy, *The School for Scandal*, which opened in 1777, gaining for Sheridan the accolade as "the modern Congreve." Sheridan's final important comedy, *The Critic*, appeared in 1779. In part to gain the protection of elected office from prosecution for debt, in 1780 Sheridan was elected to Parliament where he gained distinction as a brilliant orator, though he remained on the fringe of political power, regarded as an outsider by being an Irishman, a "poor player's son," and theatrical professional. In 1792 the Drury Lane was condemned and torn down, but Sheridan had it rebuilt before mounting his final play, a declamatory tragedy, *Pizarro* (1799). In 1809 fire destroyed the modernized Drury Lane. Asked during the fire why he remained so calm, refreshing himself at a nearby coffeehouse, Sheridan is alleged to have said: "A man may surely be allowed to take a glass of wine by his own fireside." Financial problems resulting from the fire plagued Sheridan for the rest of his life. Ousted from Drury Lane's management due to a charge of mishandling funds, Sheridan lost his seat in Parliament in 1812 (and his protection against arrest for his debts) and was imprisoned several times. His last years were spent in failing health, living in squalid conditions and ignominy at the time of his death in 1816. He was, however, honored with a grand public funeral and burial in Westminster Abbey.

For *The School for Scandal* Sheridan drew on his own experiences contending with the damaging effects of rumor and gossip during his elopement and the resulting duels, as well as aspects of his own complex temperament in the play's contrasted brothers, the profligate but good-natured Charles Surface and the scheming, secretive Joseph. Sheridan's father immediately recognized the resemblance, stating that his son "had but to dip the pencil in his own heart, and he'd find there the characters of both Joseph and Charles Surface." The play's Cain and Abel story is joined to the consequences of a May-December marriage between Sir Peter and Lady Teazle in a skillfully intertwined, complex plot turning on social deception, exposure, and the ever illusive social commodity of "reputation" under the threat of scandalmongers, such as Lady Sneerwell and her circle, who establish the play's social milieu and central themes at the outset. Lady Sneerwell, a fashionable society lady, assisted by her servant, Snake, and later joined by the other members of her "school"—Mrs. Candour, Sir Benjamin Backbite, and Crabtree—are preoccupied with intrigue, manipulation, and falsification, of blackening reputations by converting tidbits of gossip and innuendo into damaging truths. In centering the play on the scandal-loving, deceptive ethos of the *beau mondes*, Sheridan widens his range in *The School for Scandal* from his previous comedies, from exposing human foibles to exploring social values, while broadening his satire of fashionable society by treating such universal themes as the discrepancy between appearance and reality, truth and fiction, surface and substance. Lady Sneerwell is engaged in discrediting the reputation of Charles Surface, reputedly "the most dissipated and extravagant fellow in the country," to separate him from the virtuous Maria, Sir Peter's ward, for herself. She is joined by Charles's "universally well spoken of" brother, Joseph, who, like Molière's Tartuffe, disguises his selfishness and craven calculation as a holier-than-thou man of sentiment and moral platitudes. Lady Sneerwell, understanding the game of social deception, sees through his mask and dismisses one of his set speeches with "O Lud, you are going to be moral and forget you are among friends," as the pair begin to conspire in the deception of Sir Peter Teazle about Charles to help Joseph gain Maria and her fortune.

Some of the play's wittiest dialogue comes from Lady Sneerwell and her scandalous college, as in this snide comment from Sir Benjamin: "It is not that she paints so ill—but when she has finish'd her Face she joins it on so badly to her Neck that she looks like a mended Statue in which the Connoisseur sees at once that the Head's modern tho' the Trunk's antique." In our enjoyment of these witty and snide barbs, Sheridan ironically implicates the audience's own susceptibility to gossip and scandal and their cruel and cutting malice, the cost and consequences of which will form the play's many reversals and recognitions. Lady Teazle, a former unpolished country girl, comes to Lady Sneerwell's scandal school, anxious to master the social niceties of the town in gossip and flirtation. She is followed by the choleric and imperceptive Sir Peter, who is exasperated by his younger wife's modish behavior and susceptible to the deception of Joseph Surface and the slander that has tarred Charles's character partly based on his own jealousy over Charles's supposed liberties with his wife. The scenes of Sir Peter and Lady Teazle's marital tiffs are some of the most entertaining in the play, as Sir Peter threatens to explode under his wife's newly learned, complacent social poses:

> SIR PETER   . . . Recollect Lady Teazle when I saw you first—sitting
> at your tambour in a pretty figured linen gown—with a Bunch of

Keys at your side, and your apartment hung round with Fruits in worsted, of your own working—

LADY TEAZLE   O horrible!—horrible!—don't put me in mind of it!

SIR PETER   Yes, yes Madam and your daily occupation to inspect the Dairy, superintend the Poultry, make extracts from the Family Receipt-book, and comb your aunt Deborah's Lap Dog.

LADY TEAZLE   Abominable!

SIR PETER   Yes Madam—and what were your evening amusements? to draw Patterns for Ruffles, which you hadn't the materials to make—play Pope Joan with the Curate—to read a sermon to your Aunt—or be stuck down to an old Spinet to strum your father to sleep after a Fox Chase.

LADY TEAZLE   Scandalous—Sir Peter not a word of it true—

SIR PETER   Yes, Madam—These were the recreations I took you from—and now—no one more extravagantly in the Fashion— Every Fopery adopted—a head-dress to o'er top Lady Pagoda with feathers pendant horizontal and perpendicular—you forget Lady Teazle—when a little wired gauze with a few Beads made you a fly Cap not much bigger than a blew-bottle, and your Hair was comb'd smooth over a Roll—

LADY TEAZLE   Shocking! horrible Roll!!

SIR PETER   But now—you must have your coach—Vis-a-vis, and three powder'd Footmen before your Chair—and in the summer a pair of white cobs to draw you to Kensington Gardens—no recollection when you were content to ride double, behind the Butler, on a docked Coach-Horse?

LADY TEAZLE   Horrid!—I swear I never did.

SIR PETER   This, madam, was your situation—and what have I not done for you? I have made you woman of Fashion of Fortune of Rank—in short I have made you my wife.

LADY TEAZLE   Well then and there is but one thing more you can make me to add to the obligation.

SIR PETER   What's that pray?

LADY TEAZLE   Your widow.—

The couple's domestic discord is connected with the testing of the Surface brothers when their benefactor, Sir Oliver, returns to London from the East Indies. He refuses to believe the scandal about Charles or to accept the flattering reports about Joseph but will judge them both for himself, in disguise as the needy relation Stanley, to test Joseph's benevolence, and as the moneylender, Mr. Premium, to witness Charles's profligacy firsthand. Charles passes his test during one of the play's most rollicking scenes in which he auctions off the family portraits for ready cash, all except Sir Oliver's: "No, hang it! I'll not part with poor Noll. The old fellow has been very good to me, and, egad, I'll keep his picture while I've a room to put it in." Charles proves himself more than the heartless libertine that scandal has deemed him, appearing far worse than he in fact is. He shows himself deserving sympathy and reclamation, particularly assisted by Sir Oliver's vanity over his nephew's devotion that causes him to overlook Charles's youthful flaws which are shown to be far less grievous than Joseph's hidden vice.

Joseph's exposure comes in a double-barreled explosion of reversals and revelations. First he is unmasked as a hypocrite before Sir Peter in one of the most famous and skillful comic scenes in drama. Visiting Joseph in his library, Lady Teazle endures his calculated seduction, speciously arguing that if Sir Peter does not trust her, she might as well give him grounds for his suspicions. Lady Teazle sees through his argument—"So—so—then I perceive that your prescription is that I must sin in my own Defense—and part with my virtue to preserve my Reputation"—declaring that if it ever came to infidelity "It would be by Sir Peter's ill usage—sooner than your honorable Logic after all." Sir Peter's unexpected arrival begins the famous screen scene, a triumph of dramatic irony, with Lady Teazle in hiding witnessing Sir Peter's declaration to act less like her father and more like her husband by granting her financial independence as well as his hopes on behalf of Joseph's courtship of Maria, both topics that Joseph does not want Lady Teazle to overhear. Charles is next announced, sending Sir Peter into hiding in a closet after Joseph quickly invents a story about "a little French milliner" behind the screen. Now both Sir Peter and Lady Teazle overhear Charles commenting on his brother's dalliance with Lady Teazle, provoking the obtuse Sir Peter to reveal himself. To Charles's accusation that Joseph is "too moral by half," Sir Peter defends him by mentioning the French milliner, touching off the play's great explosion:

CHARLES   Oh, egad, we'll have a peep at the little milliner!

SIR PETER   Not for the world—Joseph will never forgive me.

CHARLES   I'll stand by you—

SIR PETER   Odds Life! Here He's coming—

[SURFACE enters just as CHARLES throws down the Screen.]

CHARLES   Lady Teazle! by all that's wonderful!

SIR PETER   Lady Teazle! by all that's Horrible!

It is said that a journalist, passing outside the Drury Lane just as the screen first fell and the audience exploded in laughter and applause, ran for his life for fear that the building was collapsing.

Joseph's final unmasking before Sir Oliver follows in another delightful scene turning on mistaken identity, reversal, and recognition, and Sir Peter dismisses the Scandalous College, having finally seen the light ("Fiends—Vipers!—Furies!—Oh that their own Venom would choak them—"). However, thematically the play's climax is the falling screen, a perfect metaphor in a drama about the difficulty of penetrating surfaces *and* Surfaces, of distinguishing the false from the genuine. In this delightfully contrived scene, plot and subplot combine with Joseph Surface revealed for what he truly is, a hypocritical counterfeit, and Lady Teazle finally enlightened about her husband's true character and worth. She, along with the audience, is purged of an attraction to fashionable vice and scandal in favor of the genuine and true. The scene also demonstrates clearly why *The School for Scandal* has persisted and is forever young: believable human characters, universal themes, sparkling dialogue, and thrillingly theatrical scenes.

THE PLAYBOY OF THE WESTERN WORLD

(1907)

by John Millington Synge

38

A dramatist once wrote a play
About an Irish peasant,
We heard some of the audience say
"The motive is not pleasant."
Our own opinion, we admit,
Is rather—well—uncertain,
Because we couldn't hear one bit
From rise to fall of curtain.

—Anonymous verse in a Dublin magazine, 1907

If there could be such a thing as a soundtrack for modern drama, several cuts come to mind: the door slamming behind Nora's shattering exit in Henrik Ibsen's *A Doll's House* or the chopping ax at the end of Anton Chekhov's *The Cherry Orchard* symbolizing the relentless, destructive passing of an era. A third might be the explosive outburst that initially greeted John Millington Synge's *The Playboy of the Western World* on the stage of Dublin's Abbey Theatre in January 1907. Allegedly provoked by the use of the indecorous word *shift*, audience outrage at Synge's provoking challenge to consoling notions of Irish experience and identity, as well as accepted principles of drama and language, touched off riots in Dublin through the week of the play's initial run and during an American tour in 1911–12. Synge would be castigated as a falsifier of Irish life and a defamer of the Irish character. His play, however, would eventually be recognized as Synge's masterpiece. In the words of critic Bruce M. Bigley, it is "one of the classics of modern British theater, probably the most anthologized modern full-length play written in English" and, arguably, "the finest play written in English in a couple of centuries." By his death in 1909, at the age of 37, Synge had, along with Lady Augusta Gregory and William Butler

Yeats, established an Irish national theater—the first of its kind in the world—and provided with his seven plays the core dramas for a national repertory. Of them *Riders to the Sea* (1904) is viewed by many as the greatest one-act play in English, and *Playboy* is one of the defining modern dramas that altered key operating principles for drama. By presenting the unflattering realities of Irish life as a means for reaching its poetic and mythic depths, Synge helped make Irish drama unique, relevant, and influential in the modern theater. For writer Edmund Wilson, Synge's attempts to revitalize dramatic language created "the most authentic examples of poetic drama which the modern stage has seen." Asked what playwright he had learned from, Samuel Beckett responded, "Who else but John Millington Synge?" *In The Shadow of the Glen* (1903) had introduced to the stage the eloquent tramp who would become Beckett's specialty. With *The Well of the Saints* (1905) Synge showed Beckett how two old, battered, and blind characters could hold an audience by scarcely moving from where they sat. *Riders to the Sea* and *Playboy* pioneered a dramatic minimalism in which all we see is confined to a bare room, with everything of importance happening offstage. Besides adding key dramatic resources to the modern stage, Synge, particularly in *Playboy*, established the dominant modernist dramatic genre of tragicomedy that would typify the plays of Beckett, Bertolt Brecht, and others. "The striking feature of modern art," Thomas Mann asserted, "is that it has ceased to recognize the categories of tragic and comic, or the dramatic classifications, tragedy and comedy. It sees life as tragic-comedy, with the result that the grotesque is its most genuine style." Synge's *Playboy* is one of the greatest interpretations of this grotesque, tragicomic vision, in which, as Maxim Gorky remarked, "the comical side passes quite naturally into the terrible, while the terrible just as easily becomes comic."

Synge's progress from a somewhat aimless dilettante in search of a subject and a medium to visionary playwright can be traced to his exposure to the elemental life of the Aran Islands on Ireland's west coast. Born in 1871 in the Dublin suburbs, Synge was the youngest of five children in a prosperous upper-class and devout Protestant family. Ill health as a child caused him to be tutored at home, but he earned his degree from Trinity College in 1892 where he studied the violin and music theory and won a scholarship to the Royal Irish Academy of Music. Synge left Ireland in 1893 to study music in Germany, but stage fright caused him to reconsider his aspirations to become a professional musician. Instead he shifted his focus to language and literature, studying at the Sorbonne. In Paris, in 1896, Synge first met poet and dramatist William Butler Yeats, who "had just come from Aran, and my imagination was full of those grey islands where men must reap with knives because of the stones." As Yeats later recalled their fateful meeting,

> [Synge] told me he had been living in France and Germany, reading French and German literature, and that he wished to become a writer.

He had, however, nothing to show but one or two poems and impressionistic essays, full of that kind of morbidity that has its root in too much brooding over methods of expression, and ways of looking upon life, which come, not out of life, but out of literature, images reflected from mirror to mirror. He had wandered among people whose life is as picturesque as the Middle Ages, playing his fiddle to Italian sailors, and listening to stories in Bavarian woods, but life had cast no light into his writings. He had learned Irish years ago, but had begun to forget it, for the only language that interested him was that conventional language of modern poetry which has begun to make us all weary. . . . I said: "Give up Paris. . . . Go to the Aran Islands. Live there as if you were one of the people themselves, express a life that has never found expression."

Synge heeded Yeats's directive and made four extended visits to the Aran Islands between 1898 and 1901, recording his experience in *The Aran Islands* (1907). "In writing out the talk of the people and their stories in this book," Synge explained, ". . . I learned to write the peasant dialect which I use in my plays." The islanders' rich idiom of Elizabethan- and Gaelic-inflected English gave Synge's prose the vibrancy of verse, and he adapted this dialect into a stage language that Allardyce Nicoll has called "the triumph of a new conception, where dialect . . . is used, not to form a contrast with something else, but in and for itself." He also gained from the histories, folktales, and traditions of the Aran Islanders the plot elements and themes for his plays. The core situation of *Playboy*—the sympathetic treatment of a parricide—originated from one islander's stories about

a Connaught man who killed his father with the blow of a spade when he was in passion, and then fled to this island and threw himself on the mercy of some of the natives with whom he was said to be related. They hid him in a hole—which the old man has shown me—and kept him safe for weeks, though the police came and searched for him, and he could hear their boots grinding on the stones over his head. In spite of a reward which was offered, the island was incorruptible, and after much trouble the man was safely shipped to America.

This impulse to protect the criminal is universal in the west. It seems partly due to the association between justice and the hated English jurisdiction, but more directly to the primitive feeling of these people, who are never criminals yet always capable of crime, that a man will not do wrong unless he is under the influence of a passion which is as irresponsible as a storm on the sea. If a man has killed his father, and is already sick and broken with remorse, they can see no reason why he should be dragged away and killed by the law.

Such a man, they say, will be quiet all the rest of his life, and if you suggest that punishment is needed as an example, they ask, "Would any one kill his father if he was able to help it?"

In such a story and its implications, Synge glimpsed an alternative, primal way of life that defied conventional morality and behavior, a vital existence that was ruled by the exigencies of nature and instinct, freed of the deadening artificiality and superfluity of modern civilization. In the Aran Islanders, whom he came to admire for their strength, proud self-sufficiency, and stoical resolve, Synge identified traits of a heroic, noble people that contrasted markedly from the way that the Irish—comic characters of dependable subservience, drunkenness, connivance, and belligerence—had previously been treated on stage. Absorbed by the reality of island life, its values, and dialect, Synge tapped into a deepened sense of Irish consciousness and a rich mythic and poetic reservoir of dramatic situations, characterization, and language that led him to a new kind of dramatic art. As Synge observed in his preface to *Playboy*, contrasting his dramatic subject and method with that of Henrik Ibsen and Émile Zola who deal "with the reality of life in joyless and pallid words":

On the stage one must have reality, and one must have joy; and that is why the intellectual modern drama has failed, and people have grown sick of the false joy of the musical comedy, that has been given them in place of the rich joy found only in what is superb and wild in reality. In a good play every speech should be as fully flavoured as a nut or apple, and such speeches cannot be written by anyone who works among people who have shut their lips on poetry. In Ireland, for a few years more, we have a popular imagination that is fiery and magnificent, and tender; so that those of us who wish to write start with a chance that is not given to writers in places where the springtime of the local life has been forgotten, and the harvest is a memory only, and the straw has been turned into brick.

Synge's discovery of his dramatic subject and voice fortuitously coincided with the means of expressing both in the creation of a new Irish national theater. Conceived in 1897 on a rainy afternoon while Yeats was visiting Lady Gregory at her Galway estate at Coole Park, the Irish Literary Theatre, which debuted in 1899 and was established in Dublin's Abbey Theatre in 1904, was intended as a way to "build up a Celtic and Irish school of dramatic literature." Yeats, Lady Gregory, and others imagined a theater that would contribute to restoring Irish heroic consciousness and "show that Ireland is not the home of buffoonery and of easy sentiment, as it has been represented, but the home of an ancient idealism." Drawing on subjects from Irish history, folklore, and mythology, Yeats and his associates sought to create a drama that could justify and promulgate the drive for Irish empowerment, nationalism, and independence, which was eventually achieved in 1922. It is unlikely that any other theater has played such a decisive role in affecting a people's self-definition and political destiny. Synge's treatment of traditional Irish life as a source of poetic and mythical power supplied exactly the kind of drama the Abbey Theatre hoped to cultivate; while his realism, his insistence on the authentic rather than the flattering, set him on a collision course with a politicized audience who demanded that the drama of an Irish national theater should serve the purposes of propaganda rather than truth.

The Playboy of the Western World is so inflammatory because it comically subverts sacrosanct Irish and universal pieties, most notably heroic values and the implications of hero-worship. Originally conceived as a farce called "The Murderer," the play turns the primal Oedipal crime of parricide into rollicking comedy that blends realism and fantasy into a richly symbolic drama. In a series of comic reversals an alleged murderer is treated as a hero, a male romantically becomes the pursued instead of the pursuer, and some of the most powerful classical and Christian myths are exploded. Christy Mahon, the timorous, archetypal Irish son is ordered by his domineering father to marry "a walking terror" who "did suckle me for six weeks when I came into the world." He lashes out, attacking his father with a spade. On the run, Christy, a mock Oedipus and homeless Odysseus, finds shelter on the desolate coast of Mayo in Michael James Flaherty's shebeen, or country pub, run by his attractive daughter, the independent and self-confident Pegeen Mike, who is preparing for her marriage to Shawn Keogh as the play opens. At the outset Synge stresses not the nobility of Irish rustic life but its squalor and confinement, not its elemental heroism but its frustrations and timidity. Michael James and his cronies are bound for an all-night drunk at a nearby wake, leaving Pegeen Mike unprotected. Her fiancé—the subject of Pegeen's scorn but the best of a sorry lot of marriageable men—is so enthralled to the Catholic Church that he is afraid to be with Pegeen alone without Father Reilly's permission. The outsider and fugitive Christy, therefore, arrives where he is most likely to be appreciated, among people avid for sensation and stifled by the drab inertia of their lives. His concern over the whereabouts of the "peelers" (police) sparks the villagers' curiosity, and they finally gain Christy's confession that he is a fugitive after having split his father's skull. Instead of being horrified the villagers react with wonder and admiration, and it is proposed that Christy serve as pot-boy and Pegeen's protector: "Bravery's a treasure in a lonesome place, and a lad would kill his father, I'm thinking, would face a foxy divil with a pitchpike on the flags of hell."

The comic inversion of a parricide treated as conquering hero begins the process of a deeply resonant comic transformation of Christy. "Up to the day I killed my father," he admits, "There wasn't a person in Ireland knew the kind I was . . . a quiet, simple poor fellow with no man giving me heed." With Christy now the object of attention and admiration for his daring deed, his self-confidence begins to grow. Tapping into his previously untouched resources of imagination and language, Christy begins the process of becoming in fact the dreamed-for hero, brave enough to challenge the Irish patriarchy of family, church, and state and articulate enough to refashion himself into a daring playboy. "Christy Mahon is transformed by overhearing himself," critic Harold Bloom has observed, "and his extraordinary metamorphosis in act 3 is one of the glories of modern drama." Christy becomes for Pegeen her heart's desire, "a fine handsome fellow with a noble brow," daring enough in deed and powerful enough in imagination and poetry to supply an alternative to her stifling life of predictable confinement. Pursued by the Widow Quin and other village girls, besting all comers in the village's sports, Christy's triumph as a playboy is punctured by the arrival of his undead father, Old Mahon. The Widow Quin tries to use the truth to get Christy to marry her, but Christy resists the temptation and is determined to become the daring young hero he is reputed to be and retain Pegeen's admiration by killing his father again. Committing at close range the violent assault for which he was admired by the Mayo villagers, Christy now outrages Pegeen and the locals, who turn on him and hold him for punishment. Christy, son of Mahon, first worshipped, is now betrayed and undergoes a mock crucifixion. "I'll say, a strange man is a marvel," Pegeen declares, "with his mighty talk; but what's a squabble in your back-yard, and the blow of a loy, have taught me that there's a great gap between a gallous story and a dirty deed." The ever-resilient Old Mahon reappears, as Christy says, "coming to be killed a third time," but his third "slaying" is figurative, as Christy's newfound mastery puts his formerly dominating father in his place and exits taking the spirit of romance and liberation with him:

> MAHON —[*grimly, loosening Christy.*]—It's little I care if you put a bag on her back, and went picking cockles till the hour of death; but my son and myself will be going our own way, and we'll have great times from this out telling stories of the villainy of Mayo, and the fools is here. [*To Christy, who is freed.*] Come on now.

> CHRISTY Go with you, is it? I will then, like a gallant captain with his heathen slave. Go on now and I'll see you from this day stewing my oatmeal and washing my spuds, for I'm master of all fights from now. [*Pushing Mahon.*] Go on, I'm saying.

> MAHON Is it me?

> CHRISTY Not a word out of you. Go on from this.

MAHON   —[*walking out and looking back at Christy over his shoulder.*]— Glory be to God! [*With a broad smile.*] I am crazy again! [*Goes.*]

CHRISTY   Ten thousand blessings upon all that's here, for you've turned me a likely gaffer in the end of all, the way I'll go romancing through a romping lifetime from this hour to the dawning of the judgment day. [*He goes out.*]

MICHAEL   By the will of God, we'll have peace now for our drinks. Will you draw the porter, Pegeen?

SHAWN   —[*going up to her.*]—It's a miracle Father Reilly can wed us in the end of all, and we'll have none to trouble us when his vicious bite is healed.

PEGEEN   —[*hitting him a box on the ear.*]—Quit my sight. [*Putting her shawl over her head and breaking out into wild lamentations.*] Oh my grief, I've lost him surely. I've lost the only Playboy of the Western World.

If a proper comedy should end in marriage, *Playboy* closes with a wedding in the offing but with the focus on Pegeen's grief at the prospect and her loss. Christy, the sham hero, has become one in fact. A lie has become the truth, appearance has become reality, and in the process the susceptibility of the Mayo natives (and us all) to create and destroy heroes has been rousingly exposed. Pegeen's failure of imagination to share Christy's emancipation was acted out in its first audience's rejection of the *Playboy* in one of the astounding examples of life imitating art. Just as Christy is made a scapegoat by Pegeen and the Mayo villagers, who reject and ignore core truths about their lives, Synge and his play—the most controversial in Irish history—were similarly scapegoated by an Irish audience outraged by the implications of Synge's drama. Yeats would declare that the inability of its original audience to understand and appreciate *The Playboy of the Western World* was the single serious failure of the Abbey Theatre movement. "The outcry against *The Playboy*," according to Yeats, "was an outcry against its style, against its way of seeing." Synge's triumph in the play is the freshness and the daring of its vision and the startling novelty and timelessness of its comic truths.

THE ICEMAN COMETH

(1946)

by Eugene O'Neill

39

Personally I love it [The Iceman Cometh]*! And I'm sure my affection is not wholly inspired by nostalgia for the dear dead days "on the bottom of the sea," either. I have a confident hunch that this play, as drama, is one of the best things I've ever done. In some ways, perhaps the best. What I mean is, there are moments in it that suddenly strip the secret soul of a man stark naked, not in cruelty or moral superiority, but with an understanding compassion which sees him as a victim of the ironies of life and of himself. These moments are for me the depth of tragedy, with nothing more that can possibly be said.*
—Eugene O'Neill, Letter to Lawrence Langner, August 11, 1940

If LONG DAY'S JOURNEY INTO NIGHT is Eugene O'Neill's greatest personal and dramatic achievement in exorcizing and universalizing his family demons, *The Iceman Cometh* is his most profound play, contending not with a family's tragedy but humanity's. Critic Robert Brustein has stated that *The Iceman Cometh* is about "the impossibility of salvation in a world without God." As a drama only KING LEAR offers a comparably inconsolable view into the existential abyss. In American literature the play's only rival in questioning ultimates is Herman Melville's novel *Moby-Dick*. In a sense *The Iceman Cometh* is O'Neill's version of both DEATH OF A SALESMAN and WAITING FOR GODOT. Hickey, the salesman of life without illusion, is eagerly awaited to enliven the denizens of Harry Hope's Lower Manhattan dive. As in Beckett's play, O'Neill poses the fundamental modern question, What can be believed in the impossibility of any belief? But unlike Godot, Hickey arrives. Like Willy Loman, Hickey is deceived about himself and the lesson he brings and, again like Willy, is ultimately aligned with death and the necessity of illusions. O'Neill's dark parable of nothingness is one of the starkest and most unrelenting of modern dramas. According to critic Normand Berlin, *The Iceman Cometh* "occupies a very important place in O'Neill's career, but its value as a work of dramatic art goes far beyond any considerations based on development or reputation. *The Iceman Cometh* joins *Long Day's Journey* as a masterpiece. It allows the name

O'Neill to be mentioned along with Ibsen, Strindberg, Chekhov, Shaw, and perhaps one or two others, as the giants of modern drama."

The last new play to appear on Broadway during the playwright's lifetime, *The Iceman Cometh* serves as O'Neill's summary philosophical statement after a lifelong quest for spiritual answers. A culminating work, it is also a significant new departure, the first in a remarkable series of four plays, along with *Hughie, Long Day's Journey into Night*, and *A Moon for the Misbegotten*, that crowned O'Neill's extraordinary dramatic career. In 1934 *Days without End*, a dark, spiritual meditation in which its central protagonist, wracked with religious doubts, ultimately finds peace in his Catholic faith, proved both a critical and popular failure, prompting O'Neill's withdrawal from play production, though not from playwriting. For the next five years O'Neill labored on a massive cycle of plays—"A Tale of Possessors Self-dispossessed"—a family saga tracing the decline and fall of America from the Revolutionary War through the 1930s. Although acknowledged as America's greatest dramatist with the Nobel Prize in 1936, O'Neill was widely considered a spent force, with his public silence interpreted as his having found his religious faith but lost his artistic powers. Neither was the case. In 1939, stalled in his multi-play labors, in increasing declining health from a nerve condition that would prevent his writing at all during the last decade of his life, O'Neill grew even more despairing with the war news and retreated into his past. "To tell the truth," he wrote to a friend, "like anyone else with any imagination, I have been absolutely sunk by this damned world debacle. The Cycle is on the shelf, and God knows if I can ever take it up again because I cannot foresee in this country or anywhere else to which it could spiritually belong." In desolation O'Neill told a reporter that humankind ought to be dumped down the nearest drain with the world given over to the ants. Whatever interest he could muster in the human condition was increasingly located in his own past as O'Neill began to outline two plays he "wanted to write for a long time," based on seminal events in his life. One became *Long Day's Journey into Night*; the other, the "Jimmy-the-Priest's, Hell-Hole idea," would become *The Iceman Cometh*. Both concern events in 1912. In this decisive year in O'Neill's life he narrowly survived a six-month-long bender in New York dives and a suicide attempt before being treated for tuberculosis in a sanitarium where he would rebound and commit himself to his vocation as a playwright. Having landed in October 1911 in New York City after a year and a half living as a seaman, O'Neill took up residence in cheap saloons such as Jimmy-the-Priest's and the Hell-Hole, drinking heavily, while absorbing the stories of those he recalled as "sailors on shore leave or stranded; longshoremen, waterfront riffraff, gangsters, down-and-outers, drifters from the ends of the earth" who would serve as models for the characters in *The Iceman Cometh*. There he learned that one of his closest shipmates had committed suicide by jumping overboard in mid-ocean before his roommate committed suicide by jumping from a bedroom window (much like Don Parritt in *The Iceman*). Subsequently, O'Neill tried to kill himself by swallowing an overdose of veronal tablets. Taken to a hospital and revived, O'Neill returned to his family's New London summer home. Working as a reporter on the local paper O'Neill would experience both the happy relationships that he would later describe in his comedy *Ah, Wilderness!* as well as the family traumas he would expose in *Long Day's Journey into Night.*

Probing the meanings and significance of 1912 on his life and his understanding of the human condition, O'Neill turned first to the family of drunks and outcasts he had formed in New York's saloons and flophouses before tackling his own family. "In writing *The Iceman Cometh,*" O'Neill recalled, "I felt I had locked myself in with my memories." O'Neill intended the play "as a denial of any other experience of faith in my plays," something "I want to make life reveal about itself, fully and deeply and roundly." Treating both his past and its import, O'Neill joined a realistic with a symbolic method that universalizes a graphic depiction of life at the bottom with the allegorical and representative. Set at Harry Hope's saloon, the play assembles a large, diverse cast of different nationalities, statuses, and former ways of life—an American melting pot democratized by their common defeat, alcohol, and their "hopeless hope." Their terminal, in the words of cynic Larry Slade to the newcomer Parritt, is

> the No Chance Saloon. It's Bedrock Bar. The End of the Line Café, The Bottom of the Sea Rathskeller! Don't you notice the beautiful calm in the atmosphere? That's because it's the last harbor. No one here has to worry about where they're going next, because there is no farther they can go. It's a great comfort to them. Although even here they keep up the appearances of life with a few harmless pipe dreams about their yesterdays and tomorrows, as you'll see for yourself if you're here long.

Larry introduces the key concept of the play in the pipe dream, a version of Henrik Ibsen's life-lie, the illusion that alone makes life supportable. The play will concern the ways in which human beings generate meaning in a meaningless world.

Echoing both the setting and collective protagonist method of Maxim Gorky's THE LOWER DEPTHS, as well as the concept of the life-sustaining illusion in Ibsen's *The Wild Duck, The Iceman Cometh* exceeds both plays in its depth of characterization, the daring reach of its existential vision, and its symphonic structure. As one of O'Neill's finest interpreters, director José Quintero, has argued, *The Iceman Cometh* "was not built as an orthodox play. It resembles a complex musical form, with themes repeating themselves with slight variations, as melodies do in a symphony. It is a valid device, though O'Neill has often been criticized for it by those who do not see the strength and depth of meaning the repetition achieves." Taking the form of a sequence of monologues cycling back again and again to the same core theme of the pipe dream, as well as resembling a Greek drama with chorus and three central characters—Hickey, Slade, and Parritt—*The Iceman Cometh* achieves its impressive force through its reiteration and counterpoint. In rehearsal, when an assistant director pointed out to him that he had repeated the pipe dream idea 18 separate times, O'Neill famously responded: "I *intended* it to be repeated eighteen times!" Equally intentional was the first act's thorough introduction of the bar's denizens before the entrance of Hickey at its conclusion. Adamant in resisting cuts, O'Neill wanted to build "up the complete picture of the group as it now is in the first part—the atmosphere of the place, the humor and friendship and human warmth and deep inner contentment at the bottom." Without this "you wouldn't feel the same sympathy and understanding for them, or be so moved by what Hickey does to them."

Opening in the back room of the bar, the regulars await the imminent arrival of the hardware salesman Theodore Hickman (Hickey) for his annual bender celebrating Harry Hope's birthday. They include "Jimmy Tomorrow," a former journalist; Willie Oban, a Harvard Law School graduate; Joe Mott, the onetime proprietor of a black gambling house; the "General" and the "Captain," Boer and British former adversaries; Ed Mosher, an ex–circus grifter; Pat McGloin, an ex–police lieutenant; and Hugo Kalmar, once the editor of revolutionary periodicals. They, along with Larry Slade, a disillusioned former anarchist, and Don Parritt, the son of a prominent leader of the movement, are, along with Harry, the dive's lodgers, and the 12 disciples for Hickey's reenactment of a nihilistic Last Supper. Others include three prostitutes—Pearl, Margie, and Cora—who prefer the designation "tarts"; the night bartender, their pimp, Rocky Pioggi, who prefers to be called their "manager"; and the day bartender, Chuck Morello. Most are stirred from their alcoholic stupor to reveal their present disappointments that have landed them here and the redemptive dream of tomorrow that sustains them. Until that day, as Willie declares, "Would that Hickey or Death would come!" Hickey at least promises endless free rounds and good jokes, but when he finally arrives they learn that he is on the wagon, no longer needing booze because "I finally had the guts to face myself and throw overboard the damned lying pipe dream that'd been making me miserable." Instead of the oblivion or distraction they crave Hickey brings the reality principle, which he intends to use to save them as he has been saved. "All I want," he says as the act ends, "is to see you happy."

Act 2 opens with the preparations for the midnight birthday party. Rather than the peace and contentment Hickey has promised everyone, his message of salvation through giving up pipe dreams and their attendant guilt and misery brings only dissatisfaction and dissension. Under the assault of Hickey's sobering message the regulars have retreated into their rooms and only reluctantly emerge for the celebration. Their former support of one anothers' pipe dreams is shown breaking down into enmity and accusations from the perspective Hickey has given them. As the celebration, considerably dampened by Hickey's badgering and challenges to their illusions, gets under way, Larry, referring to Hickey's old joke about his wife and the iceman, asks whether Hickey's conversion is due to his actual discovery of his wife's infidelity. Hickey responds by telling them that "my dearly beloved wife is dead." The act closes with Hickey deflecting their sympathy by asserting that "she is at peace like she always longed to be. . . . Why, all that Evelyn ever wanted out of life was to make me happy."

Act 3 begins the next morning on the fateful tomorrow in which everyone's pipe dream is to be actualized. A halting procession of the regulars makes their way downstairs, freshly attired to face the outside world, while handing in their keys and vowing never to return. Chuck and Cora are going to be married before settling on a New Jersey farm; Joe is to reopen his gambling house; Willie, Jimmy, Mosher, and McGloin are heading out for new or old jobs; the Captain and the General are bound for home. Harry Hope, the former Tammany politician who has not left his bar for the last 20 years, intends to take his long-threatened walk about the old ward. Each must force himself through the bar's swinging doors, reluctant to leave and dreading what awaits outside. Harry is the last to exit, but when Rocky predicts that he will turn back, Hickey agrees, "Of course, he's coming back. So are all the others. By tonight they'll all be back. You dumbbell, that's the whole point." Hickey reveals that he has not been helping his friends realize their dreams but their delusions with the guilt-free relief that he is certain will come from no more hopes. When Harry returns feeling "like a corpse," Larry says Hickey has brought instead the "peace of death" and demands to know how Evelyn died. Hickey reveals that she was murdered as the act ends with him trying to coerce Harry into the happiness he was sure would follow after facing the truth about himself.

By the fourth act, when the full revelations about Hickey come, it is clear how deft O'Neill has been in generating suspense in a play in which very little happens, while ironically shifting the audience's sympathy from Hickey to his congregation. As the enigmatic Hickey is revealed to be the murderer of his beloved wife, the pipe dreams that initially seemed the source of the dilemmas for the habitués of Harry Hope's are revealed to be their only viable response for the deadening realization of nothingness when illusions die. The action returns to the back room of the first act, late the following day. All the regulars have returned, their hopes shattered, like Harry's, "in a numb stupor which is impervious to stimulation." Hickey has failed to deliver his promised relief, and, as Larry asserts, "He's lost his confidence that the peace he's sold us is the real McCoy, and it's made him uneasy about his own." To disprove Larry's accusation and to offer his own story as an example for the others, Hickey begins an extraordinary monologue, the longest in O'Neill's works, confessing his past transgressions and what really happened to Evelyn. Increasingly guilty over his failure as a husband and his broken promises to reform in the face of his wife's sympathy and forgiveness, Hickey admits that "I hated myself more and more, thinking of all the wrong I'd done to the sweetest woman in the world who loved me so much. . . . So I killed her." Hickey's admission of shooting Evelyn in her sleep is followed by an even more devastating revelation:

And then I saw I'd always known that was the only possible way to give her peace and free her from the misery of loving me. I saw it meant peace for me, too, knowing she was at peace. I felt as though a ton of guilt was lifted off my mind. I remember I stood by the bed and suddenly I had to laugh. I couldn't help it, and I knew Evelyn would forgive me. I remember I heard myself speaking to her, as if it was something I'd always wanted to say: "Well, you know what you can do with your pipe dream now, you damned bitch!" . . . No! That's a lie! I never said—! Good God, I couldn't have said that! If I did, I'd gone insane! Why, I loved Evelyn better than anything in life! You've known old Hickey for years! You know I'd never—You've known me longer than anyone, Harry. You know I must have been insane, don't you Governor?

The full truth is that Hickey killed his wife not out of love but from hate, that all along he has relied on the pipe dream that he loved his wife, while his curse exposes the lie. The only way to retain the illusion that he did love Evelyn is to plead insanity. The others readily seize on Hickey's defense to protect their own dreams. As Harry explains to the detectives who have come for Hickey, "Every one of us noticed he was nutty the minute he showed up here! Bejees, if you'd heard all the crazy bull he was pulling about bringing us peace—like a bughouse preacher escaped from an asylum! If you'd seen all the damned-fool things he made us do! We only did them because—[He hesitates—then defiantly] Because we hoped he'd come out of it if we kidded him along and humored him." All readily agree. As he is led out Hickey tells the detective: "Do you suppose I give a damn about life now? Why, you bonehead, I haven't got a single damned lying hope or pipe dream left!" But he persists with the illusion: "Why, Evelyn was the only thing on God's earth I ever loved! I'd have killed myself before I'd ever have hurt her!"

Hickey's confession stimulates Parritt to confess to Larry the real motive for betraying his wanted mother to the police: Not out of patriotism as previously asserted but "It was because I hated her." The absolution Parritt seeks is delivered by Larry who orders him to "Get the hell out of life." When Parritt complies by throwing himself out of an upstairs' window, Larry sits apart from the fellowship that has returned to Harry Hope's, fueled by the restored, life-supporting pipe dreams of each of the company:

LARRY   [*In a whisper of horrified pity*] Poor devil! [*A long-forgotten faith returns to him for a moment and he mumbles*] God rest his soul in peace. [*He opens his eyes—with a bitter self-derision*] Ah, the damned pity—the wrong kind, as Hickey said! Be God, there's no hope! I'll never be a success in the grandstand—or anywhere else! Life is too much for me! I'll be a weak fool looking with pity at the two sides of everything till the day I die! [*With an intense bitter sincerity*] May that day come soon! [*He pauses startedly, surprised at himself—then with a sardonic grin*] Be God, I'm the only real convert to death Hickey made here. From the bottom of my coward's heart I mean that now!

If Larry is finally aligned to death, and to Hickey, the Iceman, who kills what his friends need to live, the others choose life, sustained by their dreams and one another. As O'Neill wrote in a letter, people must live in the "pipe dream—or die. . . . Love remains (once in a while); friendship remains (and that is rare, too). The rest is ashes in the wind!" Larry's vision, the two sides he is condemned to see—life's lacerating meaninglessness and the significance we manufacture in the dreams that forever elude us yet connect us to life and love rather than death—is finally shared by the audience through O'Neill's remarkable parable of the human condition played out in a cheap Manhattan saloon.

THE LOVE SUICIDES AT SONEZAKI

40

(1703)
by Chikamatsu Monzaemon

The Love Suicides at Sonezaki *created a new genre of Japanese theater, the sewamono, or plays about contemporary life. The Noh plays invariably dealt with the distant past, and Kabuki plays that in fact treated recent events always masked them by pretending that the story was set in the world of some centuries earlier. It goes without saying that the authorities would not tolerate criticism of the regime, but even if the treatment was favorable, no person of consequence could be represented on the stage. Tokubei and Ohatsu, however, were so insignificant in the eyes of the authorities that their stories could be enacted without censorship. . . . [Chikamatsu] seems to have been insisting that tragedy was possible even in such peaceful, humdrum times, and he emphasizes his point by choosing quite ordinary people for the heroes and heroines of various plays. The first tragedy composed in English with a common man for its hero,* The London Merchant *(1731) by George Lillo, has a preface in which the author argues that plays treating people of the middle class can be just as tragic as those that deal with people of superior rank. This was the discovery that Chikamatsu made some thirty years earlier.*

—Donald Keene, *"The Love Suicides at Sonezaki,"*
in *Masterworks of Asian Literature in Comparative Perspective*

Considered Japan's greatest playwright, Chikamatsu Monzaemon, often referred to as "the Japanese Shakespeare," expanded the boundaries of Japanese drama by incorporating a wider representation of life on stage than had previously been attempted. What makes his achievement even more remarkable is that the realism that Chikamatsu pioneered was performed in Japan's puppet theater. *Sonezaki Shinjū* (*The Love Suicides at Sonezaki*) is the first of Chikamatsu's great domestic tragedies and one of the first dramas to elevate ordinary characters to tragic status. Like Lady Murasaki whose 11th-century narrative masterpiece, *The Tale of Genji*, anticipated the realistic development of the western novel by nearly 800 years, Chikamatsu's *The Love Suicides at Sonezaki* is the earliest example of a realistic middle-class drama, which would not take hold in the West for another 150 years.

None of William Shakespeare's tragic heroes resemble in social rank or background the majority of his audience. Lower and middle-class individuals were fine for comedy, but tragedy, as Aristotle maintained, depended on individuals of high rank. Chikamatsu would alter that restriction by exploring characters from the lower orders—merchants, clerks, and prostitutes—engaged in ordinary activities, gaining for them through his great artistry an unprecedented tragic dignity.

Chikamatsu Monzaemon was born in 1653 in the province of Echizen. A member of a samurai family, Chikamatsu came to live in Kyoto after his father, for reasons unknown, lost his position as a retainer of the daimyo (feudal lord) of Echizen and became a *rōnin*, or masterless samurai. In an autobiographical account written shortly before his death, Chikamatsu summarized: "I was born into a hereditary family of samurai but left the martial profession. I served in personal attendance on the nobility but never obtained the least court rank. I drifted in the market place but learned nothing of trade." Chikamatsu's failures would be compensated by a breadth of experience taking in 17th-century Japan's three major, nonpeasant social ranks—samurai, nobility, and merchants. It was likely in Chikamatsu's service as a page among the nobility who patronized the dramatic arts that Chikamatsu had his initial exposure to the new theater that was flourishing in 17th-century Japan. Chikamatsu pursued a theatrical career during the second great flowering of Japanese drama following the development of Noh in the 15th century that produced the other enduring Japanese dramatic forms—the puppet theater (later called Bunraku) and Kabuki.

The first mention of puppetry in Japan dates from the eighth century, and throughout the Heian period (794–1185) traveling puppet performers roamed the country with their "stage," a rectangular box open at the front, carried on their backs. In the 17th century a new dramatic art form evolved from the fusion of puppetry with the recitation of storytellers, accompanied by music. The popularity of the puppet theater, called *jōruri* after the term used to designate the narrator, or chanter, during the 17th century coincided with the rise of Kabuki. A woman dancer named Okuni is credited with performing the first Japanese plays of contemporary urban life, brief playlets interspersed by singing and dance that developed into multiscene narrative plays of Kabuki in which elements of Noh drama were adapted for a wider, socially diverse audience and serving less a religious function than a secular one. The great popularity of the new dramatic forms stemmed from their contemporary relevance, initiating a realistic element in Japanese drama that reflected Japan's emerging class of merchants, traders, and artisans. In Western terms Noh drama corresponds to the medieval miracle and moralty plays, while Kabuki and the puppet theater resemble Elizabethan drama's wider interest in actuality.

Chikamatsu's career as a dramatist began in 1683, at the age of 30, when he wrote the puppet play *Yotsugi Soga* (*The Soga Successors*), which was selected by Takemoto Gidayū (1651–1714), the period's most celebrated chanter of the puppet theater, to open his new theater in Osaka in 1684. The chanter functioned as a narrator and commentator on the action, as well as providing speech for the puppets. His words were accompanied by the samisen, a guitarlike instrument introduced to Japan from China in the 16th century. The puppets in Chikamatsu's day were each operated by one man who remained visible to the spectators. A successful performance relied on an ideal balance of three elements—the play's text delivered by the chanter, the musical accompaniment, and the puppets. Chikamatsu's first major play was the heroic drama *Shusse Kagekiyo* (1684, *Kagekiyo Victorious*), which, due to its superior dramatic construction, expressive language, and considerable literary merits unprecedented in the puppet theater, is regarded by scholar Donald Keene as "so important a work that it is considered the first 'new' puppet play." Despite Chikamatsu's notoriety as a playwright for the puppet theater, between 1684 and 1695 he also produced many Kabuki plays, mainly for Sakata Tōjūrō, the leading actor of the day, a collaboration that was so successful that for the next decade (1695–1705) Chikamatsu wrote mainly for Kabuki. When Sakata retired from the stage in 1705, Chikamatsu wrote exclusively for the puppet theater until his death in 1725. Various conjectures have been advanced to explain Chikamatsu's decision to devote his artistic maturity to the puppet theater. He may have been convinced that no actor of comparable skills would follow Sakata Tōjūrō, or he may have grown frustrated by the Kabuki "star" system that privileged the actor over the text. Chikamatsu may have grown frustrated at the liberties taken by the actors and returned to the puppet theater to have his plays performed as written. This decision, however it was reached, presents the playwright with an enormous challenge, particularly one like Chikamatsu whose plays show an ambition in displaying a full range of complex human emotions and situations. Whereas live actors have the ability to alter expressions and show change and development, puppets come in types—hero, villain, and clown—with their identities firmly set in wood.

The Love Suicides at Sonezaki shows Chikamatsu simultaneously contending with the fixed conventions of the puppet theater and expanding its dramatic possibilities. In 1703 the actual suicides in Osaka of Tokubei, a shop assistant, and Ohatsu, a prostitute, had generated gossip and scandal. In contrast to the play that Chikamatsu created about this incident, their deaths were generally regarded as sordid and far from edifying, with one account sternly condemning their having "polluted the woods of Sonezaki" with their deaths disrespectfully within the precincts of a Shinto shrine. Chikamatsu's play explores what motivated these lovers' deaths. Contemporary accounts suggested that the lovers acted because they had grown tired of living; Chikamatsu invents the villain Kuheiji and a set of social circumstances with which the lovers must contend to elevate their actions to the level of the tragic, ennobled by the strength and purity of their love for each other.

The first of the play's three scenes is located at the Ikudama Shrine in Osaka on May 2, 1703, suggesting a faithful representation of events and the immediate world of Osaka. Tokubei, in contrast to a conventional stage hero, is a young clerk "with the firm of Hirano," trading in soy sauce. "Chikamatsu created in Tokubei," Keene has asserted, "a hero of a kind not found in Western drama before the twentieth century." Rather than a paragon of virtue or strength, Tokubei is a mixed character, initially characterized by his gullibility and embarrassed defeat, only eventually rising to the tragic occasion. Meeting his lover, the geisha Ohatsu, as she awaits the return of Gihei, a wealthy countryman who has secured her services, Tokubei explains his recent absence by telling how his uncle and employer had arranged for Tokubei to marry his wife's niece, securing the bargain by giving the dowry to Tokubei's stepmother. Rejecting his master's plan, Tokubei managed to retrieve the money from his stepmother but has lent it temporarily as a favor to his friend Kuheiji, who has promised to repay the loan before the deadline set by Tokubei's employer. When Kuheiji passes with his cronies, he first pretends to know nothing of the loan, and when confronted with the promissory note affixed with his seal, he cleverly declares that he had lost his seal before the date of the promissory note and accuses Tokubei of using the found seal on the note to extort money from him. Unable to disprove Kuheiji's swindle, the maddened Tokubei assaults Kuheiji but, again unlike the conventional hero, is no match for Kuheiji's entourage, who overwhelms him. As the fight rages Ohatsu is compelled to depart in Gihei's palanquin. In addition to the play's less-than-exemplary protagonist, what is novel here is the way in which money and the mundane control the destinies of the characters. For one of the first times in dramatic literature economics are at the heart of a tragedy, establishing the conflict between the characters' desires and the inflexible laws of the commercial social order. The lack of money contributes to Ohatsu becoming a prostitute and prevents Tokubei from buying her contract and loving her exclusively. Financial need establishes an unbridgeable social divide for the lovers. As Chikamatsu conceives their story, suicide becomes the only means that they can afford to overcome this divide.

The second scene is set later that evening in the brothel where Ohatsu works. Unsure what happened to Tokubei, Ohatsu sees him outside the window and goes out to him. Called back by her master, she has him conceal himself under her outer robe and hide under the porch. As Keene has observed, "Surely no hero of a tragedy has ever made a less dignified entrance!" Tokubei is now in a position to overhear and react to the arrival of Kuheiji, who abuses him. Ohatsu asserts that since her lover is unable to disprove his friend's deceit and repay the dowry Tokubei has no choice but to kill himself. When Kuheiji responds that he will take good care of her after his lover's death, Ohatsu exclaims:

Could I go on living even a moment if separated from Toku? Kuheiji, you dirty thief! Anyone hearing your silly lies can only suspect you. I'm sure that Toku intends to die with me, as I with him.

Their suicide pact is sealed by Tokubei's taking Ohatsu's foot that hangs over the edge of the porch and passing it over his throat. The gesture represents the turn in the play in which the formerly foolish Tokubei begins to earn his heroic stature by his commitment to his lover. The growing sympathy that the audience feels for Tokubei and Ohatsu is enhanced by Chikamatsu's masterfully exploiting the conventions of the puppet theater by having the lovers' journey to the place where they are to die narrated with exquisite lyricism:

> Farewell to this world, and to the night farewell.
> We who walk the road to death, to what should we be likened?
> To the frost by the road that leads to the graveyard,
> Vanishing with each step we take ahead:
> How sad is this dream of a dream!

As the lovers confront the finality and terror of their decision, they are sustained by their love and their determination to become "an unparalleled example of a lovers' suicide." After Tokubei confesses his sins and Ohatsu bids farewell to her family, she begs him to "kill me quickly!" Then in excruciatingly realistic detail, the narrator relates how Tokubei "tries to steady his weakening resolve, but still he trembles, and when he thrusts, the point misses. Twice or thrice the flashing blade deflects this way and that until a cry tells it has struck her throat." Determined to "draw our last breaths together," Tokubei kills himself, and the play concludes with the narrator's elegy:

> No one is there to tell the tale, but the wind that blows through Sonezaki Wood transmits it, and high and low alike gather to pray for these lovers who beyond a doubt will in the future attain Buddahood. They have become models of true love.

The Love Suicides at Sonezaki created a popular sensation and a vogue. Chikamatsu would follow it with several other love-suicide plays whose poetic immediacy and dramatic impact prompted imitations on stage and in life. The genre became so popular (and tempting) that the authorities considered it a social threat, banning all plays with the word *shin* (suicide) in the title. Chikamatsu's work until his death in 1725 continued to mature with an increasing diversity of incident and complexity of character built on the realistic foundation that *The Love Suicides at Sonezaki* initially established in Japanese and world drama.

EVERYMAN

41

(c. 1500)

by Anonymous

The great vice of English drama from Kyd to Galsworthy has been its aim of realism was unlimited. In one play, Everyman, _and perhaps in that one play only, we have a drama within the limitations of art. . . . It is essential that a work of art should be self-consistent, that an artist should consciously or unconsciously draw a circle beyond which he does not trespass: on the one hand actual life is always the material, and on the other hand an abstraction from actual life is a necessary condition to the creation of a work of art._

—T. S. Eliot, "Four Elizabethan Dramatists"

For T. S. Eliot the greatness of _Everyman_—the most famous medieval drama in English and the best example of the morality play—rests in its totality of vision, in its joining powerful spiritual and human insights with "ordinary dramatic interest." "The religious and the dramatic are not merely combined," Eliot asserts, "but wholly fused. Everyman is on the one hand the human soul in extremity, and on the other any man in any dangerous position from which we wonder how he is going to escape." A dramatized parable or allegory of the final judgment of a soul, _Everyman_ achieves its sustaining force by the skill with which it embodies its abstractions in the particular to reach the universal. _Everyman_ accordingly serves as a crucial prototype for Western drama and a key link between classical drama and the extraordinary flowering of Renaissance drama.

Possibly an English translation of the Dutch work, _Elckerlijc_ (or _Elckerlijk_), published in 1495 and attributed to Petrus Dorlandus, _Everyman_ may also have been adapted, along with the Dutch play, from an earlier, now-lost common source. There are no records of actual performances of _Everyman_ but printed versions of the play, first appearing in 1508, were popular through the 16th century, even as religious dramas in England became seditious during the Reformation and were banned when Elizabeth I took the throne in 1558. Although the morality play is an unmistakable influence on Elizabethan drama, _Everyman_ disappeared from view. It would not be reprinted until 1773.

In 1901, it became the first medieval play to be revived in a modern production. Directed by William Poel, the revised *Everyman* was praised for its "naïve simplicity and uncompromising sincerity," and the play became the sensation of the London theater season. William Butler Yeats and George Bernard Shaw admitted to being influenced by Poel's successful production. After seeing it German director Max Reinhardt commissioned Austrian playwright Hugo von Hofmannsthal to write a German adaptation, *Jedermann*, which was first produced in Berlin in 1911 and, after its debut in 1913 at the Salzburg Cathedral square, would ever after become a featured part of the annual Salzburg Festival. Echoes of *Everyman* are detectable in the existential plays of Jean-Paul Sartre and Samuel Beckett and in Bertolt Brecht's expressionistic dramas, and the play continues to be performed around the world, a testimony to its ability to communicate a powerful vision of the human condition that transcends the era and the doctrines of its origin.

Everyman serves as well as an essential text for illustrating the evolution of drama in western Europe in the period between the classical age and the Renaissance. What is most striking in considering the reemergence of drama in the Middle Ages is the role played by the Christian Church both in halting the classical dramatic tradition and in fostering the conditions for drama's revival. The number of theaters and performances of Roman drama reached a high point in the fourth century before significantly waning. Drama's decline to near extinction was precipitated both by the breakup of the Roman Empire and the burgeoning Christian Church's opposition to an art form with distinctively pagan roots. Theologians regarded drama as an illusionist art allied to idolatry, magic, and devilry. Church authorities actively dissuaded Christians from attending performances, threatening excommunication of anyone who went to the theater rathen than to church on holy days. Actors were forbidden the sacraments unless they foreswore their profession. The last recorded dramatic performance in the classical tradition occurred in Rome in 549, and for almost a half-millennia organized theatrical performances effectively disappeared in western Europe, with the remnants of an acting tradition fitfully maintained by traveling entertainers. Ironically the church, which had played such a decisive role in closing the theaters and halting a literary dramatic tradition, returned drama to the similar initial conditions preceeding the emergence of formal drama in Greece in the sixth century B.C. As classical comedy and tragedy originated from religious celebrations and rituals, Western drama would be restored in the Middle Ages from a comparable spiritual foundation to serve a parallel religious need. Antiphonal songs, sung responses or dialogues, like the dithyramb in Greek protodrama, were eventually incorporated into celebrations from the liturgical calendar, such as Christmas, Epiphany, and Easter. Short illustrative scenes evolved to vivify worship for a congregation that did not understand Latin, the liturgical language. First performed in the monasteries and churches around the 10th century, with clergymen or choir boys as actors, liturgical dramas would by the 13th century grow far too elaborate—with multiple scenes, actors, and stage effects—for proper staging indoors. Performances moved outdoors with nonclerical actors and secular organizations such as trade guilds producing vernacular mystery plays, scriptural dramas representing scenes from the Old and New Testament; miracle plays, dramatizing incidents from the lives of the saints; and morality plays, enacting the allegorical spiritual struggle of an average individual. Like Attic Greek plays, medieval drama therefore evolved out of religious observances, was supported by wealthy citizens or organizations to serve both a civic and religious function, and, just as the Greek choral performances in honor of Dionysus were expanded to enact the stories of multiple gods and heroes, medieval drama gradually became more secularized by incorporating aspects of familiar life and recognizable situations and characters in its performances. Enacted episodes from the liturgical calendar were joined to form complete cycles of biblical plays in increasingly more complicated productions involving realistic stage effects. Religious dramas became all-purpose moral entertainments combining serious devotional and didactic purposes with low comic, often bawdy farce. By the 15th century religious drama had established a strong, robust theatrical tradition in western Europe that would be combined with the rediscovery of the classical dramatic tradition in the Renaissance to create the greatest explosion of dramatic achievement in history.

Everyman is the best-known example of the morality play, the late-developing medieval dramatic genre that is the essential bridge between religious and secular drama. If mystery plays treated the divine as revealed in the Bible, and miracle plays, the saintly, morality plays took for their subject the spiritual struggles of representative and recognizable mixed human characters. Morality plays, which flourished between 1400 and 1550, are didactic allegories enacting the combat between Vice and Virtue for the possession of a human soul. Examples in English include *Pride of Life* (c. 1410), *Castle of Perserverance* (c. 1425), and *Mankind* (c. 1475). *Everyman* is actually atypical of the form due to its restricted scope. Instead of covering the temptations of an entire life, as do most morality plays, *Everyman* achieves its unity and intensity by concentrating only on the preparation for death, on the last act in the story of salvation or damnation. The usual enacted battle between Vice and Virtue for possession of an individual soul is over at the play's outset. Everyman is a confirmed sinner who is to be shocked into a reevaluation of his life and values. As the play opens, God, disappointed in humankind's sinfulness, in which "Every man liveth so after his own pleasure," ignoring their inevitable end and purpose on earth, proclaims a final reckoning. He orders Death to summon Everyman to "A pilgrimage he must on him take, / Which he in no wise may escape." Everyman greets this news with a range of psychologically believable reactions from incredulousness, delusion, and self-pity to rationalization that it might not be as bad as he fears, even attempting to bribe Death to "defer this matter till another day." Death is implacable but agrees to allow Everyman to gather whomever he can persuade to accompany him on his journey to the grave.

Having lost his initial battle with Death to avoid his reckoning, Everyman is next reduced to helpless, isolated despair as one by one his expected faithful and steadfast companions—Fellowship, Kindred, and Cousin—abandon him. Forced to forego human companionship from friends and relatives on his journey, Everyman next turns to his Goods, which he had valued most of all, for support. Convinced that money is all powerful, Everyman is corrected by Goods, who says that love for him is "contrary to love everlasting":

> A season thou hast had me in prosperity.
> My condition is man's soul to kill;
> If I save one, a thousand I do spill.
> Weenest though that I will follow thee?
> Nay, not from this world, verily.

If the material fails him, Everyman next turns to his virtuous accomplishments on earth, to Good Deeds, who is willing to accompanying him but is constrained by Everyman's sins, and the pilgrim is sent to Good Deeds's sister, Knowledge, to learn what he must do. At this point in the drama Everyman's spiritual journey has forced him to look from exterior support to internal resources. Knowledge provides the key to Everyman's salvation, leading him to Confession and Penance that releases Good Deeds to accompany him to his reckoning. The play thus embodies essential Christian doctrine—that a person's life on earth is fleeting and deceptive, that all must face death alone, and that good deeds are worthless without self-knowledge, faith, contrition, and absolution—in understandable human terms that invite audience identification. The play's message is delivered not through direct statement but in the interaction of a psychologically understandable Everyman with the personified and magnified abstractions that underscore a universal meaning.

No longer reluctant and despairing, with a renewed faith and self-understanding, Everyman now feels comforted and confident to undertake his journey, summoning Beauty, Strength, Discretion, and Five Wits to join Good Deeds as his companions. Doctrinally the play seems to have reached a secure moral conclusion. Everyman is no longer deceived about the world or himself and is now ready to face his final reckoning aided by worthy intrinsic companions. The play, however, delivers a surprising dramatic reversal. The companions that Everyman has counted on one by one fall away as he comes closer and closer to his journey's end at the grave. The allegory here captures an entire life in miniature in which a person's essential attributes eventually are defeated by time along life's journey: the beauty of youth fades, the strength of manhood weakens, mental acuity in maturity declines, and the senses of old age fail. In a neat, structural parallel the excuses of Fellowship, Kindred, Cousin, and Goods not to accompanying Everyman on his journey are matched by the regrets of Beauty, Strength, Discretion, and Five Wits for failing to complete the pilgrimage. Once again Everyman is stripped of support to face death alone, forced to give up his dependence not only on the externals of life but the internal faculties and attributes as well. Everyman reaches an existential moment of dreadful isolation that prompts his cry, "O Jesu, help! All hath forsaken me." But he is consoled by Good Deeds, who alone will stay with him to the end:

> All earthly things is but vanity:
> Beauty, Strength, and Discretion do man forsake,
> Foolish friends, and kinsmen, that fair spake—
> All fleeth save Good Deeds, and that am I.
> . . .
> Fear not; I will speak for thee.

Good Deeds will make the case for Everyman's salvation, and the pilgrim seeking God's mercy is shown sinking into his grave. An Angel is heard welcoming his soul to his heavenly reward:

> Now shalt thou into the heavenly sphere,
> Unto the which all ye shall come
> That liveth well before the day of doom.

Everyman converts the theological doctrine of a soul's recovery and redemption into a series of strikingly dramatic conflicts, each pushing Everyman to a greater understanding of the world and himself. What contrasts *Everyman* from other morality plays in which Vice and Virtue contend for the possession of a man's soul is that the forces that essentially divide Everyman and imperil his salvation reside within him, personified both in the external aspects of a man's life and his inherent attributes. The play takes its audience deeply into a moral and psychological arena that will increasingly form the theater to follow as religious drama gives way to the secular. Dramatic allegory is to be dressed in the costumes and traits of the particular and the individual. Notably, *Everyman* puts an average, representative man at center stage for one of the first times in theatrical history and considers his self-knowledge and salvation as its central issue. Neither a divinity nor a paragon, Everyman is made recognizable to every member of the audience—noble and peasant alike—and psychological realism, even in an allegory of contending abstractions, makes a powerful theatrical debut. *Everyman* proves triumphantly that the sufferings of someone like the rest of us can engage us emotionally and intellectually while supplying a crucial lesson on how the real, the symbolic, and insights into human nature and human existence—the key components of all drama—can be effectively combined.

ANGELS IN AMERICA: A GAY FANTASIA ON NATIONAL THEMES

42

(1991–92)   by Tony Kushner

Defiantly theatrical, unabashedly sprawling, ambitious, provocative, poignant, and hilarious, Angels proposes visions of healing through community. The seriocomic insights, emotional sweep and, in its aesthetics as "anti-illusionist Brechtian graffito," its convergence of art and activism combine to depict the emotional devastation of a sad time. Angels explores questions of tolerance and the inevitability of monumental change, crossing borders from the real to an imaginative realm in dreams, hallucinations, and fantasy to allow its real-life fears to mix with imaginative hope to offer solace. This darkly touching, ominously political, and humanly redemptive drama suggest that faith in a brighter future is essential, despite the harrowing specters of fear and doubt undermining the survival of hope. Kushner offers a beatific vision of a new America for the twenty-first century as millennium arrives.

—James Fisher, *The Theater of Tony Kushner: Living Past Hope*

Without doubt the most important drama to appear in the last decade of the 20th century was *Angels in America*, a two-part play that fundamentally challenged the conventional wisdom that had dominated contemporary theater. Tony Kushner's play demonstrated that popularity and critical acclaim are not mutually exclusive, that the marginalized could claim the mainstream stage in a drama conceived on the grandest scale. If contemporary American drama seems shrunken down to isolated, private consciousness, into what one reviewer has called "an era of apolitical American isolationist theatre," Kushner suggests a panoramic, engaged alternative. As reviewer Frank Rich asserted, *Angels in America* is "a searching and radical rethinking of the whole esthetic of American political drama in which far-flung hallucinations, explicit sexual encounters and camp humor are given as much weight as erudite ideological argument." Oversized and risky, mixing reality and fantasy, the current and the cosmological, hilarity and wrenching pain, *Angels in America* is an encyclopedia of dramatic and intellectual possibilities, a reflection of the messy contradictions of American democracy itself. Its aspirations stem from a Whitmanesque ambition to contain multitudes. Kushner has acknowledged the risk he took:

> When I started to write these plays, I wanted to attempt something of ambition and size even if that meant I might be accused of straying too close to ambition's ugly twin, pretentiousness. Given the bloody opulence of this country's great and terrible history, given its newness and its grand improbability, its artists are bound to be tempted towards large gestures and big embraces. . . . Melville, my favorite American writer, strikes inflated, even hysterical, chords on occasion. It's the sound of the Individual ballooning, overreaching. We are all children of "Song of Myself."

The young, relatively unknown playwright's attempt to elbow his way into the grand American literary tradition while treating homosexuality, the AIDS crisis, and the avowed cherished American ideals of difference and diversity in the widest possible context of American history, politics, metaphysics, and mysticism helped make *Angels in America*, in the words of scholar John M. Clum, "a turning point in the history of gay drama, the history of American drama, and of American literary culture." Critic John Lahr has argued that

> Not since Williams has a playwright announced his poetic vision with such authority on the Broadway stage. Kushner is the heir apparent to Williams' romantic theatrical heritage: he, too, has tricks in his pocket and things up his sleeve, and he gives the audience "truth in the pleasant disguise of illusion." And, also like Williams, Kushner has forged an original, impressionistic theatrical vocabulary to show us the heart of a new age.

Kushner was born in New York City in 1956. His parents, both classically trained musicians, moved their family to Lake Charles, Louisiana, when Kushner was an infant. He attributes his interest in opera and literature to his father and his passion for theater to his mother, who acted in local productions. "That's the major reason I went into the theater," Kushner reported. "I saw some of her performances when I was four or five years old and they were so powerful. I had vivid dreams afterwards." He also recollects from childhood, "fairly clear memories of being gay since I was six. I knew that I felt slightly different than most of the boys I was growing up with. By the time I was eleven there was no doubt. But I was completely in the closet." Kushner would not "come out" until his 20s. After completing high school Kushner returned to New York City to attend Columbia University, graduating in 1978 with a concentration in medieval studies. He then worked as a switchboard operator at the United Nations Plaza Hotel in Manhattan for six years before deciding to pursue a career in the theater. Kushner enrolled at New York University, where he studied with Bertolt Brecht specialist Carl Weber and earned an M.F.A. in directing in 1984. It was the year of Ronald Reagan's reelection as president, the growing AIDS epidemic, and a number of personal setbacks in which Kushner recalled, "The desolate political sphere mirrored in an exact and ugly way an equally desolate personal sphere." Around this moment in history and his life Kushner would choose to set *Angels in America*.

In 1985 Kushner left New York to become assistant director at the St. Louis Repertory Theatre for one season and saw an eclectic group of initial plays first performed. His early works include an opera, *La Fin de la Baleine: An Opera for the Apocalypse* (1983); some children's plays, including *Yes, Yes, No, No* (1985); an adaptation of Goethe's drama *Stella* (1987); *The Illusion* (1988); adapted from Pierre Corneille; and one-act and full-length original plays, including *The Heavenly Theatre* (1986), *In Great Eliza's Golden Time* (1986), and *Hydriotaphia, or The Death of Dr. Browne* (1987). Kushner's first professional production was *A Bright Room Called Day* (1985), concerning a group of friends in Germany during the early years of Adolf Hitler's rise to power. Their story is juxtaposed with commentary from a narrator who draws parallels between Hitler's regime and current politics. When it opened in New York it was called "an ambitious, disturbing mess of a play" that Frank Rich dismissed as "fatuous" and "an early front-runner for the most infuriating play of 1991." However, Oskar Eustis, the artistic director of the Eureka Theater Company in San Francisco, where the earliest version of *A Bright Room Called Day* was staged, was impressed by Kushner's talent enough to commission the playwright to write a play about the impact of AIDS on the gay community in San Francisco. This would become *Angels in America*, which grew into a seven-hour two-part drama, developed in a workshop production at Los Angeles's Mark Taper Forum in 1990 before part 1, *Millennium Approaches*, premiered in San Francisco in 1991. Part 2, *Perestroika*, premiered at the Mark Taper Forum in 1992. The first production of both parts occurred in Los Angeles before transferring to Broadway in 1993. By then Kushner had received international acclaim, and *Angels in America* was being called "the Great American Play."

The intentions and methods behind *Angels in America* reflect Kushner's influences and aims as a dramatist. An overtly socially engaged dramatist, Kushner has asserted that all drama is political and that he "cannot be a playwright without having some temptation to let the audiences know what I think when I read the newspaper in the morning. What I find is that the things that make you the most uncomfortable are the best things to write about." Unlike other American dramatists such as Clifford Odets and Arthur Miller, however, Kushner has not followed them with a predominant realistic method. Citing dramatists such as Henrik Ibsen and George Bernard Shaw as influences for the drama of ideas that interests him, Kushner also is an admirer of the lyricism and overt sexual themes of Tennessee Williams. "The first time I read

Streetcar," Kushner has asserted, "I was annihilated." Kushner's greatest influence, however, is Bertolt Brecht:

> To me, Brecht is central. Playwrights who aspire to a theater of politi-
> cal analysis and engagement and who envision the theater as a platform
> for social debate—can see in the life and work of Brecht what the mar-
> riage of art and politics has to offer. I don't think anybody interested
> in writing progressive, politically committed theater can possibly avoid
> dealing with him. His theoretical writings are incredibly important,
> not just for the theater, but for film and all the arts. Everyone seems
> to dip into him. His notion of the relationship between the means of
> production, art and the audience is fundamental. *Mother Courage* is
> my favorite play. I think he's one of the great poets of the Twentieth
> Century.

In Brecht Kushner found the conjunction of "radical, dignified left politics and
theatrical practice" that he would emulate, particularly in *Angels in America,*
which conforms in its social themes and anti-illusionist method to Brecht's
concept of epic theater.

Kushner has stated that in *Angels in America* he set out to write a play on
"AIDS, Mormons, and Roy Cohn." Linking these three disparate subjects—
the disease that was destroying and isolating gays in America, the religious
group committed to godliness but also intolerant toward gays, and the notorious conservative powerbroker who, though he persecuted gays, was himself a closet homosexual, only outed when he contracted AIDS and died in
1986—Kushner attempts to chronicle a particularly crucial moment of the
testing of American values, in a "Gay Fantasia on National Themes," featuring 30 characters played by eight actors. Set in New York City in 1985, the
play explores its era when, in the words of Yeats, "things fall apart" through
the linked narrative of two couples and the collapse of their relationships.
Joe Porter Pitt is a conservative Mormon and friend of power lawyer Roy
Cohn, married to Harper, "an agoraphobic with a mild Valium addiction."
Their marriage is dissolving because of Joe's growing awareness that he is gay.
The other couple is Louis Ironson and Prior Walter, whose relationship is
threatened by Prior's worsening health from AIDS, as Louis finds it impossible to remain with his partner. Their stories intersect and are thematically
joined in split scenes and plot developments, such as Louis becoming Joe's
lover; Belize, a former drag queen and lover of Prior's, serving as Roy Cohn's
nurse; and Joe's mother, Hannah, who comes to the aid of Prior. The play
also orchestrates its themes and connects its multiple plots and characters
with the techniques of magic realism (as when Harper and Prior participate
in a mutual dream sequence), as well as staging characters' fantasies and suffusing the narrative with ghosts, such as the spirit of Ethel Rosenberg that

haunts Cohn, and the supernatural, as in the Angel who appears to Prior at the conclusion of *Millennium Approaches.*

Kushner has stated that the play is "about people being trapped in systems that they didn't participate in creating. The point being we're now in a new world in so many ways, we have to reinvent ourselves. . . . The characters need to create their own myths to empower themselves." To achieve this new empowering myth the characters first must contend with forces that test their values and identities as the American democratic ideals of diversity and inclusion are being tested by Reaganomics and the AIDS epidemic. Joe struggles to reconcile his Mormon faith and conservative Republicanism with his actual sexual preference, while Harper copes with the collapse of their marriage by drug-assisted fantasies of global destruction and flight. The liberal Louis, racked with guilt over his betrayal of Prior, calls Joe and himself "Children of the new morning, criminal minds. Selfish and greedy and loveless and blind. Reagan's children." Perhaps the most staggering response to the trap of circumstances comes from Roy Cohn when he refuses his doctor's diagnosis of AIDS and the definitions that society forces on him:

> Roy   AIDS. Your problem, Henry, is that you are hung up on words, on labels, that you believe they mean what they seem to mean. AIDS. Homosexual. Gay. Lesbian. You think these are names that tell you who someone sleeps with, but they don't tell you that.

> Henry   No?

> Roy   No. Like all labels they tell you one thing and one thing only: where does an individual so identified fit in the food chain, in the pecking order? Not ideology, or sexual taste, but something much simpler: clout. Not who I fuck or who fucks me, but who will pick up the phone when I call, who owes me favors. This is what a label refers to. Now to someone who does not understand this, homosexual is what I am because I have sex with men. But really this is wrong. Homosexuals are not men who sleep with other men. Homosexuals are men who in fifteen years of trying cannot get a pissant antidiscrimination bill through City Council. Homosexuals are men who know nobody and who nobody knows. Who have zero clout. Does this sound like me, Henry? . . . I have sex with men. But unlike nearly every other man of whom this is true, I bring the guy I'm screwing to the White House and President Reagan smiles at us and shakes his hand. Because *what* I am is defined entirely by *who* I am. Roy Cohn is not a homosexual. Roy Cohn is a heterosexual man, Henry, who fucks around with guys.

HENRY   OK, Roy.

ROY   And what is my diagnosis, Henry?

HENRY   You have AIDS, Roy.

ROY   No, Henry, no. AIDS is what homosexuals have. I have liver
cancer.

By the end of *Millennium Approaches* the former certainties and the characters' attempts to conform to them approaches a reckoning, announced by the
Angel, whose apparition ends part 1 of the play (*"Very* Stephen Spielberg,"
Prior exclaims.). The Angel hails Prior as the new prophet of stasis and deliv-
erance from the changes and struggles that have terrified the characters and
the modern world.

Kushner has asserted that part 2 of *Angels in America, Perestroika,* "proceeds forward from the wreckage made by the Angel's traumatic entry" and
"is about the characters' learning how to change. The problems the characters
face are finally among the hardest problems—how we let go of the past, how
to change and lose with grace, how to keep going in the face of overwhelming
suffering." Opposing the otherworldly perfection of the Angel, a metaphor for
ideals that have lost touch with reality, *Perestroika* celebrates messy, imperfect,
and contradictory humanity. Belize reluctantly but compassionately nurses the
dying Cohn despite his taunts. Louis repents his abandonment of Prior and
seeks the means to make amends. Cohn's decline and death are matched by
Prior's hard-fought coping with his disease and rejecting the role of prophet
of humanity's death. Wrestling with the Angel and storming heaven, Prior
asserts to the assembled "Celestial Apparatchik/Bureaucrat-Angels" humanity's imperative: "We can't just stop. We're not rocks—progress, migration,
motion is . . . modernity. It's *animate,* it's what living things do. We desire.
Even if all we desire is stillness, it's still desire *for.*" Prior's affirmation of life,
of flux and change, despite all their pain and anguish is matched by Harper's
concluding vision of the souls of the dead rising to close the hole in the ozone
protecting the earth: "Nothing's lost forever. In this world, there is a kind of
painful progress. Longing for what we've left behind and dreaming ahead."

In the play's epilogue, set five years later, a new family and a new reflection of American democratic values have been constituted as Prior, Hannah,
Belize, and Louis assemble before the angel statue of Central Park's Bethesda
fountain. Affirming a common humanity transcending race and sexual preference, the play closes with Prior's direct address to the audience:

This disease will be the end of many of us, but not nearly all, and the
dead will be commemorated and will struggle on with the living, and we

are not going away. We won't die secret deaths anymore. The world only spins forward. We will be citizens. The time has come. Bye now. You are fabulous creatures, each and every one. And I bless you: *More Life*. The Great Work Begins.

A triumph in its moral and intellectual challenges and its avoidance of the easy, sentimental assignment of villainy and victimization, *Angels in America* is also a liberating theater experience, pointing the way for drama to reclaim a primary role as interpreter of the historical moment and the human condition.

A MIDSUMMER NIGHT'S DREAM 43

(c. 1594–95) *by William Shakespeare*

> *Nothing by Shakespeare before* A Midsummer Night's Dream *is its equal and in some respects nothing by him afterwards surpasses it. It is his first undoubted masterpiece, without flaws, and one of his dozen or so plays of overwhelming originality and power.*
> —Harold Bloom, *Shakespeare: The Invention of the Human*

A Midsummer Night's Dream is William Shakespeare's first comic masterpiece and remains one his most beloved and performed plays. It seems reasonable to claim that on any fine night during the summer at an outdoor theater somewhere in the world an audience is being treated to the magic of the play. It is easy, however, to overlook through familiarity what a radically original and experimental play this is. *A Midsummer Night's Dream* is the triumph of Shakespeare's early playwriting career, a drama of such marked inventiveness and visionary reach that its first audiences must have only marveled at what could possibly come next from this extraordinary playwright. In it Shakespeare changed the paradigm of stage comedy that he had inherited from the Greeks and the Romans by dizzyingly multiplying his plot lines and by bringing the irrational and absurd illusions of romantic love center stage. He established human passion and gender relations as comedy's prime subject, transforming such fundamental concepts as love, courtship, and marriage that have persisted in our culture ever since. If that is not enough *A Midsummer Night's Dream* makes use of its romantic intrigue, supernatural setting, and rustic foolery to pose essential questions about the relationship between art and life, appearance and reality, truth and illusion, dreams and the waking world that anticipate the self-referential agenda of such avant-garde, metadramatists as Luigi Pirandello, Bertolt Brecht, and Tom Stoppard. *A Midsummer Night's Dream* represents a kind of declaration of liberation for the stage, in which, after its example, nothing seems either off limits or impossible. In the play Theseus, the duke of Athens, after hearing the lovers' strange story of what happened to them in the forest famously interprets their incredible account by linking the lovers with the lunatic and the poet:

> One sees more devils than vast hell can hold,
> That is the madman: the lover, all as frantic,
> Sees Helen's beauty in a brow of Egypt:
> The poet's eye, in a fine frenzy rolling,
> Doth glance from heaven to earth, from earth to heaven,
> And as imagination bodies forth
> The forms of things unknown, the poet's pen
> Turns them to shapes, and gives to airy nothing
> A local habitation and a name.
> Such tricks hath strong imagination,
> That if it would but apprehend some joy,
> It comprehends some bringer of that joy:
> Or, in the night, imagining some fear,
> How easy is a bush suppos'd a bear!

A Midsummer Night's Dream similarly gives a "local habitation and a name" on stage for what madness, love, and the poet's imagination can conjure.

Shakespeare first made his theatrical reputation in the early 1590s with his *Henry VI* plays, with the historical chronicle genre that he pioneered. His early tragedies—*Titus Andronicus* and *Romeo and Juliet*—and comedies—*The Two Gentlemen of Verona, The Taming of the Shrew, The Comedy of Errors*, and *Love's Labour's Lost*—all show the playwright working within the dramatic conventions that he inherited from classical, medieval, and English folk sources. With *A Midsummer Night's Dream* Shakespeare goes beyond imitation to discover a distinctive voice and manner that would add a new dramatic species. After *A Midsummer Night's Dream* there was Old Comedy, New Comedy, and now Shakespearean comedy, a synthesis of both. To explain the origin and manner of *A Midsummer Night's Dream* scholars have long relied on a speculative story so apt and evocative that it must be believed, even though there is no hard evidence to support it. Thought to have been written in the winter of 1593–94 to be performed at an aristocratic wedding attended by Queen Elizabeth, *A Midsummer Night's Dream* therefore resembles the Renaissance masque, a fanciful mixture of allegorical and mythological enactments, music, dance, elegant costumes, and elaborate theatrical effects to entertain at banquets celebrating betrothals, weddings, and seasonal festivals such as May Day and Twelfth Night. In the words of Theseus at his own nuptial fete, the masque served "To wear away this long age of three hours / Between our after-supper and bed-time." We do know from the title page of its initial publication in the First Quarto of 1600 that the play "hath been sundry times publikely acted" by Shakespeare's company, but the notion that it had served as a wedding entertainment establishes the delightful fun-house mirroring of an actual wedding party first watching a play that included a wedding party watching a play. Such an appropriate scrambling of reality and illusion reflects the source of the humor and wonder of *A Midsummer Night's Dream*.

A Midsummer Night's Dream is one of just three plays out of Shakespeare's 39 (the other two are *Love's Labour's Lost* and *The Tempest*) for which the playwright did not rely on a central primary source. Instead Shakespeare assembled elements from classical sources, romantic narratives, and English folk materials, along with details of ordinary Elizabethan life to juggle and juxtapose four different imaginative realms, each with its own distinctive social and literary conventions and language. Each is linked by analogy to the theme of love and its obstacles. The first is the classically derived court world of Theseus, duke of Athens, who has first conquered Hippolyta, queen of the Amazons, then won her heart, and now eagerly (and impatiently) anticipates their wedding. Their impending nuptials prompt the arrival of emissaries from the natural world, the king and queen of the fairies—Oberon and Titania—to bless their union, as well as a collection of "rude mechanicals"—Bottom, Quince, Flute, Starveling, Snout, and Snug—to devise a theatrical performance as entertainment at the Duke's wedding celebration. To the world of the Athenian court, the alternate supernatural court world of the fairies, and the realistic sphere of the Athenian artisans, Shakespeare overlaps a fourth center of interest in the young lovers Hermia, Helena, Lysander, and Demetrius. Shakespeare mixes the dignified blank verse of Theseus and Hippolyta with the rhymed iambic speeches of the lovers, the rhymed tetrameter of the fairies, and the wonderfully earthy prose of the rustics into a virtuoso's performance of polyphonic verbal effects, the greatest Shakespeare, or any other dramatist, had yet supplied for the stage.

The complications commence when Hermia's father, Egeus, objects to his daughter's unsanctioned preference for Lysander over Demetrius, whom Egeus has selected for her. Egeus invokes Athenian law mandating death or celibacy for a maid's refusal to abide by parental authority in the choice of a mate. Parental objection to the choice of young lovers was a standard plot device of Greek New Comedy and the Roman comedies of Plautus and Terence that Shakespeare inherited. To the obstacles placed in the lovers' paths Shakespeare adds his own variation of the earlier Aristophanic Old Comedy's break with the normalcy of everyday life by having his lovers escape into the forest. Critic Northrup Frye has called this symbolic setting of magical regeneration and vitality the "green world." Here the lovers are tested and allowed the freedom and new possibilities to gain fulfillment and harmony denied them in the civilized world, in which duty dominates desire and obligation to parental authority and the law overrules self-interest and the heart's promptings. Critic C. L. Barber has identified in such a departure from the norm a "Saturnalian Pattern" in Shakespearean comedy in which the lovers' exile from the civilized to the primitive supplies the festive release that characterized the earliest forms of comic drama. Barber argues:

> Once Shakespeare finds his own distinctive voice, he is more Aristophanic than any other great English dramatist, despite the fact that the accepted educated models and theories when he started to write were Terentian and Plautine. The Old Comedy cast of his work results from his participation in native saturnalian traditions of the popular theater and the popular holidays. . . . He used the resources of a sophisticated theater to express, in his idyllic comedies and in his clowns' ironic misrule, the experience of moving to humorous understanding through saturnalian release.

Named for the summer solstice festival, when it was said that a maid could glimpse the man she would marry, *A Midsummer Night's Dream* celebrates access to the uncanny and the breakup of all normal rules and social barriers to display human nature in the grips of elemental passions and the subconscious. The lovers in their moonlit, natural setting, at the mercy of the fairies, act out their deepest desires and hostilities in a full display of the power and absurdity of love both to change reality and to redeem it.

Hermia elopes with Lysander, pursued by Demetrius, who in turn is followed by Helena, whom he spurns. They enter a supernatural realm also beset by marital discord, jealousy, and rivalry. Oberon commands his servant Puck to place the juice of a flower once hit by Cupid's dart in the eyes of the sleeping Titania to cause her to fall in love with the first creature she sees on awakening to help gain for Oberon the changeling boy Titania has refused to yield to him. Oberon, pitying Helena her rejection by Demetrius, also orders Puck to place some of the drops in Demetrius's eyes so that he will be charmed into love with the woman who dotes on him. Instead Puck comes upon Lysander and Hermia as they sleep, mistakes Lysander for Demetrius, and pours the charm into the wrong eyes so that Lysander falls in love with Helena when she wakes him. Meanwhile Bottom and his companions have retreated to the woods to rehearse a dramatization of the mythological story of Pyramus and Thisbe, another set of star-crossed lovers. Puck gives the exuberant Bottom the head of an ass, and he becomes the first thing the charmed Titania sees on waking. Through the agency of the change of location from court to forest and from daylight to moonlight, with its attendant capacity for magical transformation, the play mounts a witty and uproarious display of the irrationality of love and its victims who see the world through the distorting lens of desire, in which certainty of affection is fleeting and a lover with the head of an ass can cause a queen to forgo her senses and her dignity. As Bottom aptly observes, "reason and love keep little company together now-a-days." From the perspectives of the fairies the lovers' absolute claims and earnest rationalizations of such a will-of-the-wisp as love makes them absurd. The tangled mixture of passion, jealousy, rancor, and violence that beset the young lovers after Puck imperfectly corrects his mistake, causing both Lysander and Demetrius to pursue the once spurned Helena, more than justifies Puck's observation, "Lord, what fools these mortals be!"

By act 4 day returns, and the disorder of the night proves as fleeting and as insubstantial as a dream. After the four lovers are awakened by Theseus, Hippolyta, and Egeus, who are hunting in the woods, Lysander again loves Hermia, and Demetrius, still under the power of the potion, gives up his claim to her in favor of Helena. Theseus overrules Egeus's objections and his own former strict adherence to Athenian law and gives both couples permission to marry that day, along with himself and Hippolyta. Having gained the changeling boy from Titania, Oberon releases her from her spell. Puck removes the donkey's head from Bottom, who awakes to wonder at his strange dream:

> I have had a most rare vision. I have had a dream, past the wit of man to say what dream it was. Man is but an ass, if he go about to expound this dream. . . . I will get Peter Quince to write a ballad of this dream. It shall be call'd "Bottom's Dream," because it hath no bottom.

The only mortal allowed to see the fairies, Bottom is also the only character not threatened or diminished by the alternative fantasy realm he passes through. He freely accepts what he does not understand, considering it more suitable for the delight of art in a future ballad than to be analyzed or reduced by reason. Bottom coexists easily and honestly in the dual world of reality and illusion, maintaining his core identity and integrity even through his transformation, from man to ass, to fairy queen's paramour, to ordinary man again. Called by Harold Bloom "Shakespeare's most engaging character before Falstaff," Bottom is the play's human anchor and affirmation of the joyful acceptance of all the contradictions that the play has sent his way.

With the reconciliation of Oberon and Titania, Bottom's reunion with his colleagues, and three Athenian weddings, the plot complications are all happily resolved, and act 5 shifts the emphasis from the potentially destructive vagaries of love to a celebration of marriage to crown and contain human desire. Shakespeare's final sleight of hand and delightful invention, however, is the play within the play, the "tedious and brief" and "very tragical mirth" of the performance of *Pyramus and Thisbe* by Bottom and his players. In a drama fueled by the complications between appearance and reality this hilariously incompetent burlesque by the play's rustic clowns impersonating tragic lovers appropriately comments on the play that has preceded it. The drama of *Pyramus and Thisbe* involves another set of lovers who face parental objections and similarly seek relief in nature, but their adventure goes tragically awry. However, just as Hermia, Lysander, Helena, and Demetrius avoid through the stage-managing of the fairies a potentially tragic fate from their ordeal in the wood, so is the tragic fate of Pyramus and Thisbe transformed to comedy by the ineptitude of Bottom's company. The play within the play becomes a pointed microcosm for *A Midsummer Night's Dream* as a whole in its conversion of potential tragedy to curative comedy. The newlyweds, who mock the absurdity of *Pyramus and Thisbe*, fail to make the connection with their own absurd encounter with love and their chance rescue from its anguish, but the actual audience should not. In Shakespeare's comprehensive comic vision we both laugh at the ridiculousness of others while recognizing ourselves in their dilemmas. Shakespeare's final point about the inseparability of reality and illusion is scored by having the fairy world coexist with the Athenian court at the play's conclusion, decreasing the gap between fact and fancy and invading actuality itself by giving the final words to Puck, who addresses the audience directly:

> If we shadows have offended,
> Think but this, and all is mended,
> That you have but slumb'red here
> While these visions did appear.
> And this weak and idle theme,
> No more yielding but a dream.

Like the newlyweds who view a drama that calls attention to its illusion and its "tragical mirth," the audience is here reminded of the similar blending of reality and dream, the comic and the tragic in the world beyond the stage. Puck serves as Shakespeare's magician's assistant, demonstrating that substance and shadow on stage replicate both the illusion of the dramatist's art and the essence of human life in our own continual interplay of reality, dreams, and desire.

SIX CHARACTERS IN SEARCH OF AN AUTHOR

44

(1921)

by Luigi Pirandello

"Why not," I said to myself, "present this highly strange fact of an author who refuses to let some of his characters live though they have been born in his fantasy, and the fact that these characters, having by now life in their veins, do not resign themselves to remaining excluded from the world of art? They are detached from me; live on their own; have acquired voice and movement; have by themselves—in this struggle for existence that they have had to wage with me—become dramatic characters, characters that can move and talk on their own initiative; already see themselves as such; have learned to defend themselves against others. And so let them go where dramatic characters do go to have life: on a stage. And let us see what will happen."

That's what I did. And, naturally, the result was what it had to be: a mixture of tragic and comic, fantastic and realistic, in a humorous situation that was quite new and infinitely complex, a drama which is conveyed by means of the characters, who carry it within them and suffer it, a drama, breathing, speaking, self-propelled, which seeks at all costs to find the means of its own presentation; and the comedy of the vain attempt at an improvised realization of the drama on stage.

—Luigi Pirandello, Preface to *Six Characters in Search of an Author*

It can be argued that with Luigi Pirandello's *Six Characters in Search of an Author* Albert Einstein's theory of relativity arrives on stage. Called by critic Felicity Firth "the major single subversive moment in the history of modern theatre," the play is a dizzying hall of mirrors that tests the philosophical basis of the concept of reality while exposing and renewing the operating principles of the drama. The play's startling premise—the interruption of a play rehearsal by six characters conjured and then abandoned by their author who seek the means to exhibit their drama—was so shocking when the play was first performed in Rome in 1921 that the audience rioted. Catcalls and jeering led to punches. *Six Characters* would be subsequently performed internationally to great acclaim and acknowledgment as a watershed drama with its innovative treatment of philosophical themes and dazzling experimentation with dramatic structure. The impact of the play has been likened to "the effect of an earthquake," with the play's radical form compared to cubism, in which, as art historian Wylie Sypher asserts, "Pirandello 'destroys' drama much as the cubists destroyed conventional things," by not accepting "as authentic 'real' people or the cliché of the theatre any more than the cubist accepts as authentic the 'real' object [or] the cliché of deep perspective." *Six Characters* pioneered the antirealistic, self-reflexiveness that is the hallmark of modernist drama. Critic Antonio Illiano summarizes, the "sudden and unexpected appearance of live characters, who claimed to belong to the stage and could actually be seen and heard, was like a bombshell that blew out the last and weary residues of the old realistic drama." As important in the creation of modern drama as James Joyce is to modern fiction and T. S. Eliot to modern poetry, Pirandello initiated contemporary drama with its radical uncertainties, discontinuities, and undermining of the fundamental concepts of identity and reality. Pirandello's importance has been attested to by Tom Stoppard, who has asserted the "impossibility" of any contemporary Western playwright "to write a play that is totally unlike Beckett, Pirandello, [or] Kafka."

Pirandello was born in Sicily in 1867. His father was a wealthy owner of a sulfur-mining business. "I am the son of Chaos," Pirandello wrote, "and not allegorically but literally, because I was born in a country spot called by the people around *Cávusu,* a dialectal corruption of the authentic Greek word *Xáos.*" Expected to enter the family firm, Pirandello was appalled by the conditions of the mines in which men were "turned into animals by the mean, ferocious fight for gain" and turned instead to academic and artistic pursuits. Producing his first play with siblings and friends at the age of 12, Pirandello attended universities in Palermo, Rome, and finally Bonn, where he earned a doctorate in romance philology. Settling in Rome to establish himself as a writer, Pirandello agreed in 1894 to an arranged marriage to Antonietta Portulano, the daughter of one of his father's business associates. To support his wife and three children Pirandello became a literature teacher at a woman's college, where he worked for 24 years. In 1904, the same year that he gained his first critical success with the novel *Il fu Mattia Pascal (The Late Mattia Pascal)*, the failure of his father's mining business, in which Pirandello was heavily invested, resulted in the paralysis and mental derangement of Antonietta, who became obsessively jealous and delusional. Enduring constant accusations and abuse from his mentally unstable wife, Pirandello refused to have her committed until 1919, finding refuge in his study, where he produced short stories, novels, essays, and several unproduced plays, many dealing with his tormented domestic life and his fascination, prompted by his wife's condition, with the conflict between truth and illusion and the borderline between sanity and insanity.

Pirandello's early writing was strongly influenced by the Italian naturalist movement that advocated a truthful reflection of reality. Pirandello, however, came to believe that truth could be apprehended neither objectively nor scientifically and that reality itself was a problematic concept. Experience, in Pirandello's developing view, was chaotic, in constant flux, in which individuals imposed ideas, concepts, and systems of beliefs to make sense of it. Identity was not intrinsic but multiple, constructed out of the roles and responses circumstances imposed on individuals. Pirandello's evolving aesthetic principles are outlined in his book-length essay *L'umorismo* (*On Humor*), published in 1908. In Pirandello's theory of humorism, which serves as a key to his art, the comic writer exploits the opposition between appearance and reality. What is comic is the perception of this opposition, which leads both to a compassionate understanding of a character's fictive situation and a deeper insight into actuality. Pirandello's art is at its core epistemological, concerned with the problem of knowing and the embodiment of crucial philosophical ideas in a compelling human drama. Pirandello insisted:

> My works are born from live images which are the perennial source of art, but these images pass through a veil of concepts which have taken hold of me. My works of art are never concepts trying to express themselves through images. On the contrary. They are images, often very vivid images of life, which, fostered by the labors of my mind, assume universal significance quite on their own, through the formal unity of art.

By the outbreak of World War I Pirandello had established his reputation as a master of the short story and a successful novelist. During the war years he would increasingly devote himself to playwriting. "My taste for the narrative form had vanished," Pirandello recalled. "I could no longer limit myself to story telling, while there was action all around me. . . . The words would not remain on the written page: they had to explode into the air, to be spoken or cried out." In 1917 Pirandello completed *Così è (se vi pare)* (*Right You Are*), the first of his major experimentation with theatrical form and subversion of the conventions of realistic drama. Dramatizing the impossibility of objective truth, the play converts a family comedy into an ontological exploration of being and knowing. Between *Right You Are* and *Six Characters*, Pirandello wrote three plays—*The Pleasure of Honesty* (1918), *The Rules of the Game* (1919), and *All as It Should Be* (1920)—that further presented the unstable concept of identity and the conflict between reality and illusion. These themes would have their greatest expression in *Sei personaggi in cerca d'autore* (*Six Characters in Search of an Author*).

In the history of the modern theater there is perhaps no more shocking moment than the opening of *Six Characters*, in which the audience, expecting to be entertained by an illusion of real life, confronts a bare stage, "as it usually is during the daytime . . . so that from the beginning the public may have the impression of an impromptu performance." Onstage a group of actors playing actors prepare to rehearse one of Pirandello's plays. Both the stage and situation blur the distinction between illusion and reality. Trained by Henrik Ibsen and others to suspend disbelief in favor of onstage realism, Pirandello's audience is immediately reminded that they are viewing not a living room through the removed fourth wall but artifice. This radical disruption of the realistic principle is further assaulted when six characters interrupt the rehearsal—a Father, Mother, Stepdaughter, Son, adolescent Boy, and young Girl—who claim to be characters created by an author who has abandoned their story. They seek from the actors the means for self-expression. The audience, initially dealing with the notion of actors playing actors in a play that appears spontaneous, must now adjust to the more radical premise of actors playing characters who become actors in a dramatic version of their lives. The Manager and the "real" actors initially suspect the characters' sanity, but the Father makes clear, they are no less sane nor real than the rehearsing actors: "to reverse the ordinary process may well be considered a madness: that is, to create credible situations, in order that they may appear true. But permit me to observe that if this be madness, it is the sole *raison d'etre* of your profession." Having found an audience (both literally and fictively), the characters begin to tell their story. Years before, the Father, having tired of his wife, procured a lover for her with whom she lived and had three children before he died some months before. This extended family—both the Father and Mother's legitimate Son and his stepbrother and -sisters are now reunited. The Father's version of their convoluted family's history is contested both by the Mother and the Stepdaughter whose chance discovery in a brothel by the Father becomes the means for their reunion. Both Father and Stepdaughter are anxious that the scene in the brothel be dramatized to support their opposed versions of events: the Father's innocence and benevolence and the Stepdaughter's claims of his ulterior motives, including his incestuous desires. The first act ends as the Manager, having grown intrigued by the dramatic possibilities of their story, invites the characters to his office to develop a dramatic scenario. Having set in motion a play within a play, Pirandello prepares the stage for a meditation on the problematic translation of life to stage illusion and of stage illusion to life.

Act 2 opens with the Stepdaughter storming onstage outraged with the self-serving and misleading drama that the Father and the Manager are creating. The falsification of her version of reality is further undermined by the inauthenticity of actors in representing the characters. To their complaints about their "characterizations" the Manager explains: "On the stage, you as yourself, cannot exist. The actor here acts you, and that's an end to it!" The Manager, however, eventually consents to allow the characters to interpret their drama, which is then repeated by the actors and critiqued by the characters. The brothel scene is played to the point of the Father's seduction of his Stepdaughter, when the Mother, unable to control her anger and suffering any longer, acts to separate her husband and daughter forming a recognition scene. The Manager, pleased by this theatrical climax, declares it the first act curtain scene. His words are misheard by a stagehand who actually lets down the curtain to close the act. When the curtain rises again, the scene is the garden of the Father's house in preparation for the drama of the family's reunion in which the Mother is to confront her guilt over abandoning her son and he must contend with his resentment of his newly discovered siblings. The action is preceded by a lengthy discussion between the Father and the Manager on the difference between reality and illusion. As the Father observes to the Manager and his acting company, "if we [*indicating the Characters*] have no other reality beyond the illusion, you too must not count overmuch on your reality as you feel it today, since, like that of yesterday, it may prove an illusion for you tomorrow." Indeed, the Father insists that the characters are in fact truer and more real than the others:

> Our reality doesn't change; it can't change! It can't be other than what it is, because it is already fixed for ever. It's terrible. Ours is an immutable reality which should make you shudder when you approach us if you are really conscious of the fact that your reality is a mere transitory and fleeting illusion, taking this form today and that tomorrow, according to the conditions, according to your will, your sentiments, which in turn are controlled by an intellect that shows them to you today in one manner and tomorrow . . . who knows how? . . . Illusions of reality represented in this fatuous comedy of life that never ends, nor can ever end! Because if tomorrow it were to end . . . then why, all would be finished.

The Father's radical disruption of the realistic basis of existence is played out in the ensuing drama that further complicates perception. The foreground action of the Mother's attempted reunion with her resentful Son is disrupted by the revelation that the real drama was the Son's discovery of the body of the little girl in the fountain with her brother standing helplessly over her. At that moment a revolver shot rings out onstage, and the Mother and several of the actors find the prostrate body of the boy. Is he dead? Or just pretending? This radical uncertainty closes the play as the line between what is acted and what is lived onstage is obliterated, and the Manager exasperatingly cries:

> Pretense? Reality? To hell with it all! Never in my life has such a thing happened to me. I've lost a whole day over these people, a whole day!

Critic Richard Gilman helpfully summarizes the questions the play raises and the basis for the play's impact on the theater and modern culture: "What is dramatic 'reality' and dramatic 'illusion'? What does it mean to 'act' on stage? . . . What are the relationships between reality and truth, human characters and the characters of a fiction, imagination and actuality?" By calling attention to the conventions of stage realism and their implications, *Six Characters in Search of an Author* dramatically expands the possibilities of the theater that others, such as Samuel Beckett, Eugène Ionesco, Edward Albee, and Tom Stoppard, would further exploit. With Pirandello the stage is able to contain both a compelling human story and a consideration of the most profound existential questions of knowing and being. As critic Raymond Williams has argued, in Pirandello's dramas,

> The worlds of naturalism and expressionism cross and engender what is really a new form: one which has continued to be influential. Delusion, loss of identity, the reduction of personality to a role and of society to a collective impersonation: these are elements of a new kind of theatre: a use of the theatre to expose itself, and then in the double exposure to question any discoverable reality. What began as the twist of romantic drama became a decisive twist of a whole dramatic tradition. That, now, is Pirandello's importance.

MAN AND SUPERMAN

(1903)

by George Bernard Shaw

Man and Superman *is, of course, one of Shaw's major plays, though it perhaps achieves that rank from being not one play, but two. Certainly without the long third-act dialogue in Hell,* Man and Superman—*for all that it dramatizes the best known of Shaw's theories—would diminish into one of his more tractable and traditional comedies. With the Hell scene, it expands into one of the most brilliant and Shavian of them all.*

—Louis Kronenberger, *The Thread of Laughter:*
Chapters on English Stage Comedy from Jonson to Maugham

Man and Superman's subtitle, *A Comedy and a Philosophy*, perfectly encapsulates George Bernard Shaw's audacious conjunction of the 19th-century parlor comedy and a challenging drama of ideas. An early English proponent of Henrik Ibsen, Shaw adapted the Norwegian's tragic problem play as comedy designed to delight as well as instruct his audience in a provocative reassessment of human nature and the human condition. Countering the dominant aestheticism of the late 19th century, with its claim of "art for art's sake," Shaw, as he established his career in London as a reviewer and playwright, consistently insisted on art's utility in truth telling leading to self-assessment and social and moral reform. "I am convinced that fine art," he wrote in his preface to *Mrs. Warren's Profession* (1902), "is the subtlest, the most seductive, the most effective instrument of moral propaganda in the world, excepting only the example of personal conduct, and I waive even that exception in favor of the art of the stage because it works by exhibiting examples of personal conduct made intelligible and moving to unobservant, unreflecting people to whom real life means nothing." For Shaw message trumped all considerations of manner, justifying the yoking of the most heterodox elements—philosophical speculation and conventions of the well-made play—in the service of a more comprehensive understanding of the world and a call to action. As Shaw wrote in his dedicatory epistle to *Man and Superman* addressed to drama critic Arthur Bingham Walkley, who first provoked Shaw to write a Don Juan play, "My conscience is the genuine pulpit article: it annoys me to see people comfortable when they ought to be uncomfortable; and I insist on making them think in order to bring them to conviction of sin. If you don't like my preaching you must lump it. I really cannot help it."

With the exception of Shaw's massive play cycle *Back to Methuselah* (1920), *Man and Superman* is Shaw's most ambitious drama of ideas. It contains, or rather is bursting with, the philosophical and moral precepts that underpin virtually all of his work. Taking nearly eight hours to perform uncut—with the dream sequence of act 3 often performed as a separate two-hour-long play, *Don Juan in Hell*—*Man and Superman* has, as critic Archibald Henderson has stated, enough ideas for a dozen ordinary comedies. Described by critic Eric Bentley as "the supreme triumph of Shaw's dramaturgical dialectics," *Man and Superman* presents a comically inverted version of Mozart's *Don Giovanni* that begins as a satiric look at the relationship between the sexes and reaches what one critic has called, "the most searching conversation on philosophy and religion in modern English." Testing both the limits of the audience's understanding and endurance, as well as the drama's capacity to embody serious philosophical, psychological, moral, and social inquiry, *Man and Superman* is an unavoidable modern drama and one of the greatest imaginative philosophical works of the 20th century, the dramatic equivalent of Thomas Mann's *The Magic Mountain*.

It was Ibsen who provided Shaw with his fundamental model for his conception of drama and the role of the dramatist. As an iconoclast who insisted that the theater should be an arena for confronting the most difficult truths, Ibsen pioneered the dramatic revitalization that Shaw advocated. In the *Quintessence of Ibsenism*, one of the earliest English defenses of Ibsen's importance, Shaw praised Ibsen's "plays of nineteenth-century life with which he overcame Europe, and broke the dusty windows of every dry-rotten theatre in it from Moscow to Manchester." Shaw, however, would not follow Ibsen's lead in writing tragedies of ordinary life, preferring instead a comic method. Shaw's immediate predecessor, both as an Irishman who achieved dramatic success in England and as a reinterpreter of the comedy of manners, was Oscar Wilde. Reviewing Wilde's *An Ideal Husband* in 1895, Shaw observed that "In a certain sense Mr Wilde is to me our only thorough playwright. He plays with everything; with wit, with philosophy, with drama, with actors and audience, with the whole theatre. Such a feat scandalises the Englishman, who can no more play with wit and philosophy than he can with a football or cricket bat." Yet Shaw, who would rival his fellow Dubliner in the comic art of the paradox, often found Wilde's plays lacking in purpose and importance. In a famous dismissal of *The Importance of Being Earnest*, which he found "essentially hateful," Shaw asserted: "It amused me, of course; but unless comedy touches me as well as amuses me, it leaves me with a sense of having wasted my evening. I go to the theatre to be moved to laughter, not to be tickled or bustled into it."

Shaw's unique version of what he would call "corrective comedy" is a fusion of Wilde's dazzling verbal and intellectual play with the conventions of the drawing-room comedy of manners and Ibsen's problem and purpose plays. Critic Nicholas Grene has pointed out in consideration of this combination of opposites that produced a unique Shavian drama, "In being like Wilde and Ibsen simultaneously, Shaw is not the least bit like either of them."

   Man and Superman opens in the full Wildean manner with the idiom of the romantic comedy parodied and upturned. Staunchly conservative Roebuck Ramsden and the self-styled "Member of the Idle Rich Class" and professed revolutionary Jack Tanner find themselves named joint guardians of Ann Whitefield, whose father has just died. The willful and self-possessed Anne is being courted by the earnest but ineffectual poet Octavius Robinson. His sister, Violet, is discovered to be pregnant. Facing ostracism from her respectable friends, Violet claims to be married but refuses to name her husband. Tanner, the characteristic Shavian provocateur, takes subversive aim at Victorian sanctimony and hypocrisy. By the end of the act Shaw has completed a witty and startling reversal of roles and values. Violet, cast as the Victorian disgraced woman, whom Tanner sympathizes with as a victim of social conventions, reveals herself as both impenitent and dismissive of Tanner's sympathy. As she says, "I won't bear such a horrible insult as to be complimented by Jack on being one of the wretches of whom he approves." Moreover, Tanner, the play's embodiment of Don Juan, the seductive libertine, becomes the pursued by his new ward, and the radical conventionality of the play's pair of ingénues—Ann and Violet—overpowers and outmaneuvers the purported anarchist. In Shaw's drawing room women are activists, while the men are coy and elusive, and respectability is slow to conceal the unmistakable traces of the instinctual. With its gender reversal and frankness about sexual matters *Man and Superman* counters what Shaw called in his preface "the predicament of our contemporary English drama," in which dramatists have been "forced to deal almost exclusively with cases of sexual attraction, and yet forbidden to exhibit the incidents of that attraction or even to discuss its nature." Shaw sets out to dramatize "the natural attraction of the sexes for one another" as "the mainspring of the action" and the launching pad into a Shavian cosmology and morality play.

   Act 2 opens on the drive of Mrs. Whitefield's suburban estate as Tanner's chauffeur, Henry Straker, repairs his master's touring car. This is likely the first time in a serious play that an automobile had ever appeared on stage. Following the reversal of man as the pursuer and woman as pursued, Straker serves as a second major inversion concerning class. The working-class Straker demonstrates both his superiority to his master in his practical competence and his advantage over the helpless rich. As Tanner remarks, "I am a slave of that car and of you too." In the new world of technological change represented by the automobile, the engineer is king, and the conventional distinctions between master and servant are scrambled. Tanner views Straker as a new phenomenon: "Here have we literary and cultured persons been for years setting up a cry of the New Woman whenever some unusually old fashioned female came along; and never noticing the advent of the New Man. Straker's the New Man." Straker's ascendancy is only the first in a series of surprising reversals and revelations. Violet's husband turns out to be the rich young American Hector Malone, and the couple have concealed their marriage because Hector's father, a former Irish immigrant, snobbishly wants his son to marry a British aristocrat. It is Straker who breaks the news to Tanner that Ann, who has gained an invitation from her guardian to join him on a driving tour of the Continent, has set her sights on Jack, not Octavius, for her husband. Tanner, as "the destined prey," responds by flight, ordering Straker to set off immediately for North Africa.

Having exposed the conventions of gender and class as shallow and misleading, Shaw in act 3 reconstitutes and expands the battle of the sexes allegorically in a dialogue in which the characters metamorphose into archetypes as the particulars of the drama are universalized. The act opens in the Spanish Sierra Nevada, where Jack and Straker, having eluded the pursuing Ann, are seized by Spanish bandits dedicated to more equitable distribution of wealth. The bandit leader is the urbane Mendoza, a former waiter at London's Savoy Hotel. His introduction, "I am a brigand: I live by robbing the rich," is answered by Tanner: "I am a gentleman: I live by robbing the poor." Cordially agreeing to pay the demanded ransom Tanner decides to spend the night with the brigands, and they fall asleep as Mendoza recites poetry about his great unrequited love for, as it turns out, Straker's sister. As the landscape darkens and strains of Mozart's *Don Giovanni* are heard, a dream sequence commences embodying elements of Tanner's subconscious. A Spanish nobleman, Don Juan Tenorio, resembling Tanner, appears. He is eventually joined by Doña Ana, the woman Juan has seduced, her father, the Commander, whom Juan has killed defending his daughter's honor, and the Devil. The setting is hell, where Ana, to her shock, has been consigned and where her father, bored with heaven, hopes to remain. In Shaw's witty interpretation of the Don Juan story Ana becomes everywoman, afflicted by a conventional piety, who when she learns that she is damned, regrets that she was not more wicked on earth. Don Juan does not live up to his reputation as a womanizing sensualist but instead shuns women in his search for wisdom, while the Commander is recast as a hedonistic philistine who comes to hell for relief from the stultifying moral righteousness of heaven. Their dialogue, moderated by the eloquent and often persuasive Devil, begins with a reconceptualization of hell and heaven. In Shaw's *Divine Comedy* hell is reserved for self-indulgent and deluded pleasure seekers while heaven is the home of "the masters of reality." Heaven welcomes those sustained by a higher purpose beyond self, which Don Juan identifies as the Life Force that urges humankind toward perfectibility. The Devil, however, mounts the case against such an affirmative cosmic drive:

Have you walked up and down earth lately? I have; and have you examined . . . Man's wonderful inventions. And I tell you that in the arts of life man invents nothing; but in the arts of death he outdoes Nature herself, and produces by chemistry and machinery all the slaughter of plague, pestilence, and famine. . . . His heart is in his weapons. This marvelous force of Life of which you boast is a force of Death: Man measures his strength by his destructiveness.

Granting the Devil his due, Juan acknowledges Man's tendency toward destruction and violence but insists that instances of subordination to causes greater than self constitute unmistakable claims for humankind's salvation. Don Juan and the Devil next consider questions of love and woman's place in the cosmic scheme. To the Devil's relegation of women as solely the object of romantic passion, Juan recognizes a greater purpose of women in their fealty to the Life Force and their faith in the future and a higher purpose by propagating the race. The extraordinary tour de force dialogue ends as Don Juan sets off for heaven where "you live and work instead of playing and pretending," pursued by Ana who has been inspired by talk of the Nietzchean Superman. The Devil recalls the philosopher: "I had some hopes of him; but he was a confirmed Life Force worshipper. It was he who raked up the Superman, who is as old as Prometheus; and the 20th century will run after this newest of the old crazes when it gets tired of the world, the flesh, and your humble servant." Ana, earning her salvation by accepting the imperatives of the Life Force and a purpose beyond self, sets out to find "a father for the Superman."

Act 4, set in a garden of a villa in Granada, gathers the original characters to resolve the complications standing in the way of love and marriage. Having introduced the philosophical conception of the Life Force in the dream play, Shaw applies it in working out his dual love plots. Hector's father, encountering Violet, is eventually brought round to the marriage in the face of his daughter-in-law's determination and good sense. Ann confesses to Octavius that she could not live up to his romantic ideal of her and intends to marry Tanner instead. When Ann and Tanner are finally left alone, he surrenders to the power of the Life Force that has decreed their union as inevitable:

> TANNER [*despairingly*] Oh, you are witty: at the supreme moment the Life Force endows you with every quality. Well, I too can be a hypocrite. Your father's will appointed me your guardian, not your suitor. I shall be faithful to my trust.

> ANN [*in low siren tones*] He asked me who would I have as my guardian before he made that will. I chose you!

TANNER   The will is yours then! The trap was laid from the beginning.

ANN   [*concentrating all her magic*] From the beginning from our childhood—for both of us—by the Life Force.

TANNER   I will not marry you. I will not marry you.

ANN   Oh; you will, you will.

TANNER   I tell you, no, no, no.

ANN   I tell you, yes, yes, yes.

TANNER   NO.

ANN   [*coaxing—imploring—almost exhausted*] Yes. Before it is too late for repentance. Yes.

TANNER   [*struck by the echo from the past*] When did all this happen to me before? Are we two dreaming?

ANN   [*suddenly losing her courage, with an anguish that she does not conceal*] No. We are awake; and you have said no: that is all.

TANNER   [*brutally*] Well?

ANN   Well, I made a mistake: you do not love me.

TANNER   [*seizing her in his arms*] It is false: I love you. The Life Force enchants me: I have the whole world in my arms when I clasp you. But I am fighting for my freedom, for my honor, for myself, one and indivisible.

As in a Shakespearean romantic comedy, the obstacles to love and marriage are finally surmounted as the source of those obstacles—in human nature and society—are exposed. Here Shaw mounts a truly cosmic argument in which the conventions of courtship, gender, sexuality, and the meaning of existence itself are subjected to a radical and astonishing reappraisal.

PHÈDRE

46

(1677)

by Jean Racine

It would be idle to claim that all modern works of creative literature inspired by the legendary love of Phaedra for Hippolytus are indebted to Racine. . . . But Racine has put his own stamp on the legend and has contributed considerably to its attraction for the modern mind. He has been particularly influential in two quite different ways: in the exceptional clarity and intensity with which he has dramatized the conflict between the demands of conscience and the inflexible will of the gods; and in his perfectly achieved incorporation of the element of sexual jealousy into the plot and motivation of Phèdre. *While the former feature gives the play its immense tragic power, the latter, although in itself almost a seventeenth-century dramatic cliché, has offered subsequent writers opportunity for dramatic inventions to which the modern audience finds it easy to respond.*

—Edward James and Gillian Jondorf, *Racine: Phèdre*

If Molière is master of French neoclassical comedy, Jean Racine is France's preeminent neoclassical tragedian, and *Phèdre* is his essential masterpiece. It is both the culminating achievement of French neoclassical tragedy and the artistic justification for a set of stage conventions that often strikes modern audiences as overly narrow, severe, and artificial. The rules and methods of neoclassical drama that Racine commanded prescribed the strict observance of the unities of time, place, and action. Incidents needed to be confined to 12 to 24 hours in a single location. Subplots and inessential characters and scenes are eliminated, and stage action must grow out of a central, believably motivated dramatic situation. To reach the desired seriousness of purpose and elevation required for tragedy, characters needed to be of noble rank, and their language, often in long declamatory speeches, reflected their breeding and status, never descending to the crass or the common. Characters are denied physical contact, and any violence must take place offstage. As highly stylized as the Japanese Noh play, neoclassical drama seems impossibly formal and restrictive, particularly from the perspective of William Shakespeare's freedom of expression and expansiveness or compared to the graphic naturalism of modern dramatists, which spares its audience little. Racine in *Phèdre*, however, clearly shows how to make a virtue out of limitations, achieving an almost unbearable intensity and psychological penetration within the prescribed neoclassical rules that sacrificed breadth for depth, stirring action for inner conflict.

Despite abiding by the neoclassical stage conventions, Racine's dramas are marked by a radical assault on other standards of his day, particularly its melioristic humanism, and a rejection of a popular preference for tragicomedy, with its happy ending and assumed providential will in which the good are rewarded and the evil are punished. Racine returned drama to the bleak and severe tragic vision of Euripides and an examination of the often crippling paradoxes of human nature, unsupported by sustaining illusions of a benign divine order or faith in an unconquerable human will. His plays explored the darkly sinister workings of human passions and compulsions that are as irresistible as they are destructive. As a theatrical craftsman Racine was the master of dramatic intensity achieved through an economy of means. With stirring action restricted offstage, Racine concentrated interest within the characters themselves, providing an unprecedented interior view of motive and temperament. By doing so Racine pointed theater toward the modern conception of drama as inner conflict. If Molière radically altered the history of dramatic comedy, Racine accomplished the same transformation of tragedy, joining the classical and the modern into a powerful dramatic synthesis.

Racine was born in 1639 into a lower-middle-class family in a small provincial town northeast of Paris. Orphaned at age four, he was raised by his grandmother and sent in 1649 to be educated in the religious community of Port-Royal, the center of Jansenism, the austere Catholic sect akin to Calvinism that emphasized predestination and man's essentially corrupt nature. Theater was an anathema to the Jansenists, and the conflict between their spiritual teachings and more temporal, secular attractions would dominate Racine's makeup throughout his life. Racine remained at Port-Royal until he was 17, acquiring a solid education, particularly in classical literature, which equipped him well to pursue a literary career. As a university student he achieved some notoriety for his poetry, and after two years of training for the priesthood, Racine began his drama career in Paris. He was befriended by Molière, whose company performed Racine's first play, *La Thébaïde* (The Theban brothers) in 1664. It failed with audiences, but Molière persisted on behalf of the younger playwright, producing a lavish and successful production of Racine's second play, *Alexandre le Grande* in 1665. During the play's initial run Racine offended his mentor by unethically offering it to a rival company. A final break with Molière followed when Racine persuaded his mistress, one of Molière's leading actresses, to join a rival company. The two playwrights never spoke again. Despite his theatrical rivalries, quarrels with the Jansenists, and serial affairs with actresses, Racine subsequently produced the seven plays that established his reputation as the master of French classical tragedy: *Andromaque* (1667), *Brittanicus* (1668), *Bérénice* (1670), *Bajazet* (1672), *Mithridate* (1673), *Iphigénie* (1674), and *Phèdre* (1677). With stories borrowed from classical and biblical sources Racine's plays take for their themes the potentially damning effect of human passion, in which love often resembles hatred in its intensity and tendency toward self-destruction. After the production of *Phèdre* Racine experienced a religious conversion that led him to abandon the theater and to reconcile with the Jansenists. A famous quip said that after his conversion "Racine loved God as he loved his mistresses." He obtained the position of royal historiographer and spent his last 22 years chronicling the activities of the king and his court. He wrote two religious plays, *Esther* (1689) and *Athalie* (1691), before falling from the king's favor in 1698, a year before he died.

Phèdre was Racine's final secular drama, and in his own estimation, "probably the clearest and most closely-knit play I have written." Based on Euripides' *Hippolytus* (428 B.C.), *Phèdre* follows, in Racine's words, "a slightly different route from that author as regards the plot." Euripides dramatized the revenge of Aphrodite, goddess of love, on Hippolytus, Theseus's son and Phaedra's stepson for preferring Artemis, goddess of chastity. Aphrodite causes Phaedra to fall in love with Hippolytus, who rejects her advances, and Phaedra hangs herself in despair after denouncing Hippolytus as her seducer. Theseus banishes Hippolytus, who is killed fighting a bull sent from the sea to punish him. Artemis reveals the truth to Theseus, and father and son are reconciled before Hippolytus's death. As Racine's title change indicates, *Phèdre* shifts the emphasis from the chaste Hippolytus to his stepmother's monstrous passion. If Euripides dramatizes what happens when love is resisted, Racine looks at a love that is irresistible and self-destructive. In one of the stage's greatest female roles Phèdre is devoured by an uncontrollable passion that overmasters her reason and consumes her with guilt, jealousy, and self-loathing. In Racine's version of the destruction of Theseus's family the gods, who play an active role in controlling human fate in Euripides' play, are no longer central; the drama instead shifts from the clash between gods and humans to the inner conflict within the human psyche, between reason and the irrational, desire and conscience. Good and evil are not opposed in Racine's drama by representative characters but are shown battling within Phèdre herself.

As the play opens the austere and chaste Hippolytus of Euripides' play becomes, in Racine's handling, a young, guilt-ridden lover who confesses his passion for Aricie, the daughter of his father's enemy who has been condemned to celibacy. Racine's Hippolyte is therefore shown confronting a similar conflict between desire and duty that afflicts Phèdre. The power of the play is derived from the skill Racine displays in offering variations of the same theme—the potentially destructive power of passion to overbalance reason, duty, and responsibility. The most damning example is Phèdre. Unable to resist her shameful passion, Phèdre is tormented to illness and tempted by suicide. Her nurse and confidant, Œnone, describes Phèdre as "dying from a hidden malady" in which "Eternal discord reigns within her mind." Phèdre confesses to Œnone that the source of her suicidal anguish is her helpless and hateful passion for her stepson, her "adored enemy":

> I have a fitting horror for my crime;
> I hate this passion and I loathe my life
> Dying, I could have kept my name unstained,
> And my dark passion from the light of day.

Phèdre reveals herself as both wracked by guilt and heroic in her resistance to what she knows to be immoral but overpowering. She refuses to mitigate or justify her passion and is her own defendant and prosecutioner. However, news arrives that her husband, Thésée, has died, leaving open the possibility that Phèdre might overcome the illicitness of her passion and gain her desire, now, as Œnone asserts, that it is no longer shameful for her mistress to love Hippolyte. It is the first in a series of temptations that Phèdre cannot resist.

The second act opens with a third confession: Aricie's love for Hippolyte. Yet another character is struggling to control passion. Significantly for Phèdre Aricie will become a rival for Hippolyte's love, thereby adding jealousy to the mix of lust and guilt that torments Phèdre. In the act's impressive fifth scene, Phèdre finally confronts Hippolyte. In a brilliant psychological study of tentative probing and disguised wooing, Phèdre expresses her love for the son by recalling her love of the father. Describing Thésée's arrival in her native Crete when he mastered the labyrinth and slayed the Minotaur, Phèdre states:

> He had your eyes, your bearing, and your speech.
> His face flushed with your noble modesty. . . .
> Why could you not, too young, alas, have fared
> Forth with the ship that brought him to our shores?
> *You* would have slain the monstrous Cretan bull
> Despite the windings of his endless lair. . . .
> I, only I, would have revealed to you
> The subtle windings of the labyrinth.
> What care I would have lavished on your head!
> A thread would not have reassured my fears.
> Affronting danger side by side with you,
> I would myself have wished to lead the way,
> And Phèdre, with you in the labyrinth,
> Would have returned with you or met her doom.

To this Hippolyte sensibly asks if Phèdre has forgotten that Thésée is his father and her husband, and he is embarrassed and disgusted by what Phèdre's

words imply. Her response conveys her failed struggle to master her shameful
passion, and Phèdre begs Hippolyte to punish her with his sword in language
that is simultaneously masochistic, sexual, and coaxing:

> Take vengeance. Punish me for loving you.
> Come, prove yourself your father's worthy son,
> And of a vicious monster rid the world.
> I, Thésée's widow, dare to love his son!
> This frightful monster must not now escape.
> Here is my heart. Here must your blow strike home.
> Impatient to atone for its offence,
> I feel it strain to meet your mighty arm.
> Strike. Or if it's unworthy of your blows,
> Or such a death too mild for my deserts,
> Or if you deem my blood too vile to stain
> Your hand, lend me, if not your arm, your sword.
> Give me it!

Rescued by Œnone before she can take her own life, Phèdre in the third act is
alternately humiliated by Hippolyte's rejection and sustained by hope that he
will relent. Thésée's return, the reversal that sets in motion the play's climax,
presents Phèdre with the choice of revealing or concealing her love for Hippolyte. Yet again she is tempted to do the wrong thing, and the frightened
Phèdre accedes to Œnone's plan to deceive Thésée by accusing Hippolyte of
attempting to dishonor his stepmother.

In act four Thésée confronts his son with Œnone's charges, refuses to
believe his claim of innocence based on Hippolyte's avowed love for Aricie,
and banishes him, invoking the vengeance of Neptune upon his son. Phèdre,
on the brink of confessing all to Thésée and saving Hippolyte, is stunned into
silence and murderous jealousy by the revelation of Hippolyte's love for Aricie.
The news of Hippolyte's death from an encounter with the sea god Neptune
sent in response to Thésée's appeal reaches the palace. Phèdre, having taken
poison, dies onstage, in a singular violation of neoclassical conventions, after
the play's ultimate confession of her guilt to Thésée. Every attempt Phèdre
has made to overcome her passion has failed, leaving only death to resolve
her conflict. Racine comments in the play's preface that Phèdre "is neither
entirely guilty nor altogether innocent. She is involved by her destiny, and by
the anger of the gods, in an unlawful passion at which she is the very first to be
horrified. She prefers to let herself die rather than declare it to anyone. And,
when she is forced to disclose it, she speaks with such embarrassment that it is
clear that her crime is a punishment of the gods rather than an urge flowing
from her own will." Racine's mitigation of Phèdre as tragic victim is curi-
ously not a consolation that she seizes on herself. Racine's cosmology more

closely resembles the fatalistic worldview of the Jansenists than of the Greeks in which sin is the rule, not the exception. What makes *Phèdre* so powerful and so modern is its refusal to locate the source of its conflicts outside the range of human nature itself. If Molière offered in compensation for destroyed illusions a sustaining moderation and common sense, Racine indicts these as well, as hopeless against human desires. Phèdre's losing battle to control and master her passion is both heroic in her resistance and inevitable in Racine's dark vision of human limitations.

ROMEO AND JULIET

(c. 1595)

by William Shakespeare

Shakespeare, more than any other author, has instructed the West in the catastrophes of sexuality, and has invented the formula that the sexual becomes the erotic when crossed by the shadow of death. There had to be one high song of the erotic by Shakespeare, one lyrical and tragicomical paean celebrating an unmixed love and lamenting its inevitable destruction. Romeo and Juliet *is unmatched, in Shakespeare and in the world's literature, as a vision of an uncompromising mutual love that perishes of its own idealism and intensity.*
—Harold Bloom, *Shakespeare: The Invention of the Human*

Romeo and Juliet, regarded by many as William Shakespeare's first great play, is generally thought to have been written around 1595. Shakespeare was then 31 years old, married for 12 years and the father of three children. He had been acting and writing in London for five years. His stage credits included mainly histories—the three parts of *Henry VI* and *Richard III*—and comedies—*The Two Gentlemen of Verona, The Taming of the Shrew, The Comedy of Errors,* and *Love's Labour's Lost.* Shakespeare's first tragedy, modeled on Seneca, *Titus Andronicus,* was written around 1592. From that year through 1595 Shakespeare had also composed 154 sonnets and two long narrative poems in the erotic tradition—*Venus and Adonis* and *The Rape of Lucrece.* Both his dramatic and nondramatic writing show Shakespeare mastering Elizabethan literary conventions. Then, around 1595, Shakespeare composed three extraordinary plays—*Richard II, A Midsummer Night's Dream,* and *Romeo and Juliet*—in three different genres—history, comedy, and tragedy—signaling a new mastery, originality, and excellence. With these three plays Shakespeare emerged from the shadows of his influences and initiated a period of unexcelled accomplishment. The two parts of *Henry IV* and *Julius Caesar* would follow, along with the romantic comedies *The Merchant of Venice, As You Like It,* and *Twelfth Night* and the great tragedies *Hamlet, Othello, King Lear, Macbeth,* and *Antony and Cleopatra.* The three plays of 1595, therefore, serve as an important bridge between Shakespeare's apprenticeship and his mature achievements. *Romeo and Juliet,* in particular, is a crucial play in the evolution of Shakespeare's tragic vision, in his integration of poetry and drama, and in his initial exploration of the connection between love and tragedy that he would continue in *Troilus and Cressida, Othello,* and *Antony and Cleopatra. Romeo and Juliet* is not only one of the greatest love stories in all literature, considering its stage history and the musicals, opera, music, ballet, literary works, and films that it has inspired; it is quite possibly the most popular play of all time. There is simply no more famous pair of lovers than Romeo and Juliet, and their story has become an inescapable central myth in our understanding of romantic love.

Despite the play's persistence, cultural saturation, and popular appeal, *Romeo and Juliet* has fared less well with scholars and critics, who have generally judged it inferior to the great tragedies that followed. Instead of the later tragedies of character *Romeo and Juliet* has been downgraded as a tragedy of chance, and, in the words of critic James Calderwood, the star-crossed lovers are "insufficiently endowed with complexity" to become tragic heroes. Instead "they become a study of victimage and sacrifice, not tragedy." What is too often missing in a consideration of the shortcomings of *Romeo and Juliet* by contrast with the later tragedies is the radical departure the play represented when compared to what preceded it. Having relied on Senecan horror for his first tragedy, *Titus Andronicus,* Shakespeare located his next in the world of comedy and romance. *Romeo and Juliet* is set not in antiquity, as Elizabethan convention dictated for a tragic subject, but in 16th-century Verona, Italy. His tragic protagonists are neither royal nor noble, as Aristotle advised, but two teenagers caught up in the petty disputes of their families. The plight of young lovers pitted against parental or societal opposition was the expected subject, since Roman times, of comedy, not tragedy. By showing not the eventual triumph but the death of the two young lovers Shakespeare violated comic conventions, while making a case that love and its consequences could be treated with an unprecedented tragic seriousness. As critic Harry Levin has observed, Shakespeare's contemporaries "would have been surprised, and possibly shocked at seeing lovers taken so seriously. Legend, it had been heretofore taken for granted, was the proper matter for serious drama; romance was the stuff of the comic stage."

Shakespeare's innovations are further evident in comparison to his source material. The plot was a well-known story in Italian, French, and English versions. Shakespeare's direct source was Arthur Brooke's poem *The Tragicall Historye of Romeus and Juliet* (1562). This moralistic work was intended as a warning to youth against "dishonest desire" and disobeying parental authority. Shakespeare, by contrast, purifies and ennobles the lovers' passion, intensifies the pathos, and underscores the injustice of the lovers' destruction. Compressing the action from Brooke's many months into a five-day crescendo, Shakespeare also expands the roles of secondary characters such as Mercutio and Juliet's nurse into vivid portraits that contrast the lovers' elevated lyricism with a bawdy earthiness and worldly cynicism. Shakespeare transforms Brooke's plodding verse into a tour de force verbal display that is supremely witty, if at times over elaborate, and, at its best, movingly expressive. If the poet and the dramatist are not yet seamlessly joined in *Romeo and Juliet*, the play still displays a considerable advance in Shakespeare's orchestration of verse, image, and incident that would become the hallmark of his greatest achievements.

The play's theme and outcome are announced in the Prologue:

> Two households, both alike in dignity,
> In fair Verona, where we lay our scene,
> From ancient grudge break to new mutiny,
> Where civil blood makes civil hands unclean.
> From forth the fatal loins of these two foes
> A pair of star-cross'd lovers take their life;
> Whose misadventur'd piteous overthrows
> Doth with their death bury their parents' strife.

Suspense over the lovers' fate is eliminated at the outset as Shakespeare emphasizes the forces that will destroy them. The initial scene makes this clear as a public brawl between servants of the feuding Montagues and Capulets escalates to involve kinsmen and the patriarchs on both sides, ended only when the Prince of Verona enforces a cease-fire under penalty of death for future offenders of the peace. Romeo, Montague's young son, does not participate in the scuffle since he is totally absorbed by a hopeless passion for a young, unresponsive beauty named Rosaline. Initially Romeo appears as a figure of mockery, the embodiment of the hypersensitive, melancholy adolescent lover, who is urged by his kinsman Benvolio to resist sinking "under love's heavy burden" and seek another more worthy of his affection. Another kinsman, Mercutio, for whom love is more a game of easy conquest, urges Romeo to "be rough with love" and master his circumstances. When by chance it is learned that Rosaline is to attend a party at the Capulets, Benvolio suggests that they should go as well for Romeo to compare Rosaline's charms with the other beauties at the party and thereby cure his infatuation. There Romeo sees Juliet, Capulet's not-yet 14-year-old daughter. Her parents are encouraging her to accept a match with Count Paris for the social benefit of the family. Love as affectation and love as advantage are transformed into love as all-consuming, mutual passion at first sight. Romeo claims that he "ne'er saw true beauty till this night," and by the force of that beauty, he casts off his former melancholic self-absorption. Juliet is no less smitten. Sending her nurse to learn the stranger's identity, she worries, "If he be married, / My grave is like to be my wedding bed." Both are shocked to learn that they are on either side of the family feud, and their risk is underscored when the Capulet kinsman,

Tybalt, recognizes Romeo and, though prevented by Capulet from violence at the party, swears future vengeance. Tybalt's threat underscores that this is a play as much about hate as about love, in which Romeo and Juliet's passion is increasingly challenged by the public and family forces that deny love's authority.

The first of the couple's two great private moments in which love's redemptive and transformative power works its magic follows in possibly the most famous single scene in all of drama, set in the Capulets' orchard, overlooked by Juliet's bedroom window. In some of the most impassioned, lyrical, and famous verses Shakespeare ever wrote, the lovers' dialogue perfectly captures the ecstasy of love and love's capacity to remake the world. Seeing Juliet above at her window, Romeo says:

> But soft! What light through yonder window breaks?
> It is the East, and Juliet is the sun!
> Arise, fair sun, and kill the envious moon,
> Who is already sick and pale with grief
> That thou her maid art far more fair than she.

He overhears Juliet's declaration of her love for him and the rejection of what is implied if a Capulet should love a Montague:

> O Romeo, Romeo! wherefore art thou Romeo?
> Deny thy father and refuse thy name!
> Or, if thou wilt not, be but sworn my love,
> And I'll no longer be a Capulet. . . .
> 'Tis but thy name that is my enemy.
> Thou art thyself, though not a Montague.
> What's Montague? it is nor hand, nor foot,
> Nor arm, nor face, nor any other part
> Belonging to a man. O, be some other name!
> What's in a name? That which we call a rose
> By any other name would smell as sweet.
> So Romeo would, were he not Romeo call'd,
> Retain that dear perfection which he owes
> Without that title. Romeo, doff thy name;
> And for that name, which is no part of thee,
> Take all myself.

In a beautifully modulated scene the lovers freely admit their passion and exchange vows of love that become a marriage proposal. As Juliet continues to be called back to her room and all that is implied as Capulet's daughter, time and space become the barriers to love's transcendent power to unite.

With the assistance of Friar Lawrence, who regards the union of a Montague and a Capulet as an opportunity "To turn your households' rancour to pure love," Romeo and Juliet are secretly married. Before nightfall and the anticipated consummation of their union Romeo is set upon by Tybalt, who is by Romeo's marriage, his new kinsman. Romeo accordingly refuses his challenge, but it is answered by Mercutio. Romeo tries to separate the two, but in the process Mercutio is mortally wounded. This is the tragic turn of the play as Romeo, enraged, rejects the principle of love forged with Juliet for the claims of reputation, the demand for vengeance, and an identification of masculinity with violent retribution:

> My very friend, hath got this mortal hurt
> In my behalf; my reputation stain'd
> With Tybalt's slander—Tybalt, that an hour
> Hath been my kinsman. O sweet Juliet,
> Thy beauty hath made me effeminate
> And in my temper soft'ned valour's steel!

After killing Tybalt, Romeo declares, "O, I am fortune's fool!" He may blame circumstances for his predicament, but he is clearly culpable in capitulating to the values of society he had challenged in his love for Juliet.

The lovers are given one final moment of privacy before the catastrophe. Juliet, awaiting Romeo's return, gives one of the play's most moving speeches, balancing sublimity with an intimation of mortality that increasingly accompanies the lovers:

> Come, gentle night; come, loving, black-brow'd night;
> Give me my Romeo; and, when he shall die,
> Take him and cut him out in little stars,
> And he will make the face of heaven so fine
> That all the world will be in love with night
> And pay no worship to the garish sun.

Learning the terrible news of Tybalt's death and Romeo's banishment, Juliet wins her own battle between hate and love and sends word to Romeo to keep their appointed night together before they are parted.

As Romeo is away in Mantua Juliet's parents push ahead with her wedding to Paris. The solution to Juliet's predicament is offered by Friar Lawrence who gives her a drug that will make it appear she has died. The Friar is to summon Romeo, who will rescue her when she awakes in the Capulet family tomb. The Friar's message to Romeo fails to reach him, and Romeo learns of Juliet's death. Reversing his earlier claim of being "fortune's fool," Romeo reacts by declaring, "Then I defy you, stars," rushing to his wife and breaking society's rules by acquiring the poison to join her in death. Reaching the tomb Romeo is surprised to find Paris on hand, weeping for his lost bride. Outraged by the intrusion on his grief Paris confronts Romeo. They fight, and after killing Paris, Romeo finally recognizes him and mourns him as "Mercutio's kinsman." Inside the tomb Romeo sees Tybalt's corpse and asks forgiveness before taking leave of Juliet with a kiss:

> . . . O, here
> Will I set up my everlasting rest
> And shake the yoke of inauspicious stars
> From this world-wearied flesh.

Juliet awakes to see Romeo dead beside her. Realizing what has happened, she responds by taking his dagger and plunges it into her breast: "This is thy sheath; there rest, and let me die."

Montagues, Capulets, and the Prince arrive, and the Friar explains what has happened and why. His account of Romeo and Juliet's tender passion and devotion shames the two families into ending their feud. The Prince provides the final eulogy:

> A glooming peace this morning with it brings.
> The sun for sorrow will not show his head.
> Go hence, to have more talk of these sad things;
> Some shall be pardon'd, and some punished;
> For never was a story of more woe
> Than this of Juliet and her Romeo.

The sense of loss Verona and the audience feels at the lovers' deaths is a direct result of Shakespeare's remarkable ability to conjure love in all its transcendent power, along with its lethal risks. Set on a collision course with the values bent on denying love's sway, Romeo and Juliet manage to create a dreamlike, alternative, private world that is so touching because it is so brief and perishable. Shakespeare's triumph here is to make us care that adolescent romance matters—emotionally, psychologically, and socially—and that the premature and unjust death of lovers rival in profundity and significance the fall of kings.

LOOK BACK IN ANGER

(1956)

by John Osborne

I want to make people feel, to give them lessons in feeling. They can think afterward. In some countries this could be a dangerous approach, but there seems little danger of people feeling too much—at least not in England as I am writing. . . . I shall simply fling down a few statements—you can take your pick. They will be called what are often called "sweeping statements" but I believe we are living at a time when a few "sweeping statements" may be valuable. It is too late for caution.

—John Osborne, "They Call it Cricket," Declaration, 1957

Between 1945 and 1956 the British theater, caught in a post-Shavian old order, offered such fare as the drawing-room comedies of Noël Coward, Terence Rattigan's subdued dramas of repressed middle- and upper-middle class emotions, Agatha Christie's *The Mousetrap*, and the heavily nostalgic musical *The Boyfriend*. The strength of postwar British theater lay in its actors—John Gielgud, Laurence Olivier, Richard Burton, Alec Guinness, Peggy Ashcroft—whose performing genius, primarily in the classics, would become legendary. Although the revival of verse drama by T. S. Eliot, W. H. Auden, and Christopher Fry seemed to herald a new "Elizabethan Age" of theater, these plays were not powerful enough to reflect a confused post-war culture that hinted at a breakdown of class distinctions and reflected the emergence of a welfare state and the crisis of confidence resulting from Britain's loss of its empire. An influential and innovative theater of social and emotional realism had been present in American dramas by Clifford Odets in the 1930s and by such postwar playwrights as Tennessee Williams, William Inge, and Arthur Miller. On May 8, 1956, a British alternative to what one theater critic characterized as "England's aspidistra dramas" exploded onto the stage of the Royal Court Theatre with John Osborne's *Look Back in Anger*. Osborne's socially and emotionally provocative play, with its vitriolic, bitterly alienated but sensitive working-class antihero protagonist, revitalized theater in Britain and marked a revolutionary shift in dramatic energy from the old order of contemporary theater to an entirely new, more democratic style of English drama.

John Osborne belonged to a group of dissident British playwrights and novelists of the 1950s and early 1960s whom journalists dubbed the "Angry Young Men," a phrase taken from the title of the 1951 autobiography of writer Leslie Allen Paul, *The Angry Young Man*. The "Angries," who included writers such as Kingsley Amis, John Braine, John Wain, and Alan Sillitoe, produced works that expressed discontent and disillusionment with the staid, hypocritical, middle- and upper-middle-class institutions of the so-called British establishment, while at the same time articulating dissatisfaction with their own achievements. *Look Back in Anger* was the seminal work of this genre, and Osborne, perhaps the angriest and most forceful voice of this generation.

Osborne was born in 1929, in Fulham, in Southwest London, the son of a commercial artist, copywriter, and sometime publican; his mother was a barmaid who worked in pubs for most of her life. His family background was a study in contrast: His father came from a gentle, soft-spoken Welsh family, while his maternal grandparents were boisterous, reactive London publicans. The influence of his mother's side of the family led Osborne to later declare, "to become angry is to care." Osborne's childhood was marked by near poverty, frequent illnesses, and the experience of living through the war. His father, similarly delicate in health, died of tuberculosis in 1941, another event that deeply affected his son. Osborne attended state schools and at 12 became a scholarship student at a minor private school, St. Michael's in Devon, where he was expelled at 16 after the headmaster slapped his face and Osborne hit him back. He nevertheless received a general certificate of education, which ended his formal education. He went on to study at universities but was largely self-taught. He wrote for various trade journals and then accepted a job tutoring child actors in a provincial theatrical touring company, a position from which he was fired after an education inspector discovered that he was not certified to teach. However, he was asked to stay with the company as an assistant stage manager and eventually made his debut as an actor, in 1948 in Sheffield.

During his time as a repertory actor Osborne wrote, in collaboration with other actors, plays that were produced in provincial venues. *The Devil Inside Him* (written with Stella Linden and produced in 1950) concerns a young Welsh poet mistreated by his family and his village community. *Personal Enemy* (written with Anthony Creighton and produced in 1955) depicts the McCarthy era in the United States and is notable for its incoherence after the authors deleted a large portion of the play concerning homosexuality at the insistence of the Lord Chamberlain's Office, which had refused to grant a license otherwise. *Epitaph for George Dillon* (written with Creighton in 1954) portrays a young, unscrupulous actor-playwright who achieves a kind of fame when his play becomes a tawdry but artistically worthless success. The play was rejected by every theater in London but debuted in an undergraduate production at Oxford University in 1957. The following year, after the success of *Look Back in Anger*, the play was produced by the English Stage Company at the Royal Court Theatre and received mixed reviews.

The failure of *Personal Enemy* sent Osborne back to acting. He moved to London, where he endured long stretches of unemployment and spent most of his time in the public library because it was warmer than the cramped flat he shared with the first of his five wives, Pamela Lane. *Look Back in Anger*, the play he was writing at the time, reflects aspects of his failing marriage to Lane. The play was rejected by every London theatrical agent, an experience of which Osborne would later write, "The speed with which it had been returned was not surprising, but its aggressive dispatch did give me a kind of relief. It was like being grasped at the upper arm by a testy policeman and told to move on." Osborne finally submitted *Look Back in Anger* to the newly formed English Stage Company, which was advertising for new plays to offer at the reestablished Royal Court, a small theater that had been fashionable and famous earlier in the century (George Bernard Shaw had supervised productions of his plays at the Royal Court). The English Stage Company was founded by actor-manager and artistic director George Devine with the intention of promoting a writers' theater as an affordable alternative to the commercialism of West End productions. Works by Samuel Beckett, Bertolt Brecht, Jean Genet, and American playwrights would be produced at the Royal Court; *Look Back in Anger* was the first British play produced there. Devine later recorded that when he first read the play, "the text leapt to life off the page. . . . We put this play on because we thought it *had* to be put on."

On the surface *Look Back in Anger* is a conventional, realistic, three-act play. It is set in a one-room attic flat somewhere in the English Midlands and is the home of Jimmy Porter and his wife, Alison. The primary voice of *Look Back in Anger* belongs to Jimmy, a working-class young man, whose lengthy speeches set the play's polemical and emotional tone and drive the drama's action. University educated, not in one of the prestigious "red brick" Oxbridge schools, but in a newer, so-called white tile university, Jimmy runs a candy stand in an open-air market with his friend, Cliff Lewis, a good-natured young man who lives in a separate bedroom across the hall from the Porters' flat. The first act opens on a Sunday evening in April. Alison, dressed in a slip, is ironing, and Jimmy and Cliff are in easy chairs reading the Sunday papers. Jimmy, complaining that the book review he is reading in his "posh" paper is partly written in French, redirects his acid sarcasm toward Alison and Cliff, condemning his wife's middle-class inertia and taunting Cliff for his lack of education and ignorance. He rails against the soulless English middle class, singling out Alison's family, especially her brother, Nigel, "the chinless wonder from Sandhurst," a Member of Parliament whom Jimmy resents for his easy success despite his insensitivity and stupidity. He calls his wife "the Lady

Pusillanimous," attacks women in general, and complains about the noise of Alison's ironing and Cliff's rustling of his newspaper as he tries to listen to a concert on the radio. During a playful wrestling match between Jimmy and Cliff, the ironing board is accidentally turned over and Alison burns her arm. She angrily tells Jimmy to get out, and while he is gone, Cliff tends to Alison's burn and calms her. Alison reveals to Cliff that she is pregnant but is afraid to tell Jimmy, who, she fears, will think she planned it. She admits she is miserable and is thinking of leaving her husband. When Jimmy returns and Cliff leaves, Jimmy admits to Alison that he feels trapped by his love for her; he is angry that she cannot feel pain and cannot understand him, although he still wants her. The two embark on their own particular form of love play, which consists of an affectionate game of "bears and squirrels," using stuffed animals. Such regressive behavior evokes the nursery of the Edwardian era, an idealized time of innocence for which Jimmy is nostalgic. Cliff calls Alison to the phone downstairs; she returns to tell them that her actress friend, Helena Charles, is coming to stay with them. This sparks a new diatribe from Jimmy, who directs his rage once again toward Alison: "If only something would happen to you, and wake you out of your beauty sleep!" He tells Cliff, "She'll go on sleeping and devouring until there's nothing left of me."

The second act takes place two weeks later. Alison has not told Jimmy of her pregnancy. Helena's firm emplacement in the household has caused tension. Jimmy resents her influence over Alison, telling Helena, "You're determined to win her, aren't you? So it's come to this now!" He describes how he "rescued" Alison from her mother:

> Mummy and I took one quick look at each other, and, from then on, the age of chivalry was dead. . . . But even I under-estimated her strength. Mummy may look over-fed and a bit flabby on the outside, but don't let that well-bred guzzler fool you. Underneath all that, she's armor-plated—She's as rough as a night in a Bombay brothel, and as tough as a matelot's arm.

Jimmy then tells of how he sat with his father as he lay dying for months and says he "learnt at an early age what it was to be angry—angry and helpless." He is called to the phone, and while he is gone Helena tells Alison that she has telegraphed Alison's father to bring her home. Jimmy returns to report that the mother of his friend Hugh has had a stroke and that he will go to London to be with her. (She is a working-class woman who advanced the money to start the candy business.) He needs Alison to go with him, but she leaves with Helena to go to church. In the next scene it is the following evening, and Colonel Redfern, Alison's father, has arrived to collect his daughter. He was in colonial service in India for 30 years and now voices his perplexity over modern England. He is sympathetic toward Jimmy and expresses his regret at his passivity during the time his wife viciously attempted to block Alison's marriage. Alison explains that she married Jimmy because he was a challenge to her "happy, uncomplicated life," a "spiritual barbarian." After Alison and her father leave Jimmy comes in and reads the letter his wife has left for him. Helena tells him that Alison is pregnant, but Jimmy does not care; he has no pity for her after watching Hugh's mother die. He calls Helena an "evil-minded little virgin," and she slaps his face. A despairing Jimmy begins to cry, and Helena kisses him passionately.

The opening scene of act 3 reflects the setup of act 1: It is a Sunday evening; Jimmy and Cliff are reading the newspapers, and Helena is ironing. Jimmy makes fun of the stories he is reading, but the tone is light. He and Cliff go into a vaudeville routine, and Helena joins them. Jimmy and Cliff playfully wrestle, and Cliff's shirt gets dirty. When Helena goes off to wash it, Cliff tells Jimmy that he plans to give up the candy stall, move out, and perhaps find a woman of his own. Helena returns and tells Jimmy that she loves him. Alison enters, looking thin and ill; Jimmy leaves the two women alone together. Alison reveals that she has suffered a miscarriage. She does not want to come between Helena and Jimmy, but Helena realizes that the affair was wrong and is over, and she leaves. Jimmy returns to rebuke Alison for not sending flowers to the funeral. Then he softens, as he describes himself as a lonely "old bear, following his own breath in the dark forest." He remembers when they first met and tells her, "I thought I was a lost cause, but I thought if you loved me, it needn't matter." Alison collapses on the floor and, groveling before him, cries out that by failing to protect her baby, she has at last experienced the pain of living and can understand him. Jimmy tenderly comforts her, and they play "bears and squirrels" in reconciliation and in yearning for lost childhood.

Look Back in Anger, with its liberating, rhetorical power, lack of "polite" discourse (the Lord Chamberlain, in particular, took issue with Jimmy Porter's "Mummy" speech, singling out the use of the word *brothel*), and its indictment of middle-class stoicism (in a country which had just displayed that quality to the maximum in a world war), was not an immediate success, although it generated intense critical excitement. Reviewers variously characterized the play as vulgar, feverish, savage, barbaric, and even boring (one critic felt it should be called "Look Back in Whining"), while at the same time acknowledging Osborne as a playwright of great promise. Then Kenneth Tynan, the most influential theater critic of the age, weighed in on the play's merits. As he wrote in the *Observer,*

> I agree that *Look Back in Anger* is likely to remain a minority taste. What matters, however, is the size of the minority. I estimate it at roughly 6,733,000, which is the number of people in this country between the ages of twenty and thirty. And this figure will doubtless be swelled by refugees from other age-groups who are curious to know precisely what

the contemporary young pup is thinking and feeling. . . . I could not love anyone who did not wish to see *Look Back in Anger*. It is the best young play of its decade.

After a rough start, financially and critically, *Look Back in Anger* won its audience and became a staple of British theater. It was made into a well-received film with Richard Burton in the role of Jimmy Porter and continues to be performed. Its influence would be felt in the works of such playwrights as Harold Pinter, Robert Bolt, John Arden, and Peter Shaffer and novelists such as Sillitoe, the author of *Saturday Night and Sunday Morning* and *The Loneliness of the Long-Distance Runner*. This innovative group of young writers would cut across class lines to provide British literature and drama with a newly experimental and challenging voice.

THE HOMECOMING

(1965)

by Harold Pinter

Thirty-two years after its London premiere in 1965, The Homecoming . . . *still has the power to shock. It drags out of the darkness the forbidden sexual desires of fathers for their sons' wives and brothers for their brothers', showing life in an all-male family as a cauldron of anger, competition, lust and loneliness, which boils over when a woman finally arrives. The superficially unlikely, even laughable, code of behaviour by which this particular family operates is also disturbing at a deep level, because the fantasies and drives underlying it are universally recognizable.*

—Maggie Gee, Review of *The Homecoming, Times Literary Supplement,* 1997

When Harold Pinter was awarded the Nobel Prize in literature in 2005, Per Wästberg, chair of the Nobel Committee, called him "the renewer of English drama in the 20th century," a playwright who revealed "the abyss under chat, the unwillingness to communicate other than superficially, the need to rule and mislead, the suffocating sensation of accidents bubbling under the quotidian, the nervous perception that a dangerous story has been censored." The prominence and universal acclaim that Pinter now commands contrast mightily with the hostile bafflement that initially greeted his plays. When his first full-length drama, *The Birthday Party,* now regarded a classic in the modern drama repertory, opened in 1958, it was a box office and critical failure. "Sitting through *The Birthday Party,*" one reviewer observed, ". . . is like trying to solve a crossword puzzle where every vertical clue is designed to put you off the horizontal. It will be best enjoyed by those who believe that obscurity is its own reward." Another exasperatingly declared: "What all this means, only Mr Pinter knows, for as his characters speak in non-sequiturs, half-gibberish and lunatic ravings, they are unable to explain their actions." Yet, when a production of the play was broadcast in Britain in 1960 it attracted a large national audience and created a sensation. *Pinteresque* first entered the English language to describe the playwright's characteristic uncovering of threat and menace in the mundane and finding the poetry and subtext of everyday speech and silences. In subsequent plays such as *The Dumb Waiter* (1959), *The Caretaker* (1960), *The Homecoming* (1965), *Old Times* (1970), *No Man's Land* (1975), and *Betrayal* (1978), Pinter created one of the most influential body of dramatic works in English. As a modern dramatist only Samuel Beckett has attracted more critical attention. Like Beckett, Pinter's vision and methods have entered the collective consciousness. Terms such that the *Pinter moment* and the *Pinter pause*, like *Pinteresque*, are readily understood descriptors for our times. *The Homecoming* best represents Pinter's unique contribution to modern drama; it is a play whose power is undiminished after nearly half a century. Like Nora's explosive exit in Henrik Ibsen's *A Doll's House*, *The Homecoming* still provokes both an audience's unsettling fascination and critical debate over its meaning and methods.

Pinter was born in Hackney, in East London in 1930, the son of a Jewish tailor. "It was a working-class area—" Pinter recalled, "some big, run-down Victorian houses, and a soap factory with a terrible smell, and a lot of railway yards. And shops. It had a lot of shops." At the outbreak of the war Pinter was evacuated to Cornwall and to the London suburbs. Back home in 1944 Pinter experienced the German bombing: "There were times when I would open our back door and find our garden in flames. Our house never burned, but we had to evacuate several times." Pinter's wartime experiences, as well as the anti-Semitism he encountered—the sense of threat and dislocation—help explain the themes of vulnerability and menace that haunt his works. Attending Hackney Downs Grammar School, Pinter excelled at sports (football, cricket, and track) and got his first acting experience playing Macbeth and Romeo in school productions. After leaving school in 1947 Pinter worked at a variety of odd jobs, including dishwasher, waiter, and salesman. Liable for national service at 18, Pinter declared himself a conscientious objector. Tribunals twice refused Pinter's application for objector status, but instead of being jailed for his refusal to serve, a sympathetic judge merely fined him. He studied acting for a short time at the Royal Academy of Dramatic Art and later at the Central School of Speech and Drama. Pinter then toured Ireland in a Shakespearean company and worked in provincial repertory theaters throughout England.

In 1957, at the insistence of a friend, Pinter attempted his first play, *The Room*, in which a middle-aged couple's complacent domestic routine is violently and mysteriously shattered. The play foreshadows many of the themes and motifs of Pinter's subsequent dramas, most directly in the play's title. "Two people in a room—I am dealing a good deal with this image of two people in a room," Pinter later summarized. "The curtain goes up on the stage, and I see it as a very potent question: What is going to happen to these two people in the room? Is someone going to open a door and come in?" *The Room* also features Pinter's trademark realistically depicted domestic routine that is gradually supercharged with menace and mystery. The hallmarks of

Pinter's dramatic method is also established in the play's mixture of tragedy and farce; the spot-on accuracy of its dialogue, in all its trivialities, cross-talk, and avoidance of true communication; and a deliberate elimination of exposition or explicit motivation for his characters. First produced by the Drama Department of Bristol University, *The Room* received a favorable review from Harold Hobson, drama critic of the *Sunday Times*. This would lead to Pinter's first professional production of *The Birthday Party* in 1958. Set in a dingy, seaside boarding house, the play concerns the psychological deterioration of the boarder named Stanley prompted by the arrival of two sinister strangers. Why Stanley is a target and by whom are never answered. However, by eliminating conventional dramatic exposition and resolution, Pinter achieves a tension and resonance that taps into powerful anxieties of uncertainty and threat. Initially Pinter's realistic working-class characters and settings associated him with the younger generation of new social realistic playwrights, led by John Osborne, but Pinter's illogical, existential themes suggest a closer affinity with the theater of the absurd. It is actually the fusion of both—realism and absurdity—that characterizes Pinter's originality and his singular contribution to modern drama. *The Caretaker* (1960), Pinter's second full-length stage play and his first public success, concerns a tramp, Davies, who is given shelter in the home of two brothers, Aston and Mick, who quarrel over the prospect of giving Davies the job as caretaker of the house. Pinter's recurrent themes of the problems of communication and language and the struggle for dominance and power are expressed in a drama that is by turns comic, absurd, malevolent, enigmatic, and moving. As in Pinter's best work the play works simultaneously on the realistic and symbolic levels as the three characters and their circumstances are both individualized and representative of archetypes and universals.

This same mixture gives Pinter's third full-length play, *The Homecoming*, its power and energy. As critic Martin Esslin summarizes, "The play presents a sequence of realistic (or at least realistically explicable) events which at the same time could be, might well be, fantasy, a wish-fulfillment dream. On either level the play makes sense. But its poetic force lies in the ambivalence between the two." Set in a North London sitting room, the play concerns the homecoming of the eldest son, Teddy, a professor of philosophy at an American college, after an absence of six years. Teddy, who has told his family nothing about his marriage or his three sons in the United States, has brought his English wife, Ruth, whom he had married before leaving, to meet his family for the first time. The house is occupied by Max, a retired butcher, and Teddy's two brothers: the contentious and self-assured Lenny and the slow-witted, brawny Joey, who works in demolition while training as a boxer. The fourth resident is Max's brother, Sam, a hire-car driver. The play's opening scene of verbal sparring among the house's occupants sets the tone of the play in its rapidly unsettling alterations from commonplace domestic routine to brutal attack. The scene establishes that the family's matriarch, Jessie, Max's wife, is dead, along with Max's former friend MacGregor. Jessie is ambiguously recalled by her husband in both admiring and denigrating terms: "She wasn't such a bad woman. Even though it made me sick just to look at her rotten stinking face, she wasn't such a bad bitch." Max successively tangles verbally and violently with Lenny, Sam, and Joey, establishing the contradictions and menace that awaits Teddy and Ruth when they arrive after midnight in the second scene.

Nothing quite makes sense regarding their visit. Anxious that Ruth meet his family, whom he assures her are "very warm people, really. Very warm. They're my family. They're not ogres," Teddy makes no effort to wake them or announce their arrival. Ruth, who initially complains of being tired, refuses to go upstairs to bed with her husband, insisting on going for a walk instead. Teddy's first encounter with Lenny betrays no sign that either brother is pleased or surprised to see the other after such an absence. Going to bed Teddy neglects to mention Ruth who must identify herself when she returns. Lenny ignores the news, preferring to talk about his insomnia, before requesting to hold Ruth's hand. When asked why, he offers two irrelevant stories about his beating up a woman whom he would have killed except for the bother of disposing of the body and striking an old woman who had asked him to move a heavy iron mangle. Lenny's anecdotes describing acts of brutality against women imply his attempt to intimidate Ruth. She, however, coolly questions him about details of the stories while seizing the role of aggressor when Lenny proposes relieving her of the glass from which she is drinking:

RUTH   I haven't quite finished.

LENNY   You've consumed quite enough, in my opinion.

RUTH   No, I haven't.

LENNY   Quite sufficient, in my opinion.

RUTH   Not in mine, Leonard.

Pause

LENNY   Don't call me that, please.

RUTH   Why not?

LENNY   That's the name my mother gave me.

Pause

Just give me the glass.

RUTH   No.

Pause

LENNY   I'll take it then.

RUTH   If you take the glass . . . I'll take you.

Having bested Lenny in their contest of wills, Ruth goes upstairs. Their noise has woken Max. Lenny does not disclose the arrival of his brother or his wife but puts a question to his father: "That night . . . you know . . . the night you got me . . . that night with Mum, what was it like?" Enraged, Max closes the scene by shouting: "You'll drown in your own blood."

The third scene in the act takes place the next morning as Max expresses his surprise at Teddy's appearance by calling Ruth a "smelly scrubber" and a "stinking pox-ridden slut," noting that there has not been a whore in the house since Jessie died. When Joey apologizes for Max, saying he is just an old man, Max responds by striking Joey in the stomach causing him to stagger across the room. When Max begins to collapse with the exertion, Sam tries to help him, but Max hits him in the head with his cane. Max then asks Ruth if she is a mother, seems pleased when she reports that she has three boys, and invites Teddy to kiss and cuddle "your old father." When Teddy replies, "Come on, Dad. I'm ready for the cuddle," Max addresses his family: "He still loves his father!" and the act ends.

Act 1 violates virtually every sanctity of family life by revealing the compulsions and aggression uniting this family unit. The home is shown to be a winner-take-all war zone in which the mundane spontaneously combusts with verbal and physical violence, while mutuality is expressed by assertions of dominance and control. None of the characters conforms to expected behavior patterns. The aging patriarch Max insists on his virility with masculine aggression, while assuming the family's maternal role as homemaker and cook; Ruth is both passive and something of a sexual predator; the long-absent Teddy is greeted by matter-of-fact indifference. Act 2 escalates the assault on conventions while suffusing the play's naturalism with a poetic and symbolic resonance. The interactions among the six characters culminate in Teddy's abrupt insistence that he and Ruth should depart for home. Lenny, demanding a farewell dance, caresses Ruth in front of the impassive Teddy. When Joey enters he observes that "Old Lenny's got a tart in here" and joins in, eventually atop Ruth on the floor. After spending two hours upstairs with her, Joey returns to the sitting room where the men discuss arranging for Ruth to stay after Teddy's departure. Lenny solves the practical challenge of her upkeep by proposing that she be put to work as a prostitute along with "her obligations this end." The prospect of a wife and mother servicing her father-in-law and brothers-in-law while earning her keep "on the game" is shocking enough. But when Teddy calmly introduces the scheme to Ruth, she accepts after negotiating the best deal she can:

> RUTH   You'd supply my wardrobe, of course?

> LENNY   We'd supply everything. Everything you need.

> RUTH   I'd need an awful lot. Otherwise I wouldn't be content.

> LENNY   You'd have everything.

> RUTH   I would naturally want to draw up an inventory of everything I would need, which would require your signatures in the presence of witnesses.

> LENNY   Naturally.

Evidence supporting the plausibility of Ruth's acquiescence can be found in the play: in her dissatisfaction with her marriage and her discontent with her life in America, her willingness to exploit her sexuality, her past life as "a photographic model for the body." All suggest that it is actually Ruth who has come home to the fulfillment she requires in a family that conflates women's gender roles of wife, mother, and whore. Yet plausibility of motive gives way to the symbolic appropriateness of the play's final tableau. As the drama concludes, Teddy has left with Ruth's dismissive farewell: "Don't be a stranger." Sam, having revealed that the sainted Jessie had done MacGregor in the back of his cab, has collapsed on the floor. Ruth is now enshrined in Max's chair, maternally caressing Joey's head in her lap as Max collapses before her, begging a kiss and asserting "I'm not an old man," as Lenny watches. This bizarre reconstituted family grouping, with Madonna and Whore now installed and in control of the family's Oedipal longings and sexual, gender, and power compulsions, is surely one of the most disturbingly suggestive images in modern drama in which familial relationships, sexuality, dominance, and submission are interrelated as reality and fantasy intermingle, and the audience registers shock as well as recognition in a family fable for modern times.

WHO'S AFRAID OF VIRGINIA WOOLF?

50

(1962)

by Edward Albee

Who's Afraid of Virginia Woolf? *is in many important respects a "first." In addition to being the first of Albee's full-length plays, it is also the first juxtaposition and integration of realism and abstract symbolism in what will remain the dramatic idiom of all the full-length plays. Albee's experimentation in allegory, metaphorical clichés, grotesque parody, hysterical humor, brilliant wit, literary allusion, religious undercurrents, Freudian reversals, irony on irony, here for the first time appear as an organic whole in a mature and completely satisfying dramatic work. It is, in Albee's repertory, what* Long Day's Journey into Night *is in O'Neill's; the aberrations, the horrors, the mysteries are woven into the fabric of a perfectly normal setting so as to create the illusion of total realism, against which the abnormal for the first time, the "third voice of poetry" comes through loud and strong with no trace of static.*

—Anne Paolucci, *From Tension to Tonic: The Plays of Edward Albee*

The Broadway opening of Edward Albee's *Who's Afraid of Virginia Woolf?* on October 13, 1962, certainly qualifies as one of the key dates in American drama, comparable to March 31, 1945, and December 3, 1947 (the Broadway premieres of Tennessee Williams's THE GLASS MENAGERIE and *A STREETCAR NAMED DESIRE*), February 10, 1949 (the opening of Arthur Miller's THE DEATH OF A SALESMAN), and November 7, 1956 (the first U.S. performance of Eugene O'Neill's LONG DAY'S JOURNEY INTO NIGHT). A few months before it opened Albee published a scathing attack in the *New York Times* asserting that Broadway was the true theater of the absurd because of its slavish devotion to the superficial and the unchallenging. *Who's Afraid of Virginia Woolf?*, Albee's first full-length play and Broadway debut, was a direct assault on a lifeless and shallow commercial American theater, igniting a new excitement and vitality by its radical style and content. With this play American drama, as it had not had since the 1940s, regained its power and importance as an instrument of truth. *Who's Afraid of Virginia Woolf?*, in the words of critic Gilbert Debusscher, "immediately became the subject of the most impassioned controversies, the object of criticism and accusation which recall the storms over the first plays of Ibsen, and, closer to our own time, Beckett and Pinter." Few other characters on the American stage had ever gone at one another so mercilessly nor exposed their psychological core in language that drama historian Ruby Cohn called "the most adroit dialogue ever heard on the American stage." *Who's Afraid of Virginia Woolf?* propelled Albee into the front rank of American dramatists. He would go on to dominate American drama in the 1960s and 1970s, serving as the link between the previous generation of American dramatists—O'Neill, Williams, and Miller—and the next that followed him, including David Mamet, Sam Shepard, and Tony Kushner. President Bill Clinton at the Kennedy Center's honors ceremony in 1996 aptly summarized Albee's achievement by declaring to the playwright, "In your rebellion, the American theater was reborn."

Abandoned shortly after his birth in 1928, Albee was adopted by Reed and Frances Albee, heirs to the Keith-Albee theater chain fortune, founded by the playwright's adoptive grandfather and namesake, Edward Frances Albee. Growing up in a mansion in Westchester County, New York, the "lucky orphan," as Albee described himself, was raised, as one magazine reported, in a "world of servants, tutors, riding lessons; winters in Miami, summers sailing on the Sound; there was a Rolls to bring him, smuggled in lap robes, to matinees in the city; an inexhaustible wardrobe housed in a closet big as a room." Because of the family's theatrical connections, actors, directors, and producers were frequent house guests. Albee attended performances from the age of six and wrote his first play, a sex farce, when he was 12. Enrolled in and expelled from a number of boarding schools as an undisciplined and indifferent student, Albee eventually graduated from Choate in 1946 where he had begun to distinguish himself by his writing, publishing poems, short stories, and a one-act play in the school literary magazine. After attending Trinity College briefly Albee left home in 1950 determined to pursue a writing career. Supported by a trust fund that provided him with $50 a week, Albee became, in his words, "probably the richest boy in Greenwich Village." For the next decade, through his 20s, Albee worked in a succession of odd jobs—as an office-boy in an advertising agency, as a luncheonette counterman, writing music programs for a radio station, selling records and books, and delivering messages for Western Union. Most of the poetry and the long novel he wrote during this period have never been published. Searching for direction Albee was encouraged by Thornton Wilder to concentrate on drama. During his "Village decade," Albee, as his roommate William Flanagan recalled, "was, to be sure, adrift and like most of the rest of us, he had arrived in town with an unsown wild oat or two. But from the beginning he was, in his outwardly impassive way, determined to write. . . . He adored the theatre from the beginning and there can't have been anything of even mild importance that we didn't see together." Through the period, Flanagan remembered, Albee had a "thoroughly unfashionable admiration for the work of Tennessee Williams." Other influences that would impact his initial dramatic work came from European dramatists of the absurd, such as Samuel Beckett and Eugène Ionesco.

On the eve of his 30th birthday, in despair over his inability to produce anything of importance and "as a sort of birthday present to myself," Albee completed his first major play, *The Zoo Story*, a one-act, two-character drama in which two strangers—Jerry and Peter—meet in New York City's Central Park. Jerry, lonely and desperate for meaningful contact with another, provokes Peter into a fight in which he impales himself, gratefully, on the knife he has given Peter. A tour de force of compression and intensity, *The Zoo Story* serves as a kind of overture to themes that would dominate Albee's subsequent work, including the shattering of complacency, the connection between love and aggression, and the relationship between fantasy and reality. Initially rejected by American producers the play was first performed at the Schiller-Theater Werkstatt in West Berlin in 1959. It debuted in the United States in 1960 at the Provincetown Playhouse in Greenwich Village on a double bill with Beckett's *Krapp's Last Tape*, establishing the connection between Beckett and Albee that marked the younger playwright as an American proponent of the theater of the absurd. The designation initially offended Albee, but he eventually accepted the association with a characteristic contrariness. "The Theatre of the Absurd," he insisted, ". . . facing as it does man's condition as it is, is the Realistic theatre of our time; and . . . supposed Realistic theatre . . . pander[ing] to the public need for self-congratulation and reassurance and present[ing] a false picture of ourselves to ourselves is . . . really and truly The Theatre of the Absurd." He would later define the theater of the absurd as "an absorption-in-art of certain existentialist and post-existentialist philosophical concepts having to do, in the main, with man's attempt to make sense for himself out of his senseless position in a world which makes no sense—which makes no sense because the moral, religious, political and social structures man has erected to 'illusion' himself have collapsed." Albee's next three plays (*The Sandbox*, *The American Dream*, and *The Death of Bessie Smith*), all produced in 1960–61, are scathing critiques of these collapsed illusions, exposing the absurdity of American family life and racial prejudice. Like *The Zoo Story*, they counter the dominant realistic mode of American drama with antirealistic techniques derived from the European modernist dramatic tradition.

Albee's breakthrough drama, *Who's Afraid of Virginia Woolf?*, synthesizes both naturalistic and absurdist theatrical elements such that the realistic American family drama, whose precedents include *A Streetcar Named Desire*, *Death of a Salesman*, and *Long Day's Journey into Night*, is infused with the methods and existential themes derived from European postwar drama. "Like European Absurdists," Cohn argues, "Albee has tried to dramatize the reality of man's condition, but whereas Sartre, Camus, Beckett, Genet, Ionesco, and

Pinter present reality in all its alogical absurdity, Albee has been preoccupied with illusions that screen man from reality." Asked to describe his work in progress that would become *Who's Afraid of Virginia Woolf?* Albee called his play a "sort of grotesque comedy" concerning "the exorcism of a non-existent child" that deals with "the substitution of artificial for real values in this society of ours." Albee initially called the play "The Exorcism" (the title later assigned to act 3) but arrived at *Who's Afraid of Virginia Woolf?* after discovering the phrase as graffiti in a Greenwich Village bar. Albee has explicated his title with its reference to a writer centrally concerned with the nature of reality, to mean "Who is afraid of facing life without illusions?" The question serves as the play's repeated refrain and ultimatum. Set in the New England college town of New Carthage, in the living room of a history professor and his wife—George and Martha—the play depicts the boozy, late-night verbal warfare and lacerating revelations that emerge when they entertain a new faculty member and his wife, Nick and Honey.

Act 1, "Fun-and-Games," introduces the four combatants. George is a 46-year-old associate professor who has failed to realize the expectations of his wife, the daughter of the college's president, to succeed her father. Martha is "a large, boisterous woman, 52, looking somewhat younger. Ample, but not fleshly." Their continual and escalating quarrelling, which George calls, "merely . . . exercising," is rooted in their mutual dependency, frustrations, and guilt. Having returned late from a faculty party, Martha repeats the joke she has heard earlier in the evening in which "Who's Afraid of Virginia Woolf?" is sung to the tune of "Here We Go Round the Mulberry Bush" while informing George that she has invited "what's-their-names" over for a drink. Nick is a new young biology professor married to Honey, a "rather plain" blond, who arrive after George has warned Martha "don't start in on the bit 'bout the kid" to which Martha responds with a decisive "Screw You!" The act then proceeds with George and Martha's "exercising" in front of their guests. Warning Martha, who escorts Honey to the "euphemism," not to talk about "you-know-what," George evades Nick's question about whether they have children by responding, "That's for me to know and you to find out." Honey, however, returns saying that "I didn't know until just a minute ago that you had a son." Martha follows, having changed into a more provocative outfit, and begins to flirt with Nick while disparaging George's masculinity with a story about how she once boxed with him and knocked him into the huckleberry bushes. "It was funny, but it was awful," she explains. "I think it's colored our whole life. . . . It's an excuse anyway. . . . It's what he uses for being bogged down anyway." George responds by retrieving a shotgun and aims it at the back of Martha's head. As Honey screams, Martha turns to face George, and he pulls the trigger, firing a Chinese parasol. "You're dead! Pow! You're dead!" George exclaims. Martha, evidently pleased by his performance, demands a kiss, and when

George refuses her advances in front of their guests, she shifts her attention back to Nick, saying "You don't need any props, do you baby? . . . No fake Jap gun for you." Martha's taunting of her husband ("You see, George didn't have much push . . . he wasn't particularly . . . aggressive. In fact he was a sort of a FLOP!") prompts George to drown out her needling with the "Who's Afraid of Virginia Woolf?" song. Honey becomes sick and retreats down the hall, pursued by Nick and Martha, as the act ends with George alone on stage, embodying defeat and hopelessness.

Act 2, "Walpurgisnacht"—the witches' orgiastic Sabbath—both increases George's torment and creates the conditions that make a recovery possible. Locked into their marital mutually assured destruction and sustained by the illusion of a son as an embodiment of their relationship, George and Martha move toward the recognition of painful truths. Proposing a new series of games—"Humiliate the Host," "Hump the Hostess," and "Get the Guests"—George begins with the last, betraying Nick's confidence about his courtship and marriage to Honey motivated by her family fortune and a false pregnancy. Upset, Honey rushes out to pass out in the bathroom. As Nick and Martha dance and kiss, George ignores them by reading a book, but when they leave together, he flings the book hitting the door chimes. The noise rouses Honey who asks who is at the door. This gives George the idea that a messenger has come announcing the death of their son.

Act 3, "Exorcism," represents the play's dramatic turn, the casting out of the various devils—jealousy, frustration, anger, and remorse—that have condemned George and Martha to their marital hell in which their mutual destruction has replaced self-recognition. Martha enters the living room upbraiding Nick, who she renames "Houseboy," for his failed sexual performance. George arrives carrying a bouquet for Martha, echoing a scene from Williams's *A Streetcar Named Desire* (*"flores para los muertos"*) as a prelude to announcing the death of their son. He calls for one final game ("we're going to play this one to the death"). As Martha rapturously talks about their "beautiful, beautiful boy," George intones liturgical Latin before declaring "Our son is dead!" Martha reacts with horror, screaming "You cannot do that!" She demands to know why he has killed their imaginary child, and George answers that she has broken the rules by mentioning him to another. Martha responds: "I mentioned him . . . all right . . . but you didn't have to push it over the EDGE. You didn't have to . . . kill him." To which George replies with the benediction from the mass and the words, "It will be dawn soon. I think the party's over."

After Nick and Honey have gone, George and Martha are left alone on stage. Martha persists in asking George "did you . . . have to." He insists that "It was . . . time," and that their lives will be better for the truth. Martha is doubtful.

MARTHA   Just . . . us?

GEORGE   Yes.

MARTHA   I don't suppose, maybe, we could . . .

GEORGE   No, Martha.

MARTHA   Yes. No.

GEORGE   Are you all right?

MARTHA   Yes. No.

GEORGE   [*Puts his hands gently on her shoulder, she puts her head back and he sings to her, very softly.*] Who's afraid of Virginia Woolf

Virginia Woolf

Virginia Woolf?

MARTHA   I . . . am . . . George. . . .

GEORGE   Who's afraid of Virginia Woolf. . . .

MARTHA   I . . . am . . . George. . . . I . . . am. . . . [*George nods, slowly. Silence, tableau.*]

Having divested themselves of the fantasies that have ruled and sustained them, George and Martha confront themselves and their reality with sorrow for their loss and uncertainty about their future. After the preceding Sturm und Drang, the play reaches a stunned silence, and George and Martha, who have played role after role in their marital battle, settle into a final resemblance: Adam and Eve after the fall, contemplating a life without illusions. Their brave new world of existential reality is matched by the new departure for American drama that *Who's Afraid of Virginia Woolf?* made possible, in which unrelentingly honest dialogue and characterization unite to explore key human and existential issues.

THE PLOUGH AND THE STARS 51

(1926) *by Sean O'Casey*

Without a doubt, The Plough and the Stars *is O'Casey's greatest play. It is the one with the greatest intensity, the one which most ambitiously addresses the human comedy at the point where violent public events suddenly transform it into tragedy. It is the O'Casey play which tackles the greatest Irish theme, the fight for freedom, and humanizes it with searing irony to equal the greatest critiques of war and peace to be found in literature from Shakespeare's* Henry IV *to Bertolt Brecht's* Mother Courage and Her Children.
—Christopher Murray, *Sean O'Casey*

Given their similar riot-provoking Abbey Theatre openings, comparisons between John Millington Synge's THE PLAYBOY OF THE WESTERN WORLD and Sean O'Casey's *The Plough and the Stars* are inescapable. Both plays are triumphs of the modern Irish theater that were caught in the crossfire of Irish politics and identity conflict. In 1907 Synge's play was branded an "unmitigated, protracted libel upon Irish peasant man and, worse still, upon Irish peasant girlhood," while the playwright became "the most hated of all the Abbey dramatists . . . detested by nationalists of every shade and degree of political thought." Written during the Irish Literary Revival, when drama was called on to regenerate a heroic Irish consciousness and to promulgate a national destiny, Synge's comedy refused to gratify his audience with an idealized view of Irish rustic life or the Irish character. Instead it unflatteringly exposed the Irish tendency to romanticize and then betray their heroes, provoking howls of indignant protest. By 1926 when *The Plough and the Stars* debuted, Ireland had achieved a shaky, partial independence after enduring a destructive rebellion from British rule, a deadly guerrilla war, and an even more bloody civil war between those who accepted the treaty with Britain that partitioned the country and created the Irish Free State as part of the Commonwealth and Republican die-hards who held out for full independence. Who were the Irish now and whither Ireland remained crucial questions, as they had been in 1907. However, if Synge's *Playboy* assaulted sacrosanct notions of Irish identity and heroism, *The Plough and the Stars* invaded and, in the view of many of its initial audiences, desecrated a sacred Irish shrine—the Easter Rising of 1916—to expose as suspect one of the founding myths of the new Irish nation. Few dramas have dared as much or have so radically reassessed such cherished concepts as honor, patriotism, sacrifice, and justice.

Like Jonathan Swift, Oscar Wilde, and George Bernard Shaw, O'Casey is one of Ireland's great contrarians whose art targets accepted pieties to reveal challenging paradoxes. O'Casey's dissenter's viewpoint is directly attributable to his class and religious background. Born John Casey in Dublin in 1880, the youngest of 13 children, he was an anomaly from the start. A Protestant in predominantly Catholic Dublin, O'Casey grew up neither in the comfortable suburban Anglo-Irish world of Synge or Samuel Beckett nor the Protestant Ascendancy world of William Butler Yeats's big houses, but among the working class in the midst of Dublin's tenement squalor. After his clerk father died when O'Casey was six, his mother, to whom he dedicated *The Plough and the Stars* ("To the gay laugh of my mother at the gate of the grave"), battled severe poverty to keep her family together (eight of O'Casey's siblings succumbed to the conditions that produced Dublin's appalling infant-mortality rate). As a child O'Casey, often malnourished, was additionally afflicted with chronic eye disease, and he was seldom able to attend school. Instead he taught himself to read and write by the age of 13. He also became a drama enthusiast, devouring the works of William Shakespeare and the Irish 19th-century melodramatist Dion Boucicault, eventually acting in a local theater group organized by his brother. From the age of 14, O'Casey supported himself in clerical and manual labor jobs—as a stock clerk, railway laborer, navvy, hod carrier, and janitor—alongside the working-class Dubliners whose speech and mannerisms he would later draw on for his plays. In his early 20s O'Casey became an active Irish nationalist, joining the Gaelic League (changing his name to Seán O'Cathasaigh and teaching Gaelic to Dublin's poor) and the Irish Republican Brotherhood. This conventional route into radical Irish politics, however, did not serve him long. Influenced by socialist ideas O'Casey increasingly became convinced that the root cause of Irish distress was economic rather than cultural and political. He became a zealous member of Dublin's Transport Union and a lifelong admirer of its founder, James Larkin. When the union formed the Irish Citizen Army for self-protection during the violent Dublin transport strike and lockout of 1913, O'Casey was elected secretary of its council. He resigned this post in 1914, however, because of the Citizen Army's increasing collaboration with the Irish Volunteers, whose commitment to the violent overthrow of British rule O'Casey viewed as shortsighted and dangerously idealistic. In 1916 James Connolly, who had replaced Larkin as the leader of the trade-union movement and chief of the Irish Citizen Army, Pádraic Pearse, leader of the Irish Volunteers, and others spearheaded the Easter Rising in which key locations in Dublin were seized, including the General Post

Office, from which Pearse proclaimed an Irish Republic. Within days the rebellion was violently suppressed, and Pearse along with 14 other leaders, including Connolly, were executed. The rebels were originally ridiculed and dismissed by the working class of Dublin, many of whom took advantage of the chaos for a looting spree, but their executions turned them into martyrs. With its blood sacrifice on behalf of Irish freedom, which Yeats would memorialize with the phrase "A terrible beauty is born," the Easter Rising became the defining symbolic event in the modern struggle for Irish independence and the catalyst for the violence that followed. For O'Casey, who sat out the Rising nursing his dying mother, it was neither heroic nor beneficial, but needless and destructive carnage that took more lives of ordinary Dubliners than of combatants and ignored the more pressing needs of Ireland's poor, whom it victimized.

O'Casey's dissent—a pacifist during wartime, a realist in the face of blind patriotism, and a socialist rather than nationalist—would fuel his critique of the defining events of modern Irish history in his first three produced plays, his "Dublin trilogy" dramatizing the lives of the city's tenement poor against the backdrop of the Easter Rising, the war of independence, and the Irish civil war. Not since Shakespeare's history plays had a playwright mounted such a comprehensive and penetrating appraisal of the impact of political and historical forces on a country, community, and its citizens. *The Shadow of a Gunman*, presented by the Abbey Theatre in 1923 after O'Casey's first three submissions had been rejected, portrays the tragic consequences of the guerrilla warfare following the Easter Rising. *Juno and the Paycock* (1924) is set during the hostilities of the ensuing Irish civil war, during which the conflicts within an impoverished Dublin family mirror the national situation and expose the character of the Irish people. *The Plough and the Stars* looks at the period leading up to and during the Easter Rising. All three plays share O'Casey's ironic antiheroic vision that presents history not from the perspective of leaders but through the self-centered experiences of ordinary noncombatants. The trilogy explores the tragic consequences of false heroism and blind idealism and the resulting suffering and sacrifice of lower-class Dubliners. If, as it is said, history first plays out as tragedy and next as farce, O'Casey combines the two in tragicomic dramatic forms that complicate clear-cut moral categories and subvert accepted wisdom and audience expectations.

O'Casey called *The Plough and the Stars* "my most ambitious play," and it is daringly unconventional in both method and meaning. Begun in 1924 under the title, *The Easter Lily Aflame*, the play takes up the subject of the Easter Rising, which O'Casey had come to believe "was the beginning of all that happened afterward." The play's theme expanded to encompass the various political, cultural, and social forces that produced the war for independence, the civil war, as well as the current disjunction between the ideals and realities of the new Irish state. "I never make a scenario," O'Casey recalled, "depending on the natural growth of a play rather than on any method of joinery." The symbolic core of the play became the flag of the Irish Citizen Army, symbolizing workers' aspirations. "It was this flag," O'Casey declared, "that fired in my mind the title for the play; and the events that swirled around the banner and that of the Irish Volunteers . . . that gave me all the humour, pathos and dialogue that fill the play." In working out the betrayal of what this flag symbolized—the cause of labor and the goal of a better life for the working poor—by a destructively romantic patriotism, O'Casey devised a daringly experimental dramatic structure and method. *The Plough and the Stars* substitutes a collective protagonist for central characters and multiple plot lines for a central dramatic action that generate and accumulate meaning through its four acts by repetition, contrast, and ironic counterpoint.

Act 1 introduces the denizens of a Dublin tenement gathered in the flat of newly married Nora and Jack Clitheroe. As jack-of-all-trades Fluther Good puts a new lock on the Clitheroes' door, he discusses with Mrs. Gogan Nora's aspirations for a better life ("She's goin' to th' divil lately for style") and the tension between husband and wife over Jack's involvement with the Citizen Army ("for she's like a clockin' hen if he leaves her sight for a minute"). Nora's Uncle Peter dons his uniform of the Irish National Foresters, while Nora's cousin, The Covey, assaults the older man's showy, pompous patriotism with baiting insults and socialist jargon. As Nora arrives to restore peace and order in her home she is verbally assaulted by her petulant neighbor Bessie Burgess, who complains that Nora "is always thryin' to speak proud things, an' lookin' like a mighty one in th' congregation o' th' people!" Finally succeeding in gaining some separation from this congregation (symbolized by the flat's new lock), Nora achieves a private, tender moment with her husband. Jack, humiliated by being passed over as a Citizen Army officer, reaffirms his exclusive commitment to his wife by singing "their song" with the chorus: "When I first said I lov'd only you, Nora, / An' you said you lov'd only me!" Their intimate and romantic unity is broken by the arrival of the news that Jack had in fact been named a commandant of the Citizen Army in a letter Nora had never delivered. Angered, Jack reports for duty, and the act closes as a British army regiment of Irish recruits is heard singing "It's a Long Way to Tipperary" while embarking for the front and Mrs. Gogan's consumptive daughter Mollser asks, "Is there anybody goin', Mrs. Clitheroe, with a titther o' sense?"

Act 1 suggests that the play's dramatic center will be the domestic conflict between Nora and Jack Clitheroe, yet in act 2 Nora is absent, and their conflict is subsumed in the much larger context of the preparation for the rebellion and the ways multiple characters evade or succumb to outside forces. O'Casey here shifts the play's focus to the multiple relationships of his characters caught up in the historical moment. Set in a Dublin pub in which the actual words of Pádraic Pearse are heard addressing a rally outside, the act ironically juxtaposes high-minded political rhetoric ("Bloodshed is a cleansing and sanctifying thing. . . . When war comes to Ireland she must welcome it as she would welcome the Angel of God.") and the sordid reality of ordinary Dublin life as the prostitute Rosie Redmond plies her trade and the drunken squabbling between Mrs. Gogan and Bessie Burgess and Fluther and The Covey comically parodies the sacred Irish fight for freedom being eulogized outside. The low comedy counterpoints and exposes the elevated rhetoric as fatally misguided and ineffectual. The effect is like staging Hotspur's chivalric speeches in *HENRY IV, Part 1* just outside the Boar's Head Tavern in Eastcheap. The ironic undercutting of the heroic idealism by all-too-human appetites and self-interest culminates in the action that ignited the Abbey riots of 1926: Jack's arrival with his colleagues carrying into the pub the banner of The Plough and the Stars and the green, white, and orange tricolor of the Irish Republic. If Synge's use of the vulgar word *shift* served as the catalyst for the protest in 1907, O'Casey's linkage of the symbols of Irish patriotic aspiration to the sordid world of a Dublin pub and its unflattering collection of prostitutes, braggarts, drunkards, and battling mothers was positively incendiary, crystalizing the disjunction between rhetoric, idealism, illusion, and reality.

In act 3 the scene shifts to the street outside the tenement during the violence of Easter week. The "congregation" is shown now united, not by the redeeming act of the rebellion, but by the mutual advantage afforded for looting. The former combatants—Bessie Burgess and Mrs. Gogan, Peter and The Covey—now join forces in their selfishness in ironic contrast to the vision of Irish unity espoused by the speaker in act 2. When Jack and Captain Brennan arrive with the wounded Langon, in contrast to their jubilant bravado in the pub in act 2, they are dazed and frightened by their encounter with the reality of the rebellion. The act ends with Jack violently breaking free from a clinging Nora to return to battle, motivated more by his fear of being revealed a coward than by any lofty patriotic aims. The pathos of Nora's collapse under Jack's betrayal of his love and devotion to her is undercut by the arrival of the drunken Fluther, who has liberated a half-gallon jar of whiskey, singing "Fluther's a jolly good fella." As in act 2 the tragic is undercut with the farcical, producing O'Casey's antiheroic vision that submits the abstractions of love, honor, glory, sacrifice, and patriotism to a withering irony.

The final act counts the casualties and traces the consequences of Pearse's call for a sanctifying blood sacrifice. As British troops round up the rebels outside the characters take refuge in Bessie Burgess's attic rooms where the coffin of the dead Mollser is displayed. Nora, distraught over the death of her stillborn child and the uncertainty of Jack's fate, slips into insanity. In the ironic reversal of O'Casey's antiheroic vision the Falstaffian braggart, Fluther Good, rises in stature as someone capable of selfless courageous action in rescuing Nora from the deadly streets when she searches for her husband. Likewise, the termagant and outsider Bessie—Protestant Unionist amidst Catholic

Nationalists—is elevated as a truly heroic figure. Bessie risks her life trying to get a doctor for Mollser, nurses the deranged Nora, and during the play's shattering climax is shot and killed trying to protect her. In O'Casey's accounting it is ultimately the women who are the main victims of the warfare and whose commitment to the essential human values of love, life, family, and fellowship tower in comparison to the vainglorious idealism of Irish nationalism that is revealed as little more than a self-defeating death wish.

The Plough and the Stars ends with one of the most devastatingly ironic conclusions in modern drama. After the surviving men—Fluther, Peter, The Covey, and Brennan—are led off for detainment, the tenement (and stage) is occupied by British soldiers. As the red glare of a burning Dublin appears outside, they sing "Keep the Home Fires Burning," the World War I sentimental anthem justifying the sacrifice on the Western Front. Here, however, the home fires of Dublin are literally burning, and the soldiers provide a bitter mockery of the reaffirmation of order that traditionally closes a tragedy. In the ironic calculus of O'Casey's drama, Easter 1916 is not a rising but a collapse into chaos and a sacrifice of more than blood but humanity itself. Few plays have offered such a profound reassessment of our aspirations, delusions, and natures as well as their consequences for the individual, family, community, and people.

THE ALCHEMIST

(1610)

52

by Ben Jonson

Even as alchemy makes use of the most revolting ingredients . . . in order to produce gold, so Jonson in this play has employed the most sordid, the most meticulously realistic material, and defiantly extracted from it a kind of gold of the imagination. Language has not only turned a whore temporarily into the Fairy Queen, a household drudge into an officer, a beggar into a pious and frugal philosopher, and given their victims a new view of themselves; it has contracted the whole world, as it seems, and made it live fully for a few hours within the walls of a stripped and deserted house—or a theatre. There is nothing restrained, ordered or balanced about life in The Alchemist, *and no suggestions are put forward as to how any reforms in that direction might be effected. The play stares hard at chaos, with fascination far more than censure or disgust.*

—Anne Barton, *Ben Jonson, Dramatist*

One of literature's greatest comedies, *The Alchemist* is among Ben Jonson's funniest and most masterful plays. Samuel Taylor Coleridge considered it, along with *OEDIPUS* and *Tom Jones*, "the three most perfect plots ever planned," while the poet Algernon Charles Swinburne enthused that in *The Alchemist* "All the distinctive qualities which the alchemic cunning of the poet has fused together in the crucible of dramatic satire for the production of a flawless work of art, have given us the most perfect model of imaginative realism and satirical comedy that the world has ever seen." *The Alchemist*, as its title indicates, is a play about transformation. It is Jonson's *A MIDSUMMER NIGHT'S DREAM* in which the confusion between appearance and actuality, desire and reality is enacted, not in a fantastical forest outside Athens but in a townhouse in London's Blackfriars. In *The Alchemist* the agents of the play's many magical transformations are not fairies scrambling the affections of confused lovers but a trio of con artists fleecing the gullible and self-deluded. In its contemporary London setting Jonson assembles a cross-section of Elizabethan society— clerk, shopkeeper, country squire, rich widow, parson, nobleman, gamester, servant, charlatan, and prostitute. They are all frauds, either pretending to be what they are not or aspiring to become someone else. The play's gulls are shown susceptible to the promise of the cozeners that they can in fact possess all their desires largely because they are victims of their own delusions, and the play offers an unrelentingly unflattering but undeniable examination of human nature in the grips of greed, vanity, and our preference for illusion over reality. *The Alchemist*, with Jonson's broadest social canvas and its universally relevant theme of humankind's capacity for self-delusion, is arguably, the playwright's most ambitious and profound play that, along with *VOLPONE*, helped establish a new standard of dramatic construction and a realistic method and subject for the theater.

Written at the height of Jonson's dramatic powers, following two of his best comedies, *Volpone* (1606) and *Epicoene* (1609), *The Alchemist* was first performed by Shakespeare's company, the King's Men, in 1610 and stands out in marked contrast to other Elizabethan dramas. It shows Jonson turning the focus of comedy from romantic intrigue in fanciful settings that Shakespeare had patented as the standard of Elizabethan comedy to contemporary life and an "Image of the time." The play's prologue announces:

> Our scene is London, 'cause we would make known
> No country's mirth is better than our own:
> No clime breeds better matter for your whore,
> Bawd, squire, imposter, many persons more,
> Whose manners, now called humors, feed the stage;
> And which have still been subject for the rage
> Or spleen of comic writers.

Contemporary London life and "the vices that she breeds" are Jonson's subjects, and for the first time in English drama to such a degree the teeming diversity of contemporary urban life, a city's various denizens, their accents and obsessions take center stage. Countering what Jonson saw in his contemporaries' plays as violations of probabilities in characters and action, *The Alchemist* offers a new dramatic realism based on Jonson's intimate, firsthand experience of middle- and lower-class London life. Characters easily recognized on the streets inside and outside the theater, not the high-born or idealized paragons expected on stage, are shown behaving with psychological consistency in a series of motivated, plausible actions. Additionally Jonson harnesses the play's robust vitality with the disciplined structure, concentrated focus, and serious moral purpose derived from classical comedy. Set during an outbreak of the plague that has caused a London property owner, Lovewit, to escape contagion to the country, *The Alchemist* is confined to the single setting of Lovewit's abandoned house, now taken over as a base of swindling operations by a trio of cozeners: Jeremy, Lovewit's butler, known as Face; Subtle, a charlatan posing as an alchemist and necromancer; and the prostitute Doll

Common. There they lure the gullible with promises of wealth, power, and success through their mastery and demonstration of the arcane. To the play's unity of place Jonson adds a unity of action in a series of variations on the same circumstance: the cozening of the trio's succession of marks, along with a unity of time in which the play's action transpires in close to "real time," the duration of the play's performance. The result is a concentrated, intense dramatic vehicle that accelerates to a breakneck speed before its inevitable collision and catastrophe. In a sense *The Alchemist* is the prototypical modern well-made play, an artfully crafted, smoothly running dramatic machine so contrary to the often discursive multiplicity and improvisations of other Elizabethan dramas. *The Alchemist* shows what can be done on stage when, as Jonson advised, "parts are so joined, and knit together, as nothing in the structure can be chang'd, or taken away, without impairing, or troubling the whole."

The Alchemist opens with a quarrel among the play's three tricksters. Lovewit, the play's principle of law and order, has departed, and chaos, confusion, and misrule reign in his house. The servant, Jeremy, is now, as Face, the presumptive master of men, the chameleon actor of many roles, who revels in his manipulative powers. He has established the pseudo-scholarly Subtle, an expert in the jargon and processes of alchemy, palmistry, astrology, demonology, and theology in Lovewit's house, and the pair of swindlers have been so successful that they begin to believe their own con. If Subtle is unable to transmute base metal into gold as he claims, he is adept at transforming men by causing them to act out their desires and ignore or misperceive the reality of their situations and motives. Face counters Subtle's claim of priority in the scams by arguing that he has worked the greater magic by transforming Subtle from a penniless nonentity, "pinned up in the several rags / You had raked and picked from dunghills" to his present position. "I gave you countenance," Face asserts, ". . . Built you a furnace, drew you customers / Advanced all your black arts." Face and Subtle's quarrel establishes the play's central theme of self-delusion in which the characters readily ignore the reality of who they are for the far more pleasing illusion of who they would like to be. Doll Common plays peacemaker—flattering both and playing on each man's inflated self-conception, calling Subtle "Sovereign" and Face "General"—and manages to negotiate a temporary truce between the pair in the interest of their present scheming. Despite her common sense, Doll is not immune from self-deception herself and will eventually begin to believe that she can become in fact the great lady she pretends to be.

With an uneasy alliance established among the trio that could collapse at any moment due to their enmity and hubris, the play begins its parade of gulls, each arriving to profit from the illusions that the three con artists inventively supply, based on their insights into the nature of human folly and greed. Each gull, in Face's diagnosis, is afflicted with an "itch of the mind," a dissatisfaction with his or her identity and circumstance, that the trio will scratch with various promises of transformation. Jonson avoids repetition by masterfully differentiating the gulls with varying social stations, motives, and degrees of intelligence and sophistication. The first to arrive is Dapper, a young law clerk who, stifled by his dull routine, wants help in becoming a successful gambler. Exploiting Dapper's romantic sensibility as one who "consorts with the small poets of the time," Subtle claims to recognize him as a favorite nephew of the Fairy Queen who, if he will endure "a world of ceremonies," will gain an audience with his aunt and a guarantee of gambling luck. Dapper reveals himself as a victim of his own stupidity and greed and is complemented by Abel Drugger, a slow-witted young man setting up a new tobacco shop who desires to know "by necromancy" how best to arrange his shop and advertise. Drugger is easily satisfied by Subtle's nonsensical revelations from astrology and palmistry of the route to certain success in business.

Ascending the social ladder, the trio is introduced by Drugger to a country squire, Kastril, and his sister, the 19-year-old beautiful, but empty-headed wealthy widow Dame Pliant. Kastril has come up to London "to learn to quarrel, and to live by his wits," and Subtle is to provide him with the "grammar and logic / And rhetoric of quarreling." Kastril's aspirations to master city vices are revealed as springing from malice and a desire to lord over his country tenants and neighbors. Dame Pliant has come to town "to learn the fashion" and "to know her fortune." Subtle uses his crystal ball to predict "some great honor" for her, namely, his own marriage to her, and Dame Pliant becomes a contentious object of desire for more than one of the conspirators and their victims. These four somewhat simple victims of their own lack of sophistication and craven motives are contrasted with two other, more clever and distinguished gulls—the pastor of an exiled congregation of English Anabaptists, Tribulation Wholesome, and the voluptuarian Sir Epicure Mammon. For these two no simple conjuring tricks are sufficient. They require nothing less than the holy grail of transmutation, the philosopher's stone, the ultimate means to allow man to control reality. Tribulation Wholesome desires the stone as a tool for "the glorious cause," to restore "the silenced Saints" of his congregation to the pulpits of England. However, Wholesome's spiritual zeal and altruism are exposed as shams, disguising his lust for secular power. Wholesome's hypocrisy is evident as he eventually accepts Subtle's offer of the more immediate temptation of success as a counterfeiter while awaiting possession of the all-powerful philosopher's stone.

Sir Epicure Mammon, one of Jonson's greatest creations, is the most distinguished of the gulls and the most imaginative and complex in his motives. Blind to his own egotism and self-indulgence, Mammon convinces Face, Subtle, and himself that he intends to use the philosopher's stone for good, to "turn the age to gold," by eliminating all disease, restoring youth and vigor to the aged, and enriching the poor. His philanthropic rationalizations, however, do not disguise his ruling passion: to live a life of unsurpassable luxury and extravagance. In some of the most audaciously entertaining lines of the play, Mammon charts the apparently boundless nature of his desires, including possessing "a list of wives and concubines / Equal with Solomon" and a back as tough as Hercules' "to enjoy fifty a night." To Doll, whom he is introduced as a noble lady driven mad by biblical studies, he promises "a perpetuity / Of life and lust!" Mammon's magnanimity masks selfishness and a fantasy life so all encompassing that he casts Doll as the ideal noble consort for his wish fulfillment, underscoring his total lack of self-knowledge about his true motives and his preference for his outlandish desires over reality. Mammon is the one gull who has little need of the encouragement offered by the cozeners.

Both Wholesome and Mammon come accompanied by skeptical companions—Ananias, a zealous Puritan deacon, and Pertinax Surly, a gambler and man about town who prides himself on being too astute to be tricked by the likes of Face, Subtle, and Doll. Both are skeptical about the philosopher's stone, feel smugly superior to their gullible companions, and try to dissuade them from succumbing to the lures of the con artists. Both also confuse the role they assume as preservers of truth and righteousness with their reality. Ananias is far from the holier-than-thou paragon he sees himself to be and self-servingly rationalizes a justification for the counterfeiting scheme, while Surly, taking on the role of exposer of the trio's scheme, returns disguised as a Spanish grandee and shows that his "foolish vice of honesty" is just a sham to gain Dame Pliant for himself.

With seven separate gulling plots operating concurrently and requiring that no one set of characters should be aware of the others, *The Alchemist* generates a crescendo of hilarious comic situations in the best farcical manner. The play's structure has been aptly described by critic Anne Barton as driven forward "by a succession of knocks on the door," as the cozeners must juggle more and more arrivals and departures. The play becomes a tour de force of Jonson's stage-managing that pushes Face, Subtle, and Doll to the limits of their ingenious, manipulative resources. The result is some of the funniest complications ever staged, including the blindfolded Dapper being pinched and prodded by Face and Subtle speaking in fairy falsetto, Doll Common's performance as the Fairy Queen, and Surly trapped in his Spanish disguise and forced to pretend he does not understand the insults heaped upon him.

Eventually the deus ex machina arrives in the form of the unexpectedly returned Lovewit, who restores order in his house while standing in marked contrast to all the others by being immune to Face's deceptions or his own self-delusions. "No more of your tricks, good Jeremy / The truth," Lovewit commands, "the shortest way." Lovewit becomes the play's reality principle who metes out the appropriate justice on the violators. Compared to the punishment Jonson arranges for Volpone and Mosca, who have preyed on innocents, Subtle and Doll escape their fate since their prey are at best co-conspirators and victims of their own illusions. Instead they are allowed to escape direct punishment for a more sobering sentence: the man who would be sovereign over others and the woman who would be a great lady must face the reality of who they truly are: a petty cheat and a whore. Face, the protean master of men, is sentenced to subservience again as the dutiful Jeremy who helps Lovewit gain the prize of Dame Pliant. The various gulls are similarly forced to accept the reality of their circumstances and the identities that they have attempted to deny but with a final ironic suggestion that new illusions are not far away. To Lovewit's offer to return his swindled property to Sir Epicure if he "can bring certificate that you were gulled of 'em, / Or any formal writ out of a court / That you did cozen yourself, I will not hold them," Mammon replies that "I'll rather lose 'em"; that is, he prefers his illusions over facing the facts, whatever the cost.

The Alchemist, like all of Jonson's comedies, instructs through ridicule, establishing serious moral lessons behind its humor. The play makes clear that the best way to avoid succumbing to con men and self-delusion is through self-knowledge, through facing the facts about human nature and human existence. Jonson's play about transformation uses the theatrical conventions of acting and pretending to reach a serious moral truth. In the bracing wisdom of Jonson's vision the audience gains the true philosopher's stone in the form of a mirror to master our world by understanding ourselves.

TROJAN WOMEN

(415 B.C.)

53

by Euripides

The play . . . ends in total nihilism. What the Greeks felt as a subtle contradiction, the contradiction of the world in which they had to live, appears to us who see the play from the outside as a negation, a refusal. . . . Hecuba's final despair . . . answers the terrible words of Poseidon. The gods are killed with the men, and that common death is the lesson of the tragedy.

—Jean-Paul Sartre, "Why the *Trojan Women?*"
Introduction to Sartre's adaptation of the *Trojan Women*

Troades (*Trojan Women*) is one of the most harrowing plays ever staged, perhaps the darkest drama in the ancient Greek canon, and a consensus choice as one of the greatest antiwar plays ever written. Exploring the annihilating consequences of war as well as key existential truths, the play dramatizes the aftermath of the fall of Troy to the Greeks. Following the successful stratagem of the Trojan Horse, after a 10-year siege, Troy has been taken, sacked, and is being set aflame as the Greeks prepare to return home. The city's male inhabitants have all been massacred, and the women of Troy await their fate, to be distributed as booty to their new Greek masters. The history of a once grand kingdom has ended in catastrophe. Perhaps no other of Euripides' plays better illustrates the contention that he is the most modern of the classical dramatists, our contemporary in his apocalyptic, nihilistic vision. The *Trojan Women* remains an unsettling work of complex meanings and unconventional methods. In the play Euripides violates virtually every dictum of Aristotelian tragedy while establishing an alternative, revolutionary dramatic strategy whose impact can be detected in later expressionistic and symbolic drama, in the theater of cruelty and absurdist modern drama.

Critic E. M. Blaiklock has described Euripides as "the most historically significant of Greek dramatists," whose innovations helped define persistent dramatic traditions. By adapting standard mythic subjects so freely and radically Euripides brought a new kind of invention, of both plot and character, into drama. By extending the range of drama from paragons and exceptional circumstances to ordinary and complex characters in recognizable situations, Euripides enhanced dramatic realism and psychological truthfulness. Euripides would establish a precedent for Shakespearean and later tragicomedy by blurring the distinction between comedy and tragedy. Finally, in the *Trojan Women* especially, Euripides decenters his play from a focus on a single protagonist—the usual focus of a tragedy's action—to multiple centers of interest, with action virtually halted to display a central tragic situation, unified by theme and symbol. The *Trojan Women* is perhaps the most extreme example of Euripides' "flaunting of our conception of dramatic form," in the words of critic H. D. F. Kitto. In the *Trojan Women* the prescribed plot elements admired and advised by Aristotle are eliminated. The entire play is aftermath; Troy has fallen, and the time for dramatic action is essentially over. Euripides' focus shifts to what critic Jasper Griffin has called a "mournful pageant of suffering." There is neither suspense nor surprises, neither reversal of fortune nor relief by divine or human intercession or mitigation. Instead of the revelation of the tragic destiny of a central hero through a series of arranged crises and conflicts, Euripides relies on a sequence of episodic intensification, of escalating tension and misery to test the limit of endurance for both the play's characters and audience in revealing the brutality and horror of the human condition. The *Trojan Women* offers a new conception of tragedy with a collective tragic hero, the mainly offstage Greek victors, and a collective tragic victim, the Trojan survivors, who claim primacy. It also employs a radical dramatic structure in which the logic of steadily evolving action is replaced by a deepening awareness and intensification of the play's central subject of human suffering. Plot, character, and situation are conceived symbolically rather than realistically, orchestrated into a stark and terrifying tragic spectacle.

Ever the iconoclast and violator of consoling illusions, Euripides presents war stripped of any heroism except in suffering and the will to survive under the worst possible circumstances. The *Trojan Women* reverses convention by assigning dignity and compassion to the defeated and inhumanity to the conquerors. If the saying is true that history is written by the victors, Euripides counters by presenting the story of the vanquished. War is displayed devoid of any grandeur and glory as the most destructive and futile of human endeavors, brutalizing and dehumanizing winners and losers alike. Troy, symbolic of civilization itself, is wiped out in an apocalypse of flames and cruelty. Wives, mothers, and sisters are stripped of their identities and human roles, to become the chattel of their new masters, who have violated every revered human bond and source of reverence—home, family, religion, and nation. Ironically, in the background, as consequence for the Greeks' hubris, is the certain doom that awaits them on their homeward voyage. Beyond its radical challenge to the accepted heroic code of battlefield honor and glory based on enemies vanquished and prizes taken, the *Trojan Women* asked its first Greek audience to sympathize with their mythical archenemies, the Trojans, and to censure the storied accomplishments of their greatest heroes, such as Odysseus, Achilles, and Agamemnon. Moreover, Euripides fills the stage for the first time on such a scale with a predominately female cast—Hecuba, Cassandra, Andromache, Helen, and the chorus of captive Trojan women—whose collective endurance in bondage and insights offer a new definition of heroism. Euripides asks, where is the bottom to human misery? How one copes with utter defeat is Euripides' subject here. No playwright before Euripides had to such a degree explored the psychological and emotional complexity of women on stage, and in the *Trojan Women* their perspective on peace, war, life, and death takes center stage. If it is true, as some have speculated, that only men attended Athenian dramatic performances, the radical challenge Euripides poses in the play is even more obvious as males are asked to reassess central cultural standards from an alternative gender perspective that had traditionally been ignored and devalued.

When the *Trojan Women* was first staged in 415 B.C. the Athenians had been fighting a crippling war with Sparta for 16 years, and there still remained more than a decade before Athens's ultimate defeat in 404. Having written patriotic plays, such as the *Heracleidae* and the *Suppliants* at the early stages of the Peloponnesian War, Euripides, as the war futilely dragged on, increasingly dramatized its costs and consequences in the suffering of the defeated and moral corruption of the victors (in *Hecuba* and the *Trojan Women*), in its irrational causes (*Helen*), and in its destructiveness and wasteful sacrifice (in *Andromache*, *Iphigenia in Tauris*, and *Iphigenia in Aulis*). Beyond detecting disillusionment over the course of the Peloponnesian War some scholars have identified an even more immediate context for the *Trojan Women* in Euripides' response to Athens's siege and destruction in 414 B.C. of the neutral island state of Melos in which Athenians slaughtered all the men and enslaved the women and children. Thucydides would regard the event as a tipping point in the moral decline of Athens. Such an ignominious use of Athenian might must have contributed to Euripides' skepticism about the concept of a just and ennobling war, and he subversively refracts the circumstances of the recent victims of Athens's brute force to the mythical nemeses of the Greeks, the Trojans, and the Greeks' most celebrated military triumph.

The *Trojan Women* opens with a prologue by the god Poseidon, who surveys the ruin of the city that he had helped to build. "Nothing remains for me," he declares, "but to abandon my shrines and altars in this city . . . bitter enemies of Troy have prevailed." The Greeks have triumphed in large measure because of the divine assistance they have received from the goddess Athena, who joins Poseidon and shocks him with her request for his assistance in punishing the Greeks on their homeward voyage. Angered that the virgin priestess of Apollo, Cassandra, has been dragged by Ajax from Athena's altar and violated, the goddess now wants to punish the Greeks for their transgressions and "fill their journey home with pain." Poseidon readily agrees, delivering a final judgment on the Greeks: "Blind is the man who sacks cities with temples and tombs . . . himself so soon to die." The two gods depart having established the play's situation, sympathy for the Trojans, and central irony that the Greeks' triumph offends the gods and their well-known disastrous homecomings will result. Although Poseidon and Athena ally to punish the Greeks' offenses, they offer neither aid nor comfort to the prostrate figure of Hecuba, queen of Troy, below them, or the other Trojan victims. Hecuba has witnessed the death of her husband and two sons, Hector and Paris, and has fallen further, from queen to slave, than any other Trojan woman. She will serve as the human reference point for the drama, onstage from beginning to end, and will reflect the escalating suffering that surrounds her. Described by Poseidon as the "queen of grief," Hecuba, the classical archetype for tragic misfortune, is recalled by Hamlet as he measures the misery of one of the players: "What's he to Hecuba, or she to him, / That he should weep?" Hecuba invites the chorus of Trojan women captives to join her in a lament for their past lives while summoning their courage and forbearance to accept their fate. The play begins, therefore, with the proud assertion of Hecuba's fortitude, and it will proceed by successive, escalating assaults on her resolve and her conception of the limits of human despair.

A Greek herald, Talthybius, enters to carry out the order of distributing the Trojan captives to their new masters. One of the play's most disturbing and modern touches is keeping the agents of the play's agony offstage, with their decisions delivered by one who is only following orders. Hecuba's daughter, Cassandra, is to be the concubine of Agamemnon; her sister Polyxena is "to serve at Achilles' tomb." We know, through Poseidon, that Polyxena has already been sacrificed, news that will be later revealed to Hecuba by her daughter-in-law Andromache, who has been given to the son of her husband's slayer, Achilles' son Neoptolemus. Hecuba herself is to be the prize of Odysseus, who conceived the wooden horse and therefore is the man most responsible for Hecuba's fall from power and most hateful to her. Cassandra enters with a bridal torch in hand, singing to Hymen, the goddess of marriage, in a terrible parody of the marital rites that here links marriage and murder. As a seer fated not to be believed, Cassandra breaks her mother's heart in her presumed madness in joyfully celebrating her enslavement and death, though she actually reveals sinister truths. As Agamemnon's concubine she will become the agent of his and her own death and the destruction of his entire family. The victims here, she asserts, are not the Trojans, whose sacrifice in defense of family and home is noble, but the Greeks, and Cassandra's ultimate consolation is her awful prediction of mutually assured destruction. "Let us get on with it," she declares on exiting to her fate. "I am a bride—but a bride of death."

Cassandra's joyful embrace of her own destruction crushes Hecuba. She is revived by the thought that she still has another daughter left to her. That consolation is removed with the arrival of her daughter-in-law Andromache with her grandson Astyanax, amid Hector's possessions as trophies of war. Andromache tells Hecuba of Polyxena's death but argues that dying is better than living as Andromache must, as the most loyal of wives who must now commit the ultimate disloyalty to her husband's memory by giving herself to another. Hecuba counsels survival, urging Andromache to yield to the forces beyond her control in order to raise her son "to be a hero of Troy once again." This glimmering hope in Troy's future through Astyanax is extinguished as Talthybius returns to announce that the Greeks, convinced by Hecuba's new master Odysseus, have decided that the child must be killed, thrown from the city walls, thereby ending the Trojan royal line. "This scene," critic Gilbert Murray has stated, "with the parting between Andromache and the child which follows, seems to me perhaps the most absolutely heart-rending in all the tragic literature of the world. After rising from it one understands Aristotle's judgment of Euripides as 'the most tragic of the poets.'" Andromache is made to learn what is worse than disloyalty to a dead husband: the fate of her child whom she cannot protect. His grandmother's response is the stark, despairing realization: "There is nothing now. No justice."

However, Hecuba is roused for a final assertion to gain some justification for the pain and suffering endured by her, her family, and her kingdom as Helen is brought onstage for a reckoning. Invoked frequently up to this point as the cause of the Trojan's misery, Helen is tried, with Hecuba serving as the prosecutor. In the words of critic Eric A. Havelock, Euripides here succeeds in carrying "disillusionment one stage further" to expose "the sheer vacuity of normal moral pretensions." If someone is to blame, if there is a consequence and responsibility for human actions, Hecuba's prosecution suggests the existence of some moral order and justice in the world. Helen's "acquittal" will deal Hecuba a final, ultimate blow to the justification for the queen's and Troy's suffering. Menelaus has resolved to take Helen home to be killed there in punishment for the deaths her infidelity has caused. Hecuba tries to convince him to bring Helen to justice immediately in Troy. Helen defends herself by evading her complicity and blaming everyone from Aphrodite to Paris and Hecuba herself for her actions in a bravado performance of self-serving equivocation. Hecuba fails to rouse Menelaus to immediate punishment, and Helen departs, allowing her the opportunity to reverse her husband's death sentence through her wiles and sexual attractions. Ironically the one woman who gains a happy future in Euripides' play is the woman most responsible for the war in the first place. Hecuba is left realizing that Helen has triumphed and that there is no moral order in the universe.

The *Trojan Women* ends with a final heartbreak for Hecuba as the lifeless, broken body of Astyanax is carried in on Hector's shield. Hecuba delivers a concluding lament, judged by many the most moving speech Euripides ever wrote. Like Lear cradling the dead Cordelia, Hecuba has been taken from worse to worst, and the audience is presented with an ultimate nullity of human hopes and illusions that Hecuba bitterly summarizes as the final burning of Troy commences and the captives depart:

> The man who believes his Fortune is secure is blind.
> Fortune knows no reason.
> She is mad, giving and taking at will.
> No one controls one's own happiness.

SAINT JOAN

(1923)   *by George Bernard Shaw*

54

The unique power of Saint Joan *arises from its stress on factors which would seem to con-flict with the legend of a saint, yet which undergird the legend through giving it a fresh, contentious, and broad context. Shaw subjects mysticism to rationalism, heroism to skepti-cism, villainy to understanding, and sanctity to humor, piercing traditional stereotypes with an irreverent, unrelenting scrutiny. The myth, far from being destroyed, is tested, and as it ultimately triumphs it emerges with a new energy and strength, having been rendered both credible and poignant on grounds which appeal to the modern imagination. The tale of Joan is vividly presented, but more intriguing is Shaw's penetrating conceptualization of the intrinsic nature of Joan, of the complex society in which she lived, and of their nearly epic interrelationship. While qualifying the supernatural with the human, Shaw links the human to great abstractions. He thereby vitalizes both myth and history with a twofold thrust, rendering them movingly alive through convincing human denominators and memorably significant through timeless social and spiritual implications. His undertaking, combining the immediacy of drama with a sensitive view of myth and a broad philosophical perspective of history, is a heroic attempt at a heroic totality. It incorporates both tragedy and comedy, which ultimately fuse in terms of compassionate understanding.*
—Charles A. Berst, *"Saint Joan*: Spiritual Epic as Tragicomedy,"
in *Bernard Shaw and the Art of Drama*

Few playwrights have understood the human and philosophical dimensions of historical and cultural mythmaking as well as George Bernard Shaw. The high-minded sensibilities present in many of Shaw's characters—heroism, social utopianism, romantic idealization—are counterbalanced by characters representing antiheroism, individualism, and pragmatism, all of whom force consideration of the conundrums present in varying points of view with an end toward reaching a realistic and compassionate understanding of human nature and society. In *Saint Joan* saintliness, spirituality, questions of individual conscience, nationalism, and theology are added to the Shavian philosophical mix in a play concerning one of history's most heroic figures.

316

Shaw had established himself as a popular and critically successful playwright during the 1904–07 seasons at the Royal Court Theatre, which featured 988 performances, of which 701 were plays by Shaw. These included *MAN AND SUPERMAN* (1904), *MAJOR BARBARA* (1905), and *The Doctor's Dilemma* (1906). The second phase of Shaw's career as a dramatist solidified his reputation with three works produced between 1911 and 1914. *Fanny's First Play* (1911) set a first-run box-office record of 622 performances. *Androcles and the Lion* (1912), a philosophical farce about early Christianity, explores a recurring theme in Shavian drama: that there are causes worth dying for. *Pygmalion* (1913), loosely inspired by Ovid's story of a sculptor who brings a lovely statue to life, further popularized as a 1938 film, earned Shaw an Academy Award for his screenplay and undergoing an adaptation, six years after his death, became the hit Broadway musical *My Fair Lady*.

After two decades of struggle Shaw was now Britain's leading playwright. However, he did not write any dramas immediately after the outbreak of World War I in August 1914. Instead he produced a long pamphlet, with Swiftian overtones, titled *Common Sense About the War*, which appeared in November 1914 and sold nearly 75,000 copies. In it Shaw contended that Britain and its allies were as much to blame for the war as the Germans, characterized the hostilities as inevitably ruinous for all participants, and called for peace and negotiation. The pamphlet made Shaw internationally notorious. It proved to be a boon for German propaganda. In Britain, with patriotic fervor running high, Shaw was castigated as a traitor, the prime minister even going so far as to publicly express the view that he should be shot. His antiwar speeches were censored by British newspapers; he was turned away from the Dramatists' Club, although he had been its most eminent member; and he suffered a further diminishment in his popularity when, in 1915, he publicly dismissed the sinking of the *Lusitania* by a German U-boat. By 1917 public opinion had shifted and even some in the British government recognized the validity of Shaw's earlier arguments against the war. He was asked to report from the front in Flanders for the *Daily Sketch* and produced a series of articles that were reprinted in the 1931 volume *What I Really Wrote About the War*. By 1918 his reputation had been restored, and he was looked upon by many as the only public figure who had understood the futility of the war from the start.

Shaw emerged from his wartime experiences with a considerably more somber perspective on humanity. He also produced what many critics consider to be three of his greatest plays. *Heartbreak House* (1920), an examination of the prewar spiritual impoverishment that contributed to the outbreak of the war, called by Shaw his *KING LEAR*. *Back to Methuselah* (1922), a five-part cycle of plays in which Shaw begins with Adam and Eve and develops a theory of creative evolution to attempt to explain and resolve humanity's "evolutionary appetite," played out in the human tendency toward self-destructiveness. Neither *Heartbreak House* nor *Back to Methuselah* was received with enthusiasm; it would take the third play in Shaw's postwar canon, and his third full-length historical play, *Saint Joan*, to restore him fully to a public perception of dramatic greatness. He would receive the Nobel Prize in literature in 1925.

The writing of *Saint Joan* was a project Shaw apparently intended to pursue as early as 1913 (Joan had been beatified in 1909); he mentions the idea of doing "a Joan of Arc play some day" in a letter to Mrs. Patrick Campbell, written from Orléans in September of that year. His creative energies, exhausted after the strenuous effort put into *Back to Methuselah*, were revived after Joan's canonization in 1920, and he decided to pursue the writing of a chronicle play about her. Although set during the Hundred Years' War (1337–1453) between the French and the English over disputed French territory, *Saint Joan* reflects aspects of post–World War I culture, such as new views concerning gender roles, science versus religious faith, and unthinking English chauvinism and imperialism. Creative evolution plays a role in *Saint Joan*, and his charismatic title character embodies Shaw's earlier philosophy of a "life force" that keeps evolving and producing extraordinary individuals throughout history who contest outworn methods within an existing social order.

Saint Joan contains six scenes and an epilogue. The first scene takes place at the castle of Vaucouleurs on a spring morning in 1429, where Squire Robert de Baudricourt is chiding his steward for not providing eggs for his breakfast, a situation the steward attributes to "an act of God." The hens will not lay, he claims, as long as Joan the Maid is kept waiting at the door. After the squire shouts out the window for her to come up, Joan appears. Shaw describes her as "an ablebodied country girl of 17 or 18, respectably dressed in red, with an uncommon face" and "normally a hearty coaxing voice, very confident, very appealing, very hard to resist." Joan astonishes de Baudricourt by stating simply that the Lord has directed her, through Saint Catherine and Saint Margaret, whose voices she hears every day, to obtain from him a horse, armor, and soldiers to accompany her to the Dauphin, hiding out in Chinon Castle. He, in turn, will provide her with more soldiers so that she can raise the English siege at Orléans, after which victory, she will see the Dauphin crowned king at Rheims. Joan, with a mixture of logic and faith, argues that if the divided French forces will abandon their fear and their mercenary aims and learn from her to fight for a higher purpose, in this case, "the will of God," they will unite and drive the English from French soil. The squire is won over and agrees to Joan's requests. The steward rushes in to report that the hens have begun laying again.

The second scene is set in the throne room of Chinon Castle where Tremouille, the Lord Chamberlain and the army's commander, discusses with the Archbishop the lack of royal funds. The two attempt to bully the craven, excitable Dauphin, Charles, into refusing to admit Joan. A courtier, Gilles de Rais ("Bluebeard") suggests he impersonate Charles to see if Joan can penetrate the disguise; if she can, it will prove she has been sent by God. Joan easily identifies the Dauphin, kneels before him, and reveals her mission. The Archbishop, now convinced of her piety, affirms her right to speak to Charles alone. Joan responds to "Charlie's" litany of financial woes by earnestly stating, "I tell thee that the land is thine to rule righteously and keep God's peace in, and not to pledge at the pawnshop as a drunken woman pledges her children's clothes." Carried away by Joan's assertion that he will become "the greatest king in the world as [God's] steward and His bailiff, His soldier and His servant," Charles gives command of the army to her, to the ire of Tremouille.

More evidence of Joan's simple faith in God and her ability to inspire even experienced soldiers and to provoke miracles occurs in the third scene. Outside of Orléans, the army's commander, Dunois ("the Bastard"), is skeptical that Joan can mount an attack, given the lack of a favorable wind that will allow the soldiers to cross the Loire upstream. He wants Joan to go to church and pray for a west wind; when she cries out that she will go and pray to St. Catherine, the wind changes. Dunois says that God has spoken and he will follow Joan "for God and Saint Dennis!"

Theology, military strategy, and politics converge from the opposition's point of view in the fourth scene. The French have scored several victories, and in a tent at the English camp, the Earl of Warwick, his chaplain, and Peter Cauchon, the Bishop of Beauvais, discuss the inevitable crowning of Charles. Warwick rationalizes Joan's military successes as the workings of a sorceress, but Cauchon believes she is not a witch but a heretic whose soul must be saved to save the English cause. Warwick wants to "burn the woman" to destroy "the cult of the Maid" that threatens to overwhelm the social order of Europe; Cauchon reviews the history of famous heretics who presumed to follow their "voices" and to ignore the authority of the nobles and the religious establishment. Joan acts as if she, herself, were the church and must be saved from her individualism, which Cauchon labels "Protestantism." Since the church only recognizes one realm, the kingdom of Christ, Joan, he argues, is committing another form of heresy by appealing to the people's sense of nationalism. Finally, she is rebelling against Nature by wearing men's clothes. All agree she must be captured; Warwick tells Cauchon, "if you will burn the Protestant, I will burn the Nationalist."

The play and its central character reach a decisive turning point in scene five, set in the cathedral at Rheims after Charles's coronation. In response to Joan's assertion that she will return to the farm once she has taken Paris, Dunois chides her for her naiveté in believing that the men of the court, who are jealous of her military success, will support her. The king wants a treaty with the Burgundians to end the fighting, and the Archbishop condemns Joan's spiritual hubris and warns of tragic consequences if she falls into the hands of Cauchon. She will not be ransomed and will be disowned by them all. The Archbishop tells her: "You stand alone; absolutely alone, trusting to your own conceit, your own ignorance, your own headstrong presumption, your own impiety in hiding all these sins under the cloak of a trust in God." Joan cries out that she has always been alone, like France and God himself; this loneliness is God's strength, and "In his strength I will dare, and dare, and dare, until I die." Comforted by the love she receives from the common people, which will repay her for the hatred of the court, she goes out, leaving the men of the court to express their various feelings about her. Charles, perhaps, speaks for them all when he says, "If only she would keep quiet or go home!"

Scene six, set in 1431, resolves the climax that was reached in the previous scene and contains a more detailed discussion of the theological issues with regard to Joan's crime of heresy introduced in the fourth scene. Captured by the Burgundians nine months earlier at Compiègne, Joan has been brought by Warwick to the ecclesiastical court at Rouen to stand public trial for heresy. This is her seventh, and last, trial, and Joan responds to the intense questioning with spirit and confidence in the validity of her own spiritual judgment. However, when she sees the executioner standing behind her, ready to lead her to the stake, she recants in fear and is sentenced to "perpetual imprisonment." For Joan this verdict is worse than death, and she tears up the recantation, proclaiming that she does not dread the fire "as much as the life of a rat in a hole." Her voices, she claims, were right, that by wanting to take "the light of the sky and the sight of the fields and flowers" from her "or from any human creature," she knows that "your counsel is of the devil, and that mine is of God." Her fate is sealed; she is burned as a relapsed heretic in an execution that gives no one joy. The executioner reports that only her heart would not burn but that Warwick has seen the last of her. Warwick smiles wryly and wonders aloud if he has.

There is a tragicomic and symbolic dream epilogue to *Saint Joan* that represents the rehabilitation of Joan of Arc that began in 1456. The scene is set in the bedroom of Charles VII, 25 years after Joan's execution. A flash of lightning reveals the silhouette of Joan in the window. Charles tells Joan of her victory in receiving justice that day and tries to convince her that it was his doing. They are joined by Cauchon, Dunois, Warwick, Warwick's chaplain, the executioner, and an English soldier now in hell, all of whom respond, according to their own sense of politics and theology, to Joan's execution and rehabilitation. A clerical-looking gentleman dressed in the fashion of 1920 appears, to the mirth of the others, to announce the elevation of Joan to sainthood. By now the Archbishop and the inquisitor are on hand, and all kneel to an enraptured Joan, offering her praise in the name of the people, the soldiers, the wicked, the foolish, the unpretending, and the heroic. Joan asks if she should work another miracle and come back from the dead. This provokes consternation from the men, each of whom offers apologies and excuses that reveal that they all prefer her to be dead. They steal away, and the king goes back to bed, leaving Joan alone, at the stroke of midnight, bathed in a white, radiant light, and asking, "O God that madest this beautiful earth, when will it be ready to receive Thy saints? How long, O Lord, how long?" The addition of the epilogue frames *Saint Joan* in the context of history and in Shaw's "life force" philosophy, articulated in Joan's last, anguished question. In his extensive preface to the published version of the play, Shaw, with characteristic sly humor, explains that, "As to the epilogue, I could hardly be expected to stultify myself by implying that Joan's history in the world ended unhappily with her execution, instead of beginning there." The preface performs a similar function, comparing the historical Joan of Arc with the legendary martyr. For Shaw Joan, although a Catholic, is "one of the first Protestant martyrs," following her conscience in defiance of official authority. A blend of common sense and innocence, Joan of Arc is less a figure of romance than a visionary reformer destroyed by an inflexible system. At its core *Saint Joan* is a philosophically powerful drama of the Middle Ages, in which a teenage country girl who is by turns courageous, miraculous, and unbearable and men possessed of both credulity and certainty vie, tragically and comically, for the soul of a complicated era.

BLOOD WEDDING

(1933)

by Federico García Lorca

*Lorca said once that the only hope for happiness lies in "living one's instinctual life to the full." *Blood Wedding* can be understood as a gloss on that belief. In it the poet succeeded in creating a medium that allowed him to express the deepest elements in his personality while at the same time to deploy his multiple talents.*

—Ian Gibson, *Federico García Lorca: A Life*

In his poetry and plays Federico García Lorca opened up Spanish literature to accommodate elements of European modernism without losing any of the forces of tradition and place from which his works derive so much strength. Through his intense analysis of himself and his world García Lorca contributed to a redefinition of Spanish identity and consciousness while grappling with issues that transcend national borders and strictly contemporary issues. As a poet his artistry grew from his earliest poetry of adolescent longing to the more mature achievement of the *Romancero gitano* (*Gypsy Ballads*) in which a highly personal style emerges with a fusion of traditional poetic elements and striking modern images. In his breathtaking sequence *Poeta en Nueva York* (*Poet in New York*), García Lorca abandoned traditional poetic forms for a succession of surreal images capturing the chaotic nightmare of modern urban life and the poet's anguish as he confronts it. García Lorca's plays are filled with the same intensity, daring imagery, and preoccupations that mark his poetry. His plays appeal to a large popular audience yet resonate with a poetic intensity and lyricism that much modern drama has jettisoned or failed to realize. His best plays explore psychological and social forces in which human instincts collide with society's restraints and are meant to be instructive. "The theatre is a school of weeping and of laughter," García Lorca observed, "a rostrum where men are free to expose old and equivocal standards of conduct, and explain with living examples the eternal norms of the heart and feelings of man." At his best García Lorca achieves the fusion of lyric and dramatic effects that William Butler Yeats and T. S. Eliot struggled with mixed results to join in a revitalized poetic drama. García Lorca's rich blend of folk tradition, contemporary social analysis, and deeply personal exploration of universal themes is simultaneously timeless, sophisticated, and authentic. As critic Francis Ferguson has asserted, García Lorca "writes the poetry of the theater as our poets would like to do." Of all his plays *Bodas de sangre* (*Blood Wedding*) is recognized as his masterpiece, his most performed play worldwide and a summation of the theatrical methods and particular genius of one of the great originals in dramatic expression in the 20th century.

García Lorca's inspiration and artistic power originate in his background and the influence of his native Andalusia, with its rich blend of Moorish, Gypsy, and rural Spanish tradition. Born in 1898 in a small village west of Granada, García Lorca was the son of a prosperous farmer and a former schoolteacher who encouraged her precocious son in his reading and musical ability. His interest in drama was stimulated early when entertainers came to the village and performed a puppet show. Enchanted with the performance, García Lorca eventually constructed his own set of marionettes and presented original performances for the neighbors. An accomplished pianist and guitarist, García Lorca first intended to become a musician and composer; instead, yielding to the wishes of his practical father, he began to study law at the University of Granada but left for Madrid in 1919. He lived at the Student Residence of the University of Madrid for 10 years, while he read widely, wrote, and associated with a circle of young intellectuals and artists who included future film director Luis Buñuel and artist Salvador Dalí. He also met such international figures as François Mauriac, H. G. Wells, and Igor Stravinsky and was exposed to the avant-garde movements of dadaism and surrealism. García Lorca incorporated modern artistic techniques into traditional poetic forms, performing his poetry like a troubadour in cafés and night clubs. In 1920 his friendship with Gregorio Martínez Sierra, director of Madrid's Eslava Theater, led to the production of García Lorca's first play, *El maleficio de la mariposa* (*The Butterfly's Evil Spell*), a symbolic fable in which a cockroach's earthbound existence is challenged by the appearance of a butterfly. He would achieve his initial theatrical success with *Mariana Pineda* (1927). Set in the 1830s, the play is the first of García Lorca's portraits of heroic, suffering women, in which the title character is executed for her revolutionary activity. Following the publication of *Gypsy Ballads* in 1928, García Lorca became famous. In 1929, seeking relief from severe depression and emotional distress, which may have been caused by his growing awareness of his homosexuality, he went to New York, where be studied briefly at Columbia University. His experience in a different culture, so antagonistic to his native and regional values, produced an emotional crisis and self-exploration of his identity and homosexuality in the nightmarish visions of *Poet in New York*, published posthumously in 1940.

García Lorca, who would say that "The theater was always my vocation," returned to Spain in 1930 to concentrate on drama and the revitalization of the Spanish theater. Endorsing the social function of drama as a reform agent, he wrote that "a theater that is sensitive and well oriented in all of its branches, from tragedy to vaudeville, can in a few years change the sensibility of a people; and a shattered theater, in which hoofs substitute for wings, can debase and benumb an entire nation." His initial dramatic efforts during this period were experimental pieces in the surrealist manner, although such works as *Amor de don Perlimplín con Belisa en su jardín* (*Don Perlimplin and Belisa in the Garden*), *La zapatera prodigiosa* (*The Shoemaker's Prodigious Wife*), and *Doña Rosita la soltera* (*Dona Rosita the Spinster*) show him attempting to balance elements derived from the Spanish dramatic tradition with his characteristic lyricism and theatrical innovations that joined farce with serious themes and incorporated music and dance. In 1932 the fledgling Spanish Republic advanced educational and cultural reforms by funding the University Theater, popularly known as La Barraca, with García Lorca as one of its directors. Its mission was to employ university students to provide theater and other cultural opportunities for the underprivileged in the country's isolated villages. Traveling across rural Spain in a truck loaded with props and sets, the company, under García Lorca's direction, performed classic dramas of Félix Lope de Vega, Miguel de Cervantes, Pedro Calderón de la Barca, Tirso de Molina, and others to appreciative rural audiences. The experience of adapting classic Spanish texts to entertain large, unsophisticated audiences, while reconnecting with Spain's peasant culture, proved to be formative in García Lorca's development as a playwright when he began his masterworks, the "rural trilogy," initiated with *Blood Wedding* in 1933, followed by *Yerma* (1934), and *La casa de Bernarda Alba* (*The House of Bernarda Alba*), produced posthumously in 1945. In 1936 anti-Republican forces under Francisco Franco revolted, setting off the Spanish civil war. García Lorca's connections with the Republican government made him a target in the purges mounted by Franco's troops. He sought protection in the house of a friend near Granada but was arrested and executed by a firing squad at the age of 38. As Chilean poet Pablo Neruda lamented, "Those who in shooting him wanted to hit the heart of his people made the right choice."

Blood Wedding, in which García Lorca attempted to represent that heart, originated from a newspaper account of a murder committed before a wedding near the Andalusian town of Níjar, in the province of Almería. The dead man was the previous lover of the bride, who, after running away with her the night before the wedding, had been killed by the groom's cousin. This notorious case provided the basis for the themes of García Lorca's play in its tragedy of thwarted love and passion crippled by social conventions and avarice. As García Lorca's biographer Ian Gibson summarizes, "In the Níjar tragedy the poet found a powerful metaphor. . . . Leonardo and the Bride, like their real-life prototypes, have experienced a passionate adolescent love which lasted for three years, a love frustrated by economic considerations and almost forgotten by their neighbors. Nature had 'made' the two for each other, but society frustrated her designs. Tragedy is the inevitable outcome." García Lorca would transform the facts of the case with a highly stylized, symbolic method to universalize the drama.

Set in rural Andalusia, *Blood Wedding* opens in the home of the Mother and her son, who informs her of his intention to marry. Her husband and other sons have been killed in a blood feud, and the Mother is sorry to lose her only surviving son, but she orders him to buy presents for the Bride as custom dictates. From a neighbor the Mother learns that the Bride was once wooed by her cousin, Leonardo, before his marriage to another three years before. Leonardo is also a member of the family who had killed her loved ones. To emphasize the social forces and representative nature of the characters only Leonardo is given a name; all the other characters are designated by their societal position or role. The second scene takes place at Leonardo's house. As Leonardo's Wife and Mother-in-law are rocking a baby to sleep, he is asked whether he has been riding "on the far side of the plains," where the Bride lives. Leonardo denies it, and the conversation shifts to the news of the upcoming marriage of the Bride and Bridegroom, while Leonardo's neglect of his wife and child is suggested. The final scene of the act takes place at the Bride's home. The Mother of the Bridegroom and the Father of the Bride formalize the match, each praising the worthiness of their offspring and their good fortune in consolidating their property through the marriage. The Bride is quiet and respectful in company, but once alone with her Servant expresses her impatience and frustration with the wedding planning and her future life. Told that it looks as if she did not want to be married, the Bride bites her hand in anger. She denies having heard a horse late the previous night or seen its rider, but when the Servant identifies the rider as Leonardo, the Bride sees him on horseback outside her window.

The second act takes place at the Bride's house as the Servant prepares the Bride for the ceremony. The Bride reacts to the promised bliss that will follow her marriage by throwing her wreath of orange blossoms to the ground. Leonardo, his Wife, and his Mother-in-law are the first guests to arrive, and Leonardo and the Bride manage a private meeting to speak of their past love, its betrayal by Leonardo's marriage, and his warning about the action the Bride is taking:

> To burn with desire and keep quiet about it is the greatest punishment we can bring on ourselves. What good was pride to me—and not seeing you, and letting you lie awake night after night? No good! It only served to bring the fire down on me! You think that time heals and walls hide things, but it isn't true, it isn't true! When things get that deep inside you there isn't anybody can change them.

The Bride persists in her intention of marrying and forgetting Leonardo and their past, as wedding songs are heard. In the second scene the guests have returned from the wedding ceremony. Amidst the bustle of drinking and dancing the Bride resists the Bridegroom's embrace and announces that she wishes to rest and asks to be left alone. When the Bridegroom later goes to find her, she has disappeared. It is discovered that she and Leonardo have ridden away on his horse. The humiliated Bridegroom, anxious for revenge, gathers a posse of his relatives to pursue them.

   The climactic third act shows García Lorca's brilliance in joining striking stage effects with a symbolic method that expands the plays conflict into a collision of elemental, universal forces. The act shifts from its previous interior daytime settings to a forest at night and from prose, periodically broken by verse—such as the lullaby in the second scene of act 1 and the wedding songs of act 2—to mainly verse. The act begins with a chorus made up of woodcutters, who anticipate the bloody result of the lovers' actions while underscoring the play's central theme:

> FIRST WOODCUTTER   When the moon comes out they'll see them.
>
> SECOND WOODCUTTER   They ought to let them go.
>
> FIRST WOODCUTTER   The world is wide. Everybody can live in it.
>
> THIRD WOODCUTTER   But they'll kill them.
>
> SECOND WOODCUTTER   You have to follow your passion. They did right to run away.
>
> FIRST WOODCUTTER   They were deceiving themselves but at the last blood was stronger.
>
> THIRD WOODCUTTER   Blood!
>
> FIRST WOODCUTTER   You have to follow the path of your blood.
>
> SECOND WOODCUTTER   But blood that sees the light of day is drunk up by the earth.
>
> FIRST WOODCUTTER   What of it? Better dead with blood drained away than alive with it rotting.

Ironically, by properly following one's blood—instincts and desires—a wedding of blood, of death, results when social conventions are violated. This blood wedding, following the actual wedding, is further orchestrated by the symbolic figure of the Moon, appearing as a young woodcutter with a white face and presaging Death, which appears in the guise of a Beggar Woman who becomes the Bridegroom's guide in his pursuit. Leonardo and the Bride are given a final recognition scene together in which they consider what they have done and its consequences, finding themselves trapped between their destructive passions and societal retribution. The scene ends with García Lorca's inspired stage direction, integrating sight and sound into a stunning tableau:

> The Moon appears very slowly. The stage takes on a strong blue light. The two violins are heard. Suddenly two long, ear-splitting shrieks are heard, and the music of the two violins is cut short. At the second shriek the Beggar Woman appears and stands with her back to the audience. She opens her cape and stands in the center of the stage like a great bird with immense wings. The Moon halts. The curtain comes down in absolute silence.

The final scene of the play opens with two girls winding a skein of red wool, suggesting human fate. Leonardo's Wife and Mother-in-Law and the Bridegroom's Mother await news, and they eventually learn that the Bridegroom has died at the hands of Leonardo, who is also dead. The Bride appears seeking the vengeance of the Mother, who is inconsolable, as the bodies of Leonardo and the Bridegroom are brought in to be mourned by the bereaved women. The play concludes with a catharsis of pity and terror as stark and unmitigated as any Greek tragedy, which the power of García Lorca's poetry and stagecraft have made possible.

THE MARRIAGE OF FIGARO

56

(1784) *by Pierre-Augustin Caron de Beaumarchais*

That the two plays are now known to the English stage only through Rossini and Mozart is our loss. The repertory of classic comedies does not contain so many works of a like order than we can afford to ignore The Barber *and* Figaro. *In the European theatre they still hold their place and they have something to say on issues which retain a contemporary interest. Beneath the fun and frivolity there is a quality which is not to be confused with indifference. A man who must laugh at the world lest he should weep is a figure only the happier ages of history can ignore. An ironic awareness of values other than those of conventional society is revealed only in flashes in* The Barber; *in* Figaro *it is implicit, a continuing accompaniment to the comic theme. It is a challenge that the agents of tyranny have rarely failed to detect. Louis XVI, after hearing a reading of* Figaro, *said that such a play could never be allowed to appear on the stage. . . . Napoleon's grim comment on Beaumarchais was that in his time such a fellow would have been clapped into jail. And presumably kept there! The restored Bourbons had their censors delete from the plays all reference to censorship. Most recent censors have acknowledged in* Figaro *one who, when speaking of Liberty, does not take that name in vain.*

—John Wood, Introduction to the Penguin edition of *The Barber of Seville* and
The Marriage of Figaro

Pierre-Augustin Caron de Beaumarchais's *Le Mariage de Figaro* (*The Marriage of Figaro*), the most popular play of 18th-century France, celebrates the exhilaratingly insubordinate triumph of a servant over a nobleman that anticipates the assault on the social and class system in the French Revolution. The play is surely as subversive as anything Voltaire or Thomas Paine ever wrote. Louis XVI is reported to have denounced the play by fuming, "It is hateful, it will never be played. . . . That man mocks everything that is to be respected in government." Georges-Jacques Danton claimed that the play "killed the nobility," and Napoleon would later assert that it portrayed "The Revolution in action." Baroness Oberkirch, an aristocrat who attended a performance and was angry at herself for being amused by it, wrote that the "nobility showed a great want of tact in applauding it, which was nothing less than giving themselves a slap in the face. They laughed at their own expense . . . They will repent it yet." With Figaro, one of the great comic figures of the Western literary tradition, Beaumarchais promotes the impudent and resourceful servant—a stock figure of comedy from the Greeks and Romans—from supporting to the primary role. A character who was conventionally employed to clear away the obstacles to love among his betters not only gets the girl but deserves her more than his well-born rival, who, despite his rank and authority, is exposed as inferior to his self-made and self-sustaining underling. Dramatizing the coup of ability over birthright, the common man over the aristocrat, and the claims of the marginalized—illegitimates and women—over the status quo, Beaumarchais's comedy provided a powerful brief for the subsequent social revolution that would create the modern world and a radical new dramatic art. It, perhaps more so than any other play, helped democratize French drama, while injecting a social critique into the theatrical experience and initiating a significant shift in subject and manner that subsequent European drama would absorb and expand.

Beaumarchais's remarkable career as artisan, musician, courtier, businessman, secret agent, pamphleteer, and playwright echoes in interesting ways that of his most famous creation, Figaro, the former barber of Seville, who proves his worth against the rich and powerful in multiple roles and situations. Born Pierre-Augustin Caron in Paris in 1732, Beaumarchais was the son of a master watchmaker with whom Beaumarchais apprenticed from the age of 13. When he was 20, Beaumarchais invented an innovative watch mechanism that was recognized by the Academy of Sciences, and he was invited to Versailles to demonstrate his invention before Louis XV. This proved to be the start of Beaumarchais's next career as a courtier and entrepreneur. Commissioned to design a watch for Madame de Pompadour, the king's mistress, Beaumarchais traded on his connections to proclaim himself the "king's watchmaker." He gained a minor court position as an officer of the king's pantry and a more substantial sinecure as a royal auditor and ceremonial waiter at the king's table while he curried favor with the king's daughter by his harp playing. He eventually married a wealthy widow through whom he acquired holdings in the village of Beaumarchais, from which he derived his name. Growing rich from his contacts and financial ventures he was able to purchase the title of Secretary to the King and entered the rank of the hereditary French nobility. Beaumarchais had by the age of 30, through multiple talents and determination, managed to leap the considerable chasm between the ranks of the artisan and mercantile classes and the highest levels of French society.

His literary activities began in the late 1750s with his composition of comic sketches, derived from the Italian commedia dell'arte, for the private entertainment of Madame de Pompadour's house guests. His professional theatrical career began in 1767 with the production by the Comédie Français of *Eugénie,* a sentimental drama inspired by the ideas of Denis Diderot that replaced the loftier neoclassical tragic and comic subjects with contemporary situations treated with a new authenticity. Beaumarchais defended his dramatic intentions in *Essai sur le genre dramatique sérieux* (*An Essay on Serious Drama*) in which he asserted that his new dramatic genre "shatters at last the barriers of prejudice and shoots beyond known boundaries." Citing the influence of Samuel Richardson's novels and Jean-Jacques Rousseau's *Julie, ou La Nouvelle Héloïse,* Beaumarchais defines a play as "a faithful picture of human actions" that seeks to stir emotions and improve morals. "It is the essential aim of the serious drama," he asserted, ". . . to offer a more powerful interest and a morality which is more relevant than that of heroic tragedy and more profound than that of gay comedy." As critic Joseph Sungolowsky summarizes, Beaumarchais's *drame,* or the *genre sérieux,*

> presents a touching situation with which one can always identify. Its heroes are always honest and common people whose misfortunes not only arouse our compassion but force us to look into our own hearts. As an intermediate genre between tragedy and comedy, drama can be as sublime as the former since it also portrays man's struggle with life and does so more effectively than the latter, which presents only perplexities in which he is caught up.

In his conception of bourgeois drama Beaumarchais attempted to transfer fiction's new psychological realism and recognizable characters and situations to the stage. Serious drama, he asserted, should be "true as nature itself," jettisoning the verbal artificiality and restricted rules of neoclassical decorum for a "living language, urgent, fragmented, tumultuous, and truly passionate." Beaumarchais's next play, *Les Deux amis, ou le Négociant de Lyon* (1770; *The Two Friends, or the Merchant of Lyon*) furthers the goals of this bourgeois drama by treating middle-class provincial businessmen in a plot derived from their financial dealings.

Beaumarchais's own bourgeois drama during this period was even more "fragmented, tumultuous, and truly passionate" than his dramatic inventions. In 1773 a violent quarrel with the duke of Cahulnes led to his being incarcerated for two and a half months. In 1774 Beaumarchais was caught up in a notorious legal and bribery case. His account of the affair brought him international notoriety but left him bankrupt, branded a criminal, and deprived under French law of his civil rights. In pursuit of a royal pardon Beaumarchais offered his services as the king's agent in Britain to suppress a scandalous account of Madame du Barry, but Louis XV died before Beaumarchais could be rewarded. Instead he continued working as a secret agent in England for Louis XVI, helping to secure aid for the American forces in the opening phase of the Revolutionary War. Even while chasing across Europe, in the best tradition of a picaresque romance, a mysterious adventurer who was attempting to publish a scurrilous pamphlet attacking the French Crown and libeling Queen Marie Antoinette, Beaumarchais managed to complete *Le Barbier de Séville* (*The Barber of Seville*), which debuted in 1775. Originally conceived as a comic opera in 1772 that was rejected by the Opéra Comique, it was reworked first as a five-act comedy that was hissed at when it premiered. Two days later it reopened as a four-act play that became a triumphant success. The comedy—in which Count Almaviva enlists the aid of the resourceful barber and apothecary Figaro in his courtship of Rosine over the objections of her guardian, Dr. Bartholo—presents the standard New Comedy situation of the obstacles to love with an updated, witty ingenuity and craftsmanship. Beaumarchais entertainingly mixes burlesque and farce along with a sophisticated comedy of manners and social critique that echo Molière. Anchoring the play is Figaro, whom Beaumarchais called *"le machiniste"* (the scene shifter), who "instead of being a villain is a funny chap, a carefree man, who laughs equally at the success or failure of his enterprises." The ever adaptable, resourceful, and worldly wise Figaro steals the play and became a great audience favorite, and he would be brought back in Beaumarchais's masterpiece, *The Marriage of Figaro*, in 1784.

Having served as Count Almaviva's co-conspirator and ally in *The Barber of Selville*, Figaro now must oppose his master when the nobleman has designs on Figaro's fiancée, Suzanne, lady's maid to the Countess. Three years after the events of the first play, the Count has tired of his wife, and in his official capacity as corregidor, or first magistrate, of Andalusia, wants to reinstate the droit du seigneur, the right of a feudal lord to sleep with any woman in his domain on her wedding night. Faced with this abuse of aristocratic powers Figaro schemes to outwit and outmaneuver his master while also contending with the scheming of Marceline, the Count's housekeeper to whom Figaro has pledged marriage if he is unable to repay the money she has lent him. Suzanne and the Countess also launch their own plan to protect Suzanne's virtue and salvage the Countess's marriage. With so many plots and counterplots the comedy presents an unflagging series of exciting entrances and exits, surprising reversals, mistaken identities, and barely averted catastrophes in the best French farce tradition. All is unified thematically by the foolishness and contradictions committed on behalf of love. The Count, for example, dismisses the young page, Chérubin, for his effrontery in becoming infatuated with the Countess, overlooking his own foolishness in pursuit of Suzanne. To expose the Count's violations in the name of love and his responsibilities as a nobleman Figaro plots to dress Chérubin in Suzanne's clothing and send him to keep the demanded rendezvous, while diverting the Count's attention with an anonymous letter suggesting that the Countess has a lover. Meanwhile, Marceline demands that the Count rule on her claim—Figaro's money or his hand. In another abuse of power the Count self-servingly declares that Figaro must either repay the money (thereby pressuring him to accept the dowry the Count is willing to provide Suzanne for her services) or marry Marceline immediately (and eliminate his rival for Suzanne). The complications collapse in a series of breathtaking reversals. Marceline discovers that Figaro is in fact her long-lost illegitimate son by Figaro's old nemesis, Dr. Bartholo. When the Countess and Suzanne spring their trap to undo the Count they exchange clothing, and Figaro witnesses his supposed betrothed (actually the Countess) willing to be wooed by his rival. Enraged at Suzanne's apparent duplicity, Figaro confronts the supposed Countess (Suzanne in disguise) to inform her, only to recognize Suzanne's voice. He then decides to turn the tables on Suzanne by pretending to woo her as the Countess. The Count arrives to see Figaro apparently making love to his wife, seizes his servant, and places him under arrest. Ultimately, the revelation that the woman the Count took for Suzanne in his wooing was the Countess makes clear that the Count has been tricked. Realizing the attractions of his wife that had captivated him in the first place, the Count relents in his infidelity, chastened by his treatment: "I thought I was being clever and they've treated me like a child." The play ends with the marriage of Figaro and Suzanne and the besting of the all-powerful nobleman by a bastard and a lady's maid. The comedy has wittily both exposed human follies and subverted the accepted social order that privileges birth over abilities, power over ingenuity, and deference over self-assertion.

The play's powerful social theme is perhaps best expressed in Figaro's long monologue in act 5 that expresses a kind of comic version of Benjamin Franklin's *Autobiography* and the Declaration of Independence:

No, My Lord Count, you shall not have her, you shall not have her! Because you are a great nobleman you think you are a great genius. . . . Nobility, fortune, rank, position! How proud they make a man feel! What have you done to deserve such advantages? Put yourself to the trouble of being born—nothing more! For the rest—a very ordinary man! Whereas I, lost among the obscure crowd, have had to deploy more knowledge, more calculation and skill merely to survive than has sufficed to rule all the provinces of Spain for a century! Yet you would measure yourself against me. . . . Could anything be stranger than a fate like mine? Son of goodness knows whom, stolen by bandits, brought up to their way of life, I become disgusted with it and yearn for an honest profession—only to find myself repulsed everywhere. I study Chemistry, Pharmacy, Surgery, and all the prestige of a great nobleman can barely secure me the handling of a horse-doctor's probe! . . . A great nobleman comes to Seville and he recognizes me. I get him safely married, and as a reward for my trouble in helping him to a wife he now wants to intercept mine! . . . Oh! Fantastic series of events! Why should they happen to me? Why these things and not others? Who made me responsible? Obliged to follow a road I set out on, all unknowing, and one I shall come to the end of, willy nilly, I have strewn it with such flowers as my high spirits have permitted: I say my high spirits without knowing whether they are any more mine than the rest or who is this "me" that I'm worrying about: a formless aggregation of unidentified parts, then a puny stupid being, a frisky little animal, a young man ardent in the pursuits of pleasure with every taste of enjoyment, plying all sorts of trades in order to live—now master, now servant, as fortune pleases, ambitious from vanity, industrious from necessity, but lazy from inclination! Orator in emergency, poet for relaxation, musician when occasion demands, in love by mad fits and starts.

Figaro, the self-made man of many parts, is crowned the master of situations in Beaumarchais's play, and the drama needed to contain him would bring down the neoclassical rules and release the energy of both the Revolution and the Romantic movement that would reshape the life and art that followed. After Figaro, the deluge.

THE GLASS MENAGERIE

(1944)

by Tennessee Williams

57

Being a "memory play," The Glass Menagerie can be presented with unusual freedom of convention. Because of its considerably delicate or tenuous material, atmospheric touches and subtleties of direction play a particularly important part. Expressionism and all other unconventional techniques in drama have only one valid aim, and that is the closer approach to truth. When a play employs unconventional techniques, it is not, or shouldn't be, trying to escape its responsibility of dealing with reality, or interpreting experience, but is actually or should be attempting to find a closer approach, a more penetrating and vivid expression of things as they are. . . . Everyone should know nowadays the unimportance of the photographic in art: that truth, life, or reality is an organic thing which the poetic imagination can represent or suggest, in essence, only through transformation, through changing into other forms than those which were merely present in appearance. These remarks are not meant as a preface only to this particular play. They have to do with a conception of a new, plastic theater which must take the place of the exhausted theatre of realistic conventions if the theatre is to resume vitality as part of our culture.
> —Tennessee Williams, Production Notes for *The Glass Menagerie*

With the above words Tennessee Williams articulated a dramatic credo and a new direction for American drama. His call for a new, poetic "plastic theatre" to replace "the exhausted theatre of realistic conventions" would be embodied in Williams's first major stage achievement, *The Glass Menagerie*, a play signaling both the arrival of a powerful new dramatic voice and ushering in an unsurpassed creative period for American drama. Acknowledging his debt to Williams in general and *The Glass Menagerie* in particular, Arthur Miller asserted:

> [It] seemed to me a triumph of fragility, a play utterly at odds with standard Broadway fare. Seeing it was like stumbling on a flower in a junkyard. I suppose the most striking thing about that play at the time was that one knew it had been *written* rather than having been overheard in

somebody's kitchen; its lines were fluent and idiomatic but at the same time rhythmically composed. Playwriting . . . was at the time regarded as something close to engineering, structure and its problems taking first place in all consideration of the art. *Menagerie* appeared to have no structure or at best the structure of a lyric. . . . Its heart was on its sleeve. It was still a time when the convention was to suspect Chekhov's plays as real dramas because in them "nothing happened." . . . [T]he Broadway play emphasized plot, while Williams had pushed language and character to the front of the stage as never before, in America anyway.

Others have seconded Miller in regarding *The Glass Menagerie* as a breakthrough and milestone in American drama. Critic Brooks Atkinson described it as "a revelation of what superb theater could be," stating that "Williams's remembrance of things past gave the theater distinction as a literary medium." Critic Joanne Stang has summed up the play's impact by observing that "the American theater, indeed theater everywhere, has never been the same" since the premiere of *The Glass Menagerie.*

Williams's route to *The Glass Menagerie* was a creative and personal search for a distinctive subject and voice. Born Thomas Lanier Williams in Mississippi in 1911, Williams had an overprotective mother and an often absent father who relocated his family to St. Louis, Missouri, when Williams was eight. Echoing the characters in *The Glass Menagerie,* Williams's mother, like Amanda Wingfield, was a southern belle who relied on her memories of home and the past to sustain their far less genteel life in St. Louis. Williams, like Tom Wingfield, worked for a time in a shoe warehouse; while his beloved older sister, Rose, was, like Laura Wingfield, disabled, in Rose's case with schizophrenia that led to her being institutionalized. Writing, which began for Williams when his mother gave him an old typewriter when he was 11, served the shy and often bullied Williams as consolation and compensation for his feelings of being trapped in an uncongenial home life and hostile outside world. "I write from my own tensions," Williams once told an interviewer. "For me, this is a form of therapy."

After graduating from college in 1938 Williams pursued a bohemian life as a struggling, itinerant writer. In Chicago he tried unsuccessfully to work for the Federal Writers' Project of the Works Projects Administration, but his writing was deemed lacking in "social content." In 1939 he submitted a collection of one-act plays, called *American Blues,* for a prize offered by the Group Theatre; it won a special $100 award. Through the support of one of the judges Williams managed to secure an agent who helped him gain a grant and scholarship to the New School in New York City, where he began work on *Battle of Angels,* the first of Williams's full-length plays to show his subsequent characteristic dramatic trademarks. Set in the South, the play explores the psychology of repressed passions in the context of both religion and sex, a combination that led, after a disastrous opening night in Boston in 1940 in which an excessive smoke effect during the play's final lynching scene drove the gasping audience from the theater, to the play being banned. Dejected by the failure, Williams retreated to New York where he worked for a time as a theater usher, elevator operator, and waiter-entertainer. In 1943 Williams managed to secure a scriptwriting contract from a Hollywood studio. Struggling through his first assignment—a feature starring Lana Turner, which Williams referred to as "The Celluloid Brassiere"—Williams refused his next project, a film starring child actress Margaret O'Brien. He then presented an original idea for a film script, an outline for a work entitled "The Gentleman Caller," based on an early short story called "Portrait of a Girl in Glass" (published in 1948 in the collection *One Arm*). It was rejected, and when the studio suggested that Williams stay away from his office for the remainder of his contract, he developed his outline into a stage play that he renamed *The Glass Menagerie*.

The play premiered in Chicago in December 1944, gaining considerable attention due to the return to the stage of the much-admired actress Laurette Taylor as Amanda Wingfield. It opened to enthusiastic reviews in New York in 1945, winning the New York Drama Critics Circle Award and running for two years on Broadway. In *The Glass Menagrie* Williams replaced the convoluted and sensational southern gothic elements that had marred *Battle of Angels* with a far simpler, more authentically felt story derived from Williams's family background. The play's setting—a dingy St. Louis apartment during the depression—directly corresponds to Williams's family situation, while the Wingfield family triangle—Amanda and her son Tom and daughter Laura—resembles Williams's relation with his mother and sister. Tom Wingfield, the frustrated writer and Williams's surrogate, who serves both as a participant in the drama and its narrator and interpreter, announces to the audience at the outset the play's reversal of stage conventions: "Yes, I have tricks in my pocket, I have things up my sleeve. But I am the opposite of a stage magician. He gives you illusion that has the appearance of truth. I give you truth in the pleasing disguise of illusion." The play accepts all the distortions, selectivity, and subjectivity of recollection. "Being a memory play," Tom insists, "it is dimly lighted, it is sentimental, it is not realistic." Underscoring the notion that the play is Tom's retrospective projection, Williams undermines realism with various expressionistic and lyrical stage techniques. "The lighting in the play is not realist," Williams explains in his production notes. Instead, he insisted, the stage should be dim and shadowy with characters suddenly illuminated as "in religious paintings, such as El Greco, where the figures are radiant in atmosphere that is relatively dusky." Music is to be used "to give emotional emphasis to suitable passages," serving "as a thread of connection and allusion between the narrator with his separate point in time and space and the subject of his story." Most radically, Williams originally proposed projecting "images or titles" onto the wall of the Wingfield apartment, such as "Où sont les neiges," preceding Amanda's nostalgic recollections of her girlhood in scene 1, or "Annunciation" in scene 5 when Tom announces the coming of the gentleman-caller. The purpose, Williams declared, was "to give accent to certain values in each scene," strengthening "the effect of what is merely allusion in the writing and allow the primary point to be made more simply and lightly than if the entire responsibility were on the spoken lines." All of these elements—the narrator's direct address to the audience, lighting, music, and interpretive captions for the scenes—shift the focus from surface illusion to the inner reality of the characters and situation.

There are, as Tom initially announces, five characters in his memory play: Tom; his mother, Amanda; his sister, Laura; a gentleman-caller, "the most realistic character in the play, . . . an emissary from a world of reality that we were somehow set apart from"; and the "larger-than-life-size photograph over the mantel" of Tom and Laura's father—"a telephone man who fell in love with long distances" and abandoned his family to fend for themselves—who serves as an ironic absent presence throughout the play, reflecting both the past and the threat of Tom's following in his father's footsteps. The play opens with scenes exploring Amanda and her relationship with her two adult children. Amanda, a fading southern belle, is, in Williams's description, "a little woman of great but confused vitality clinging frantically to another time and place," who compensates for her present diminished circumstances by harkening to her girlhood triumphs back in genteel "Blue Mountain." Tom, feeling trapped by his job and his family obligations, mightily enforced by his mother, dreams of breaking free for a life of fulfillment and adventure, which he indulges in vicariously through nightly trips to the movies. Laura, left crippled by a childhood illness and painfully shy and self-conscious of the brace on her leg, has since high school withdrawn further and further to the private refuge of old phonographic records and her collection of tiny glass animals. As Williams points out, "Laura's separation increases till she is like a piece of her own glass collection, too exquisitely fragile to move from the shelf." The dramatic action centers on Amanda's efforts to secure her daughter's future. Although she refuses to accept Tom's characterization of her daughter as crippled and "peculiar," Amanda realizes that Laura cannot survive on her own. When Amanda's schemes to equip her daughter with job skills by enrolling her in a business school end disastrously, Amanda responds with a final hope that a husband can be found who will provide for and protect Laura, and asks Tom to find a suitable young man among his associates at the warehouse. Tom invites Jim O'Connor to dinner, and Amanda is delighted with the prospect of a much anticipated gentleman caller for Laura, which stirs her memories of her own former suitors, making clear that Amanda is vicariously reliving her own past through her daughter.

When Jim arrives, he proves to be everything Amanda could have desired: well-behaved, personable, and ambitious, enrolled in self-improvement courses, and readying himself for a future in television. He also turns out to be Laura's former high school classmate for whom she has secretly pined ever since. Laura is terrified by his visit and becomes physically ill when he arrives. After dinner, however, Jim and Laura are left alone, and he gradually is able to put her at ease, encouraging her self-confidence by urging her to "think of yourself as *superior* in some way!" As music from the Paradise Dance Hall across the alley plays, they dance, bumping against the table that holds Laura's most prized possession, a glass unicorn, which falls breaking its horn. The accident changes the mood from exuberance to tenderness, ending in a kiss. Apologizing, Jim explains that he cannot call again because he is engaged to be married. He leaves abruptly, taking the unicorn, Laura's gift to him as a "souvenir."

Jim's departure and the news of his engagement shatter Amanda's great expectations. "Things," she says, "have a way of turning out so badly." She lashes out at Tom for the cruel joke she accuses him of playing on his family by bringing home a gentleman caller who is some other girl's fiancé. Despite his protest of ignorance of Jim's engagement, Amanda continues to attack Tom's betrayal of the family while exposing long unstated truths about them all. "You live in a dream," Amanda insists. "You manufacture illusions!" For the first time verbalizing the full truth about Laura and their circumstances, Amanda taunts the departing Tom:

> AMANDA   Go to the movies, go! Don't think about us, a mother deserted, an unmarried sister who's crippled and has no job! Don't let anything interfere with your selfish pleasure! . . .

> TOM   All right, I will! The more you shout about my selfishness to me the quicker I'll go, and I won't go to the movies!

> AMANDA   Go, then! Then go to the moon—you selfish dreamer!

As Amanda is seen comforting her daughter, the play concludes with Tom's soliloquy revealing that he has followed in his father's footsteps as a wanderer though still tormented by guilt at having abandoned his sister:

> I didn't go to the moon. I went much further—for time is the longest distance between two places . . . I traveled around a great deal. The cities swept about me like dead leaves that were brightly colored but torn away from the branches. I would have stopped, but I was pursued by something. . . . Perhaps I am walking along a street at night, in some strange city, before I have found companions. I pass the lighted window of a shop

where perfume is sold. The window is filled with pieces of colored glass, tiny transparent bottles in delicate colors, like bits of a shattered rainbow. Then all at once my sister touches my shoulder. I turn around and look into her eyes.

Onstage Laura is seen blowing out the candles, ending Tom's address to the ghostly presence of his sister and the play:

Oh, Laura, Laura, I tried to leave you behind me, but I am more faithful than I intended to be! I reach for a cigarette, I cross the street, I run into the movies or a bar, I buy a drink, I speak to the nearest stranger—anything that can blow your candles out!

[Laura bends over the candles]

—for nowadays the world is lit by lightning! Blow out your candles, Laura—and so good-bye. . . .

[She blows the candles out]

Rarely before or since has an American play achieved such poetry and pathos. *The Glass Menagerie* manages in its stagecraft, language, and vision a delicate balance between illusion and reality, between showing the fragility and failure of human dreams and their necessity, through a complex blend of symbolism, realism, and expressionism that would open new dramatic prospects for American drama.

THE GOOD PERSON OF SETZUAN *58*

(1943) *by Bertolt Brecht*

Shen Te, unlike Puntila and Mother Courage, realizes the futility of self-deception. Unlike the gods on whom Brecht pours his sarcasm she is unable to preserve the utopian optimism which ignores the split between good intentions and evil means. Shen Te cannot, in the end, share the ideology of the gods that she herself had hoped to foist on her son—the ideology of idealism which evades and suppresses the truth. Because Shen Te does not succumb to the fraudulent idealism of the gods she, unlike them, is not a comic but a tragic figure. In her final despairing gesture she represents humanity in its tragic greatness: impotent, helplessly caught in the web of circumstances, in the perennial frustration of human aspirations, but honestly facing the truth instead of hiding behind make-believe, and therefore great.
   —Walter H. Sokel, "Brecht's Split Characters and the Sense of the Tragic"

Der gute Mensch von Sezuan (The Good Person of Setzuan, also often titled *The Good Woman of Setzuan)* is Bertolt Brecht's master parable and an encapsulation of the epic theater concepts he pioneered. Imitating the methods of highly stylized Japanese and Chinese drama, Brecht moves from history in *Mother Courage* and biography in *Galileo* to fable, staging a central moral drama about how good can survive in a corrupt world. As critic John Fuegi has stated, "The profound metaphysical question of why evil is permitted, indeed encouraged, in the world has seldom been asked with such force." Written during the war years when the conflict between the forces of good and evil was far from metaphysical and its outcome far from certain, *The Good Person of Setzuan* is Brecht's summary statement about human psychology, the human condition, and the dramatic form he required for their enactment.

In 1933 when Adolf Hitler came to power, Brecht, marked for liquidation for his unpatriotic writings and anti-Nazi statements, departed Germany for what would become 15 years of exile, "Changing more countries than shoes," as the playwright ruefully observed. His first stop with his wife and children was Austria, then Czechoslovakia, Switzerland, France, Denmark, Sweden, Finland, and, finally, via the Trans-Siberian Railroad across the Soviet Union to the United States in 1941, where he remained for the duration. Despite the dislocations, the continual threat of the war catching up to him, and enormous family and financial pressures, Brecht managed to complete his greatest work during these exile years. Ironically Brecht's years out of Germany, freed from political and theatrical responsibilities that had formerly absorbed him, gave him both the time to devote himself exclusively to his writing and the distance that widened his perspective. As critic Martin Esslin summarizes,

> From 1937 onwards Brecht had thrown off the shackles of political pro-paganda and had begun to write a series of plays which showed his talent not only undiminished, but considerably matured and purged of the more puerile antics of his *enfant terrible* period: *The Life of Galileo* (1937–38); *The Trial of Lucullus* (1938); *The Good Soul of Setzuan* (1938–40); *Mother Courage* (1938–9). It is significant that all these plays were produced at a time when the situation had grown so bad that political pamphleteering had become quite clearly futile, when war was imminent, and when the alliance between the Nazis and Stalin had damped the spirit of even the most ardent German Communists.

Characteristically Brecht responded to the historical moment with the distanc-ing he felt was needed for understanding and action. In *Mother Courage* Brecht frames his meditation on war by the more distant events and characters of the Thirty Years' War; in *Galileo* he treats the conflict between conscience and authority using scenes from the Renaissance scientist's life and times. In both cases contemporary issues are universalized by finding current relevance in the past. After completing *Galileo* Brecht resumed work on a play first conceived in the late 1920s under the name "Die Ware Liebe" (love as merchandise), noting in his diary, "it gives me the chance to develop the epic technique and, finally to reach my standard again. No concessions are needed for the desk drawer." Finding too many compromises in the restriction of a particular his-torical era or biographical subject, Brecht sought a different approach. What would become *The Good Person of Setzuan* took shape as Brecht freed himself of the limitations imposed by a particular time, place, or biography. His first conception was a story of a prostitute who disguises herself as a man. Taking place in Germany, it was to be a strictly economic study of the relationship of prostitution to the capitalist system. The play would be transformed, however, by Brecht's incorporation of elements of the Japanese and Chinese drama.

For Brecht the conventions of Asian drama embodied the anti-illusionist, antinaturalistic epic theater principles he was striving to create. Stage real-ism, according to the playwright, was over-individualized, too focused on the particular and the absorbing special case to reach the universal principles that, when altered, would make change possible. Brecht believed that the audience in the illusionist theater is lulled into identification rather than provoked into criticism. His conception of the epic theater sought to change the fundamental relationship between the audience and what happened onstage. By deliberately avoiding contemporary subjects and lifelike presentation, Brecht sought to "make strange" stage action, employing distancing effects that called attention to the theatricality of the stage experience to encourage an audience's critical attitude. In the conventions of the Japanese and Chinese theater Brecht discovers exactly the techniques to serve this purpose. In Asian drama scenery is usually minimal or suggested by a stylized picture or prop. There is little attempt to create a realistic locale, situation, or psychology. Distancing between stage action and reality is further established by the use of masks, musicians present onstage, and, in the case of the Japanese puppet theater, with the puppeteer clearly visible. Formally Japanese and Chinese drama resemble the Western epic tradition in which narrative passages combine with dialogue, and the plays range widely in time and space with the supernatural mixing with domestic and historical scenes. Recitation and recapitulation are common. Songs and verse passages interrupt and comment on stage action. All of these elements find their way into *The Good Person of Setzuan.*

Resembling a fable or parable, the play has a generalized Chinese setting that is both ancient and modern, in which gods and airmen coexist. In a preface Brecht asserted that the province of Setzuan stood for any place where people exploit one another. The setting is, in Brecht's phrase, a "half Europeanized" China, both familiar and strange. The play opens with a prologue in which Wang, an impoverished water seller, encounters three gods who have come to Earth on a quest. If they can find at least one truly good human being, then the world as it is will be allowed to continue. Confirming the futility of the gods' mission, no one except the poor prostitute Shen Te is willing to put them up for the night. The gods, relieved to claim success for their mission, declare Shen Te the good person they have been seeking, to which she counters:

> I'm not at all sure that I'm good. I'd like to be good of course, but how am I to pay my rent? Well, I'll confess it to you: I sell myself in order to live, and even so I can't get along. . . . It would be pleasant to attach myself to one man and be faithful to him. I too should like not to exploit anyone, not to rob the helpless. But how? How? Even when I break only a *few* of the commandments, I can hardly survive.

More anxious to end their tiring quest than to deal with Shen Te's dilemma, the gods merely exhort her only to continue to be good without supplying any answers about how this is to be done. However, the payment they leave for their lodging is great enough for Shen Te to buy a small tobacco shop. Determined to use her unexpected prosperity to secure her future and do good for her neighbors, she is nevertheless immediately beset by opportunists taking advantage of her good nature. The former shop owner begs for rice and money, and an elderly couple who took Shen Te in but evicted her when she could not pay them beg for shelter for themselves and six relatives. Worried that her charity will bankrupt her, Shen Te is told by the elderly couple that she is far too nice and that she should put people off by claiming that a relative actually owns the store. This idea materializes as Shen Te disguises herself as her ruthless male "cousin," Shui Ta, to drive the hard bargains that her good nature resists. Shui Ta orders the family of eight out of the shop, and when they ignore his order he has them arrested. Having previously, in both *Mother Courage* and *Galileo*, dealt with individuals divided between the personal and political, by economic and historical necessity, Brecht here embodies the split personality in Shen Te and her alter ego. In Brecht's fable good and evil are shown as mutually dependent, with evil necessary for survival in a world of parasites and gulls. The metaphysical and ethical dilemma posed by the play is commented on in short scenes in which the gods receive updates on Shen Te's progress from Wang and in the various songs performed by several of the characters. An example is Shen Te's "Song of the Defenselessness of the Gods and Good Men," in which she laments:

> Good men
> Cannot long remain good in our country.
> Where the plates are empty, the dinner guests fight.
> Alas, the commandments of the gods
> Are no use against want.
> Oh, why don't the gods do the buying and selling
> Injustice forbidding, starvation dwelling?
> Oh, why don't the gods do the buying and selling?

Both the interludes with the gods and the songs serve to conceptualize the action and establish a critical context for the issues raised.

With Shui Ta's shrewdness and willingness to exploit rather than help those around him, the shop thrives. Shen Te, in a park one evening, encounters an unemployed pilot, Yang Sun, whose inability to find work has pushed him to the brink of suicide. The soft-hearted Shen Te immediately comes to his aid and falls in love with this man in distress. They become lovers and plan to marry, but after Shen Te lends him money to secure a job, Yang Sun makes clear to Shui Ta that he has no intention of marrying Shen Te and is only interested in what he can gain from her. Finding herself pregnant, Shen Te is forced to remain Shui Ta longer and longer, determined to provide for her child. Inevitably Shen Te's long absence arouses rumors and suspicion, and Shui Ta is eventually arrested and put on trial for her murder. In the play's concluding courtroom scene, the three gods appear as judges whose interrogation of Shui Tai eventually leads to the truth. Shen Te confesses:

Your former injunction to be good and yet to live
Tore me like lightning in halves.
I don't know how it happened.
To be good to others and to myself—
I couldn't do both at the same time.
To help others and to help myself was too hard. . . .
Condemn me: everything I did I did to help my neighbor,
To love my lover, and to save my little son from want.
For your great plans, O Gods, I was too poor and small.

To her question of how she can go on being a good person given what she faces, the gods offer only platitudes, underscoring their ineffectuality and indifference to the practicality of the morality they espouse. "You can do it," one of the gods insists. "Just be good and everything will turn out well!" To Shen Te's plea, "But I need my cousin!" the gods rule that she may rely on him "Not too often"—only once a month. The gods depart singing the praises of "The good, good person of Setzuan," as Shen Te cries for help.

With the dilemma Shen Te faces unresolved, the play closes with an epilogue in which one of the actors addresses the audience directly:

Ladies and gentlemen, don't be angry! Please!
We know the play is still in need of mending.
A golden legend floated on the breeze,
The breeze dropped, and we got a bitter ending.
Being dependent on your approbation
We wished, alas! Our work might be commended.
We're disappointed too. With consternation
We see the curtain closed, the plot unended.
In your opinion, then, what's to be done?

Inviting the audience to supply the resolution that the gods and the open-ended play have failed to answer, the actor concludes with some suggestions:

Change human nature or—the world? Well: which?
Believe in bigger, better gods or—none?
How can we mortals be both good and rich?
The right way out of the calamity
You must find for yourselves. Ponder, my friends,
How man with man may live in amity
And good men—women also—reach good ends.
There must, there must, be *some* end that would fit.
Ladies and gentlemen, help us look for it!

Completed in 1941, *The Good Person of Setzuan* debuted in Zurich, Switzerland, in 1943. Brecht again employed the Chinese-inspired theatrical model for his last major play, *The Caucasian Chalk Circle* (1948), set in Soviet Georgia in the aftermath of World War II. It, like *The Good Person of Setzuan*, poses a central moral question: How is justice possible? Both plays push Brecht's stage innovations to their logical conclusions, turning the theater into an arena where the largest human questions can be debated.

SHE STOOPS TO CONQUER

59

(1773)

by Oliver Goldsmith

Convention and conviction and an unquestioned standard of values seem to support the large, airy world of his invention. Nothing could be more amusing than She Stoops to Conquer—*one might even go so far as to say that amusement of so pure a quality will never come our way again. . . . To mistake a private house for an inn is not a disaster that reveals the hidden depths or the highest dignity of human nature. But these are questions that fade out in the enjoyment of reading—an enjoyment which is much more composite than the simple word amusement can cover. When a thing is perfect of its kind we cannot stop, under that spell, to pick our flowers to pieces. There is a unity about it which forbids us to dismember it.*

—Virginia Woolf, "Oliver Goldsmith," *Collected Essays*

In the prologue to Oliver Goldsmith's *She Stoops to Conquer*, written by the illustrious 18th-century English actor-manager David Garrick, a mourner takes the stage to announce: "The Comic Muse, long sick, is now a-dying!" After "the sweet maid is laid upon the bier," only "a mawkish drab of spurious breed, / Who deals in sentimentals, will succeed!" The mourner laments that the current fashion for sentimental, or crying, comedy has forsaken laughter. Yet hope remains:

> A Doctor comes this night to show his skill.
> To cheer her heart, and give your muscles motion,
> He, in Five Draughts prepar'd, presents a potion:
> A kind of magic charm—for be assur'd,
> If you will swallow it, the maid is cur'd:
> But desperate the Doctor, and her case is,
> If you reject the dose, and make wry faces!
> This truth he boasts, will boast it while he lives,
> No poisonous drugs are mixed in what he gives.
> Should he succeed, you'll give him his degree;

If not, within he will receive no fee!
The College YOU, must his pretensions back,
Pronounce him Regular, or dub him Quack.

"Doctor" Goldsmith has arrived to prescribe a comic curative in the play that follows: *She Stoops to Conquer*. It is Goldsmith's remarkable bid to restore and revitalize the health of English comedy by reintroducing audiences to laughter. The prudish moralism that led Jeremy Collier to attack the plays of William Congreve and his fellow Restoration dramatists as too debauched and overly concerned with vice rather than virtue in 1698 had developed by the mid-18th century into a cult of sentimentalism and genteel propriety that had banished lower-class characters, coarse language, and broad comedy from the stage as vulgar and indecorous. As Goldsmith observed in his dedication of the play to his friend and patron Samuel Johnson, "Undertaking a comedy not merely sentimental was very dangerous." Goldsmith risked financial ruin and critical humiliation in going against the fashionable sentimental vogue by attempting to revive the comic methods of Shakespeare and the Restoration playwrights and reintroducing exuberant comedy and belly laughs to audiences primed for pathos and tears. The manager of London's Covent Garden Theatre was dubious about the propriety of *She Stoops to Conquer*, and three members of the acting company withdrew their services in protest over the unrefined parts they were being asked to play. On opening night Goldsmith's distinguished friends, including Dr. Johnson, Sir Joshua Reynolds, and Edmund Burke, were on hand to encourage the audience's applause, but they were not needed. *She Stoops to Conquer* was an immediate and resounding popular success. It has gone on to be performed regularly ever since, one of the triumphs of the 18th-century stage that continues to elicit the delight Dr. Johnson first experienced when he declared that it "answered so much the great end of comedy—making an audience merry."

In an all too brief but remarkable literary career of 15 years, Goldsmith excelled in every established literary genre of the day—essays, letters, biography, poems, the novel, and drama—justifying Johnson's eulogy that there was no form of literature that Goldsmith had not put his hand to, and whatever he had attempted, he had made elegant. Goldsmith produced two of the best-known and most admired long poems of the 18th century, *The Traveller* and *The Deserted Village*; one of the most beloved 18th-century novels in *The Vicar of Wakefield*; and in *She Stoops to Conquer* one of drama's most enduring comedies. The writer's route to a literary career is marked by both accident and necessity. The year and exact place of Goldsmith's birth are uncertain, probably in 1728 or 1730 in County Longford, Ireland. He grew up in Lissoy, Westmeath, where his father was an impoverished Anglican clergyman. Goldsmith would later base his put-upon but good-natured cleric Dr. Primrose, in *The Vicar of Wakefield*, on his father, and Lissoy served as the model for the idyllic "sweet Auburn" of *The Deserted Village*. Smallpox at age eight or nine left ugly pockmarks, which, along with a protrusive brow, receding chin, and stocky figure, gave Goldsmith a lasting conviction of his own ugliness and a corresponding social awkwardness. As a student Goldsmith purportedly had the experience that would supply the central plot of *She Stoops to Conquer*. Traveling home from his boarding school Goldsmith mistook a local squire's house for an inn and spent the night there before realizing his mistake. Goldsmith entered Trinity College, Dublin, as a menial sizar, or "poor scholar," waiting on his better-off fellow students at table and sweeping floors. He earned his degree in 1750, and, after working briefly as a private tutor, he missed his boat to immigrate to America and gambled away the money to allow him to study law in London. Goldsmith instead went to Edinburgh to study medicine. In 1754 he traveled through Holland, France, Switzerland, and Italy, in great poverty, paying for his board and lodging by playing his flute and engaging in lively debates at local monasteries along his route. In 1756 Goldsmith arrived in London, alternating between teaching and practicing medicine, adopting the title "Doctor," despite never having earned his medical degree. He stumbled into a professional writing career by producing reviews, translations, and a series of popular social commentaries—the "Chinese Letters," published later in book form as *The Citizen of the World*—from the point of view of a Chinese man in London. The work brought Goldsmith to the attention of the capital's literary and artistic elite including Johnson, James Boswell, Burke, Reynolds, William Hogarth, and Garrick. Despite his notoriety chronically poor money management drove Goldsmith to hack writing for survival, and the drudgery of continual efforts to raise money with his pen would eventually result in failing health and his death in 1774 at the age of 44. Johnson rescued his insolvent and improvident friend from debtor's prison by arranging for the publication, in 1766, of the manuscript Goldsmith was working on—*The Vicar of Wakefield*—to satisfy the claims of Goldsmith's landlady. Although it would become one of the enduring classics of English fiction, the novel was initially only a modest success.

Goldsmith turned next to the theater to make his fortune, and his first stage success, and financial prosperity, came in 1768 with his comedy *The Good Natur'd Man*. In part a burlesque on the conventions of sentimental comedy, the play challenged genteel stage conventions by introducing a scene involving a decidedly low-class Cockney bailiff and his Irish assistant. It provoked hisses from the gallery and loud cries of "Low" and "Damned Vulgar," and Goldsmith was forced to cut their parts during the play's run. Restored in the play's published version, their low comedy was justified in Goldsmith's preface as part of an earlier distinguished comic tradition "when the term *genteel comedy* was . . . unknown among us," allowing the pursuit of true humor in "the recesses of the mean." Before his second comedy, *She Stoops to Conquer*, premiered in 1773, Goldsmith helped prepare the ground for its reception by anonymously publishing "An Essay on the Theatre; or, A Comparison between Laughing and Sentimental Comedy," which argued that the aim of comedy was to provoke laughter by "ridiculously exhibiting the Follies of the Lower Part of Mankind." "Weeping Sentiment Comedy," he argued was inferior to "Laughing and even Low Comedy" because it is both less amusing and less instructive, since it causes the audience to sympathize with the possessors of faults. "In these Plays almost all the Characters are good," he asserts, "and exceedingly generous . . . and though they want Humour, have abundance of Sentiment and Feeling. If they happen to have Faults or Foibles, the Spectator is taught not only to pardon, but to applaud them, in consideration of the goodness of their heart; so that Folly, instead of being ridiculed, is commended." Goldsmith instead advocates on behalf of the wisdom and benefit of laughing comedy, contending that the dramatist in search of humor and truth must be willing to explore all levels of society, must be willing to stoop to the "low" by presenting humorous characters from the inferior levels of society, setting scenes in such unfashionable locations as taverns, and realistically incorporating into the comic action the rowdy and indecorous activities associated with such locations.

She Stoops to Conquer served as the application and proof of Goldsmith's comic theory, a demonstration that the traditional comic resources could still delight and instruct. The play is a marvel of comic methods, of mistaken identities and miscommunication, illustrating the clash between town and country values, shallow sentiment and genuine human feelings, self- and social deception and the need to see clearly. Two young suitors from London journey to the Hardcastles' country home. Marlow is the son of Mr. Hardcastle's old friend and the intended match for Hardcastle's daughter Kate. He is "one of the most bashful and reserved young fellows in the world." Paralyzed by the over-elaborate demands of fashionable sentiment, he is hopelessly shy with young ladies but is at his ease with wenches. Marlow is joined by his friend Hastings, who is anxious to court Constance Neville, the Hardcastles' ward. Losing their way they seek directions at an ale-house from Mrs. Hardcastle's son by her first marriage, the irrepressibly mischievous but good-natured boor Tony Lumpkin. He has been called both "one of the most objectionable brats in dramatic literature" (Brooks Atkinson) and "a booby who lays booby traps for others" who makes the play "not farce, but comedy of continuous incident" (Oscar James Campbell). Lumpkin stands below only Sir John Falstaff as comic drama's most entertaining character. Serving as the play's Lord of Misrule, he directs Marlow and Hastings to his stepfather's house but, for a cod, describes it as an inn run by an eccentric who fancies himself a gentleman. Arriving at their destination the pair encounters Mr. Hardcastle, their host, whom they treat imperiously and condescendingly with scant courtesy as an innkeeper. This initial deception leads to a breathless and entertaining series of misunderstandings and contretemps as the order and proprieties of the

Hardcastle's residence suffer the disruption of Tony Lumpkin's playful inversion of home to public house. The centerpiece in the comedy is the wooing of Marlow and Kate Hardcastle, a heroine whose ingenuity, resourcefulness, and wit recalls Viola in *Twelfth Night* and Rosalind in *As You Like It*. As the fashionable daughter of a country squire, Kate must endure the halting and frigid sentiment of the bashful, tongue-tied, and eye-averting Marlow, causing her to declare in exasperation, "Was there ever such a sober, sentimental interview?" But dressed in simple country attire to gratify her father's rustic values, Kate is misperceived by Marlow as the inn's barmaid and is subjected to a far more spirited wooing that reveals Marlow's attraction as a suitor. Realizing Marlow's deception, his mistaking her home for an inn and its residents as menials, Kate, formerly the pursued, now becomes the pursuer, deciding to stoop to a lower station to draw Marlow out by assuming first the role of the barmaid, then that of a poor relation of the Hardcastles. The multiple roles of the main lovers—young lady of fashion and serving girl; sentimentalist and flirt—provide the central amusing tangle. The other is the blocked effort of Constance and Hastings to elope with her jewels that Mrs. Hardcastle is determined to retain. Again, Tony Lumpkin plays the central role, like Puck in *A Midsummer Night's Dream*, in confounding the schemers by taking the jewels from his mother and setting them on their comic way in and out of the possession of multiple characters.

Resolution of the main plot and subplot comes with the arrival of Hardcastle's friend, Sir Charles Marlow, and a reassertion of order and propriety. The confusion over Marlow's misperception of Hardcastle as innkeeper is revealed to the master of the house, and Kate, to convince her father and Sir Marlow that the chronically bashful Marlow earnestly loves her, stages an overheard lovers' interview in which Marlow professes his passion for Kate the serving-girl, offering his hand if only the differences in their social classes could be overcome. Kate's true identity solves the dilemma, and Marlow is consequently cured of his sentimental affliction that has restricted authentic passion to subservient women and sententiousness and genteel artificiality to a "modest woman" of his own class. The fate of the second courtship between Hastings and Constance is finally resolved after Tony Lumpkin delivers his mother and Constance, after a hair-raising wild goose chase, not to Aunt Pedigree's house where Constance is to be taken to keep her from eloping but back to the Hardcastles' home. Mrs. Hardcastle's scheme to have her son marry Constance to keep her fortune in the family is foiled when it is revealed that Tony has been of age all along and free to refuse Constance, whom he does not love, enabling her to marry Hastings. The play ends with both couples—Marlow and Kate and Hastings and Constance—ready to wed in classic Shakespearean romantic comic fashion, and the audience is delightfully instructed through this comedy of errors resulting from human foibles and failings to applaud and approve the genuine over the artificial, real feeling over sentimentality, truth over deception.

It is rarely critically profitable to analyze jokes, or, as Virginia Woolf puts it, "to pick our flowers to pieces." *She Stoops to Conquer* is one of the stage's most enjoyable jokes and most satisfying boquets. Beyond the sheer delightful entertainment of the play, however, are some lessons of importance. *She Stoops to Conquer* matters in its signaling a new kind of comedy in which ingenious stage complications involve and are motivated by believable human characters, in which the often cynical comedy of the Restoration dramatists is softened by an affirming humanity. Goldsmith opposed not feeling but its posturing in a sentimental drama that restricted so much of life and human nature from the stage. *She Stoops to Conquer* shows Goldsmith redirecting comedy back to the source of its power in play since Aristophanes: the creation of interesting, believable characters tested by situations that point out the inconsistency of human nature and society in the gaps between appearance and reality, surface and substance, truth and illusion.

MURDER IN THE CATHEDRAL

(1935)

by T. S. Eliot

60

> Murder in the Cathedral *is a play which, as Eliot explains in "Poetry and Drama," is designed "to bring poetry into the world in which the audience lives and to which it returns when it leaves the theater." But the drama is much more than a formal exercise in poetic language; it is designed to bring the saint's play of the past into the present and to make it relevant to the full range of human experience in our time.*
>
> —Clifford Davidson, "*Murder in the Cathedral* and the Saint's Play Tradition"

T. S. Eliot dominated literature in the period between the world wars of the 20th century, spearheading a revolution in literary taste in poetry, criticism, and drama. "It is very likely that when the literary history of our times come to be written," critic Thomas Lask has observed, "it will be characterized as the Age of Eliot, just as we now speak of the Age of Pope or Tennyson." The publication of *Prufrock and Other Observations* in 1917 has been compared to the appearance in 1798 of William Wordsworth and Samuel Taylor Coleridge's *Lyrical Ballads.* Both publications signaled the arrival of a new conception of poetry and the commencement of a new poetic era. In *The Waste Land,* Eliot produced what fellow poet William Carlos Williams called "the atomic bomb of poetry," the modern epic that epitomized the spirit of the age and the characteristic methods and concerns of literary modernism. Eliot's poetry defined modern disillusion and the search for moral and spiritual values to challenge the void and cultural barrenness left after the Great War. Beginning largely as a social critic and satirist, Eliot would move from doubt to faith while attempting to embody his own pilgrim's progress in a revitalized poetic drama. His first complete dramatic work, and his best, *Murder in the Cathedral* is a morality play for modern times. "Of the greatness of *Murder in the Cathedral,*" David E. Jones, author of *The Plays of T. S. Eliot,* has asserted, "there can be no doubt—it may be the greatest religious drama ever written." The critic John Gross has argued that "It is Eliot's one indubitable theatrical triumph and the one English addition to the classic repertoire since Shaw."

Thomas Stearns Eliot, who would eventually define himself as a "classicist in literature, royalist in politics, and anglo-catholic in religion," began his journey toward orthodoxy in St. Louis, Missouri, where he was born in 1888. His grandfather had come west from Harvard Divinity School to found St. Louis's first Unitarian church and Washington University. Eliot's father was a prosperous brick manufacturer, and his mother was a woman of literary tastes. The Eliot family spent summers on the Massachusetts coast, and Eliot returned to the East for college, graduating from Harvard in only three years. He stayed on as a graduate student in philosophy before going to Oxford to complete his dissertation on the philosopher F. H. Bradley. Eliot completed his thesis but never received his degree, rejecting an expected academic career for life in England as a writer. In 1915 Eliot married Vivien Haigh-Wood, a woman prone to mental illness, and their 17-year marriage was a test of Eliot's emotional and physical stamina. He supported himself by teaching in an English grammar school, lecturing, writing reviews and criticism, and holding a position in Lloyd's Bank for eight years. Fastidious and reserved, Eliot suffered a mental breakdown in 1921 and was treated in Lausanne, Switzerland. In 1922 he published his landmark poem, *The Waste Land*, which baffled critics but created a sensation, particularly among the young, who regarded Eliot as the poetic voice of the modern age.

The state of English poetry that Eliot had inherited and would help to transform was largely exhausted and moribund. The innovation of personal exploration introduced by the Romantics had atrophied into the stately cadences and moralizing pronouncements of the Victorians, supporting a set of traditions invalidated by the experience of the Great War. At the core of Eliot's poetics was the search to invest in language a new means to capture and affirm the modern experience. "Our civilization comprehends great variety and complexity," Eliot observed, "and this variety and complexity, playing upon a refined sensibility, must produce various and complex results. The poet must become more and more comprehensive, more allusive, more indirect, in order to force, to dislocate if necessary, language into meaning." Eliot therefore pursued a strategy of dislocation, using the concrete image as his basic component, or what he called the "objective correlative," a physical detail to evoke thought and feeling. Eliot's first major poem, "The Love Song of J. Alfred Prufrock," written in 1910 but not published until 1915, set his poetic method and characteristic concerns. Confronting the modern scene in all its vulgarity and sordidness while plumbing the depths of private emotion and feeling, Eliot creates a dramatic monologue in which Prufrock reveals his consciousness in a series of startling images of a disconnected mind trapped by its own inadequacies. Eliot's technique is presentative and cinematic, surveying the landscape of Prufrock's neuroses, not through analysis, but through images exposing his deepest fears. *The Waste Land* both widens and deepens this approach. Again the poem's core is dramatic, creating a symphony of voices, scenes, and images adhering around the central question of what can be believed in the absence of the possibility of belief. Lacking the expositions and transitions of a linear narrative, the poem is a series of intense moments of great pressure in which it is the reader's responsibility to reassemble the "heap of broken images" and the "fragments shored against my ruins" into coherence.

In 1925 Eliot left Lloyd's to become an editor at the publishing house Faber and Faber, a position he would hold for the rest of his life. He also became a British citizen and, to the shock of many, converted to Anglicanism in 1927. His subsequent creative efforts increasingly turned from poetry to drama. *Murder in the Cathedral* (1935), *The Family Reunion* (1939), *The Cocktail Party* (1950), *The Confidential Clerk* (1955), and *The Elder Statesman* (1959) show him attempting to revitalize poetic drama infused with the search for spiritual meaning expressed in his poetry. Eliot had long been an advocate of the power and popular appeal of the Elizabethans, whose verse dramas were the best means, in Eliot's view, for treating the spiritual in human experience. Onstage, inner and abstract feelings and ideas could be objectified, with poetry rather than prose serving as the appropriate medium of expression. "The human soul," Eliot observed, "in intense emotion, strives to express itself in verse. . . . The tendency . . . of prose drama is to emphasize the ephemeral and superficial; if we want to get at the permanent and universal we tend to express ourselves in verse."

Eliot's first experiment in writing for the stage was *Sweeney Agonistes: Fragments of an Aristophanic Melodrama*, written in 1926 and first performed in America in 1933 and in England the following year. In it Eliot dramatizes the spiritual dryness of contemporary life with a verse form enlivened by speech and jazz rhythms and song and dance elements derived from the music hall. Eliot would next accept a commission from E. Martin Browne, director of religious drama for the London diocese of the Anglican Church, to collaborate on a religious pageant play to raise money for church construction. The result was *The Rock*, performed in London in 1934. In scenes representing the challenges faced by a succession of church builders through history, Eliot experimented with various choral elements, updating the traditional Greek chorus and liturgical devices of medieval religious drama. Subsequently Eliot was asked to write a play for the Canterbury Festival of 1935. Eliot chose as his subject the martyrdom of Thomas Becket, archbishop of Canterbury, whose quarrel with his former friend King Henry II led to his murder in 1170 as he prayed in Canterbury Cathedral. Becket would be canonized three years later with his tomb in the cathedral becoming a major pilgrim's destination, most famously celebrated in Chaucer's *Canterbury Tales*. Eliot's play, initially called "The Archbishop Murder Case" and "Fear in the Way" before becoming *Murder in the Cathedral*, was performed in the Chapter House of Canterbury, a few yards from where Becket had been killed, before beginning a year-long London run and becoming the first successful religious play of the 20th century.

Murder in the Cathedral opens with a Chorus of the women of Canterbury, who express their apprehension over the upheaval that they fear will result from the archbishop's return from an exile of seven years: "Some presage of an act / Which our eyes are compelled to witness, has forced our feet / Towards the cathedral." Three priests enter to discuss the dispute that led to Becket's exile and its implications, introducing the play's central conflict between worldly and spiritual power. Their discourse is interrupted by a herald announcing Becket's imminent arrival. The priests are divided in their reactions as the Chorus repeats its foreboding at the coming conflict. After the women are told by one of the priests to cease "croaking like frogs" and disperse, Becket arrives to chide the priest for scolding the women, while sounding the key themes of the play:

> They know and do not know, that acting is suffering
> And suffering is action. Neither does the actor suffer
> Nor the patient act. But both are fixed
> To an eternal action, an eternal patience
> To which all must consent that it may be willed
> And which all must suffer that they may will it,
> That the pattern may subsist, for the pattern is the action
> And the suffering, that the wheel may turn and still
> Be forever still.

The relationship between suffering and action, between individual will and divine plan, will be central concerns in the play's exploration of the reasons behind Becket's return and the retaliation he provokes by his actions. Although a historical drama, Eliot replaces expected reliance on historical, political, and social details with a focus on the inner struggle of Becket as he contends with the conflict between the secular power of the king and the spiritual force of conscience. Underscoring his inner dilemma, Becket is visited by four tempters representing alternatives to his duty to the church that his conscience is struggling to resolve. The first urges Becket to return to the worldly pleasure and success he had before becoming archbishop and quarreling with the king. The second offers him enhanced political power in the restoration of Becket's former position as chancellor. The third urges him to "fight for liberty" and overthrow the king and wield temporal power himself. All three tempters are easily resisted by Becket, who asks, "Shall I, who keep the keys / Of heaven and hell, supreme alone in England, / Who bind and loose, with power from the Pope, / Descend to desire a punier power?" Becket refutes all of their enticements with assertions of his faith in God's will. The fourth tempter, however, proves more formidable. Advising Becket to "think of glory after death," he argues that by persisting in his present course Becket would become a martyr and saint, gaining his eternal reward in heaven and immortality on earth:

> When king is dead, there's another king.
> And one more king in another reign.
> King is forgotten, when another shall come:
> Saint and Martyr rule from the tomb.
> Think, Thomas, think of enemies dismayed,
> Creeping in penance, frightened by a shade,
> Think of pilgrims, standing in line
> Before the glittering jewelled shrine,
> From generation to generation
> Bending the knee in supplication.

"Who are you, tempting me with my own desires?" Becket responds indicating that the fourth tempter's argument is the most seductive. Wrestling with his conscience, Becket ultimately determines that courting one's fame through martyrdom is an act of "sinful pride." He manages to refute the fourth tempter's argument with one of the most memorable lines of the play: "The last temptation and the greatest treason / Is to do the right deed for the wrong reason." Martyrdom, Becket concludes, if it comes, must be God's will and not his:

> I shall no longer act or suffer, to the sword's end.
> Now my good Angel, whom God appoints
> To be my guardian, hover over the swords' points.

A prose interlude follows as Becket preaches his Christmas sermon on the Christian message of peace, arguing that Christ's peace is "not as the world gives," that is the lack of political strife, but spiritual solace. Four knights (usually played by the actors who appeared as the four tempters) next arrive, charging Becket with being "in revolt against the King" since he "sowed strife abroad." Ordered to absolve those bishops that he had previously excommunicated, Becket refuses, explaining that "It is not Becket who pronounces doom, / But the Law of Christ's Church." Priests guard the archbishop inside the cathedral, but Becket insists "I will not have the Church of Christ, / This sanctuary, turned into a fortress" and commands that the knights be allowed entrance. The door is unbarred, and the knights enter. After refusing to recant any of his former actions, Becket prays: "Now to Almighty God. . . . I commend my cause and that of the Church." The knights fall upon him and kill him as the Chorus laments the curse that has descended on their land and their lives.

The four Knights now directly address the audience. "We know that you may be disposed to judge unfavorably of our action," one explains. "Nevertheless, I appeal to your sense of honor. You are Englishmen, and therefore will not judge anybody without hearing both sides of the case." The other three then take turns justifying their actions, stressing that they acted in a "perfectly disinterested" manner, not to benefit from the murder. They insist that Becket was far from the moral paragon he appeared to be in the play. Having been appointed by the king, Becket betrayed his former friend to become the king's rival for power and source of the kingdom's strife. "No one regrets the necessity for violence more than we do," one of the knights contends. "Unhappily, there are times when violence is the only way in which social justice can be secured." To the question "Who killed the Archbishop?" the only logical response, a knight reasons, given Becket's egomania and his deliberate pursuit of martyrdom, would be to "render a verdict of Suicide while of Unsound Mind." From the ridiculousness of the knights' self-serving equivocation the play shifts to the sublime as the Chorus proclaims to God that "the blood of Thy martyrs and saints / Shall enrich the earth, shall create the holy places." Seeking God's forgiveness for doubting his "blessing," they seek the intercession of a new protector: "Blessed Thomas, pray for us."

Given the serious issues it raises regarding faith and belief *Murder in the Cathedral* is an impressive and moving theatrical experience that lifts a 12th-century bloody dispute to universal relevance. If all are unable to follow Eliot to orthodoxy, Becket's testing of belief and principle still retains its urgency. As a modern dramatist Eliot establishes what subsequent playwrights would be quick to learn from him: that past dramatic forms can still serve current needs. As critic Francis Ferguson has argued, "Any study of drama must discover a more particular debt to Eliot: he has been over this ground before; he is one of the very few contemporary writers in English who are directly concerned with drama as a serious art."

THE BALD SOPRANO

61

(1950)
by Eugène Ionesco

In The Bald Soprano, *which is a completely unserious play where I was concerned with solving purely theatrical problems, some people have seen a satire on bourgeois society, a criticism of life in England, and heaven knows what. In actual fact, if it is criticism of anything, it must be of all societies, of language, of clichés—a parody of human behavior, and therefore a parody of the theatre too. I am thinking both of the commercial theatre and the theatre of Brecht. In fact, I believe that it is precisely when we see the last of economic problems and class warfare (if I may avail myself of one of the most crashing clichés of our age) that we shall also see that this solves nothing, indeed that our problems are only beginning. We can no longer avoid asking ourselves what we are doing here on earth, and how, having no deep sense of our destiny, we can endure the crushing weight of the material world.*

—Eugène Ionesco, "The World of Eugène Ionesco,"
New York Times, June 1, 1958

If French existentialist thought as articulated by Jean-Paul Sartre and Albert Camus dominated post–World War II philosophy and literary culture, the embodiment of these ideas and the creative expression of the senselessness of life in light of the war experience were represented principally in drama. The novel and poetry were the dominating genres expressing the spirit of the age in the 19th and early 20th centuries. In the wartime and postwar period drama would achieve a striking revival and cultural primacy. Both Sartre and Camus wrote plays to illustrate their concepts, while an emerging French drama, later identified as the theater of the absurd, staged the irrationality and purposelessness that the existentialist attempted to explain. The drama associated with Eugène Ionesco, Samuel Beckett, Arthur Adamov, Jean Genet, and others who pioneered postwar experimental theater responded to a purposeless universe stripped of the former consolations of religious faith and coherence. "Absurd" became the fundamental operating principle of the contemporary world. "Absurd is that which is devoid of purpose," Ionesco observed. "Cut off from his religious, metaphysical, and transcendental roots, man is lost; all his actions become senseless, absurd, useless." Existentialism as presented in the works of Sartre and Camus derived from an attempt to deal with this sense of absurdity. Yet, as Martin Esslin points out in his groundbreaking critical study *The Theatre of the Absurd,*

> these writers differ from the dramatists of the Absurd in an important respect: they present their sense of the irrationality of the human condition in the form of highly lucid and logically constructed reasoning, while the Theatre of the Absurd strives to express its sense of the senselessness of the human condition and the inadequacy of the rational approach by the open abandonment of rational devices and discursive thought. While Sartre or Camus express the new content in the old convention, the Theatre of the Absurd goes a step further in trying to achieve a unity between its basic assumptions and the form in which these are expressed.

Ionesco's *La Cantatrice chauve* (*The Bald Soprano*) is one of the earliest and enduring examples of the theater of the absurd, a play that set the themes and methods for the experimental drama that would dominate the theater throughout the second half of the 20th century. The story of its origin and development is one of the great shaggy dog stories in literary history.

Its creator, Eugène Ionesco, was born in Slatina, Romania, in 1909. His father was a Romanian municipal official, and his mother was the daughter of a French civil engineer employed by a Romanian railroad company. The family moved to Paris when Ionesco was two years old. One of his earliest memories was of the Punch and Judy performances at the Luxembourg Gardens. "It was the spectacle of the world itself," Ionesco recalled, "which, unusual, improbable, but truer than truth, presented itself to me in an infinitely simplified and caricatured form, as if to underline its grotesque and brutal truth." When Germany declared war on Romania in 1916, Ionesco's father returned to Bucharest, severing contact with his family until Ionesco was 13. Having secretly divorced his wife and remarried, Ionesco's father gained legal custody of his son and daughter when his mother was unable to care for them, and Ionesco was uprooted from his French home and mother to live with his father in Romania. This traumatic displacement, in which Ionesco was forced to cope with a new language, an unfamiliar culture, and unfamiliar parental authority, anticipates the often grotesque and unsettling transformations that would appear in his plays. Although his father was determined that his son should become, in Ionesco's words, "a bourgeois, a magistrate, a soldier, a chemical engineer," the son immersed himself instead in literature and wrote poetry, influenced particularly by his discovery of the French surrealists and his fellow Romanian, Tristan Tzara, a founder of the dada movement. Leaving home at the age of 17 and supporting himself as a French tutor, Ionesco entered the University of Bucharest to study French literature in 1928. There he published poetry and criticism. From 1936 to 1938 he taught French in secondary schools while witnessing Romania's slide into fascism. With a grant to complete a thesis on "the themes of sin and death in French poetry after Baudelaire," Ionesco managed to return to Paris for the first time since 1922. However, the outbreak of the war forced Ionesco back to Romania where he continued to teach while fearing persecution for his antifascist views. He eventually managed to secure an exit visa to France in 1942, and Ionesco and his wife survived the war living in extreme poverty hiding outside Marseilles. At war's end Ionesco returned to Paris where he found work as a proofreader for a publisher of medical and legal books.

Ionesco's career as a playwright began accidentally and as absurdly as any of his future plays. His childhood fascination with the theater had eventually grown into dislike. "Having acquired a critical sense," he observed, "I became aware of the strings, the crude strings of the theater." Ionesco sensed the disjunction between "two planes of reality—the concrete, material, impoverished, empty, limited reality of these living, everyday human beings, moving about and talking on stage, and the reality of the imagination, the two face to face and not coinciding, unable to be brought into relation with each other; two antagonistic worlds incapable of being unified, of merging." Despite his hostility to the theater, his first play, which became *The Bald Soprano*, was born out of his experience teaching himself English. In 1948 Ionesco acquired a language primer that taught English through the rudimentary dialogue between an English married couple, the Smiths, and their younger friends the Martins. As Ionesco recalled:

> I set to work. Conscientiously I copied whole sentences from my primer with the purpose of memorizing them. Rereading them attentively, I learned not English but some astonishing truths—that, for example, there are seven days in the week, something I already knew; that the floor is down, the ceiling up, things I already knew as well, perhaps, but that I had never seriously thought about or had forgotten, and that seemed to me, suddenly, as stupefying as they were indisputably true. . . . To my astonishment, Mrs. Smith informed her husband that they had several children, that they lived in the vicinity of London, that their name was Smith, that Mr. Smith was a clerk, that they had a servant, Mary— English like themselves. . . . In the fifth lesson, the Smiths' friends the Martins arrive; the four of them begin to chat and, starting from basic axioms, they build more complex truths: "The country is quieter than the big city. . . ."

In simply transcribing their inane dialogue his play began to take shape, and then "a strange phenomenon took place. I don't know how—the text began imperceptibly to change before my eyes, and in spite of me. The very simple, luminously clear statements I had copied diligently into my . . . notebook, left to themselves, fermented after a while, lost their original identity, expanded and overflowed." The dialogue began to comment on itself, parodying both the speakers and language itself, while the series of pointless and absurd dialogues and situations exposed the stale and stilted theatrical conventions of the drawing room comedy. It became "a parody of human behavior, and therefore a parody of the theatre too." When he read his "antiplay" to a group of friends, they found it funny, which surprised Ionesco who thought he had written a serious work on "the tragedy of language." One of his friends, an actor, showed the manuscript to the avant-garde director Nicolas Bataille, who agreed to stage the play. First called "L'Anglais sans peine" and later "L'Heure anglaise," the play found its eventual title by accident during rehearsal. During a run-through the actor playing the part of the Fire Chief mistakenly substituted the words "*institutrice blonde*" (blond school teacher) with "*cantatrice chauve*" (bald soprano), and Ionesco declared the phrase to be the title. The play also went through several possible endings before its debut. In one, after the final quarrel between the two couples, extras from the audience were to start booing and protesting, prompting the theater manager and police to come onstage and "machine-gun" the audience. This ending was rejected because it required too many additional actors. Ionesco next planned to let the maid introduce the "author" at the height of the quarrel who would berate the audience. Considered "too polemical," this ending eventually gave way to no ending at all, simply starting the play over at its end, substituting the Martins for the Smiths.

The Bald Soprano opened at the Théâtre des Noctambules in Paris in 1950 to mainly empty seats and hostile criticism. Without funds for publicity the company, along with the playwright, donned sandwich boards to announce each performance, several of which attracted fewer than three customers. After six weeks the play closed. For Ionesco, however, the experience of bringing his ideas to life was transformative, committing him to a dramatic career. "To incarnate phantasms," Ionesco declared, "to give them life, is a prodigious, irreplaceable, adventure to such extent that I myself was overcome when, during rehearsals of my first play, I suddenly saw characters move on the stage who had come out of myself. I was frightened. By what right had I been able to do this? Was this allowed? . . . It was almost diabolical." *The Bald Soprano* was revived in 1952 by Bataille's company on a double bill with Ionesco's next play, *La Leçon* (*The Lesson*), to considerable acclaim. Again revived in 1957, at the Théâtre de la Huchette, the double bill has been continually performed there ever since, one of the longest runs in theater history.

Ionesco's assault on conventional behavior and expectation is sounded in the initial stage directions for *The Bald Soprano:*

> Scene: A middle-class English interior, with English armchairs. An English evening. Mr. Smith, an Englishman, seated in his English armchair

and wearing English slippers, is smoking his English pipe and reading
an English newspaper, near an English fire. He is wearing English spectacles and a small gray English moustache. Beside him, in another English
armchair, Mrs. Smith, an Englishwoman, is darning some English socks.
A long moment of English silence. The English clock strikes 17 English
strokes.

The inane conversation of this representative, respectable bourgeois couple
is undermined by contradictions and veers toward incoherence. The Smiths
are interrupted by Mary, the maid, who announces the arrival of their dinner
guests, Donald and Elizabeth Martin. After the Smiths exit to dress for dinner Mary leads in the Martins, who behave as if they have never met. Their
interrogation of each other leads to their startling revelation that since they
both live in the same room, sleep in the same bed, and both have a daughter
who seems to be the same child, they must be married. As they kiss, gratified
at having found each other again, Mary returns to announce to the audience
that the Martins' deductions are incorrect:

> It is in vain that he thinks he is Donald, it is in vain that she thinks she is
> Elizabeth. He believed in vain that she is Elizabeth. She believes in vain
> that he is Donald—they are sadly deceived. But who is the true Donald?
> Who is the true Elizabeth? Who has any interest in prolonging this con-
> fusion? I don't know. Let's not try to know. Let's leave things as they are.
> [*She takes several steps toward the door, then returns and says to the audience*]
> My real name is Sherlock Holmes.

The Smiths, dressed exactly the same as in the first scene, return, and the
couples fill an awkward silence by describing shocking incidents—a man on
the street who bent down to tie his shoe lace; a man on the Metro reading a
newspaper—as the doorbell repeatedly rings, but no one is at the door. Mrs.
Smith concludes, "Experience teaches us that when one hears the doorbell ring
it is because there is never anyone there." But her deduction is contradicted
when the doorbell rings a fourth time, and the Fire Chief is discovered on the
doorstep. An old family friend, the Fire Chief eventually admits that he had
previously rung the doorbell and hidden as a prank. In search of a fire the Fire
Chief says that he does not have time to sit, only to remove his helmet, while
sitting down with his helmet untouched. He participates with the Smiths in a
series of incongruous stories that fall short of resolutions and coherence. Mary
enters, recognizing the Fire Chief as a former lover, and recites a nonsensical
poem in his honor. Exiting because "in exactly three-quarters of an hour and
sixteen minutes, I'm having a fire at the other end of the city," the Fire Chief
asks about the bald soprano. An embarrassed silence is then broken by Mrs.
Smith, who reports that "She always wears her hair in the same style."

Left alone the Martins and the Smiths begin a heated series of bizarre assertions:

MRS. MARTIN   I can buy a pocketknife for my brother, but you can't buy Ireland for your grandfather.

MR. SMITH   One walks on his feet, but one heats with electricity or coal.

MR. MARTIN   He who sells an ox today, will have an egg tomorrow.

MRS. SMITH   In real life, one must look out of the window.

MRS. MARTIN   One can sit down on a chair, when the chair doesn't have any.

Their increasingly enraged chatter degenerates into a chorus of nonsense words, phrases, and sounds hurled back and forth:

MR. SMITH   The pope elopes! The pope's got no horoscope. The horoscope's bespoke.

MRS. MARTIN   Bazaar, Balzac, bazooka!

MR. MARTIN   Bizarre. Beaux-arts, brassieres!

MR. SMITH   A, e, i, o, u, a, e, i, o, u, a, e, i, o, u, i!

MRS. MARTIN   B, c, d, f, g, l, m, n, p, r, s, t, v w, x, z!

MR. MARTIN   From sage to stooge, from stage to serge!

MRS. SMITH   [*imitating a train*]   Choo, choo, choo, choo, choo, choo, choo, choo, choo, choo, choo!

MR. SMITH   It's!

MRS. MARTIN   Not!

MR. MARTIN   That!

MRS. SMITH   Way!

MR. SMITH   It's!

MRS. MARTIN   O!

MR. MARTIN   Ver!

MRS. SMITH   Here!

The stage goes dark. "It's not that way, it's over here!" is repeated before the lights come up again to reveal Mr. and Mrs. Martin seated like the Smiths at the beginning of the play, repeating the same lines from the first scene.

The Bald Soprano detonates social conventions and theatrical expectations. As in the work of other absurdist dramatists the play mocks both bourgeois social conventions and the theater traditions used to reflect them. Long before Jerry Seinfeld, Ionesco presents a play about nothing in which the commonplace routines and utterances of daily life are revealed as empty, banal, and absurd. In Ionesco's version of the drawing room comedy wit degenerates to clichés, non sequiturs, and eventually meaningless babble. The Aristotelian series of arrivals and departures lead nowhere and resolve nothing. Beginnings, middles, and ends are replaced by pointless repetition. Personal identity itself is unstable, multiple, and indistinguishable. Mary morphs into Sherlock Holmes. Donald and Elizabeth Martin are and are not Donald and Elizabeth. "You can put Martin in place of Smith and vice versa," Ionesco insisted, "no one will notice." Language itself frustrates communication, with dialogue—the core of drama—reverting back to meaningless sounds, a verbal equivalent of the irrationality Ionesco finds in experience. In a perfectly tuned blending of theme and form The Bald Soprano plunges its audience into the absurd vortex, making the search for coherence and meaning a participatory rather than a spectator sport.

THE GHOST SONATA

62

(1907)

by August Strindberg

Strindberg was the precursor of all modernity in our present theater. . . . Strindberg still remains among the most modern of the moderns, the greatest interpreter in the theatre of the characteristic spiritual conflicts which constitute the drama, the life-blood of our lives today. . . . It is only by means of some form of "super-naturalism" that we may express to the theatre what we comprehend intuitively of that self-obsession which is the particular discount we moderns have to pay for the loan of life.

— Eugene O'Neill, Program Note for the Provincetown Playhouse's production of *The Ghost Sonata*, 1923

August Strindberg's *Spöksonaten* (*The Ghost Sonata*) is perhaps the greatest achievement of his antirealistic, symbolic, dream-influenced plays that closed the dramatist's remarkable career. If *MISS JULIE* (1888) represents Strindberg's response to Ibsenian realism and the naturalistic technique promulgated by Émile Zola that refined and expanded both methods, *The Ghost Sonata* shows Strindberg's remarkable mid-life creative regeneration that pioneered an alternative to representational drama. It is a groundbreaking play that anticipates the concerns and techniques of the expressionists in the 1920s and the theater of the absurd and theater of cruelty in the 1950s, and in its blurring the distinctions between actuality and fantasy forecasts the innovations of Luigi Pirandello, Georg Kaiser, Eugene O'Neill, Samuel Beckett, Eugène Ionesco, Harold Pinter, Edward Albee, and many others. "Three things in especial Strindberg did," British literary historian Allardyce Nicoll has noted.

First, in the supreme concentration of the dramas of his middle period, he showed how much even the closely packed realistic plays of Ibsen lacked of essential dramatic economy. Secondly, he came as near as any man towards creating a modern social tragedy. And, thirdly, in his latest works he achieved what might have seemed impossible producing theatrical compositions that in effect are wholly subjective. In the long range of his writings his hands touch now the early romantics, now the realists and naturalists, now the expressionists, now the surrealists, and now the existentialists. There is no author whose range is wider or more provocative. In him the entire history of the stage from 1800 to the present day is epitomized.

Strindberg's extraordinary artistic development—his recasting of his own personal torment and search for spiritual and existential answers into new dramatic forms—is one of the most fascinating stories in modern literary history. Having set out with *Miss Julie* to revolutionize the theater with an enhanced conception of stage realism, Strindberg followed it with a series of naturalist-influenced dramas—*Den stakare* (*The Stronger*), *Fordringsägare* (*Creditors*), and *Leka med Elden* (*Playing with Fire*)—that like *Miss Julie* dramatize the naturalist's slice of life but at a decisive moment of crisis and conflict that exposes aspects of the human psyche and condition closed off by a narrower restriction to the details of ordinary life advocated by more doctrinaire naturalists. Like *Miss Julie*, these plays similarly advanced Strindberg's notions of how life and character should be presented on stage: in realistic settings and with production and acting styles that reinforce his interest in exploring complex and paradoxical characters in the grip of the forces of heredity, the environment, and instinctual and unconscious psychological drives. Strindberg's fascination with characters in distress, with abnormal states and the repressed origins of motive and behavior eventually required an entirely new dramatic approach that left the conventions of the realistic stage behind.

This new dramatic method would emerge out of Strindberg's so-called Inferno crisis of the 1890s, a period of lacerating self-doubt and mental and emotional torment. By 1892 Strindberg had reached a personal and professional dead end. He could neither get his plays produced nor support himself by his writing; his first marriage had dissolved, and his second would end in a separation after only a few months. Strindberg wound up in Paris, summarizing his condition in a letter: "I detest mankind and I cannot be alone—thus, bad company, alcohol, late nights, Chat Noir [a cabaret in Montmarte], despair and the lot—above all, paralysis." Abandoning playwrighting for alchemical research, which came to represent for him a search for spiritual and existential meaning, Strindberg spiraled to a psychological breakdown that has been variously diagnosed as schizophrenia, manic depression, paranoia, and absinthe poisoning. He managed to halt his decline with medical help, a change of locale from Paris to Sweden and Austria, and a spiritual conversion to what he called a "creedless Christianity." Strindberg chronicled and analyzed his spiritual and emotional struggles in the autobiographical novel *Inferno* (1898), which has been called by biographer Michael Meyer perhaps his best non-dramatic work and "an extraordinarily powerful and convincing portrait of the interior of a distraught mind, worthy to stand beside the self-portrait of

Van Gogh, the poems of Hölderlin or the novels of Dostoevsky." In January 1898 Strindberg began his first play in five years, *Till Damascus* (*To Damascus*), which eventually became part of a trilogy dramatizing aspects of Strindberg's own spiritual struggle. With it Strindberg discovered a means to embody a complex inner psychological world by having the protagonist—the Stranger— encounter personifications of his own fears and anxieties on his quest, which becomes a descent into his unconscious. According to critic Maurice Valency, the result is "a quasi-medieval work that was to furnish the blue-print for the most advanced drama of the twentieth century."

Strindberg, therefore, emerged from his Inferno crisis, in his words, hav- ing "regained the grace of being able to write for the theater," producing a series of pioneering plays, including *Dödsdansen* (1900; *The Dance of Death*) and *Ett Drömspel* (1902; *The Dream Play*), whose 1906 preface provides Strindberg's articulation of his antirealistic, symbolic methods and a theoretical basis for expressionistic drama. He states: "the writer has tried to imitate the disjointed but apparently logical form of a dream. Anything may happen: everything is possible and probable. Time and space do not exist. . . . The characters are split, doubled, and multiplied: they evaporate and are condensed, are diffused and concentrated." Strindberg rejects Aristotelian dramatic conventions and the representational on stage for a subjective projection of inner reality in which characters become archetypes and aspects of certain universal condi- tions, in which causality gives way to contrast, juxtaposition, and repetition of images and ideas, and the recognizable is disrupted by the fantastical. By erasing the boundary between reality and fantasy, between conscious thought and dream logic, between rational truth and the irrational, Strindberg opened up new possibilities for dramatists such as George Bernard Shaw, Pirandello, O'Neill, Beckett, and others to exploit. Strindberg showed that whatever could be imagined could be powerfully dramatized on stage.

Among the dramas written in Strindberg's visionary, experimental mode, *The Ghost Sonata* is one of his "chamber plays," dramas constructed along musi- cal principles and produced for the 161-seat Intimate Theatre that Strindberg opened in Stockholm in 1907. The play excavates the buried secrets that exist beneath the surface of conventional behavior. Set in an alternative world in which dream and reality meet, the conventional laws of space and time are replaced by the terrifying logic of a nightmare. Inspired by Beethoven's piano sonata in D minor, op. 21, no. 2, and its three-part structure of thematic state- ment, development, and recapitulation, *The Ghost Sonata* opens in the first of its three movements, or scenes, in a recognizably realistic setting that quickly gives way to the extraordinary and macabre. Set on a respectable city street beside a fashionable apartment building, the play begins on the day after a fatal house collapse where a poor Student, Arkenholz, has spent the night tending the wounded and dying. At a drinking fountain he encounters a Milkmaid whom only Arkenholz, a "Sunday child" with special visionary powers, is able to see. Nearby is an Old Man in a wheelchair, Jacob Hummel, who observes the Student's apparent conversation with no one. Arkenholz learns that the Old Man was connected with the bankruptcy and ruination of his father. The Old Man claims to have contrived Arkenholz's heroism to facilitate his meeting and eventually marrying the Colonel's daughter, who lives in the nearby apartment building that the Student has long admired and dreamed as the ideal realization of a happy and successful life. The inhabitants, as described by the Old Man, include the Colonel's wife, a once lovely young lady and the Old Man's former fiancée, who now is a half-crazed recluse called the Mummy; a Lady in Black, who awaits her aristocratic lover; and a former consul, whose dead body is laid out upstairs. He, however, is seen by the Student inspecting his mourners. After seeing the Colonel's beautiful daughter, Arkenholz is determined to comply with the Old Man's plan for him to meet her and gain an invitation to their home. From the Old Man's servant, Johansson, Arkenholz learns that Hummel is "like the god Thor himself. He looks at houses, pulls them down . . . sneaks through windows, plays havoc with human destinies, kills his enemies—and never forgives." The Old Man's sinister power is confirmed when the Milkmaid returns, making motions like a drowned person, and now seen by both Arkenholtz and Hummel.

The initial scene establishes the dominant themes of the play in the persistence of death, fraud, lies, and deceit that exists beyond the respectable facades of buildings and individuals that the play's symbolic and fantastical disruptions reveal. In its second scene the play moves inside the fashionable building for a full exposure of the dislocations and secrets alluded to in the first scene. As Strindberg described his play in a letter, "It is horrible, like life, when the veil falls from our eyes and we see things as they are. Secrets like these are to be found in every home. People are too proud to admit it; most of them boast of their imagined luck, and hide their misery." Arkenholz has secured an invitation to the "ghost supper," hosted by the Colonel and his family. It is called a ghost supper because, according to the servant Bengtsson, the diners "look like ghosts. And they've kept this up for twenty years, always the same people saying the same things or saying nothing at all for fear of being found out." The Old Man arrives uninvited to complete his mission of unmasking and revenge. Opposing him is the Old Man's former lover, the Mummy, whose daughter is the result of their affair. The Mummy emerges from her closet, and her parrot-like babbling warns Hummel that if he harms the Colonel he will die. Hummel persists in his revenge on the Colonel for having taken his fiancée from him by gaining control of all the Colonel's debts. The Old Man strips the Colonel of his belongings and everything he values, revealing that even his claim to a noble title is a fraud. The Old Man orders the ghost supper to proceed as planned to complete his mission of exposure. With all assembled, he reveals his intention "to pull up the weeds, to expose the crimes, to settle all accounts, so that those young people [Arkenholz and the Girl, the Colonel's daughter] might start afresh in this home, which is my gift to them." The counterstroke comes from the Mummy who emerges from her penitential isolation to retaliate by revealing the Old Man's own crimes. "We have erred and we have sinned," she declares to Hummel. "We are not what we seem, because at bottom we are better than ourselves, since we detest our sins." The Old Man by contrast denies his sins and pretends to be virtuous. However, his perfidy is revealed, including his murder of the Milkmaid, whom he had lured to her drowning death to conceal his crimes. Crushed by the weight of these revelations, the Old Man, now babbling like a parrot, crawls into the closet the Mummy has occupied for 20 years to use the rope he has often used to strangle the life of others and hang himself.

If the play's second scene provides the play's moral climax in which all the crimes of the past and secret guilt and deception are brought to the surface, and the play's avenging angel—the Old Man—is forced to confront his own past sins, the final scene supplies a spiritual expansion of the themes of crime, punishment, repentance, and redemption to the innocent second generation, represented by the Girl and the Student. A few days after the Old Man's funeral, the Student and the Girl are shown together in the house's Hyacinth Room, filled with the flowers that are described "a replica of the universe." Although the room looks beautiful and perfect it is really a "room of ordeals," in which the Girl is afflicted by a maid who dirties the house more than she cleans it and a cook, from "the Hummel family of vampires," who boils out all of the nourishment of the family's food before serving it and leaves them only the watery broth. All, including the innocent Girl, are thereby punished for their sins, and there is no escaping "illusion, guilt, suffering and death." To rescue her from this poisonous environment Arkenholz proposes marriage and expresses the hope that beauty and truth might be attainable somewhere in the world. As the formerly idealistic young Student expresses his achieved understanding of life's horrors, however, the Girl withers and collapses, and he greets her death in these words:

> The Liberator is coming. Welcome, pale and gentle one. Sleep, you lovely, innocent, doomed creature, suffering for no fault of your own. Sleep without dreaming, and when you wake again . . . may you be greeted by a sun that does not burn, in a home without dust, by friends without stain, by a love without flaw. You wise and gentle Buddha, sitting there waiting for a Heaven to sprout from the earth, grant us patience in our ordeal and purity of will, so that this hope may not be confounded.

With the sounds of harp music, the light fades, the room disappears, and is replaced by Arnold Böcklin's painting, *The Island of the Dead*. The play closes, therefore, on an apocalyptic note suggesting a tenuous redemption reserved for those who fully face the truth of self and the world and whose suffering leads to enlightenment.

The Ghost Sonata, in a series of intensely compressed scenes, unleashes the forces of guilt and deception lurking beneath the facade of respectability, while formulating an understanding of the human condition in terms wide enough to encompass truth without easy or unearned consolations. Few plays risk so much in their conceptions of the self and the world or embody so powerfully our anxieties and our nightmares. The play's process is ultimately therapeutic in facing down the worst that can be imagined. "What has saved my soul from darkness during this work," Strindberg wrote in a letter, "has been my religion, the hope of a better life to come, the firm conviction that we live in a world of madness and delusion from which we must fight our way free."

THE INSPECTOR GENERAL

63

(1836)

by Nikolai Gogol

[The Inspector General] is a work of enormous scale, at one extreme an entertaining comedy of errors and, at the other, an illuminating drama of corruption. No single inter-pretation encompasses all its meaning. . . . It is a play of great originality that contains the inexhaustible riches of all great art. Its theme is universal and it speaks to the eternal human condition. Its laughter is directed at what is essential and permanent in man. It transcends its own time and people, belonging to all ages and all people. It has justly earned for itself the name of immortal comedy.

—Michael Beresford, Introduction to *The Government Inspector:
A Comedy in Five Acts,* 1996

Vladimir Nabokov judged Nikolai Gogol's *Revizor* (*The Inspector General*) to be "the greatest play ever written in Russian (and never surpassed since)." It can be argued that Gogol's masterpiece serves a comparable role in Russia as Miguel de Cervantes's *Don Quixote* does in Spain as the foundation work of a national literature. Critic Thomas Seltzer has called Gogol's play "a national institution" and has asserted:

> There is no other single work in the modern literature of any language that carries with it the wealth of associations which the Inspector-Gen-eral does to the educated Russian. The Germans have their Faust; but Faust is a tragedy with a cosmic philosophic theme. In England it takes nearly all that is implied in the comprehensive name of Shakespeare to give the same sense of bigness that a Russian gets from the mention of the Revizor.

Russian drama before *The Inspector General* was imitative of foreign models. Gogol took up a distinctively Russian subject while challenging audience expectations about what a comedy could be. Gone are the standard idealized characters and romance plot as well as the expected poetic justice in which virtue is rewarded and vice punished. Instead Gogol places at the center of his comedy recognizable mixed human characters in unflattering situations that turn his comedy into a substantive critique of Russian life and human nature. By so doing Gogol, who has been called "the father of Russian realism," established a representational and critical tradition that Russian writers—from Ivan Turgenev through Feodor Dostoevsky, Leo Tolstoy, Anton Chekhov, Maxim Gorky, and others—have followed ever since. *The Inspector General* brought within comic range for the first time the ways in which Russian society and government actually works, in all its petty corruption and ineptitude, while embodying in his characters key national traits—archetypes that continue to serve the Russian imagination and collective consciousness.

Born in 1809 into a modest Ukrainian landowning family, Gogol formed an interest in literature and drama while attending boarding school, where he acted in amateur theatricals. Failing to gain employment as an actor or recognition for his initial literary work, Gogol worked as a civil servant in St. Petersburg where he eventually gained a reputation as a writer of promise with his comic folktales based on Ukrainian life. In 1835 Gogol published, in the volume *Arabesques*, the first of his Petersburg Tales, which would include the classic short stories "The Nose" and "The Overcoat." While in St. Petersburg, Gogol also began his first work for the theater, an unfinished satire on the civil service, *Vladimir of the Third Class*, and a two-act comedy of manners, *The Wedding*, begun in 1833 and completed nine years later. In his *Author's Confession* (1847) Gogol credited the inspiration for his next play, *The Inspector General*, to Aleksandr Pushkin. Gogol wrote to his friend complaining about his lack of funds and solicited the poet's help by suggesting "some anecdote, humorous or not, but purely Russian. My hand trembles from eagerness to write a comedy. Do me a favor, give me a subject; I will instantly make a five-act comedy of it and it will be funnier than hell." Pushkin obliged by telling Gogol how during a provincial journey he had been mistaken for a government inspector by the local officials and had amused himself by encouraging the mistake. Gogol seized upon the suggestion for his plot, further influenced by Gregory Kvitka's 1827 comedy, *The Newcomer from the Capital*, from which he borrowed some details. However dependent on others for his initial theme, setting, and characters, Gogol made the subject of the false inspector uniquely his own, combining realism, farce, and fantasy in the story of a stranded, impecunious traveler named Khlestakov, who is mistaken for an expected official, is bribed and feted, attempts to seduce the mayor's wife and daughter, and departs shortly before the town's residents learn of their mistake and await the arrival of the real government inspector.

With its provocatively unflattering epigraph "If your face is crooked, don't blame the mirror," it is a wonder that *The Inspector General* was cleared for production at all in the repressive Russia of the 1830s. *The Inspector General* was nonetheless first performed in St. Petersburg before Czar Nicholas I himself, after the emperor had the comedy read to him and overruled the imperial censor. Nicholas found the play not seditious but delightfully amusing. At the premiere, the czar laughed heartily and was quoted as saying that "everyone got his due, and I most of all" and ordered all his ministers to see the play. The audience's reaction was far less generous or benign. Critic Pavel Annenkov would later recall the opening night audience's mixed reception:

> Even after the first act everyone looked bewildered as if they could not decide what to make of it. And yet certain features and scenes in this "farce" were so realistic that once or twice, especially where the conventional idea of comedy was not contradicted, there were gusts of laughter. In the fourth act the reaction was quite different: there was still laughter rippling occasionally across the theater, but it was rather timid and stopped as soon as it began; there was barely any applause; but the concentration of the audience on the development of the action and the dead silence in the hall manifested the deep impression that the play was making on the spectators. At the end of it, bewilderment gave way to general indignation that was loudly expressed in the fifth act. Some called for the author because they thought he had written a comic masterpiece, others thought some of the scenes showed talent, most applauded because it had made them laugh. The unanimous opinion of the select public, however, was that "this is impossible, this is libel, this is farce."

Reviews were no less mixed. Some praised the play as a new type of social drama that dispensed with the traditional theme of romantic love for a dissection of important social issues. Others accused it of being a slander on Russia and its social order, as well as a grotesque distortion by a caricaturist with "not a single noble feature seen of the human heart."

Gogol defended his play in the important early theoretical justifications of drama in Russia, *After the Play*, which takes the form of various recorded audience reactions to *The Inspector General*. While skewering the obtuseness of Petersburg theatergoers, Gogol also asserts the striking originality of his production in its comic realism, lack of idealized character and action, and its thematic unity in which "Everyone is a hero; the movement of the play sets all the pieces of the machinery in motion and no part of it becomes rusty, so to speak, or remains inactive." After debating the moral benefit of presenting vice as well as virtue on stage, the playwright offers an explicit declaration about his comic method and intention:

> No one has seen the honest character in my play. It is laughter. It is noble because it has appeared in spite of the low esteem in which it is held. . . . Laughter is more meaningful than people think. Not the laughter that is evoked by a passing irritation and a morbid, jaundiced disposition,

nor that trivial laughter that is meant to amuse and entertain, but the laughter which comes from man's serene nature . . . that deepens every-thing, points to what might have passed unnoticed and without whose penetrating force man would have been disheartened by life's frivolity and emptiness.

Stung by the criticism of his play, Gogol began a self-imposed European exile from Russia for the next 12 years, during which he completed his equally groundbreaking comic novel *Dead Souls*, an epic expansion of many of the themes of *The Inspector General*, published in 1842. Gogol died at the age of 42 in 1852, having literally starved himself to death in mortification of the flesh from religious zeal.

The Inspector General develops its prodigious comic energy, verbal play, and social critique from a simple plot line of mistaken identity. The opening line immediately sets the play in motion as Anton Antonovich Skvoznik-Dmukh-anosky, the governor of a small provincial town, announces to the assembled municipal officials, including the judge, the superintendent of schools, the director of charities, the town doctor, and a local police officer: "I have called you together, gentlemen, to tell you an unpleasant piece of news. An Inspec-tor General is coming." The commotion this causes among the corrupt town officials allows Gogol to satirize the provincial milieu and its leaders, who are marked by a craven self-interest, mismanagement, and timidity. Warned that the inspector is to arrive incognito to assess the town's administration, the assembly strategizes about what should be done to conceal their corruption and incompetence. The governor is advised to hide the evidence of bribes; the hospital manager is urged to issue clean nightcaps and remove the patients' tobacco; the judge is told to spend less time hunting; the assessor is cautioned to eat garlic to cover up the smell of liquor on his breath, and so on. Amidst the finger pointing, word arrives that a mysterious stranger from St. Peters-burg is staying at the inn. Convinced that he must be the inspector, the group scatters to do what they can to conceal the evidence of their dishonesty and ineptitude.

Act 2 is set in the room of the suspected inspector, Ivan Alexandrovich Khlestakov, whose servant, Osip, reveals that his master is a young govern-ment clerk of the lowest grade journeying to his provincial home who has lost all his money gambling, and is unable to pay his bill at the inn. Khlestakov is far from the expected dramatic hero of rank and ability, but is described in Gogol's stage directions as "A skinny young man of about twenty-three, rather stupid, being, as they say, 'without a czar in his head,' one of those persons called an 'empty vessel' in the government offices. He speaks and acts without stopping to think and utterly lacks the power of concentration." When the governor greets him deferentially, Khlestakov is convinced that he is being arrested for debt, and the cross-purpose dialogue exploits each character's mistaken understanding and motives to the limits of the absurd. Confusing the governor's ingratiating offer for Khlestakov to stay at his home with a threat of being jailed, Khlestakov promises to pay up though he presently lacks a "single kopek." The governor, however, hears his truthful admission as a solicitation for a bribe and presents him with 400 rubles to pay his 200-ruble bill. In a delightful irony Khlestakov's acceptance of the bribe confirms the mayor's conviction that he must be the high official since bribery is the understood currency of officialdom, while the feckless Khlestakov reciprocates characteristically by not questioning a gift horse. The farcical comedy of cross-purposes is thereby exquisitely blended with the personality and values of each man.

The action shifts in act 3 to the governor's house where, in what Nabokov has called "the most famous scene of the Russian stage," Khlestakov begins to act up to the expectations of his fawning, toadying audience, including the governor's wife and daughter, by boasting of his importance and his fashionable life in St. Petersburg:

> Ah, St. Petersburg! What a life, to be sure! Maybe you think I am only a copying clerk. No, I am on a friendly footing with the chief of our department. He slaps me on the back. "Come, brother," he says, "and have dinner with me." I just drop in the office for a couple of minutes to say this is to be done so, and that is to be done that way. There's a rat of a clerk there for copying letters who does nothing but scribble all the time—tr, tr—. They even wanted to make me a college assessor, but I think to myself, "What do I want it for?" And the doorkeeper flies after me on the stairs with the shoe brush. "Allow me to shine your boots for you, Ivan Aleksandrovich," he says.

In Gogol's satirical treatment of identity Khlestakov manufactures a lifestyle, temperament, and set of values just vulgar enough to satisfy the crude expectations of his audience; while the others, in trying to conceal themselves in self-praise and bravado, as surely reveal their true selves. Collecting tribute from all, Khlestakov next turns his attention to the governor's daughter and wife, flirting with both in turn, and proposing marriage to Marya, the daughter, when the mother catches him on his knees in front of the younger woman. The expected romantic sentiment of previous comedies is here revealed as meaningless clichés and posturing by the feckless Khlestakov, who is gratefully accepted as the governor's future son-in-law before departing.

In act 5 the governor now exults in anticipation of a grand future with the inspector general as a member of his family, and husband and wife receive the envious congratulations of their friends. Their complacency and delusion are shattered by the arrival of the postmaster, who has opened the letter Khlestakov sent to his friend describing his amusing situation as the purported inspector general. Calling himself a fool for falling for Khlestakov's deception, the governor suddenly turns on the assembly (and the theater audience), stating, "What are you laughing at? You are laughing at yourself, oh you!" This realization is brilliantly underscored by the play's final "silent scene," provoked by a policeman's announcement that "An official from St. Petersburg sent by imperial order has arrived, and wants to see you all at once. He is stopping at the inn." Gogol's stage direction reads: "All are struck as by a thunderbolt. A cry of amazement bursts from the ladies simultaneously. The whole group suddenly shifts positions and remains standing as if petrified." The actors are instructed to hold their "same position of rigidity for almost a minute and a half" before the curtain falls. It is a shattering dramatic effect, ending the comedy on a sobering and crashing note of self-realization that has transformed an absurd case of mistaken identity into a delightful and sobering instrument of social and human truth telling.

THE CRUCIBLE

64

(1953)

by Arthur Miller

I was drawn to write The Crucible *not merely as a response to McCarthyism. It is not any more an attempt to cure witch hunts than* Salesman *is a plea for the improvement of conditions for traveling men. . . . The* Crucible *is, internally,* Salesman's *blood brother. It is examining the questions I was absorbed with before—the conflict between a man's raw deeds and his conception of himself; the question of whether conscience is in fact an organic part of the human being, and what happens when it is handed over not merely to the state or the mores of the time but to one's friend or wife. The big difference, I think, is that* The Crucible *sought to include a higher degree of consciousness than the earlier plays. . . . For me* The Crucible *was a new beginning, the beginning of an attempt to embrace a wider field of vision, a field wide enough to contain the whole of our current awareness.*

—Arthur Miller, "Brewed in *The Crucible*," *New York Times*, March 9, 1958

It is possible that around the world more theatergoers know about American life from its depiction in just two American communities: Grover's Corners, New Hampshire, in Thornton Wilder's *Our Town* and Salem, Massachusetts, in Arthur Miller's *The Crucible*. These are unquestionably among the most popular and most performed American plays, offering two distinctive attempts to illuminate American history and American values in the conflict between the individual and the social group. Both are thoroughly local in time and place but have managed to universalize their message ensuring a persistent relevance. For Miller *The Crucible* connects the events of the Salem witch trials in the 17th century with McCarthyism of the 1950s, while transcending both eras with larger questions regarding dissent, oppression, and conscience in an atmosphere that William Butler Yeats prophetically diagnosed in his poem "The Second Coming": "The best lack all conviction, while the worst / Are full of passionate intensity." Critic Robert A. Martin has observed, the play "has endured beyond the immediate events of its own time. . . . As one of the most frequently produced plays in the American theater, *The Crucible* has attained a life of its own; one that both interprets and defines the cultural and historical background of American society."

Miller entered the 1950s as one of the foremost American dramatists and a target. *All My Sons* and Death of a Salesman firmly established Miller's importance as a playwright and a social critic, earning both great praise and censure for his critique of American life and values. *Death of a Salesman* in particular was attacked by conservatives as "a time bomb expertly placed under the edifice of Americanism," and in the ensuing red scare that gripped America in the 1950s Miller was frequently branded that "pinko playwright." As Miller recalled,

> If the reception of *All My Sons* and *Death of a Salesman* had made the world a friendly place for me, events of the early fifties quickly turned that warmth into an illusion. It was not only the rise of "McCarthyism" that moved me, but something which seemed much more weird and mysterious. It was the fact that a political, objective, knowledgeable campaign from the far Right was capable of creating not only a terror but a new subjective reality, a veritable mystique which was gradually assuming even a holy resonance.

In Miller's view America's most cherished principles of personal liberty and the protections of conscience were under attack:

> It was as though the whole country had been born anew, without a memory even of certain elemental decencies which a year or two earlier no one could have imagined could be altered, let alone forgotten. Astounded, I watched men pass me by without a nod whom I had known rather well for years; and again, the astonishment was produced by my knowledge, which I could not give up, that the terror in these people was being knowingly planned and consciously engineered, and yet that all they knew was terror. That so interior and subjective an emotion could have been so manifestly created from without was a marvel to me. It underlies every word in *The Crucible*.

Miller became interested in writing about the 1692 Salem witch trials after reading Marion Starkey's 1949 book *The Devil in Massachusetts* and decided in April 1952 to write a play about the events having discovered a "living connection between myself and Salem, and between Salem and Washington." An additional powerful link occurred two days before he was to leave for research at the Salem Historical Society when Miller learned that Elia Kazan, who had directed *All My Sons* and *Death of a Salesman*, had been subpoenaed by the House Un-American Activities Committee and was planning to name those suspected of communist sympathies to save his career. "Oddly enough,"

Miller reported, "I was not filling up with hatred or contempt for him; his suffering was too palpable for that. It was the whole hateful procedure which had brought him to this, and I believe it made the writing of *The Crucible* all but inevitable. . . . the concept of an America where such self-discoveries were mandated, pressed out of people, was outrageous and a frightening contradiction of any concept of personal liberty." In Salem, examining the court records, Miller became fascinated by the testimony of a farmer, John Procter, his wife, Elizabeth, and their servant, Abigail Williams, who, after being dismissed from the Procters' service, had accused Elizabeth but not John of witchcraft. "It was the fact that Abigail," Miller later wrote, "their former servant, was their accuser, and her apparent desire to convict Elizabeth and save John, that made the play conceivable for me." The public, social drama of the mass hysteria of the Salem trials became in Miller's mind connected with a psychologically rich human story of this domestic triangle in which Elizabeth's discovery of John's adultery provided Abigail with a motive that would fuel the witch hunt. Although extensively researched and fact-based, *The Crucible*, as Miller's note on historical accuracy in the published text makes clear, "is not history in the sense in which the word is used by the academic historians." Miller raises Abigail's age and fuses several characters, but he insists that "the reader will discover here the essential nature of one of the strangest and most awful chapters in human history."

Set in the spring of 1692, the play opens with the Reverend Samuel Parris confronted by his 10-year-old daughter Betty's apparent coma after he has discovered her, his teenage niece Abigail Williams, and other village girls dancing "like heathens" in the forest. As concerned with protecting his reputation as restoring his daughter's health or discovering the truth about the girls' actions, Parris eventually accepts the allegations that witchcraft is the cause when Ann and Thomas Putnam report their daughter is similarly afflicted. Abigail, who had been dismissed as a servant of John and Elizabeth Proctor, meets separately with Mercy Lewis and Mary Warren, and the girls discuss what really happened in the forest. When she is shaken into consciousness by Abigail, Betty reveals: "You drank blood, Abby! . . . You drank a charm to kill John Proctor's wife!" Breaking free and threatening to fly from the window, Ruth is restrained by Abigail, who threatens all the girls if they reveal the truth.

Arriving to fetch Mary home, John Proctor speaks privately with Abigail, and she confesses that the uproar has nothing to do with witchcraft. They reveal their past relationship as the remorseful Proctor resists Abigail's advances:

I know how you clutched my back behind your house and sweated like a stallion whenever I come near! Or did I dream that? It's she put me out, you cannot pretend it were you. I saw your face when she put me out, and you loved me then and you do now!

To which John replies: "Abby, I may think of you softly from time to time. But I will cut off my hand before I'll ever reach for you again."

With the arrival of the Reverend John Hale, who has been called in as an expert in the manifestation of witchcraft, Abigail deflects blame by accusing the Parris's family slave, Tituba, of summoning the Devil in the forest and making her drink blood. To save her life Tituba admits to consorting with the Devil and begins to name others as witches, with more accused by Abigail and the other girls. The act ends with arrest orders being given.

Act 2 begins eight days later at the Proctors' home. As the community disintegrates in a frenzy of accusations there are now 14 being held in jails facing hanging unless they confess to witchcraft and name their co-conspirators. John tells Elizabeth that Abigail confessed to him that witchcraft had nothing to do with what happened in the forest, and Elizabeth, knowing that Abigail wishes her harm, urges him to go to the authorities with this information. John, however, realizes that he risks his reputation by coming forward and revealing his adultery. They are interrupted by the arrival of Reverend Hale who has come to test their religious faith. Marshals of the court subsequently arrive to arrest Elizabeth based on Abigail's testimony. Despite John's resistance and Hale's suspicions that the charge is fraudulent, Elizabeth is taken away in chains. The act ends as John tries to persuade Mary to admit the girls' inventions while implying his willingness to admit his adultery to end Abigail's power over the court and free his wife: "We are only what we always were, but naked now. Aye, naked! And the wind, God's icy wind, will blow!"

Act 3 is set in the vestry of the Salem meeting house, now serving as the anteroom for the court, presided over by Deputy Governor Danforth, whom Miller called "the rule-bearer, the man who always guards the boundaries which, if you insist on breaking through them, have the power to destroy you. His 'evil' is more than personal, it is nearly mythical. He does more evil than he knows how to do; while merely following his nose he guards ignorance, he is man's limit." Before him come Francis Nurse, Giles Corey, and John who each try to save their condemned wives. Nurse presents a petition testifying to Rebecca Nurse's good character, prompting Danforth to order all who signed to be seized for questioning. Corey charges that Putnam was witnessed coaching the girls in their accusations but refuses to name his source and is jailed. John offers Mary Warren's testimony, which Abigail rebuts by charging her as the Devil's agent. Finally John admits to his adultery with Abigail, revealing her motive for accusing Elizabeth, swearing that Abigail had been dismissed as the Proctors' servant when Elizabeth had discovered the affair: "She thinks to dance with me on my wife's grave! And well she might, for I thought of her softly. God help me, I lusted, and there *is* a promise in such sweat. But it is a whore's vengeance, and you must see it; I set myself entirely in your hands. I know you must see it now." Danforth calls Elizabeth to corroborate John's story, but unaware that he has already confessed his infidelity, she protects her husband and denies that John ever committed "the crime of lechery." Elizabeth's lie, ironically a testimony to her love for and faith in her husband, condemns John as a perjurer. His charges escalate when Mary breaks down and joins in the other girls' accusations, charging him with being the "Devil's man." Ordered to answer this charge John in despair responds: "I say—I say—God is dead! . . . A fire, a fire is burning! I hear the boot of Lucifer, I see his filthy face! And it is my face, and yours, Danforth! For them that quail to bring men out of ignorance, as I have quailed, and you quail now when you know in all your black hearts that this be fraud—God damns our kind especially, and we will burn, we will burn together!" The only one who understands John's curse for what it is, an accusation of all in their community's destruction, is Hale, who is finally convinced that personal vengeance has been behind the witchcraft accusations.

The final act opens several months later as the initial hysteria has subsided and the community is growing resentful against the trials and the impending execution of such respected citizens as Rebecca Nurse and John Proctor. Moreover, Abigail has run away with Reverend Parris's money, casting doubt on the principal accuser. The trials, ironically established to restore moral order in the community, have torn it apart. As Hale summarizes, "There are orphans wandering from house to house; abandoned cattle bellow on the highroads, the stink of rotting crops hangs everywhere, and no man knows where the harlot's cry will end his life." Danforth, however, is adamant that the executions go forward since any hesitation calls into doubt the 12 who have already been hanged. He presses for confessions that would validate the proceedings, while Hale urges the accused to lie to save themselves. Elizabeth is summoned to convince John to confess. Left to speak with her husband alone, Elizabeth tells John that Rebecca Nurse remains adamant in asserting her innocence while Giles Corey has died while being coerced to name Putnam's accuser. John, however, is tempted to lie to save his life, adding only an additional sin to the adultery that has caused his predicament. "I cannot mount the gibbet like a saint" he declares. "It is a fraud. I am not that man. My honesty is broke, Elizabeth; I am no good man. Nothing's spoiled by giving them this lie that were not rotten long before." Declaring that "I will have my life," John agrees to confess, to the delight of his accusers, but changes his mind when he is asked to name others and hand over his signed confession for public display. Asked to explain why, John answers: "Because it is my name! Because I cannot have another in my life! Because I lie and sign myself to lies! Because I am not worth the dust on the feet of them that hang! How may I live without my name? I have given you my soul; leave me my name!" John's assertion of personal integrity in the face of death is the play's great tragic moment. It is, in Miller's words, "that moment of commitment . . . that moment when, in my eyes, a man differentiates himself from every other man. . . . the less capable a man is of walking away from the central conflict of the play, the closer he approaches a tragic existence. In turn, this implies that the closer a man approaches tragedy the more intense is his concentration upon the fixed point of his commitment." Opting for truth and personal integrity even at the cost of his life, John is sent to his hanging with Elizabeth's final tribute:

> HALE   Woman, plead with him! Woman! It is pride, it is vanity. Be his helper!—What profit him to bleed? Shall the dust praise him? Shall the worms declare his truth? Go to him, take his shame away!

> ELIZABETH   He have his goodness now. God forbid I take it from him!

The play's final irony is that John is able to regain his life—his identity and integrity—by sacrificing his life. The significance of the play's title is not just the witch's cauldron out of which the events are brewed or the melting pot of American life with its inherent challenge between the one and the many, but the purgative conflicts in which core values are tested and self-discovery is achieved. As intriguing as *The Crucible* is as a dramatization of a moment of American history and as a reflection of another challenge to American liberty and conscience, the play ultimately claims its audience by its psychological and moral questioning of what is worth dying for and living to protect.

MARAT/SADE

65

(1964)
by Peter Weiss

Starting with the title, everything about this play is designed to crack the spectator on the jaw, then douse him with ice-cold water, then force him to assess intelligently what has happened to him, then give him a kick in the balls, then bring him back to his senses again. It's not exactly Brecht and it's not Shakespeare either, but it's very Elizabethan and very much of our time.

Weiss not only uses total theater, that time-honoured notion of getting all the elements of the stage to serve the play. His force is not only in the quantity of instruments he uses: it is above all in the jangle produced by the clash of styles. Everything is put in place by its neighbour—the serious by the comic, the noble by the popular, the literary by the crude, the intellectual by the physical: the abstraction is vivified by the stage image, the violence illuminated by the cool flow of thought.

—Peter Brook, Introduction to the published version of the play

Peter Weiss's complex, innovative political drama concerning revolution, anarchy, individualism, and despotism is an example of the kind of confrontational theater that was a vital feature of the stage during the 1960s and 1970s. Provocative and frequently experimental, theater during that iconoclastic era made use of a variety of dramatic methods to express the deepest human awareness and emotion, to drive home political viewpoints, and to shake audience expectations of how drama could—and should—be performed. As auteur stage director and filmmaker Peter Brook observes, *Marat/Sade*'s ability to provoke and disconcert begins with its full title, which, translated from the original German to English, usually appears as *The Persecution and Assassination of Jean-Paul Marat as Performed by the Inmates of the Asylum at Charenton under the Direction of the Marquis de Sade*. While the shortened version of the title cleverly suggests a dialogue and debate between the two central characters, the full title reads like an announcement, telling us that an ordinary historical event is going to be presented in an extraordinary manner. What follows is a multilayered drama that combines dramatic devices ranging from the doggerel and balladry of Elizabethan theater and the irony of *The Beggar's Opera* to Brechtian epic theater of alienation, the theater of the absurd, and Antonin Artaud's theatre of cruelty.

A painter, filmmaker, novelist, and journalist, as well as a playwright, Peter Ulrich Weiss was born into a wealthy bourgeois family in Berlin in 1916 and spent his childhood in the capital and in Bremen. His father, a textile manufacturer of Czechoslovakian descent, was a convert from Judaism to Lutheranism, and his mother, a former actress and a Swiss Gentile, had abandoned her career to care for her six children. Throughout his life Weiss retained strong feelings of alienation, which, while growing up, he worked to overcome by rejecting the conventional expectations of his parents and seeking a sense of identity through artistic expression. He would later recall his youth as a frustrating time, when he felt stifled by his parents' values of conformity, propriety, and success and disappointed that even his mother would not support his artistic aspirations. He was nevertheless able to gain permission from his parents to attend the Academy of Art in Prague and enrolled in 1937. There Weiss met the socialist writer Max Barth, who would become his intellectual mentor. He also corresponded with and visited the novelist Hermann Hesse, who lived in Switzerland. Weiss viewed Hesse as an encouraging father figure whom he greatly admired for his work as well as for his dedication to reclusive individualism. In 1939, after the German occupation of the Sudetenland, Weiss fled to Zurich and then to Sweden, where his parents had found refuge from the Nazis. He worked as a fabric designer at his father's textile mill until 1942 and then took odd jobs as a lumberjack and farm laborer. In 1945 he became a Swedish citizen, and in 1947 he returned to Berlin to report on life in the divided city for a Swedish newspaper.

Weiss's early writings were in Swedish, but he returned to the German language around 1950. His first work is dominated by surrealistic images of isolation, imprisonment, eroticism, and cruelty punctuating his principal theme of human despair. His first collection of short prose, *Frän ö tillö* (1947; *From Island to Island*), received critical acclaim and was followed by prose works that established his reputation in the Swedish postwar literary avant-garde. In 1949 he joined a group that had started an experimental cinema studio at the university in Stockholm. Weiss would go on to make 14 films between 1952 and 1960, most of them short documentaries influenced by surrealism.

Weiss's first play, *Der Turm* (*The Tower*), was produced in 1949. An existentialist parable, the play concerns a protagonist struggling for liberation from a hostile universe. *Die Versicherung* (*Insurance*), written in 1952 but not performed until 1971, shows the influence of German expressionism, dadaism, and French surrealism. A multimedia production including film footage of street riots and natural disasters, the play attempts to show the absurdity of bourgeois society's ability to protect itself from disaster and the failure of revolution to resolve the anarchy and violence inherent in capitalistic society. *Nacht mit Gästen* (*Night with Guests*), performed in 1963, is a one-act play written in doggerel verse, with techniques borrowed from Kabuki theater and Punch-and-Judy shows. In it a robber holds a family hostage while the husband digs up a chest of gold as ransom. The parents, the robber, and a neighbor are killed. The children survive but discover that the chest contains nothing but turnips.

Weiss's autobiographical novels, *Abscheid von den Eltern* (1961; *Leavetaking*) and *Flachtpunkt* (1962; *Vanishing Point*) established him as a German author of consequence, and he was invited to gatherings of Group 47, an association of progressive German writers. At a meeting of the group in the fall of 1963 Weiss, beating on a drum he held between his knees, recited his new play, *Marat/Sade*. He had begun the play in 1962 and revised it to reflect his changing views toward the hedonistic, self-indulgent, intellectual individualist the marquis de Sade and the radical revolutionary populist ideologue Jean-Paul Marat, and to refine the political versus antipolitical and body versus mind antagonism that characterizes the two within the confines of the drama. The historical marquis de Sade and Marat never met, but Sade did deliver the eulogy at Marat's funeral. From 1801 until his death in 1814, Sade actually was confined at the Charenton Asylum, where he produced and directed plays among the patients and appeared as an actor himself. In his "Author's Notes on the Historical Background to the Play," Weiss writes, "In exclusive Paris circles it was considered a rare pleasure to attend Sade's theatrical performances in the 'hiding-place for the moral rejects of civilized society.'" These "rejects" included social undesirables such as prostitutes and persons with medical conditions poorly understood at the time, as well as the truly mentally ill.

Marat/Sade resembles a Chinese puzzle box in its technique: There is a play (showing the assassination of Marat by Charlotte Corday), performed as a play (written and staged by the marquis de Sade, who appears as himself in his own play), within a play (an allusion to parallels between the Napoleonic empire and postwar Europe, written by Weiss). There is also an audience (the asylum's director, Coulmier, and his wife and daughter) watching Sade's play, as well as an audience watching Weiss's play. Thus, when the asylum bell tolls, signaling the start of the play, the curtain rises, and Coulmier and his family take their seats; the wider audience in effect becomes part of Weiss's play.

Marat/Sade is a two-act drama divided into 33 scenes set in the bath hall of the asylum on July 13, 1808, exactly 15 years after the Girondist Charlotte Corday stabbed the Jacobin Jean-Paul Marat to death. It is a time when the revolutionary spirit has been replaced by the enlightened despotism of the Napoleonic era. A portion of the dialogue is in rhyme, and there are songs that were composed for the first British production of the play by Richard Peaslee. The first act begins with "Assembly," during which the members of the cast take their places. The "Prologue" has Coulmier welcoming the audience to "this salon," where Sade, he tells us, has "produced this play for your delectation and for our patients' rehabilitation." Coulmier describes his asylum: "We're modern enlightened and we don't agree / with locking up patients. We prefer therapy / through education and especially art / so that our hospital may play its part / faithfully following according to our lights / the Declaration of Human Rights." In "Preparation" and "Presentation," as the orchestra begins to play, the cast completes its opening tableau, and the Herald, part-Harlequin, part-jester, introduces the "lucky paranoiac" playing Marat and a patient with narcolepsy and melancholia portraying Corday. Like the real Marat, who suffered from a debilitating skin disease and required immersion in warm water, the actor playing Marat sits in a bathtub. He is attended to by a patient playing his mistress, Simonne Evrard. Also portrayed are Corday's lover, Duperret, a Girondist deputy, who gropes Corday whenever possible, and the radical priest Jacques Roux, played by a patient in a straitjacket.

The cast pauses for an "Homage to Marat," a sung catalogue of the attitudes and grievances of the masses, which ends with a refrain that will be repeated throughout the play: "Marat we're poor and the poor stay poor / Marat don't make us wait any more / We want our rights and we don't care how / We want our revolution NOW." The patients-actors become agitated, and Coulmier calls on Sade to control his cast. Corday is introduced, and she sings of her intent to "murder Marat and free all mankind." Marat claims "I am the Revolution." Corday, using the deceit that she will promise to betray the Girondists of her city, Caen, makes her first attempt to see Marat; Simonne reminds her that she must come three times before gaining admittance. Four balladeers-patients describe Corday's first visit to Paris, during which she witnesses a crowd performing a dance of death as they proceed to the guillotine. The patients mime an execution, kicking and throwing the severed head, prompting Coulmier to protest once again.

Sade and Marat discuss the meaning of life and death, in which Sade compares violent death to the indifference he has observed in "passionless" Nature, merely an example of the survival of the fittest. Marat responds that Sade's view results from a lack of compassion; Sade maintains that compassion belongs to the privileged classes who use it contemptuously. Marat claims that he uses action to defeat "Nature's silence." He indicts the church for keeping the poor in their place by encouraging them to view suffering as a spiritual honor. The patients mime a church service; one of them, a former abbott, offers a frenzied prayer to Satan and is restrained by male nurses. Sade describes the horrific violence he has seen and insists that he does not know whether he is "hangman or victim," while Marat claims that people are more repressed now than when the revolution began. Corday discusses her plans with Duperret, who continually touches her and must have his attention refocused on his lines. He fails to dissuade her from her goal and waits for France to "speak the forbidden word / Freedom." Sade tauntingly questions Marat on the validity of the revolution, insisting he (Sade) only believes in himself. In a scene that Coulmier insists was to be cut, Jacques Roux attempts to rouse the masses-patients to continued revolution and calls upon Marat to "come out and lead the people," and is restrained. Philosophic belief and sadomasochistic excess come together as Sade delivers a long monologue while Corday whips him (in some productions, with her hair). He confronts his own criminality and claims that the revolution has led "to the withering of the individual man." Corday makes her second visit to Marat with a letter requesting his aid and is turned away. The first acts ends with "The Faces of Marat," a scene in which Marat's life is mocked and ridiculed by characters representing his youth, science, the army, the church, the nouveaux riches, and historical figures, including Voltaire. Roux defends Marat and the revolution. The Herald announces an interval so that the audience can consider and debate what has just taken place and what might happen next.

The second act opens with an imaginary scene in the National Assembly, in which Marat questions the actions of those currently in power and attempts to rally the people to continue the revolution according to his views. The fickle crowd cheers and denounces him at the same time. Duperret deplores Marat's attempts to rouse the masses, while Roux interrupts and further incites the patients. Disorder ensues until stopped by Sade, who raises his hands, causing the entire cast to freeze. Marat returns to his bathtub to write down his thoughts, while Sade scornfully suggests he abandon his futile "scribbling," as he himself did "when the Bastille fell." Marat insists that his writing was always a prelude to action; Sade counters that it is too late and that the revolution is lost. Marat lies in his bathtub exhausted and confused. The patient playing Corday is awakened and given the dagger for her third and final visit. Sade refers to Corday's beauty to interject his ideas about sensuality and suggests that the masses will only revolt with the promise of a direct and personal reward. He stirs the patients to sing "And what's the point of a revolution / without general copulation." Corday knocks at Marat's door and is invited to enter. The murder is interrupted by a musical history of the revolution, highlighting events that have taken place during the "fifteen glorious years" between Marat's assassination and the time of Sade's play. Marat is finally killed and poses in his bathtub as in the famous painting by David. The Epilogue has Coulmier insisting that with the rule of Napoleon, "today we live in far different times / We have no oppressors no violent crimes / and although we're at war anyone can see / it can only end in victory." The patients are aroused and march in a frenzy around the stage, prompting Coulmier to instruct the nurses to violently strike them down. The last lines belong to Jacques Roux, who admonishes the audience, "When will you learn to see / When will you take sides."

Weiss prepared five versions of *Marat/Sade* before it premiered in West Berlin in April 1964 and in East Germany in March 1965. The award-winning play became an international success in the English-speaking world after Peter Brook produced it for the Royal Shakespeare Company in 1964. Brook also directed a film version of *Marat/Sade* in 1967 and an opera of the play premiered in Kassel, Germany, in 1984. The success of *Marat/Sade* made Peter Weiss the most respected playwright working in the German language.

An epic circus of ideas and techniques, *Marat/Sade* is a remarkable piece of drama: the most innovative stage work since the advent of Bertolt Brecht's post–World War I theater. Weiss, a moralist who once insisted that "art should be so strong that it changes life," was working in a late post–World War II climate dominated by the clash between communism and capitalism. But in *Marat/Sade* the past is closely allied with the present. The philosophical dilemma presented in the play is the clash between the possibility of a perfect society (Marat) and the conviction that humanity cannot be perfected (Sade). At the center is what Weiss perceives to be the ultimate failure of revolutions, from the French Revolution to 19th- and 20th-century liberation movements, as well as the Russian Revolution. Using a full array of dramatic techniques in the kind of political drama that is rarely, if ever, seen now, Weiss achieves a singular theatrical experience, as he asks his audience to consider, discuss, and debate the possibility of establishing a more humane world.

TRANSLATIONS

66

(1980)

by Brian Friel

Brian Friel has by now produced a more significant body of work than any other play-wright in Ireland, and it is time that he was, as it were, translated. . . . His recent plays—
Aristocrats *and* Faith Healer *last year, and now* Translations—*show him in the grip of a major theme. He has come in from different angles but with a constant personal urgency upon the need we have to create enabling myths of ourselves and the danger we run if we too credulously trust to the sufficiency of these myths. In the opening moment of* Transla-tions, *a girl who has been mute is being taught by Manus to say: "My name is Sarah." Nothing can stop her now, Manus assures her, she can say who she is so she is safe. Towards the end of the play, however, when the English captain demands who she is, his command and strangeness scare her: "My name . . . my name is . . ." is all she can manage. It is as if some symbolic figure of Ireland from an eighteenth-century vision poem, the one who once confidently called herself Cathleen Ni Houlihan, has been struck dumb by the shock of modernity. Friel's work, not just here but in his fourteen preceding plays, constitutes a powerful therapy, a set of imaginative exercises that give her the chance to know and say herself properly to herself again.*

—Seamus Heaney, Review of *Translations*,
Times Literary Supplement, October 24, 1980

Among contemporary playwrights few have produced as rich, challenging, or more compelling a body of dramatic works than Brian Friel. His plays are simultaneously thoroughly local in drawing on Irish history and culture and profoundly universal in their implications. As critic Frank Rich has asserted, "Mr. Friel makes the Irish condition synonymous with the human condition." Perhaps none of Friel's dramas better displays his skill in irradiating a particu-lar time and place with timeless relevance than *Translations*, a recognized clas-sic of modern Irish drama and one of the great plays of the last quarter of the 20th century. In the words of fellow countryman Seamus Heaney, "That play went intravenously into the consciousness of the audience and the country."

The play was written purposefully to allow the Irish to "talk to ourselves"; by now the rest of the world has listened in and been caught up in the debate.

The play is set in 1833, as British soldiers of the first Ordnance Survey of Ireland arrive in a small, rural Irish-speaking community in County Donegal to map the country and Anglicize Irish place-names. At the same time the newly instituted state-run national schools, to be taught in English, are about to replace the Irish-speaking "hedge schools," the often clandestine, informal classrooms open to the Irish peasantry. The play depicts, in Friel's phrase, "the meeting of two cultures," in which a traditional Irish way of life is dying—"no longer quickened by its past, about to be plunged almost overnight into an alien future." *Translations* shows the beginning of the end of a viable and vital Irish language, native traditions, and an indigenous Irish cultural identity as well as the genesis of modern divided Ireland in search of its soul and its autonomy. "The play found expression in the issue of actual place names," Friel asserted, "but I think in some way my concern is more with the whole problem that the writers in this country experience: having to handle a language that is not native to them." As critic Helen Lojek points out, "*Translations* excavates the layers of language in Ireland. . . . And it reflects the confusions and divisions of an area split by language and colonialism." The Irish locale and historical moment serve to dramatize global and persistent themes of the ways language shapes and distorts human communication, as well as the complex antagonisms of nationalism and colonialism that have defined much of modern history.

Friel as both an international literary artist and an Irishman is not an exceptional case. Despite its history, size, and location (James Joyce called Ireland the "afterthought of Europe"), Ireland has produced a disproportionate share of writers who have dominated modern literary expression. William Butler Yeats is the consensus choice for the 20th-century's greatest poet, Joyce towers over modern fiction, and modern drama has an unmistakable Irish accent with Oscar Wilde, Yeats, John Millington Synge, George Bernard Shaw, Sean O'Casey, Samuel Beckett, and Brendan Behan exerting an unavoidable impact. Why such a small country with its long history of political and cultural suppression should have produced such an oversized influence on modern literature is an intriguing paradox. In a sense Ireland through its turbulent history in many ways has been on the cutting edge of historical, cultural, and political developments—from its colonial repression and nationalistic aspirations, through its violent war of independence, civil war, and ongoing sectarian conflict—that have dominated modern debate giving Irish writers seeking to come to terms with Irish history a worldwide relevance. Friel's career as a playwright and his achievement with *Translations* underscore this point.

Brian Friel was born in 1929 near Omagh, County Tyrone, a member of the first generation of the Northern Irish Catholic minority born into the partition that divided Ireland following its violent break from British rule and an even bloodier civil war. Friel's father, a primary school teacher and principal, moved his family in 1939 to Derry, a city where Catholics were in the majority yet were denied basic civil rights by the Protestant minority. Friel's grandparents were Irish speakers from across the border in County Donegal, where he spent part of his school vacation every year. The area would inspire the setting for many of Friel's plays—his fictional Donegal community of Ballybeg (in Irish, "small town"), which Friel has called the "edge of the known world." After attending St. Columb's College in Derry from 1941 to 1946 Friel enrolled in a seminary but abandoned his plans to enter the priesthood, moving on instead to St. Joseph's Teacher Training College in Belfast. From 1950 to 1960 Friel worked as a teacher in Derry while publishing short stories and writing radio plays. Supported by a contract with the *New Yorker* Friel quit teaching to write full time. In 1963 the "33-year-old ex-schoolmaster" and author of three unpublished plays, only one of which had been performed onstage, declared to a Belfast newspaper his ambition to write a "great Irish play" in which "the author can talk so truthfully and accurately about people in his own neighbourhood and make it so that these folk could be living in Omagh, Omaha or Omansk." The same year Friel spent six months as an "observer" at the Tyrone Guthrie Theater in Minneapolis. Friel called the time spent there "some kind of explosion in the head." "I learned that the playwright's first function is to entertain," he has stated, "to have audiences enjoy themselves, to move them emotionally, to make them laugh and cry and gasp and hold their breath and sit on the edge of their seats." Friel's rededication to the craft of the theater culminated in his first internationally successful play, *Philadelphia, Here I Come!*, initially performed at the Dublin Theater Festival in 1964 and subsequently appearing to great acclaim in New York and London. It concerns the conflicting thoughts and memories of a young Irishman before he immigrates to America and is a psychologically rich and clear-eyed look at contemporary Irish life. It employs the innovation of having a second actor play the private side of the protagonist Gar O'Donnell, seen and heard only by Gar and the audience. Since 1964 Friel has produced a remarkable series of plays that have been staged in Ireland, London, and New York, including *The Loves of Cass McGuire* (1966), *Lovers* (1967), *The Freedom of the City* (1972), *Volunteers* (1975), *The Faith Healer* (1979), *Aristocrats* (1979), *Making History* (1988), and perhaps his most famous play besides *Translations*, *Dancing at Lughnasa* (1991). It is a dramatic canon that supports the commonplace contention that Friel is the "heir apparent" of such towering figures as O'Casey and Synge, the greatest living Irish playwright and a preeminent contemporary dramatist.

Translations serves as one of the crucial texts not only in Friel's canon but, in the words of more than one critic, as "a watershed in Irish theatrical history." Friel has described his early plays, including *Philadelphia, Here I Come!*, as "attempts at analyzing different kinds of love" through individual, family, and community relationships. Beginning in the 1970s the politics and history of Ireland, particularly the violence in the North and the consequences of Ireland's cultural dispossession, became central focuses of his work. Beginning with *Translations* Friel began to reflect contemporary themes in the wider context of Irish history, myth, and cultural conflict. The play represents a significant turning point, both in Friel's career and in Irish literary history. In central ways its production history is as important as the play itself, in keeping with the Irish dramatic tradition of the collision of playwright, play, audience, and times that marked the premieres of Yeats's *The Countess Cathleen*, Synge's THE PLAYBOY OF THE WESTERN WORLD, and O'Casey's THE PLOUGH AND THE STARS. With *Translations* reconciliation rather than riots became the main feature of the play's first performances.

In 1979 Friel and Belfast-born actor Stephen Rea created the Field Day Theatre Company in Derry, and *Translations* became its first production. In the midst of the worst days of the sectarian violence in Northern Ireland, Field Day set out "to contribute to the solution to the present crisis by producing analyses of the established opinions, myths and stereotypes which had become both a symptom and a cause of the current situation." By basing their company in Derry, Friel and Rea hoped to challenge the theatrical hegemony of Dublin, Belfast, London, and New York. "Apart from Synge," Friel has remarked, "all our dramatists have pitched their voices for English acceptance and recognition. . . . However, I think that for the first time this is stopping. . . . We are talking to ourselves as we must and if we are overheard in America, or England, so much the better." Strikingly the premiere of *Translations* took place in Derry's Guildhall, a longtime symbol of Unionist repression that Friel had formerly used as the setting for *The Freedom of the City*, where civil rights demonstrators seek shelter from the violence outside and eventually emerge to their deaths. Instead of a symbol of division and oppression the Guildhall became a meeting ground for both sides at the premiere of *Translations* on September 23, 1980, in which Unionists and Republicans both acclaimed a modern Irish masterpiece. The *Times* critic declared of the subsequent London production, "I have never been more certain of witnessing the premiere of a national classic."

Translations opens in a hedge school in Baile Beag (before it is Anglicized to Ballybeg) run by the classical scholar and alcoholic Hugh O'Donnell, as his son Manus is teaching Sarah, a mute young peasant girl, to say her name. It is a striking opening image in a play in which language, names, and identity all will become central themes. Also striking is the theatrical premise that these are Irish speakers using English, a language they do not understand. Their words have been translated for an English-speaking audience, vividly emphasizing the language loss to come as English asserts its power and control. Manus's success in getting Sarah to say her name—to experience language for the first time and begin the process of communication—prompts his exultant cry,

"Nothing'll stop us now! Nothing in the wide world!" The phrase will turn decisively ironic as the outside forces that will stop Manus, Sarah, and the rest make their appearance. Hugh's other son, Owen, arrives with the news that he is involved with the British engineers as a translator. When the British appear—represented by Captain Lancey and Lieutenant Yolland—Owen must deal with the difficulty of translating Lancey's words into Irish and the community's response back into English, while coping with the misunderstandings and misperceptions of both sides. This initial clash of cultures makes clear that true communication and true understanding face enormous linguistic, cultural, and historical barriers.

In act 2 the work of Anglicizing the place-names begins, and Yolland, who is falling under the spell of Irish life, begins to understand that finding English equivalents for Irish place-names is no simple matter. As Hugh comments, "Yes it is a rich language, Lieutenant, full of mythologies of fantasy and hope and self-deception—a syntax opulent with tomorrows. It is our response to mud cabins and a diet of potatoes; our only method of replying to . . . inevitabilities." At risk, therefore, is more than a language but a way of seeing and understanding the world that is threatened with extinction both from within and without. The linguistic dilemma is embodied in the second scene of the act in which Yolland's and the young Irish girl Maire's lovemaking becomes a sequence of miscommunications. Only by reciting the Irish place-names that Yolland has been charged to replace do they manage a mutual understanding that culminates in a nonverbal act of communion: a kiss. Sarah, who witnesses the act and judges it a betrayal of Maire's suitor, Manus, will ironically use her newly discovered speech against the lovers and provoke the tragedy to come.

Act 3 explores the aftermath and consequences of the various errors of miscommunication and understanding. Yolland is missing; Manus, humiliated by Maire's betrayal but unable to bring himself to challenge his rival, is readying his departure. The community is plunged into the cycle of violence and retaliation that sets the terms for Ireland's future history. Lancey arrives to announce forced evictions "and leveling of every abode in the following selected areas" but needs Owen now to translate the newly Anglicized place-names back into Irish to be understood. Sarah is intimidated back into silence, and the play concludes with more questions than answers. One of the most pointed is Hugh's final comments about the nature of language itself and the historical moment. Here, as elsewhere in the play, Friel resists the temptation of easy nostalgia about the now-lost Irish past or the usual dichotomy between victims and victimized for a more charged confrontation with an actuality in which all are culpable. Hugh asserts that language (and culture) is neither permanent nor absolute. "We like to think we endure around truths immemorially posited, but we remember that words are signals, counters. They are not immortal. And it can happen . . . that a civilization can be imprisoned in a linguistic contour which no longer matches the landscape of . . . fact."

Language, according to Hugh, is a continual translation between historical circumstance and human needs. Accordingly, Hugh insists, "We must learn those new names. . . . We must learn where we live. We must learn to make them our own. We must make them our new home." In the course of *Translations* Friel has himself brilliantly translated the historical moment and historical necessity into compelling human terms in the lives of ordinary people with a critical perspective that serves past, present, and future.

THE BEGGAR'S OPERA

67

(1728)

by John Gay

The Beggar's Opera *shows what can happen when mock-heroic irony is applied with some consistency to a character: the final effect is not so much to direct the satire to the thieves' betters as to dramatize social classes on the move upward and thus produce a comedy of manners. We observe the highwayman who sees himself as an aristocrat, flaunting his gentility and generosity, and the thief-takers and jailers who see themselves as merchants, with ledgers always at hand and talk of responsibility and duty on their lips.*

—Ronald Paulson, "Mock-Heroic Irony and the Comedy of Manners"

On January 29, 1728, one of the most original works in the history of the English stage opened in London, at the Lincoln's Inn Fields Theatre. *The Beggar's Opera* featured a dashing highwayman, an ingenue, a wronged lover, thieves, whores, and informers. It was overlaid with political and social satire aimed at the court of George II and the corrupt Whig administration of Prime Minister Robert Walpole, mocked the class structure of the time, and ridiculed sentimental, pastoral, and romantic themes. It also introduced a new genre: the ballad opera, a play with numerous songs set to familiar tunes, here with John Gay's words, including numerous double entendres. *The Beggar's Opera* became an instant and unprecedented success, remained hugely popular for the rest of the century, and went on to inspire adaptations and imitations, most notably the 1928 Bertolt Brecht–Kurt Weill masterpiece, *The Threepenny Opera.* Its influence is seen in such diverse literary and theatrical talents and genres as Henry Fielding, Gilbert and Sullivan, and American musical comedy.

Gay's fame rests primarily on *The Beggar's Opera,* which represents the high point of his talent and career. Gay's achievements have historically been overshadowed by the greater accomplishments of his contemporaries, the literary giants Alexander Pope and Jonathan Swift. His milieu was not the court, where he failed to secure a lucrative appointment and thus lacked the success necessary for widespread popularity, but rather the life of the London streets.

His accessibility was therefore to the common reader and playgoer. In his *Lives of the Poets* (1779), Samuel Johnson observes that Gay's many friends "regarded him as a play-fellow, rather than a partner, and treated him with more fondness than respect." Recent scholars and critics have looked beyond Gay's flippant humor, such as his self-composed epitaph—"Life is a jest; and all things show it. / I thought so once; but now I know it."—to recognize the ironic and ambiguous quality of truth telling that informs his poetry and plays.

Born in Barnstaple, Devon, in 1685, Gay was the youngest of four surviving children in a family that included tradesmen, clergymen, and soldiers. When Gay was 10, his parents, William and Katherine Hammer Gay, died, and he went to live with his uncle Thomas Gay. He attended the local grammar school in Barnstaple, where he received an excellent education that included the performance of plays and the translating of classics into English verse; among Gay's efforts was a copy of Horace, with Gay's annotations, which still survives. Because Gay lacked both wealth and land he was unable to pursue the life of an independent gentleman, and at 17 he was apprenticed to a silk merchant in London. By 1706 he had negotiated a release from his articles, possibly because of bad health, and he returned to Barnstaple to live with another uncle, John Hammer, a dissenting minister. After Hammer's death in 1707 Gay made his way back to London, securing a position there as secretary to his school friend, Aaron Hill, a minor playwright and magazine editor, who possessed the money and connections to help support Gay's literary ambitions and his entrée into literary circles. In 1708 Gay anonymously published his first poem, "Wine," a high-spirited blank-verse Miltonic burlesque with shifts of tone ranging from jesting ridicule to lyrical sincerity as it explores the virtues and vagaries of the title beverage. Hill's subsequent tenures as manager of the Theatre Royal Drury Lane, and the Queen's Theatre opera house provided Gay with an opportunity to learn how the London theater world functioned, and Hill's collaboration with composer Georg Friedrich Handel on *Rinaldo*, Handel's first opera in England, gave Gay a first taste of opera and a preliminary understanding of the concept of integrating words and music. Gay himself would later write the libretto for Handel's short pastoral opera, *Acis and Galatea*, completed in 1722 but not produced until 1732, the year of Gay's death.

During his career Gay supported himself through the wealthy patronage of such aristocrats as Richard Boyle, Lord Burlington; Charles and Catherine Douglas, the duke and duchess of Queensbury; and Anne Scott, duchess of Monmouth, for whom he became domestic steward and secretary in 1712. The same year, in response to the demands of London theatergoers for short dramas, Gay presented to the managers of the Drury Lane theater, *The Mohocks*, a one-act tragicomical farce in three scenes to be used as an afterpiece. The play concerns a gang of London street toughs called Mohocks (a name bowdlerized by Londoners after a group of Mohawk Indians who had visited the city in 1710). In the play the Mohocks, ruled over by an "emperor," capture members of the night watch, disguise themselves in their clothes, and bring the captives before the justices of the peace, who charge the watch with being the gang. A version of the truth is eventually revealed, and the play ends with a dance. The issue of marauding Mohocks became politicized, with Whigs and Tories accusing one another of "Mohocking." This, together with Gay's large cast, led the cautious Drury Lane management to reject *The Mohocks*, although Gay did have the play published. More important, Gay's first play contained a contraposition of values that would later feature in *The Beggar's Opera*.

Gay followed *The Mohocks* with, *The Rural Sports* (1713), a long poem contrasting city and country life, which was dedicated to his lifelong friend Pope, and *The Fan* (1713), a long poem about the values and concerns of polite and fashionable society that has suffered in comparison with Pope's much more successful mock heroic, *The Rape of the Lock* (1714). At this time, despite his early assertion that he "never cared one farthing either for Tory or Whig," Gay publicly went over to the Tory side, associating himself with Pope, Swift, Dr. John Arbuthnot, a Scottish author and court physician to Queen Anne, and the Tory lord treasurer Robert Harley, the earl of Oxford, in the Scriblerus Club, a literary club founded to mock "all the false tastes in learning." Gay's position as the club's secretary solidly placed him at the center of prestigious London literary society, and the members' collaborative penchant for the burlesque form influenced his playwriting.

Gay's first major success was *The Shepherd's Week* (1714), a long mock pastoral poem derived from his youth in Devon, in which he made extensive use of folklore and folk dialect and customs. In 1716 he shifted his focus from country to town in the poem, *Trivia: or, The Art of Walking the Streets of London*. Both poems express Gay's ambiguous feelings concerning his former rural life and the city life he had chosen. His subsequent best-known works of poetry include the anthology *Poems on Several Occasions* (1720) and *Fables* (1727), a series of moral tales in verse, a second volume of which was published posthumously in 1738.

The first of Gay's plays to be produced was *The Wife of Bath* (1713), a reflection on marriage, femininity, and pedigree, set in Chaucer's England as Gay imagined it. As in *The Mohocks*, Gay used songs throughout the play, one of which, "There was a Swain full fair," became a popular air and shows Gay's emerging power as a lyricist. Gay's next, and more popularly successful effort, *The What d'ye Call It* (1715), is a tragicomic pastoral farce featuring a modestly convoluted plot and an infusion of literary satire, an influence of Gay's association with the Scriblerus Club. With its perception that in a class-dominated society rich and poor are essentially alike, *The What d'ye Call It* contains the seeds of what would become *The Beggar's Opera*. Gay's sense of satire became more focused and sophisticated with his next play, *Three Hours after Marriage* (1717), a farce about infidelity featuring pretense, disguise, and satiric barbs at current literary figures, the identities of whom have remained open to speculation. Gay next turned to tragedy with *Dione* (1720), a pastoral tale of unrequited love in Arcadia in rhymed pentameter couplets that was never produced, and *The Captives*, a heroic tragedy produced in 1724. Although *The Captives* was financially profitable for Gay, who read it to the princess of Wales, neither it nor his subsequent *Fables* resulted in the preferment at court he had long desired. The tragedy form was also not one with which he felt comfortable, and he never attempted the genre again. Instead Gay returned to burlesque, with an idea that had first been suggested by his fellow Scriblerians. In 1716 Swift had written to Pope about a possible project for Gay: "What think you of a Newgate pastoral, among the whores and thieves there?" Gay's "Newgate pastoral," became a mock pastoral, in which he drew on English and French theatrical traditions, the commedia dell'arte, the folklore and argot of the London underworld, and popular and formal music. The result, *The Beggar's Opera*, was a sexual, social, political, and literary burlesque that would join Pope's *The Dunciad* and Swift's *Gulliver's Travels* as the third great satirical work of the decade.

The Beggar's Opera begins with an Introduction, in which the playwright, a beggar, explains to one of the players: "Throughout the whole piece you may observe such a similitude of manners in high and low life, that it is difficult to determine whether (in the fashionable vices) the fine gentlemen imitate the gentlemen of the road, or the gentlemen of the road the fine gentlemen." His characters are amoral rather than immoral; "honor" is a virtue to be treated with irony. We meet Peachum, a fence for a group of London thieves and a police informer, both honorable occupations in his view, since the former affords him a living and the latter disposes of those rogues who are unproductive. Peachum's song, the opening ballad, sets the tone and theme of the play suggested earlier by the beggar-playwright:

> Through all the Employments of Life
> Each Neighbour abuses his Brother;
> Whore and rogue they call Husband and Wife;
> All Professions be-rogue one another.
> The Priest calls the Lawyer a Cheat,
> The Lawyer be-knaves the Divine;
> And the Statesman, because he's so great,
> Thinks his Trade as honest as mine.

Peachum and his wife discover that their daughter, Polly, has married Captain Macheath, a handsome highwayman (a character inspired by Jonathan Wild, the leader of a gang of London thieves). The Peachums fear that their new son-in-law will learn family secrets, have them hanged, and thus gain the fortune intended for their daughter. The two try to persuade Polly to betray her husband to the authorities, but she warns Macheath of the danger, and he decides to go into hiding with his gang until Polly's parents relent. He stays behind at a tavern, while his men go about their thieving business, to pay his respects to his women. Jenny Diver, one of this motley crew of female pickpockets and whores, betrays Macheath to Peachum, who arrives with the constables to arrest the highwayman and take him to Newgate Prison. There, Peachum and Lockit, the Newgate warder, reflect on the subject of bribery and vice, and the delicacy of their positions in the wider context of satire:

> When you censure the age,
> Be cautious and sage,
> Lest the Courtiers offended should be:
> If you mention vice or bribe,
> 'Tis so pat to all the tribe;
> Each cries—That was levell'd at me.

The two quarrel over who should receive the reward and question each other's honesty, then agree to split the take, both knowing full well that each has the power to hang the other. Macheath encounters the warder's daughter, Lucy, whom he had earlier promised to marry. She agrees to help him buy off her father in exchange for lighter fetters (Macheath: "Money, well tim'd, and properly apply'd, will do anything") if he will swear that the rumor of his marriage to Polly in false. Enter Polly, who squabbles with Lucy, prompting Macheath's famous lament:

> How happy could I be with either,
> Were t'other dear charmer away!
> But while you thus teaze me together,
> To neither a word will I say.

An angry Peachum arrives and carries off Polly. Lucy relents and helps Macheath to escape, but he is betrayed once again, this time by Diana Trapes, a procuress, who innocently tells Peachum and Lockit that the highwayman is with one of her girls. At Newgate again, Macheath is condemned to the gallows. Polly and Lucy beg their fathers to spare Macheath's life, but neither parent is moved. Resigned to his fate, Macheath reflects ironically that the rich can escape the gallows but the poor man must swing. The player and beggar-playwright reappear, the former protesting that to let Macheath hang would be to turn the opera into "a downright deep tragedy." The latter responds: "Your objection, Sir, is very just; and is easily removed. For you must allow, that in this kind of Drama, 'tis no matter how absurdly things are brought about—So—you rabble there—run and cry 'a Reprieve'—let the prisoner be brought back to his wives in triumph." Macheath is reprieved, gallantly chooses Polly as his lawful wife and vows to give up the vices—if not the follies—of the rich.

Gay first presented *The Beggar's Opera* to eminent actor-manager Colley Cibber, who, to his everlasting chagrin, declined to produce it. John Rich, of the Theatre Royal, took it reluctantly. His fears of a flop proved unwarranted; the play proved to be a popular and financial success, leading to the quip that *The Beggar's Opera* "made Gay rich and Rich gay." Gay quickly responded with a sequel, *Polly* (1729), but the production of the new play was prohibited by the lord chamberlain, acting on the king's instructions and probably under Walpole's influence. However, the play sold well in book form, and although it definitively ended Gay's hopes of court patronage, *Polly* ironically ended his lifelong financial insecurity. Gay died of a fever in December 1732 while in the midst of arranging the production of his opera *Achilles*. He is buried in Westminster Abbey, next to Chaucer's tomb. Together with his self-written epitaph is one by Pope: "In wit, a man; simplicity a child."

Gay's achievement in *The Beggar's Opera* was to create a sharply satirical yet simply plotted work with a jocularity and bawdiness that, unlike the Restoration comedies of manners and the burlesques and farces popular at the time, does not contain complicated and interwoven subplots to divert attention. Moreover, the play can be enjoyed and appreciated by audiences unfamiliar with the politics, society, and theater of the playwright's own time. With its tone of absurdity *The Beggar's Opera* was adapted perfectly by Brecht and Weill for the alienated, expressionistic sensibilities of post–World War I Weimar German culture in *The Threepenny Opera*. The influence of *The Beggar's Opera* has been wide reaching, from the mock pastoral of Henry Fielding's *Tom Jones* and the operettas of Gilbert and Sullivan to the American musical comedy and the ballad musicals of Andrew Lloyd Weber, all of which owe much to Gay's masterpiece of irony and ambiguity.

AMPHITRYON

(c. 186 B.C.)

by Plautus

68

The Amphitruo *is a resoundingly comic and healthy response to man's dilemma in the face of the caprices of the gods. Plautus takes the dark despair of the* Bacchae *and converts it into a celebration of the powers of comic theatre. . . . The object of this joyous celebration is the traditional Roman theater itself, with its adultery plots, clever slaves, and mass confusion. Plautus dethrones Dionysos and puts in his place the benevolent genius of comedy.*
—Niall W. Slater, *"Amphitruo, Bacchae,* and Metatheatre," in *Oxford Readings in Menander, Plautus, and Terence*

Amphitryon (Amphitruo in Latin) is the masterwork of the Roman dramatist Plautus, who has been hailed as the father of European comedy and farce. In this exuberantly bawdy, topsy-turvy tale of mistaken identity and intrigue, Jupiter dupes the Theban general Amphitryon by impersonating him to bed Amphitryon's wife, Alcmena, while Mercury complicates matters by assuming the likeness of Amphitryon's slave, Sosia. The story of Amphitryon and Alcmena stands behind only that of Oedipus and Medea as the most popular classical dramatic subjects, and Plautus's version is the only extant example of mythological travesty in Roman comedy. The play has been reworked and adapted in subsequent eras, by Molière, John Dryden, and Heinrich von Kleist, and in modern versions by Jean Giraudoux (*Amphitryon 38*, 1929) and by Harold Pinter (*The Lovers*, 1963). Even though William Shakespeare relied mainly on Plautus's *Twin Menaechmi* (the first ancient play to be translated into a modern European language and put on stage in Italy in 1486) for *The Comedy of Errors*, he had the precedent in *Amphitryon* for identical twin servants and the exclusion of Antipholus from his own house while his twin was inside. Plautus's drama has served as a storehouse of comic effects—of clever wordplay and farcical situations—and one of the most influential of all comedies that helped to establish Plautus as a contentious but unavoidable dramatist. "Of all the Greek and Roman playwrights," classicist Erich Segal has asserted, "Titus Maccius Plautus is the least admired and the most imitated. 'Serious'

scholars find him insignificant, while serious writers find him indispensable."
The first known professional playwright, Plautus left the largest corpus of
classical dramatic works (20 extant complete plays), and he is, along with Terence, the principal source for our understanding of the development of drama
from the Attic to the Roman stage and from classical to modern European
theater.

Little is certain beyond legend regarding Plautus's life and career. Believed
to have been born in the Umbrian city of Sarsina c. 254 B.C., Plautus is said
to have gained a fortune in connection with the theater, possibly as an actor,
which he subsequently lost on a failed mercantile venture. Tradition has it that
he was then forced to subsist as a worker in a flour mill. During this time, at
the age of 50, he wrote his first surviving comedies. He would amass a second
fortune from the stage and become the most popular and successful of all
Roman playwrights, with as many as 130 plays attributed to him, including
The Pot of Gold, The Capives, The Braggart Warrior, and *Pseudolus.* Plautus's success in pleasing a diverse (and often unsophisticated) popular audience with
rollicking farce and bawdy language drew the ire of such literary custodians
as Horace, who criticized the playwright for breaking all the rules of proper
dramatic construction and decorum to please and to profit. Subsequent critics
have echoed Horace's high-minded condescension regarding Plautus's pandering to the vulgar demands of his audience. Plautus is intriguing and significant,
however, as the first dramatist to depend solely on his audience's approval for
economic survival. His works therefore provide instructive examples of popular Roman entertainment, showing how, like Shakespeare in a similar era of
commercial theater, a dramatist could cater to, modify, and transform popular
taste. Plautus is best appreciated as a dramatic pioneer who in gratifying his
audience's tastes discovered many of the essential methods, situations, and
characters of comic drama that have persisted for more than two millennia.
After Plautus died in 184 B.C., Cicero is said to have memorialized him with
these words: "After Plautus has met his death, Comedy goes into mourning,
the theater is deserted; then Laughter, Sport and Jest, and Immeasurable Measures with one accord have burst into tears."

To understand *Amphitryon* and Plautine dramatic achievement it is instructive to consider the drama that he inherited. Tradition dates the beginning of
Roman drama to 240 B.C. when a Greek from Tarentum, a Greek settlement
in southern Italy, named Livius Andronicus first presented Latin translations
of Greek plays at the Ludi Romani, the annual festival in Rome of games
and entertainments. If Livius Andronicus is credited with introducing the
first "plays with plots" to a Roman audience and the first to expose Romans
to the Greek dramatic tradition, preliterary, indigenous dramatic forms had
previously flourished in Italy. Horace traced the origin of Roman theater
back to the Etruscan Fescennine songs—improvised satrical and bawdy choral performances of masked singers at harvest and wedding celebrations—

associated with the Etruscan city of Fescennium. Livy pointed to another Etruscan source in the 364 B.C. arrival at Rome of Etruscan musical and dancing performers. Improvised dialogue was subsequently added to these performances, first by amateurs and later by professionals, and according to Livy, the Romans derived their term for actors (*histriones*) from the Etruscan word *ister* for player, affirming an Etruscan basis for Roman drama. As adapted by the Romans, Livy called these early theatrical entertainments *satura*, or medleys of song, dance, and dialogue. Another native source for Roman drama is the so-called *fabula Atellana*. Named for the town in Compania where they are thought to have originated, these were short farces performed by masked actors representing, as in the commedia dell'arte, stock characters such as the clown Maccus (from whom Plautus's middle name may have derived), the glutton or braggart Bucco, the gullible old man Pappus, and the trickster Dossennus. The Roman drama that Plautus inherited, therefore, was an amalgam of Greek New Comedy models and indigenous farcical, satirical, musical, dance, and bawdy elements.

Roman plays, like the Greek's, were performed in connection with festivals several times a year but not, like the Athenian drama competitions, as the centerpiece of a celebration. Roman stage plays instead had to compete with other forms of popular entertainment, including athletic competitions, gladiatorial fights, chariot races, and animal baiting for audience share. Roman playgoers lacked the sophisticated appreciation of dramatic tradition acquired by the Greeks and restively demanded diversion and entertainment over edification or challenge to immediate gratification. There were no permanent theaters in Rome before 55 B.C., so plays were performed on temporary wooden stages made to resemble a city street. Most actors were slaves owned by a theatrical company's manager or freedmen of notoriously low esteem who could be beaten for a bad performance, as Mercury reminds the audience in the prologue to *Amphytron*. Something of the knockabout, carnival quality of Roman theater is captured in the prologue to Plautus's *The Carthaginian* in which the audience is instructed in proper decorum:

> Let no worn-out harlot sit in front of the stage, nor the magistrate or his rods make a sound, nor the usher roam about in front of people or show anyone to a seat while the actor is on the stage. Those who have had a long leisurely nap at home should now cheerfully stand, or at least refrain from sleeping. Keep slaves from occupying the seats, that there will be room for free men, or let them pay money for their freedom. . . . And let the nurses keep tiny children at home and not bring them to see the play, lest the nurses themselves get thirsty and the children die of hunger or cry for food like young goats. Let matrons view the play in silence, laugh in silence, refrain from tinkling tones of chatter; they should take home their gossip, so as not to annoy their husbands both here and at home.

And, now, as to what concerns the directors of the games, no actor should receive the prize unjustly, nor should any be driven out through favoritism so that inferior actors are preferred to the good ones. And there's this point, too, which I had almost forgotten: while the show is going on, lackeys, make an attack on the bakery; rush in now while there is an opportunity, while the tarts are hot.

Plautus conjures a theater that is a vital, unruly, raucus meeting place for all comers—freedman and slave alike—who were easily distracted, hard to please, easy to displease, and a challenge for the dramatist to subdue and master.

All of Plautus's comedies are believed to be adaptations of lost Greek New Comedy originals, begging the question of Plautus's innovations and genius. Plautus's craftsmanship and orginality were, however, decisively confirmed with the discovery in 1958 of the first complete text of a comedy by Menander, *Dyskolos* (*The Grouch*), and in 1969 of 42 lines from Menander's *Dis Exapaton* (*The Double Dealer*), a play that Plautus adapted as *Bacchides*. Comparison with both Menandrian sources makes it clear that Plautus should be credited with far more genius than just ability as a translator. Plautus demonstrates his gifts as a comic craftsman who transformed his subdued, decorous, and somewhat threadbare New Comedy sources into a robust and rollicking situational comedy of ingenious invention and clever wordplay. He eliminated the chorus used in Greek comedies and thereby abandoned Attic drama's episodic division between dialogue and song, shifting the force of his dramas to nonstop action. Plautus also integrated the musical elements associated with the chorus throughout his plays. It is believed that about two-thirds of each of Plautus's works were accompanied by music, causing Plautine drama to resemble modern musical comedy with some scenes spoken and others sung to musical accompaniment. Like Greek New Comedy, Plautus's comedies steer away from political and social issues to concentrate on everyday, domestic situations surcharged with sufficient bawdiness and slapstick to hold the widest possible audience.

Amphitryon shows Plautus's comic inventiveness and stagecraft at his innovative and daring best. If Plautine comedy is ruled by comic misunderstandings and fueled by mistaken identities, misunderstood motives, and deliberate deceptions, all three are ingeniously featured in Jupiter's duping of Amphitryon and Alcmena. All of Plautus's comedies begin with a prologue to clarify the background of the dramatic action, identify the performers, and, in a sense, let the audience in on the jokes to come. The prologue of *Amphitryon* is delivered by Jupiter's son, Mercury, who, taking the form of Sosia, Amphitryon's slave, prepares the audience for the play's comic inversions. Mercury makes clear that the greatest of the gods, Jupiter, will here take the part of an actor in a play of his own devising. Impersonating Amphitryon, returning after an absence on the battlefield, Jupiter will enjoy a "reunion" with the Theban general's wife, Alcmena. The presence of gods on stage as an adulterer is far from a laughing matter, and Mercury conjures a new hybrid dramatic genre to justify both as subjects for the audience's amusement:

> Now first I'll tell you what I come to say;
> And then explain the plot, which underlies
> This tragedy; but why contract your brows,
> When I say tragedy? For I'm a god
> And soon can change it; if you like I'll make
> These selfsame verses be a comedy.
> Shall I or not? But sure I am a fool,
> Being a god, and yet not knowing what you wish.
> Ah, yes! I know your mind; and I will make it
> A tragicomedy; for it is not right
> To make a play where kings and gods do speak
> All comedy. But since a slave takes part
> I'll make it for you tragicomedy.

Amphitryon begins then with a cosmic and aesthetic reversal. Gods are usually not shown conspiring to cuckold a valiant general; nor should the potentially tragic themes of the gods' relationship with humankind as well as the revered Roman value of marital chastity be mixed with the practical joke of duping master, mistress, and servant. Subversively, Plautus collides tragedy and comedy and daringly subjects the sacrosanct to unsettling and liberating misrule.

Sosia, whose arrival threatens to interrupt Jupiter's lovemaking, confronts his own likeness in the form of the disguised Mercury. The scene, one of the comic triumphs of the classical stage, has been called by the critic Niall W. Slater, "the *locus classicus* of the Doppelgänger (double) theme," in which Sosia begins to doubt his own identity: "Tell me where I've lost myself. Where was I transformed? Where did I misplace my face?" Sosia retreats in disarray to his master, and Jupiter and Alcmena emerge from their long night of lovemaking. Jupiter exits, propitiating Alcmena for his sudden departure by giving her the golden cup awarded to Amphitryon for his noble war service. With the arrival of the real Amphitryon and Sosia, it is now the master and mistress's turn to be baffled. Alcmena is shocked by her husband's sudden return, and her references to their lovemaking cause Amphitryon to suspect her fidelity. Despite the evidence of the golden cup to substantiate Alcmena's account, Amphitryon continues to doubt his wife and leaves for a witness to substantiate his having spent the past night aboard his ship. Jupiter returns again as Amphitryon and tries to soften Alcmena's anger at her husband's accusations. The frustrated Amphitryon comes back to his home to find his door barred against him, his servant (the disguised Mercury) abusing him, and Jupiter in his own likeness treating the former master with contempt. Escalating humiliation of Amphitryon concludes with the revelation that Alcmena has given birth to two sons, one by Amphitryon, and the other, Hercules, by Jupiter. In a witty use of the deus ex machina Jupiter the trickster becomes the cosmic restorer of order, explaining to Amphitryon what has happened and exonerating Alcmena from blame. Amphitryon dutifully accepts the divine will, and domestic peace is restored.

With its freewheeling fantasy, its breaking of dramatic illusion with direct addresses to the audience, and its irreverent mixing of the sacred and profane, *Amphitryon* recalls Aristophanes rather than the more staid, domestic New Comedy. Synthesizing both Old and New Comedy elements, challenging decorum, and extending comic boundaries, *Amphitryon* cleverly displays the resources of both the comedy of manners and the absurdist, self-reflexive modern dramas of Luigi Pirandello, Bertolt Brecht, Samuel Beckett, and others, while more than justifying a description of its author as a progenitor of Western comic drama.

NO EXIT

69

(1944)   *by Jean-Paul Sartre*

It is a sort of living death to be surrounded by the ceaseless concern for judgments and action that one does not even desire to change. In fact, since we are alive, I wanted to demonstrate, through the absurd, the importance for us of liberty, i.e. the importance of changing our acts by other acts. Whatever the circle of hell in which we live, I think we are free to break out of it. And if people do not break out, they stay there of their own free will. In this way they choose to live in hell.

—Jean-Paul Sartre, Preface to the Deutsche Gramaphon recording of *No Exit*

Although drama was only a small part of Jean-Paul Sartre's remarkable oeuvre that included the central texts of French existentialism—the philosophical movement that he named and spearheaded—in the forms of novels, essays, and an almost continual stream of articles, Sartre is unique among philosophers in illustrating his ideas in literary works. Of his nine plays *No Exit* is centrally important both as a crucial text applying the philosophical precepts that dominated the post–World War II era and as a formulation of a new kind of drama that significantly influenced the theater in the second half of the 20th century. Scholar Robert Solomon has called *No Exit* "one of philosophy's most profound contributions to the theater," while Irish critic Vivien Mercier has suggested that all of Samuel Beckett's major plays, and by extension the theater of the absurd, ultimately derive from it. *No Exit* therefore commands attention as a vehicle for its influential ideas and its dramatic methods that established new possibilities for the drama.

No Exit and the ideas that gave birth to it derived from Sartre's attempt to make sense of the moral and metaphysical implications of the German occupation of France during World War II. Born in Paris in 1905, Sartre was the only son of a naval officer who died when Sartre was only 15 months old. His mother, a second cousin of the German-born theologian, musicologist, humanitarian, and Nobel laureate Albert Schweitzer, raised her son with the help of her grandparents. One of Sartre's earliest intellectual influences was his grandfather Charles Schweitzer, a professor of German, who educated his grandson and stimulated Sartre's love of literature and intellectual ambition. The central trauma of Sartre's childhood came when his mother remarried in 1916 to a man Sartre despised. Sartre would feel both abandoned and dispossessed in his home, feelings that would later figure prominently as the existential anguish of a purposeless life. Sartre attended the École Normale Superieure where he studied philosophy and met fellow philosophy student Simone de Beauvoir, with whom he would maintain a lifelong personal and intellectual relationship. Sartre spent much of the 1930s teaching philosophy and studying the works of German philosophers Edmund Husserl and Martin Heidegger, who, along with Friedrich Nietzsche and Søren Kierkegaard, anticipated many of the key concepts of existentialism. Sartre's prewar philosophical writings reflect the influence of Husserl's phenomenology and focus on the workings and structure of consciousness. Sartre's first novel, *La nausée* (1938; *Nausea*), depicts a man's reaction to the absurdity of existence, and his story collection *Le mur* (1939; *The Wall*) offers various explorations of relationships, sexuality, insanity, and the implication of human action—scenarios that prefigure an analysis of the human condition Sartre would evolve in existentialism.

With the outbreak of the war Sartre joined the army, was captured by the Germans, and spent nine months in a prison camp. There he began his career as a playwright, writing, directing, and acting in a Christmas play for his fellow prisoners of war, *Bariona, ou Le Fils du tonnerre* (*Bariona, or The Son of Thunder*). The play adapts the nativity story as a context to illustrate the imperatives of human freedom and the necessity of resistance to oppression. Sartre would later insist that his experience as a prisoner of war was a crucial and positive experience in his personal and philosophical evolution, and the play anticipates a new sense of engagement that began to dominate Sartre's thinking. Released in 1941 Sartre returned to occupied Paris and joined the Resistance. While at work on the fundamental existential treatise *L'Etre et le néant* (*Being and Nothingness*) in 1942, Sartre conceived his second play, *Les Mouches* (*The Flies*), like his first, on the theme of freedom and resistance but based on a reinterpretation of Aeschylus's *The Libation Bearers*. In Sartre's version the community of Argos, plagued with flies as divine punishment for having permitted the murder of Agamemnon and accepted the tyranny of Aegisthus, is redeemed and liberated by Orestes, who defies supernatural authority and accepts responsibility for his vengeance on his mother and her lover. Sartre would later argue that his interpretation of the Orestes story was intended to provide moral support to Resistance fighters while reflecting a critique of the French moral dilemma under occupation that would provide the key concepts of existentialism. Responding to the sense of helplessness and despair felt by the French under the German occupation, existentialism recognizes that even in the worst circumstances humans still have choices and therefore freedom.

Human consciousness, Sartre argues, acquires meaning through choices, and all are responsible to consider the ramifications of choices made or not made and fully accept the consequences. Evasion results in inauthentic action, delusion, or what Sartre calls "bad faith." An encouragement toward action and responsibility under an oppressive regime that negated both, existentialism as articulated by Sartre and fellow writer Albert Camus, whom Sartre first met at a performance of *The Flies*, would serve as a compelling response to the horrors of the war that diminished free will and responsibility.

Sartre's next play, *No Exit*, is a forceful parable embodying the key concepts of existentialism. In it Sartre made a virtue of the conditions governing French theater under the occupation. Censorship restricted what could be said on stage, and practical considerations, including the curfew and limited resources, constrained how. The actress Gaby Sylvia, who played the role of Estelle in *No Exit*'s first performance, recalled that the play originated when Camus asked Sartre for a short play for four characters that could be performed in the home of friends:

> What do you find in any living room? A sofa, a small table, arm chairs, a mantel piece and sometimes a Barbedienne bronze sculpture. So much for the set. There would be no intermission, because of the curfew. Next necessity. There had to be a reason that these four characters are together in a living room and unable to leave it. "Let's shove them into hell," Sartre said to himself. And in two weeks at a table at the [Café] Flore he wrote *No Exit*.

Sartre's own account, recollected many years after the fact, differs slightly:

> When one writes a play, there are always chance circumstances and deep needs. The chance circumstance when I wrote *No Exit* in 1943 or the beginning of 1944 was the fact that I had three friends for whom I wanted to write a play, without giving any one of them a larger part than the others. In other words, I wanted them to be together on the stage all the time, because I said to myself: "If one of them leaves the stage, he'll think that the other two have better parts in his absence." So I wanted to keep them together, and I said to myself: "How can one put three characters together without an exit, and keep them there on stage to the end of the play, as though eternally?" That's when the idea came to me to put them in hell and make each one of them the torturer of the other two. That's the circumstantial cause.

Initially called "Les Autres" (The others), about characters trapped in a cellar during a bombardment, Sartre shifted the setting to hell, which resembled the Paris hotel room where the play was first rehearsed. Directed by Camus, who also, initially, played the role of Garcin, No Exit eventually premiered with a different cast and director at the 335-seat Théâtre du Vieux-Colombier on the eve of the Normandy invasion to largely hostile reviews. One critic observed that "The play censors itself because it is so boring," while others used adjectives such as "scandalous," "rotten," "venereal," and "lugubriously unhealthy" to describe it. After Paris was liberated in August 1944, the play reopened to considerable more appreciation as a challenging drama representative both of the wartime zeitgeist and a new kind of drama.

Sartre would describe this new French drama in a 1946 lecture he delivered in the United States, "Forgers of Myths," in which he called for the replacing of the 19th-century psychological theater of "caractères" (personalities) by "un théâtre de situations":

> Since the situation is what we care about above all, our theater shows it at the very point where it is about to reach its climax. We do not take time out for learned research, we feel no need of registering the imperceptible evolution of a character or a plot: one does not reach death by degrees, one is suddenly confronted with it—and if one approaches politics or love by slow degrees, then acute problems, arising suddenly, call for no progression. By taking our dramatis personae and precipitating them, in the very first scene, into the highest pitch of their conflicts we turn to the well-known pattern of classical tragedy, which always seizes upon the action at the very moment it is headed for catastrophe.

In what can serve both as an encapsulating description of No Exit and many of the plays that would follow it, Sartre summarizes:

> Our plays are violent and brief, centered around one single event; there are few players and the story is compressed within a short space of time, sometimes only a few hours. As a result they obey a kind of "rule of the three unities," which has been only a little rejuvenated and modified. A single set, a few entrances, a few exits, intense arguments among the characters who defend their individual rights with passions—this is what sets our plays at a great distance from the brilliant fantasies of Broadway.

No Exit opens with the South American journalist Garcin being led by a valet into a windowless, brightly lit drawing room in which three couches are positioned before a mantel with a heavy bronze statue on it. Garcin asks where are the "racks and red-hot pincers," and it soon becomes clear, despite the respectable furnishings and solicitude of the valet, that this is hell, where Garcin has been consigned for eternity. He is soon joined by Inez, a lesbian, and Estelle, a fashionable socialite. Each takes a seat on one of the sofas and relates the cause of his or her death: Estelle by pneumonia, Inez from the fumes of a gas stove, and Garcin by 12 bullets. To pass the time Garcin suggests that they should speculate why they have been damned. Estelle says that, though married to an older man, she has had an affair, and Garcin, who ran a pacifist newspaper, claims to have been executed for his treasonous views. Inez accuses them both of not telling the full truth, insisting that "We are criminals—murderers—all three of us. We're in hell, my pets; they never make mistakes, and people aren't damned for nothing." Perceptively Inez suggests that they are to be one another's torment. To counter this possibility Garcin proposes that "each of us stays put in his or her corner and take no notice of the others" and that way "we'll work out our salvation looking into ourselves." However, each is forced to an awareness of mutual dependence, though in a triangular relationship that guarantees their suffering. Inez is attracted to Estelle, who has long depended on men to validate her self-worth. Drawn accordingly to the formerly womanizing Garcin, Estelle (and Garcin) will be continually frustrated by the scorned and man-hating Inez. Realizing the futility of their situation and seizing on the opportunity for self-understanding, Garcin proposes that they should earnestly confess why they have been condemned. He admits that he had been abusive to his wife and that he was shot not because of his pacifist principles but because he had tried to save himself by running away; Inez confesses to having betrayed her cousin by seducing his wife and torturing her with his death; Estelle admits that she had a baby with her lover whom she murdered, causing her lover's suicide.

Faced with the shared knowledge of these shocking truths about themselves, each craves escape and release from the others' censure, yet when suddenly the drawing room door is opened, they take no action to leave. Garcin declares that he must stay to prove himself to Inez and reverse her judgment on his cowardice: "Only you two remain to give a thought to me. She—she doesn't count. It's you who matter; you who hate me. If you'll have faith in me I'm saved." Brought to the brink of self-knowledge and undeluded self-acceptance, Garcin manages a shattering understanding that concludes with the most famous line in the play:

> So this is hell. I'd never have believed it. You remember all we were told about the torture-chambers, the fire and brimstone, the "burning marl." Old wives' tales! There's no need for red-hot pokers. Hell is—other people!

When validation and identity derives from others, others become hell, a state where torture is not meted out by devils but self-inflicted and inescapable. As Sartre observed, "Relations with other people, encrustation, and freedom . . . are the three themes of the play. I should like you to remember this when you hear that hell is other people."

No Exit, as an intense and compressed dramatic parable, presents the core existential truth that each individual must ultimately face self-truth and consequence, forced to an inescapable encounter with others who provide the measure for moral judgment. In the enclosed space of the stage that mirrors the enclosed self Sartre presents a modern morality play, while forecasting the themes and methods that emerge from the implications of an absurd universe and a search for new meaning.

A RAISIN IN THE SUN

70

(1959)
by *Lorraine Hansberry*

A moving testament to the strength and endurance of the human spirit, A Raisin in the Sun *is a quiet celebration of the black family, the importance of African roots, the equality of women, the vulnerability of marriage, the true value of money, the survival of the individual, and the nature of man's dreams. A well-made play,* Raisin *at first seems a plea for racial tolerance or a fable of man's overcoming an insensitive society, but the simple eloquence of the characters elevates the play into a universal representation of all people's hopes, fears, and dreams.*

—Ann Cheney, *Lorraine Hansberry*

Lorraine Hansberry's groundbreaking play of a struggling working-class African-American Chicago family of the 1950s is an important and enduring work in the canon of classic American family dramas of the 20th century. First produced in an era when issues of segregation and integration were rising to the forefront of American consciousness and the civil rights movement that would reach its zenith in the next decade was taking shape, *A Raisin in the Sun* is a pre-1960s evocation of the African-American experience. Adding to its distinctiveness is the fact that it was the first play written by a black playwright and featuring African-American characters to appear on Broadway, the first Broadway play to be written by a black woman playwright, and the first to be directed by an African American.

Hansberry, justly known as the foremother of African-American drama, was a phenomenon at a time when successful women playwrights were rare and black women playwrights even more uncommon. She was born in Chicago in 1930, the youngest of four children of Carl Hansberry, a successful real estate agent, and Nannie Perry Hansberry. In 1938 the Hansberrys purchased a home in a white neighborhood, an event that caused racial tension in legally segregated Chicago. In an episode that was the genesis of *A Raisin in the Sun,* black family friends helped guard the house against white neighbors, one of whom had thrown a brick through the window, narrowly missing Lorraine.

After the family was evicted by the Illinois courts, Carl Hansberry, with the help of lawyers of the National Association for the Advancement of Colored People took the case to the Supreme Court. The landmark case, *Hansberry v. Lee*, resulted in a Court decision prohibiting racially restrictive covenants, but the family remained subjected to, as Lorraine Hansberry later described, "a hellishly hostile white neighborhood." Nevertheless, the Hansberry house was visited by such prominent African Americans and Harlem Renaissance figures as poet Langston Hughes, W. E. B. DuBois, Duke Ellington, and actor Paul Robeson, whom Lorraine had seen in *OTHELLO*. Hansberry attended a mostly white high school, where she excelled in English and history and was president of the debating society.

Hansberry went on to the University of Wisconsin and in 1950, after two years of college, left for New York City. There she took courses at the New School and supported herself by writing for the *Young Progressives of America* magazine and working on the staff of *Freedom* magazine, a radical black monthly published in Harlem by Robeson. Contributors to *Freedom* included DuBois, noted artist Charles White, and Alice Childress. Promoted to associate editor in 1951, Hansberry wrote articles for the magazine on such diverse topics as women's rights, the arts, social issues in New York, and African history and politics. She worked on behalf of civil rights issues, traveling to Mississippi with a delegation of women to present to the governor a petition with signatures gathered from around the world protesting the execution of a young black man, went to Uruguay to deliver a speech to a banned peace congress on behalf of Robeson, whose passport had been revoked, and attended the Sojourners for Truth Conference in Washington, D.C. In 1953 Hansberry married Robert Nemiroff, whom she had met on a picket line at New York University when Nemiroff was a graduate student there. The couple separated in 1957 and divorced in 1964, although they continued to collaborate. Hansberry died in 1965 at the age of 34 after a short battle with pancreatic cancer. Nemiroff, an editor, writer, lyricist, and producer, would produce Hansberry's second play, *The Sign in Sidney Brustein's Window* (1964), and *To Be Young, Gifted and Black* (1969), a play he adapted from many of her writings. He completed Hansberry's play, *Les Blancs*, which opened in 1970.

After marrying Nemiroff, Hansberry resigned from *Freedom* and took a series of jobs while she worked on three plays, including *The Crystal Stair*, which was begun in 1956. The title would be changed to *A Raisin in the Sun*, which is taken from Langston Hughes's "Harlem," a poem in his collection, *Montage of a Dream Deferred*. In 1956 Nemiroff scored a financial success with a hit song, "Cindy, Oh Cindy," which allowed Hansberry the freedom to write full time. In 1957 she read the first draft of *Raisin* to Philip Rose, a music publisher and family friend, who optioned the play for Broadway and spent the next year and a half attempting to get it produced. The outlook for the production of a play featuring African-American characters and written by an unknown black woman playwright seemed bleak at first, as did a play that ran for nearly three hours as originally written. Rose finally managed to secure some financial backing from the well-known actor-singer Harry Belafonte and other black cultural leaders. Lloyd Richards was hired as director and Sidney Poitier was convinced to star in the play. Hansberry cut some significant scenes from the first production, some of which have been included in later renditions of the play. After a successful tryout in New Haven, Connecticut, *A Raisin in the Sun* played to critical acclaim in Philadelphia and then had a successful run in Chicago before moving to Broadway, where it premiered on March 11, 1959.

The three-act play is set in the small, dreary one-bedroom apartment occupied by the Younger family in the working-class South Side area of Chicago. That the Youngers are poor is shown by the "tired" furniture, the fact that the family shares a hall bathroom with other tenants on their floor, and the cramped sleeping arrangements. Lena, the mother, is a retired domestic whose overworked husband has died, leaving her with an insurance policy worth $10,000. Lena's son, Walter Lee, is in his 30s. He works as a chauffeur for a rich white man and is disgusted with his job. He is married to Ruth, a housekeeper to a white family, and the couple have a 10-year-old son, Travis. Walter's highly intelligent, outspoken sister, Beneatha, is a college student who wants to become a doctor. The first act begins with the family having breakfast and arguing over how to spend the insurance money that is due to arrive the next day. Lena wants to put a down payment on a house in the suburbs, where they can all have a better life. Walter wants to invest the money in a liquor store with two friends, a scheme his mother opposes on religious grounds. Walter tells Beneatha, who knows her mother will use some of the money for her medical school tuition, that she should become a nurse or a wife "like a normal woman." He leaves for work, complaining that all black women belong to "the world's most backward race of people and that's a fact." The next morning Joseph Asagai, who has recently returned from his native Nigeria, brings Beneatha a traditional African gown and headdress, criticizes her for straightening her hair, which he views as racial assimilation and an aspiration to white values, and asserts that she should seek fulfillment as a wife. Beneatha likes the Yoruba nickname he has given her, *Alaiyo*, meaning "One for Whom Bread-Food Is Not Enough." As the first act ends Walter arrives in a state of excitement with the liquor store contracts and is bitter when Lena refuses to give him the money. His mother reveals that Ruth is pregnant and considering an abortion and urges him to convince her to have the baby. Walter, angry over the refusal of money and upset at the prospect of another mouth to feed, storms out of the house.

In the second act Beneatha is visited by another suitor, George Murchison, who is from a well-to-do African-American family. He has encouraged her to separate herself from her heritage and to be less serious about her studies. George views her African gown with derision and calls her "eccentric." Walter derides George in turn, making fun of his "faggoty-looking white shoes." Lena arrives with the news that she has bought a house in Clybourne Park, an all-white neighborhood. Walter is outraged and accuses his mother of destroying his dream. He misses three days of work and begins to drink heavily, causing his mother to rethink her decision and to offer him some of the money for his venture. The Youngers learn from a neighbor that there have been bombings of houses belonging to black families in white neighborhoods. The family's enthusiasm for the move remains strong, even when Karl Linder, a white man from the New Neighbors Orientation Committee arrives with an offer to buy the house from the Youngers at a profit. Although he presents himself as reasonable rather than as a racist, it is clear that his real goal is to keep black families from integrating Clybourne Park. The family refuses his offer and Walter throws him out. The family celebrates their impending move, and Lena is presented with a pair of gardening tools. The Youngers' joy is destroyed by the arrival of Bobo, Walter's friend and business partner, who tells them that their other partner, Willy, has absconded with the money. Walter has lost everything, including the money his mother gave him, which was to be deposited in the bank and used for Beneatha's schooling. The Youngers' dreams have been completely crushed.

The third act consists of one scene, in which Joseph Asagai asks Beneatha to return with him to Nigeria and shares with her his dream of a politically independent Africa freed from colonialism. Beneatha questions whether new regimes would be as corrupt and violent as the old, but Asagai argues that independence is worth fighting and dying for and that such questions are for the future. (This interchange shows remarkable perspicacity on the part of Hansberry, given the political and sectarian turmoil that has defined many African states after independence was gained.) A humiliated Walter offers to sell the house to Linder, but Lena objects to taking the money to "tell us we ain't fit to walk the earth. . . . We ain't never been that poor. We ain't ever been that—dead inside." When Linder appears to close the deal Walter has a change of heart. He speaks eloquently of his father's hard work and the family's pride and introduces his sister as a future doctor and his son as the sixth generation of American Youngers. They will not sell the house but rather move to Clybourne Park as planned. Lena tells Ruth that her son has finally come into his manhood that day. The family leaves for better, if uncertain circumstances in their new neighborhood.

A critical and popular success, *A Raisin in the Sun* ran for nearly two years and earned for Hansberry the added achievement of becoming the youngest playwright and the first black playwright to win the New York Drama Critics Circle Award, no small honor in a season that included plays by Eugene O'Neill and Tennessee Williams. Hansberry wrote the screenplay for the well-received 1961 film version of her play, which also starred Sidney Poitier and which earned Hansberry a nomination from the Screen Actors Guild. A Tony Award–winning musical adaptation of the play, *Raisin*, with a musical book by Robert Nemiroff, played on Broadway from 1973 to 1975.

Noted critic Kenneth Tynan, in his review of the play for the *New Yorker* magazine, wrote: "I was not present at the opening, twenty-four years ago, of Mr. Odets' *Awake and Sing!*, but it must have been a similar occasion, generating the same kind of sympathy and communicating the same kind of warmth." Tynan's reference to Clifford Odets's drama of the depression is certainly relevant in that both plays focus on the tightly constructed set of relationships that define a family, the outside forces that affect those relationships, and the end result of liberation from constricting circumstances. Similarly both plays illuminate the struggle to find one's place in society. But unlike the Bergers of *Awake and Sing!*, the Youngers find their strength—and their liberation—in family unity. Each character represents individual and collective aspects of the black experience of the 1950s, a point of view that audiences at the beginning of America's civil rights movement needed to see and understand.

OUR TOWN

71

(1938)   *by Thornton Wilder*

Our Town *is not a philosophical drama in the sense that it presents in dialogue form the explanation, discussion, or development of metaphysics. Wilder does have ideas, but they appear in the way the characters are presented, in the stage image. Wilder's experience and his philosophical thinking are transformed to a large degree by his imagination. There is no easy dilemma to be solved. The picture itself of American living is Wilder's idea. He is in the tradition of Walt Whitman. He is a defender and explainer of American idealism.... The way the American thinks about his living and his world are Wilder's subject.... Our* Town *is one of those rare modern works that is both meaningful and for everybody.*

—Donald Haberman, Our Town: *An American Play*

In the postwar era of the 1920s such playwrights as Eugene O'Neill, Elmer Rice, Philip Barry, and Sydney Howard brought a new gravity and dramatic energy to American theater. American drama would continue to evolve throughout the 1930s, exploring, often with a radical, leftist viewpoint, political and social themes in response to the rise of fascism in Europe and the economic difficulties caused by the Great Depression. The Group Theatre collective of New York City and the Works Progress Administration's Federal Theatre Project dominated the stage with such dramas of social realism as Clifford Odets's *Awake and Sing!* and Marc Blitzstein's *The Cradle Will Rock*. These dramas of the 1920s and 1930s, together with musical comedy, which came of age in the 1940s, began to form a uniquely American canon of theater.

The most innovative and vivid American drama of the 1930s was *Our Town*, a play of simple clarity and exquisite form of expression. Thornton Wilder was a playwright who eschewed the theatrical realism and utopian answers offered in other dramas of the decade in favor of a focus, like that of Jane Austen's, on the small in order to illuminate the universal and to affirm, through family and community relationships, the joy and pain experienced in life and the sadness and inevitability of death. One proof of the power of *Our Town* lies in its popularity: It has been the most performed American play of the 20th century, in repertory and particularly in schools, where it is appreciated because it has a large cast, features straightforward American colloquial language, and, with its minimum of sets, is easy to produce. However, *Our Town* is not as simple in style as it would appear on the surface. Though set in the traditionally halcyon early years of the 20th century, it is, at its core, a very modern play that owes much to the highly theatrical stagecraft of Luigi Pirandello and Jean Cocteau and, unlike most American dramas of its era, is a work that, like its author, defies easy categorization.

Wilder was a writer of considerable originality and eclectic intellect. He first attained literary success as a novelist but asserted in 1938, "Everything I have written has been a preparation for writing for the stage. . . . For the drama, it seems to me, is the most satisfying of all art-forms." He was born in 1897 in Madison, Wisconsin, the second son in a family that would eventually include three girls (Wilder had a twin who died at birth). His father, Amos Wilder, who had earned his doctorate in political science from Yale University, was the editor of the *Wisconsin State Journal* and a devout Congregationalist; his mother Isabella, the daughter of a Presbyterian minister, was well read in world literature and accomplished in music. In 1906 the family moved to Hong Kong, where Amos Wilder had been appointed consul general in Hong Kong under the Theodore Roosevelt administration. After six months his wife returned to the United States with the children and settled in Berkeley, California. The Wilder children attended public schools until 1909, when they relocated to Shanghai, where Amos had been transferred. After a year and a half in China, Isabella and the children went back to California permanently. Wilder attended the Thacher School in Ojai and graduated from Berkeley High School in 1915. He had early developed an interest in the theater, performing with his brother and sisters in his own plays at home and as an extra in the Greek dramas produced by a university theater at Berkeley. While in high school he frequently attended plays at the Liberty Theatre in Oakland.

Wilder attended Oberlin College for two years, during which time some of his writings appeared in the college literary magazine. When his father was relocated to New Haven, Connecticut, to become executive secretary of the Yale in China program, Wilder was sent to Yale. During his first year there he published short plays and essays in the *Yale Literary Magazine*. In 1928 a collection of very short dramatic pieces, most of which were written at Oberlin and Yale, was published as *The Angel That Troubled the Waters and Other Plays*. After spending eight months with the Coast Artillery Corps in Rhode Island, from 1918 to 1919 (his poor eyesight prevented active service in World War I), Wilder returned to Yale to complete his senior year. Before graduating in 1920 he published his first full-length play, *The Trumpet Shall Sound*, serially, in four issues of the *Yale Literary Magazine*. A tragedy in four acts, the play features a plot borrowed from Ben Jonson's *The Alchemist* and has as its allegorical reference point the second coming of Christ and Judgment Day when, at the play's finish, the criminally minded characters are either forgiven or punished accordingly. *The Trumpet Shall Sound* would go on to have its only New York production in 1926 at the American Laboratory Theatre, where it ran in repertory for 30 performances. During this time Wilder met actor-teacher Richard Boleslavsky, whose ideas on improvisational acting would affect Wilder's writing of *Our Town*.

After college, while spending several months in Rome studying archaeology at the American Academy, Wilder composed character sketches, which he called "Memoirs of a Roman Student." These sketches would result in his first novel, *The Cabala*, the story of Roman aristocrats faced with the decline of the old European order. A section of the novel, "Three Sentences," appeared in the New Orleans *Double Dealer* in 1924. The following year Wilder, who had been teaching French at the Lawrenceville School in Princeton, New Jersey, a position his father had secured for him, left to study for a master's degree in French at Princeton University and to finish *The Cabala*, which was published to good reviews in 1926. Wilder's next novel, *The Bridge of Saint Luis Rey*, appeared in 1927 and won for its author the first of three Pulitzer Prizes. The character-driven novel explores issues of destiny and death relating to the lives of five disparate types of people prior to their fall from a broken bridge in Peru. Wilder produced two novels in the 1930s, *The Woman of Andros* (1930) and *Heaven's My Destination* (1935).

Wilder's first dramatic effort of the 1930s was *The Long Christmas Dinner and Other Plays in One Act*, published in 1931. A well-received collection of six pieces, five of which depict middle-class Americans who represent different professions, character traits, or family roles, particularly the role of the mother, the plays prefigure the technique of *Our Town* in their colloquial language, stage directions (which call for a bare stage), the blending of the realistic and nonrealistic, and an emphasis on the continuity of life and death. Wilder next turned his dramatic attention to translation, adapting André Obey's *Le Viol de Lucrèce* for the stage in 1931 and Henrik Ibsen's *A Doll's House* in 1937. The latter production is particularly significant in that it paired Wilder with highly regarded producer-director Jed Harris, who had been a classmate of Wilder's at Yale and with whom he would work on *Our Town*.

Our Town, with its abrogation of traditional fourth-wall realism, amply illustrates what Wilder contended was one of the primary functions of drama: "A play visibly represents pure existing." With almost pastoral simplicity Wilder gives us the fictional community of Grover's Corners, New Hampshire, loosely based on the real town of Peterborough, New Hampshire, during the years 1901 to 1913. The stage directions call for "No curtain. No scenery. The audience, arriving, sees an empty stage in half-light." Visual completeness is supplied by the characters and their interactions with one another, a few set props introduced to suggest the homes of the central characters' families, and the audience's imagination and collective memory and experience. Each of the three acts has its own title and is introduced by the Stage Manager, who serves as the omniscient narrator, takes on several different but key roles within the play, and knows the past, present, and future of each character, including when and how each will die.

In act 1, "Daily Life," the Stage Manager describes the town and introduces the two families that make up the central characters: Doctor Gibbs, his wife, Julia, and their children, George (16) and Rebecca (11); Mr. Webb, editor of the town newspaper, the *Grover's Corners Sentinel*, his wife, Myrtle, and their children, Emily (16) and Wally (11). The Stage Manager guides the audience through a typical day in Grover's Corners: the Gibbses and the Webbs pursue their daily routines of meals, work, school, chores, choir practice, and homework; Professor Willard, a long-winded historian, and Mr. Webb talk about the town; the women gossip about Simon Stimson, the church organist, who is considered eccentric and is reputed to be a drunkard; George and Emily discuss George's academic problems at school, a scene that suggests a future relationship between the two. The audience is reminded of the macrocosm in which small towns, no matter how self-centered and parochial, exist, when, at the end of act 1, Rebecca reads to her brother the address on a friend's letter from her minister; the address names not only the person, farm, town, county, and state, but also the country, continent, hemisphere, planet, solar system, universe, and the "Mind of God." Rebecca wonderingly remarks that the postman delivered the letter despite this address.

At the start of act 2 the Stage Manager, in his relaxed, homespun manner, informs the audience that this act is called "Love and Marriage" and that "There's another act coming after this: I reckon you can guess what that's about." It is three years later and George and Emily's wedding day, although the action also flashes back to the couple's senior year in high school, when they realized that they were in love with each other. George and Emily are anxious about marriage, feeling that they are not ready, but both regain their composure and are wed by the Stage Manager in the role of the parson.

Act 3, which takes place nine years later, is never named, but the Stage Manager's hint at the start of the second act, together with the setting—the town graveyard—makes it clear that death is the subject but conjoined, as the audience will see, with what it means to be alive. The dead sit in straight-back chairs that suggest gravestones and stare unseeingly ahead. Emily, who has died giving birth to her second child, is being buried today. The dead include Mrs. Gibbs, Wally Webb, and Simon Stimson, who has hanged himself in his attic and is full of bitterness. The living, he asserts, "move about in a cloud of ignorance; to go up and down trampling on the feelings . . . of those about you." Emily arrives and describes her death, prompting one of the dead women to remark with a sigh, "My, wasn't life awful—and wonderful." Emily discovers that she can relive moments in her life, and Mrs. Gibbs, after advising against this, suggests that she choose a seemingly unimportant day. With the help of the Stage Manager, Emily chooses to revisit her 12th birthday. It is a joyful experience at first, but Emily weeps as she comes to understand that most people are unaware of the value of being alive, even in the mundane existence of daily routine: "Oh, earth, you are too wonderful for anybody to realize you." The Stage Manager agrees and proposes that perhaps only saints and poets realize the day-to-day and minute-to-minute importance of living. After Emily returns to her grave, the Stage Manager closes the play with a short speech comparing the continuity of town life with the movement of the heavens, remarks on the strain of daily living and the need for people to rest, and tells the audience to "get a good rest, too."

Our Town opened in New York in February 1938 and was a great success, running for 336 performances and earning Wilder the Pulitzer Prize for drama. Reviews were mixed, with critics citing the mundane content and abstract quality of the play, an unusual dramatic combination for the theater of the time. Critics have since noted the importance of Our Town in the development of modern American theater and recognized the play as more than merely an exercise in American sentimentalism. American values and history are an important feature of Our Town: Key events from the past, present, and future (up to World War I) that would have traditionally appeared in any child's textbook are mentioned. Yet the history, lifestyle, and culture that make up the play are not, in a wider context, uniquely American. When Emily says her farewell to life, she is mourning the kind of simple daily details that make up existence: her parents, "clocks ticking," flowers, "new-ironed dresses," eating, sleeping, and waking. Such simple living has been common to all communities throughout time. As critic Rex Burbank observes in Thornton Wilder, "In making the little American town a mythical representation of civilized human life everywhere in all ages, [Wilder] accomplished what he and Gertrude Stein conceived to be the main achievement of a literary masterpiece—the use of the materials of human nature to portray the eternal and universal residing in the collective 'human mind.'" Wilder, who died in 1975, reminds us that Grover's Corners and communities like it represent nothing less than the center of all creation.

THE COUNTRY WIFE

72

(1675) *by William Wycherley*

With his third play, Wycherley hit the jackpot. The King's Company produced at Drury Lane in January 1675 The Country Wife, the first of the great Restoration comedies. Many critics think it the best; certainly it is one of the great comedies of all time. With it, Restoration comedy came of age.
> —Norman N. Holland, *The First Modern Comedies*

William Wycherley's *The Country Wife* is in many ways the defining Restoration comedy, capturing in its boldness, wit, and vitality the spirit of the age during the reign of Charles II and representing that age's most distinctive contribution to the dramatic tradition. When the English monarchy was restored in 1660, one of the king's first acts was to reopen the theaters, which had been closed since 1642. Charles granted patents to Thomas Killigrew and Sir William Davenant to form companies to mount productions. Killigrew formed the King's Company, Davenant, the Duke's Company, and both added actresses to their casts and constructed new indoor theaters to cater to an audience mainly of the court and the higher levels of London society. Initially the theaters depended on the earlier works of William Shakespeare, Ben Jonson, Francis Beaumont and John Fletcher, and others, but gradually new dramatic forms emerged to gratify the aristocratic tastes of Restoration audiences—heroic verse drama and the comedy of manners. "Written for a coterie with clearly defined standards (the court circle and those who imitated them)," critic Katherine M. Rogers explains, "Restoration comedy was preoccupied with fine social distinctions. The audience was keenly aware of manners and affectations, and it valued wit above all things. It considered repartee 'the very soul of conversation' and therefore 'the greatest grace of Comedy.' . . . Accordingly, the conversation of witty, sophisticated ladies and gentlemen was better developed in Restoration comedy than ever before or since." Wycherley became one of the first masters of the new form, best expressed in his masterpiece, *The Country Wife*. In its brilliant construction, witty dialogue, satiric thrust, and underlying moral seriousness, *The Country Wife* is the paradigmatic Restoration drama and one of the greatest comedies in English.

Wycherley's life before his initial stage success in 1671 is shadowy and filled with gaps in the biographical record. Wycherley's father, Daniel, was the high steward in the household of John Paulet, marquess of Winchester, at Basing House in Hampshire, where he met and married Bethnia Shrimpton, lady-in-waiting to the marchioness. The eldest of six children, William was probably born in 1641. When civil war broke out, less than two years later, Basing House was seized by parliamentary forces under Oliver Cromwell. While the marquess was imprisoned for the duration of the interregnum, Wycherley's father acted as his deputy, acquiring a law degree and sufficient fortune to buy property in Shropshire. It has been speculated that his father's dual obsessions—acquiring land and litigation—provoked his son's attacks in his plays of social climbers and figures such as Sir Jasper Fidget of *The Country Wife*, whose sole "pleasure" is "business," and the litigious Widow Blackacre in *The Plain Dealer*. Befitting a son of an ardently Royalist family, Wycherley, at the age of 15, was sent to France for his education. There he became closely associated with Julie d'Angennes, marchioness of Montausier, who introduced him to the brilliant world of French intellectual and social life. Her husband, Charles de Sainte-Maure, was the inspiration for Molière's rigidly honest Alceste in *THE MISANTHROPE*. Wycherley's time in France would be crucial in exposing him to ideas and dramatic influences that would find their way into his plays. We know little for sure about Wycherley's subsequent activities between the ages of 15 and 30, before his return to England early in 1660. It is generally believed that he spent some time in Madrid in the household of the poet-ambassador Sir Richard Fanshawe. This may explain the influences from Spanish drama in general and from Pedro Calderón de la Barca in particular in his first two plays. Back in England Wycherley spent a few months at Queen's College, Oxford, before enrolling as a law student in London's Inner Temple. It is doubtful that he ever completed his legal training or ever practiced law.

In 1669, his first work, a verse burlesque of the Hero and Leander story, was published anonymously. Two years later, his first play, *Love in a Wood; or, St. James's Park*, was performed by the King's Company at the Theatre Royal. Wycherley's comedy of lovers contending with the fortune hunters, social climbers, and the bawds of contemporary London handles the conventions of the Restoration comedy of manner with a robust humor that succeeded with his audience. The play made Wycherley famous and resulted in a relationship with Barbara Palmer, the duchess of Cleveland, one of the king's mistresses, which in turn led to Wycherley's being accepted as one of the court wits who were King Charles's favored companions. Wycherley's second play, *The Gentleman Dancing-Master*, appeared in 1672 and failed with Restoration audiences. It features a more simplified farcical story of a wealthy merchant daughter's foiling her father's plan to marry her to a rich fool and winning the gentleman of her choosing. Wycherley's third play, *The Country Wife*, combines the wider social panorama of his first play with the more controlled dramatic focus of his second to become his masterpiece, showing him in full control of dramatic construction and the humor that is unified by a central thesis: the failure of contemporary marriage arrangements.

The conceit that drives the comedy is the notorious womanizer Harry Horner's scheme to circulate the rumor that a cure for venereal disease has left him impotent. This ingenious ruse (possibly borrowed from Terence's the *Eunuchus* in which a young man poses as a eunuch to gain entry to a girl's room to rape her), playing on the sexual hypocrisies of fashionable London society, is to provide Horner with access to wives whose husbands now no longer perceive him as a threat. Moreover, by exposing women's lasciviousness by their aversion to his supposed condition he can identify likely targets for seduction. Horner's deception reveals the various sexual duplicities and marital mismanagements among fashionable London society, while setting in motion a complex, interlocking series of situations that are both hilarious and richly satirical. Scholar Norman N. Holland has described *The Country Wife* as a "right-way-wrong-way play" that shows the "contrast and interaction of three closely woven lines of intrigue. Two of these intrigues define a 'wrong way,' a limited, half-successful way of life. The third defines a 'right way' that contrasts with the limitations of the other two." The first of these wrong ways is represented by Sir Jasper and Lady Fidget who visit Horner after receiving news of his affliction. Sir Jasper, more interested in his political affairs than attending to his wife, is only too happy to unload her on the unthreatening, unmanned Horner. Lady Fidget's irritation over Horner's condition reveals her considerable sexual appetite beneath her respectable veneer and highly moral platitudes. As Horner remarks, "She that shows an aversion to me, loves the sport . . . your women of honour . . . are only chary of their reputations, not their persons, and 'tis scandal they would avoid, not men." The sophisticated town values of the Fidgets are all about appearances, and Sir Jasper is deceived by the appearance of Horner's disability while Lady Fidget's profession of high-minded rectitude merely conceals her baser instincts.

The contrasting "wrong way" is represented by Jack Pinchwife and his new wife Margery. Pinchwife is an aging rake, often betrayed by his lovers, who has married an innocent country girl whom he hopes to dominate and control to insure her faithfulness. In contrast to Sir Jasper's indifference to his wife, Pinchwife is jealous, tyrannical, and brutal and conceives his marital role as whoremaster. Unaware of Horner's condition, Pinchwife does everything he can to keep Margery away from him and the temptations of the town, while confirming Horner's contention that "a foolish Rival and a jealous Husband assist their Rival's Designs; for they are sure to make their Women hate them, which is the first step to their love, for another Man." In confirmation, every

attempt Pinchwife makes to keep Margery away from Horner and enticements pushes her closer to him and seduction. Margery's unsophisticated and
open nature contrasts with Lady Fidget's hypocritical pretense, and she is both
charming and refreshing in her candor, one of the great comic stage heroines.
"Mrs. Margery Pinchwife," the essayist William Hazlitt asserted in her praise,
"is a character that will last for ever, I should hope; and even when the original
is no more, if that should ever be, while self-will, curiosity, art, and ignorance
are to be found in the same person, it will be just as good and just as intelligible as ever in the description." Margery's eventual betrayal of her husband
is mitigated both by Pinchwife's foolishness and brutality. Disparaging all that
his country wife has missed in town—plays, dinners, parties, and dances—he
stimulates Margery's appetite for what he has denied her. Eventually agreeing
to take her to the theater, Pinchwife insists that she dress as a man, thereby
displaying her figure to Horner's delighted gaze and provoking Horner, who
sees through the ruse, into kissing the young "gentleman" and delivering the
message through "him" that he is in love with Mrs. Pinchwife. Instructing his
wife in the art of letter writing to discourage Horner's attention, Pinchwife
provides the means for Margery to openly communicate with Horner when
she substitutes a love letter for the cold dismissal Pinchwife brutally dictates:
"Write as I bid you, or I will write Whore with this Penknife in your Face."
It is not surprising that Margery, given her treatment, contracts what she calls
the "London disease they call Love":

> I am sick of my Husband, and for my Gallant; I have heard this distem-
> per, call'd a Feaver, but methinks 'tis liker an Ague, for when I think of
> my Husband, I tremble and am in a cold sweat, and have inclinations
> to vomit, but when I think of my Gallant, dear Mr. Horner, my hot fit
> comes, and I am all in a Feaver, indeed, & as in other Feavers my own
> Chamber is tedious to me, and I would fain be remov'd to his, and then
> methinks I shou'd be well.

The third intrigue, and the "right way" of love and eventual marriage is
represented by Pinchwife's sister, Alithea, and her lover, Harcourt. Alithea, a
sophisticated and intelligent young woman of principle, contrasts both with
the concealed baseness of the town wife, Lady Fidget, and the open feelings
of the country wife. She is engaged to marry the fop Sparkish because he has
shown no jealousy, and she can thereby avoid Margery's fate of marrying a
tyrannical husband. However, Sparkish's lack of jealousy is actually indifference since he is merely marrying a fortune. Alithea, however, stands by her
decision provided Sparkish maintains his trust even when the better man,
Harcourt, declares his love and urges her to marry him.

With the various contrasting husbands, wives, and lovers in play, Wycherley arranges a series of hilarious predicaments and reversals. Horner, gaining

unobstructed access to Lady Fidget and her female friends, reveals his ruse, and they are only too anxious to enjoy his favors under the protection of his presumed disability. In one of the wittiest scenes in English comedy Lady Fidget's assignation with Horner at his lodgings is interrupted by the unexpected arrival of Sir Jasper. Her alibi is that she has come for some of Horner's china, which, in a riot of double entendres, comes to stand for the sex that ensues in the next room as Sir Jasper patiently waits. Emerging from the room with a piece of china in her hands, Lady Fidget addresses her husband and her friend Mistress Squeamish, who has also arrived to sample Horner's "wares":

> LADY FIDGET   And I have been toiling and moiling for the prettiest piece of china, my dear.

> HORNER   Nay, she has been too hard for me, do what I could.

> MISTRESS SQUEAMISH   Oh Lord, I'll have some china too, good Mr. Horner—don't think to give other people china, and me none. Come in with me too.

> HORNER   Upon my honour, I have none left now.

> MISTRESS SQUEAMISH   Nay, nay, I have known you deny your china before now; but you shan't put me off so. Come—

> HORNER   This lady had the last there.

> LADY FIDGET   Yes indeed, madam; to my certain knowledge he has no more left.

> MISTRESS SQUEAMISH   Oh, but it may be he may have some you could not find.

> LADY FIDGET   What, d'y' think if he had had any left, I would not have had it too? For we women of quality never think we have china enough.

When Pinchwife discovers his wife writing another love letter to Horner, Margery claims that she was writing for Alithea who has fallen in love with Horner. Reckoning that by marrying Alithea to Horner he can protect his wife from the rake, Pinchwife agrees to allow them to meet. Disguised as Alithea, Margery is unsuspectingly delivered by her husband to her lover. When Pinchwife leaves to get a clergyman to marry the couple, he encounters Sparkish, who on learning of his betrayal, jealously confronts the real Alithea. She now has grounds to break her engagement and accept Harcourt, who believes her guiltless despite the evidence against her. "I will not only believe your innocence myself," he declares, "but make all the world believe it." Harcourt loves Alithea generously, not as an investment, diversion, or a possession to be jealously guarded. Their relationship, based not on sexual appetite but on trust and mutual respect, serves as the moral alternative to the other relationships. Announcing the play's central moral Alithea concludes: "Love proceeds from esteem." Despite the victory of love over lust achieved by Alithea and Harcourt, the far less ideal world of dupes and gulls remains firmly functioning as the drama closes. On the brink of being unmasked, Horner is saved by Alithea's servant who takes responsibility for all the confusion and by his quack doctor who reaffirms the impotency diagnosis. His conquests manage to silence the ever-unsophisticated Margery's denial of the doctor's opinion. Husbands are reunited with their wives, happily unaware that they either have been cuckolded or will likely be. Only Margery is unsatisfied: "And I must be a country wife still too, I find, for I can't (like a city one) be rid of my musty husband, and do what I list."

Wycherley would produce only one additional play, *The Plain-Dealer* in 1686. In it the moral seriousness that coexists with the comedy in *The Country Wife* predominates. It failed with Restoration audiences but anticipated the more sober moral comedies that would dominate the English stage in the 18th century. Wycherley would live on until 1715, more and more on the fringe of the society he dominated during his short five-year run as a leading dramatist. *The Country Wife*, in its delicate balance of the real and the ideal, farce and satire, sentiment and bawdiness, remains the classic expression of an age that derived pleasure and instruction from a clever and unabashed look at the way of the world.

73

TRAVESTIES

(1974)   *by Tom Stoppard*

Travesties . . . mediates upon its own dramatic origins and at the same time dramatizes questions concerning the proper relation of politics to art. The stylistic and thematic ventures proceed in tandem, as Stoppard harks back to the plays of Oscar Wilde and George Bernard Shaw. He defines his most serious concerns against theirs and raids their arsenal of techniques and characters. Glittering in borrowed finery, he creates a distorted likeness of their plays called travesty. And in so doing he writes a new chapter in the history of the comedy of ideas.

         —Margaret Gold, "Who Are the Dadas in *Travesties?*"

For nearly half a century now Tom Stoppard has established himself as an unavoidable dramatist. His plays are bravura verbal and intellectual happenings that have restored and reinvented what Stoppard has called the "High Comedy of Ideas." "Stoppard is that peculiar anomaly—a serious comic writer born in an age of tragicomedy and a renewed interest in theatrical realism," critic Enoch Brater has observed. It can be argued that between them Stoppard and Harold Pinter have had joint custody of modern British drama since the 1960s, offering two contrary dramatic approaches with which all other playwrights have had to contend. Pinter's specialty is super-realistic minimalism, characterized by the unspoken and the inexplicable. Stoppard embraces an exuberant theatricality, the dialectic, and a verbal torrent. "I think it is impossible," Pinter has stated, ". . . to start writing a play from any kind of abstract idea. . . . I start writing a play from an image of a situation and a couple of characters involved, and these people always remain for me quite real; if they were not, the play could not be written." By contrast, Stoppard is preeminently an idea man. "I am a playwright," he has confessed, "interested in ideas and forced to invent characters to express those ideas." Stoppard pursues his ideas in defiance of any realistic or naturalist dramatic norm. The theater itself becomes an epistemological opportunity in which Stoppard's plays comment on their own violations of verisimilitude and the search for meaning and significance. No modern playwright has done more to restore the stage as both an entertaining and intriguing arena for contending ideas. Of all his plays *Travesties*, described by critic Susan Rusinko as "the most intoxicating reinvention of language on the modern English stage," is virtuoso and vintage Stoppard at his most outrageous and instructive.

Born Tomáš Straüssler in 1937 in Zlín, Czechoslovakia, Stoppard was the second son of Martha and Eugen Straüssler, a physician who worked for a shoe manufacturer. The day the Nazis invaded Czechoslovakia his family fled to Singapore. (Stoppard would later be surprised to learn from a Czech relative that his family had been Jewish, and several of his relatives perished in the Holocaust.) Prior to the Japanese invasion of Singapore he was evacuated with his mother and brother to Darjeeling, India. His father, who stayed behind, was killed. In India his mother remarried a major in the British army, Kenneth Stoppard, who moved the family to England in 1946. By the age of nine, therefore, Tomáš Straüssler had became Tom Stoppard, acquiring a new name, nationality, and language, changes that Stoppard and others have cited as explaining much about his artistry. Stoppard has attributed his fascination with language with "the fact that I was actually brought up to speak two languages at least, in that I was born in Czechoslovakia . . . [M]y attitude to the English language is one of awe and admiration." A director of his plays has stated that "You have to be foreign to write English with that kind of hypnotized brilliance." Others have suggested that Stoppard's background helps to explain a sense of detachment in his plays that avoids the personal or explicit social and political criticism. As dramatist James Saunders has observed, Stoppard is "basically a displaced person. Therefore, he doesn't want to stick his neck out. He feels grateful to Britain because he sees himself as a guest here, and that makes it hard for him to criticize Britain."

Educated at English public schools in Nottinghamshire and Yorkshire, Stoppard, the most erudite of playwrights, became "Thoroughly bored by the idea of anything intellectual . . . totally bored and alienated by everyone from Shakespeare to Dickens." Leaving school at 17, Stoppard went to work as a journalist in Bristol for the *Western Daily Press* in 1954 and the *Evening World* in 1958, where his interest in theater began. It was the period of first performances of Samuel Beckett and the English stage revolution set off by John Osborne's LOOK BACK IN ANGER. "Like a lot of other people I started writing plays not very long after being moved to tears and laughter by *Look Back in Anger*," Stoppard recalled. "After *Look Back in Anger* young writers tended to be young playwrights, not because what they had to say I think was particularly suited to dramatic form but because the theater was clearly the most interesting and dynamic medium." Coming to London in 1962, Stoppard joined the staff of a short-lived magazine, the *Scene*, reviewing 132 plays during a seven-month period. Stoppard's career as a playwright began with a staging of *A Walk on the Water* on television in 1963 and the radio broadcasts in 1964 of two plays. In Berlin on a grant for aspiring young playwrights, Stoppard wrote a Shakespearean pastiche, *Rosencrantz and Guildenstern Meet King Lear*, which, in 1966, retitled *Rosencrantz and Guildenstern Are Dead*, premiered at the Edinburgh Festival before being staged by the National Theatre in London. It became a sensation. Stoppard's exuberant comic parody that writes its way into the world's most famous play is also a deeply philosophical work presenting such recurrent themes as identity, fate, death, and the nature of theatrical reality. Filled with his trademark brilliant wordplay and concept-juggling, his first major drama set the Stoppard prototype. His plays are literary and intellectual echo chambers in which dissonance and reverberation are more important than any clear message or finality. Stoppard, who has called his distinguishing mark, an "absolute lack of certainty about almost anything," has described the structure of his plays as "firstly, A; secondly minus A"; that is, one character takes up a concept that conflicts with another's, setting up what the playwright has called "infinite leapfrog." The essence of Stoppard's drama is not necessarily to win the argument but to extend the debate by presenting a range of different views, all delivered fairly. "I characteristically write plays for two voices," Stoppard has stated. "Obviously I try to be as persuasive as possible on both sides." *Rosencrantz and Guildenstern* would be followed by the one-act plays *The Real Inspector Hound* (1968) and *After Magritte* (1970) and his second full-length drama, *Jumpers*, in 1972.

The departure point for Stoppard's third major play, *Travesties*, is the historical convergence of three prominent revolutionaries who shaped 20th-century art and politics—James Joyce, Lenin, and dadaist poet and theorist Tristan Tzara—as residents of Zurich during World War I. *Travesties* brings the three together in the recollections of one Henry Carr, a British consular official, who actually took part in a wartime production of Oscar Wilde's THE IMPORTANCE OF BEING EARNEST with Joyce as the business manager. Echoing the subtitle of Wilde's play, *A Trivial Comedy for Serious People*, *Travesties* shreds history, literature, and biography—great figures during great times—and reconstitutes all into a crackbrained version of Wilde's comedy-cum-debate on the nature of art and the role of the artist in our times. The play opens in the Zurich public library as Henry Carr's younger sister, Gwendolen, is taking dictation from Joyce during the composition of *Ulysses*. Cecily, a librarian, is similarly engaged, assisting Lenin with his great work on imperialism. Tzara is occupied cutting words out of a newspaper and randomly arranging them into a dadaist composition. The manuscript folders of both Joyce and Lenin are inadvertently switched, echoing the lost handbag of Wilde's comedy, as Lenin's wife arrives to announce that the Russian Revolution has begun. The scene then changes to Henry Carr's apartment as the elderly Carr recalls his wartime experiences in Zurich. Since, as Stoppard's stage directions explain, "Most of the action takes place within Carr's memory," his "various prejudices and delusions" cause his account to "jump its tracks" and "has to be restarted at the point where it goes wild." Transformed into his younger self in the past, Carr jumbles his recollections with the part he played in *The Importance of Being Earnest* ("not Ernest, the other one"), and the play proceeds, after multiple stops and restarts, in the line of the first act of Wilde's comedy. Tzara, assuming the role of John Worthing, arrives to propose to Gwendolen, who has accompanied Joyce who recruits Carr to play Algernon in the upcoming production.

The play's ingenious echoing of *Earnest* alternates with a debate over modern art and the responsibility of the artist. Carr takes the conventional bourgeois position that "it is the duty of the artist to beautify existence." Joyce's art for art's sake position is countered by Tzara who asserts that "you've turned literature into a religion and it's as dead as all the rest, it's an overripe corpse and you're cutting fancy figures at the wake. It's too late for genius! Now we need vandals and desecrators, simple-minded demolition men to smash centuries of baroque subtlety, to bring down the temple, and thus finally, to reconcile the shame and necessity of being an artist!" Joyce responds:

> An artist is the magician put among men to gratify—capriciously—their urge for immortality. The temples are built and brought down around him, continuously and contiguously, from Troy to the fields of Flanders. If there is any meaning in any of it, it is in what survives as art, yes even in the celebration of tyrants, yes even in the celebration of nonentities. What now of the Trojan War if it had been passed over by the artist's touch? Dust. . . . But it is we who stand enriched, by a tale of heroes, of a golden apple, a wooden horse, a face that launched a thousand ships— and above all, of Ulysses, the wanderer, the most human, the most complete of all heroes—husband, father, son, lover, farmer, soldier, pacifist, politician, inventor, and adventurer. . . . It is a theme so overwhelming that I am almost afraid to treat it. And yet I with my Dublin Odyssey will double that immortality, yes by God *there's* a corpse that will dance for some time yet *and leave the world precisely as it finds it.*

Joyce's notion of the artist as magician, as resurrectionist, is precisely the role Stoppard plays in *Travesties* as these historical corpses are set dancing. Like *Ulysses* in which an epic is refracted from the trivial details of an ordinary day in the life of Dublin, *Travesties* similarly conflates epic events of history and its major figures and serious questions of art and politics with the trivial in the scraps of Carr's petty memories and the borrowed plot and dialogue from Wilde's play.

If art dominates the debate in the first act, politics rule the second. Stoppard has asserted that *Travesties* poses the question "whether an artist has to justify himself in political terms *at all.*" In the play's second act the aesthetic questions raised in act 1 are considered in relationship to the social and political change shaped by war and revolution. The act opens at the library with Cecily delivering a long, humorless lecture on Marxism. Stoppard, who has described his plays as "ambushes for the audience," has confessed: "I thought it would be quite nice" "if [the audience] all went out thinking 'oh this is fun isn't it,' came back, and [I] just hit them with this boring thing, as though they'd come back into the wrong theatre." Carr, mercifully, returns in the role of spy to discover Lenin's plans about returning to Russia to lead the revolution, and the *Earnest* plot is reengaged, echoing the second act of Wilde's comedy. Tzara has concealed his true identity to avoid a conflict with Lenin, who is contemptuous of the dadaists, by calling himself Jack Tzara. Carr, assuming the identity of "the decadent nihilist" Tristan, courts Cecily, who admits that it has been her girlish dream to reform him since she heard about him from Jack. Lenin joins the debate over art by arguing its essential didactic function. Cecily, who becomes Lenin's mouthpiece in the play, insists that "the sole duty and justification for art is social criticism." The high seriousness of Lenin's position, made tedious in the context of what has come before, serves as its own critique on the incompatibility between dogma and art. When Lenin and his wife depart for Russia, the older Carr defends his failure to stop them and changing the course of history because he was preoccupied with Cecily, and, after all, *"he wasn't Lenin then!"* The confusion over the identity of Jack and Tristan Tzara is finally resolved; the switched manuscript folders are exchanged, and the reconciled couples are paired off to dance out of view. Old Carr dances back onstage with an Old Cecily, who corrects a number of points in his recollections, including her assertions that he was never close to Lenin, that Bennett was not his servant but the British consul, that she never worked with Lenin, and that the woman who married Tzara was named Sophia, not Gwendolen. Dismissing Cecily as a "pedant," Carr concludes the play in indeterminacy: "I learned three things in Zurich during the war. I wrote them down. Firstly, you're either a revolutionary or you're not, and if you're not you might as well be an artist as anything else. Secondly, if you can't be an artist, you might as well be a revolutionary . . . I forget the third thing."

Echoing Carr's faulty memory and contradictions, *Travesties* operates by affirming the messy mutuality of art and history, style and substance, the trivial and the serious. Few other plays or playwrights provide such an entertaining or mind-stretching exercise in verbal gymnastics or intellectual and artistic brinkmanship.

THE LOWER DEPTHS

(1902)

by Maxim Gorky

> The Lower Depths . . . *is a remarkable play for a relatively inexperienced dramatist. It entertained but confronted, challenged and divided the auditorium. The Moscow Arts Theatre and arguably Russian theater were never to be the same again.*
> —Cynthia Marsh, *"The Lower Depths," in Reference Guide to Russian Literature*

Na dne, meaning literally, "On the Bottom," but translated into English as *The Lower Depths,* is the single work by which Maxim Gorky is known outside Russia. Only the second of Gorky's 15 plays, which in total represent but a small portion of the writer's considerable output of novels, short stories, memoirs, and essays, *The Lower Depths,* both in its themes and methods, has exerted an oversized significance and an important legacy for subsequent dramatists internationally. In Russian literary history *The Lower Depths* is noteworthy as the first time that society's outcasts—prostitutes, thieves, casual laborers, and the destitute and the derelicts—took center stage in a drama. Anton Chekhov, who served as Gorky's mentor, provided the younger writer with a dramatic method and technique that Gorky applied to a lower-class, urban milieu into which Chekhov's plays never ventured. In claiming importance and humanity for a class that the Russians call *bosyák* (vagabonds, or literally "barefoot") and that Gorky described as "ex-people" and "creatures who were once men," he both opened up a new dramatic subject and moved Russian drama into the political and social arena that would lead to revolution and the ongoing debate over the role and purpose of literature as a reflection of contemporary sociopolitical issues and an agent of social reform. *The Lower Depths* has been variously viewed as one of the groundbreaking realistic and naturalistic works of modern literature that gave voice and stature to the marginalized and invisible, as a visionary and spiritual affirmation and negation of human and social perfectibility, and as effective propaganda for multiple (and contradictory) philosophical and social positions. Its creator is no less contentious. Gorky's declaration, "I came into the world in order to disagree" can well stand as the motto of his life and works. He has been both heralded as a crucial Russian revolutionary and dismissed as a party apologist who sacrificed his genius (and conscience) for the Soviet state. Regarded by many of his compatriots as the greatest Russian writer of the 20th century, Gorky was canonized by the Soviets as the Walt Whitman of Russia, its revered proletarian bard. To honor him his place of birth was renamed for him, as was the Moscow Arts Theatre, so crucial in the productions of Chekhov's groundbreaking plays. Yet Gorky's significance beyond Russia is far less secure. In the West he is more a mystery than a national literary force, with his considerable opus remaining mainly unknown and untranslated. *The Lower Depths* alone has sustained his reputation internationally, a play deservedly considered a classic work of modern drama.

Born Alexei Maximovich Pyeshkov in 1868 in the Volga river town of Nizhniy Novgorod, Gorky would rechristen himself, in 1892, "Maxim the Bitter," as commentary on his brutalized childhood and rough-and-tumble development. His father, a carpenter, died of cholera when his son was four, and Gorky was grudgingly raised by his maternal grandparents, proprietors of a dye works, who alternately subjected their grandson to brutal beatings and pietistic sermonizing. The irony did not escape him, with the disjunction between high-minded idealism and reality forming one of Gorky's persistent themes. By the age of 10, Gorky was largely fending for himself in a succession of menial jobs, including work as a shopkeeper's errand boy, a dishwasher on a Volga steamer, and an apprentice to an icon maker, who taught him to lie about the age and value of the religious images to enhance sales. Almost completely self-educated, Gorky tried to enter the university at Kazan, without success, but stayed there to work for a baker whose association with radical politics marked the beginning of Gorky's own raised political consciousness. At the age of 19, convinced that he had no prospects for a better life, Gorky fired a bullet into his left side but missed his heart. After recovering Gorky would spend the next several years working in a fishery on the Caspian Sea and as a railway watchman as well as tramping about Russia, contracting tuberculosis and attracting the attention of czarist police for subversive activities protesting working conditions.

In 1898 Gorky published two volumes of sketches and stories that forcefully and intimately offered an insider's view of the lifestyle and oppression of Russia's outcasts and derelicts. They brought him immense acclaim as a cult figure. Imprinted on the popular imagination in his characteristic rustic Russian blouse, worker's boots, and walking stick, Gorky became the embodiment of his subject, setting the style for romantic individualism and disenchantment with repressive social norms. "Everywhere one could see his picture" observes critic Alexander Kaun, "—on postal cards, cigarette- and candy-boxes, and in endless cartoons. Shady characters stopped citizens in the street and asked for, or rather demanded, 'a bottle of vodka in the name of Maxim Gorky.'"

Gorky was befriended by Leo Tolstoy and Chekhov, who found in Gorky's works much to admire. To refine the young writer's sometimes ornate writing style, Chekhov sent him plays, such as August Strindberg's *Miss Julie*, to encourage a greater economy of expression. Chekhov also introduced him to the Moscow Art Theatre company. On the basis of an outline Gorky had described at their first meeting in 1900, its director, Konstantin Stanislavky, solicited Gorky's first play. This work, which would become *The Lower Depths*, initially concerned an ex-waiter whose prized possession was his dress clothes, mementos of his former respectability. The play was set in a flophouse, and, as Stanislavsky recalled in *My Life in Art*,

> The second act finished with an unexpected police raid, at the news of which, the whole anthill came to life, trying to hide stolen goods. In the third act came the spring, the sun; nature bloomed again; the inhabitants of the foul-smelling lodging came out into the clean air to work on a farm; they sang songs under the sun, forgetting their former hatred of each other.

Reworking his original conception, Gorky failed to deliver the completed play on time. Instead, in 1901 the Moscow Art Theatre rushed into production another Gorky play, *Meshchane* (variously translated as *The Petty Bourgeois*, *The Philistines*, and *The Smug Citizens*). In place of Gorky's popular lower-class subject matter, the play was a scathing attack on middle-class complacency that disappointed audiences. Chekhov considered the play immature but with an important subject. "Gorky's strength as a dramatist," Chekhov declared, "is not that audiences like him, but that he is the first in Russia and in the world generally to speak out with contempt and disgust against the philistine—and that he did so just when society was ready to hear such criticism."

By the 1902 season Gorky had completed *The Lower Depths*, and the company of the Moscow Art Theatre, to achieve authenticity in their depiction of Russia's criminal and indigent subculture, visited the foul-smelling shelters where beggars, thieves, and tramps lived. When asked by the actors what effect he wanted the play to have on his audience, Gorky answered: "I'll be satisfied if you can shake the audience so much that they can't sit comfortably in their seats." Cleared by the censor largely because Gorky's first play had failed and officials expected no more for this second effort, *The Lower Depths* proved to be a triumphant success, with its formerly unseen lower-class underworld brought to vivid and violent life onstage. Acclaim for the play and its creator brought government censure, with one establishment newspaper condemning the "mob" that "wildly applauds the stench, filth, and vice of revolutionary propaganda . . . while the leader of the derelicts, Maxim Gorky, using his pen as a lever, shakes the ground on which that society was built. What a dangerous writer! How wretched and blind are his admirers, readers, and spectators!"

Banned in working-class theaters and prohibited from being translated into other languages of the empire, the play still managed to be performed and read widely. When it was published, the first edition of 40,000 copies sold out in two weeks; a second edition of 35,000 was gone in under a year. Productions were mounted in Berlin, London, and New York that would establish Gorky's reputation internationally and influence subsequent dramatists such as Bertolt Brecht and Eugene O'Neill, who called *The Lower Depths* "the great proletarian revolutionary play" and whose THE ICEMAN COMETH directly imitates.

The four-act drama opens in a "cavelike basement" of a cheap urban rooming house, lit by a single small window and filled with plank beds and a collection of human wreckage—drunken derelicts, thieves, laborers, misfits, and the desperate—a microcosm of life at the bottom of society. The denizens include Bubnov, a capmaker; Klestch, a locksmith, and his consumptive, battered wife, Anna; Nastya, a prostitute; Vassya Pepel, a young thief; the Actor and the Baron, both in decline from their former positions; and the cardsharp Satin. The lodging is run by Kostylyov, a fence, and his wife, Vassilisa, who jealously brutalizes her sister Natasha, who is her rival for Vassya's affections. Act 1, set on a morning in early spring, presents the lodgers' routine of facing another day of uncertain and desperate prospects. Through their preoccupations and bickering they reveal their values and the conditions of their lives. A catalyst in their confessions is Luka, a 60-year-old tramp, who arrives with a philosophy of consolation and the expectations of a better life. Reactions to Luka and his message divide the inhabitants into opposing camps of the hopeful and the realists. Luka comforts the failing Anna that death will finally bring her peace, encourages the Actor to seek a cure for his alcoholism, and persuades Vassya to make a fresh start in Siberia. Those sustained by a hope for a better life are opposed by others such as the Baron, who mocks the prostitute Nastya for her romantic fantasies; Bubnov, who claims to revere only the truth but whose cynicism justifies his indifference to others and his own paralysis; and Satin, whose more positive advocacy of truth will dominate the play's final act.

Employing a similar "collective hero" as in Gerhart Hauptmann's *The Weavers* and Chekhov's polyphonic dramatic structure of overlapping characters and dialogue joined thematically, *The Lower Depths* pushes its characters to ever more revealing extremes. In act 2 Anna dies, and Vassilisa offers money and Natasha to Vassya if he will free her from her burdensome husband. Act 3 ends with a brawl between Vassya and Kostylyov that ends in the latter's death. Although Vassya has rejected Vassilisa's proposal and has acted only to protect Natasha, killing Kostylyov accidentally, Natasha accuses Vassya and her sister of the conspiracy, and both are jailed. The play concludes with the aftermath of the violence. Luka, who has dominated the first three acts, offering the others what Gorky would later describe as the "consoling lie," has disappeared, as have most of the prospects he has offered to sustain hope. The play's philosophical spokesperson in act 4 is Satin, who represents an alternative both to the delusions some have taken from Luka's consoling message and the cynical despair of the mockers. Ridiculing Luka's remedies as "soft bread to the toothless," Satin advocates truth, but he also defends Luka and the lies that inspire and confirm man's self-respect and worth:

> The old man is not a faker. What's truth? Man—that's the truth! He understood this. . . . Certainly he lied—but it was out of pity for you, the devil take you! There are lots of people who lie out of pity for others—I know it—I've read about it. They lie beautifully, excitingly, with a kind of inspiration. There are lies that soothe, that reconcile one to his lot. There are lies that justify the load that crushed a worker's arm—and hold a man to blame for dying of starvation—I know lies! People weak in spirit—and those who live on the sweat of others—these need lies— the weak find support in them, the exploiters use them as a screen. But a man who is his own master, who is independent and doesn't batten on others—he can get along without lies. Lies are the religion of slaves and bosses. Truth is the god of the free man.

The truth that Satin offers recognizes the necessity of hope and its delusions as an ultimate affirmation of humanity. In one of Gorky's most quoted passages, Satin, clear eyed but confident, declares:

> What is man? It's not you, nor I, nor they—No, it's you, I, they, the old man, Napoleon, Mohammed—all in one. You understand? It's tremendous! In this are all the beginnings and all the ends. Everything in man, everything for man. Only man exists, the rest is the work of his hands and his brain. Man! It's magnificent; it has a proud ring to it! A man has to be respected! Not pitied . . . don't degrade him with pity. . . . You've got to respect him!

The final test of pity and respect comes with the revelation that closes the play: The Actor, in despair of gaining a cure for his drunkenness, has hung himself. The news interrupts the lodgers' drunken revelry and prompts Satin's final comment: "Ah, spoiled the song—the fool!"

Gorky's existential drama shocks with the vividness of its characters and the world it portrays, in allowing the marginalized and misfits of society to supply an often profound critique on human possibilities and motives. The play's strengths—its graphic realism and daring mixture of sociology, psychology, and philosophy—do not come without flaws. One of the plays earliest critics of these was Chekhov. After receiving a copy just after Gorky finished the play, Chekhov praised it but noted: "You have excluded the most interesting characters (except for the Actor) from the fourth act, and now mind lest nothing comes of it. That act could seem boring and unnecessary, especially if with the departure of the stronger and more interesting actors only the so-so remain." Chekhov's criticism has been repeated by others, who have similarly complained of Gorky's odd dramatic structure in which act 4 seems more an afterthought as well as of the ideological positions of Luka and Satin that at times seem contradicted by the play's action. Gorky himself later decided he had failed to embody fully his conception of his characters, particularly Luka's selfishness and the destructiveness of his philosophy. Ultimately *The Lower Depths* works neither as a social message nor as a satisfying philosophy but as a powerful psychological drama of life at the bottom. *The Lower Depths* presents, in KING LEAR terms, "unaccommodated man" in which we are instructed, like Lear, "to feel what wretches feel."

PRIVATE LIVES

(1930)   *by Noël Coward*

The Depression put an end to the question of which set of values would prevail. Private
Lives *(1930), a triumph of personality and pace, caught the mood of dissolution. The
bright, breezy veneer of its cross-talk hid disenchantment with a smile. The old narrative
stage conventions had disappeared as well as anything remotely resembling the old values.
Romance is a put-on, honour a masquerade, loyalty hardly an issue, communication a kind
of truce between flying lamps. . . . Minimal as an art deco curve,* Private Lives' *form
matched its content: a plotless play for purposeless people.*

—John Lahr, Coward the Playwright

The comedy of manners, which flourished during the Restoration and High
Georgian periods with the plays of William Wycherley, William Congreve,
Oliver Goldsmith, and Richard Brinsley Sheridan, was revived in the 1890s by
Oscar Wilde and reappeared in the works of Noël Coward. If Wilde, particularly in THE IMPORTANCE OF BEING EARNEST, set the comedic and satiric tone for
sophisticated irresponsibility at the dawn of Edwardian high society with his
epigrammatic verbal acrobatics and "bunburying," Coward, in *Private Lives*,
is, as dramatist Edward Albee has observed "a dramatic mountain goat," scal-
ing, with perfect equipoise and symmetry, heights of moral ambiguity and
wit coupled with vitriol in what is essentially a drawing-room comedy of bad
manners set among the hyper-stylish privileged classes during the years of
disillusionment between the two world wars.

In the second half of the 19th century Wilde created an English persona
for himself and his characters out of an Irelander's sensibility; the quintessen-
tially English Coward, with only slightly less flamboyance, brought a conge-
nial British cynicism and an understated nonchalance to 20th-century theater.
Born in 1899, Coward began his long and diverse career as a precocious child
acting and singing talent and by the time of his death, in 1973, had become
world famous as not only an actor but a playwright, director, producer, composer, lyricist, screenwriter, nightclub entertainer, novelist, poet, memoirist,

and highbrow A-list performing arts celebrity. The second of three sons, he was born in Teddington, England, a small, inelegant suburb of London, to Violet and Arthur Coward. His father was a clerk in a music publishing house who doubled as a piano salesman. It was early determined by Violet that Noel would seek a career in the theater, and in 1911, the opportunity arrived in the form of the leading role in an all-children's fairy play, *The Goldfish*. Coward continued to win child and young-adult roles, appearing from 1913 to 1915 as Slightly in J. M. Barrie's *Peter Pan* and playing Charley Wykeham in the perennial comedy *Charley's Aunt* in 1916. While on tour in the north of England in 1913, he had met another teenage actor, Gertrude Lawrence, who became a close friend and would go on to have a glittering stage career.

In 1917 Coward played an adult role in *The Saving Grace*, a comedy directed by venerable actor-manager Charles Hawtrey. Coward looked upon Hawtrey as a mentor from whom he learned both comic acting and playwriting techniques. The following year Coward was called up for military duty in the British army but suffered a concussion during training and resultant recurring headaches led to his discharge. He turned to playwriting and in 1919 completed his first effort, *I'll Leave It to You*, a comedy concerning a legacy, which was commissioned by American producer George Miller. The play was performed at a matinee in Manchester in 1920 and was a moderate success. Unable to get subsequent plays performed over the next few years because he was an unknown writer, Coward, in 1923, contributed songs and sketches to a revue show, *London Calling!* His first great critical and financial success came in 1924 with the production of *The Vortex*, a somewhat risqué play concerning a drug addict's obsession with his nymphomaniacal mother. Now in great demand, Coward followed the success of *The Vortex* with *Fallen Angels* (1925), a three-act comedy about two middle-aged women who slowly get drunk while anxiously waiting for a mutual lover to arrive, and *Hay Fever* (1925), one of Coward's best-known and most durable comedies, in which four insufferable family members, including an aging actress, insult one another's weekend guests. From the mid- to late 1920s Coward turned out revues, for which he composed such songs as the popular "A Room with a View," and several plays. *Bitter Sweet*, a romantic operetta, for which Coward wrote the book, music, and lyrics, was produced in 1929 and became one of his most successful works.

Coward had promised the starring role in *Bitter Sweet* to Gertrude Lawrence, but it soon became apparent that her voice was not strong enough for the constant singing required for the operetta. He vowed that his next play would be for her. While on a cruise to Asia in 1929 Coward composed his most famous song, "Mad Dogs and Englishmen," and in four days in a hotel room in Tokyo also wrote *Private Lives*. Completed in December, it was, as Coward later observed, "typed, revised, and ready for production" by February of the following year. The three-act, four-character play was produced by

Coward at the Phoenix Theatre on September 8, 1930, and starred Lawrence and Coward. Also in the cast was 23-year-old Laurence Olivier, who would become the most famous actor of the 20th century.

The first act of *Private Lives* begins in a hotel in Deauville, where Elyot Chase and Amanda Prynne, once married to each other and divorced for five years, are with new spouses Sybil and Victor. The couples are beginning their honeymoons. Sybil and Victor are dull, conventional types, convinced they know how to handle their respective spouses (much to Amanda and Elyot's considerable annoyance). Sybil and Victor demand reassurance that they are the chosen love objects (Amanda tells Victor, "I love you . . . calmly") and to that end disparage their predecessors. Amanda, according to Sybil, was "uncontrolled, and wicked, and unfaithful"; Elyot, says Victor, was "a cad." Amanda and Elyot, in contrast to Victor and Sybil, are irritable, often violently quarrelsome bohemian eccentrics in essential harmony with each other, as the action of the play demonstrates. The irony of the play's title begins to become clear as Coward creates an elaborate coincidence by having the couples occupy adjacent hotel suites. When Elyot and Amanda step onto their respective balconies and are shocked to see each other, both try to convince their spouses to leave. Elyot will not tell Sybil why; Amanda tells her husband the truth, prompting this interchange:

> VICTOR   I'm damned if I can see why our whole honeymoon should be upset by Elyot.
>
> AMANDA   My last one was.

After heated arguments with their new spouses, Amanda and Elyot find themselves alone together on Elyot's balcony. As they verbally spar with each other the orchestra plays the same refrain over and over again, leading Amanda to recite one of Coward's best lines: "Extraordinary how potent cheap music is." The scene ultimately results in a declaration of love between the two, and, after agreeing on a catchphrase to use together with a cooling-off period whenever they start to bicker, the couple runs off together. Victor and Sybil meet, share a cocktail, and toast absent friends.

Act 2 takes place a week later in Amanda's Paris apartment, where she and Elyot have been blissfully cohabitating; so far, they have managed to check their quarrels with the password *Sollocks* and five-minute silences while they cool down. However, minor verbal skirmishes concerning the morality of their arrangement, the issue of sex too soon after dinner, Amanda's previous liaisons, and the fact that she refuses to turn off the gramophone get out of hand and not even the magic "Sollocks!" works to restrain them. The two become physically violent, wrestling on the floor and knocking over tables and lamps in the process. Amanda extricates herself and rushes offstage left, slamming the door, and Elyot does the same, stage right, just as Victor and Sybil apprehensively enter the room and sink onto the sofa.

The third act takes place the next morning, as the four characters endeavor to establish their positions for the final battle. In keeping with their personalities, Elyot is amusingly flippant, Amanda is high handed, Victor is unimaginatively upright and proper, and Sybil is wounded and weeping. The men and the women, as well as the spouses, all have heated exchanges with one another and finally agree to divorce, although there is a slight, convoluted disagreement on exactly how to effect these divorce arrangements. Since table manners must be observed at all times, the four enjoy a brief desultory, somewhat absurd respite from squabbling during breakfast, as they discuss the pleasures of travel, especially to the south of France. Amanda's raptures about traveling—". . . arriving at strange places, and seeing strange people, and eating strange foods"—is interrupted by Elyot, who says, "and making strange noises afterwards," a reference to their lovemaking. Amanda chokes on her food at this riposte, prompting Victor and Sybil to begin to quarrel, first over the merits and demerits of having a sense of humor and then more violently, in the manner of Elyot and Amanda. The latter wink at each other across the table and laugh silently. As Victor and Sibyl's quarrel continues to escalate Elyot and Amanda get up quietly and, hand in hand, go toward the front door. Seeing themselves thus mirrored in Victor and Sybil, they exit, smilingly, with their suitcases to a new love venue.

In *Private Lives* reason and convention collide with anarchy, silliness, and improbability in a farcical manner, but as critic Robert Kiernan observes:

> This final tableau announces the triumph of frivolity: the demon of temper in Amanda and Elyot has relocated itself in Sybil and Victor, and Elyot and Amanda take their leave as innocent of involvement in the quarrel as of concern for their spouses. It is an audacious vision—farcically symmetrical but too morally ambiguous for farce, exactly suited to a comedy of manners that proclaims contemporary manners *are* a farce. Victor and Sybil's quarrel actually gives us hope for them, for their bad behavior is a measure of their potential for loving each other in Coward's emotionally symmetric world.

Farce relies on the return of characters to their more conventional personas once the comic chaos has subsided, yet the characters in *Private Lives* are too sophisticated for the play to fit the genre. The socially rebellious Elyot and Amanda are essentially unconventional characters for whom anarchy is a way of life and love; Victor and Sybil similarly abandon all pretenses toward socially acceptable behavior. Although their battles are childish, Elyot and Amanda, especially, possess a sense of self-awareness and a serious appreciation of the frivolous that belies the silly innocence of farce. Coward's view of romantic love in *Private Lives* is certainly cynical, but his explication of relationships is, beneath the superficial brittleness and improbability of farcical comedy, realistic and knowing.

At least one authority figure would have been happy to see *Private Lives* reduced to the status of simple farce. Like so many playwrights before him, Coward had to suffer the censure of the Lord Chamberlain, who, while the play was in its second week of rehearsal, objected to the love scene in the second act on the grounds that it was too risqué for the morality of the times. Coward responded by reading the play in its entirety to him, acting out all the parts, and managing to persuade him that the scene would be acceptable if it were directed with dignity. Decorum notwithstanding, *Private Lives* established Coward as the great comic genius of his generation and continues to be popular in revival.

While *Private Lives* was enjoying its first London success, Coward wrote a famous parody of the play, titled *Some Other Private Lives*, which was performed at a charity matinee at the Hippodrome. The play featured the four principal actors from the Phoenix Theatre production playing characters named Fred (Elyot), Flossie (Amanda), Elsie (Sybil), and Alf (Victor); the setting was a lower-middle-class lodging house. Coward's parody had a touch of the prophetic about it. His brand of English drawing-room comedy featuring the free-thinking, socially unbound privileged classes between the wars would give way to the postwar dramas of such playwrights as Harold Pinter and John Osborne, whose disillusioned and constricted middle- and lower-middle-class families in their semi-detached houses, attic flats, and kitchens struggle to communicate with one another in the hopes of reaching, as in *Private Lives*, an enchanted and delicate balance.

FOOL FOR LOVE

76

(1983)   *by Sam Shepard*

Everything about Fool for Love *suggests a controlled hallucination. Nothing is certain, least of all incest, since the Old Man insists he see nothing of himself in either of the lovers. Nor can we believe anything that May and Eddie say about one another. We can be certain that they inspire obsessiveness, each in himself or herself and in the (more-or-less) beloved. . . . Shepard's people are lyrical selves, desperately seeking a stable identity. They are not going to find it. Their dramatist remains our major living visionary, stationed at the edge of our common abyss.*

—Harold Bloom, Introduction to *Sam Shepard*

In his critical study *American Dreams: The Imagination of Sam Shepard*, Michael Earley observes that Shepard "seems to have forged a whole new kind of American play," bringing to his work "a liberating interplay of word, theme, and image that has always been the hallmark of the romantic impulse. His plays don't work like plays in the traditional sense but more like romances, where the imaginary landscape (his version of America) is so remote and open that it allows for the depiction of legend, adventure, and even the supernatural." The author of more than 40 plays and 15 screenplays, Shepard, in the words of critic Jack Kroll, has "overturned theatrical conventions and created a new kind of drama filled with violence, lyricism and an intensely American compound of comic and tragic power." There is perhaps no better example of Shepard's particular theatrical power and originality than *Fool for Love*, in which the iconic American isolated individual, the family, and American myth—Poe-derived gothic and western frontier images—collide in a shabby motel room on the edge of the Mojave Desert. *Fool for Love* has been described by reviewer Frank Rich as an "indoor rodeo" and "a western for our time" in which "We watch a pair of figurative gunslingers fight to the finish—not with bullets, but with piercing words that give ballast to the weight of a nation's buried dreams." *Fool for Love* is, in the words of critic Douglass Watt, "Sam Shepard's purest and most beautiful play. An aching love story of classical symmetry, it is . . . like watching the division of an amoeba in reverse, ending with a perfect whole." In significant ways Shepard's *Fool for Love* is a culmination of the playwright's vision and dramatic innovations, which have secured his place as one of the most important contemporary American writers and dramatists.

Born Samuel Shepard Rogers in 1943 in Fort Sheridan, Illinois, Shepard is the son of a career army officer who spent his early childhood moving from base to base before his family settled, after his father's retirement from the military, on a ranch in Duarte, California, where they grew avocados and raised sheep. There Shepard enjoyed the ranch work and began playing his father's drum set, the start of his continuing fascination with rock and roll. After graduating from high school Shepard spent three semesters studying agriculture at the local community college with the intention of becoming a veterinarian. His father's abusive drinking, however, made his family situation intolerable. "Everything just got so hysterical in my family," Shepard remembered, that "I fled the scene." Having been introduced to plays by reading Samuel Beckett's *Waiting for Godot*, which he did not understand, and acting in campus productions, Shepard left home to tour with a repertory company. In 1963, after a few months of performing in church halls throughout New England, at the age of 19, he changed his name to Sam Shepard and headed to New York City. He landed a job at the Village Gate, a downtown jazz club, where he met Ralph Cook, the founder of the Off-Off-Broadway Theatre Genesis, who encouraged him to switch from the poetry he was writing to playwriting. Shepard's first efforts—*Cowboys* and *The Rock Garden*—were first performed at St. Mark's Church in the East Village. "When I arrived in New York," Shepard later recalled, "there was this environment of *art* going on. I mean, it was really tangible. And you were right *in* the thing, especially on the Lower East Side. La Mama, Theatre Genesis . . . all those theaters were just starting. So that was a great coincidence. I had a place to go and put something on without having to go through a producer or go through the commercial network. All of that was in response to the tightness of Broadway and Off-Broadway, where you couldn't get a play done." Between 1965 and 1970 Shepard completed more than 14 plays, mixing striking verbal and visual images derived from popular culture—B-westerns, sci-fi and horror films, country and rock music. Shepard has called his early works "survival kits" and "explosions that were coming out of some kind of inner turmoil in me that I didn't understand at all." Shepard's originality and experimentation found an audience in New York City's burgeoning Off-Off Broadway theater scene in the 1960s. His first major uptown production, *Operation Sidewinder*, first performed at Lincoln Center in 1970, is a surrealistic fantasy set in Hopi Indian country of the American Southwest about the attempts to control a huge, mechanical rattlesnake originally designed to trace unidentified flying objects. A mixed-media experience assaulting the audience's senses, one reviewer observed: "Everything about Sam Shepard's *Operation Sidewinder* is important to our theater. More than any recent major production, it is built upon exactly the style and the mentality energizing the youth movement in America today."

From 1971 to 1974 Shepard lived in London, explaining the move by saying that "the difference between living in New York and working in New York became wider and wider. . . . And also I was into a lot of drugs then. . . . I didn't feel like going back to California, so I thought I'd come here—really to get into music, you know. . . . I had this fantasy that I'd come over here and somehow fall into a rock 'n' roll band. It didn't work." Instead he managed to write a series of plays—*Angel City*, *Geography of a Horse Dreamer*, and *The Tooth of Crime*—dealing with the various seductions of the artist and a new consideration of the American experience. "It wasn't until I came to England that I found out what it means to be an American," Shepard has stated. "Nothing really makes sense when you're there, but the more distant you are from it, the more the implications of what you grew up with start to emerge." In the mid-1970s Shepard returned to California, becoming playwright-in-residence at the Magic Theatre in San Francisco where he produced some of his most important plays—*Buried Child, Curse of the Starving Class*, and *True West*. Having long avoided traditional American realistic drama in the mode of Eugene O'Neill's *Long Day's Journey* or Tennessee Williams's *Cat on a Hot Tin Roof,* Shepard explained that "I always did feel a part of that tradition but *hated it*. I couldn't stand those plays that were all about the 'turmoil' of the family. And then all of a sudden I realized, well that was very much a part of my life, and maybe that has to do with being a playwright, that you're somehow snared beyond yourself." Shepard's take on the American family drama shifts the emphasis from sociological realism to the tormented psychology underlying family relationships in which the particularity of time and place morphs into the mythic, and characters becomes archetypes.

Fool for Love, first produced at the Magic Theatre in San Francisco in 1983 under Shepard's direction before moving to New York's Circle Repertory the same year, illustrates the playwright's reinterpretation of the American family drama. Meant to be "performed relentlessly without a break," as stated in Shepard's stage directions, the play is set in a "stark, low-rent room on the edge of the Mojave Desert," as two characters—Eddie and May—face off. May, in her early 30s, sits on the bed "legs apart, elbows on knees, hands hanging limp and crossed between her knees, head hanging forward, face staring at the floor," embodying defeated and vulnerable desolation. Eddie, a rodeo stunt-man, with a body that is "aged long before his time," dressed in his cowboy gear, sits at a table insisting that he's "not goin' anywhere." When he moves closer to stroke her hair, May squeezes his leg, then pushes him away, accusing him of smelling like he has been with another women, which Eddie denies. These apparently reunited, battling lovers are not alone in the motel room. An

Old Man, attired like Eddie and suggesting a resemblance that will be developed in the play, is seated on a rocker, drinking whiskey from a Styrofoam cup. In Shepard's stage directions, he "exists only in the minds of May and Eddie." Having written as many as 16 drafts struggling to present his lovers and their situation, Shepard finally struck on the notion of introducing the spectral presence of the Old Man, which shifted the play from a conventionally romantic confrontation between long-separated lovers to a more expansive, deeper psychological drama suspended between fantasy and reality. By employing the Old Man as a kind of chorus and projection of the protagonists (or they of him), Shepard breaks realistic conventions, suggesting that the play is simultaneously naturalistic and symbolic in which the characters must be regarded both in actuality and as figments of consciousness. This is made clear in the Old Man's first words to Eddie. Directing his attention to a nonexistent picture on the wall of singer Barbara Mandrell, he asks Eddie "would you believe me if I told ya' I was married to her?" After Eddie replies, "No," the Old Man responds: "Well, see, now that's the difference right there. That's realism. I'm actually married to Barbara Mandrell in my mind. Can you understand that?" The distinction prepares the way for the audience to expect different planes of reality in a play that incorporates the unseen and fantastical.

The Old Man's words are delivered after May has kissed Eddie and then kneed him in the groin, dramatizing their combat that gravitates between attraction and repulsion—fight or flight. Having retreated to the bathroom, she reenters with a red dress and heels, announcing that she has a date. Eddie leaves, returning with a bottle of tequila and a shotgun, playing the role of the jealous lover and accusing May of forgetting their "pact" and reminding her that she will never be able to replace him. After he leaves again May begins to weep, and the Old Man tells a story of traveling with her when she was a child. Because May would not stop crying, he took her into a herd of mooing cattle in total darkness, which silenced her. This story comforts her, and she begins drinking from Eddie's bottle. When he returns they resume their quarrel, with Eddie alternately denying that May's date exists and threatening to "nail his ass to the floor." May responds by calling Eddie a "jealous, little snot-nosed kid," as their argument takes on the appearance of a sibling squabble. Headlights shine through the window. Assuming that her date has arrived May opens the door but sees a woman sitting in a black Mercedes staring back at her. She is identified as the "countess," Eddie's ex-lover who has tracked him down. Gunshots ring out, and after the car drives off Eddie reports that the windshield of his truck has been shot out. He urges May to forget the past and leave with him. As both stand looking at each other, the Old Man comments that neither of them resembles him, causing him to doubt his paternity. Eddie asserts his faithfulness, while May complains that he has manipulated her for 15 years. Headlights again shine in the room. Eddie attempts to push May into the bathroom as she tries to break free to confront the countess. Instead

Martin, May's date, crashes through the door and pulls Eddie to the ground. May stops the fight by introducing Eddie as her cousin, which Eddie denies, and blocks Martin's exit insisting that they have a drink.

Eddie explains to Martin that May is his half sister. Their father, a rambler, lived alternately and secretly with each of their mothers. Eddie then recounts to Martin the night he first met May as a teenager. Joining his father on one of his nocturnal walks, Eddie ended up at May's mother's house where he first encountered the young May: "We can't take our eyes off each other. It was like we knew each other from somewhere but we couldn't place where. But the second we saw each other, that very second, we knew we'd never stop being in love." May calls Eddie a liar and counters with her version of the story in which her mother's desperate search for her father, who has disappeared, finally led to the town where he was living with his other family. "The funny thing was," May explains, "that almost as soon as we'd found him—he disappeared. . . . Nobody saw him after that. Ever. And my mother—just turned herself inside out." Ignoring the pain of her mother's obsession and the threat that Eddie would become like his father—irresistible but restless and unfaithful—May fell hopelessly in love with Eddie. May's mother urges Eddie's mother to separate the lovers, but she responds by blowing her brains out. The Old Man protests that May's version of the past could not be true and demands that Eddie balance May's account with "the male side of things. You gotta represent me now. Speak on my behalf. . . . Tell her the way it happened. We've got a pact. Don't forget that." Eddie refuses, confirming May's story, while embracing her. As the pair ignores the Old Man who tries to part them, the sound of an explosion and shattering glass is heard. Eddie's ex-lover has returned to torch his truck and set free his horses. As Eddie exits, promising to return, May begins to pack. Martin offers her a ride if she needs one, expecting her to leave with Eddie, but May tells him Eddie has already gone and then follows him out of the room. The Old Man closes the play by pointing to the imaginary picture of Barbara Mandrell on the wall and saying, "Ya' see that picture over there? Ya? see that? Ya know who that is? That's the woman of my dreams. That's who that is. And she's mine. She's all mine. Forever."

In Shepard's version of ROMEO AND JULIET, the warring families dividing the lovers are the same family, and each of the star-crossed lovers is the projection of the other's deepest needs and fears. Psychology, heredity, and the environment unite to make love toxic, as fated as it is self-destructive. In the end all that is left are illusions. The vestiges of the American myth of limitless possibility and transcendent freedom have narrowed to the claustrophobic four walls of a motel room in which a tormented present battles a distorted past to a draw as Shepard's lovers wrestle with the ties of blood and passion that are inescapable. By subverting the confines of realistic drama Shepard finds a dramatic arena for his lovers' combat in which fantasy contends with reality, love with hatred, the mundane with the mythic.

A FLEA IN HER EAR

(1907)

by Georges Feydeau

Farce is tragedy played at about a hundred and twenty revolutions a minute. The story of Othello and the plot of Feydeau's Puce à l'Oreille *have a striking similarity. Desdemona's lost handkerchief and Victor Emmanuel Chandebise's missing braces both give rise to similar misunderstandings, undeserved jealousies and accumulating catastrophe. Othello's mistake is the stuff of tragedy, Madame Chandebise's leads to events which move so quickly that we are left helpless with laughter and nobody dies.*

—John Mortimer, Introduction to *Georges Feydeau: Three Boulevard Farces*

Georges Feydeau is the modern master of farce. Regarded by some as the greatest French dramatist since Molière, others have only granted him the dubious achievement of perfecting the commercially seductive bedroom farce, that somewhat tawdry drama of quick entrances and exits and bed-hopping run amok. Historically no French playwright dominated or better represented his era—France during *la belle époque*—than Feydeau, capturing in his plays the pleasure-loving, halcyon years before the cataclysm of the Great War. Although his plays can be read as period pieces, their persistence suggests a greater appeal and relevance. Feydeau's dramas are, first and foremost, marvels of dramatic and comic construction that continue to perform wonderfully well. While hilarity is certainly its own justification, it can be argued that his farces anticipate the concerns that would dominate 20th-century experimental theater, particularly the theater of the absurd. For the existentialists Feydeau's often blameless characters trapped in ridiculous situations beyond their control seemed emblematic of the absurd. Eugène Ionesco claimed a kinship. "I was astonished to see there was great resemblance between Feydeau and myself," he observed, ". . . not in the themes or subjects of the plays, but in the rhythm and their structure. The development of a play like *La Puce*, for example, demands a pace that rapidly quickens to a dizzy climax, the movement lies in a kind of lunatic progression; there I seem to recognize my own obsession with proliferation." As critic Manuel A. Esteban has observed,

Well before Ionesco and Beckett, and in similar fashion, Feydeau had underlined the absurdity of social institutions, the stupidity of ordinary speech and small talk, the impossibility of true communication despite constant talking, the incompatibility of the sexes, as couples destroy and strip each other of their dignity, the ultimate isolation of the individual and the fate of man as a simple puppet, the plaything of inexorable forces and a capricious fate.

While never daring the more radical violations of audience expectation and coherence provided by absurdist dramatists, Feydeau's farces—particularly his most performed and best-known play worldwide, *Une Puce à l'oreille* (*A Flea in Her Ear*)—manage to reach beyond sheer entertainment and justify representation in a listing of great drama.

Georges-Léon-Jules-Marie Feydeau was born in Paris in 1862. His father, Ernest, was a stockbroker who gained notoriety by writing the sensational novel *Fanny*. His mother was a Polish beauty who became the subject of rumored affairs. She would deny the allegation that Napoleon III was the real father of her son by saying, "How could you believe that such an intelligent child could be the son of that imbecile!" Influenced by his father's literary interests and association with such notable writers as Théophile Gautier, Gustave Flaubert, and Edmond and Jules Goncourt, Feydeau began writing plays by the age of 10. Submitting an early effort to the French dramatist Henri Meilhac, he was allegedly told, "My child, your play is stupid. And it is theatrical. You will be a great man of the theater." After his father's death in 1873, Feydeau's mother remarried a well-known journalist, and the couple, to dissuade Feydeau from pursuing a theatrical career, secured him a clerical position in a law firm. Feydeau persisted in his theatrical interests, however, attending the theater regularly and writing. He performed a comic monologue, "The Rebellious Young Lady," at a social gathering, and it proved so popular that he wrote several others that were performed by leading comedians of the day. His first play, the one-act comedy *Par la fenêtre* (*Wooed and Viewed*), was produced in 1881; his first full-length play, *Tailleur pour dames* (*Fittings for Ladies*), appeared with great success in 1886. Several poorly received plays followed, and in 1890 Feydeau stopped writing for two years to study the techniques of the leading French dramatic masters and discover a formula for success.

Feydeau's theatrical options in the 1890s included the experimental symbolist dramas provided by Lugné-Poe's Théâtre de Œuvre, which opened in 1893 with Maurice Maeterlinck's hauntingly symbolic *Pelléas et Mélisandre* and would cause a scandal with Alfred Jarry's shocking *King Ubu* in 1896. Naturalistic drama was on display at André Antoine's Théâtre Libre, founded in 1887. Both experimental theaters were alternatives to the dominant commercial theater of the boulevards that still specialized in well-made plays mastered by Eugène Scribe and his successor, Victorien Sardou. Scribe had transformed vaudeville, the unsophisticated French popular entertainment that mixed sentiment, comedy, and song into an ingeniously constructed dramatic form that dominated the French stage from the mid-19th century. Critic Leonard C. Pronko summarizes:

> Essential to the well-made play is its logical structure—indeed, the well-made play in Scribe's hands at least is almost nothing *but* structure, and action is its focal point: not action in a philosophical sense, but intrigue neither pure nor simple. Beginning at a point near its climax, the action rises and falls in a ceaseless movement following the fortunes and misfortunes of the hero and heroine, punctuated by reversals and surprises, and ending in a moving or thrilling "obligatory scene" (*scène à faire*) in which a secret, known to the audience but withheld from certain characters, is finally revealed, and the true character of one or more personages is made clear.

Feydeau would master the construction principles of Scribe and his imitators for his return to the stage, infusing the stock characters and situations of the well-made play with a new freshness and frisson by drawing both more directly from life. "I noticed that *vaudevilles* were invariably built on obsolete plots," Feydeau recalled, "with conventional, ridiculous, false characters, puppets." Feydeau would base his comedies on believable characters in outlandish, but at least identifiable situations. "Each of us in life," Feydeau explained, "gets mixed up in farcical situations without necessarily losing our individuality in the process. That was all I needed. I started to search for my characters in real life, determined to preserve their personalities intact. After a comic explosion, I would hurl them into burlesque situations." Feydeau emerged from his hiatus with a dramatic prescription—"a gram of imbroglio, a gram of libertinage, a gram of observation"—that he used in a unbroken string of highly successful plays, including *Champignol malgré lui* (1892; *Champignol in Spite of Himself*), *Un Fil à la patte* (1894; *Not by Bed Alone*), *L'Hôtel du libre échange* (1894; *Hotel Paradiso*), *Le Dindon* (1896; *The Dupe*), *La Dame de chez Maxim* (1899; *The Lady from Maxim's*), *Le Bourgeon* (1906; *The Sprout*), *A Flea in Her Ear* (1907), *Occupe-toi d'Amélie* (1908; *Keep an Eye on Amélie*), and *Je ne trompe pas mon mari* (1914; *I'm Not Deceiving My Husband*). Feydeau reigned as the king of the boulevard theater until World War I altered the dramatic landscape. Despite enormous success from a seemingly bottomless reservoir of comedy, Feydeau's personal life was marked by considerable sadness and setback. His marriage was unhappy, and in 1909, he left his home to reside in a hotel for the next 10 years, living a largely nocturnal and increasingly isolated life. In 1919, after contracting venereal disease, he was institutionalized for madness. He died in 1921.

A Flea in Her Ear perfectly represents Feydeau's dramatic genius and the satisfying formula he employed to produce his breathlessly energized comedies. The comic explosion that ignites the farce is the "flea" of jealousy that infects Raymonde, whose loving husband, Chandebise, has recently been unable to fulfill his conjugal duties. When she opens a package addressed to her husband from the Hôtel du Minet-Galant containing his suspenders, Raymonde is convinced that Chandebise is having an affair. She devises a plan to catch him in the act by having her friend, Lucienne, write an anonymous letter to him requesting a rendezvous. When he comes to the hotel for the assignation, Raymonde will be waiting for him. What she does not know is that Chandebise is under doctor's orders treating his condition and that the suspenders had been given to his nephew, Camille, who left them at the hotel when he was last there with the maid Antoinette. Marital deception is the staple of Feydeau's comedies with infidelity (real or imagined) of either husband or wife fueling mounting complication that turns on some secret, mistake, misjudgment, or lie. When Chandebise receives the note, he assumes it has reached him by mistake and shows it to his friend, Tournel, a dashing young man secretly attempting to seduce Raymonde. Later Chandebise shows the letter to Lucienne's fiery-tempered husband, Homenides, who recognizes his wife's handwriting and threatens Chandebise. He defends himself by revealing that it is Tournel who is going to the assignation, sending the murderous Homenides in hot pursuit and his servant, Emile, Antoinette's husband, to warn Tournel.

In act 2, all converge at the shady Hôtel du Minet-Galant. "When writing a play," Feydeau stated, "I seek among my characters the ones who should not run into each other. And they are precisely the ones I bring into a confrontation as soon as possible." Here the confrontations are further complicated by two special features of the hotel. To cater to their clientele's illicit affairs, a room in the hotel is equipped with a bed on a turntable in which, in case of the unexpected arrival of a suspicious spouse, when a button is pushed, the bed and a section of the wall turn and are replaced by the bed in the next room, occupied by the owner's old uncle, Baptisin, whose job is to lie in bed reading. The other feature is the uncanny resemblance between Chandebise and Poche, the drunken hotel porter (both parts are played by the same actor who astounds the audience with quick costume changes and precisely timed entrances and exits). Raymonde arrives in the room, and while she is in the adjacent washroom, Tournel enters and sits on the bed, hidden by a curtain. When Raymonde returns, she slaps Tournel, believing he is her husband. Once he is recognized, Tournel tries to convince her to become his lover, but she resists. As he goes to lock the door, the frightened Raymonde presses the button to summon help. Tournel turns back from the door and leaps onto the bed, showering Baptisin with kisses. Next door, Raymonde flees, seeing Poche in the hall and believes he is her husband. When the button is pushed again, the original bed returns with Poche sitting in it, indifferently hearing the pleas of both Tournel and Raymonde for forgiveness, in a perfect reversal of the initial situation in which Chandebise's infidelity was to have been exposed. Both are shocked when Ferraillon, the hotel owner, comes in and repeatedly kicks "Chandebise."

When Camille arrives with the maid, Antoinette, they flee from Poche, also thinking him Chandebise. Camille winds up the next occupant on the revolving bed, while Antoinette seeks refuge in another guest's room, that of a violent, sex-starved Englishman who proceeds to undress her. Etienne, who has come to warn Lucienne about Homenides, enters to discover his wife with the Englishman. Lucienne arrives, having agreed to help Raymonde confront Chandebise, who follows in advance of the murderous Homenides. In the escalating chaos of Feydeau's masterfully timed entrances and exits and escalating misunderstandings, Ferraillon mistakes Chandebise for Poche, kicking him and forcing him to wear Poche's livery. Poche puts on the clothes discarded by Chandebise. Raymonde, encountering her husband, believes him to be Poche; Lucienne runs into Poche believing him to be Chandebise, and they take refuge in Baptisin's room. When the furious Homenides arrives in the empty room next door, he shoots at the button, and the bed turns, revealing Poche (whom he takes for Chandebise) and his wife together as he first suspected. The act ends in magnificent chaos as everyone flees from the hotel.

In act 3, in a kind of distorted mirrored version of the previous act, Antoinette, Raymonde, Lucienne, and Tournel have returned to Chandebise's home and anxiously await his arrival. Instead Poche arrives to deliver Chandebise's clothing. They believe him to have gone mad since he insists he is not Chandebise but Poche. When the actual Chandebise appears, Camille thinks he has gone mad since he has just put his uncle to bed. Ferraillon next appears and again begins to kick Chandebise, believing him to be Poche. After Homenides threatens him with his gun, Chandebise is finally convinced of his own madness when he sees "himself" in his own bed. Poche finally jumps out of the window to avoid being shot by Homenides. Having pushed his characters and their situation to lunacy, Feydeau next restores order by clearing up all the misunderstandings and mistaken identities. Finding the first version of his wife's love letter to Chandebise written by Raymonde, Homenides is now prepared to believe her explanation, forgive his wife, and help convince Chandebise why he found Raymonde in the arms of Tournel at the hotel. Raymonde finally confesses her suspicion of Chandebise's infidelity, to which he replies:

CHANDEBISE   Good heavens! Why? Whatever gave you that idea?

RAYMONDE   Well, because you—because . . .

CHANDEBISE   No! Not for such a little . . .

RAYMONDE   But *because* there was such a little . . .

CHANDEBISE   Oh—well!

RAYMONDE   I know. I was very silly. The fact is—I had a flea in my ear!

CHANDEBISE   [*putting his arm round her*] All right! I'll squash that flea, tonight!

RAYMONDE   You?

CHANDEBISE   Yes. That is—[*he lets her go*]—well, at least I'll try!

Like an amusement park thrill ride, *A Flea in Her Ear* leaves its audience breathless as spectators to a nonstop series of barely averted catastrophes in which our most trusted assumptions about identity, time, and space are comically undermined. Feydeau's farces expose the chaos underneath the conventional. Paradoxically the playwright's meticulously logical dramatic construction of finely timed entrances and exits demonstrates ultimately the underlying absurdity and irrationality of life. Feydeau's comedies ultimately affirm not order but our often tenuous grip on normalcy. All comedy takes aim at our pretensions, but few comedies mount a more effective assault on our most sacred assumptions that we are in control of our destiny than *A Flea in Her Ear*.

GLENGARRY GLEN ROSS

78

(1983) *by David Mamet*

Like Mamet's other plays, Glengarry Glen Ross *can be viewed on several different, even contrasting levels: it can be seen as a black comedy, a thriller, a morality play with serious political overtones, a straightforward account of the world of real estate sales, and a study of male companionship and competition. Its chief value, however, lies in Mamet's superb use of language; the play is an unsurpassed demonstration of linguistic skill by a playwright already lauded for his dialogue. His interest in storytelling reaches its zenith in this work—his salesmen are both fabulators and consummate actors who are able to set up a fictional "reality" with ease. But it is not merely their ability to construct stories that make Mamet's salesmen interesting; it is why they choose to do so. They sell not only real estate but also hope and consolation, as much to themselves as to their hapless clients. So alone in the world are they that they need words to construct alternative worlds. It is their tragedy that they have subverted language to such a degree that they can barely articulate genuine needs and emotions. Selling is their whole lives, and they do not really exist outside of the workplace. Despite their corruption, they are worthy of our sympathy; a ruthless, capitalist society has set them on the wheel, and for them there is no turning back.*
—Anne Dean, David Mamet: Language as Dramatic Action

Virtually all critical appreciations of playwright David Mamet begin with his ear, in praise of his remarkable ability to characterize through dialogue that seems both spot-on street smart and revelatory. English critic Robert Cushman has asserted that "Nobody alive writes better American," while the critic Jack Kroll has called Mamet "that rare bird, an American playwright, who is a language playwright. . . . the first playwright to create a formal and moral shape out of the undeleted expletives of our foul-mouthed time." Discussing Mamet's most acclaimed play, *Glengarry Glen Ross*, reviewer Frank Rich observed that "the strange and wonderful thing about the play . . . is Mr. Mamet's ability to turn almost every word inside out. The playwright makes all-American music hot jazz and wounding blues out of his salesman's scatological native lingo. In the jagged riffs of coarse, monosyllabic words, we hear and feel both the exhilaration and sweaty desperation of the huckster's calling." In tapping into both the American vernacular and zeitgeist, Mamet is the direct descendant of other American playwrights, such as Tennessee Williams and Edward Albee, who revitalized stage language with a breakthrough lyricism and realism, as well as Eugene O'Neill and Arthur Miller, who used drama as a penetrating instrument to explore American identity and the American dream. *Glengarry Glen Ross* in its subject, ambition, and thematic reach forces a comparison with Miller's THE DEATH OF A SALESMAN. Both plays link the pursuit of the American dream with the salesmen who purvey it, men who are in turn consumed and corrupted by the dreams they sell. Compared to the tragic dimensions of Miller's play, however, Mamet has called *Glengarry Glen Ross* "a kind of bastard play. It's formally a gang comedy in the tradition of *The Front Page* or *Men in White*. And the first act is episodic, although like a detective story, almost gothic. The second act is a very traditional formal last act of a comedy drama." Mamet has defined a "gang comedy" as "a play about revealing the specific natures and the unifying natures of a bunch of people who happen to be involved in one enterprise." That enterprise is American business, encapsulated in *Glengarry Glen Ross* by the shady and cut-throat dealings of pitchmen peddling dubious land development schemes in Arizona and Florida. Drawing a distinction between his play and Miller's, Mamet asserts: "*Death of a Salesman* is really not concerned with big business. That is the difference. *Death of a Salesman* is a tragedy. The gang comedy is really concerned with the effects of the specific environment, which in a gang comedy is almost always the work place, on the people engaged—whereas in *Death of a Salesman* Miller is concerned with the family. It is a tragedy about a man who happens to be a salesman." The power of *Glengarry Glen Ross* comes from its stripping away all the humanizing alternates to the profit motives that drives the characters. The drama, therefore, takes on the qualities of a frightening version of the American Dream, in which family is replaced by the firm and transcendence has devolved into the pitch with no option to separate reality from illusion.

Mamet's progress in tapping into the American vernacular and the American experience began in Chicago, where he was born in 1947. Both of his parents—his father who worked as a labor lawyer and his schoolteacher mother—were children of Jewish immigrants who downplayed their ancestry and heritage to assimilate and succeed as Americans. Mamet would attribute his early fascination with language to his father, an amateur semanticist, who often insisted that his son find the exact word to express himself. When his parents divorced in 1958, Mamet first lived with his mother in the Chicago suburbs but eventually moved into the city with his father, transferring to a private school where he first took drama classes and played his first lead role in a school musical. His interest in the theater was further stimulated by working backstage at the Hull House Theater and as a "general dogsbody" for the improvisational-comedy Second City Company. Mamet would later credit the fast-paced, improvised, and satirical sketches he saw performed at Second City as crucial in his development as a dramatist. From 1965 to 1969 Mamet attended Goddard College in Vermont as a literature and drama major, spending his junior year in New York City at the Neighborhood Playhouse, a Stanislavsky-oriented company under the direction of Sanford Meisner, a founding member of the Group Theatre of the 1930s. Mamet would value his experiences there in teaching him the degree to which "the language we use, its rhythm, actually determines the way we behave rather than the other way around."

Mamet's first play, a Second City–style revue called *Camel*, served as his thesis for his Goddard degree. After graduating Mamet divided his time between theater work as an actor, dancer, and stage manager and a number of part-time jobs in Chicago as a cabdriver, short-order cook, and busboy. For almost a year Mamet worked as an office manager in what he has called "a fly-by-night operation which sold tracts of undeveloped land in Arizona and Florida to gullible Chicagoans." He would eventually bring the office and its staff to life in *Glengarry Glen Ross*. In 1970 he served a one-semester appointment as an acting teacher at Marlboro College in Vermont, and in 1971 he was invited back to Goddard to teach in the theater program. There he completed the initial drafts of *Duck Variations*, vignettes of two old men musing on a park bench, and *Sexual Perversity in Chicago*, concerning relationships of young urban singles. Both were initially performed in Chicago, the first of Mamet's plays to be produced commercially. Mamet's breakthrough play, *American Buffalo*, followed, opening on Broadway in 1977. Set in a dilapidated junk shop, it deals with the efforts of the store owner and two associates to steal a valuable American buffalo nickel. Their scheme comes to nothing, and, as critic John Lahr observes, "In these bumbling and inarticulate meatheads, Mamet has found a metaphor for the spiritual failure of entrepreneurial capitalism." Featuring Mamet's trademark staccato language that trails off into pauses and profanity, the play jettisons major plot action for character revelation in a minimalist naturalistic drama that still manages a telling critique of American myth and reality. As Edith Oliver observed in her review, "What makes [the play] fascinating are its characters and the sudden spurts of feeling and shifts of mood—the mounting tension under the seemingly aimless surface, which gives the play its momentum." Many of the play's themes and methods—its all-male cast, its robbery plot, its uncensored street argot, and its indirect critique of American capitalist society—would be reworked six years later in *Glengarry Glen Ross*.

Mamet has written that *Glengarry Glen Ross* "is about a society based on business . . . a society with only one bottom line: How much money you make." In this society, "It becomes legitimate for those in power in the business world to act unethically. The effect of the little guy is that he turns to crime. And petty crime goes punished; major crimes go unpunished." To embody his theme Mamet shifts his concern from the petty thieves of *American Buffalo* to a group of salesmen vying with one another to sell the most parcels of Florida land developments, including the seductive-sounding Glengarry Highlands and Glen Ross Farms. Initially unsure about the play's unconventional two-act structure in which the audience is immediately confronted with the insider language of real estate and must puzzle out relationships and circumstances with no concessions to explanations and exposition, Mamet sent his play to Harold Pinter for a reaction. Pinter responded by arranging for a production at London's National Theatre, where it premiered in 1983. The American premiere followed in Chicago before transferring to Broadway the same year, winning the Pulitzer Prize for 1984.

Glengarry Glen Ross opens with a series of three two-character scenes in separate booths of a Chinese restaurant. In the first, Shelly "the Machine" Levene, a former top salesman on a losing streak, meets with the real estate office manager John Williamson to intimidate, beg, and finally bribe him into releasing the good leads (contact information of promising customers). Levene's urgency and desperation are explained in context, as details are gleaned from the first two scenes: the company's downtown bosses, Mitch and Murray, have established a sales contest in which the top earner will win a new Cadillac, the runner-up gets a set of steak knives, and the others get fired. The "A-list" leads—the Glengarry leads— are reserved for the those at the top of the "board," with Shelly and the others forced to make do with played-out prospects. "You're giving me toilet paper, John," Levene insists. "I've *seen* those leads. . . . They're *broke*, John. They're cold. They're deadbeats." Williamson eventually agrees to violate Mitch and Murray's edict by giving Levene some of the premium leads for a percentage of his sales, but the deal breaks down when he further insists on an upfront payment of 50 dollars a lead, forcing Shelly to do the best he can with the "B list."

In the second scene, in another booth in the restaurant, two of the other salesmen—Dave Moss and George Aaronow—discuss their frustration at being forced to get results from the worthless leads they have been given. Moss floats the idea of staging a fake break-in at the office to steal the premium leads, selling them to a competitor, and eventually going to work for him. In a brilliant example of Moss's manipulation, beginning with "just talking," he winds up threatening to name Aaronow as an accomplice before the fact if he does not steal the leads:

> AARONOW Why are you doing this to me, Dave. Why are you talk-
> ing this way to me? I don't understand. Why are you doing this at
> *all* . . . ?
>
> Moss That's none of your fucking business . . .

AARONOW   Well, well, well, *talk* to me, we sat down to eat *dinner*, and here I'm a *criminal* . . .

Moss   You *went* for it.

AARONOW   In the abstract . . .

Moss   So I'm making it concrete.

AARONOW   Why?

Moss   Why? Why *you* going to give me five grand?

AARONOW   Do you need five grand?

Moss   Is that what I just said?

AARONOW   You need money? Is that the . . .

Moss   Hey, hey, let's just keep it simple, what I need is not the . . . what do *you* need . . . ?

AARONOW   What is the five grand? [*Pause.*] What is the, you said that we were going to *split* five . . .

Moss   I lied. [*Pause.*] Alright? My end is *my* business. Your end's twenty-five. In or out. You tell me, you're out you take the consequences.

AARONOW   I do?

Moss   Yes. [*Pause.*]

AARONOW   And why is that?

Moss   Because you listened.

In the third scene Richard Roma, mentioned in passing in the first scene as the salesman at the top of the board, is in conversation with another solitary drinker named Jim Lingk. Roma's near-monologue asserting his existential life philosophy of "acting each day without fear" that glides effortlessly into a sales pitch has been described by critic Stanley Kaufman, in its "conversational start through pungent musings to the sheer ecstasy of selling," as "one of the finest Dionysian swirls in twentieth-century American drama." Seducing both Lingk and the audience Roma offers an intimacy that becomes nothing more than a sales strategy, making Mamet's point that these salesmen will violate every human need to get a sale.

Act 1 establishes the obsessed and ruthless world of these salesmen, sets the play in motion with its robbery plot, and creates a perfect paradigm for American business. "American capitalism comes down to one thing," Mamet has observed. "The operative axiom is 'Hurrah for me and fuck you.' Anything else is a lie." The company's competition with its unequal distribution of a Cadillac, steak knives, or a sacking perfectly encapsulates a system in which success, defined by results, is rewarded, and failure is not tolerated. Under such intense pressure and such a system, it is not surprising that Moss proposes a robbery as the means to success, given that the sales themselves of dubious land parcels are just another form of criminality inherent in business. Moreover, in Roma's remarkable monologue, Mamet makes clear that these salesmen are wordsmiths, role players, and brilliant performers, selling not land parcels but their customers' need to dream and trust.

Act 2 deals with consequence. Set in the ransacked real estate office the next morning, the act takes on the conventional outlines of a whodunit as a detective uses the inner office to interrogate each salesmen about the burglary. Roma arrives demanding to know if his contract for the sale of property to Lingk has been filed or stolen. Waffling, Williamson eventually insists that it was filed before the burglary, putting Roma "over the top" and making him the winner of the Cadillac. As Aaronow nervously awaits his turn with the detective Levene arrives announcing that he has closed a big deal. Moss stalks out after being abused by the detective; Levene celebrates his euphoria over his sale by belittling Williamson for having "no balls" and trumpeting his own prowess as a closer. His improvisational skill is tested when Lingk enters to cancel his deal, urged by his wife to exercise his legal right to back out within three days of the contract being filed. Playing a rich investor, Levene assists Roma in delaying the matter with Lingk as Roma insists that, since the contract has not yet been filed, there will still be sufficient time when they next can meet to cancel within the prescribed three days. Thinking he is being helpful, Williamson blurts out that the contract has been filed. Roma is, thereby, caught in a lie, sending the frightened Lingk off to get legal assistance to cancel the deal. Incensed, Roma attacks Williamson for costing him his commission and the Cadillac. "You want to learn the first rule you'd know if you ever spent a day in your life," Roma says to Williamson before being led into the inner office, "you never open your mouth till you know what the shot is. You fucking *child*."

Levene continues to attack Williamson for killing Roma's deal and lacking the basic skills of the salesmen Williamson manages, setting in motion the play's final series of reversals. Inadvertently Levene, who ignores his own advice to the office manager to keep his mouth shut, reveals that he knows Williamson was lying about having sent in the contract, intelligence only known if Levene had seen the contract on Williamson's desk when he broke into the office to steal the leads. Levene admits to the robbery, consoled by the breaking of his losing streak with the deal he has just closed: "So I wasn't cut out to be a thief. I was cut out to be a salesman. And now I'm back, and I got my *balls* back." Before handing him over to the detective, Williamson delivers the coup de grâce: Levene has closed a deal with a couple whose checks are worthless, who "just like talking to salesmen." Levene, headed to prison, loses everything, including his self-worth. On emerging from his interrogation, Roma delivers the play's epitaph, addressed to Shelly as a respected peer:

> I swear . . . it's not a world of men . . . it's not a world of men, Machine . . .
> it's a world of clock watchers, bureaucrats, officeholders . . . what it is, it's
> a fucked-up world . . . there's no adventure *to* it. Dying breed.

Like Charley's eulogy for Willy Loman as "a man way out there in the blue, riding on a smile and a shoeshine," Roma celebrates the salesman as America's frontiersman and adventurer in a diminished world: the last American dreamer and peddler of a debunked and lethal American dream that corrupts and destroys both buyer and seller.

79

KING UBU

(1896)
by Alfred Jarry

The players are supposed to be dolls, toys, marionettes, and now they are all hopping like wooden frogs, and I can see for myself that the chief personage, who is some kind of King, carries for a scepter a brush of the kind that we use to clean a closet. Feeling bound to support the most spirited party, we have shouted for the play, but that night at the Hôtel Corneille I am very sad, for comedy, objectivity, has displayed its growing power once more. I say: "After Stéphane Mallarmé, after Paul Verlaine, after Gustave Moreau, after Puvis de Chavannes, after our own verse, after all our subtle colour and nervous rhythm, after the faint mixed tints of Conder, what more is possible? After us the Savage Gods."
—W. B. Yeats, *The Trembling Veil,*
commenting on the first performance of *King Ubu*

If the slammed door in Henrik Ibsen's *A Doll's House* sounded the onset of modern drama, the opening word of Alfred Jarry's *Ubu roi* (*King Ubu*)—"*Merdre!*"—opened another kind of door for drama. (*Merde*, the French word for "shit," was purposefully given an extra "r" in Jarry's script to slightly alter the scandalous word.) The play's debut in Paris on December 10, 1896, was as explosive and as indicative of a fundamental artistic shift as the premiere of Victor Hugo's *Hernani* had been in 1830 when it signaled the romantic challenge to classicism. As scholar Claude Schumacher has asserted, "In *Ubu roi* all the basic dramaturgical conventions are deliberately subverted, and it is the iconoclastic nature of the play that makes it such an important landmark in contemporary world drama." Before the curtain rose, the 23-year-old Jarry took the stage to address the packed house at the Théâtre de l' Œuvre to prepare the audience for what was to come, concluding:

In any case we have a perfect décor, for just as one good way of setting a play in Eternity is to have revolvers shot off in the year 1000, you will see doors open on fields of snow under blue skies, fireplaces furnished with clocks and swinging wide to serve as doors, and palm trees growing at the foot of a bed so that little elephants standing on bookshelves can browse on them. . . . As to the orchestra, there is none. Only its volume and timbre will be missed, for various pianos and percussion will execute Ubuesque themes from backstage. The action, which is about to begin, takes place in Poland, that is to say: Nowhere.

The curtain parted to reveal a set designed by Jarry in collaboration with artists Pierre Bonnard, Édouard Vuillard, Henri de Toulouse-Lautrec, and Paul Sérusier, described by audience member Arthur Symons as follows:

> The scenery was painted to represent, by a child's conventions, indoors and out of doors, and even the torrid, temperate, and arctic zones at once. Opposite you, at the back of the stage, you saw apple trees in bloom, under a blue sky, and against the sky a small closed window and a fireplace . . . through the very midst of which . . . trooped in and out the clamorous and sanguinary persons of the drama. On the left was painted a bed, and at the foot of the bed a bare tree and snow falling. On the right there were palm trees . . . a door opened against the sky, and beside the door a skeleton dangled. A venerable gentleman in evening dress . . . trotted across the stage on the points of his toes between every scene and hung the new placard on its nail.

At the play's opening obscenity, spoken by the grossly vulgar Père Ubu, the audience exploded. As critic Roger Shattuck relates in his study of the French avant-garde before the Great War, *The Banquet Years*,

> several people walked out without hearing any more. The rest separated into two camps of desperately clapping enthusiasts and whistling scoffers. Fist fights started in the orchestra. . . . Jarry's supporters shouted, "You wouldn't understand Shakespeare either." Their opponents replied with variations of the *mot* of the evening. . . . The actors waited patiently, beginning to believe that the roles had been reversed and they had come to watch a performance out front.

The audience quieted long enough for the grotesque Père and Mère Ubu, in farcical parody of *Macbeth*, to seize the throne of Poland and wreak havoc on their subjects until the next "*merdre*" set off the audience again. The initial run of the play would be just two performances, but the impact of *King Ubu* was registered in the war of words that followed in the press during what became known as the "Year of Jarry," in which *Ubu roi* and its creator became notorious. Nothing like Jarry's direct assault on good taste, theatrical illusion, causal logic, and coherence had ever been seen on stage before. "No event marks more clearly than this," Shattuck states, "the close of one era and the imminence of another." Called the "Father of the Theater of the Absurd" and the acknowledged precursor of the dadaists, surrealists, expressionists, the theater of cruelty, and Bertolt Brecht's epic theater, Jarry, according to scholar Martin Esslin, "must be regarded as one of the originators of the concepts on which a good deal of contemporary art, and not only in literature and the theater, is based."

Born in Laval, France, in 1873, Alfred-Henri Jarry was the son of a traveling salesman for a textile manufacturer who had married the daughter of a Brittany magistrate. Indulged by his eccentric mother, Jarry came to loathe his father, later calling him "a worthless joker—what you call a nice old fellow." When he was 12 Jarry moved with his mother and older sister to Brittany, where he first began writing poems and skits in the manner of Victor Hugo. In 1888 Jarry entered the lycée in Rennes, where he was described by one of his classmates as "a brilliant student with all the marks of the worst kind of troublemaker. . . . He delighted in attacks on our modesty." He was soon initiated in the school tradition of tormenting the well-meaning but ineffectual professor of physics, Félix Hébert, known as Père Hébé, who became the prototype for Père Ubu. Jarry and classmate Henri Morin collaborated on a play featuring a grotesque caricature of their hapless professor as a gluttonous, blundering king of Poland. This Ur-Ubu was first performed by a marionette. Jarry's schoolboy satire on his teacher would expand to encompass all the perceived bourgeois violations of the age and would include an absurd alternative physics, "Pataphysics," which would in turn grow into a worldview and aesthetic theory. Père Hébé became Père Ubu, the dominating figure in Jarry's subsequent imaginary creations, a spokesperson and an alter ego who would eventually subsume his creator's identity.

In 1891, Jarry, aged 17, went to Paris to study at the Lycée Henri IV to prepare for the competitive exam for acceptance to the prestigious École Normale Supérieure. In Paris he cultivated an increasingly outlandish appearance and behavior that gained him the attention of impressionist painters, musicians, and symbolist writers, such as Paul Valéry, Stéphane Mallarmé, Toulouse-Lautrec, Maurice Ravel, and Jean-Jacques Rousseau, into whose artistic and intellectual circles Jarry joined. The poet Henri de Régnier would later describe Jarry during the period as

A short stocky man, with a large head and broad shoulders, planted on bowlegs. In a pale face, with fine contracted features and a thin brown moustache, brilliant eyes shone with a metallic glare. At the bottom of knee-breeches, calves ringed in garters ended in feet shod in rubber-soled shoes. . . . His pockets bulged with cycling tools, among which one could see the butt of an old revolver, at once sordid and disquieting.

Failing the entrance exam three times, Jarry abandoned his academic aspirations to pursue a career as a *homme des lettres*. He would later recall this period when the writings of Friedrich Nietzsche, the lectures by Henri Bergson, symbolism, occultism, and anarchism animated Parisian salons and café society as a time "when a revelation took place; even a verse from the Apocalypse is not too grandiloquent: 'The sky opened and rolled back like a scroll.'" Jarry's initial contribution to the ferment was the first appearance of Père Ubu in the fragmentary dialogues recycled from the Rennes material called "Guignol," appearing in a monthly review in 1893. A year later, his first book, *Les Minutes de sable mémorial* (*Minutes of Memorial Sand*), a selection of prose, poetry, and woodcuts was published combining Ubu material with new symbolist elements. Jarry wrote in a tiny garret room that he named "Dead Man's Calvary," decorated with censers, crucifixes, live owls, and a marionette theater. He fueled his fantasies with a steady stream of absinthe and ether and set himself up as a provocation and alternative to conventionality.

After a disastrous few months of military service ended with a medical discharge, and the publication of his second book in 1895, *César-Antéchrist* (*Caesar Antichrist*), Jarry began his professional theatrical involvement in 1896 when Aurélien-Marie Lugné-Poe, the director of the Théâtre de l'Œuvre, invited Jarry to become *secrétaire-régisseur* of his company. At the same time a completed version of *King Ubu* first appeared in print, and Jarry campaigned successfully to convince Lugné-Poe to mount a production. Jarry's play and his instructions for its staging constituted a radically new conception of dramatic form and technique. French theater before *King Ubu* provided reassuring entertainment to a mainly bourgeois audience, following the traditions of the well-made play in which psychological plausible characters engaged in a coherent sequence of action, ending in a satisfying resolution. Jarry sought to violate each of these elements to provoke and shock a complacent audience. Realistic stage illusion would be shattered, character would become caricature, suggesting not psychological depth but disturbing archetypes, and coherence would give way to the irrational and illogical—all to provoke and undermine audience expectation. He explained after the play's first performance:

> I intended that when the curtain went up the scene should confront the public like the exaggerating mirror in the stories of Madame Leprince de Beaumont, in which the depraved saw themselves with dragons' bodies, or bulls' horns, or whatever corresponded to their particular vice. It is not surprising that the public should have been aghast at the sight of its ignoble other self, which it has never before been shown completely. This other self, as Monsieur *Catulle Mendès* has excellently said, is composed "of eternal human imbecility, eternal lust, eternal gluttony, the vileness of instinct magnified into tyranny; of the sense of decency, the virtues, the patriotism and the ideals peculiar to those who have just eaten their fill."

King Ubu would, therefore, be a distorted mirror to reveal inner and hidden human truths.

The play opens with Pa Ubu, a monstrous clown, typifying all imaginable vulgarity, cowardice, and cruelty, conspiring with the shrewish Ma Ubu and Captain Bordure to kill the king of Poland and seize his throne. Poland, that much partitioned, contested, noncountry, serves as a kind of universal Everywhere, with Ubu as a particularly virulent and terrifying Everyman whose greed, vulgarity, cruelty, aggression, cowardliness, and violence make him equally ridiculous and absurd as either hero or villain. In the second act Ubu and his men attack and kill the king and two of his sons, but the youngest, Bougrelas, escapes to a mountain cave where his dead ancestors appear and demand vengeance. Ubu solidifies his power by throwing gold coins to the Polish mob. He so enjoys the violent scramble that ensues that he arranges another violent race for prizes before inviting his subjects into his palace for an orgy. In the third act Ubu liquidates the nobility with his "disembraining machine," a toilet brush, distributing their wealth to his subjects that he then reclaims through taxation. Now secure on the throne, Ubu betrays Captain Bordure and imprisons him. Bordure escapes, however, and takes refuge in Russia, where he joins the forces of Czar Alexis and the usurped Bougrelas, which attack. While Ubu leads his army into battle, Ma Ubu searches the crypts that hold the remains of the former kings of Poland for treasure. Bougrelas advances on Warsaw as Ubu meets the czar in battle in the Ukraine. Eventually defeated, Ubu retreats to a cave in Lithuania where his cowardice is exposed when he and his two remaining retainers are attacked by a bear. In the final act Ma arrives at the cave while Ubu is sleeping. Impersonating the angel Gabriel she compels her husband to confess his sins but hears instead a steady stream of complaints about her. Interrupting the ensuing violent squabbling of husband and wife, Bougrelas and his army arrive. Soundly beaten, the Ubus just manage to escape to a ship on the Baltic where Ubu intends to make for Paris to get himself named minister of finance and begin again his quest for money and power.

Jarry managed two sequels—*Ubu enchaîné* (*Ubu Enchained*) and *Ubu cocu* (*Ubu Cuckolded*)—but no one was willing to invite more controversy by producing them. Instead Jarry took Ubu to the streets, more and more mimicking the speech and jerky walk of Ubu and blurring the distinction between creator and creation. Jarry continued to write, publishing two novels *Messaline* (1900; *The Garden of Priapus*) and *Le Surmâle* (1902; *The Supermale: A Modern Novel*). A third, *Gestes et opinions du docteur Faustroll, pataphysicien* (*The Exploits and Opinions of Dr. Faustroll, Pataphysician*), was published posthumously in 1911. Jarry died, weakened by malnutrition and years of substance abuse, in 1907. With a line that could easily have appeared in *King Ubu*, Jarry's final words were a request for a toothpick. At the time of his death he was remembered less as a significant dramatist or influential writer and more as a bizarre drunken or drugged figure declaiming on the streets of Montparnasse. His literary reputation was revived in 1927 when Antonin Artaud and Roger Vitrac founded the Théâtre Jarry to recognize the playwright's importance to modern drama, which had caught up with the innovations Jarry had pioneered. In 1948 a group of French writers and artists, including Eugène Ionesco, Raymond Queneau, and Marcel Duchamp, expressed their indebtedness to Jarry's groundbreaking work by establishing the Collège de Pataphysique. Branches of the "college" have spread worldwide. The most famous reference to Jarry's pseudoscience occurs in the Beatles' "Maxwell's Silver Hammer" in which Joan who "was quizzical / studies pataphysical science in the home." In *Dr. Faustroll* Jarry defined Pataphysics as "the science of imaginary solutions, which symbolically attributes the properties of objects, described by their virtuality, to their lineaments." This can also serve as a summarizing definition of the modern, antirealistic drama that *King Ubu* first expressed. As critic Martin Esslin has asserted, it is a "definition of a subjectivist and expressionist approach that exactly anticipates the tendency of the Theatre of the Absurd to express psychological states by objectifying them on the stage." Jarry's alternative to the Aristotelian and realistic theater served as a liberation for the drama that followed. After *King Ubu* anything that could be imagined could be staged.

CLOUD NINE

80

(1979)

by Caryl Churchill

One of the things I wanted very much to do, in Cloud Nine . . . *was to write a play about sexual politics that would not just be a woman's thing. I felt there were quite a few women's groups doing plays from that point of view. And gay groups. . . . There was nothing that also involved straight men. Max [Stafford Clark], the director, even said, at the beginning "Well shouldn't you perhaps be doing this with a woman director?" He didn't see that it was his subject as well.*

—Caryl Churchill, Interview in *Ms.*, May 1982

Of all the plays of the 1970s and 1980s that offered a radical and daring reassessment of sex, race, and gender, *Cloud Nine* by Caryl Churchill is certainly one of the most innovative and timeless in treating its subjects in the widest possible context of power politics, patriarchy, and modern identity. Churchill would emerge from a group of politically engaged British playwrights working in the radical theater movement who challenged the dominance of the social realistic drama pioneered by John Osborne and the psychological theater of Harold Pinter to become one of the most performed and admired contemporary playwrights. With Churchill, as critic Benedict Nightingale once commented, "We can no longer patronise women playwrights as peripheral." *Cloud Nine*, first performed in Britain in 1979 and in New York in 1981, was Churchill's breakout play, gaining her international recognition as an accomplished and unavoidable force in modern drama. A succession of powerful and challenging plays have followed, including *Top Girls* (1982), *Fen* (1983), *Serious Money* (1987), *Mad Forest* (1990), and *Far Away* (2000), but *Cloud Nine* has retained its lead position as essential Churchill: a summary statement of the playwright's amazing theatrical resources and brilliant repossession of the Shavian drama of ideas.

Churchill was born in 1938 in London. Her father, a cartoonist, would have a major impact on her future dramatic work. "Cartoons are really so much like plays," Churchill has said, "an image with somebody saying something.

I grew up with his cartoons of the war—of Goebbels and Mussolini." Her mother, who left school at 14, worked as a secretary, model, and film actress. Churchill's first exposure to the theater was the Christmas pantomimes she attended and then imitated to entertain her parents at home. After spending the war years in London, when she was 10 Churchill and her family moved to Montreal, where she was educated in a private school before returning to England in 1957 to attend Oxford. Having begun writing short stories as a schoolgirl, Churchill would spend one summer helping to paint sets for a summer theater, but she did not "put the two things together"—writing and the stage—until her studies at Oxford and exposure to the works of Samuel Beckett, John Osborne, Harold Pinter, T. S. Eliot, and Bertolt Brecht, all of whom she has acknowledged as important influences. She wrote her first play in response to a friend's need for something to direct. "It was a turning point," as she recalled. "I realized I preferred things as plays. It has something to do with . . . liking things actually *happening*." Churchill has attributed the relative scarcity of women playwrights to the upbringing of girls, who are encouraged to be passive rather than active and are taught to avoid conflict, which "lends itself much more readily to the letter, the diary—to the reflective form." Churchill's first two plays, *Downstairs* (1958) and *Having a Wonderful Time* (1960), were produced at Oxford, where she received a B.A. in English in 1960.

Churchill married the barrister David Harter in 1961 and spent the decade at home raising three sons. As she recalled, "I didn't really feel a part of what was happening in the sixties. During that time I felt isolated. I had small children and was having miscarriages. It was an extremely solitary life. What politicised me was being discontent with my own way of life—of being a barrister's wife and just being at home." During the period Churchill wrote radio dramas, but a new life of engagement in social issues began when her husband left his job to work for a legal aid group in 1972. "We did not want to shore up a capitalist system we did not like," Churchill has asserted. The same year Churchill's first major stage play was produced at London's Royal Court Theatre, *Owners*, about a woman's growth toward independence from her coarse husband that incorporates issues of gender and class. "I wrote it in three days," she said. "I'd just come out of the hospital after a particularly gruesome late miscarriage, still quite groggy and my arm ached because they'd given me an injection that didn't work. Into [the play] went for the first time a lot of things that had been building up in me over a long time, political attitudes as well as personal ones." *Objections to Sex and Violence*, exploring the connection of sexuality, violence, and power followed in 1975. The next year the feminist company, Monstrous Regiment, commissioned Churchill to write a play about witches. The result was *Vinegar Tom*, set in England in the 17th century. This would initiate a period of working closely with others in a workshop setting that resulted in some of Churchill's finest work. "You don't collaborate on writing the play," she has explained, "you still go away and write it your-self. . . . What's different is that you've had a period of researching something together, not just information, but your attitudes to it, and possible ways of showing things." Also in 1976 Churchill began an association with London's Joint Stock Theatre Group, a corps of actors, directors, and playwrights com-mitted to the creation of experimental drama, which resulted in *Light Shining in Buckinghamshire*, a play depicting the ordinary men and women who made the English revolution in the 17th century, and *Cloud Nine.*

The usual production method of Joint Stock was for the writer, director, and actors to spend three to four weeks in a workshop researching a subject, followed by the writer completing the play and six weeks of rehearsal and revi-sions before performances. The starting point for *Cloud Nine* was the topic of "sexual politics" suggested by Churchill. "We formed a company considering their sexual as well as acting experience. . . . [W]ith *Cloud Nine* we started from ourselves, moving out from that to a more general context." The company was selected on the basis of sexual diversity, gender, sexual orientation, and marital and sexual history. Improvising scenes dramatizing characteristic expressions of sexual and gender relations, the company deliberately tested assumptions by having men's parts played by women, and vice versa, straight roles played by gay actors, and vice versa. Gathering insights from these sessions Churchill then wrote the play. "I originally thought it would all be set in the present like the second act," she has explained, "but the idea of colonialism as a parallel to sexual oppression, which I first came across in Genet, had been briefly touched on in the workshop. When I thought of the colonial setting the whole thing fell quite quickly into place. Though no character is based on anyone in the company, the play draws deeply on our experiences, and would not have been written without the workshop." First performed at Dartington College of Arts in 1979, a revised version of *Cloud Nine* opened at the Royal Court Theatre in 1980 and then in New York in 1981. It would become the most popular and most performed "feminist" drama of the decade.

The play's exploration of sexual politics commences in act 1 in a British African colony "in Victorian times." Clive, the colonial administrator and pater familias who represents the conjunction of the patriarchal values of the empire and Victorian family, supplies the opening introductions:

> This is my family. Though far from home
> We serve the Queen wherever we may roam
> I am father to the natives here,
> And father to my family so dear.

Intoning the fundamental gender assumptions of the Victorians, Clive's wife, Betty, declares: "I am a man's creation as you see, / And what men want is what I want to be." Clive's "boy," the African servant Joshua, proclaims, "What white men want is what I want to be," while Clive's son Edward asserts, "What father wants I'd dearly like to be." Having sounded the patriarchal credo, the play proceeds to exploit the difference between the Victorian sexual and gender norm and its reality as expressed by who these characters truly are and what they do: Clive is committing adultery; Betty yearns for masculine adventure and is in love with the glamorous visiting explorer Harry Bagley; the governess, Ellen, is a closet lesbian in love with Betty; Edward who would rather play with the doll of his sister, Victoria (who is actually played by a doll), has a crush on Harry, who in turn will proposition both Joshua and Clive. The conflict and confusion between code and violation, appearance and reality, are further underscored by the play's cross-racial and cross-gender casting. Betty, who longs to experience the world of adventure open only to men, is played by a man; Joshua, who longs to be white, is played by a Caucasian actor; Edward, whose inclinations are conventionally attributed to females and repressed in males, is played by a woman. Each therefore reflects the race and gender of his or her aspiration and inner nature. The casting, moreover, challenges the artificially restrictive demarcation of gender and power roles that the play explores generally. As the act proceeds the conflict between enforced roles and actual identities causes both the family and the colonial outpost to fall apart at the seams. As each character moves closer to his or her true self and actual desires, Clive, who is disgusted by Harry's sexual advance, tries to enforce a return to normalcy by contriving the traditional comedic happy ending in arranging a marriage between the homosexual Harry and the lesbian Ellen. As the act concludes Clive proposes the wedding toast:

> Harry, my friend. So brave and strong and supple.
> Ellen, from neath her veil so shyly peeking.
> I wish you joy. A toast—the happy couple.
> Dangers are past. Our enemies are killed.
> —Put your arm round her, Harry, have a kiss—
> All murmuring of discontent is stilled.
> Long may you live in peace and joy and bliss.

Clive's proclamation is vividly undercut by the long repressed and self-hating Joshua who raises a gun to shoot Clive. He is seen only by Edward, who does nothing to warn the others but puts his hands over his ears before the stage goes black.

Act 2 takes place 100 years later in London with some of the same characters from the first act, who have aged only 25 years. Betty is preparing to leave Clive, who appears only for the play's final words. Edward is a gay park gardener with a lover named Gerry; Victoria, no longer a doll, is a theoretical feminist, married to Martin. Victoria's lesbian friend Lin is divorced with a five-year-old named Cathy, who is played by a man (the only cross-gender casting in the act). Clive's absence and the return of the appropriate gender casting suggest that the Victorian standards have been swept away. The gender and sexual frustrations under the restrictions exposed in act 1, now seem poised in the more enlightened present-day world for fulfillment to reach the sexual utopia suggested in the play's title, *Cloud Nine*. However, the struggle for sexual freedom and self-definition of the two principal characters of act 1—Betty and Edward—continue unabated, now joined by Victoria. They confront many of the same sexual and gender role restrictions, complexity, and contradictions in different forms. In the utopia of true gender equality that the modern age nominally accepts, what gender assumptions should now apply? Lin, rejecting feminine stereotyping, encourages her daughter, Cathy, to act in stereotypically masculine ways by playing with toy guns and beating up boys (this gender reversal is intensified by having Cathy played by a man). Lin is therefore shown imposing her views of gender and sexuality on Cathy in the same way that Clive had imposed them on Betty and Edward. Neither Edward, Victoria, nor Betty reaches Cloud Nine despite the progress they have made toward independence and gender and sexual empowerment. Edward struggles to achieve the domestic security of marriage with his lover, Gerry, who prefers a lifestyle of casual sex rather than commitment to Edward. Victoria and her husband have similar problems despite their open and seemingly liberated relationship. The newly independent Betty, having always depended on men to define her, faces the terrifying world of singledom and self-determination. The closest to Cloud Nine that Churchill imagines is when Betty in a remarkable closing monologue expresses her satisfaction and empowerment in her rediscovery of the joy of masturbation and the self-knowledge it brings. Recalling her shame and pleasure at touching herself, Betty declares:

> I felt myself gathering together more and more and I felt angry with Clive and angry with my mother and I went on and on defying them, and there was this vast feeling growing in me and all round me and they couldn't stop me and no one could stop me and I was there and coming and coming. Afterwards I thought I'd betrayed Clive. My mother would kill me. But I felt triumphant because I was a separate person from them. And I cried because I didn't want to be. But I don't cry about it any more.

Betty is able to claim sexual pleasure without guilt, a first step in accepting herself on her own terms and reconciling her past and her present. Her triumph and consummation of her newly integrated identity is played out under Clive's disproving critique:

> You are not that sort of woman, Betty. I can't believe you are. I can't feel the same about you as I did. And Africa is to be communist I suppose. I

used to be proud to be British. There was a high ideal. I came out onto the verandah and looked at the stars.

As Clive exits, the actor who had played the past Betty from the first act enters and embraces the actress playing the present Betty in a new gender synthesis resolving the polarities of Victorian / contemporary, passive / active, male / female. The play's ingenious time and gender bending have produced a remarkable reassessment both of past and present sexual assumptions and the challenges that persist even when patriarchy gives way to liberation. The strength of *Cloud Nine* rests on its going beyond the polemical tendency to illustrate gender, racial, and power conflict by shallow categories of victim and victimizer. The play is far more knowing in its ability to stretch the conventions of both stagecraft and ideology into a new synthesis of possibilities.

AT THE HAWK'S WELL

81

(1916)

by William Butler Yeats

All imaginative art remains at a distance, and this distance once chosen must be firmly held against a pushing world. Verse, ritual, music and dance in association with action require that gesture, costume, facial expression, stage arrangement must help in keeping the door. Our unimaginative arts are content to set a piece of the world as we know it in a place by itself, to put their photographs, as it were, in a plush or plain frame, but the arts which interest me, while seeming to separate from the world and us a group of figures, images, symbols enable us to pass for a few moments into a deep of the mind that had hitherto been too subtle for our habitation.
—W. B. Yeats, Introduction to *Certain Noble Plays of Japan* by Pound and Fenollosa

Although William Butler Yeats is widely regarded as the greatest English-language poet of the 20th century, his contribution to modern drama is far less recognized or appreciated. Yeats asserted in 1917, following his composition of one of his most important plays, *At the Hawk's Well*, that "I need a theatre. I believe myself to be a dramatist. I desire to show events and not merely tell of them . . . and I seem to myself most alive at the moment when a room full of people share the one lofty emotion." Yeats was the author of some 30 plays, and the creative and practical challenges of the theater dominated much of his professional life. Drama for Yeats served both private self-expression and a political and cultural end. The cofounder of Ireland's Abbey Theatre, Yeats helped to restore a heroic Irish cultural identity that made the Irish national-ist and independence movement possible. He was also at the center of the violent reaction to the premieres of John Millington Synge's THE PLAYBOY OF THE WESTERN WORLD and Sean O'Casey's THE PLOUGH AND THE STARS, pub-licly defending both playwrights and their works against Irish philistinism and censorship. Yeats's own plays differed markedly from the regional naturalism of Synge and O'Casey in their nonrepresentational, poetic alternative to the realistic domination of the modern stage. Yeats sought in his plays "a deeper reality than any that can be reached by observation, for it is the reality of the imagination and comes from the withdrawal of the poet's mind into itself, not from the effort to see and record." His search for such an inner, expressive dramatic form would result in more than 30 years of experimentation to fuse poetry and drama. T. S. Eliot declared that in Yeats's plays "the ideas of the poetic drama was kept alive when everywhere else it had been driven underground." His experiments would incorporate elements from the classical theater, from the symbolists, from Celtic folklore, and Japanese Noh drama, pioneering formal methods that would later become standard elements in the works of later playwrights. Fellow Irishman Samuel Beckett, for example, could see in Yeats's plays the possibilities of minimalism, of stripping dramatic components to express a core intensity. To emphasize language over action in performance Yeats even proposed putting actors in barrels to restrict their unnecessary movements, a strategy that Beckett would subsequently employ. Yeats's play *The Cat and the Moon* pairs a blind man and a lame man that recalls Beckett's interdependent tramps in *Waiting for Godot*, and the depiction of frustrated waiting in *At the Hawk's Well* anticipates the central situation of Beckett's groundbreaking play. In both his formal innovations and visionary, poetic expression Yeats expanded dramatic possibilities and restored drama's lyrical capacity.

Yeats was born in Dublin to an Anglo-Irish family in 1865. His father gave up a legal career to become a struggling and often impoverished portrait painter in Dublin and London. His mother came from a merchant-shipping family from Sligo, on Ireland's northwest coast, where Yeats spent his childhood summers and school holidays and where he was first introduced to Irish folklore and peasant superstitions. Sligo became for Yeats the "Land of Heart's Desire," a landscape of both great beauty and poetic possibilities, in stark contrast to the often grim and restricted life the young Yeats led in London. His father was a free thinker and religious skeptic, very much under the influence of Charles Darwin and others who toppled Victorian faith and whose artistic interest resided exclusively in the visible world. He provoked a contrary reaction in his son. Yeats felt caught between his father's skepticism and the need for belief—between reason and the imagination—with no way to bridge the gap. "I am very religious," Yeats later recalled, "and deprived by Huxley and Tyndall, whom I detested, of the simple-minded religion of my childhood, I had made a new religion, almost an infallible church of poetic tradition." His search for a compensating imaginative realm led him first to romantic poets such as William Blake and Percy Bysshe Shelley, then to the French symbolists and to the Celtic past and mysticism from various sources in theosophy, spiritualism, neo-Platonism, and finally his own created symbolic system to give pattern and coherence to the expression of his thoughts and need for belief. The dreamy and ethereal quality of Yeats's earliest poems and plays eventually gave way to works more grounded in the details and concerns of Irish life. It was Ireland that ultimately asserted itself in Yeats's mind and saved him from becoming a derivative 19th-century aesthete. In the folklore that he picked up during his visits to Sligo and in the rediscovered myths and legends of the Celtic past Yeats found fresh subject matter, and in the peasant speech of Irish country people he absorbed a fresh and vigorous poetic diction and rhythm. It became clear to Yeats that only by defining his relation to his native country, by putting the symbols of Ireland in order could he achieve the kind of creation he was groping toward that joined the real and the ideal. Drama would increasingly become his means toward that end.

The decisive event in Yeats's dramatic career occurred in 1899 when Yeats, Lady Augusta Gregory, and playwright Edward Martyn conceived the notion of an Irish national theater, declaring their intention

> to build up a Celtic and Irish school of dramatic literature. We hope to find in Ireland an uncorrupted and imaginative audience trained to listen by its passion for oratory, and believe our desire to bring upon the stage the deeper thoughts and emotions of Ireland will ensure for us a tolerant welcome, and that freedom to experiment which is not found in theatres of England, and without which no new movement in art or literature can succeed. We will show that Ireland is not the home of buffoonery and of easy sentiment, as it has been represented, but the home of an ancient idealism.

The Irish Literary Theatre debuted with a performance of Yeats's verse play *The Countess Cathleen*, concerning a woman who sells her soul to the devil to assist her tenants during the Irish famine. Criticized as blasphemous, it would be the first of Yeats's tangles with Irish audiences over what was appropriate for the stage, particularly one dedicated to fostering an Irish heroic identity. The most important of Yeats's early plays, *Cathleen Ni Houlihan* (1902), is his most direct nationalistic call to arms. Set in the west of Ireland during the French landing in support of the 1798 Rebellion, a young man, about to be married, hears an old woman express her "hope of getting my beautiful fields back again" and "of putting the strangers out of my house" and decides to forgo his obligations to his family and fiancée to join the rebellion. The old woman, a symbol of Ireland, is imaginatively revitalized by the young man's devotion to her cause into a young girl with "the walk of a queen." Yeats's stirring call to blood sacrifice would be most dramatically answered in the Easter Rebellion of 1916 that touched off the Irish War of Independence. Yeats would later ponder, "Did that play of mine send out / Certain men the English shot." By 1904 the national theater Yeats had helped create was housed at the Dublin's Abbey Theatre, which opened with a performance of Yeats's *On Baile's Strand*, the first of Yeats's five plays devoted to the legendary Irish warrior Cuchulain. As a director of the Abbey Theatre Yeats would devote more than two decades dealing with the practical day-to-day running of the theater. Increasingly wearied by the public criticism, most violently expressed in the *Playboy* riots of 1907, and the demands implicit in establishing a national theater when the Irish nation was itself being formed, Yeats began to shift his playwriting focus away from appealing to a popular audience to more private themes and experimental methods of production.

Ezra Pound, who served as Yeats's secretary from 1913 to 1916, introduced the playwright to Japanese Noh drama, through Pound's collaboration with translator Ernest Fenollosa that produced the collection *Certain Noble Plays of Japan*. The plays were a revelation to Yeats, who admired their concentration of stylized action with their complex interrelationships of language, masks, mime, song, and dance to express core emotional and spiritual truths. *At the Hawk's Well* became the first of Yeats's plays to incorporate what he learned from the Noh plays, fused with classical, Christian, Celtic, and symbolist elements. Having long wished to write plays "free from the demands of commercialism, whose words could be restored to their sovereignty over gesture and scenery, and the element of ritual in drama rediscovered," Yeats found in the aesthetic of Noh the way toward the creation of "an image of nobility and strange beauty." With this synthesis of dramatic elements Yeats declared that he had created "Theatre's anti-self," a new dramatic form that was "distinguished, indirect, and symbolic, and having no need of mob or Press to pay its way—an aristocrat form."

To suit his intention *At the Hawk's Well* was first performed in Lady Cunard's London drawing room before a select audience, including T. S. Eliot, Sir Thomas Beecham, and Pound. It was played on a small platform without special lighting, with the audience seated on three sides, and featured the Japanese dancer Michio Ito, with music and costumes by artist Edmund Dulac. Set during the Irish heroic age, the play begins with three masked musicians, serving as both chorus and accompanists on flute, gong, and zither, who enter and ritualistically unfold a black cloth as one addresses the audience to conjure, in the "eye of the mind," a desolate hilltop and "a well long choked up and dry" that is attended by a Guardian, a figure covered by a black cloak, and an Old Man who has been waiting 50 years to drink from its miraculous waters to gain immortality. Each time the water has bubbled out he has been cheated from drinking by the "deceivers," the guardians of the well, whose "unfaltering, unmoistened eyes" he is terrified to see. He is joined by a Young Man, who identifies himself as the legendary warrior Cuchulain. On a quest also to gain the water's immortal powers Cuchulain, with the confidence of youth, is convinced that the water must soon flow, despite the discouraging words of the Old Man:

O, folly of youth,
Why should that hollow place fill up for you,
That will not fill for me? I have lain in wait
For more than fifty years, to find it empty,

Or but to find the stupid wind of the sea
Drive round the perishable leaves.

Dominated by a mood of defeat and disillusion, the play contrasts Cuchulain's
assurance that his quest will be realized and the Old Man's despair. Cuchulain's
test comes as the Guardian of the well assumes the appearance of a hawk that
lures him away from the well with its dance, as the Old Man, cowering from
the terrifying hawk's gaze, falls into a helpless sleep. Entranced by the hawk's
performance Cuchulain pursues, proclaiming "Run where you will, Grey bird,
you shall be perched upon my wrist." While giving chase Cuchulain misses
the opportunity to drink the water that has come and gone in the well. Awakening, the Old Man realizes his missed chance and curses the shadows that
"have deluded me my whole life through." Cuchulain returns, having failed
to capture the hawk, to be called to battle and the destiny that awaits him. In
the Old Man's words, "never till you are lying in the earth / Can you know
rest." Thwarted once again, the Old Man exits the stage, and the play closes
with the black cloth unfolded and folded again and the musician's closing song
contrasting the failed quest for the unobtainable with the quiet contentment
of ordinary life:

> Come to me, human faces,
> Familiar memories;
> I have found hateful eyes
> Among the desolate places,
> Unfaltering, unmoistened eyes.

> Folly alone I cherish,
> I choose it for my share;
> Being but a mouthful of air,
> I am content to perish;
> I am but a mouthful of sweet air.

> O lamentable shadows,
> Obscurity of strife!
> I choose a pleasant life
> Among indolent meadows;
> Wisdom must live a bitter life.

With a haunting lyrical beauty Yeats stages a meditation on human aspirations and the human condition registered by the play's archetypal characters
and situation. By restricting his drama to a single situation—the dual disappointment of Old Man and Young to gain what they seek—in a stylized and

ritualized enactment, Yeats achieves a desired universality, intensity of effects, and fusion of poetry and drama.

At the Hawk's Well is the first of a sequence of Noh-inspired dramas followed by *The Only Jealousy of Emer*, *The Dreaming of the Bones*, and *Calvary*, which were published as *Four Plays for Dancers* (1921). Yeats would go on to write several subsequent plays, including *The Cat and the Moon* (1924), *The Words upon the Window* (1933), *Purgatory* (1938), *The Herne's Egg* (1938), and *The Death of Cuchulain* (1939). All are marked by the same combination of formal experimentation and visionary depth that Yeats first realized on stage with *At the Hawk's Well*.

ORPHEUS

82

(1926)   by Jean Cocteau

Theatrically speaking, Orpheus *is an exciting work. Objects become ritualistic symbols, virtual protagonists. Divested of their customary functions, these objects (doors, mirrors, gloves, glass) acquire new and startling meanings. Gloves are not merely used to keep hands warm or for reasons of fashion; they become mysterious entities. When worn by Death, they give audiences the impression of witnessing an actual operation. Later, they seem to turn into religious talismans, endowed with the power to ensure safe passage from one world to the next. . . . Mirrors likewise assume a different function. Habitually, they reflect man's image, permitting him to indulge his narcissistic bent. [In] Cocteau's* Orpheus, *however, the mirror becomes an instrument by which one sees Death's daily works. . . .In this mirror, man faces his own aging and decaying self as does Dorian Gray in the painting and Raphael Valentin in the shrinking magic skin. Cocteau's mirror, like Alice's looking glass, becomes a door that leads to the other world—life's counterpart. It is a mysterious and mystical instrument.*

—Bettina L. Knapp, Jean Cocteau

Described by its author as "half farce, half meditation upon death," *Orpheus* is a tragicomedy of the post–World War I creative avant-garde, an era of experimentation in the arts and synonymous with such figures as Pablo Picasso, composer Erik Satie, and the writers Virginia Woolf and Gertrude Stein. In *Orpheus,* inspired theatrical technique joins with wordplay to reinvent Greek myth and explore themes relating to the creative imagination and the destiny of the poet. Jean Cocteau did not ally himself with any one "school" of dramatic thought, but with *Orpheus* he nevertheless combines dadism, surrealism, futurism, and the theater of the absurd to examine the magical and mysterious world of the artist, using symbolism and imagery to create a complete theatrical experience.

Cocteau, a filmmaker, as well as a poet and playwright, is probably best known to film historians and cinema aficionados as the director of the hauntingly beautiful and visually dazzling 1946 live-action film version of the fairy tale *La Belle et la bête* (*Beauty and the Beast*), one accessible and engaging example of the fantasy, mystery, and theatrical dynamism that informed Cocteau's artistic sensibility. He was born in 1889 at the Cocteau family's summer home at Maisons-Laffitte, near Paris, one of three children in a wealthy bourgeois family that included stockbrokers, lawyers, and military officers. In 1899 Cocteau's father committed suicide after a financial failure, and his mother brought the children to Paris. Cocteau preferred Paris, once declaring "I was born a Parisian, I speak Parisian, my accent is Parisian." The force of imagination that characterizes Cocteau's work was developed early in a sensitive childhood and adolescence spent playing by an 18th-century castle in Maisons-Laffitte, among the art treasures in his grandparents' Paris home, in the fascination he developed for the theatre and its glittering performers, and in his love for the music hall, the circus, and the ballet. He disliked the dismal and, what he later referred to as the "sinister," atmosphere of the school he attended before his mother brought him home to be taught by private tutors.

Cocteau's first medium was poetry, and his talent, together with his good looks, affability, and graceful cosmopolitan demeanor, attracted numerous friends in the literary and theatrical worlds. In 1906 celebrated actor Édouard de Max arranged for a public reading of Cocteau's poetry at the Théâtre Femina, which was attended by well-known actors and actresses of the day and received good reviews. The same year Cocteau cofounded a literary magazine, *Schéhérazade*, with Maurice Rostand, son of the dramatist Edmond Rostand. Cocteau's first published volume of verse was *Lampe d'Aladin* (1909; *Aladdin's Lamp*), which was quickly followed by two more collections, *Le Prince frivole* (1910; *The Frivolous Prince*) and *Le Danse de Sophocle* (1912; *Sophocles' Dance*). In 1912 Cocteau moved out of his mother's house to the Hôtel Biron, whose famous occupants included the sculptor Auguste Rodin and the poet Rainer Maria Rilke. His circle of friends eventually widened to include ballet impresario Serge Diaghilev, Erik Satie, Igor Stravinsky, Picasso, Amadeo Modigliani, Guillaume Apollinaire, and Max Jacob. After a trip to Switzerland with Stravinsky in 1913 Cocteau published *Le Potomak*, a collection of drawings, poems, and prose dialogues, which he dedicated to the composer. Rejected from the French army during World War I, he served illegally as an ambulance driver on the Belgian front until he was discovered and sent back to Paris. Out of this experience came the 1922 novel *Thomas l'Imposteur* (*Thomas Imposter*). In 1917 Cocteau collaborated with Diaghilev, Satie, and Picasso on *Parade*, an ambiguous and musically atonal ballet-scenario of the title event. Disliked by audiences at the time and considered an artistic failure, *Parade* is now generally regarded as one of the most innovative ballets of the 20th century, a modern work of the theater that foreshadowed postwar experimentalism in the arts.

Cocteau's artistic vision was transformed after he began a love relationship with the much younger writer Raymond Radiguet in 1919. His work began to show a more mature appreciation for classical, simple, and direct expression in contrast to the modern sensibilities of the time. His output increased and included a pantomime, *Le boeuf sur le toit* (1920; *The Do-Nothing Bar*), which featured masks and sets by Raoul Dufy and music by Darius Milhaud; a play, *Les maires de la Tour Eiffel* (1921; *The Wedding on the Eiffel Tower*); a novel, *Le grand écart* (1923; *The Great Split*); and a volume of poetry, *Plain-chant* (1923). In 1923 Radiguet died of typhoid fever, sending Cocteau into a depression that he endeavored to alleviate with opium. After a 60-day rehabilitation in a sanatorium in Paris Cocteau cured himself of his drug habit and continued to write, producing the poems *Opera* (1925) and *L'Ange Heurtebise* (1925; *The Angel Heurtebise*), as well as an oratorio, *Oedipus Rex* (1925), written in collaboration with Stravinsky. In 1925 Cocteau also completed *Orphée* (*Orpheus*), which had its debut at the Théâtre des Artes on June 17, 1926.

Cocteau had been interested in writing a play based on the legend of Orpheus for several years. In the Greek myth Orpheus, the son of Apollo and the muse Calliope, is a Thracian poet and musician whose instrument is the lyre. Distraught after his wife, Eurydice, dies from a snake bite while fleeing from the attentions of the shepherd, Aristeus, Orpheus journeys to hell to try to get her back. His music softens the hearts of Hades and Persephone, rulers of the underworld, who agree to let Eurydice return with him to earth under the condition that he walk in front of her and not look back. However, the anxious Orpheus breaks his vow, and Eurydice vanishes from his sight. He receives permission to try again, but the ferryman refuses him passage to the underworld. Orpheus is eventually torn apart and decapitated by a mob of howling bacchantes and his head and his lyre thrown into the river. He is joined with Eurydice in the underworld.

Cocteau was less intrigued by the love story of Orpheus and Eurydice than with the original focus of the Orphic myth: the transformative power of poetry and art. A link between Greek and Christian lore stemming from the appearance of Orpheus in early Christian tomb paintings in Rome also appealed to Cocteau, who had been influenced by the Catholic poet Jacques Maritain, and first conceived of a five-act Orpheus play that would blend Christian and Greek lore, incorporate the Incarnation, and feature Mary, Joseph, and Gabriel, the angel of the Annunciation. Although he kept the concept of a guardian angel (the character of the glazier, Heurtebise), Cocteau abandoned the Incarnation idea as too complex and chose instead to create a simpler work containing a prologue, 13 scenes, and an interval. Cocteau is very detailed concerning costume, scenery, and production, indicating exactly how the many and significant props should be used and how the characters should enter and exit (through a mirror). The actor playing Orpheus delivers the Prologue, asking the audience to refrain from expressing their feelings on the play until the end, because "we are playing at a great height, and without a safety-net. The slightest untimely noise and the lives of my comrades and my own may be imperiled."

Orpheus is set in Thrace, in a room in Orpheus's villa. The characters are dressed in the fashion "at the time of the performance," Cocteau instructs, and the room is "strange . . . rather like the room of a conjuror. In spite of the April-blue sky and the clear light, one suspects that it is surrounded by mysterious forces. Even familiar objects have a suspicious air." Orpheus is seated across from Eurydice, here portrayed as a selfish wife, jealous of her husband's love for his poetry, which she cannot understand. To her annoyance Orpheus is focused on the tapping of a white horse in a circus box in the center of the room; the head of the horse sits atop a man in tights. The horse taps out the word *hell*, and then *hello*, which enchants Orpheus, who sees it as a tactful response to an earlier message, "Orpheus hunts Eurydice's lost life." Orpheus has submitted this sentence to the Thracian poetry competition, where he hopes it will become immortal. Eurydice expresses her doubt regarding these messages and complains of neglect. She provokes Orpheus, who accuses her of nagging him and of smashing windowpanes to attract the attention of Heurtebise. Orpheus breaks a windowpane to continue the pattern and exits to attend the competition.

The guardian angel / glazier Heurtebise enters with a lump of poisoned sugar for the horse and an envelope for Eurydice. The latter is from her friend, Agloanice, a bacchante hated by Orpheus. When Eurydice places a letter into the envelope and seals it, she dies from the poison Algoanice has placed on the flap. As she is dying, she sends Heurtebise for Orpheus. Death, played by a woman in an evening dress and wearing rubber gloves, enters, together with two "surgeons." Death gives the poisoned sugar cube to the horse, which disappears, and performs a series of measurements and calculations with mechanical devices, including a watch supplied by a member of the audience. A dove, Eurydice's soul, flies off. Death exits without her gloves. When Orpheus reenters and finds Eurydice dead, Heurtebise shows him how to reach her in Hades—by professing to return the gloves Death has left behind. The angel tells him: "Mirrors are the doors through which Death comes and goes." Orpheus steps through the mirror into the underworld and returns with Eurydice, who has received permission to remain on earth as long as Orpheus does not look at her. However, they soon begin bickering again, Orpheus looks at Eurydice, and she disappears into the mirror. Orpheus claims he looked at her on purpose and seems unmoved. He opens a letter left by the postman and holds it up to the mirror, since it was written backwards. The letter warns Orpheus that the bacchantes have decided that his poem for the contest is a hoax (the first words he submitted were "O Hell!") and are coming to exact revenge. Orpheus goes out to the balcony to defend his ideas, is stoned to death, torn to pieces, and his head flies through the window. Heurtebise places the head on a pedestal. In the last scene Heurtebise leads Orpheus and Eurydice to Paradise, where they are reborn. As the three prepare for a leisurely lunch in their new villa Orpheus offers a prayer thanking

God for Heurtebise, for "having saved Eurydice, because, through love, she killed the devil in the shape of a horse, and in doing so she died. We thank thee for having saved me because I adored poetry, and thou art poetry. Amen."

Historically significant as one of the first in a series of modernizations of Greek myths by French playwrights—including Jean Giraudoux's *Amphitryon 38* (1929) and Jean-Paul Sartre's *Les Mouches* (1943; *The Flies*)—*Orpheus* stunned its first-night audience of poets, artists, and musicians, who debated the meaning and content of the play, its characters, its theatricality, and whether it was tragedy or comedy, or both. Audiences had been thrust into a new theatrical world, where established constructs and values had lost validity and meaning. But the visual unorthodoxy of Cocteau's play does not obscure the basic themes he dramatized in *Orpheus*: the universal and eternal conflict between men and women, the source for poetic and artistic expression, death as a magical substitution for life, and the capacity to be reborn in paradise. Familiar objects and the mechanical deftness with which they are used, as well as the function of such minor characters as the postman and police commissioner, point to an exploration of the myth of machine and the machinery of the state. Cocteau, who died in 1963, used Greek myth and theatrical wizardry to examine other, more modern forms of myth in a postwar culture of crisis and doubt that is as relevant today as it was in 1926.

"MASTER HAROLD" ...
AND THE BOYS

83

(1982)

by Athol Fugard

["Master Harold" ... and the Boys] is a "history" play—a family "history" play written, like O'Neill's Long Day's Journey into Night, *as an exorcism of the tormented ghosts of [Fugard's] childhood; but it is also a phase of South African "history," an anachronistic backward glance to a time when black men in their stoical optimism still dreamed of social change and when white boys might have been able to grasp the implications of "Whites Only" benches and choose to walk away from them. It deals with a rite of passage clumsily negotiated, a failure of love in a personal power-struggle with political implications.*

—Errol Durbach, *"Master Harold and the Boys*: Athol Fugard and the Psychopathology of Apartheid"

In 1989 *Time* magazine called Athol Fugard, "the greatest active playwright in English." He is certainly the best-known and most performed African playwright, a white South African whose explorations of his country's complex race relations during and after apartheid has led to his being described as "the literary conscience of Africa" and South Africa's "most eloquent anti-apartheid crusader abroad." A groundbreaking force in the establishment of a black and integrated South African theater, Fugard's early plays were performed for small private audiences rather than in public theaters since apartheid laws forbade white actors appearing on stage with black actors and "mixed" audiences. Considered subversive and threatening by the white ruling majority, Fugard's plays were often restricted and censored. It was not until *"Master Harold"* . . . *and the Boys* debuted outside South Africa in 1982 that the world became aware of Fugard's works and an international appreciation began. One of Fugard's most confessional works, *"Master Harold"* is based on the playwright's upbringing and draws on a specific incident from his past. Brilliantly incisive in capturing the psychological enslavement of apartheid, *"Master Harold"* is neither a polemic against a failed policy nor now outdated given the sweeping changes that have transformed South Africa since the abandonment of apartheid in the 1990s. The play continues to hold and speak to audiences as a universal drama of human relationships tested by societal and psychological forces.

Fugard has asserted that his plays are ultimately derived "from life and from encounters with real people." Born in South Africa in 1932, Harold Athol Fugard was raised in Port Elizabeth, an industrial city on the Indian Ocean that would become the setting for many of his plays. His father was the son of Anglo-Irish immigrants; his mother was the daughter of Dutch-speaking Afrikaners. His father's disability as an amputee forced his mother to support the family by managing a tearoom and boardinghouse. Fugard has described his father as a man "full of pointless, unthoughtout prejudices," while he has credited his mother's "outrage over the injustice of [South African] society" for encouraging his moral development and critical social view. "I think at a very early age," Fugard has observed, "I became suspicious of what the system was trying to do to me . . . conscious of what attitudes it was trying to input in me and what *prejudices* it was trying to pass on to me." Despite this awareness Hally (as Fugard was known during his boyhood) insisted on being called "Master Harold" by the family's black employees and has confessed to spitting in the face of an older Basuto waiter named Sam Semela, whom Fugard called the "most significant—the only—friend" of his youth. Fugard's sense of guilt and shame over his behavior and the incident would provide the impetus for *"Master Harold."*

Attending a Catholic Marist Brothers college before beginning his secondary education at a local technical college, Fugard went on to the University of Cape Town, studying philosophy and anthropology, but dropped out before his final exams in 1953 to embark on a hitchhiking trek through Africa. Reaching Port Sudan, Fugard signed on as the only white crewmember of a British tramp steamer headed to Asia. Fugard has credited his 10-month experience at sea, living and working with men of different races, with finally liberating him from the prejudices endemic in his South African background. Returning home he worked for a time as a freelance journalist for the *Port Elizabeth Evening Post* before being transferred to Cape Town, where he married the actress Sheila Meiring in 1956. His wife's theatrical involvement led Fugard into acting and writing his initial plays, which he now dismisses as "some rather pretentious little pieces." His mature work began when the Fugards moved to Johannesburg in 1958. There Fugard found work as a clerk in a Native Commissioner's Court that prosecuted "nonwhite" violators of South Africa's repressive Pass Laws, which restricted blacks to specific areas and out of whites-only areas. "I knew the system was evil," Fugard recalled, "but until then I had no idea of just how systematically evil it was. That was my revelation." Fugard began to associate with a group of black writers and actors who broadened his understanding of life for blacks under apartheid, which he began to embody in plays dealing directly with issues of race and identity under the apartheid regime.

His first major theatrical success was *The Blood Knot* (1961), which explores the relationship between two nonwhite half brothers, one of whom is light skinned enough to pass for white. Fugard took this role, while the other brother was played by actor Zakes Mokae, the beginning of a long collaboration with Fugard that would include originating the role of Sam in *"Master Harold."* The premiere, featuring the country's first mixed-race cast, "sent shock waves through South Africa," according to critic Derek Cohen. "Those who saw the initial performance knew instinctively that something of a revolution had taken place in the stodgily Angloid cultural world of South Africa. Whites, faced boldly with some inescapable truths about what their repressive culture and history had wrought, were compelled to take notice." *The Blood Knot* set the pattern for most of Fugard's subsequent plays in which a two- or three-character cast is presented in relationships that embody social and personal tensions. *Boesman and Lena* (1969) considers a homeless couple who turn their fury over the racial system against each other. *Sizwe Banzi Is Dead* (1972) concerns a man who exchanges identity with a corpse to evade the Pass Laws. *The Island* (1975) features black prisoners who put on a production of *Antigone*, finding in the play correspondences to the political repression they have experienced. *A Lesson from Aloes* (1978) deals with the corrosive effects of apartheid even on a group of liberal activists. Firmly rooted in the Henrik Ibsen tradition of realistic social protest drama, Fugard's plays avoid the merely polemical by being so closely based on felt experience and wider, more universal implications. All his plays, Fugard has asserted, are forms of protest: "My object is to defy. I am protesting against the conspiracy of silence about how the next man lives and what happens to groups other than our own."

In *"Master Harold" . . . and the Boys* Fugard uses his own past to explore the casualties and consequences of South Africa's racial system. Based on Fugard's family circumstances and the incident he had long been ashamed to reveal, *"Master Harold"* is set on a rainy afternoon in 1950 in the St. George's Park Tea Room in Port Elizabeth. Two 45-year-old black waiters (the boys of the title), Sam and Willie, pass the time in the empty restaurant tidying up and practicing dance steps for an upcoming contest. Sam, learning that Willie has beaten his partner, Hilda, urges him to apologize to her and restore their partnership for the competition. "Tapdance or ballroom," Sam says, "it's the same. Romance. In two weeks time when the judges look at you and Hilda, they must see a man and a woman who are dancing their way to a happy ending." The men are joined by the 17-year-old student Hally, or Master Harold, the white son of the owners of the restaurant, who has a long-standing relationship with the two men, particularly Sam who has been like a surrogate father to him. Hally's own father, a crippled, often abusive alcoholic, has been hospitalized, and Hally is disturbed by the news delivered by Sam that his mother is bringing his father home. Sitting down to his lunch, Hally and Sam discuss Hally's problems at school, which include a paddling for drawing an irreverent picture of a teacher, causing Sam to describe the caning prescribed for blacks by the judicial system. "I've heard enough, Sam!" Hally exclaims.

"Jesus! It's a bloody awful world when you come to think of it. People can be real bastards." Hally is comforted by the thought that "things will change, you wait and see. One day somebody is going to get up and give history a kick up the backside and get it going again." After each nominates individuals who have made the greatest contribution to humankind, Hally recalls former days when his family ran the Jubilee Boarding House. "Those years are not remembered as the happiest ones of an unhappy childhood," Hally confesses. His happiest memory is when Sam made a kite for him out of tomato-box wood, brown paper, and one of his mother's old stockings. "A little white boy in short trousers," Hally recalls, "and a black man old enough to be his father, flying a kite." At first embarrassed by the contraption Hally was shocked and exhilarated to find that the kite flew. The questions why Sam left him alone in the park with the kite tied to a bench and why Sam made the kite in the first place are left for the play's climax.

Their reminiscences are interrupted by a phone call from Hally's mother confirming that his father is being released from the hospital. Hally attempts to persuade her to keep him in the hospital longer. After hanging up Hally's irritation with his parents extends to Sam and Willie, whom he orders to get back to their work, and when they make too much noise as Sam helps Willie with his dance steps, Hally strikes Willie on the rear with a ruler and disparages "your ballroom nonsense." Rejecting Hally's contention that danc-ing is simple-minded with no real goal—just participants bumping into each other—Sam insists that "it's like being in a dream world without collisions . . . and it's beautiful because that is what we want life to be like." When Hally's mother calls again to say his father has been released, Hally reveals his deep resentment of his manipulative father: "You know what it's going to be like if he comes home. . . . I'm not being disrespectful but I'm sick and tired of emptying stinking chamberpots. I'm warning you now: when the two of you start fighting again, I'm leaving home." Hanging up the phone he remarks: "So much for a bloody world without collisions."

Transferring his hostility against his parents, while exercising the only power he can command, Hally lashes out at Sam who chastises him for speak-ing derogatorily about his father. "It's a terrible thing to mock your father, Hally . . . even if he is a cripple, he is your father," Sam says. Hally counters: "Mind your own business and shut up! Just do what you're paid to do. My mother is always warning me about allowing you to get too familiar . . . this time you have gone too far. . . . You're only a servant in here, and don't forget it." Insisting that Sam begin calling him "Master Harold," Hally widens the gap between the former friends and his surrogate father by repeating one of his father's racist jokes: "What isn't fair? A nigger's arse." Shocked and disappointed Sam replies that the punch line should have been "Sam's arse . . . because that's the one you're trying to kick," and dropping his trousers presents his backside for Hally's inspection: "Have a good look. A real Basuto

arse . . . which is about as nigger as they can come." Hally retaliates by spitting in Sam's face. Calling Hally a coward who wants to spit in his father's face
but uses his "because you think you're safe inside your fair skin," Sam recalls
the time they had to retrieve Hally's drunken father from the floor of Central
Hotel Bar, as people gathered to watch a black man carrying his drunk master
on his back and Hally, shamefaced, carrying his father's crutches: "I felt for
that little boy . . . Master Harold. I felt for him." Sam then reveals that this
is why he made the kite: "I wanted you to look up, be proud of something, of
yourself . . . and you certainly were that when I left you with it up there on
the hill." Sam next reveals why he left Hally: "I couldn't sit down there and
stay with you. It was a 'Whites Only' bench. You were too young, too excited
to notice then. But not anymore. If you're not careful . . . Master Harold . . .
you're going to be sitting up there by yourself for a long time to come, and
there won't be a kite in the sky." Sam proposes that they should "try again"
and fly another kite. "It worked once," he says, "and this time I need it as
much as you do." Hally responds weakly that "You can't fly kites on rainy days,
remember?" and states that "I don't know anything anymore." Sam responds
by saying:

> You sure of that, Hally? Because it would be pretty hopeless if that was
> true. It would mean nothing has been learnt in here this afternoon, and
> there was a hell of a lot of teaching going on . . . one way or the other.
> But anyway, I don't believe you. I reckon there's one thing you know. You
> don't *have* to sit up there by yourself. You know what that bench means
> now, and you can leave it any time you choose. All you've got to do is
> stand up and walk away from it.

Instead Hally walks away from the restaurant, too proud or embarrassed to ask
forgiveness or to accept the challenge Sam offers, leaving the waiters to close
up. Willie, however, reveals that he has learned a lesson from Sam, that he will
apologize to Hilda and will stop beating her to "relax and romance with her,"
and win the dance contest as "promising newcomers." Using his bus fare to
play Sarah Vaughan's "Little Man You're Crying" on the jukebox, Willie says
"Let's dream," and the two men dance together to the music.

   Beautifully modulated by its expansive symbols of the kite flying and the
dance, *"Master Harold" . . . and the Boys* explores both the contamination of
race prejudice and its defeat. Driven by a sense of atonement and moral repa-
ration over an adolescent violation of a human bond, Fugard makes clear that
the whites in South Africa's racial system are victims of their own weaknesses,
compensating for their own vulnerabilities and inadequacies by control and
dominance over the blacks. Here, it is a black character, the dehumanized
object of contempt, who asserts the moral and humane standard, who undermines force and coercion by empathy, compassion, and a vision of a "world

without collisions." That the youth Hally would grow into a playwright who profited from the lesson learned in the St. George's Tea Room is perhaps the most hopeful aspect of the play. By making reparations with the past Fugard finds a way forward out of South Africa's apartheid regime. In Fugard's version of James Joyce's *A Portrait of the Artist as a Young Man*, his coming of age drama in the age of apartheid likewise aspires to Stephen Dedalus's impossible dream of forging "the uncreated conscience of my race."

THE WELL-CURB

84

(c. 1420)

by Zeami Motokiyo

*Many people believe [*The Well-Curb*] is his greatest play, and one authority (Kōsai Tsutomu) called it frankly "a masterpiece among masterpieces." It is admired as a model of the yōgen (depth and grace) that was Zeami's own ideal and that the modern schools of nō proudly uphold.*

—Royall Tyler, *Japanese Nō Dramas*

Zeami Motokiyo is the leading playwright and principal codifier of Noh, the classical drama of Japan. As the greatest playwright, critic, and actor of his age Zeami embodies in the history of Japan's classical drama, by Western standards, the combined stature of William Shakespeare, Aristotle, and Richard Burbage. Zeami's plays form the major part of the Noh repertory and have been continually performed since their creation more than 500 years ago. In the West, Noh drama has exerted a significant influence, particularly in modern drama, as the basis for a genuine poetic drama and as an example of how the most abstract ideas and powerful emotions can be presented in the most economical and suggestive ways. Of all his works, Zeami regarded *Izutsu* (*The Well-Curb*) written in his 60s at the height of his powers after a lifetime perfecting his craft, as "the highest flower." It is an ideal play to illustrate the power of Noh drama and Zeami's remarkable achievement as its greatest practitioner.

The origin of Noh has many parallels with that of ancient Greek drama. Both arose out of religious rites; both combined music and dance and included a chorus; both evolved solo parts and dialogue involving male, masked actors; and both employed traditional myths and stories adjusted to the rigid conventions of their theatrical forms. However, whereas Greek and Western drama moved closer to realistic representation, Noh has retained its highly stylized and ritualized form in its pursuit of *yōgen*, a complex term denoting beauty, mystery, and depth—literally, an object concealed from view—that Noh attempts to reveal. Like Zen Buddhism, whose philosophy is essential to Noh, the drama's aesthetics proceed from the fundamental notion that outward reality is an illusion and inner truth is reached by contemplating the essence beneath the surface of things. Noh derives its power and beauty from its concentration in which all its elements—music, verse, costumes, and motion—unite to produce a single, clarified impression of some primary human relation or emotion. If Western drama depends on conflict and the primacy of the individual, Noh drama is unconcerned with the assumptions that produce either tragedy or comedy in a Western sense. Noh is not primarily concerned with dramatic action; instead it expresses a situation in lyrical form. The action that determines the Noh play's present situation occurs in the past, and the actors—reduced to a principal figure, the *shite*, and the *waki*, or companion—embody the emotions that the play dramatizes and represent an aspect of the human psyche, magnified in time and space and revealed through speech and gesture. To produce Noh's desired goal of illumination depends on the highest skills of the actor to reveal profound significance with an economy of method and within a prescribed limitation of theatrical effects.

Noh plays are performed on a standardized raised, roofed platform about 20-feet square, with the audience seated on three of its sides. The rear of the stage is a panel on which an aged pine tree is painted. To the left a bridgeway (the *hashigarkari*) leads to a curtained doorway, the entrance and exit points for the principal actors. In a shallow backstage area, visible to the audience, four musicians of drums and flute sit. The Chorus, seated along the left edge of the stage sings, speaks for or as the leading actor, moralizes, and narrates. A complete Noh program consists of three to five plays (each usually shorter than a Western one-act play) in several categories: *kamimono*, plays praising the gods; *shuramono*, plays about warriors; *kazuramono*, plays about women; *zatsu*, miscellaneous plays often about deranged persons (often women who have suffered the loss of a child or husband); and *kirimono*, plays about demons or other supernatural beings. Performed in this sequence a Noh program suggests a pattern moving from the innocence and peace of the world of the gods through human struggle and error to repentance and redemption and a final restoration of peace and harmony. The object of a Noh play is to capture the essence of a situation and emotion with climaxes signaled by extremely stylized gestures or bodily attitudes held for emphasis. During a performance every movement and intonation follow set rules and carry great significance. All Noh plays culminate in a dance with the action that precedes it serving mainly to establish the circumstances that motivate it. It was principally Zeami, over a lifetime in the theater, who established the goals and methods of Noh that continue to sustain the world's oldest continuously performed dramatic form.

Zeami, born in 1363, was the eldest son of Kannami, a distinguished actor who is credited with initiating the refinement of the popular form of theater that combined music, dancing, and mimicry, known as *sarugaku* ("monkey music") into the more refined and disciplined Noh drama, which his son perfected. In

1374, after Kannami's troupe performed for the 17-year-old shogun Ashikaga Yoshimitsu, the shogun, captivated by Zeami's beauty and charm as an actor, became the patron of his father's troupe. The rural and folk elements out of which Noh was derived were thereby refined to reflect the spirit and beliefs of the samurai culture of Noh's upper-class patron. When Kannami died in 1384, Zeami, at the age of 21, assumed leadership of the troupe. In 1400 he wrote the first of his treatises on Noh, *Fūshikaden*. In it Zeami formulates an aesthetic for the theater, specifies the training necessary for an actor, categorizes types of Noh plays and characters, and lists the philosophical principles that underlie Noh. *Fūshikaden* and the treatises that followed were not meant for a wide audience but as instruction for his fellow professionals. They also reveal the values Zeami considered essential in his plays and performance. He makes clear that a play's text must be viewed like an opera's libretto, only a single part of a much more complex joining of elements, including music and movement, depending on the intricate skill of the actor, whose lifelong training eventually leads to mastery of the traditions and the possibilities of the form. With Yoshimitsu's death in 1408 Zeami's preeminence began a long, slow decline, as Yoshimitsu's sons gradually withdrew the privileges Zeami and his troupe had received. In 1432 Motomasa, Zeami's eldest son, who had succeeded to the leadership of the troupe, suddenly died. It has been speculated that he may have been assassinated on the orders of the shogun Yoshinori, who also exiled Zeami to Sado Island in the Japan Sea in 1434. It is believed that before his death in 1443 Zeami was pardoned and allowed to return to the mainland.

One distinction of Zeami's genius, compared to other Noh playwrights, is the formal unity of his dramatic effects; another is the deepened exploration of the individual's emotions and humanistic concerns that emerge. Zeami's plays trace the complex nature of human identity and the profound recesses of the human psyche. As one of the principal scholars of Zeami's artistry, Thomas Blenham Hare has asserted: "Zeami's plays concentrate attention on the essential nature of an individual experience; the goal of their aesthetic is the lyric exfoliation of identity." Zeami's aesthetic and mastery are fully displayed in *The Well-Curb*. The play is based on an episode in the *Ise monogatari* (*Tales of Ise*), a 10th-century collection of short tales and poems considering various aspects of love. The episode that Zeami dramatizes in *The Well-Curb* concerns a boy and a girl who lived next door to each other and played by a nearby well. When they grew up the young man courted the girl, and they were married. He was unfaithful but, due to his wife's great devotion, he eventually overcame his infatuation with his mistress and was reconciled with his wife. In Zeami's version the play commences with a priest on pilgrimage who comes upon an old well-curb (the wooden platform atop a well), the meeting spot of the two lovers in the ancient tale—the woman, Ki-no-Aritsune and the man, Ariwara-no-Narihira. As the priest performs religious rites "for the sake of those twin souls," a maiden, wearing a young woman's mask, enters, singing

Autumn nights are lonely anywhere,
Yet even lonelier
Is this old temple rarely visited,
When the autumn winds sound through the garden pines.
The moon sinking westward,
The drooping eaves o'ergrown with waving ferns—
All reminds me of the past
Alas! How long must I still live
And naught to hope for in the future!
Each thing that happens leaves its mark upon the mind;
Such is our mortal world.

The maiden, joined by the Chorus, tells the lovers' story:

Here in this province long ago
Two households once lived side by side;
The children, boy and girl, were playmates.
Leaning over the well-curb beyond the gate,
They peered together down the well
Where mirrored lay their faces cheek to cheek,
Their sleeves hanging o'er each other's shoulder.
Thus used those bosom friends to play.
In time they grew reserved and shy,
Till the faithful-hearted youth
Sent her a letter with a poem
Telling his flower-like love
In words like sparkling dew drops.

A villager then comes forward to continue the story of Narihira's mistress and Aritsune's lack of jealousy, which caused him to suspect she had a lover as well. Setting off for his mistress as usual Narihira secretly returned to spy on his wife. Instead of uncovering her lover he hears Aritsune's undiminished profession of her love for him. Marveling that any man could have so true a wife, Narihira renounces his mistress and reunites with his wife.

In the play's second part, the priest awakes to discover that the maiden is actually the ghost of Narihira's wife. Attesting to her continuing love for her husband, she peers into the well and sees his face in her reflection. As morning dawns the ghost retreats, and the Chorus closes the play:

The garden pines awaken with the breeze;
And like the torn leaves of the basho tree
The priest's dream is shattered and day dawns,
The priest's dream is shattered and day dawns.

Exquisite in its simplicity and suggestiveness, *The Well-Curb* achieves its impact by a radical paring down to a lyric core all its dramatic element, in which deep emotion finds form through the integration of story, verse, music, and dance. Using his borrowed lovers' story, Zeami manages to ring the changes on central human emotions while brilliantly in the single image of the reflected faces in the well water establishes an equally important theme. As Thomas Hare has asserted,

> Zeami's plays are . . . ruminations on the problem of identity. . . . The characters he creates have little faith in the efficacy of human action. A tortured but inescapable absorption in the self, an inability to escape the ties of a past life, love, hate, longing, and pride—these characteristics persecute Zeami's shite. Yet they are the very characteristics that can give birth to a great performance and provide an opportunity for the uninhibited individual expression of an actor's attainment.

It is no wonder that the rediscovery of Noh drama in the West by such writers as Ezra Pound and William Butler Yeats proved to be so revelatory. In works such as *The Well-Curb* Westerners glimpsed the possibilities of a poetic drama that achieved the most from the least.

THE OTHER SHORE

85

(1986)

by Gao Xingjian

Gao Xingjian's plays are characterized by originality, in no way diminished by the fact that he has been influenced both by modern Western and traditional Chinese currents. His greatness as a dramatist lies in the manner in which he has succeeded in enriching these fundamentally different elements and making them coalesce to something entirely new.
—Göran Malmqvist, Presentation Speech for the 2000 Nobel Prize in literature

Gao Xingjian, the only Chinese writer to have received the Nobel Prize in literature, was a controversial choice by the Swedish Academy. As a playwright, critic, and novelist Gao is a prominent leader of the avant-garde movement in fiction and drama that emerged in China following the Cultural Revolution. Although called in 2000 by critic Howard Goldblatt, "a major figure in world drama, and the most innovative, if not the most famous playwright China has produced in this century," Gao was at the time largely unknown both in the West and in China, where his work had been banned. Reaction from China to the Nobel announcement was vituperative. "This shows that the Nobel Prize for Literature has virtually been used for political purposes and thus has lost its authority," the director of the Chinese Writers Association declared. "China boasts many world-famous literary works and writers, about which the Nobel Committee knows little." China's Foreign Ministry called the award a political maneuver and not an occasion for national pride. However, with the award more of Gao's works became available, justifying his recognition as a writer of great distinction. His novel *Lingshan* (*Soul Mountain*) has been praised as one of the singular achievements in modern Chinese fiction, while his plays have opened up new territory and techniques for Chinese drama. *Bi'an* (*The Other Shore*) provides the best example of Gao's unique combination of European modernist and traditional Chinese dramatic elements.

   Classical Chinese drama that took shape following the Mongols' conquest of China in the 13th century had largely become an operatic form by the 17th century, evolving into the Beijing opera that became dominant by the

19th century. Primarily a theatrical rather than a literary form, Beijing opera privileged performance over a play's text, with story little more than a vehicle for the performer to demonstrate rigidly controlled conventions of acting, dancing, and singing. Western-style "spoken" or "new" drama entered China after the demise of the Chinese empire in 1912. Beginning as translations and adaptations of foreign plays by William Shakespeare, Anton Chekhov, George Bernard Shaw, Henrik Ibsen, and others, drama in this new style eventually was created by native playwrights incorporating Chinese subjects and themes. The best known of these playwrights is probably Cao Yu, who, in plays such as *Thunderstorm* (1933), *Sunrise* (1935), and *The Bridge* (1945), dealt with contemporary social problems. After the Communists assumed control in 1949, both Beijing opera and the spoken drama were retooled to conform to party doctrine and to extol the virtues of the revolution. New works were mainly ideological melodramas showing the triumph of party principles over the enemies of the revolution. During the Cultural Revolution traditional Chinese drama was suppressed, and professional theater in China largely ceased to exist except for the production of a few "model" plays. Not until the end of the Cultural Revolution and the death of Mao Zedong in 1976 was greater freedom of theatrical subjects and conventions again permitted.

Gao Xingjian's life and artistic development fully reflects the political and cultural shifts that has affected modern Chinese literary and dramatic expression. Born in 1940 in Ganzhou in eastern China, Gao, during his childhood, contended with both the Japanese invasion and the civil war won by the Communists in 1949. Gao's father was a banker; his mother was an amateur actress. His family kept a sizable library of Chinese and Western literature, and Gao was early on introduced both to traditional Chinese literature and performing arts and European works. He attended the Beijing Foreign Languages Institute from 1957 to 1962 where he studied French language and literature, absorbing the ideas of French existentialist thinkers and the dramatic works of such figures as Samuel Beckett, Eugène Ionesco, Jean Genet, and Antonin Artaud, whom he would later translate into Chinese. After graduation Gao worked as a translator and editor of the French edition of the magazine *China Reconstructs* and began secretly writing plays, stories, and essays to avoid sanctions against any writing that did not serve the state. His wife eventually denounced him to government officials, and Gao was sent to rural China for six years of "reeducation" as a farm laborer and teacher. He eventually returned to Beijing in 1975 and went to work for the Chinese Writers Association. In the more moderate atmosphere following the Cultural Revolution he began to publish his work regularly. His first four books were *A Preliminary Discussion of the Art of Modern Fiction* (1981), *A Pigeon Called Red Beak* (1985), *Collected Plays* (1985), and *In Search of a Modern Form of Dramatic Representation* (1987). In 1981 he was assigned to work as a writer for the Beijing People's Art Theater, and his first play, *Juedui xinhao* (*Absolute Signal*), about a failed train robbery, was produced in 1982. It employs an innovative multiple perspective technique and flashbacks to explore its characters. His next play, *Chezhan (Bus Stop)*, followed in 1983. Drawing upon Beckett and the techniques of the theater of the absurd, the play deals with several characters representing a cross-section of Chinese society who wait for a bus that never stops. Government officials declared the play subversive, and Gao left Beijing to avoid a prison sentence. Misdiagnosed with terminal cancer he embarked on a 10-month walking tour across rural China. His experiences would form the basis for his acclaimed novel *Soul Mountain* (1989). Gao's next play, *Yeren (Wilderness)*, depicts a journalist who travels into the wilds of China in search of a legendary creature who is part-man, part-monkey. Its episodic, elliptical structure is interspersed with traditional Chinese song, dance, and music. *The Other Shore* was the final work Gao wrote in China before his political exile. Traveling to Paris on an artistic fellowship, Gao sought political asylum in France after denouncing the suppression of the student protests in Tiananmen Square in 1989. Gao's play about the massacre, *Taowang (Fleeing)*, appeared in 1992 and caused Chinese officials to ban all his works. He became a naturalized French citizen in 1998. Continuing to write in both French and Chinese, Gao has stated: "I don't consider myself to have cut myself off from my roots. But China remains an authoritarian state, and I don't plan on returning while I'm alive."

Encapsulating many of the themes and techniques of his works, *The Other Shore* began as an exercise for actors in "pure drama" to test their versatility in assuming multiple roles in several situations, unassisted by costume or stage scenery. The one-act play breaks dramatic conventions by presenting a series of isolated episodes without a clear plot of dramatic complications and resolutions or apparent character development. Thematic links provide the play's coherence. The play begins with a small group of actors asked to play a game with ropes. Each holds onto an end of a rope and then is instructed by the Lead Actor to give an end to him. "This way you'll be able to establish all kinds of relationships with me," he tells the group, "some tense, some lax, some distant, and some close, and soon your individual attitudes will have a strong impact on me. Society is complex and ever-changing, we're constantly pulling and being pulled." The exercise establishes the play's major themes of the relationship between the individual and the collective and the amount of freedom and autonomy that is possible in the social and human condition. While *The Other Shore* is not overtly political, it certainly can be read as a commentary on life under the Communist Party in China, symbolized as a web in which each individual is bound collectively, and each movement affects all. After a time the Lead Actor instructs them to let down the ropes and imagine a river in front of them. Invoking the Buddhist concept that enlightenment, or nirvana, is reachable on the other shore after crossing the river of life, the actors enact this journey. Expressing both anxiety and exhilaration during the crossing, when they arrive they experience, not enlightenment on the other shore, "only oblivion." Replacing Buddhist beliefs with a more existential philosophy the play suggests that the search for enlightenment leads not to perfect fulfillment but continual struggle. On "the other shore" an archetypal battle between the individual and the collective ensues.

The actors become members of a Crowd who have lost their language and their memories. A Woman emerges from the oblivion and walks among them, teaching the Crowd words and helping them to learn how to differentiate themselves from one another. As the Crowd grows confident in its use of language and power it turns on the Woman and threatens her. A Man intervenes but fails to prevent them from strangling her. With the emergence of the Man in conflict with the Crowd the dramatic focus of the play—the relationship between the individual and the mass—is fully engaged. Invited by the Crowd to lead them the Man refuses. When they meet a Card Player he realizes that the game is rigged, but when he tries to help the Crowd realize the truth they abuse and humiliate him. Briefly transformed into his younger self, he meets his mother, his young girlfriend, and his father. They supply neither answers for the Man nor provide any relief. Taunted relentlessly by the Crowd and others who accuse him of being a troublemaker, he asserts: "I'm going my way! I'm not bothering anybody, and nobody's bothering me, okay?" Blocked by a man named Stable Keeper, the Man is invited to crawl through his crotch. Doing so, he picks up a key that he uses to unlock an imaginary door. Inside mannequins are brought to life under his control, forming "a gigantic collective pattern. . . . As they move about the pattern keeps changing slowly yet unstoppably." After a process of "constant discovery, renewal, rediscovery, and further renewal" the mannequins cease to respond to his commands, and he gradually becomes weaker, crawling out of the room "like a worm, utterly exhausted." Shadow, the representation of the Man's inner life, takes up the narration of the man's increasingly debilitating journey: "You have long lost your faith in people, your heart has grown old and it will not love again. Your only wish is to go walking among the trees in the forest until you are totally exhausted. Then you will collapse somewhere, hoping never to be found." Accused of self-pity by his Shadow the Man cannot escape the Crowd that has materialized from the trees in the forest, and they accompany him offstage along with his "drooping, blind, and deaf heart."

The actors reappear onstage as themselves, commenting on the play they have just enacted, about dinner plans, someone's kitten, and other fragments of trivial conversation. The sounds of a baby crying and a car engine starting are heard, and one of the actors says:

> How are you going to get back?
> It's so bad, what kind of stupid play is this anyway?
> Are you doing anything tomorrow? Shall we have dinner together?

Bicycle bells, running water, the car running, and an ambulance's siren close the play. Having begun with an exercise to stress the forces restraining and controlling each individual, followed by a series of symbolic encounters that underscore the struggles of the individual to achieve autonomy and fulfillment, the play closes with fragmented images from actuality, suggesting that the journey and its lessons persist.

Working on multiple levels *The Other Shore* can be described as an experimental theater class, a political allegory, and, in the words of critic Rob Kendt, a "series of individuation psychodramas." Despite its radical style that subverts conventional dramatic expectations the play achieves a suggestive power by harnessing elements of Chinese and existential philosophy and fusing the stylized, nonrepresentational aspects of traditional Chinese drama with aspects of the theater of the absurd. Rejecting the Buddhist promise of nirvana for the righteous, Gao stages an alternative view of man's fate as a continual struggle between self and other. A series of ostensibly disjointed encounters, absurd dialogue, and nightmarish imagery express humans' inner torment and social discontents. Man, exhausted under the weight of anxiety, outside threat, and despairing loneliness, muddles on, tethered by a web of relationships that he cannot evade. Like Jean-Paul Sartre's *No Exit*, *The Other Shore* makes clear both that "Hell is other people" and that the testing is the one constant of human existence. There is no escape from the suffering of this world, no other shore of blissful respite or consoling illumination. By fusing Chinese and Western ontological concepts, political commentary, and methods derived from the theater of the absurd *The Other Shore* becomes a powerful and provoking modern existential fable.

THE LITTLE FOXES

(1939)   *by Lillian Hellman*

Craft, and more than craft, is here at work. For the very plainness of the situation, the single-mindedness with which it is pursued, reflects a way of thinking, a habit of handling bonds and psyches as though they were equally negotiable, that once did exist . . . and may continue to characterize an age for some time to come.
    —Walter Kerr, Review of a 1967 revival of *The Little Foxes*

Acknowledged as a classic of the American theater, *The Little Foxes* is the most frequently performed of Lillian Hellman's plays. It is a taut, precisely crafted three-act work that focuses on rapacious mercantile interests, life-destroying greediness, and sibling rivalry in a southern family at the turn of the 20th century, aspects of life in the South that are rarely seen onstage. Adding to the play's uniqueness and importance is the presence of a female protagonist, Regina Giddens (née Hubbard), who is both shocking and compelling in her limitless ambition and ruthlessness. Portrayed most memorably by Tallulah Bankhead in the original stage production and by Bette Davis in the 1941 film version, Regina may be a less complex character than many of her sisters in southern literature, but her transparent single-mindedness, her viciousness, and, most notably, her refusal to allow herself to be victimized because she is a woman serve to give her a stature equal to and even greater than that of the men in the play.

In her 1973 memoir, *Pentimento*, Hellman revealed that her mother's family, wealthy southerners who had left Alabama for the moneymaking possibilities offered by the industrial North, had inspired the Hubbards of *The Little Foxes* and its prequel, *Another Part of the Forest* (1941). Born in New Orleans on June 20, 1905, Hellman was the daughter of Max Hellman and Julia Newhouse. Her father owned a shoe store on Canal Street in New Orleans until his partner made off with the store's funds and bankrupted him. He took his wife and daughter to New York to make a fresh start when Hellman was five. Max's business interests took him back and forth between New York and New

Orleans, and Hellman spent half of each year in the city in which she was born. She completed her education in New York, which included three years at New York University (NYU) and some study at Columbia, but her experience of the South is reflected in many of her works. After she left NYU she worked as a publisher's reader, book reviewer, and theater publicist and subscription manager, and in 1925 she married Arthur Kober, a press agent who would later become a successful playwright and screenwriter. The couple went to Paris, where Kober edited an English-language magazine, *The Paris Comet*, in which Hellman published two short stories. Hellman later called these early stories, including a third, which appeared in a French magazine, "lady-writer stories." Hellman and Kober were divorced in 1932.

Hellman was encouraged to write plays by her longtime companion, detective novelist and screenwriter Dashiell Hammett, whom she met in Hollywood while she was working as a scenario reader. Hammett would become a major influence on Hellman's work until his death in 1961. While working as a play reader for New York producer Herman Shumlin, for whom she discovered the play *Grand Hotel*, Hellman began to write her own play, *The Children's Hour*, the subject of which was suggested by Hammett and was based on a Scottish court case. Hellman completed *The Children's Hour* in 1934, and Shumlin produced it on Broadway the same year. The play concerns two women who own and operate a girls' school and who are emotionally devastated and financially ruined when a spoiled and vicious student publicly accuses them of lesbianism. Because of its homoerotic subject matter, well-known actresses refused to appear in the play, and it opened with a cast of unknowns. Nevertheless, the play became a Broadway sensation (it was banned in Boston—a cliché, but an appropriate one, since the setting is a New England town), and Hellman achieved instant celebrity. She then went to Hollywood to work on the screenplay for *The Children's Hour*, which was released in 1936 under the title *These Three*. At the same time Hellman completed *Days to Come*, a play centering on strikers and strikebreakers at a brush factory in a small Ohio town. *Days to Come* opened on Broadway in 1936 and closed after a week's run. Hellman herself later described the play as "an awful failure" that was punctuated by a distinguished member of the audience, newspaper mogul William Randolph Hearst, "getting up in the middle of the first act and leaving with his party of ten."

Her confidence shaken, Hellman abandoned playwriting for a time to write the screenplay of Sidney Kingsley's play *Dead End* (1937). She then went to France, Russia, and Spain, which was in the midst of its civil war. When she returned to the United States Hellman wrote a column on her impressions of the war at the suggestion of Walter Winchell. The Hearst newspapers called her account "Loyalist propaganda" and refused to run it, but the article was eventually published in the *New Republic*. She continued her antifascist activities, forming Contemporary Historians, Inc., with John Dos Passos, Archibald

MacLeish, and Ernest Hemingway in order to have the celebrated Dutch film-maker Joris Ivens direct *The Spanish Earth*, a war documentary (1937). Hellman also helped to raise money for the Loyalist cause, as well as for Loyalist refugees and refugees from Adolf Hitler's Europe.

Hellman was determined to eradicate the failure of *Days to Come* with a third play that would recapture the success of *The Children's Hour*. She chose to re-create a turn-of-the-century southern family whose money is obtained through deceitful business practices and opportunism and whose lives are defined and ultimately taken over by material acquisition and arrogance. She filled several notebooks with the results of her careful research on the era, particularly the American South and American business practices, and rewrote the play nine times. The outcome of her labors was *The Little Foxes*, a title suggested to Hellman by Dorothy Parker, and which referred to a verse from the biblical Song of Solomon: "Take us the foxes, the little foxes, that spoil the vines, for our vines have tender grapes." In *Pentimento* Hellman revealed that *The Little Foxes* was "the most difficult play I ever wrote. . . . Some of the trouble came because the play has a distant connection to my mother's family and everything I had heard or seen or imagined had formed a giant tangled time-jungle in which I could find no space to walk without tripping over old roots, hearing old voices speak about histories made long before my day." *The Little Foxes* opened on Broadway on February 15, 1939, and was a commercial and critical success.

The Little Foxes is set in the spring of 1900 in a small southern town. The action takes place primarily in the elegant and expensively furnished living room of Horace and Regina Giddens, a room Hellman describes as reflecting "no particular taste. Everything is of the best and that is all." Individual taste is clearly not a commodity held by the characters to be of any particular importance. As the play opens Regina and her brothers are entertaining William Marshall, a Chicago businessman, who is negotiating with them to build a local cotton mill to be controlled by the Hubbards if they can raise enough money to buy 51 percent of the company. The project stands to earn millions for the Hubbards and Regina, and each foresees the attainment of his or her heart's desire. Ben wants a stable of thoroughbreds, Oscar, a new home. Regina, "a handsome woman of forty" who feels trapped in a loveless marriage, plans to go to Chicago, which she sees as offering her the fashionable cosmopolitan life she lacks. The genteel, timid Birdie, Oscar's wife, whom he married for her father's cotton fields and who mistreats her, yearns to see her family's plantation, Lionnet, returned to its former grace. To complete the partnership the family needs Regina's one-third of the money to come from her banker husband, Horace, who has spent five months being treated at Johns Hopkins for a heart ailment. Horace has not responded to the deal, and when Oscar and Ben pressure Regina, she craftily extracts a promise from Ben for a greater share of the profits if she can get Horace home within two weeks. When Oscar objects Ben suggests that Alexandra might marry Oscar's son, Leo, a dissipated young man who works for Horace Giddens, to keep the money in the family. Regina is not overly attracted to the idea of the marriage but agrees to consider the plan. She sends her gentle 17-year-old daughter, Alexandra, to bring her father home.

At the start of act 2, Horace and Alexandra have not yet arrived and the deadline for the transaction is approaching. The restive Hubbard brothers secretly send Leo to "borrow" Horace's railroad bonds from his safe deposit box as collateral for Marshall. When Horace returns home he refuses to give Regina the money for her share of the partnership: "I'm sick of you. . . . I'm sick of your brothers and their dirty tricks to make a dime. . . . Why should I give you the money? To pound the bones of this town to make dividends for you to spend? You wreck the town, you and your brothers, *you* wreck the town and live on it." An infuriated Regina counters maliciously, "I hope you die soon. I'll be waiting for you to die." By act 3, Horace has discovered the theft. He informs his wife that he will call the theft a loan and change his will so that Regina inherits the bonds but cannot make money from the partnership. However, before he can put this plan into action, he suffers a heart attack and breaks his bottle of medicine. As Regina cruelly looks on Horace dies while trying to go upstairs for his second bottle. Regina confronts her brothers with the theft and threatens to expose them unless she receives the majority of the profits. She has apparently won, but at the end of the play Alexandra wonders why her father was found on the stairs. This detail interests Ben, who suggests that in the future he may use the information to get the better of his sister. Regina tries to reach out to her daughter, but a completely disillusioned Alexandra announces that she is leaving. She echoes Addie, the Giddens's wise black maid, when she tells her mother: "Addie said there were people who ate the earth and other people who stood around and watched them do it. And just now Uncle Ben said the same thing. . . . Well, tell him for me, Mama, I'm not going to stand around and watch you do it. Tell him I'll be fighting as hard as he'll be fighting some place where people don't just stand around and watch." The curtain descends on Regina as she climbs the stairs alone.

The Little Foxes lends itself to various interpretations. It can been seen as the final violation of the South by carpetbagging northern industrial interests that have arrived, as Horace complains, to exploit its cheap black labor, a condition that will further worsen race relations. In contrast to the mercantile interests of the Hubbards are Horace, Birdie, and Addie, who stand for the values of the Old South. Written and first produced toward the end of the Great Depression but set squarely in the South of Jim Crow, *The Little Foxes* raises many questions concerning these older and ostensibly more genteel values. Ben and Oscar speak disparagingly of the "niggers"; Birdie, trapped in the past, insists to Oscar that her family always treated their "people" well. Horace is gentle, loving, and honorable, and because he is a morally upright, "good" character in contrast to the "bad" Hubbards we want to believe that he has a more highly evolved view of southern blacks.

Given Hellman's antifascist views and her left-leaning sensibilities, many critics thought that she was attacking capitalism. Hellman's emphasis on social responsibility, as well as the development of well-meaning but ineffectual characters who allow evil to succeed, is a feature of her plays, but she discounted critics' assertions that she was attacking capitalism or the changing South. In *Pentimento* she wrote that she "had meant the audience to recognize some part of themselves in the money-dominated Hubbards. I had not meant people to think of them as villains to whom they had no connection." There is melodrama—Leo's pilfering of the bonds, the threat of an arranged marriage, Horace's fatal heart attack—but there is humor and irony as well, a feature Hellman insisted was an important aspect of the play. Ben Hubbard is laughably avuncular, spouting wornout, meaningless clichés; the childlike Birdie runs over to the Giddens to greet Horace in her bathrobe and later becomes comically tipsy as she plays the piano and reminisces about her youth at Lionnet; Regina at various times attempts to be agreeable, but her gaiety is often absurd. For Hellman *The Little Foxes* was a play about greedy, unscrupulous, hot-tempered people, straightforward and uncompromising in their aspirations and their sibling rivalry, and she deliberately leaves her characters' future ambiguous. The Hubbards, she told the *New York Herald Tribune* in 1939, "are just starting to get on in the world in a big way, but their various futures I like to think I leave to the imagination of the audience. I meant to be neither misanthropic nor cynical, merely truthful and realistic."

FENCES

87

(1985)   *by August Wilson*

For the new play, I wanted to explore our commonalities of culture. What you have in
Fences *is a very specific situation, a black family which the forces of racism have molded
and shaped, but you also have husband-wife, father-son. White America looks at black
America in this glancing manner. They pass right by the Troy Maxsons of the world and
never stop to look at them. They talk about niggers as lazy and shiftless. Well, here's a man
with responsibilities as prime to his life. I wanted to examine Troy's life layer by layer and
find out why he made the choices he made.*
　　　　—August Wilson, Interview with Dennis Watlington, *Vanity Fair,* 1989

One of the most ambitious projects ever undertaken by an American dramatist
is August Wilson's 10-play Pittsburgh Cycle. Each play is set in a different
decade of the 20th century to chronicle the black experience in America. "I'm
taking each decade," Wilson said about his work in progress, "and looking at
one of the most important questions that blacks confronted in that decade
and writing a play about it. Put them all together, and you have a history."
Beginning with *Ma Rainey's Black Bottom* in 1984, the cycle was completed
with *Radio Golf,* which opened only a few months before Wilson's death from
liver cancer in 2005. It has been described by critic Lawrence Bommer as "the
most complete cultural chronicle since Balzac wrote his vast *Human Comedy,*
an artistic whole that has grown even greater than its prize-winning parts."
In a playwriting career of a little more than 20 years, Wilson dominated the
American stage as few other dramatists have ever done. Since 1984 no Ameri-
can playwright had more productions on Broadway than Wilson. Two of them,
Fences, in 1987, and *The Piano Lesson,* in 1990, won both the Pulitzer Prize and
the Tony Award for best drama. He received seven New York Drama Critics'
Circle Awards for best play. Since the award was inaugurated in 1936, only
Tennessee Williams, who won it four times, had ever won it more than twice.
His plays' critical acclaim and wide popularity are also unique and significant.
"His audience appeal," critic John Lahr has observed, "almost single-handedly

broke down the wall for other black artists, many of whom would not otherwise be working in the mainstream." As a dramatist Wilson set out to change the ways "white America looks at blacks, and the way blacks look at themselves." Author Toni Morrison has called her efforts of bearing witness to previous generations' racial experiences "re-membering," that is, revivifying and embodying what has been lost in the past as too painful to recall. Wilson's plays function in a similar way. "What I want to do," he told an interviewer in 1987, "is place the culture of black America on stage, to demonstrate that it has the ability to offer sustenance, so that when you leave your parents' house, you are not in the world alone." *Fences* epitomizes Wilson's efforts to dramatize the reality of the black experience in America while probing its depths and complexity.

The search for self-definition and a sustaining racial heritage that dominates Wilson's plays is also reflected in his background and development. Born Frederick August Kittel in 1945, Wilson grew up in Pittsburgh's black ghetto known as the Hill. Wilson's white father abandoned the family when Wilson was a child. His mother, Daisy Wilson Kittel, worked as a cleaning woman to support her six children, who lived in a two-room apartment above a grocery store. Wilson would later take his mother's maiden name to honor her and his African-American heritage. When Wilson was 12, his mother remarried, and the family moved to the predominantly white working-class suburb of Hazelwood, where they were the target of racial abuse. At 14, Wilson was the only black student at Central Catholic High School. He subsequently transferred to a vocational school and then to a public high school, where he was falsely accused of plagiarism. Disgusted by the injustice and the racism he experienced, Wilson dropped out of school at age 15, spending his time at a public library where he educated himself, reading all he could of writers such as Richard Wright, Ralph Ellison, and Langston Hughes.

In 1965 Wilson moved out of his mother's home to a rooming house and began to associate with a group of local young black intellectuals and writers. Around this time, Wilson first heard Malcolm X speak and discovered the blues in the records of Bessie Smith. Both would have an important impact on his development. Wilson has called the black pride and power message of Malcolm X and the Nation of Islam "the kiln in which I was fired," while he has described the blues, with its complexity and distinctness as an African-American folk expression, as the wellspring of his art. In 1968 Wilson cofounded with Rob Penny the Black Horizons community theater in the Hill. In operation until 1978, the theater served as a forum for his first plays and exposure to the works of other black dramatists, such as Amiri Baraka, Ed Bullins, and Lonnie Elder. Wilson's evolving dramatic aesthetic would differ from that of other black dramatists of the period by avoiding an overt political and didactic take on the African-American experience. Although also dealing with confrontations with whites, as critic Mark William Rocha has explained, "in Wilson's plays the confrontation occurs off-stage so that the emphasis is placed not so much on the confrontation itself, but on how the black community invests itself in that face-to-face encounter." Moreover, contrary to the often racially exclusionary aesthetic of members of the black arts movement, Wilson embraced a cross-cultural diversity of influences. "When I sat down to write," Wilson recalled about his first experience as a playwright, "I realized I was sitting in the same chair as Eugene O'Neill, Tennessee Williams, Arthur Miller, Henrik Ibsen, Amiri Baraka, and Ed Bullins."

Wilson's career as a dramatist began in 1978 when he took a job writing dramatic skits for the Science Museum of Minnesota, in St. Paul. There, far away from Pittsburgh and the Hill, he discovered his dramatic voice recalling situations and characters from his hometown. Among his early plays, *Jitney* is a realistic drama set at a Pittsburgh gypsy-cab stand in the 1970s. *Fullerton Street*, a play set in the1940s on the night of a famous Joe Louis prizefight, followed. In 1981 Wilson began submitting his plays to the National Playwrights Conference of the Eugene O'Neill Center in Connecticut. Four were rejected, but a fifth, *Ma Rainey's Black Bottom*, was accepted for a staged reading. This began Wilson's long association with Lloyd Richards, who directed the play at the Yale Repertory Theatre before it came to Broadway in 1984. This would set the model for most of Wilson's subsequent dramas, directed by Richards and premiering first at Yale before going on to Broadway. Set in a Chicago recording studio in 1927, *Ma Rainey's Black Bottom* treats the historical blues singer Gertrude "Ma" Rainey and four male members of her backup band and the racial exploitation and frustration they experience. Reviewer Frank Rich declared Wilson "a major find for the American theater," who "sends the entire history of black America crashing down upon our head" through the play's "searing inside account of what white racism does to its victims."

Wilson has acknowledged that he never set out to write a play cycle by decades, but after completing *Ma Rainey* he realized: "I've written three plays in three different decades, so why don't I just continue to do that?" The scheme "gave me an agenda, a focus, something to hone in on, so that I never had to worry about what the next play would be about. I could always pick a decade and work on that." For his next play Wilson chose the 1950s and set *Fences* in his hometown. Wilson has described the play as "the odd one, more conventional in structure with its large character." As he recalled its genesis, "I kept hearing *Ma Rainey* described as oddly constructed and I thought, 'I can write one those plays where you have a big character and everything revolves around him.'" In *Fences* that character is 53-year-old garbage collector Troy Maxson, the patriarch of a large, extended family living in a tenement in Pittsburgh in 1957. Gradually, through the play's nine scenes, Troy's complex makeup based on his past experiences and his relationships are revealed.

As the play opens Troy and his friend Jim Bono are sitting on the front porch of Maxson's home discussing Troy's challenge to his employer and the union over being denied the same opportunities as whites on the job. Troy's strength of character in insisting on fairness and justice to provide for his family is balanced by Bono's accusation that Troy has been unfaithful to his wife, Rose, by seeing a woman named Alberta. When Lyons, Troy's son by a previous marriage, arrives to borrow money from his father, Troy urges him to get a job, to which Lyons replies: "I don't wanna hear all that about how I live. . . . If you wanted to change me, you should have been there when I was growing up." Troy's conflict with Lyons is repeated in his relationship with his younger son, Cory. Annoyed that his son is neglecting his job at a supermarket to play high school football in the hopes of winning a college scholarship, Troy has informed the football coach that he has forbidden Cory to play any longer. The reasons behind Troy's actions are revealed in the details of his past that gradually are made clear. His own father was selfish, insensitive, and angry at the world. His mother ran off when he was eight. Beaten by his father, Troy left home, resorting to crime to survive. Accidentally killing a man in a robbery, Troy was sent to prison where he learned to play baseball and, after his release, became a star in the Negro Leagues. He was too old, however, to take advantage of the integration of the Major Leagues and is still resentful that he was denied the opportunity for success because of his race. Rather than compensating vicariously through his son's success, Troy insures that Cory will repeat his disappointment. When Cory is given the chance to play football in college on a scholarship, Troy does not see the social change that could result in his son's betterment but rather his own past denial. Racism makes Troy into both a victim and a victimizer in which the pain and resentment he has experienced become the principal legacy that he passes on to his family.

In the second act the consequences of Troy's nature escalate. Confessing to Rose that he has been seeing another woman and that she is going to have his baby, Troy explains his betrayal by Alberta's letting him forget his family responsibilities. In baseball terms, Troy says:

> I done locked myself into a pattern trying to take care of you all that I forgot about myself. . . . Rose, I done tried all my life to live decent . . . to live a clean . . . hard . . . useful life. I tried to be a good husband to you. In every way I knew how. Maybe I come into the world backwards. I don't know. But . . . you born with two strikes on you before you come to the plate. You got to guard it closely . . . always looking for the curveball on the inside corner. You can't afford to let none get past you. You can't afford a call strike. If you going down . . . you going down swinging. Everything lined up against you. What you gonna do. I fooled them, Rose. I bunted. When I found you and Cory and a halfway decent job . . . I was safe. Couldn't nothing touch me. I wasn't gonna strike out no more. . . . Then when I saw that gal . . . she firmed up my backbone. And

I got to thinking that if I tried . . . I just might be able to steal second. Do you understand after eighteen years I wanted to steal second.

The baseball analogy appears as well in the metaphor of the fence that Rose has asked Troy to complete around their property. For Rose the fence represents protection and security for her family; for Troy fences have restrained him all his life, and as a power hitter his goal has always been to clear the fences. The climax for metaphor and man comes after Alberta has died in childbirth and Troy brings the infant, Raynell, home to be raised by Rose. She agrees, extending compassion to the innocent baby, but tells her husband, "I'll take care of your baby for you . . . this child got a mother. But you a womanless man." Troy's control over the people in his life is slipping away, culminating in his climactic confrontation with Cory who stands up to his father: "You ain't never done anything but hold me back. Afraid I was gonna be better than you. All you ever did was try and make me scared of you." Troy advances to strike his son, but Cory defends himself with his father's baseball bat. Taunted by his father to "put me out," Cory swings and misses twice before Troy retrieves his bat and orders Cory out of his house. As his son departs, Troy exults: "I can't taste nothing. Helluljah! I can't taste nothing no more." Assuming his batting stance, he taunts Death to get a fastball by him: "Come on! It's between you and me now! Come on! Anytime you want! Come on! I be ready for you . . . but I ain't gonna be easy."

The final scene is set in 1965 on the morning of Troy's funeral. Rose is devoted to the seven-year-old Raynell and to involvement in her church. Lyons is serving time for cashing other people's checks. Cory arrives as a Marine corporal, determined not to attend his father's funeral. Rose, however, comes to Troy's defense:

> Your daddy wanted you to be everything he wasn't . . . and at the same time he tried to make you into everything he was. I don't know if he was right or wrong . . . but I do know he meant to do more good than he meant to do harm. He wasn't always right. Sometimes when he touched he bruised. And sometimes when he took me in his arms he cut.

Rose's muted elegy for her flawed husband serves to reconcile Cory sufficiently that he relents. The play closes, emphasizing the fences that divide and protect. "At the end of *Fences* every person," Wilson has stated, "with the exception of Raynell, is institutionalized. Rose is in church. Lyons is in a penitentiary. . . . Cory's in the marines. The only free person is the girl, Troy's daughter, the hope for the future."

Wilson would continue documenting the past and suggesting a basis for the future in a remarkable series of plays, including *Joe Turner's Come and Gone* (1988), *The Piano Lesson* (1990), *Two Trains Running* (1992), *Seven Guitars*

(1996), *King Hedley II* (2001), and *Radio Golf* (2005). All, in a sense, deal with the central issue of *Fences* as Wilson explained it:

> I was trying to get at why Troy made the choices he made, how they have influenced his values and how he attempts to pass those along to his son. Each generation gives the succeeding generation what they think they need. One question in the play is "Are the tools we are given sufficient to compete in a world that is different from the one our parents knew?" I think they are—it's just that we have to do different things with the tools. That's all Troy has to give. Troy's flaw is that he does not recognize that the world was changing.

THE DYBBUK

88

(1920)   *by S. Ansky*

The particular setting of The Dybbuk *is the world of Hasidic pietism which grew out of one sage's intense sense of the goodness and accessibility of God and out of his profound conviction, therefore, of the necessity for joy and exaltation. . . . On the one hand it is a world that has not purged itself of faith in magic making, a world tarnished by superstition; on the other hand it is a world pervaded by a mystic sense of the immediacy of divinity, of the omnipresent miraculous, and of the power of man, in Martin Buber's phrase, "to compel the upper world." In such a world the natural and the supernatural, the quick and the dead, commingle in continual relationships, and daily reality is often only a symbol of daily eternity.* The Dybbuk *is not at all a play about the powers of darkness, as Joseph Wood Krutch referred to it in his review of the 1925 Neighborhood Playhouse production; it is a play about the powers of Light and their immediacy in the world of men.*
—Joseph C. Landis, *The Dybbuk and Other Great Yiddish Plays*

A revolutionary drama of its time, *The Dybbuk* is the most famous play from the second golden era in Yiddish theater. Set in the vanished, mystically religious world of the 19th-century eastern European Hasidim, it is a complex and meticulously crafted tragedy in which two lovers, betrothed before they have been conceived and denied earthly communion, are ultimately bound together for all eternity. *The Dybbuk* is one of the few dramas from what author Irving Howe described as the "brief, stormy, vivid, and ambiguous" history of Yiddish theater that has universal appeal and has endured as a viable work for the American stage.

Yiddish theater is a distinct genre that has been as influential as Greek drama, commedia dell'arte, and the medieval passion play in the evolution of Western theater. Written in the day-to-day language of the Ashkenazi Jews, who reserved Hebrew for religious observances, Yiddish theater first appeared in the Jewish communities of France and Germany and in the shtetlach of eastern Europe, and originated from weddings and Purim celebrations. In the 11th century Jewish wedding entertainments began to feature masquerades, which included dancers and monologues by masked speakers, known as jesters (*lets, marshaliks,* or *badkhns*). From the 15th century well into the 20th century, jesting was a well-established professional occupation, often hereditary. The compositions of jesters resulted in a unique repertoire of Yiddish theatrical material, including songs for the bride and groom, riddles, parodies, and general serious and comical songs. The singing of cantors in synagogues was another influence, as were the Purimspiels, satiric improvisations featuring parodies of biblical passages, sermons, and deathbed confessions that enlivened Purim festivities and were frequently performed by a wandering yeshiva student. By the 16th century it was customary for Jewish communities to feature Purim plays with a Purim king as the central character. Also figuring in the development of Yiddish theater was the rich Sephardic tradition from 12th-century Spain of dialogues in Jewish poetry known as Tahkemoni, which included discussions between believer and heretic, husband and wife, day and night, land and ocean, wisdom and foolishness, and avarice and generosity. The scope of Yiddish theater, tied to the evolution of Jewish literary culture in general, widened in the wake of the Haskalah, the Jewish enlightenment of the late 18th century, with the exposure to European society and secular theater traditions.

The professional Yiddish theater grew out of variety entertainments initially offered by singers (who often doubled as cantors in synagogues) in taverns where men gathered after work or business. These entertainers, called Brody singers after a town in the western Ukraine, described the substance or difficulties of different kinds of occupations in Jewish society and impersonated the characters in their songs. There were some professional and amateur Yiddish theater productions in Poland in the early and mid-1800s, but there was no established Yiddish theater until 1876, when Russian-born playwright Abraham Goldfaden and two Brody singers formed a professional touring troupe that added plot continuity to songs, with comic dialogue improvised in the manner of commedia dell'arte. Initially all-male, Goldfaden's troupe soon featured actresses and even families, a tradition that would be carried on in the American Yiddish theater. Goldfaden's repertoire of musical theater—the precursor to American vaudeville—was later brought to America by immigrant members of his company. Adding to the musicals and melodramas that saturated the Yiddish theater in New York City after the first large-scale waves of immigration in the 1880s and 1890s were the realistic dramas of Jacob Gordin. Inspired by European literature and featuring probability of plot and dialogue suited to the characters, Gordin's dramas, which included *The Jewish King Lear* (1892), *God, Man, and Devil* (1900), and *The Kreutzer Sonata* (1902), replaced the declamatory, stilted, and often tawdry melodrama and comedy of popular Yiddish theater. Other dramatists who would influence 19th- and early 20th-century Yiddish theater were Sholem Asch, Sholem Aleichem, and Peretz Hirshbein, who would go on to form his own troupe that toured Russia. The most prominent offspring of Hirshbein's company was the Vilna Troupe, which began in 1916 with a play by Sholem Asch. Even given the mass immigrations to the United States through the first decades of the 20th-century, the Yiddish theater in Europe thrived until the virtual extinction of Yiddish culture in Poland by the end of World War II and in the postwar Soviet Union.

In the United States the Yiddish theater, based in New York City, featured an impressive group of star actors and entertainers who appeared in Gordin's plays, as well as dramas written by new playwrights on topical themes such as the condition of Jewish workers in sweatshops and the problems of assimilation in the New World, comedies, operettas on Jewish religious and secular themes, and Shakespeare plays. The first generation of performers, many of them immigrants, included David Kessler, Zigmund Mogulesco, Boris Thomaskevsky, Jacob Adler, and Bertha Kalisch. In 1917 actor-manager Maurice Schwartz, at the suggestion of actor Jacob Ben-Ami, who had been with the Hirshbein Troupe, founded the Jewish Art Theatre, opening with three successful Hirshbein comedies. Schwartz's company would dominate the Yiddish stage in the United States for two decades, and Schwartz himself would go on to play the title role in the 1939 film *Tevye*, based on the stories of Sholem Aleichem. *Tevye*, in turn, would become the hugely successful Broadway musical *Fiddler on the Roof*. The post–World War I Yiddish theater continued to reflect traditional Jewish concerns and sensibilities, but it also displayed a new dedication to literary form, acting technique, and theatrical cohesion, as well as a consciousness of the experimentalism and boldness that marked postwar European theater. This consciousness was evident in productions of such plays as Ossip Dymov's comedy *Bronx Express* (1919).

By the late 1930s Yiddish theater was on the decline, as the aging immigrant audiences grew too small to sustain interest in serious theater in the genre and their assimilated children, no longer speaking their families' native tongue, turned to the aesthetics of English literature and mainstream American theater and film. But the styles of performance, ebullient creativity, and liveliness that characterized Yiddish theater would be seen in the dramas offered by the Group Theatre, a company that was critical to the evolution of American theater; in the work of actors and playwrights who went on to careers on Broadway and in Hollywood; in Jacob Adler's daughter, Stella Adler, an actor and teacher of acting, who influenced an entire generation of actors; and in the inspired brashness of performers, ranging from the Marx Brothers to the tummlers of the Catskills to the stand-up and sketch comedians of today.

In the pantheon of Yiddish drama *The Dybbuk* stands out as one of the most original and powerful plays in the genre. It is the creation of Shloyme Zanvil Rappoport, whose pseudonym is recorded variously as S. Ansky, S. Anski, Sholom Ansky, and Solomon Ansky. A folklorist (he was the first Jewish folklorist to undertake large-scale fieldwork) as well as a writer, he was born in 1863 in Vitebsk, Belorussia (some sources say Lithuania), and worked as a secretary to Russian populist journalist and intellectual Peter Lavrov, led cultural field expeditions in Ukrainian provinces and in Kiev from 1911 to 1914, and was a relief worker in Russia during World War I. In 1917 he was elected to the Constituent Assembly in Russia. He immigrated to Poland in 1918 and died in Warsaw two years later. Ansky's writings include poetry, political and cultural articles and essays, and a four-volume account of World War I, titled *The Destruction of Galicia*. Besides *The Dybbuk* he authored the one-act plays *Father and Son* (1906) and *The Grandfather* (1906) and an unfinished play, *Day and Night* (published in 1921). Ansky's poem "The Vow" became the official anthem of the Jewish Workers Party of Poland.

Ansky's conception of *The Dybbuk* began in 1911 and coincided with his interest in Hasidic folklore. By 1914 the work had evolved into a four-act play, initially written in Russian and later in Yiddish, which Ansky subtitled in the first edition, *A Dramatic Legend*. Subsequent versions of the play include the subtitle *Between Two Worlds*, an appropriate description of a drama in which the spiritual and mystical world of the Hasidim coexists with—and ultimately transcends—the world of the physical and the material. During the course of the play, which takes place variously in the old wood synagogue in the town of Brinnits, in the town square, and in Miropolye at the house of Reb Azrielke, a *Tsaddik* (righteous man and judge), we learn that Khonnon, a young rabbinical student, is in love with Leye, the daughter of a prominent townsman, Sender, but he cannot marry her because he lacks the wealth that Leye's father seeks for her. To the horror of his fellow students, he mounts an argument in favor of holiness in sin, asserting, "All that God had created has within it a spark of holiness" and that this is so since God created Satan. He thus invokes Satan's help in winning his beloved. At the moment he learns that Leye has been betrothed to a wealthy young man, a despairing Khonnon has a mystical experience during which he sees by "what powers" he can prevent the marriage, cries out "I have won!" and falls down dead. Leye, distraught at the death of Khonnon, whom she has always loved, goes unwillingly to be married to the wealthy Menashe, but just as she is about to be wed, she is possessed by a dybbuk, a spirit that in Jewish folklore is believed to be the dislocated soul of someone who is dead. A soul that has not been able to fulfill its role during its lifetime looks for an opportunity to do so after death in the form of a dybbuk (from the Hebrew for "attachment") and will leave a body, with help, once its goal has been realized. The dybbuk speaks in Khonnon's voice and cries out, "You buried me! But I have come back to my destined bride, and I will not leave her." Leye / Khonnon approaches the prospective father-in-law, Nakhman, and shouts in his face, "Murderer!"

Leye, together with her nurse, Frade, and her father, is taken to Reb Azriekle's house to have the dybbuk expelled by the rabbi and a *minyan* (quorum of 10 men). The dybbuk refuses to leave, even when threatened with excommunication. Reb Azrielke shifts his attention to Sender, telling him that the rabbi of the city, Reb Shimshon, has had dreams in which a long-dead friend of Sender's, Nissen ben Rivke, appeared three times. The spirit of Nissen has demanded that Sender be called before a rabbinical court to answer charges for a wrong he has done his old friend. During the course of the trial it is revealed that Sender and Nissen had betrothed their unborn children, Leye and Khonnon. Nissen died soon after his son was born. Although Khonnon was a young man with a "lofty soul," Sender refused to acknowledge him and to honor the betrothal, insisting instead on a rich husband for his daughter. He has forgotten the duties of a *Tsaddik* (righteous person) in his thirst for wealth. The court punishes Sender, sentencing him to give away half his wealth and to light a candle and say kaddish (the prayer for the dead) for Nissen and Khonnon on the anniversary of their deaths as long as he lives. The dybbuk is expelled willingly from Leye's body and begins its journey toward redemption. The court orders that Leye be led to the bridal canopy to marry Menashe, but before the bridegroom arrives Khonnon's voice is heard. He has left Leye's body to return to her soul, the act of which has broken the barrier between them. Khonnon and Leye declare their love for each other, and Leye goes toward her destined bridegroom. She dies, her spirit joined to Khonnon's forever.

In 1914 actor-director-teacher Konstantin Stanislavsky considered *The Dybbuk* for the Moscow Art Theatre. Although Stanislavsky decided not to stage the play, he suggested that Ansky add the key role of a celestial Messenger, who, as a Greek chorus, establishes the mood, comments on the action to come, and indicates the presence of the supernatural. The Messenger provides the theme of the play at the start of the first act with an anecdote about a rich and stingy Hasid and a rabbi who gives the Hasid a lesson in seeing others rather than only himself. Ansky did not live to see his play in performance. *The Dybbuk*, in Yiddish, was first produced by the Vilna Troupe at the Elysium Theatre in Warsaw on December 9, 1920, 30 days after the traditional mourning period that followed Ansky's death on November 8. Two years later Maurice Schwartz produced the play in New York and simultaneously in Moscow, where it was performed by the Habima Company in Hebrew. In 1921 the Yiddish Art Theatre mounted the first New York production in Yiddish, and in 1925 *The Dybbuk* made its debut in English, in a production at New York City's Neighborhood Playhouse. Since then the play has been frequently revived. *The Dybbuk* has, through the decades, inspired both admiration for its magical, romantic quality and spiritual enchantment and debate over its meaning. The play is an evocation of the mystical world of shtetl Hasidim, which makes it a drama about a culture that was vanishing even when Ansky was exploring its customs and folklore. It is also a heartbreaking and poignant love story that exists side by side with the twin themes of the human capacity for redemption dependent upon a holy law that determines individual conduct and the inexorability of justice in a divine and immutable universe.

THE VISIT

89

(1956)   *by Friedrich Dürrenmatt*

Tragedy presupposes guilt, despair, moderation, lucidity, vision, a sense of responsibility. In the Punch-and-Judy show of our century . . . there are no more guilty and also, no responsible men. It is always, "We couldn't help it" and "We didn't really want that to happen." And indeed, things happen without anyone in particular being responsible for them. Everyone is dragged along and everyone gets caught somewhere in the sweep of events. We are all collectively guilty, collectively bogged down in the sins of our fathers and of our forefathers. . . . That is our misfortune, but not our guilt: guilt can exist only as a personal achievement, as a religious deed. Comedy alone is suitable for us. . . .

But the tragic is still possible even if pure tragedy is not. We can achieve the tragic out of comedy. We can bring it forth as a frightening moment, as an abyss that opens suddenly.

—Friedrich Dürrenmatt, "Problems of the Theatre"

Friedrich Dürrenmatt's view of the theater as a vehicle for moral revelation and universal relevance is reflected in *Der Besuch der alten Dame* (*The Visit*), a tragicomedy combining expressionistic devices and elements of Brechtian epic theater with an inspired sense of the shocking and grotesque. At its core the play is a serious exploration of humanity's dark side in its conviction that economics determines morality, an idea that is found in drama as early as the 1830s, with the opening scene of Georg Büchner's *Woyzeck*. In *The Visit* the tragedy is that an entire community is caught in a sweep of events that leads to a murder by the masses; Dürrenmatt's genius is to present what is a tragedy of commission into a work of unsettling humor.

In Friedrich Dürrenmatt the attributes of the dissident intellectual coalesced with those of the rural villager, the result of a family situation in which strict Protestant training coexisted with unorthodoxy. Dürrenmatt was born in 1921 in the Swiss village of Konolfingen in the canton of Bern, the older of two children of Reinhold and Hulda Zimmerman Dürrenmatt. His father was the Protestant pastor of the town church and his paternal grand-

518

father, Ulrich, was an eccentric, who had been active in 19th-century Swiss politics. A fanatically conservative newspaper publisher, Ulrich was proud to have spent 10 days in jail for composing a viciously satiric poem he printed on the front page of the paper. His grandson was also affected by the tales his father told him from classical mythology and the Bible tales recounted by his mother, all of which would later provide material for his works. Dürrenmatt's first ambition was to become a painter, and while attending secondary school in a nearby village he spent his spare time in the studio of a local painter. He continued to paint and draw as an adult, and his first published plays were accompanied by his illustrations. In 1935 the family relocated to the city of Bern, where Dürrenmatt attended the Frieies Gymnasium, a Christian secondary school. He was adept at classical languages but was otherwise a poor student, and after two and a half years there he was asked to leave. He was then sent to a private school from which he often played hooky. Rejected from the Institute of Art, Dürrenmatt studied at the University of Zurich and the University of Bern, where he tutored in Greek and Latin to earn money. After a stint in the military and a return to the University of Zurich, a bout with hepatitis sent him home to Bern, where he studied philosophy at the university and considered writing a doctoral dissertation on Søren Kierkegaard and tragedy.

Dürrenmatt began his literary career in the early 1940s with fictional sketches and prose fragments, and in 1945 he published a short story echoing the intense style of German writer Ernst Jünger. He failed in his attempt to become a theater critic as well as a cabaret sketch writer, although the latter efforts displayed his gift for social satire. In 1946 he married Lotti Geissler, an actress, and the following year the couple relocated to Basel. His first play, *Es steht geschrieben* (*Thus It Is Written*), performed in Zurich in 1947, is a parody of Western history in the guise of a panoramic historical drama with Brechtian influences. Set in the 16th century the 30-scene play concerns Anabaptists, their transformation of Münster into a New Jerusalem, and the destruction of the city by a coalition of Catholic and Protestant troops. At once solemn, passionate, prophetic, religious, existential, cynical, and apocalyptic, the play is unwieldy in execution, with a large cast and dialogue ranging from the biblically hymnic to the absurd. It drew boos from its first-night audience; however, reviewers praised Dürrenmatt's potential, and he was awarded a cash prize from the Welti Foundation as an encouragement to continue writing plays. Twenty years later Dürrenmatt reworked the play as a comedy, *Die Wiedertäufer* (*The Anabaptists*), which was more stageworthy but failed equally with audiences. A similar fate greeted his second play, *Der Blinde* (1948; *The Blind Man*), considered to be a pretentious, heavy-handed blend of theology and philosophy.

Dürrenmatt's first theatrical success was *Romulus der Grosse* (*Romulus the Great*), performed in 1948. It is a Shavian-like tragicomedy, in which the title ruler, personifying deliberate irresponsibility and inaction, accepts that the power and tyranny of Rome must give way to truth and humanity. He refuses to try to halt the barbarian destruction of Rome and ultimately accepts a pension from the German conqueror that will allow for a comfortable retirement. In 1949 *Romulus the Great* became the first Dürrenmatt play to be performed in Germany, where it became a standard offering in German theater. Nevertheless, Dürrenmatt continued to suffer financially, and to help support his family, which had grown to three children, he turned to writing detective novels, which were a great success, as were his radio plays. The royalties from the latter allowed him to purchase a home near Neuchâtel in 1952, where he lived until his death in 1990. He completed the manuscript for his next play, *Die Ehe des Herrn Mississippi* (*The Marriage of Mr. Mississippi*), in 1950. A panorama of violence and intrigue, with expressionistic touches, in which the title character destroys himself and everyone around him with his determination to impose absolute Mosaic justice, the play was rejected by Swiss theaters but was produced in 1952 at the Intimate Theatre in Munich and established Dürrenmatt as an avant-garde dramatist. *Ein Engel kommt nach Babylon* (*An Angel Comes to Babylon*), also produced at the Intimate Theatre in 1952, is a satire of power and bureaucracy that validates, through the hero, the beggar-artist Akki, the values of innocence and ingenuity over institutional power and corruption.

The philosophical, theological, and social themes that Dürrenmatt explored in his previous plays are highly developed, straightforward, and sardonically and grotesquely amusing in *The Visit*, first performed in Zurich in 1956 and from then on a mainstay of Western theater. *The Visit* is set in Guellen, a small town somewhere in German-speaking central Europe. The once-prosperous Guellen, where "Goethe spent a night" and "Brahms composed a quartet," has decayed in recent years to the point where it is almost completely impoverished (the name in German translates to "liquid manure"). *The Visit* begins and concludes with a parody of a chorus like that of a Greek tragedy, which serves to give the play a classical symmetry, that heightens its sense of irony. The first act opens at the ramshackle railroad station, where four unemployed citizens sit on a bench and interest themselves in "our last remaining pleasure: watching trains go by," as they recite a litany of woes:

MAN THREE   Ruined.

MAN FOUR   The Wagner Factory gone crash.

MAN ONE   Bockmann bankrupt.

MAN TWO   The Foundry on Sunshine Square shut down.

MAN THREE   Living on the dole.

MAN FOUR   On Poor Relief Soup.

MAN ONE   Living?

MAN TWO   Vegetating.

MAN THREE   And rotting to death.

MAN FOUR   The entire township.

This chorus of men, together with Guellen's mayor, schoolmaster, priest, and shopkeeper, gather to meet a train and greet its famous passenger, Claire Zachanassian (née Wascher), daughter of Guellen's builder, who is visiting her hometown after 45 years. Now 63, she is the richest woman in the world, the widow of the world's richest man, and the owner of nearly everything, including the railways. She has founded hospitals, soup kitchens, and kindergartens, and the Guelleners plan to ask her to invest in their town:

MAYOR   Gentlemen, the millionairess is our only hope.

PRIEST   Apart from God.

MAYOR   Apart from God.

SCHOOLMASTER   But God won't pay.

The mayor appeals to the shopkeeper, Alfred Ill (sometimes translated as Anton Schill), who was once Claire's lover, to charm her into generosity. For his part Ill knows that if she were to make the expected financial gift, he will be victorious in the next mayoral contest. Madame Zachanassian arrives. She is a *grande dame*, graceful, refined, with a casual, ironic manner. She is accompanied by an unusual retinue: a butler, two gum-chewing thugs who carry her about on a sedan chair, a pair of blind eunuchs (who, as Dürrenmatt states in his postscript to the play, can either repeat each other's lines or speak their dialogue together), her seventh husband, a black panther, and an empty coffin. When Claire and Ill greet each other, Ill calls her, as he used to, "my little wildcat" and "my little sorceress." This sets her, as Dürrenmatt's stage notes indicate, purring "like an old cat." Eventually, the two leave the fulsome (and transparently false) cordiality of the town behind to meet in their old trysting places. In Konrad's Village Woods, the four citizens from the first scene play trees, plants, wildlife, the wind, and "bygone dreams," as Ill tries to win Claire over. When he kisses her hand, he learns that it is made of ivory; most of her body is made of artificial parts. Nevertheless, he is convinced that he has beguiled her into making the bequest. At a banquet in her honor that evening Claire sarcastically contradicts the overly flattering testimonial offered by the mayor of her unselfish behavior as a child, but declares that, "as my contribution to this joy of yours," she proposes to give 1 million pounds to the town. There is, however, one condition: Someone must kill Alfred Ill. For her 1 million, Claire maintains, she is buying justice: Forty-five years earlier she brought a paternity suit against Ill, who bribed two witnesses to testify against her. As a result she was forced to leave Guellen in shame and to become a prostitute in Hamburg. The child, a girl, died. The two witnesses are the eunuchs, whom Claire tracked down, blinded, castrated, and added to her entourage. The butler was the magistrate in the case. The mayor indignantly rejects the offer "in the name of humanity. We would rather have poverty than blood on our hands." Claire's response: "I'll wait."

The second and third acts chronicle the decline of Guellen into temptation, moral ambiguity and complicity. In the weeks that follow the banquet, Madame Zachanassian, who, it is revealed, intentionally caused Guellen's financial ruin, watches with grim satisfaction as the insidiousness of her proposal manifests itself in the town's behavior. She also marries three more times; husband number eight is a famous film star, played by the same actor as husband number seven. At first gratified by the town's loyalty to him, Ill becomes increasingly uneasy when the Guelleners, including his family, begin to buy expensive items on credit, even from his own store, and there comes into being the kind of night life and social activities found in a more prosperous town. Guelleners are clearly expecting their financial positions to change, and with this expectation comes a withdrawing of support for Ill and collective outrage for his crime of long ago. Claire's black panther, who symbolizes Ill, is shot and killed in front of Ill's store. Fearing for his life Ill tries to leave town on the next train but is surrounded on all sides by Guelleners. The citizens insist they are just there to wish him luck on his journey, but a terrified Ill is convinced they will kill him if he tries to board the train. He faints as the train leaves without him. The play reaches a crescendo, with the finale becoming a grand media event, when reporters and broadcasters arrive. Ill faces up to his guilt and publicly—and heroically—accepts responsibility for his crime and the judgment of the town, despite the support of the schoolmaster, the only citizen who attempts to question Guellen's willingness to abdicate its responsibility as "a just community." Ill is murdered by the crowd. The death is ruled a heart attack; the mayor claims Ill "died of joy," a sentiment echoed by reporters. The mayor receives the check for 1 million, and Claire Zachanassian leaves with Ill's body; the coffin now has its corpse. A citizen chorus descries "the plight" of poverty and praises God that "kindly fate" has intervened to provide them with such advantages as better cars, frocks, cigarettes, and commuter trains. All pray to God to "Protect all our sacred possessions, / Protect our peace and our freedom, / Ward off the night, nevermore / Let it darken our glorious town / Grown out of the ashes anew. / Let us go and enjoy our good fortune."

In his postscript Dürrenmatt makes clear that "Claire Zachanassian represents neither justice . . . nor the Apocalypse; let her be only what she is: the richest woman in the world, whose fortune has put her in a position to act like the heroine of a Greek tragedy: absolute, cruel, something like Medea." Guellen is the main character and Alfred Ill its scapegoat, ritually murdered so that the community can, at the same time, purge itself and justifiably accept a portion of Claire Zachanassian's bounty. They are not wicked, claims Dürrenmatt, but, tragically, "people like the rest of us," concerned with sin, suffering, guilt, and the pursuit of justice and redemption in an ostensibly alien and indifferent universe.

THE WEAVERS

90

(1892)

by Gerhart Hauptmann

Seen in the context of Hauptmann's work and of the contemporary literary situation, Die Weber *was indeed a unique contribution. For its author it represented a first application of Naturalist theory and technique to documented, historical subject matter, and for the German stage it was a major step away from the traditional "classical" or "closed" form of drama to a more "open" indeed "epic," form. As a Naturalist play it epitomizes the favorite ideas and techniques of the movement. The inherent determinism of milieu is all-pervasive—to the extent that the weavers' very bodies have been deformed by endless labor in cramped postures behind their looms. On the one hand, the sheer uniformity of their lot—constant hunger, inadequate light and lack of sunshine, dusty working conditions, the necessity of constant work by all members of the family to keep from starving—imposes a terrible sameness of appearance and outlook on Hauptmann's workers. On the other hand, through extensive, careful stage directions and an almost microscopic attention to detail— especially linguistic detail—the author manages to imbue all but the most peripheral of his characters with unique personalities. . . . The result is a portrait of the masses that differs radically from similar efforts which preceded and were soon to follow it. . . . Hauptmann elevates his masses from the status of stage extras, designed to enhance the atmosphere of revolution, to a central role, the "collective hero."*

—Warren R. Maurer, *Gerhart Hauptmann*

Gerhart Hauptmann's *Die Weber* (*The Weavers*) is commonly regarded as the first revolutionary proletarian play in German literature as well as the greatest of all naturalist dramas. Based on events that took place in 1844 among Silesian weavers who violently protested their dire working conditions that the Industrial Revolution had brought to eastern Germany, *The Weavers* orchestrates documentary sources and interviews with participants into what has been called by critic James Huneker a "symphony in five movements with one grim, leading motive—hunger." According to the critic Hugh F. Garten, *The Weavers* is "the supreme achievement of Naturalistic drama, at the same time transcending all aesthetic theories by its dramatic power and emotional impact." Hauptmann's play is revolutionary both in its message and its form. When it was first performed in Berlin in 1892 it sparked the most notorious political censorship trials in the history of German literature and gained international notice. Its social message and methods would set the prototype for the modern drama of social protest. Translated into Russian by Lenin's sister, *The Weavers* would become not only an influential force in Russian literature but a factor in the Russian Revolution itself. Praised and condemned as socialist agitprop, *The Weavers* evades being easily reduced to the level of propaganda. Despite its being heralded and branded as an incitement to socialist revolution *The Weavers* has also puzzled and disappointed Marxist critics with its ambiguous, muted conclusion. As powerful and paradoxical as its message is, *The Weavers* is also a breakthrough in dramatic form. Adapting the thematically related, loosely connected tableaux of Georg Büchner's *Woyzeck*, *The Weavers* achieves an epic magnification centered for one of the first times in dramatic history not on a conventional protagonist but on a collective hero, as indicated by the play's title. Moreover, it replaces the accepted continuities of previous dramatic structure with a strategy of dislocation, of argument by analogy, contrast, juxtaposition, and leitmotif. All would serve as important elements in the formation of modern drama.

    The Weavers synthesized Hauptmann's background and artistic development, as well as European philosophical and aesthetic thinking in the latter half of the 19th century, and changed theatrical conditions to reflect those ideas. Born in 1862 in Salzbrunn in Silesia, Hauptmann was the son of an innkeeper and the grandson of a weaver. His father, who had witnessed the storming of the barricades in Paris in 1848, and was called by his neighbors "the red Hauptmann," contributed to his son's heightened political and social conscience, while his mother's piety stimulated in her son both a religious fervor and faith in human ennoblement. An undistinguished student, Hauptmann took up an apprenticeship in agriculture from 1880 to 1882 before pursuing his interest in sculpture at the art institute in Breslau and in Rome. In Berlin in 1884 Hauptmann continued his scientific and social studies at the university, saw performances of Henrik Ibsen's plays, and became involved with a group of young German intellectuals who were attempting to spread and apply the new theory of naturalism formulated by Émile Zola in France. Naturalism extended the movement toward realism—the accurate representation of ordinary life—in literature that had been developing throughout the 19th century in the novels of Stendhal, Gustave Flaubert, Charles Dickens, William Thackeray, George Eliot, Leo Tolstoy and others, and onstage especially in the works of Ibsen. To the realism's faithful depiction of recognizable experience, naturalism added a new scientific exactitude supported by ideas derived from Charles Darwin and Karl Marx that heredity and environment are the key factors determining human behavior. Zola first articulated the principles of naturalism in his preface to the dramatization of his novel *Thérèse*

Raquin in 1873 and in *Naturalism in the Theatre* and *The Experimental Novel* (1881). He asserted that the naturalist dramatist should seek to uncover the "inevitable laws of heredity and environment" observable in human behavior and then record that behavior with the same clinical detachment and objectivity of a scientist in pursuing truth. "Instead of imagining an adventure," Zola declared, "complicating it, preparing stage surprises, which from scene to scene will bring it to a final conclusion, one simply takes from life the history of a being, or of a group of beings, whose acts one faithfully records." Advocating a completely objective dramatic method, Zola and his supporters urged that drama should represent a slice of life, unobstructed and unmitigated by idealization and distortions imposed by an artful manipulation of experience into pleasing symmetries or calculated resolutions.

Zola's radical theory of literary and dramatic expression initially resulted in few successful plays embodying naturalist principles. To do so a complementary change in theatrical practices was needed. Since naturalism began to be associated with depravity owing to its focus on raw and unidealized experience, censorship seriously curtailed the mounting of plays created to the new naturalist standards. André Antoine, however, created in Paris in 1887 the Théâtre Libre, a private subscription theater that was exempt from existing censorship laws. The Théâtre Libre would produce many formerly banned realistic and naturalistic plays, including works by Zola, Ibsen, and August Strindberg, while pioneering experimental production techniques that emphasized minutely rendered realistic settings and a natural acting style that eschewed the stylized and declamatory. The German equivalent of the Théâtre Libre was Berlin's Freie Bühne (Free Stage), organized in 1889 under the leadership of Otto Brahm. Mounting its productions on Sunday afternoon, when the professional actors of Berlin's legitimate companies were free to participate, the Freie Bühne, like its French counterpart, was able to evade the censorship of the established theaters and offered opportunities for new playwrights such as Hauptmann to apply the theory of naturalism to the stage.

Hauptmann's first play *Vor Sonnenaufgang* (*Before Dawn*) became in 1889 the first drama by a German playwright to be performed by the Freie Bühne. Set in a rural mining community, it is a brutally frank anatomy of the destruction of two lovers trapped by their environment and alcoholism that represent the implacable power of heredity. The play established Hauptmann's reputation as the "dramatic Zola," in which he extended the realistic subjects and methods of Ibsen both by its sexual explicitness and its working-class milieu. Two more plays followed—*Das Friendensfest: Eine Familienkatastrophe* (*The Coming of Peace: A Family Catastrophe*) and *Einsame Menschen* (*Lonely Lives*)—before Hauptmann produced his naturalist masterpiece, *The Weavers*, in 1892.

With the subtitle *A Play of the Eighteen-Forties*, a striking innovation of *The Weavers* is its historical subject, which naturalism had avoided in favor of an emphasis on current conditions. Hauptmann, however, uses his depiction of the circumstance of the Silesian weavers on the verge of their 1844 rebellion to establish the continuity between the past and the present. The weavers' revolt was brutally suppressed, and conditions had changed little a half-century later as Hauptmann took up their cause. Abiding by the scientific principles of naturalism, Hauptmann traveled to the scene of the revolt and interviewed survivors. Supplementing firsthand observation of current conditions with his recollections from childhood Hauptmann declared: "What was revealed in these huts of the weavers was . . . misery in its classical form." To convey it Hauptmann replaced a conventional plot with a presentation of the weavers' conditions from a variety of perspectives and escalating tensions leading up to the explosive revolt. *The Weavers* also forgoes a central protagonist, with only one relatively minor character appearing in all five acts. Instead the play combines multiple scenes and characters in an objective, documentary fashion to examine an entire community as the sum of various human parts.

Act 1 is set in the business offices of the exploitative mill owner Dreissiger where the region's weavers have come to deliver and be paid for what they have woven in their homes. As Hauptmann's stage directions indicate, the weavers "have a stark, irresolute look—gnawing, brooding faces. Most of the men resemble each other, half-dwarf, half-schoolmaster. They are flat-chested, coughing creatures with ashen grey faces . . . their women folk . . . are broken, harried, worn out." Several complain to the manager, Pfeifer, that they are unable to keep their families from starving with the pittance they are given. Pfeifer, a former weaver himself, deflects their pleas with platitudes— "He who weaves well, lives well"—or with explicit threats to take it or leave it. Only the younger weaver Baecker refuses to submit and demands his rights, prompting Pfeifer to summon Dreissiger. Baecker is denied further employment, prompting him to respond that "It's all the same to me whether I starve behind the loom or in a ditch by the side of the road." Their escalating confrontation is interrupted when an eight-year-old boy, sent to collect his parents' pay, collapses from hunger. Dreissiger uses this crisis to excoriate the irresponsibility of the weavers for neglecting their children, while threatening to depress wages even more by hiring 200 additional weavers.

Having presented the suffering weavers collectively, act 2 shifts from macro- to microcosm, presenting the family life of one of the weavers on hand in the previous act, Old Baumert. As the act opens Baumert's wife, daughters, deranged son, ragged grandson, and a recently discharged soldier, Moritz Jaeger, await his return with his pay. The family has slaughtered the starving family dog for the rare treat of meat for their dinner. From them Jaeger learns more of the hardship and disintegration of the community since he has been away. Baumert is unable to keep down the unaccustomed rich fare, and Jaeger reads aloud the banned "Dreissiger's Song" that serves to focus and foment the weavers' resentment and revolutionary fervor:

Here a bloody justice thrives
More terrible than lynching.
Here sentence isn't even passed
To quickly end a poor man's life.

Men are slowly tortured here,
Here is the torture chamber,
Here every heavy sigh that's heard
Bears witness to man's misery.

The song will serve as the play's principal leitmotif, expressing the rising passion of the weavers and connecting the various stages of their rebellion.

Act 3 shifts the scene to the principal tavern in Peterswaldau, where a traveling salesman is instructed in the local conditions and a group of young rebels, led by Baecker and Jaeger, express their discontent. Incited by the blacksmith Wittig, they begin to sing the banned song despite the efforts of the policeman Kutsche to prevent them. The act ends with the protesters taking to the streets as Old Baumert is left with the innkeeper Welzel and the ragpicker Hornig, who utters the play's most famous line:

WELZEL   Are you goin' to join up with such madness?

OLD BAUMERT   Well, you see Welzel, it ain't up to me. A young man sometimes may, and an old man must.

HORNIG   It'll sure surprise me if things don't come to a bad end here.

WELZEL   Who'd think the old fellows would completely lose their heads?

HORNIG   Well, every man has his dreams.

In yet another contrasting setting act 4 takes place in Dreissiger's luxuriously furnished drawing room, shifting the focus from victims to victimizers and dramatizing the complicity between capitalism and the church in protecting their mutual vested interests. Dreissiger is joined by Pastor Kittelhaus, who respond to the challenges voiced by Weinhold, the young tutor of Dreissiger's children, that the growing unrest among the weavers is the expression of "hungry, ignorant men" who "are expressing their dissatisfaction in the only way they know how." Weinhold is summarily dismissed, and an apprehended Jaeger is brought in to be interrogated as a ringleader of the uprising. Announced by their song, the rebels storm the house. Dreissiger, his family, and Pfeifer barely escape, while the rebels set about the destruction of Dreissiger's home. Baecker incites the mob to greater effort: "Once we're through here, we'll really get goin'. From here we'll go over to Bielau—to Dittrich's—he's the one who's got the steam power looms. . . . All the trouble comes from those factories."

The play's concluding act draws back from the explosive violence of act 4 to the perspective of the weaver Old Hilse in his tiny, dismal room. Breaking dramatic conventions by introducing a significant new character in the final act, Hauptmann offers an alternative to the play's previous victim-victimizer conflict in Old Hilse's rejection of the materialism that dominates both the capitalists and the workers. Hilse regards his lot as providentially ordered, with its suffering as a precondition to spiritual salvation. His faith and piety, however, cannot insulate him and his family from the troubles outside. When his granddaughter brings home a silver spoon found among the rubble left by the rioters, the family is split over whether to keep what could provide them with several weeks of sustenance. Ultimately Hilse is abandoned by his family when the rebels call their comrades to join them, remaining at his loom, where he is killed by a stray bullet. Ending on this ominous and ambiguous note *The Weavers* continues to spark critical debate in which Hilse has been interpreted both as a deluded victim of the opiate of religion and a heroic visionary sacrificed in a senseless cycle of violence in which the victims become victimizers. Hauptmann in turn has been viewed as both an advocate of revolution and acquiescence, of social change and spiritual reform. By adding a metaphysical and spiritual dimension to his naturalistic drama Hauptmann succeeds in elevating his historical chronicle and social protest play, in the words of critic Paul Schlenther, to the level of a "modern fate drama."

LE CID

91

(1637)

by Pierre Corneille

Le Cid *is a powerful work, but it lacks what the clumsiest sixteenth-century tragedy had: a concentration on a single tragic meaning. We have instead, a play which (for the first time in French drama) successfully attains seriousness by means of a clearly articulated plot arousing suspense and surprise and resting on the psychological conflicts of characters portrayed as human beings. . . . It looks forward to the see-sawing emotional effects of much of later drama, through the piece bien faite to Ibsen and beyond. That is,* Le Cid *points forward (in this, and in its use of realistic and non-tragic elements) to a more naturalistic type of drama. It marks the beginning of something new: but this new element has little to do with the methods of the Greek and Latin dramatists, and still less to do with tragedy.* Le Cid *marks the beginning of a form of naturalistic piece bien faite whose ghost still haunts our stages. It marks a break from the efforts in France to continue the classical tradition of tragedy.*

—Gordon Pocock, *Corneille and Racine: The Problems of Tragic Form*

Pierre Corneille's *Le Cid* has been described by critic Burns Mantle as "the first smash hit in the history of French drama." It would establish the playwright as 17th-century France's preeminent dramatist, *le grand Corneille*, who, along with Molière and Jean Racine, became one of the undisputed masters of French neoclassical drama. Voltaire, in his preface to *Le Cid*, argued that in contrast to the undisciplined extravagance of the Spanish and English playwrights, Corneille was the first writer to produce tragedies that were "sufficiently regular to move the audience to tears." The beauty and excellence of the verses and the sentiment of *Le Cid* prompted the coinage of the proverbial expression *"Cela est beau comme Le Cid"* ("That is lovely, like *Le Cid*"), while the controversy surrounding the play produced the 17th-century's greatest literary debate—the Querelle du Cid (Quarrel of *Le Cid*)—that helped establish the theory and practices of neoclassical drama, which would dominate the stage for the next two centuries. *Le Cid* became the exception that proved the rule. Its supposed violations of admired values of verisimilitude and decorum led to the assertion and ascendancy of neoclassical dramatic ideals as well as France's greatest period of dramatic achievement.

Born in Rouen in 1606, Corneille was educated to pursue a legal career. As a student in a Jesuit school from 1615 to 1622 he excelled in Latin translation and versification and acquired his first exposure to classical drama. After receiving his law degree in 1624, Corneille served in important administrative positions in Rouen, then the second largest city in France. Rouen attracted visiting theatrical troupes from Paris, and it is conventionally believed that Corneille met the actor Montdory on a visit and presented him with his first play, the comedy *Mélite, ou Les Fausses Lettres* (*Mélite, or the Forged Letters*), which was performed by Montdory's company in Paris in 1629. Corneille described his play as "the portrayal of social intercourse among people of good breeding." This early form of the French comedy of manners, with its lifelike situations and refined language, later prompted the playwright to assert:

The novelty of this kind of comedy, unprecedented in any language, and the natural style which produced a portrait of the manners and speech of gentlefolk, were no doubt the reason for the success and reputation of the play. It was unknown for a comedy to provoke laughter without ridiculous characters such as clownish servants, parasites, braggart captains, pedant doctors, and so forth. This one achieved its effect by the vivacious mood of characters of a higher social rank than those one sees in Plautus and Terence, who are merely shopkeepers.

Corneille began his dramatic career attempting to elevate comedy with an unprecedented imitation of actual life, while extending comedy's range to include the higher-ranking characters usually reserved for tragedy. These refinements of genre and presentation would have a significant impact on the evolving neoclassical dramatic standards in both comedy and tragedy. *Clitandre* (1631), a tragicomedy; four more comedies; and his first tragedy, *Médée* (1635) followed. During this period Corneille attracted the attention of the powerful Cardinal Richelieu, who enlisted him as a member of the Society of Five Authors, who composed plays under Richelieu's direction and with whom he contributed the third act of their joint effort, *La comédie des Tuileries* (*The Comedy of a Tuileries*), in 1635. Corneille would break from the group and Richelieu, which became a factor in the criticism that surrounded *Le Cid*, as two of the society's members—Jean Mairet and Georges de Scudéry—were particularly outspoken against their rival. Another factor was Corneille's resistance to courting the favor of the influential by remaining throughout his career in Rouen. Corneille, the foremost celebrator of the heroic in drama, preferred his bourgeois life in the provinces. Unlike most of his contemporaries in the theater, Corneille neither worked for nor was involved with the running of a theater or acting company. Following the Querelle du Cid, which lasted until 1740,

Corneille responded to charges that he had violated neoclassical standards with his most admired tragedies—*Horace* (1640), *Cinna* (1641), and *Polyeucte* (1642)—models of the accepted subject, tone, and structure of neoclassical tragedy. In the 1650s Corneille wrote commentaries on his plays and produced the 17th century's most important dramatic treatises, *Discarse du poème dramatique, De la tragédie*, and *Des trois unités* (*Discourse on poetic drama, On Tragedy, On the Three Unities*), in part as further replies to the criticism of *Le Cid*. None of Corneille's later plays, with the exception of *Oedipe* in 1659, earned the same degree of critical acclaim or popular success as his earlier work, and the title as the age's premier tragedian passed to the younger Racine, who had begun his career in imitation of the older playwright. Corneille retired from the theater in 1674 and died in relative obscurity 10 years later.

Le Cid is an adaptation of *Las Mocedades del Cid* (The youthful exploits of the Cid) by the Spanish dramatist Guillén de Castro, first published in 1618. Its subject is the most popular figure in medieval Spanish legend, the 11th-century Castilian nobleman Rodrigo Díaz de Vivar. Despite being exiled Rodrigo returned to defend his country against the Moors, earning from his enemy the honorific of *el Cid* ("the lord") as a mark of respect for his battle prowess. Ballads and romances subsequently celebrated his real and imagined exploits, and the legend developed that Rodrigo married, on the king's order, the daughter of a man he had killed. Castro embellished this story by suggesting that Rodrigo's eventual bride had previously loved him before her father's death and afterward, to serve her family honor, demanded the death of the man she loved. Castro's focus on one of the central themes of the Spanish *comedia*—the conflict between love and honor—is lost in the interest of his overloaded chronicle play, which, in the words of critic Claude Abrahams, resembles "a long, rambling dramatic poem in which the tragic rubs elbows with the comic, the trivial with the epic, and the tasteless with the sublime." Corneille's version reduces all to the essential conflict between the two lovers—Rodrigue and Chimène—while adhering to the *règles* (rules) derived from Aristotle's *Poetics* that his era increasingly considered essential for serious drama. Corneille observes the unity of place by restricting Castro's multiple locations to the Spanish court at Seville. He preserves the unity of time by limiting the duration of the action to a single day and enforces a unity of action by eliminating subplots and inessential characters to focus on the internal crises of the two central protagonists. The result is a concentration and intensification of characters' emotional and moral inner lives that was unprecedented in French drama.

The play opens with Chimène happily anticipating the approval by her father, the count of Gormas, of her choice of Rodrigue as her suitor. However, a quarrel between her father and his older rival, Rodrigue's father, Don Diègue, occurs. The feeble Don Diègue, unable to claim satisfaction himself when he is struck by the Count, calls on his son to uphold the family honor.

In act 2, Rodrigue manages to overcome his conflict between his love for the Count's daughter and his obligation to his father and name by challenging and killing the Count in an offstage duel. Chimène, learning of her father's death, now faces the same conflict between love and honor that beset Rodrigue, and she too chooses to do her duty to her father at the risk of her love by demanding vengeance from the king. In the third act Rodrigue and Chimène, in the first of two emotional meetings in the play, grapple with their conflict as he offers her his life to satisfy her honor. Chimène's love for Rodrigue prevents her from accepting his sacrifice, but she is compelled to continue her pursuit of vengeance. Their impasse is interrupted by the attack of the city by the Moors, and Rodrigue rushes to the defense. After an offstage battle Rodrigue appears before the king in triumph as the city's savior. Chimène, realizing that the king will not help her exact vengeance on such a hero, invokes the tradition of single combat and offers to marry the champion who will slay Rodrigue. The king agrees but, suspecting that Chimène still loves Rodrigue, stipulates that she must wed whoever is victorious. In the final act Rodrigue again meets Chimène and gains her admission that she wishes him to survive the combat but that her honor forces her to risk his life. Rodrigue defeats her champion but pardons him, sending him back to Chimène with the news. She, believing she is meeting Rodrigue's killer, reveals her grief and love for Rodrigue. The king asserts the play's comic conclusion by decreeing that Rodrigue and Chimène have both acted nobly, that honor has been satisfied, and that the lovers can hope to be united in time.

Corneille's play marks an important dramatic shift from external to internal stage action in which circumstances push his characters to extreme conflicts to reveal their inner resources and values. By concentrating attention on his two protagonists and by forcing Rodrigue and Chimène to reconcile the competing demands of love and honor, Corneille dramatizes the meaning of both in human, moral, and emotional terms. Drama, in Corneille's handling, became less centered on plot and more on character and the sentiment that the circumstances provoked. *Le Cid* proved to be both an extraordinarily popular success and a target. Literary critics and rival playwrights, in a pamphlet war, attacked Corneille and the play's perceived transgressions of decorum, realism, and morality. The playwright Scudéry was one of the most outspoken in a detailed attack that concluded with the charge that the play's "subject is worthless, that it violates the principal rules of dramatic poetry, that it has many bad verses, that all its beauties are plagiarized." Scudéry's most damning complaint, however, centered on Corneille's presumed violations of verisimilitude and morality in allowing Chimène to love her father's murderer. Corneille's defense rested on claims of historical truth and the play's classically derived tone and structure. A war of words escalated into vicious personal attack, and the quarrel was finally appealed to the newly formed Académie Française for arbitration. After six months, the magisterial *Sentiments de l'Académie sur Le*

Cid appeared. Largely the work of scholar Jean Chapelain, with the approval if not the input of Cardinal Richelieu, the treatise supplied a point-by-point critique of Scudéry's charges as well as a scene-by-scene analysis of the play assessing questions of believability and "regularity." Although Chapelain took issue with many of Scudéry's complaints, he agreed with him that in attempting to follow the unities Corneille had shown too much action for a single day. This offense of verisimilitude, however, was minor compared to the play's most serious transgression. By depicting "a girl introduced as virtuous" who consents to marry her father's murderer, the play offends, Chapelain asserted, both verisimilitude and morality. For Chapelain a drama cannot be called good, "however pleasing it may be to the common folk," unless the required precepts of decorum, verisimilitude, and propriety are observed. Corneille's defense that the story was historically true was insufficient and misguided, in Chapelain's view: "There are monstrous truths which must be repressed for the good of society," and "It is primarily in these cases that the poet should prefer verisimilitude to truth." For Chapelain Chimène is "too susceptible a lover and too unnatural a daughter" to be plausible.

The lasting significance of the Querelle du Cid was the impact of its widespread public debate on the ends and means of drama that tested and popularized neoclassical ideals. The debate would establish France as the European center for dramatic theory, and French critics would dominate and define the understanding and practices of drama for the next century and a half. The controversy brought attention both to the limitations and benefits of the classically derived stage principles that governed how a play should be presented, as well as the degree to which truth could be in conflict with the desire to edify and instruct an audience. Chapelain, advocating the emerging neoclassical ideals, had earlier asserted that the end of drama was "to move the soul of the spectator by the power and truth with which the various passions are expressed on the stage and in this way to purge it from the unfortunate effects which these passions can create in himself." To do so drama must replicate the conditions of real life, and hence the performance must be "accomplished and supported" by verisimilitude. *Vraisemblance*, in the evolving conception of neoclassical drama, was in turn supported by the unities of time, place, and action and the principles of decorum that reserved the stage for the noble and banned vulgar characters or details. Corneille had shown in *Le Cid* the force and psychological and emotional possibilities that could be achieved by adhering to certain neoclassical conventions, even if he fell short of others. By concentrating dramatic interest on the human psyche and passions in distress, Corneille helped establish verisimilitude, or believability, as well as its limits, as crucial measures of a drama's success. The legacy of *Le Cid* is the challenges and the achievements of later dramatists, such as Molière and Racine, who tried to abide by and profit from the neoclassical ideals that Corneille's play had helped define and popularize.

THE ROVER

92

(1677)

by Aphra Behn

With Mrs. Behn we turn a very important corner on the road. We leave behind, shut up in their parks among their folios, those solitary great ladies who wrote without audience or criticism, for their own delight alone. We come to town and rub shoulders with ordinary people of the streets. Mrs. Behn was a middle-class woman with all the plebeian virtues of humor, vitality, and courage; a woman forced by the death of her husband and some unfortunate adventures of her own to make her living by her wits. She had to work on equal terms with men. She made, by working very hard, enough to live on. . . . here begins the freedom of the mind, or rather the possibility that in the course of time the mind will be free to write what it likes. For now that Aphra Behn had done it, girls could go to their parents and say, You need not give me an allowance; I can make money by my pen. . . . Thus, toward the end of the eighteenth century a change came about which, if I were rewriting history, I should describe more fully and think of greater importance than the Crusades or the Wars of the Roses. The middle-class woman began to write.

—Virginia Woolf, *A Room of One's Own*

Aphra Behn is not the first woman dramatist, but she is almost certainly the earliest to gain sufficient popular success to allow her to succeed as a professional playwright and writer. The author of some 20 plays, Behn was surpassed by only John Dryden as the most prolific Restoration dramatist. She mastered virtually every literary genre of her age—poetry, fiction, and translations—demonstrating for the first time in literary history that a woman could compete on the same footing with men as a literary professional. Neither was Behn the only Restoration woman playwright, but she was the notable exception: a woman writer who openly flaunted her gender and expected the same treatment—in remuneration and critical reception—accorded to male writers. As she wrote in the preface of one of her plays, "All I ask, is for the privilege for my masculine part, the poet in me . . . to tread in those successful paths my predecessors have long thrived in. . . . If I must not, because of my sex, have this freedom, but that you will usurp all to yourselves; I [will] lay down my

Quill and you shall hear no more of me." By asserting gender equality and, as a woman, openly associating with the theater, Behn faced scurrilous accusations that she violated sacrosanct social and moral proprieties. By writing as frankly about sexual subjects as male playwrights, Behn was condemned as little more than a prostitute for her moral laxity and expecting payment for her work. Despite these attacks Behn gained an eminence unknown by other women of her day in which she was praised as the "English Sappho" for her considerable artistic gifts. Yet she never quite lost her association with the unseemly. Dryden, for example, advised another prospective woman writer to avoid "the license which Mrs. Behn allowed herself, of writing loosely, and giving . . . some scandal to the modesty of her sex." Alexander Pope would later famously critique Behn under her pen name, Astraea: "The stage how loosely does Astraea tread, / Who fairly puts all characters to bed." The charges of unladylike sexual explicitness in her work and the presumed corresponding looseness of her character continued into the Victorian age, when Behn was condemned along with other Restoration writers for licentiousness and castigated as "a mere harlot, who danced through uncleanness," as "one of the original corrupters and polluters of the stage." Interest in Behn and her work, as well as a renewed respect for her achievement as a woman, was stimulated by women writers in the early 20th century, most notably, by Vita Sackville-West, who published a 1927 appreciative biography called *Aphra Behn: The Incomparable Astrea*. For Sackville-West's close friend Virginia Woolf, Behn was the founding figure of women's literary consciousness and expression, the first to demonstrate that a woman could support herself by her writing. "All women together," Woolf declared, "ought to let flowers fall upon the tomb of Aphra Behn . . . for it was she who earned them the right to speak their minds."

Renewed interest in Behn's career and accomplishments has been further accelerated (and frustrated) by both what we know and do not know of her life. Her birth date and maiden name remain a mystery, and her parentage is a subject of much speculation. Tradition has it that she was born in 1640, and it has been claimed that she was the daughter of a Kent barber, John Amis. An alternative view is that she may have been the natural or foster child of a Canterbury gentleman named Johnson in the service of Lord Willoughby, who appointed him lieutenant general of Suriname. Nothing is known for certain how she gained the considerable learning that is evident from her works. It is believed that in 1663 Aphra accompanied Johnson, his wife, and a young boy, mentioned as Behn's brother, on a voyage to take up residence in the West Indies. Johnson, however, died on the way, and, it is believed, Aphra lived for several months in Suriname. Her most famous novel, *Oroonoko* (1688), is believed to be based on her experiences there. On her return to England in 1664, she either married or took the name of a Dutch merchant named Behn, who died, possibly in the plague of 1665. Left without funds, Mrs. Behn, as she would subsequently be known, accepted an assignment as a secret agent for Charles II in Antwerp during the war against the Dutch (1665–67). Neither the king nor his government, however, responded to Behn's repeated requests for payment for her services. She returned to London penniless and was in 1668 incarcerated in debtor's prison. The circumstances of her release are unknown, but in 1670 her first play, *The Forc'd Marriage*, was produced in London, and Behn subsequently earned her living as a playwright, poet, and novelist until her death in 1689. She is buried in the cloister of Westminster Abbey, not in Poet's Corner to Virginia Woolf's chagrin, with the gravestone epitaph: "Here lies a proof that wit can never be / Defence enough against mortality."

As a woman, Behn's career as a professional writer is exceptional; as a theater professional, it is remarkable. Behn grew up in the England of the Puritan Commonwealth that closed the theaters in 1642, effectively putting an end to the greatest period of theatrical achievement in English history. When Charles II was restored to the throne in 1660, he brought the theater back with him, having developed a love for the stage during his years of exile on the Continent. The restored theater, sponsored by the king, would feature London's first public performance by an actress (in the role of Desdemona in a production of *Othello* in December 1660). The previous Elizabethan and Jacobean prohibitions on women performing on the commercial stage gave way, though the moral opprobrium attached to actresses remained strong. However, the novelty of women onstage may have contributed to the subsequent acceptance of women playwrights, which Behn exploited in establishing her dramatic career. Behn forcefully defended her works in the prefaces and epilogues to her plays, countering the charge that her dramas could not be any good because they were by a woman and consequently were lacking in erudition and training in classically derived dramatic principles. Behn argued not only that women could equal men in learning if they had equal educational opportunities, but even more radically that schooling and scholarship were not essential for creating entertaining dramas. In staking out a place for women dramatists Behn contended: "Plays have no great room for that which is men's great advantage over women, that is Learning." Drama, according to Behn, deals in experience, not scholarship, and the theater is, therefore, within the range of women writers, as it was for the self-taught William Shakespeare and Ben Jonson.

Behn's provocative challenges to gender assumptions as well as the originality and vitality of her unconventional perspective are evident in her most successful and accomplished play, *The Rover; or, The Banished Cavaliers*, first performed in 1677. Set during the Puritan interregnum, it concerns a roistering group of displaced Royalists—Willmore (the Rover), Belvile, Frederick, and Ned Blunt—awaiting the restoration of Charles II in Naples during Carnival. An adaptation of Sir Thomas Killigrew's 10-part closet drama, *Thomasa, or the Wanderer, The Rover* displays Behn's considerable dexterity in stage-craft, condensing a sprawling story and joining a large cast to a swiftly paced intrigue plot. The comedy at the same time offers a knowing look at the battle of the sexes from a woman's perspective that exposes the double standard and the constricted and precarious prospects for women in a patriarchy. The play opens with two sisters—Hellena and Florinda—discussing their dismal fate. The younger, Hellena, is to be sent to a nunnery, while her sister, who has fallen in love with the English colonel Belvile, is being offered in marriage by her father to a wealthy old man and by her brother to one of his friends for his own advantage. The sisters decide to seize the opportunity afforded by the Carnival's masquerading to enjoy a final spree of independence and flirtation before surrendering to their onerous fates. The theme of the arranged or forced marriage, a favorite in Behn's plays, is immediately established, and the play will wittily dramatize the perilous course of love in an environment in which women are the commodities and playthings of men. Aiding this theme, the Carnival's masquerade scrambles the distinctions of class and produces the satirical equation between well-born lady and whore in a tangled plot based on concealed identities and gender reversals.

The lively, outspoken Hellena, who is contrasted with her more virtuous and dutiful sister Florinda, meets her match in the charmingly irresponsible Willmore, the archetypal cynical Restoration rake hero who regards virtue as "an Infirmity in Women" and who asks "What the Devil should I do with a virtuous Woman?" Hellena's bringing of Willmore to heel (and the altar) supplies the play's main courtship plot that collides and crosses purposes with the frustrated wooing of Florinda and Belvile, with Willmore's affair with the famous courtesan Angellica Bianca, and with the other pairings involving Frederick with the sisters' cousin Valeria and Ned Blunt's transactions with the harlot Lucetta. The respectable Hellena takes on the disguise of a Gypsy whore to attract Willmore, while the actual whore Angellica falls in love with him as well. Despite her professional calculation in matters of the heart, Angellica sides with constancy and the ideal claim of love over the practical, and in a witty reversal Behn turns the good girl bad and the bad girl good, giving Hellena an unmistakable robust sexual appetite and Angellica a vulnerable "virgin heart." Both women reverse the expected role of females as the pursued to become pursuers of Willmore, who is naively convinced that men are the buyers and women are the sellers. Angellica points out that men are just as likely to act the prostitute, holding out for the highest bidder and exchanging sex for a handsome dowry. The confusion and complexity of gender assumptions escalate dangerously as Angellica grows violently jealous of Willmore's attentions to Hellena, and Florinda tests Belville's faithfulness by courting him in disguise. While awaiting her lover Florinda is almost raped by the drunken Willmore, who takes her for a common whore, and the confusion continues as Blunt and Frederick at the last minute hesitate to violate Florinda on suspicion that she may be well born. "Two'd anger us vilely to be truss'd up for a Rape upon a Maid of Quality," Frederick reasons, "when we only believe we ruffle a Harlot." He exposes the double standard in operation in which forced sex with a woman of quality is rape and has consequence, while the same act with a whore is mere harmless play.

Unable to bring herself to shoot Willmore after failing to secure his constancy, Angellica consoles herself with another paying customer, and the play concludes with a witty love negotiation between Willmore and Hellena. She holds out for marriage, while he argues that love requires no vows:

> WILLMORE Hold, hold, no bug words, child. Priest and Hymen? Prithee add a hangman to 'em to make up the consort. No, no, we'll have no vows but love, child, nor witness but the lover: The kind deity enjoins naught but love and enjoy. Hymen and priest wait still upon portion and jointure; love and beauty have their own ceremonies. Marriage is as certain a bane to love as lending money is to friendship. I'll neither ask nor give a vow, though I could be content to turn gypsy and become a left-handed bridegroom to have the pleasure of working that great miracle of making a maid a mother, if you durst venture. 'Tis upse gypsy that, and if I miss I'll lose my labor.

> HELLENA And if you do not lose, what shall I get? A cradle full of noise and mischief, with a pack of repentance at my back? Can you teach me to weave incle to pass my time with? 'Tis upse gypsy that, too.

> WILLMORE I can teach thee to weave a true love's knot better.

> HELLENA So can my dog.

> WILLMORE Well, I see we are both upon our guards, and I see there's no way to conquer good nature but by yielding. Here, give me thy hand: One kiss, and I am thine.

> HELLENA One kiss! How like my page he speaks! I am resolved you should have none, for asking such a sneaking sum. He that will be satisfied with one kiss will never die of that longing. Good friend single-kiss, is all your talking come to this? A kiss, a caudle! Farewell, captain single-kiss.

> WILLMORE Nay, if we part so, let me die like a bird upon a bough, at the sheriff's charge. By heaven, both the Indies shall not buy

thee from me. I adore thy humor and will marry thee, and we are
so of one humor it must be a bargain. Give me thy hand.

Hellena finally wins Willmore by matching his wit and sidestepping his gender expectations. She brings him to the altar ultimately by proving herself
more interesting as a person than as a sex object or pawn or plaything for a
male. Indeed all the women in the play succeed in evading male authority
and control. Hellena and Florinda overturn parental and filial authority to
gain the men of their choice; Lucetta tricks Blunt out of his trousers; even
Angellica, though bested in the contest to gain Willmore, awards her heart
as she chooses. *The Rover* wittily rewrites the masculine-dominated Restoration comedy into a drama of female empowerment that, as critic Jane Spencer
argues, "manages to subject masculine figures to a female gaze." It is this same
female gaze, by one of the first major woman playwrights, that extends the
range and possibilities of drama.

AWAKE AND SING!

93

(1935)

by Clifford Odets

The Berger family are on the verge of the middle class and as such are especially vulnerable. To deny the reality of the American dream is ostensibly to condemn themselves to permanent deprivation. The constant image is one of flight, escape. They look to escape the reality of their situation through marriage, through luck, through a desperate commitment to political or social myths, through a sardonic humour, through self-deceit, or even, most desperately, through suicide, albeit a suicide which, like that which was to send Willy Loman to his death in Death of a Salesman, *is designed to liberate the next generation.*

—C. W. E. Bigsby, "The Group Theatre and Clifford Odets,"
in *A Critical Introduction to American Drama*, Volume 1: *1900–1940*

There can be stability and safety in constriction, as the sweet round of life that defines the existence of the small-town families in OUR TOWN demonstrates. Thornton Wilder's characters may catch tantalizing glimpses of a world outside Grover's Corners, but they do not seek liberation from the unchanging universe they inhabit. Their immovability is their strength. Although written in the same decade as *Our Town*, Clifford Odets's *Awake and Sing!* stands in stark social contrast to Wilder's lyrical evocation of small-town America. Odets's struggling urban Jewish Berger family has risen from immigrant poverty to a working-class plateau in the midst of the Great Depression, where the prevailing reality is emotional, economic, and cultural stagnation and dislocation. Through the Bergers Odets spoke to the need for Americans in the 1930s to escape from economic deprivation and to break free from idealized political and social solutions and stultifying and volcanic family relationships to move up toward a more stable place in society.

Odets once wrote in the New York *World-Telegram*, "Understand that I am supposed to confess how I came to write 'Awake and Sing!' I was sore; that's why I wrote the play. I was sore at my whole life." Odets, an unhappy and marginally talented actor before he became a playwright and the new voice of social drama in the 1930s, claimed that he had attempted suicide three times before the age of 25. Certainly his early life and career were marked by struggle. The oldest of three children, Odets was born in 1906 in Philadelphia, where his father, Louis, a Russian Jewish immigrant, held down jobs selling newspapers and peddling salt, and his mother, Pearl, worked in a factory. When Odets was six the family moved to the Bronx. There Louis Odets worked his way up from a job as a feeder in a printing plant to owner of the company. The family later resettled in Philadelphia, where Odets's father became vice president of a boiler company and owned an advertising agency. Despite his family's rise from the working class to the prosperous middle class, Odets described himself as a "melancholy kid." He had a difficult relationship with his father, who wanted him to enter his advertising business rather than pursue his intention to become an actor. Odets dropped out of high school after his sophomore year and tried his skill at poetry, further angering his father, who smashed his son's typewriter. Louis Odets eventually replaced the machine and gave his permission for Clifford to attempt an acting career.

During the late 1920s Odets acted with an amateur theater group, worked as an announcer for a small Bronx radio station, wrote radio plays, recited poetry on the air, performed in vaudeville for $1 a night, and acted in melodramas produced by a stock company. His entrance onto the Broadway stage was as an understudy for Spencer Tracy in a forgotten play titled *Conflict*. From there Odets moved to the Theatre Guild, an influential 12-year-old theater collaborative that produced noncommercial American and foreign plays on Broadway. The year 1931 marked the beginning of Odets's actual career, when he joined the Group Theatre, a new theater collective formed by Harold Clurman, Cheryl Crawford, and Lee Strasberg, who would go on to found the prestigious Actors Studio. The Group Theatre, which lasted for 10 years, had a major impact on the American theater. Derived from the "method acting" teachings of Konstantin Stanislavsky and the naturalistic acting of the Yiddish theater's David Kessler, whom Strasberg had seen perform when he was a child, the Group was conceived as an ensemble theater company producing socially relevant, sometimes leftist dramas. A training ground for actors, the Group Theatre emphasized naturalistic, forceful, and disciplined artistry and pioneered what would become the unique American acting technique known simply as the "method."

Odets played a few minor roles for the Group Theatre, beginning with the company's first production, Paul Green's *The House of Connelly*. However, he remained unnoticed by reviewers and became frustrated by his lack of advancement to better roles. In 1933 he managed to secure a leading role as a patriotic Russian husband in *They All Came to Moscow*. Odets turned to playwriting in 1932 with a play about Beethoven, about which he noted in his diary, "Here I am writing the Beethoven play, which when it is finished may not even be about Beethoven. Why not write something about the Greenberg family, something I know better, something that is closer to me?"

During the winter of 1932–33, while living in a tiny room of the community apartment shared by the financially poorest members of the Group Theatre, Odets wrote *I Got the Blues*. Greenberg was changed to Berger, and the title eventually became *Awake and Sing!* In 1934 Odets joined the Communist Party for eight months "in the belief, in the honest and real belief, that this was some way out of the dilemma in which we found ourselves." At the same time he wrote *Waiting for Lefty*, the revolutionary work that would establish his career as a playwright. Inspired by the New York taxi strike of February 1934, *Lefty* is very much a play of its time. In seven vignettes, each separated by a blackout, the theater becomes a union hall, where cabbies meet to plan a strike for higher wages as they anticipate the arrival of Lefty Costello, their elected chairman, who will support them. A play of "originality and fire," as Clurman described it, *Waiting for Lefty* was an indictment of capitalism and a statement of the right of every individual and family to have dignity and self-worth. The play debuted in January 1935 and was an immediate sensation when it reached Broadway in March 1935; by July it was playing in 30 cities. *Lefty*'s status as a hit contributed to the Group Theatre's decision to produce Odets's earlier play, *Awake and Sing!*, which opened at the Belasco Theatre on February 19, 1935.

A conventionally structured three-act drama, *Awake and Sing!* takes its title from a line in Isaiah 26:19: "Awake and sing, ye that dwell in dust." Set in the Berger's Bronx tenement apartment, the play explores the family's relationships, ambitions, and frustrations with intensity but also with humor. Bessie Berger, characterized as the archetypal Jewish mother, is the play's antagonist. In her struggle to keep the family fed, clothed, and sheltered, she has developed as a strong-willed, autocratic, possessive, and materialistic woman committed to preserving the respectability of her family at all costs. Her husband, Myron, has worked as a clerk for 30 years. He is a dignified and likable but weak-willed "born follower," who lives in the past and in denial of the failure that has been his lot in life. The family circle includes Bessie and Myron's grown children, Ralph and Hennie, and Bessie's wise old immigrant father, Jacob, a faded Marxist idealist and antimaterialist, and the family's conscience. Finally, there is Uncle Morty, Bessie's brother, a shrewd, cynical clothing manufacturer, who lives well, drives a big car, and contributes $5 a week toward the support of his father, whom he calls "a nut." Ralph, naive and romantic, works as a clerk and complains that all he wants is "a chance to get to first base." Hennie, beautiful, proud, self-contained, and pregnant by a man who cannot be located, has several suitors, including Schlosser, the janitor, whose wife ran away with another man and whose daughter left him to become a chorus girl in burlesque. She is also courted by the sensitive but ineffectual Sam Feinschreiber and Moe Axelrod, who boards with the Bergers and, it is discovered, was Hennie's first love. A petty racketeer who lost a leg in the war, Moe brings a vital and masculine life-affirming presence to the household.

The dramatic center of the play is the attempt by Ralph and Hennie, to break free from their stifling environment. Their support in this endeavor comes from Moe and especially Jacob, who is constantly at odds with his daughter: "This is a house? Marx said it, abolish such families." He urges Ralph to "Go out and fight so life shouldn't be printed on dollar bills." Bessie's acidulous response to her father's politics is "Go fight City Hall." She forces Hennie to marry Sam and to let him think the child is his, and when she learns that Ralph is interested in a girl, she breaks up the relationship so that the family will not lose the weekly salary check he brings home. Hennie's marriage is predictably unhappy, and after a year, she tells Sam the truth about the child, thus precipitating the climax of the play. Ralph is outraged when he learns of the deception and confronts his mother with her guilt in the matter. Bessie responds to her son's reproaches by turning angrily on Jacob and breaking the cherished opera records that are the aesthetic and spiritual center of her father's life. Jacob gives Ralph a last piece of advice: "Do what is in your heart and you carry in yourself a revolution. But you should act. Not like me. A man who had golden opportunities but drank instead a glass tea." He goes up to the roof, ostensibly to exercise the dog, Tootsie, but instead takes his life by falling to his death. A dazed Bessie asks Moe to call Morty with the news. He refuses, and she hesitantly dials the number.

During the last scene of the play, which takes place a week later, Ralph learns that he is the beneficiary of his grandfather's insurance policy and declares his independence by refusing to share the money with the family. Despite the heinous act Bessie committed against her father, which precipitated his suicide, she inspires our sympathy and commands for herself a certain stature during her last speech to her son:

> Ralphie, I worked too hard all my years to be treated like dirt. It's no law we should be stuck together like Siamese twins. Summer shoes you didn't have, skates you never had, but I bought a new dress every week. A lover I kept, Mr. Gigolo! . . . Or was Bessie Berger's children always the cleanest on the block?! . . . Here, I'm not only the mother but also the father. The first two years I worked in a stocking factory for six dollars while Myron Berger went to law school. If I didn't worry about the family who would? . . . here without a dollar you don't look the world in the eye. Talk from now to next year—this is life in America.
>
> "Mom, what does she know? She's old-fashioned!" But I'll tell you a big secret: My whole life I wanted to go away too, but with children a woman stays home. A fire burned in *my* heart too, but now it's too late. I'm no spring chicken. The clock goes and Bessie goes. Only my machinery can't be fixed.

After Bessie goes wearily off to bed, Moe announces that he is leaving for a new life in Cuba and declares his love for Hennie. She agrees to abandon her husband and child to go with him. Ralph decides not to take the money: "Let Mom have the dough. I'm twenty-two and kickin'! I'll get along. Did Jake die for us to fight about nickels? No! . . . I saw he was dead and I was born!" Hennie and Moe leave, and Ralph watches them go, standing "full and strong in the doorway seeing them off as the curtain slowly falls."

Like *Waiting for Lefty, Awake and Sing!* debuted at a pivotal moment in American history—1935 was the bleakest year of the Great Depression and also the year in which New Deal measures instituted by the Roosevelt administration began to move the nation slowly toward economic recovery. The rise of fascism in Europe and the American tendency toward isolationism were causes for concern, the latter most prominently among liberals and leftists. *Awake and Sing!* contains a fair amount of Marxist propagandizing, in keeping with the social and political preoccupations of its author and its time, but the play's real strength is in Odets's creation of robust and interesting characters and their interactions with one another. *Awake and Sing!* is an intimate play and, like all effective drama in which the characters are fighting for survival, raises as many questions as it answers. The play ends on an optimistic note, but the fates of Ralph and Hennie remain ambiguous. Despite the courage Hennie shows in replacing sullen acquiescence with positive action in choosing to go away with the man she loves, she has flouted morality and acted irresponsibly by leaving her husband and especially her baby behind. It is unclear whether the idealistic Ralph will get what he wants from life, or whether he will succumb to the unrealistic romanticism that defines his father. But Odets makes clear that action for its own sake is better than perpetual stagnation. Wilder's characters in *Our Town* may speak to a universal nostalgia for certainty needed in the midst of difficult times, but Odets reminds us of the need to look outward and move forward, breaking the grip of family limitation, honoring American dreams, and achieving liberation for future generations.

THE BROTHERS

94

(160 B.C.)

by Terence

With its well-knit plot, lifting the usual farce motifs into a high comedy of character, and with searching analysis of the eternal problem of the education of youth, The Brothers *combines intrigue with intellectual interest, and is the most richly stimulating of the Roman comedies.*

—Joseph T. Shipley, *Guide to Great Plays*

The two great Roman comic dramatists, Plautus and Terence, provide a study in contrasts, while together they mark out the shape and boundaries of classical comedy that would significantly influence the development of modern European drama. Plautus is the great master of invention, of broad farcical situation and extravagant verbal effects; Terence perfected the comedy of character, putting his more carefully plotted and more restrained humor to the service of a deeper exploration of human nature and actuality. Plautus's comedies are shaped and sustained by his audience's demand to be continually entertained. In his plays, the joke, prank, and pratfall are paramount, and at times Plautus shows an indifference to contradictions and irrelevancies and neglects joining his many comic elements into a unified, coherent whole. Terence, staying closer in tone and texture to the Greek New Comedy originals they both adapted, replaces Plautus's comic improvisations and irrelevancies with concentrated action and a unity of purpose in which all contribute to advancing his plots, shaping his themes, and individualizing his characters. Terence ingeniously ties together multiple story lines and generates his incidents from the nature and plausible motives of his characters. Plautus's characters are rarely more than functional types and convenient passengers for the playwright's wild ride; Terence populates his dramas with individuals whose motives and temperament drive their stories. Plautus's comedies were preferred by Roman audiences, while Terence, whose plays make few concessions to contemporary taste and required closer attention to appreciate his more subtle and sophisticated effects, endured popular failure and required patronage for support in challenging contemporary dramatic conventions. In comparing the achievements of the playwrights noted classical scholar George E. Duckworth summarizes:

> Both worked from the social drama of the New Comedy, Terence in the direction of subtlety and elegance, Plautus toward bustling vivacity and boisterous humour. Both were limited by the forms and conventions of their originals, but both deserve great credit as independent and creative dramatists. Terence remolded the Greek plays so as to reveal his interest in human character and his perfect control of dramatic structure. Plautus transformed the more serious works of the Greeks and produced laughable comedies to delight the audiences of his day.

Both playwrights would serve as influential models in the development of European drama. If Plautus assembled a valuable storehouse of comedic elements—plots, character types, and gags—Terence offered subsequent playwrights the example of drama's potential in harnessing and controlling its many elements in aid of drama as a truth telling instrument.

Regarded as one of the premier Latin stylists of the second century B.C., Terence was admired and his work studied throughout the Middle Ages, serving as an important bridge figure spanning the period between classical drama and the beginning of drama in the Renaissance. In the 10th century the Saxon nun Hrotsvitha composed pious comedies in imitation of the manner of Terence, risking, as she declares in the preface to her plays, "being corrupted by the wickedness of the matter." During the 16th century Terence's works served as models for teaching Latin to schoolboys, and there were more than 446 complete editions of his plays available before 1600. Niccolò Machiavelli translated Terence's *Andria* in 1517; Molière would adapt two of Terence's plays (*The School for Husbands* is based on *The Brothers; The Trickeries of Scapin*, on *Phormio*); William Congreve would call Terence "the most correct writer in the world." "What man of letters has not read his Terence more than once and does not know him almost by heart?" asked the French critic Denis Diderot. "Who has not been struck by the truth of his characters and the elegance of his diction?" Diderot would go on to assert, "Young poets, alternately turn the pages of Molière and of Terence. Learn from one to draw, from the other to paint." Oscar Wilde's doubling plot in *The Importance of Being Earnest* as well as George Bernard Shaw's conjoining the structure of the well-made play with the exploration of social problems both show more than a trace of Terence's abiding influence.

Publius Terentius Afer, Anglicized as Terence, is believed to have been born in Carthage around 195 B.C. and brought to Rome as the slave of the Roman senator Terentius Lucanus. Educated and eventually freed by his master, Terence formed a friendship with the young Roman noble Publius

Cornelius Scipio Aemilianus and became a member of his literary and philosophical group known as the Scipionic Circle, united by a shared admiration of
Greek art, literature, and culture. Terence's more faithful adaptation of Greek
New Comedy models compared to Plautus's would have been encouraged
by Scipio and others who helped finance productions of his plays and were
alleged as Terence's collaborators. In the prologue to *The Brothers* Terence
neither admits nor rejects such assistance but regards the charge "as his greatest merit, that he has it in his power to please those, with whom you, and the
whole people of Rome, are so much pleased." His first play is said to have been
initially read to the aging comic master Caecilius for his approval. Dressed in
tatters and relegated to a lowly stool as the dinner entertainment, the young
dramatist made such a favorable impression after the first few lines that he was
invited to join the company at table. Terence's six surviving plays—*Andria, The
Self-Tormentor, The Eunuch, Phormio, The Mother-in-Law*, and *The Brothers*—
were produced between the years 166 and 160 B.C. Terence's struggle for audience approval is best captured in the prologue of *The Mother-in-Law*, in which
the play's leading actor recounts the plays multiple failures with the restive and
easily distracted Roman theater audience:

> On the first occasion when I began to act it, the great renown of some
> boxers (expectation of a tight-rope walker was thrown in), friends getting
> together, a clatter of conversation, women's penetrating voices, made me
> leave the theater all too soon. . . . I brought it on again: the first act was
> liked, and then there came a rumor that gladiators were on the program;
> the people came flocking in, rioting, and shouting, fighting for places:
> when that happened, I could not keep *my* place.

After staging *The Brothers* Terence left Rome for a tour of Greece. There he
collected additional plays by Menander, but his adaptations were apparently
lost in a shipwreck. The playwright either perished with them on his return
voyage or died of an illness in Greece in 159 B.C.

The Brothers demonstrates the innovations that characterize all of Terence's
works as well as the exceptional characteristics that justify it being regarded as
his masterpiece. Based on a play by Menander (*Adelphoi*), as are three others
of Terence's six plays (the other two are by Menander's disciple, Apollodorus),
The Brothers borrows a situation (Aeschinus's abduction of a slave girl) from a
play of Diphilus, which had previously been presented by Plautus. The borrowing and modification of his sources demonstrate Terence's characteristic
fleshing out of the often thin New Comedy plots with multiple storylines
from different sources, producing the most intricately plotted of all surviving ancient drama. *The Brothers* combines the two most common situations
in Greek New Comedy—a young man who needs money for his mistress
and a young man who conceals his involvement with a poor but respectable

girl. The young men, Aeschinus and Ctesipho, are the natural sons of the authoritarian Demea, whose more easygoing brother Micio is entrusted with the raising of Aeschinus. The play, therefore, juggles the affairs of two sets of brothers and multiple contrasts for the father-son theme, the standard topic of New Comedy. Terence, however, innovatively shifts emphasis from the young lovers to the contrasted attitudes and values of the older brothers who try to bring up the young men in their image. The standard New Comedy love intrigue is thereby in *The Brothers* put to a larger serious purpose of testing and evaluating contrasting philosophies of upbringing and parental authority. As critic M. S. Dimsdale points out, the play's interest "is educational and ethical as much as dramatic." *The Brothers* can therefore be regarded as one of the earliest social problem comedies.

The Brothers, like all of Terence's plays, opens with a prologue, the handling of which again underscores the playwright's originality and challenge to audience expectations. It was customary for the prologues of comic dramas to alert the audience to the characters and situations to come. Terence, however, rejecting the expository prologue, chooses to deal not with the play's content but with criticisms of his works, becoming in effect the first playwright to offer a critique and justification of his intentions at the play's outset. The prologue to *The Brothers*, while raising and dismissing the allegation by "malicious critics" of undue influence from Terence's influential patrons, counters a charge of theft for importing the incident of the slave girl's adduction from another, non-Menandrian source. Terence argues against a slavish adherence to sources with the proof of the effectiveness of his modifications in the performance. "As to what remains," the prologue concludes, "do not expect now to hear from me the subject of the play; the two old men, who come on first, will partly explain it, and the rest will gradually appear in representation." Terence makes clear that he intends to develop his characters and situations internally. Without foreknowledge of the play's circumstances and outcome Terence's audience must be alert to an enfolding drama in which suspense and surprise is increased. Once the play commences the actors resist the repeated device employed by Plautus of direct address to the audience, reinforcing a heightened dramatic realism.

In the play's opening monologue Micio establishes the fundamental contrast of *The Brothers* in his and his brother's opposed parental philosophy. Demea interrupts Micio's complacent reflections with the news that Micio's charge, Aeschinus, has broken into another's house, forcibly carried off a slave girl, and beaten her master, the pimp and slave dealer Sannio. Demea uses Aeschinus's scandalous behavior to criticize Micio's parental laxity and to contrast Micio's rearing of the evidently wild libertine Aeschinus with his own strict regime that has produced Ctesipho, the very model of a thrifty and assiduous young man. While Micio has encouraged openness and liberality with his charge to achieve right action through choice rather than fear of punishment, Demea favors intimidation and restraint. Aeschinus has actually abducted the girl that Ctesipho has secretly fallen in love with but cannot afford to buy, having agreed to procure her for his brother to shield Ctesipho from Demea's expected censure. Terence takes great pains in these early scenes to individualize both pairs of brothers through contrast: the tolerant Micio versus the pompous authoritarian Demea; the self-reliant, decisive Aeschinus with the timid Ctesipho. Terence designs his plot to monitor their reactions and to reveal their temperaments and values under the pressure of adversity.

News of the abduction reaches the poor Athenian widow Sostrata and her daughter Pamphilia, who is about to be delivered of Aeschinus's child. Aeschinus has concealed his liaison with Pamphilia from Micio, and therefore, both sons have kept their affairs from their fathers. Neither educational philosophy, indulgence nor restraint, has produced the desired outcome of honest, trustworthy sons, and both Micio and Demea are left ignorant of what their sons are truly like. Demea, while searching for Ctesipho, whom he has learned was involved in the abduction, discovers from a kinsman of Sostrata Aeschinus's apparent desertion of Pamphilia and sets out to deliver this crushing news to Micio. Meanwhile, Micio, having gained the truth regarding the abduction and the relationship between Aeschinus and Pamphilia goes to Sostrata's house to explain everything. Encountering Aeschinus on the same mission Micio tests the moral worth of his ward and Aeschinus's true feeling for Pamphilia by pretending to represent another suitor for Pamphilia's hand. Aeschinus's agony at the prospect of losing the woman he loves confirms that he had no intention of abandoning Pamphilia, and Micio agrees to the match.

Demea's revelations about Ctesipho and the impact on his parental philosophy close the play and establish an ongoing critical debate over Terence's handling of his plot and thematic intention. Finally learning that his iron-fisted rule has turned Ctesipho into a role-playing sneak, Demea is eventually persuaded by Micio that his severe regime has forced his son to disguise his true feelings and identity from his stern father. Urged to try tolerance and generosity, Demea resolves on a change of heart in a monologue reviewing his life that neatly parallels Micio's opening monologue. "Come, come now," he convinces himself, "let me see whether I can speak gently or behave kindly, since my brother challenges me to do so." The play ends, however, not with Demea's acceptance of Ctesipho's foibles and Micio's superior philosophy but with Demea's asserting his change of heart by urging Micio to practice what he preaches and by forcing him into more and more absurd concessions to Aeschinus's wishes, even to the point of marrying Sostrata. Demea's "hasty fit of prodigality" at his brother's expense is finally revealed as Demea's testing of the limits of Micio's permissiveness. "Your passing for an easy agreeable man is not genuine," Demea tells Micio, "or founded on equity and good sense, but is due to your overlooking things, your indulgence, and giving them whatever they want." Instead of fully endorsing Micio's lenient philosophy, the play ends at the moderate mean between overindulgence and authoritarian strictness.

Demea's transformation and the humiliation of Micio has been called by critic J. W. Duff "the drollest thing in Terence," and by the classical scholar Gilbert Norwood, "the legitimate fruit of the whole play, the perfectly sound result of that collision between Micio and Demea which has created and sustained the whole wonderful drama." Others, including Diderot, Gotthold Lessing, and Goethe, have been troubled and disappointed by the play's conclusion, seeing in Demea's turnaround the sacrifice of a character's plausibility and in his testing of Micio Terence's desire for a curtain lowering dramatic reversal at the expense of the play's previously earned ethical values. What matters most in evaluating the conclusion of *The Brothers* may be the degree to which Terence complicates the simpler moral conclusion that Micio's openness and generosity are preferred to Demea's restraint. Both elements—trust and discipline—are valuable in childrearing, and Terence's play makes it clear that either in extreme or without the other produces the complications that *The Brothers* enact. Moreover the issue of Demea's change of heart, as measured by a criterion of plausibility, suggests a new standard of truthfulness that Terence helped establish in drama.

THE BALCONY

95

(1956)

by Jean Genet

His plays are concerned with expressing his own feeling of helplessness and solitude when confronted with the despair and loneliness of man caught in the hall of mirrors of the human condition, inexorably trapped by an endless progression of images that are merely his own distorted reflections—lies covering lies, fantasies battening upon fantasies, nightmares nourished by nightmares within nightmares.

—Martin Esslin, "Jean Genet: A Hall of Mirrors," in *The Theatre of the Absurd*

Jean Genet, one of the genuine revolutionaries of modern literature, was a dominating force in the experimental theater of the mid-20th century. A poète maudit in the French tradition of François Villon, Arthur Rimbaud, and Lautréamont, Genet was, in the estimation of Jean-Paul Sartre, who titled his appreciation of Genet's life and works, *Saint Genet: Actor and Martyr,* the embodiment of the existential hero who fully embraced his status as criminal and outcast that society deemed him and in so doing transcended all social and moral boundaries. Through Genet's vision the marginalized and the alienated take center stage, and society's most sacred truths are radically reassessed. As a playwright Genet the thief is still clearly in evidence, since his plays rob his audience of reassuring truths. Theater, for Genet, should be an assault, meant to disturb and provoke. Among his plays *Le Balcon (The Balcony)* is his most expansive view of the world as he saw it: a brothel dubbed the House of Illusions in which fantasies of power and control are enacted as a violent revolution explodes outside. The play blurs all distinctions between the real and the imagined, social and psychic, real life and theatricality in such a way that an audience has no choice but to confront the imperatives of power and illusion that define our lives. In fundamental ways *The Balcony* is a play about plays and the ways in which the theater is the ruling metaphor for the human condition.

Born in Paris in 1910, Genet was abandoned at the age of seven months to the public welfare system, then raised by a carpenter and his family in France's

Morvan region. Genet knew nothing about his origin until he was given his birth certificate when he turned 21, which indicated that his mother, Camille Gabrielle Genet, was single and a governess (she died in 1918). His father was not named. According to Sartre's biographical account, Genet was a good student and member of the church choir who was caught stealing from his foster mother's purse and called a thief. Considering the charge unjust Genet responded by taking pride in the designation and becoming a thief in earnest. Sartre regarded this as a defining existential decision. Genet himself analyzed his development by stating that "Abandoned by my family, I found it natural to aggravate this fact by the love of males, and that love by stealing, and stealing by crime, or complicity with crime. Thus I decisively repudiated a world that had repudiated me." Confined to the correctional facility of Mettray as a teenager, Genet joined the army in 1929 to gain an early release. In 1936, after serving in Syria, Morocco, and Algeria, he deserted and traveled as a vagabond through Italy, Yugoslavia, Austria, Czechoslovakia, Poland, Nazi Germany, and Belgium, surviving as a male prostitute, pimp, smuggler, and petty thief. Returning to France in 1937 he spent the next seven years in and out of prisons, where he began to write. Reading the "idiotic and self-pitying" poems of a fellow convict, Genet "declared that I was able to make poems just as good. They dared me and I wrote the *Condamné à Mort*," an elegy to the memory of a convict executed for murder. A powerful lyric combining Genet's characteristic reversal of conventional morality and sanctification of the sordid and profane, the poem was published at Genet's expense and came to the attention of Jean Cocteau, who became the first of Genet's literary mentors and served as his advocate. Four narrative works followed—*Notre Dame des fleurs* (1943; *Our Lady of the Flowers*), *Miracle de la rose* (1946; *The Miracle of the Rose*), *Pompes funèbres* (1947; *Funeral Rites*), and *Querelle de Brest* (1947; *Querelle of Brest*)—all published clandestinely and in limited editions. They have been described by scholar Martin Esslin as "erotic fantasies of a prisoner, the daydreams of a solitary outcast of society, who is resolved to live up to the pattern he feels society has imposed upon him" and "a curious mixture of lyrical beauty and the most sordid subject-matter." With the exception of *Journal du voleur* (1949; *The Thief's Journal*), his fictionalized memoir, Genet concentrated almost exclusively on drama for the remainder of his career. He died in 1986.

Genet's first work for the stage was *Haute Surveillance* (*Deathwatch*), begun in 1943, published in 1947, and first performed in 1949. Set in a prison cell, the play explores the perverse hierarchy among the convicts based on their crimes and their acceptance (or rejection) of the core truths revealed about their identity and integrity. Genet's first produced play, *Les Bonnes* (*The Maids*), in 1947, is based on the actual murder of an upper-class mistress by her female servants. In Genet's treatment two sisters assume the roles of sadistic employer and submissive maid to enact ritualized fantasies of power and control. When their attempts to kill their real mistress fail, the sisters must satisfy themselves with killing her image, and the play ends with one sister, assuming the role of mistress, drinking the poisoned tea prepared for her actual employer. As Genet biographer Edmund White has commented, "*The Maids* represents a real departure in modern theater: a new interest in ritual, exalted language, and the portrayal of psychological violence that may or may not stand for a veiled political struggle." *The Maids* shows Genet moving beyond the prison setting of his previous work and expanding his exploration of sexuality and power in the context of the illusory nature of social roles and the relationship between fantasy and reality.

Genet's most ambitious treatment of these themes is his third play, *The Balcony*, first published in 1956 and first performed in London in 1957. As the play opens a man dressed in the religious vestments of a bishop addresses a "penitent" wearing a lace dressing gown and another woman. The décor of the room suggests a sacristy, though a mirror reflects an unmade bed and an armchair on which pants, a shirt, and a jacket have been placed. The audience only gradually realizes that the woman is Madame Irma, proprietress of the Grand Balcony, a brothel catering to her customer's various fantasies; the penitent is one of her prostitutes; and the bishop is a gas worker. Madame Irma's "house of illusions" supplies the settings, furnishing, costumes, actors, and actresses for her customers to enjoy sexual fulfillment in the power scenarios they crave. Three other tableaux are enacted in other rooms. A judge crawls on his belly toward a half-naked woman who instructs him to lick her extended foot. Beside them a male employee of the brothel named Arthur is attired as an executioner to carry out the judge's sentence on the "thief." In another room a client playing a general rides his horse, played by a woman in black corset and stockings. In another room a client acts out his fantasy as a tramp, studying his reflection in three mirrors and completing the illusion by donning a wig with fleas. In all the scenarios images of power are enacted with an emphasis on the externals—costume, makeup, setting—that create the illusion of authority and command. Genet stressed that his play was not a satire but the "glorification of the Image and the Reflection." According to the playwright, authority derives from externals wielded by those in power and the complicity of those without. The play shows, in Genet's words, that "power cannot do without theatricality. . . . Power shelters behind some kind of theatricality, whether it is in China, the Soviet Union, England or France. . . . There is only one place in the world where theatricality does not hide power and that is in the theater." Theatricality as the essence of power is the basis for Madame Irma's establishment, as she clarifies in the play's fifth scene in which she discusses her operation with one of her employees, Carmen. Justifying her elaborate staging of her customer's fantasies, Irma explains:

> They all want everything to be as true as possible. . . . Minus something indefinable, so that it won't be true. . . . Carmen, it was I who decided to call my establishment a house of illusions, but I'm only the manager.

Each individual, when he rings the bell and enters, brings his own scenario, perfectly thought out. My job is merely to rent the hall and furnish the props, actors, and actresses. My dear, I've succeeded in lifting it from the ground—do you see what I mean? I unloosed it long ago and it's flying. I cut the moorings.

Breaking the illusion that Madame Irma assiduously labors to create are sounds of machine-gun fire and explosions signaling the revolution that is taking place outside, threatening both the operation of the Grand Balcony and the authority figures who play such a prominent role in the customers' fantasies. The importance of those fantasies are underscored by Irma's lover, the Chief of Police, who arrives to inquire whether anyone has requested to play him, the confirmation of his secure hold on power in the public's imagination. Irma disappoints him with the news that "your function isn't noble enough to offer dreamers an image that would console them. . . . You have to resign yourself to the fact that your image does not yet conform to the liturgies of the brothel."

The play's sixth scene, the only one that takes place outside the Grand Balcony, shows the revolutionaries who are intent on challenging the ruling authority figures and thereby breaking their psychic hold on the citizenry. Yet even they are unable to proceed without their own substitute images of power. Roger, a leader of the revolt, is shown arguing with his lover, Chantal, one of Madame Irma's girls who has left because she could no longer stand playing her assigned roles and wants instead to live in so-called reality. The revolutionaries, however, claim that Chantal is needed for their cause as a symbol representing liberty, self-sacrifice, and heroism. Having played her parts in the house of illusion, Chantal is offered but another instead of the reality she craves. Rather than overthrowing the symbols of power that coerce and repress the revolutionaries are simply replacing them with other images equally unreal. Chantal accepts her new role knowing that by doing so she not only must give up her lover but her life as well. "In order to fight against an image," Roger bitterly realizes, "Chantal has frozen into an image. The fight is no longer taking place in reality, but in a closed field. . . . It's the combat of allegories. None of us know any longer why we revolted." The unbreakable hold of images on the populace is made clear when, after the palace has been blown up and the queen and her administration have perished, a surviving Court Envoy, to halt the revolution, requests that Madame Irma take on the role of the queen herself and her customers should play their roles as bishop, judge, and general in "reality" to reassure the populace that the symbols of authority and power remain intact. On the balcony Irma and her clients, appropriately attired, show themselves to the crowd. After a Beggar shouts, "God Save the Queen," Chantal appears on the balcony and is shot dead, signaling the defeat of the revolution.

In the play's final scene all retreat back inside the Grand Balcony to review the parts they have played and the challenge of actually becoming the people they have pretended to be. The Chief of Police arrives confident that now with his victory over the revolutionaries someone will want to impersonate him. To assist he is having a giant mausoleum built. "I want my image to be both legendary and supreme," he asserts. "I have been advised to appear in the form of a gigantic phallus." By completing the link between sex and power upon which the Grand Balcony depends, the Chief of Police will not be "the hundred-thousandth-reflection-within-a-reflection in a mirror, but the One and Only, into whom a hundred thousand want to merge." His prediction is realized when Madame Irma announces that Roger has arrived and asked to impersonate the Chief of Police. Donning the Chief's uniform, Roger proceeds with the scenario of empowerment, declaring that "I've got a right to lead the character I've chosen to the very limit of his destiny . . . no, of mine . . . of merging his destiny with mine." In a gesture both of violation and self-sacrifice, Roger subverts the expected scenario by castrating himself. The Chief of Police, watching the enactment, is, however, delighted by what he sees: "Well played. He thought he had me. . . . Though my image be castrated in every brothel in the world, I remain intact." Rather than destroying the Chief of Police's power and authority Roger has secured them by his action, a martyr to authority's total control. The Chief of Police then descends into the tomb he has constructed claiming, "I've won the right to go and sit and wait for two thousand years. You! Watch me live and die. For posterity. . . . I've won!" The play closes with a burst of machine-gun fire suggesting that the revolution has recommenced and the cycle of order and disorder has resumed. Madame Irma is left alone readying her establishment for the next day's business. "In a little while," she says, "I'll have to start all over again . . . put all the lights on again. . . . Dress up . . . ah, the disguises! Distribute roles again . . . assume my own." She then addresses the audience directly: "You must now go home, where everything—you can be quite sure—will be falser than here. . . . You must go now. You'll leave by the right, through the alley. . . . It's morning already."

In Genet's phantasmagorical allegorical fable, the distinctions between substance and shadow, reality and illusion, power and pretense are subverted. William Shakespeare's contention that all the world's a stage is underscored in the distorted mirror world of *The Balcony*. Different from Samuel Beckett's *reductio absurdum*, Genet offers a proliferation of fantasies, a dizzying performance in which the disorientation is primary. All the components of the theatrical experience in *The Balcony* unite to drive home the point that role-playing and our susceptibility to illusion are inescapable. Instead of Beckett's minimalist void, Genet's version of the absurd is, in Sartre's phrase, a "whirligig of reality and illusion."

ACCIDENTAL DEATH OF AN ANARCHIST

96

(1970)

by Dario Fo

Next to such esteemed Nobel laureates as Samuel Beckett and Luigi Pirandello, Mr. Fo seems like an alien, even an accidental choice. His response was characteristic: He said that to be in their company gave him "a certain sensation." One can imagine that the sensation was a combination of disbelief and pride, seasoned by a hearty Fovian laugh, an awareness of the irony of it all. By recognizing Mr. Fo, the Swedish Academy expands the boundaries of literature and underscores the immediacy of theater. It legitimizes the world of performance and recognizes the contribution of comedy, and, in particular, of political satire. All outspoken monologuists, clowns and cartoonists should be aware of the importance of the award. Jonathan Swift takes his position in the pantheon with Shakespeare.

—Mel Gussow, "The Not-So-Accidental Recognition of an Anarchist,"
New York Times, October 15, 1997

Woody Allen famously asserted "Humorists always sit at the children's table." The awarding of the Nobel Prize in literature to Dario Fo in 1997 was certainly an elevation of the comedian to the grown-ups' table, bestowing respectability and gravitas to a playwright who has relished his role as jester-provocateur. Justifying the choice, the citation of Swedish Royal Academy stated:

> Fo emulates the jesters of the Middle Ages in scourging authority and upholding the dignity of the downtrodden. For many years, Fo has been performed all over the world, perhaps more than any other contemporary dramatist, and his influence has been considerable. He, if anyone, merits the description of jester in the true meaning of the word. With a blend of laughter and gravity he opens our eyes to abuses and injustices in society. . . . Fo's strength is in the creation of texts that simultaneously amuse, engage, and provide perspectives.

The Swedish Academy's recognition has highlighted the considerable achievement of Fo, long regarded as "Europe's most popular political satirist." In Fo the possibilities of comedy as a powerful instrument of truth have been renewed and revitalized. "Clowns," Fo has asserted, "are grotesque blasphemers against all our pieties. That's why we need them. They're our alter egos." Fo's characteristic synthesis of clowning and serious social satire is best expressed by his most performed play, *Morte accidentale di un anarchico* (*Accidental Death of an Anarchist*). The play and Fo's career make clear that to include the jester at the grown-ups' table, expect some broken plates and shattered etiquette.

Fo was born in 1926 in the northern Italian village of San Giano. His father was a stationmaster; his mother grew up on a farm where Fo spent his childhood vacations. The playwright would later cite his grandfather's storytelling ability as a significant influence. Another came when the family moved in 1936 to Porto Valtraglia, on the shores of Lake Maggiore. In his Nobel acceptance speech Fo paid tribute to the *fabulatori* he learned from there: "They were the old storytellers, the master glass-blowers who taught me and other children the craftsmanship, the art, of spinning fantastic yarns. We would listen to them, bursting with laughter—laughter that would stick in our throats as the tragic allusion that surmounted each sarcasm would dawn on us." In 1940 Fo began commuting daily to Milan to study at the Brera Art Academy. In 1944, after Mussolini was ousted from Rome and retreated to Salò, on Lake Garda, as his new capital, Fo was conscripted into the army of Mussolini's Salò Republic. He deserted and spent several months in hiding in an attic storeroom. After the war ended Fo resumed his studies of art and architecture in Milan. During his daily journeys to Milan he began to entertain fellow commuters and his classmates with the tall tales he had heard in his childhood and stories and songs of his own. His skill at performing improvisational monologues caught the attention of Franco Parenti, actor and manager of a local theater company, and in 1950 Fo began performing in the company's reviews. A fellow company member was the actress Franca Rame, whom Fo married in 1954. She would become his lifelong collaborator, whom Fo called "Mrs. Nobel" after receiving news of his award.

A series of Fo's monologues were aired on Italian radio in 1951–52, and his first plays—*Il dito nell'occhio* (1953; A poke in the eye) and *I sani da legare* (1954; Madhouse for the Sane), cutting and uproarious social satires—gained Fo notice as a controversial and provocative playwright. In 1958 husband and wife established the theater company, Compagnia Fo-Rame with Fo as writer, actor, director, and stage designer. The company performed both Fo's farces and one-man shows, called *guillarate*, in which Fo relied on improvisation and audience participation in the manner of medieval Italy's roving street performers whose techniques were first brought to the stage by the commedia dell'arte troupes in the 16th century. The most famous of Fo's *guillarata* is *Mistero buffo* (1969), a burlesque of the medieval mystery plays that mixes broad physical comedy and slapstick with stinging attacks on religious and governmental targets. In 1968, after considerable success on stage and television, Fo and Rame formed a new troupe, Nuova Scena, under the sponsorship of the Italian Communist Party. "We were tired of being the jesters of the bourgeoisie," Fo recalled, "on whom our criticisms had now the effect of an alka-seltzer, so we decided to become the jesters of proletariat." Fo's subsequent plays became more explicitly political, ridiculing the church, army, and big business and performed mainly for working-class audiences. Fo's subsequent burlesque of the Communist Party, *L'operatio conosce 300 parole, il padrone 100, per questo lui è il padrone* (1969; *The Worker Knows 300 Words, the Boss 1000; That's Why He Is the Boss*), led to the breakup of Nuova Scena and the formation of a new, independent company in a warehouse in a working-class area of Milan, where *Accidental Death of an Anarchist* was first performed in 1970.

The play deals with one of the most contentious and defining events in modern Italian history. Italy in the late 1960s was in turmoil, under assault from radicals on both the right and the left in a series of increasingly violent strikes and protests. On December 12, 1969, a bomb went off in the Banca Nazionale dell'Agricoltura in Milan's Piazza Fontana. Sixteen were killed, and 90 were injured. The incident, the first of its kind in Italy on such a scale, targeting innocent bystanders, signaled a decisive escalation in violence that came to represent a monstrous benchmark. "The degeneration of our democratic system began with Piazza Fontana," Italian philosopher Norberto Bobbio asserted, while journalist and author Giorgio Bocca called the bombing the event "which changed the lives of generations." Outrage and retaliation precipitated a rush to judgment as police quickly announced that an anarchist group was responsible. Among the suspects seized, Giuseppe Pinelli, a railroad worker, was subjected to 72 hours of interrogation before falling to his death from a fourth-floor window of the Milan police station. Officials ruled it an accident, but contradictions and inconsistencies in testimony of those involved called their assessment into question exposing a police and judicial cover-up of the truth. Subsequent investigations determined that the bombing was most likely the work of right-wing extremists in Italy's military and secret service agencies meant to discredit the Italian Communist Party, and that the innocent Pinelli was pushed to his death after being manhandled and possibly tortured.

Fo has explained the genesis of his play dealing with the incident as follows:

> In spring 1970, some comrades who attended our plays . . . asked us to write a full-length play about the Milan bombs and the Pinelli killing which would treat the causes and the political consequences. The reason for this request was the terrifying lack of information surrounding the

problem. Once the initial shock had passed, the press fell silent. . . . there was an expectation that "light would be shed," that people should wait, and not create mayhem. . . . This was not enough.

Accidental Death of an Anarchist challenged the authorized version of the incident. "It is essential to cause mayhem," Fo has stated, "and with every means available, so that people who are forgetful, who read little and badly, and who read only those things which come easily to hand, should get to know how the state organized the massacre and controlled the mourning, the anger, the distribution of medals to orphans and widows, the funerals with policeman lining up and taking the salute." Fo based his play on material gathered from the two official inquiries, which are quoted, sometimes verbatim, as dialogue in the play. His means "To unleash the comedy and satire" is the invented character of the Maniac, who is seen entering the window of police headquarters at the beginning of the play. The Maniac, based on the disrupting iconoclastic Arlecchino, or Harlequin, in commedia dell'arte, is, in Fo's words, an "anarchic character *ante litteram*, who has no sympathy with current moral rules, the rules of authority . . . a free spirit, a prevaricating, violent and scurrilous outsider who continually provokes the audience." Through "the logic of wild paradox," the Maniac "attempts to unhinge the logic of sane people. So as it happens the real madmen turn out to be the 'normal' folk."

The Maniac has entered the office of Inspector Bertozzo, who confronts the intruder with his file in which his compulsion to pass himself off as others is documented. The Maniac's defense is a zany stream of doubletalk displaying his considerable verbal dexterity, which exasperates the ponderous and plodding Bertozzo. Escorted out of the office the Maniac manages to return alone to answer a phone call from another Inspector, whom he insults pretending to be Bertozzo. From the caller the Maniac learns of the imminent arrival of a judge from Rome charged with reexamining police conduct in the death in custody of the anarchist and bombing suspect. The Maniac decides to pass himself off as the judge, and the scene ends with the return of Bertozzo, cluelessly assaulted by the enraged Inspector whom the Maniac had insulted over the phone.

The second scene shifts to the Inspector's office on the fourth floor where the anarchist had been interrogated, with the Maniac playing the judge and summoning the Superintendent. Indignant over such a command, the Superintendent enters, becoming unctuously deferential when he learns that a high-ranking judge is on the scene. The Maniac then asks the officers to reenact their interrogation with the anarchist, and in the process they reveal that they had fabricated evidence to frame him and force a confession. Fearing that they are to be made scapegoats the officers are consoled by the Maniac, who explains that he intends to help them devise a more plausible cover-up. The Maniac suggests that instead of abusing the anarchist they offered him compassion and sympathy. Because the officers played with trains as children, the

Maniac suggests, the railway anarchist was received warmly. When the Superintendent balks, however, at the Maniac's suggestion that they joined voices with the anarchist in a sing-along, the Maniac responds by saying:

> Do you have any idea what people out there think of you? That you are liars and scum. Who do you think is ever going to believe you again? Apart from the judge who called off the inquiry, of course. And do you know basically why people don't believe you? Because your version of the facts is well, it's complete crap for one thing, and it lacks any human understanding or warmth. . . . The public would weep with joy and shout your names from the rooftops at hearing such a story! So please, do yourself a favor . . . Sing!

The act closes with the Maniac and the officers rehearsing a number of possible songs.

Act 2 begins with the officers still singing and the Maniac resuming his inquiry that underscores the various inconsistencies in the official version of the incident: the anarchist's dubious motivation for suicide, why the window in the office was open on one of the coldest nights of the year, how a policeman could claim that he had grabbed the anarchist to prevent his fall, pulling off a shoe, when the body on the ground was fully shod. The various absurd rationalizations offered both from the officers and from the ingeniously nonsensical Maniac are interrupted by the arrival of a journalist to interview the Inspector. The Maniac, donning a disguise of eye patch, wooden leg, and false mustache, helps the Inspector fend off the journalist's probing questions regarding the anarchist's death and the bombing investigation. The interview is interrupted by the arrival of Bertozzo, who instantly recognizes the Maniac but is prevented from unmasking him in front of the journalist by his colleagues. In desperation Bertozzo handcuffs them all before exposing the Maniac's identity. The Maniac responds by claiming to have recorded everything and threatens to release the tape to the press. The lights go out, and when they come on again the Maniac has disappeared. In the courtyard people gather around a body that has inexplicably fallen from a window, prompting the officers to come up with invented and ridiculous versions of what must have happened. A bearded man (instantly recognizable as the actor who had played the Maniac) enters and is set upon by the police. They learn that he is the real high court judge who has come to conduct the inquiry into the supposed accidental death of the anarchist. Fo's final stage directions read: "The four policemen look unwell . . . Slow fade to black."

With comic brio and inventiveness Fo's play exposes authority's "new clothes" while causing officialdom and the powerful to slip on as many banana peels as possible. Fo takes up comedy's traditional role as a scourge to the powerful. His version of the farce becomes an instrument of political action and truthtelling, with its mayhem servings as both purge and curative.

THE HOSTAGE

(1958)   *by Brendan Behan*

It has been suggested that in The Hostage *Brendan Behan is trying to "open up the stage." This is an understatement. He would like to hack the stage to bits, crunch the proscenium across his knee, trample the scenery underfoot, and throw debris wildly in all directions. Like his various prototypes—Jack Falstaff, Harpo Marx, W. C. Fields, and Dylan Thomas—Behan is pure Libido on a rampage, mostly in its destructive phase; and if he has not yet achieved the Dionysian purity of those eminent anarchists, he is still a welcome presence in our sanctimonious times.*

—Robert Brustein, "Libido at Large," in *Seasons of Discontent*

Like his fellow Irishman Oscar Wilde who declared that he put his genius into his life and only his talent into his work, Brendan Behan invested his genius on his public and pub persona as the brawling, much-quoted Dubliner on a bender, obscuring a considerable talent as a dramatist. By his early death at the age of 41 from alcohol-induced diabetes in 1964, Behan had become a legend, notorious for his drunken antics, youthful activities in the Irish Republican Army and imprisonments, defined by squandered promise rather than for actual accomplishment. As fellow writer Flann O'Brien remarked, Behan "is much more a player than a playwright." Books on Behan fall into two groups: recollections and critical studies of his works, with the former considerably outpacing the latter. As a dramatist Behan deserves better recognition for his achievement and influence. Like Sean O'Casey, who served as a major influence, Behan would help revitalize Irish theater by universalizing aspects of Irish history and Dublin slum life. Again, like O'Casey, Behan extended his plays' realism with experimental innovations. Like Wilde and George Bernard Shaw before him, Behan made his reputation in Britain as an iconoclast, mounting a full-frontal attack on literary conventions and the sacred cows of mainstream society. A product of his nothing-is-sacred attitude, *The Hostage* is Behan's masterpiece, one of the earliest and best examples of the theater of the absurd in English that provided a new direction and new possibility for the socially realistic drama that dominated the English stage during the post–World War II period. With Behan there is an alternative to the constricted minimalism of playwrights such as John Osborne and Harold Pinter and a precedent for the dazzling inventiveness of subsequent playwrights such as Tom Stoppard and Caryl Churchill.

Brendan Behan's background is central to the persona he adopted and the values and attitudes that dominate his works, which are all drawn from his personal experiences. Behan was born in Dublin in 1923 during the civil war following the Irish War of Independence, and his life would from the start be dominated by an association with the Republican cause that opposed the partition of Ireland and allegiance to the British Crown, which were the conditions for Irish autonomy in 1922. Behan's father, a Dublin house painter, was a Republican prisoner in Kilmainham Gaol at the time of his son's birth. His mother had been previously married to a veteran of the Easter Rising of 1916 who died in the influenza epidemic of 1918. Despite his subsequent depiction of growing up in working-class squalor that suited a more proletarian self-image, Behan actually was raised in a highly cultured home. From his mother Behan acquired his Catholicism, a fine voice, and a theatrical personality; from his father he inherited an irreverent agnosticism, exposure to literature, first encountering the works of William Butler Yeats, John Millington Synge, and O'Casey in his father's library, and sympathy with the aspirations of Irish nationalism and the working class. Behan's formal education in Catholic schools ended at age 14 when he apprenticed as a house painter. Having joined the Fianna Éireann, the Republican youth organization from which the IRA recruited members, at the age of eight, Behan embraced the cause of militant nationalism, and in 1939, when he was 16, he set out on a one-man bombing mission to blow up a British warship in Liverpool. Arrested for possession of explosives, Behan was sentenced to imprisonment for two years in a reformatory in Borstal, England. His experiences would be vividly recounted in his memoir *Borstal Boy* (1958). After his release he was arrested again, in Dublin in 1942, in a drunken shootout with police. Serving three years of a 14-year sentence in Dublin's Mountjoy Prison and the Curragh Military Camp, Behan acquired the experiences he would draw on for his prison drama *The Quare Fellow*, while becoming proficient in Irish through the instruction of a fellow prisoner. During his imprisonment Behan published his first significant prose, wrote his first play, *The Landlady*, based on the eccentric life of his grandmother, and decided to pursue a literary career. On his release in 1946 Behan resumed work as a house painter while mixing with the Dublin literary community, publishing poetry and short stories in literary periodicals.

The first public performance of Behan's dramatic work occurred in 1952 when a producer of Radio Éireann asked him to write a comedy series that became the two playlets, *Moving Out* and *The Garden Party*, based on Behan's family's experiences when his family was relocated from its tenement rooms to a new suburban housing estate. He followed these by work on a play based on an execution that had occurred while he was in prison. Initially called "The Twisting of Another Rope," it became *The Quare Fellow*, first performed in Ireland in 1954 and in London by Joan Littlewood's avant-garde Theatre Workshop in 1956, two weeks after the legendary first performance of Osborne's *Look Back in Anger.* The play brought Behan his first acclaim and identification as one of the new dramatists—the "Angry Young Men" or "working-class realists"—who were revolutionizing British theater. Critic Kenneth Tynan famously praised Behan and *The Quare Fellow* by declaring that "It is Ireland's sacred duty to send over every few years a playwright who will save the English theater from inarticulate dumbness." Behan's prison drama takes place during the hours leading up to the execution of the title character, a convicted murderer who never appears onstage. It is striking in its challenge to conventional staging by employing a chorus of various inmates instead of a central protagonist and a dramatic structure that avoids or undercuts any expected crisis or climax. Behan instead offers what has been described as "absolute realism," with a closely observed depiction of the prison routine and a convincingly authentic characterization of inmates who had never before been brought to life on an English stage. The play offers a chilling portrait of the dehumanization of prison life and indifference to suffering and violence, made particularly striking by the play's mordant humor in which paradox and comic reversals expose the absurd values of the prison community.

Behan responded to his notoriety from the success of *The Quare Fellow* by the drunken antics that would make him a celebrity. Back in Dublin in the spring of 1957 he was approached by Gael Linn, a society promoting Irish language and culture, for a new work. As he had for *The Quare Fellow*, Behan based his new play on actual events, drawing on the case of a British soldier kidnapped during the IRA's recent "Border Campaign" of reprisals conducted in Northern Ireland. Although the soldier was eventually released unharmed, Behan later recalled: "The incident moved me and remained in my mind because I thought it was tragic for young fellows from England to be stuck in Northern Ireland." Written in Irish, *An Giall* was first performed in Dublin in 1958 before Joan Littlewood asked Behan to translate it into English for the Theatre Workshop. *The Hostage* emerged not as a literal translation of *An Giall* but as a radical reworking of Behan's formerly more naturalistic drama into a much more experimental, absurdist work. Although the story line of a British soldier held in a Dublin tenement to be killed in retaliation for an Irishman being executed in Belfast is the same, *The Hostage* adds the songs, dances, bawdy humor, and other elements that function in the manner of Bertolt Brecht to alienate the audience and call attention to the theatricality rather than the verisimilitude of the performance. The play was thereby transformed into its most original and striking feature: the mixture of a serious story with a farcical, music-hall style.

Set in "an old house in Dublin that has seen better days," *The Hostage* repopulates the setting for O'Casey's Dublin Trilogy—*THE PLOUGH AND THE STARS*, *Juno and the Paycock*, and *The Shadow of a Gunman*—for an updated reassessment of Irish identity and history. As critic Benedict Kiely has asserted, the play's rundown lodging house that doubles as a brothel is "heroic Ireland down in the dumps; it is the world in a mess." As the play opens "pimps, prostitutes, decayed gentlemen and their visiting 'friends' are dancing a wild Irish jig." Left alone, the caretaker, Pat, a formerly committed Irish nationalist and IRA soldier, and his consort, Meg, hear the sounds of "an off-key bagpiper," Monsewer, the addled-brained owner of the tenement who, as Pat explains, "has taken it into his head to play the Dead March for the boy in Belfast Jail when they hand him in the morning . . . for his I.R.A. activities." Undercutting the play's opening exuberant hilarity is the play's dark catalyst: the impending execution that demands retribution. Monsewer is an Anglo-Irishman who "converted" to the Irish cause, a veteran of the Easter Rising of 1916 who continues soldiering on, absurdly commanding his "troops" of outcasts who occupy his lodging house. Pat, who plays along with Monsewer's delusions, asserts privately to Meg that "This is nineteen-fifty-eight, and the days of the heroes are over this thirty-five years past. Long over, finished and done with. The I.R.A. and the War of Independence are as dead as the Charleston." As Pat and Meg squabble over Irish history and the present state of Ireland Behan introduces the core theme of the play: the nature of Irish identity and the disjunction between high ideals and sordid reality. Although Meg eulogizes the condemned young Irishman in Belfast for having done "his duty as a member of the I.R.A.," proving that "the old cause is never dead," Pat is far more cynical and fatalistic, although not immune to nostalgia over his own past actions during the War of Independence and the Irish Civil War. The play juxtaposes the defining myths of modern Irish identity—heroic blood sacrifice and a commitment to the "old cause" of Irish nationalism—with the actuality of life in a brothel in which the only Irish speaker is the former Englishman Monsewer, the self-righteous Miss Gilchrist and the drunken Mulleady pray for divine forgiveness for their "fall from grace," while continuing to fondle each other, and the servant girl Teresa is deemed safer working in a brothel than in her respectable position with "a clerical student in the house." Underscoring the contrasts between the Irish self-image and reality, between the serious and the comic, dialogue is interrupted by the characters breaking into songs that ironically comment on the proceedings. Act 1 concludes with the hostage, Leslie, a British soldier who is to be executed in retaliation for the prisoner in Belfast, led in by two IRA guards, and all sing:

SOLDIER There's no place on earth like the world,
There's no place wherever you be.

ALL   There's no place on earth like the world,
    That's straight up and take it from me.

WOMEN   Never throw stones at your mother,
    You'll be sorry for it when she's dead.

MEN   Never throw stones at your mother,
    Throw bricks at your father instead.

MONSEWER   The South and the north poles are parted,

MEG   Perhaps it is all for the best.

PAT   Till the H-bomb will bring them together,

ALL   And there we will let matters rest.

Act 2 develops the relationship between Leslie and the inhabitants, most notably in his romance with Teresa. In a comic echoing of Romeo and Juliet's situation, Leslie and Teresa come together despite differences of religion and the feud that has divided their two countries. The play opposes a persistent political death wish and paralysis by the past with sheer human vitality expressed in the songs and dances and, most especially, in Teresa and Leslie's passion. "The two young people are concerned with life and the present," critic Ted E. Boyle has noted. "Everyone else in the brothel is concerned with death and the past. In the midst of unimaginable sterility—commercial sex, homosexuality, destructive chauvinism—the young people assert life. If Behan had intended a 'modern morality play,' the moral he intended seems aptly expressed by Meg: 'What's wrong with a bit of comfort on a dark night?'" The counterstroke to this comfort is sounded when Leslie is informed that he is to be shot if the Belfast prisoner is executed. The act ends, however, undercutting any sympathy for Leslie's fate with his song:

I am a happy English lad, I love my royal-ty,
And if they were short a penny of a packet of fags,
Now they'd only have to ask me.
I love old England in the east, I love her in the west,
From Jordan's streams to Derry's Walls,
I love old England best.
I love my dear old Notting Hill, wherever I may roam,
But I wish the Irish and the niggers and the wogs,
Were kicked out and sent back home.

Tensions mount as the execution approaches in the third act, and the characters begin to realize that they are all condemned by pointless ideals into an absurd situation that they can neither control nor change. Leslie's death as payback serves no purpose other than to prove that "an Englishman can die as well as an Irishman or anybody else in the world." The pathos of Leslie's situation, however, is undermined by slapstick as police burst into the house and in the confusion shoot and kill the hostage they intended to rescue. Teresa rejects Pat's offered consolation ("It's no one's fault. Nobody meant to kill him.") with her own accusation and eulogy:

> It wasn't the Belfast Jail or the Six Counties that was troubling you, but your lost youth and your crippled leg. He died in a strange land, and at home he had no one. I'll never forget you, Leslie, till the end of time.

Teresa's sentiment collides with the play's concluding vision of the resurrected Leslie singing the play's final song:

> The bells of hell,
> Go ting-a-ling-a-ling,
> For you but not for me,
> Oh death, where is thy sting-a-ling-a-ling?
> Or grave they victory?
> If you meet the undertaker,
> Or the young man from the Pru,
> Get a pint with what's left over,
> Now I'll say good-bye to you.

In the absurdist calculus of *The Hostage* sing-along trumps sting-a-ling as death and the intractable cycle of destructive violence that has ruled Irish history are overcome both by an irrepressible life wish and a dramatic vision that liberates by the sheer force of its comic invention.

THE HEIDI CHRONICLES

(1988)

by Wendy Wasserstein

I know The Heidi Chronicles *was a controversial play among many feminists. It was a play where some people thought I had sold out, because she had a baby at the end and I was saying that all women must have babies—run out and adopt a Panamanian tonight! I know that this happened, but from my point of view, what's political is that this play exists. What's political is that we can talk about this play that's about us—like it, don't like it; it's there, it exists, and that's the forward motion.*

—Wendy Wasserstein, *The Playwright's Art: Conversations with Contemporary American Dramatists*

Wendy Wasserstein's *The Heidi Chronicles* is an insightful tour of 25 years in the life cycle of the baby boom generation. It is more, however, than a time capsule. Wasserstein succeeded in making stage worthy the perspectives of college-educated women who came of age in the late 1960s as feminism was beginning to redefine and reshape gender assumptions. She drew both comedy and pathos from these women's attempts to reconcile the demands of professional careers with their traditional roles as wives and mothers. Prior to Wasserstein plays had neither treated these issues nor created her brand of serious comedy. "Serious issues and serious people can be quite funny," Wasserstein once stated. Before the feminist movement most women onstage, as in life, were cast solely in a supporting role. "In Wendy's plays women saw themselves portrayed in a way they hadn't been onstage before—wittily, intelligently, and seriously at the same time," André Bishop, artistic director of Lincoln Center Theater has observed. "We take that for granted now, but it was not the case 25 years ago. She was a real pioneer." An acute observer of the zeitgeist and the psychic and emotional dilemmas it created, Wasserstein brought women's intellectual and emotional development to center stage, while finding humor and compassion in the knottiest problems of gender and identity. With *The Heidi Chronicles* she became the first woman ever to win a Tony Award for best play. It also received the Pulitzer Prize and the award for best new play from the New York Drama Critics Circle. Heidi Holland, its protagonist, is the prototype for all the Carrie Bradshaws and Bridget Joneses who would follow in novels, films, and plays. *The Heidi Chronicles* is both the defining play of Wasserstein's art and for the generation it celebrates and criticizes.

The Heidi Chronicles and all of Wasserstein's work, as she has freely admitted, draw on aspects of her own life. "My plays tend to be autobiographical or come out of something that's irking me," she explained, "and it's got to irk me long enough for me to commit to spend all that time writing and then turn it into a play." Wasserstein was born in Brooklyn in 1950. Her father was a prosperous textile manufacturer and the inventor of velveteen; her mother was an amateur dancer. Named for the character in J. M. Barrie's *Peter Pan*, Wasserstein attended theater regularly, although she also was struck by the something missing in the Broadway plays she saw. "I remember going to them and thinking," she recalled, "I really like this, but where are the girls?" Although fascinated by the theater Wasserstein did not begin to write for it until, while attending Mount Holyoke College, she was persuaded by a friend to enroll in a writing class at nearby Smith College so they could take advantage of shopping possibilities in Northampton, Massachusetts. Wasserstein has credited the professor, Leonard Berkman, as "the first person who made me feel confident with my own voice." After graduating in 1971 with a bachelor's degree in history, Wasserstein became one of the first students in a new creative writing program at City College of the City University of New York that featured small classes with distinguished writers. Wasserstein studied with novelist Joseph Heller and playwright Israel Horovitz before receiving her master's degree in 1973. Her first produced work was her thesis, a play called *Any Woman Can't*. Unsure about her next step Wasserstein applied to both Columbia University's business school and the Yale School of Drama. Accepted by both, she opted for Yale, where she earned her master of fine arts degree in 1976.

Her first widely known play, *Uncommon Women and Others* (1977), grew from a one-act play she wrote at Yale. Involving a group of Mount Holyoke students who consider their relationships with men and their futures, it deals with the impact of the arrival of feminism on college campuses in the late 1960s and its dual legacy of liberation and guilt. Empowered, the women in Wasserstein's play are both torn between their career ambitions and expectations as wives and mother. As one of the characters pointedly summarizes their dilemma,

> God knows there is no security in marriage. You give up your anatomy, economic self-support, spontaneous creativity, and a helluva lot of energy trying to convert a male half-person into a whole person who will eventually stop draining you, so you can do your own work. And the alternative—hopping onto the corporate or professional ladder is just

as self-destructive. If you spend your life proving yourself, then you just become a man.

Wasserstein's following play, *Isn't It Romantic* (1981), grew out of her realization that many woman of her generation as they approached 30 were suddenly desperate for marriage at any cost. "Biological time bombs were going off all over Manhattan," she reported. "It was like, it's not wild and passionate, but it's *time.*" In a series of short scenes the play perceptively explores how and why women choose a husband, a career, or a lifestyle.

The Heidi Chronicles, her next major work, took shape in Wasserstein's mind from the image of a contemporary woman confessing her sense of frustration and unhappiness to an assembly of other women. The speaker became Dr. Heidi Holland, an art history professor, who finds herself adrift and isolated despite her generations' social gains and her successful, independent life. Wasserstein tells Heidi's story—how she got to her present dilemma—in a series of flashbacks from the late 1960s through the 1980s. The play opens in a lecture hall at Columbia in 1989 as the 40-year-old Heidi delivers a lecture on three accomplished women artists from the past—Sofonisba Anguissola, Clara Peeters, and Lilly Martin Spencer—who are virtually unknown today. An example of Spencer's works reminds Heidi of "One of those horrible high-school dances. And you sort of want to dance, and you sort of want to go home, and you sort of don't know what you want. So you hang around, a fading rose in an exquisitely detailed dress, waiting to see what might happen." Establishing a connection between artists and lecturer and the cost to women of achievement, the action flashes back to a high school dance in 1965 where the 16-year-old Heidi, paired with her best friend Susan Johnston, negotiates the complex gender dynamics of the "mixer." As Susan pursues a boy who can twist and smoke at the same time, Heidi retreats to read her copy of *Death Be Not Proud* and meets Peter Patrone. Observing, "You look so bored you must be bright," Peter, the second of the three recurring characters who serve as foils to Heidi, succeeds in getting Heidi out on the dance floor. The next scene is a 1968 Eugene McCarthy party for campaign volunteers in New Hampshire where Heidi, now a committed social activist, meets the supremely self-confident, already world-weary, radical journalist Scoop Rosenbaum, who sizes up the idealistic Heidi as "one of those true believers who didn't understand it was just a phase." Despite being irritated at Scoop's assaults on her convictions Heidi becomes his lover.

The next scene takes place in 1970 during a women's consciousness-raising session in a church basement in Ann Arbor, Michigan, where Heidi is visiting the ever-adaptable Susan, who has now embraced feminism. The other attendees are Fran, a 30-year-old lesbian, and 17-year-old Becky, who is living with her abusive boyfriend. Initially aloof and withdrawn, Heidi is drawn into their dialogue of empowerment and manages her own feminist epiphany about her relationship with Scoop. "The problem is me," she confesses. "I could make a better choice. I have an old friend, Peter, who I know would be a much better choice. But I keep allowing this guy to account for so much of what I think of myself. I allow him to make me feel valuable. And the bottom line is, I know what's wrong." In the next scene, set during a protest at the Chicago Art Institute in 1974 over the paucity of women artists represented, Peter, a medical intern, reveals that he is homosexual, while Heidi confesses that she is not involved with Scoop anymore. "I just like sleeping with him," Heidi explains. Scoop eventually marries, and the following scene takes place at his wedding reception in 1977 where he explains to Heidi his decision to marry someone less accomplished and demanding than Heidi:

> Let's say we married and I asked you to devote the, say next ten years of your life to me. To making me a home and a family and a life so secure that I could with some confidence go out into the world each day and attempt to get an "A." You'd say "No." You'd say "Why can't we be partners? Why can't we both go out into the world and get an "A?" And you'd be absolutely valid and correct.

He goes on to explain that his bride, Lisa, is not an "A+" like Heidi, "But I don't want to come home to an 'A+,' 'A-' maybe, but not 'A+.'" Scoop goes on to predict an unhappy life for Heidi because she expects too much from it. "If you aim for six and get six," he says, "everything will work out nicely. But if you aim for ten in all things and get six, you're going to be very disappointed. And, unfortunately, that's why you 'quality time' girls are going to be one generation of disappointed women. Interesting, exemplary, even sexy, but basically unhappy. The ones who open doors usually are."

Act 2 confirms Scoop's prediction. As the "Greed Is Good" 1980s descend, the generation that believed that it would change the world are shown changed by it, and the solidarity among women and their challenge to traditional gender roles recede in the face of increasing conformity and divisive competition to "have it all." The first scene, following another excerpt from Heidi's art lecture at Columbia in 1989, takes place in 1980 at a baby shower for Scoop's wife, Lisa, in the aftermath of the news of John Lennon's death and the symbolic end of the 1960s. Since Lisa and Scoop's wedding Heidi has lived for a number of years in Europe where she has left a man she was planning to marry to accept her position at Columbia. Scoop has gone from the *Liberated Earth News* to running the successful lifestyle magazine *Boomer*. Susan has taken a job as an executive of a television production company that "wanted someone with a feminist and business background. Targeting films for the twenty-five to twenty-nine-year-old female audience." Peter is being touted as "The Best Pediatrician in New York Under Forty."

In the next scene Heidi, Scoop, and Peter are reunited in a television panel discussion on the baby boom generation. Both men misrepresent themselves—Scoop, who is a womanizer, as the quintessential family man and Peter by dodging the truth about his homosexuality—while they shamelessly talk over Heidi and prevent her from discussing the issues that matter to her. The scene suggests that males continue to control the dialogue. Two years later, in 1984, Heidi has lunch with Susan at a trendy New York restaurant where her friend is too busy networking to engage seriously with the crucial issue that is troubling Heidi: "Susie, do you ever think that what makes you a person is also what keeps you from being a person?" Susan responds, "I'm sorry, honey, but you're too deep for me. By now I've been so many people, I don't know who I am. And I don't care." Asked to serve as a consultant on a situation comedy that Susan is developing exploring professional women in their 30s who "don't want to make the same mistakes we did," Heidi replies: "I don't think we made such big mistakes. And I don't want to see three gals on the town who do." For Susan feminism is a passé trend. As in the play's opening scene Susan's adaptability leads to success, while, increasingly, Heidi's high-minded principles leave her isolated and out-of-step.

The thematic core of the play is the next scene in which Heidi is the featured speaker at a luncheon for alumna of Miss Crain's School. Asked to address the topic "Women: Where Are We Going," she first offers a self-portrait as a woman who has it all—fulfilling career, marriage, and children—before denying any resemblance. Instead she compares herself to other women at an exercise class who seem to be competing with one another in a display of accomplishments and who make her feel inadequate and unhappy. "I don't blame the ladies in the locker room for how I feel," she concludes. "I don't blame any of us. We're all concerned, intelligent, good women. [*Pause*] It's just that I feel stranded. And I thought the whole point was that we wouldn't feel stranded. I thought the point was we were all in this together." The emotional core of the play occurs in the next scene, set on Christmas Eve 1987, as Heidi has come to tell Peter good-bye after having accepted a teaching position in the Midwest. She explains that she is leaving because she has no reason to stay, no life in New York because she has no love interest there. Peter is upset that Heidi in abandoning the emotional connections and kinship she has had with him, which is even more important to him now as a gay man in the age of AIDS. With so much death around him, Heidi's angst seems trivial in comparison. His accusation finds its target, and Heidi agrees to postpone becoming someone else and accept the consequences of her decisions.

A year later Scoop visits Heidi in her new apartment with the news that his settling for a life that is only a six has not worked. He has decided to sell his magazine, enter politics, and go for a 10 inspired in part by his desire not to be remembered by his children "as basically a lazy man and a philanderer" who had "a nose for Connecticut real estate," and by the news that Heidi has adopted a baby. Both, by their choices, affirm a better future. "Scoop, there's a chance, just a milli-notion," Heidi asserts, "that Pierre Rosenbaum and Judy Holland will meet on a plane over Chicago. . . . And he'll never tell her it's either / or baby. And she'll never think she's worthless unless he lets her have it all. And maybe, just maybe, things will be a little better. And, yes, that does make me happy." The play closes with Heidi rocking her baby and singing Sam Cooke's "You Send Me."

Although the play closes on a note of liberation for both men and women, Heidi's finding fulfillment in a traditional role as mother and investing her future in her child drew strong criticism from feminists. The playwright responded by saying that Heidi was "a woman who wants a baby. I think it takes enormous courage to do what she does." Wasserstein herself would later follow Heidi's example into single motherhood by giving birth to a daughter at the age of 48. Professionally, several plays followed *The Heidi Chronicles*, including *The Sisters Rosensweig* (1992), *An American Daughter* (1997), *Old Money* (2002), and *Third* (2005). She also published essays in *Bachelor Girls* (1990) and *Shiksa Goddess; or, How I Spent My Forties* (2001). A first novel, *Elements of Style*, was published following her death in January 2006. All share elements that made *The Heidi Chronicles* such an effective drama: a perceptive sense of the forces of generation, family, and past that form identity and the serious comedy of those who settle and those who search.

THE KING'S THE BEST MAGISTRATE

_99_

(c. 1620)

by Lope de Vega

> _Lope is like ten brilliant minds inhabiting one body. An attempt to enclose him in any formula is like trying to make one pair of boots to fit a centipede._
>
> —Ezra Pound, _The Spirit of Romance_

Any gathering of the world's greatest dramatists must find room for the over-sized and voluminous Lope de Vega, the foundation figure of Spanish drama who established the _comedia nueva_, the full-length Spanish secular play, and initiated the flowering of a century of Spanish Golden Age drama from the 1580s to the 1680s. As Ezra Pound once observed, "Lope de Vega gave Spain its theater, and Spain in turn gave her theater to Europe." Called by Miguel de Cervantes _"un mónstruo de naturaleza"_ (a monstrosity of nature) for his superhuman productivity and extravagant, profligate imagination, Lope de Vega has been described, again by Pound, as "not a man, he is a literature." Essayist José Martínez Ruiz has asserted:

> Lope is the real world. Everything is to be found in Lope. The four corners of the earth . . . and the nations of Europe in particular; and Greek antiquity; and Roman antiquity; and Christianity; and the lives of saints; and the most haloed heroes in the universe; and the mountains; and the rivers; and the forests; and the cities. Lope's genius has fluttered around over everything on earth. Neither time nor space has held secrets for him. His strength is pliant, light, smooth: an immense poet's strength, prodigious, titanic, yet appearing as simple as a child's.

It is easy to understand Martínez Ruiz's sense of Lope as boundless and all encompassing simply by considering his astonishing output. "No other writer in the world's history," literary historian George Tyler Northrup has claimed, "even remotely approaches his record of productivity." Lope's first biographer calculated 1,800 three-act plays to his credit. Lope's own reckoning went as high as 1,500, claiming that many of them, with their complex plots and varied metrical forms were completed in 24 hours or less. As critic Francis C. Hayes summarizes, "He tapped almost every literary source known to seventeenth century Spain and wrote enough dramas, considered quantitatively, for a whole nation of playwrights." It has been estimated that Lope created between 17,000 and 20,000 characters and produced 1.5 million lines of verse dialogue. About 500 of his plays survive, and if we conservatively accept 600 plays as a likelier number of his completed full-length plays, to reach even that number he would have had to produce a new play every month over his 50-year career. These astounding numbers become truly staggering when you consider that his dramatic output was almost equaled by his nondramatic writings—epics, lyrics, ballads, romances, short stories, and thousands of letters—over a turbulent lifetime with enough reversals and romantic adventures to fill one of his most sensational cape-and-sword dramas.

Born Félix Lope de Vega Carpio in 1562, the son of a Madrid embroiderer, Lope de Vega was a literary prodigy who was said to have translated Latin poetry at the age of five and produced his first play at 12. After a Jesuit education in Madrid and possibly study at the University of Alcalá de Henares, he worked in the household of the bishop of Ávila, where he is thought to have composed his earliest plays. In 1583 he both began his career as a professional dramatist and joined a two-month naval expedition to quell a rebellion in the Azores. On his return to Madrid he gained notoriety as a brawler and a philanderer and had an affair with a married woman whose family objected and denounced him to the authorities. In 1588 Lope was arrested and banished to Valencia under a sentence of eight years of exile from Madrid. Within a few months, however, he illegally returned to the capital and eloped with the 17-year-old Isabel de Urbina. A few days after his marriage he joined the Spanish Armada and, after the Spanish defeat, returned to exile in Valencia with his wife to begin his most productive period of literary work, which continued until his wife died in 1595. Finally pardoned, Lope returned to Madrid where he had an affair with an actor's wife and married the daughter of a rich butcher. After she died in 1613 Lope was ordained a priest, but his multiple affairs with married women continued. It is said that he fathered 11 offspring by his two wives and some of his many lovers. One of them, Marta de Nevares, became the love of his life and bore him a daughter in 1617. However, when Marta's husband died in 1620, Lope refused to marry her because of his vow of celibacy. Despite declining health, Lope continued his remarkable creative vigor and literary productivity until his death in 1635.

The Spanish theater that Lope transformed during his lifetime had barely emerged from its medieval and crude folk traditions when he began his dramatic career. Classical drama, introduced by the Greeks and the Romans to the Iberian Peninsula, gave way to the liturgical dramas of the Middle Ages with secular theater barely kept alive by traveling entertainers and performers in short farces. Spaniards traveling to Italy brought back the *comedias humanísticas* of the Renaissance, and performances of classically inspired dramas were supplemented by Italian theatrical troupes that came to Spain in the mid-16th century. Plays were performed at the royal court, in aristocratic households, and in open courtyards (*corrales*). The first permanent open-air theater was established in Madrid in 1579, when Lope was 17. Performances were given by daylight with a stage ordinarily representing the two-story facade of a house with balconies on a Madrid street. As in the Elizabethan theater there was a pit for the groundlings, and the upper windows of the surrounding houses served as boxes. Women spectators were segregated in an area known as *la cazuela* (the stewpan), but onstage women's parts were played by actresses.

It was Lope who formulated a new dramatic form, the *comedia nueva*, that broke with the Aristotelian formulation of the classical dramatic tradition as interpreted during the Renaissance, which dictated a strict separation of comedy and tragedy within a five-act structure and a restricted number of dramatic characters and situations. Lope instead pioneered a flexible and varied dramatic form aimed at appealing to his audiences. In his dramatic treatise *Arte nuevo de hacer comedias en este tiempo* (1609; *The New Art of Writing Plays*) Lope declared his artistic independence from the established rules of dramatic decorum and expounded a liberated dramaturgical method. Lope insisted that his plays were based on an assimilation and refinement of classical rules and the Spanish popular tradition. According to Lope, the action of the *comedia* should be confined to three acts encompassing exposition, complication, and denouement, with a premium of sensation and suspense. He eschewed a highly stylized and allusive poetic style and narrow, prescribed subjects, preferring an expressive method aimed at capturing the richness of everyday life. "When I set out to write a play," he observed, "I lock up all the rules under ten keys, and banish Plautus and Terence from my study. . . . For I write in the style of those who seek the applause of the public, whom it is but just to humor in their folly, since it is they who pay for it." If art imitates nature, Lope asserted, the variety of nature is infinite and so should be the subjects represented onstage. To supply the variety his audiences demanded Lope mixed the comic and the tragic, allowed noble characters to interact with the humble, and violated the unities of time and place, asserting that a Spanish theatergoer grows impatient if he is not shown in two hours "all human history from Genesis to the Last Judgment."

Unapologetic in his catering to his audiences' often unsophisticated taste, Lope viewed his plays as inferior to his other writings, dashed off for money. All show signs of haste and repetition, and if few of them rise to the level of Shakespearean depth and profundity in the complexity of their characterization or ideas, they still serve an important liberating function in the history of Western drama. To reach his audience Lope turned drama into a stirring vehicle for embodying an age's values in a form flexible enough to incorporate stories from ancient mythology, the Bible, the lives of the saints, legends, ancient and Spanish history, and the social life of contemporary Spain. On Lope's stage kings mix with commoners, and both are entitled to comic or tragic treatment. Lope transformed the often crude Spanish dramatic folk tradition with a new artistry, while he expanded the rigidly prescribed neoclassical drama by his genius and the breadth of his vision into an all-purpose entertainment that could both give pleasure and mount an effective criticism of life. As literary historians Richard E. Chandler and Kessel Schwartz summarize, Lope's eminence "derived from the fact that he breathed the essence of national life into his drama, identified totally with the popular mind, adapted folk poetry to the stage, dramatized ballads, and wrote what the audience wanted. He was the voice of the people and the echo of a dynamic, proud, vigorous, active nation."

Lope propagated for the theater of his day multiple new genres and refinements of older forms, producing religious plays, pastoral dramas, mythological plays, historical dramas derived from past and contemporary events, and plays of intrigue and adventure turning on jealousy and revenge. Of the several of Lope's plays that have entered the canon of world dramatic literature, including *El acero de Madrid* (*Steel in Madrid*), *Peribáñez y el comendador de Olmedo* (*The Knight from Olmedo*), *El castigo sin venganza* (*Punishment without Revenge*), *El perro del hortelano* (*The Dog in the Manger*), and *Fuente Ovejuna, El mejor alcalde, el rey* (*The King's the Best Magistrate*) is the best choice to illustrate both the strengths and the limitations of the playwright's art. It is an example of Lope's historical *comedia*, set during the 12th-century rein of Alfonso VII. Sancho, "hidalgo born, though humbly poor," is in love with the beautiful peasant Elvira. On the eve of their wedding Sancho seeks the approval of the region's overlord, Don Tello de Neira. The nobleman is at first gracious and generous and insists on seeing the bride to seal his approval of the nuptials. However, overwhelmed by her beauty, Don Tello stops the wedding and has Elvira kidnapped to his castle, ignoring Sancho's heartbroken pleas for her release. As Elvira struggles to protect her honor from Don Tello's lustful advances, Sancho seeks justice from the king and travels to his court in León. After sympathetically hearing Sancho's story the king reprimands Don Tello and orders that Elvira be immediately restored to Sancho, but his command is ignored. As Don Tello asserts, "I reign here, and here I do my will as the king does his in his Castile. My forebears never owed this land to him—they won it from the Moors." Alfonso next decides to go himself to render justice, declaring that "The king's the best magistrate." Arriving in disguise he first verifies Sancho's story, is abused by the haughty nobleman, and then confronts Don Tello as the king only to find that he is too late. Elvira, dramatically coming on stage with clothes torn and hair disheveled, reveals that she has been forcibly taken, and she recounts her disgrace in moving verse. The king responds by ominously ordering a "priest and a hangman." He commands Don Tello to marry Elvira, restoring her honor, and immediately after has Don Tello executed. As his widow Elvira now has a rich dowry for her second husband, Sancho. Justice is served on the level of the state, in which the duty of a liege lord to his king is affirmed; in the community, in which the rights of the victims of the powerful are protected;, and at the personal level, in which mutual love is shown as the basis of marriage. Alfonso displays the ideal quality of kingship in the responsibility he takes on to serve the interests of even the most humble of his subjects.

The play is a tragicomedy, mixing a romantic love story and intrigue with realistic details of Spanish peasant life. It incorporates as well standard elements of the pastoral with the historical. Despite Sancho and Elvira's idealized love for each other, their less-than-naturalistic speeches, and the poetic justice of the play's conclusion, there is a striking realism to the plot in Lope's refusal to preserve Elvira's chastity, as she is raped before the king can restore her to her proper lover and redeem her honor. Moreover, the play's pathos surrounding the entitlement of love over class deference and its moral about the proper working of justice are firmly set in the wider context of new social forces operating among the peasants, a feudal lord, and the king. If depth of character generally gives way in Lope's plays for the demands of plot, it is the thematic purposes that the plot serve that make his dramas more than trivial entertainments and give them relevance that transcends their culture and time. For all its sensational circumstances and suspense the play enacts the breakup of a feudal society, its replacement by a nation-state, and its core values of love, charity, and justice. Don Tello's supremacy as a feudal lord is replaced by the peasant's protection under the law of the state as represented by the monarch. The gratification of the lust of the powerful is bested by the triumphant passion of the humble. Commoners, who previously were depicted onstage as comic clowns, here claim the moral and emotional high ground, worthy of a king's respect. Lope's persistent advocacy on behalf of the claims of the lower class and the poor has caused many to see in his plays one of the earliest instances of a proletarian drama. An additional strong case can be made that Lope de Vega in Spain, like William Shakespeare and the Elizabethan dramatists in England, played a crucial role in widening the reach of Western drama to consider the claim of monarch and commoner alike.

PETER PAN

(1904)

James M. Barrie

The secret of Peter Pan *seems to be that it is not merely a children's entertainment but a great play in its own right, a memorable theatrical experience, differing only in the nature of its appeal to the adult playgoer or to the child. And so it seems worth studying, not only for its remarkable stage history, but also as a piece of great literature: its background as a story as well as its foreground as a play. Like the other great stories of its kind, it was told first to a particular child or a group of children—but like them also it was invented to please the author and drew from the unsuspected depths of his memory and of his own deepest personality.*

—Roger Lancelyn Green, *Fifty Years of Peter Pan*

James M. Barrie wrote several plays for adults, the best known of which are *The Admirable Crichton* (1902), *Quality Street* (1902), *What Every Woman Knows* (1908), and *Dear Brutus* (1917), as well as the theatrical version of his most celebrated novel, *The Little Minister* (1897). Barrie's works for the stage were popular in their day, and some were later filmed (with varying degrees of success), but by the 1930s his plays had begun to seem less like the charming pastiches they were and more as quaint relics of middle-class Victorian and Edwardian sentimental sensibilities, lacking the intellectual and sociological heft of works by such contemporaries as George Bernard Shaw. Barrie's plays are infrequently revived now. Only *Peter Pan*, the first important play written for children and in many ways the most sentimental of Barrie's work, has, for the more than 100 years since it was first performed, continued to enchant both children and adults in numerous dramatic and musical stage, film, and television productions. *Peter Pan* has attained the status of what one critic has called a "legendary creation," and the play and its central character have survived to confer upon Barrie and his "Boy Who Would Not Grow up" (the play's subtitle) a reputation similar to that of Lewis Carroll and his Alice. Barrie's particular Wonderland, which he called Neverland, with its pirates, Lost Boys, Indians, lagoons, and dueling captains, Hook and Peter Pan, has continued to work its magic on audiences not only because it is a world embodied in productions that are entertaining spectacles but also because this adventurous, storybook milieu is juxtaposed with a sweet idealization of family life and the tenderness and pain of parenthood to speak to a sense of childhood lost. In 1929 the *Boston Transcript* characterized *Peter Pan*'s appeal as an adult, as well as a children's, play: "It is middle age's own tragicomedy—the faint, far memories of boyhood and girlhood blown back in the bright breeze of Barrie's imagination."

The inspiration for *Peter Pan* grew out of several singular experiences in Barrie's life, as well as from his imagination. The ninth of 10 children in a family that lived in one small cottage, James Matthew Barrie was born on May 9, 1860, in Kirriemuir, Scotland. His father, David, was a handloom weaver; his mother, Margaret Ogilvy, the daughter of a stonemason, was known by her maiden name, according to Scottish tradition. She was the strongest influence on her third son, who would later produce a series of popular newspaper articles about her, as well as a titular biography, published in 1896, a year after her death. Although David Barrie had been poorly educated, he was hardworking, ambitious, and determined that his children should have every opportunity to receive an education. With careful planning the Barries were able to send their children to private schools and to college. Barrie's eldest brother, Alexander, eventually became a bursar at Aberdeen University and one of the first of Her Majesty's Inspector of Schools, and four of Barrie's five sisters to survive childhood were schoolteachers before they married.

During his childhood Barrie played with a friend's toy theater and acted out improvised dramas in the family's little brick washhouse, a building he later identified as the original of the little house the Lost Boys build for Wendy in *Peter Pan*. He enjoyed Penny Dreadfuls—penny-a-number magazines featuring sensational fiction in serialized form—although when he later read a condemnation of this class of fiction in the morally conscientious children's magazine *Chatterbox*, he buried his supply of them in a field. A turning point in Barrie's life came at the age of seven, when his 14-year-old brother, David, a brilliant boy and his mother's favorite, died in a skating accident while attending a private school run by Alexander Barrie. Margaret Ogilvy was inconsolable over the loss and became, in Barrie's words, "delicate from that hour." Young James attempted to take the place of his elder brother and spent much time in his mother's room listening to her reminisce about her childhood. Margaret Ogilvy's mother had died young, and the eight-year-old Margaret had been, as Barrie later wrote, "mistress of the house and mother to her little brother." The young Margaret would become Barrie's first model for Wendy Darling, the girl who mothered Peter Pan and the Lost Boys. At the same time, in Margaret Ogilvy's memory, the dead son, David, was always the golden child who never grew up. The idea of youth frozen in time would inspire Barrie years later in the creation of *Peter Pan*. Mother and son also read together, beginning with *Robinson Crusoe* and continuing with other adventure stories, including the historical novels of Sir Walter Scott and James Fenimore Cooper, as well as R. M. Ballantyne's *The Coral Island*, a tale of shipwrecked sailors and pirates. When the supply of books at the local library and bookshop was exhausted Barrie began writing his own adventure tales to entertain his mother.

At 13 Barrie was sent to Dumfries Academy, where he joined a make-believe pirate crew of boys and founded a school dramatic society. He wrote and produced an original drama, "Bandelero the Bandit" (1877), the style of which was based on the Penny Dreadfuls and Cooper stories he had read. The production caused a minor controversy when a local clergyman denounced the piece as "grossly immoral," a pronouncement that only served to bring welcome publicity to the drama society. At 17 Barrie left Dumfries Academy determined to become a writer, but his parents insisted he attend university and become a minister, as David would have done had he lived. With the help of his brother Alexander a family compromise was reached whereby James would study literature at Edinburgh University. Shy and self-conscious about his short stature of five feet, two inches, Barrie was unhappy during his first few terms at Edinburgh, but he eventually found a welcome niche as a freelance drama critic for a local newspaper. After graduating with an M.A. in 1883 Barrie wrote for the *Nottingham Journal* for a time and then went to London to try to earn a living as a freelance writer. His first popular success was with a series of semi-fictionalized articles of life in Kirriemuir, later collected in three volumes, *Auld Licht Idylls* (1888), *A Window in Thrums* (1889), and *The Little Minister* (1891). Barrie's first commercially successful play was *Walker, London*, a comedy produced in 1892. In the cast was a young actress, Mary Ansell, whom Barrie married in 1894. The marriage was a childless and unhappy one, and the couple eventually divorced in 1909.

The spark that would result in the creation of *Peter Pan* was kindled by the friendships Barrie developed with various children, most notably the five sons of Arthur and Sylvia Llewelyn Davies, whom he had met while walking his St. Bernard (the prototype for the nursemaid character of Nana in the play) in Kensington Gardens. Barrie, with his flair for playacting and storytelling, became a great favorite of the boys, especially after the death of their father in 1907. Barrie's close relationship with the Llewellyn Davies boys has led to questions of inappropriateness, but as his biographer Andrew Birkin has pointed out, Barrie was "a lover of childhood, but was not in any sexual sense the pedophile that some have claimed him to have been." He was certainly, in his platonic way, in love with Sylvia Llewelyn Davies, the daughter of the writer George du Maurier and the sister of actor Gerald du Maurier, who would play the first Mr. Darling and Captain Hook in *Peter Pan*. When Sylvia died in 1910, Barrie became the boys' guardian.

In 1902 Barrie published *The Little White Bird*, a novel that chronicles his growing friendship with the oldest Llewellyn Davies boy, George, in the character of David, the son of a penniless young couple. Barrie appears in the novel as Captain W, a lonely bachelor who plays the anonymous fairy godfather to the couple. Most important, the novel introduces the figure of Peter Pan, named for George's baby brother, Peter. The character is featured in a story within the story and concerns a baby who flies out of its nursery to the island of the birds. When Peter returns home he finds the window barred against him and another baby in his place. Wendy also makes her first appearance in the novel, as Maisie, a little girl who stays in Kensington Gardens at night to watch Peter Pan and the fairies at play. Despite her temptation to live on the island with Peter she returns to her mother. At around this time the pirate games Barrie and the Llewellyn Davies boys played at the Barries' country home, Black Lake Cottage, resulted in a self-published book, *The Boy Castaways of Black Lake Island*, which featured photographs of the boys. Barrie, in his introduction to the first published version of *Peter Pan* in 1928, dedicates the play "To The Five," and credits the Black Lake games he played with the boys for inspiring the work: "I suppose I always knew that I made Peter by rubbing the five of you violently together, as savages with two sticks producing a flame. That is all he is, the spark I got from you."

Barrie was inspired to work on a fairy play of his own after taking the boys to see *Bluebell in Fairyland*, a work written and performed by Seymour Hicks (another future Mr. Darling/Hook). Although not very successful as art, the piece was an innovation in that it was an original play for children rather than an adaptation of a book or a pantomime (a comic spectacle with songs and speeches taken from fairy tales and nursery rhymes). In November 1903 Barrie began the first draft of what he initially titled "Anon, A Play." After several changes and refinements (which continued up to the play's opening and even in subsequent productions while Barrie was alive), Barrie took *Peter Pan* to actor-producer Herbert Beerbohm Tree, whom he visualized as Captain Hook. Tree disliked the play and told Barrie's manager and backer, the American impresario Charles Frohman: "Barrie must be mad. He's written four acts all about fairies, children, and Indians running through the most incoherent story you ever listened to; and what do you suppose? The last act is to be set on top of trees!" Tree would later say ruefully that he would probably be known to posterity as the producer who had refused *Peter Pan*. Certainly when the play opened on December 27, 1904, it was a spectacle of theatrical trickery, with stage flight attempted for the first time, as well as a variety of other special effects and elaborate scenery and staging. *Peter Pan* was an instant success in London and in New York, where it was produced in 1905 with Maude Adams in the title role.

The story of *Peter Pan: Or The Boy Who Would Not Grow Up* concerns the titular motherless, half-magical boy, who, the audience learns, has frequently peered into the night nursery of the Darlings in Bloomsbury to watch the family life within. During one visit he has left his shadow behind; when Mr. and Mrs. Darling go out for the evening he comes back with his fairy friend, Tinker Bell, to retrieve it. The Darling daughter, Wendy, awakens and sews the shadow on for him. Despite the warning barks of the dog nursemaid, Nana (whom Mr. Darling had sent to the doghouse over the protestations of his wife), who fears the influence of the boy at the window, Peter teaches Wendy and her brothers, Michael and John, to fly and takes them to the Neverland, where Wendy becomes the mother of the Lost Boys who live underground and in the hollow trunks of trees. (Peter: "They are the children who fall out of their prams when the nurse is looking the other way. If they are not claimed in seven days they are sent far away to the Neverland. I'm captain.") The children have adventures with Indians and pirates, the latter of which is led by dastardly Captain Hook, named for the steel hook he wears in place of the right hand that was bitten off by a crocodile, who, as Hook explains, "liked my arm so much . . . that he has followed me ever since . . . licking his lips for the rest of me." There is a war between the pirates and the children, during which Hook and his men capture Wendy and the boys and imprison them on the pirate ship. Hook tries to poison Peter, but Tinker Bell drinks the draught and nearly dies. To save her Peter appeals to the audience to clap their hands if they believe in fairies. As the audience applauds, Tinker Bell's light grows bright again, and Peter rushes off to save Wendy and the boys. The pirates walk the plank, the crocodile dispatches Hook, and the Darling children return home to their sorrowing parents. Mr. and Mrs. Darling adopt the Lost Boys, but Peter refuses to stay: "I don't want to go to school and learn solemn things. No one is going to catch me, lady, and make me a man. I want always to be a little boy and to have fun." Realizing that Peter "does so need a mother," Wendy convinces her mother to allow her to go to Peter each year for spring-cleaning at the little house the Lost Boys built for her that now nestles in the treetops. In a coda to *Peter Pan*, titled "An Afterthought," first presented in 1908 and featured as an extra chapter, "When Wendy Grew Up," in the 1911 novel, *Peter and Wendy*, the adult Wendy sadly realizes she can no longer go with Peter and instead sends her daughter Jane with him to do the spring-cleaning. For his part Peter has forgotten the adventures he has had with Wendy: for him there is neither a past nor a future, only the joy of the present moment.

Barrie's genius in creating *Peter Pan* was to synthesize the fairy tale and the adventure tale—the two basic elements of popular children's literature—

into a single work that uses the entire space of the stage to create an exciting, but ultimately benevolent, fantasy world juxtaposed with the safe and secure world of the family. The emotional and psychological conflicts within the play, sensed by children and understood by adults, concern the struggle for possession of Wendy as a mother, a daughter, and a spouse (Wendy and Peter play mother and father to the boys) and the contradictory human desire to be both free from responsibility and part of a family and society. *Peter Pan* speaks to these truths, even as it joyously captures the elemental child in each of us.

PLAYS BY YEAR OF PUBLICATION

1933	*Blood Wedding*, Federico García Lorca
1935	*Awake and Sing!*, Clifford Odets
	Murder in the Cathedral, T. S. Eliot
1938	*Our Town*, Thornton Wilder
1939	*The Little Foxes*, Lillian Hellman
1941	*Mother Courage and Her Children*, Bertolt Brecht
1943	*The Good Person of Setzuan*, Bertolt Brecht
1944	*The Glass Menagerie*, Tennessee Williams
	No Exit, Jean-Paul Sartre
1946	*The Iceman Cometh*, Eugene O'Neill
1947	*A Streetcar Named Desire*, Tennessee Williams
1949	*Death of a Salesman*, Arthur Miller
1950	*The Bald Soprano*, Eugène Ionesco
1953	*The Crucible*, Arthur Miller
	Waiting for Godot, Samuel Beckett
1956	*The Balcony*, Jean Genet
	Long Day's Journey into Night, Eugene O'Neill
	Look Back in Anger, John Osborne
	The Visit, Friedrich Dürrenmatt
1957	*Endgame*, Samuel Beckett
1958	*The Hostage*, Brendan Behan
1959	*A Raisin in the Sun*, Lorraine Hansberry
1962	*Who's Afraid of Virginia Woolf*, Edward Albee
1964	*Marat/Sade*, Peter Weiss
1965	*The Homecoming*, Harold Pinter
1970	*Accidental Death of an Anarchist*, Dario Fo
1974	*Travesties*, Tom Stoppard
1979	*Cloud Nine*, Caryl Churchill
1980	*Translations*, Brian Friel
1982	*"Master Harold" . . . and the Boys*, Athol Fugard
1983	*Fool for Love*, Sam Shepard
	Glengarry Glen Ross, David Mamet
1985	*Fences*, August Wilson
1986	*The Other Shore*, Gao Xingjian
1988	*The Heidi Chronicles*, Wendy Wasserstein
1991–92	*Angels in America: A Gay Fantasia on National Themes*, Tony Kushner

A SECOND HUNDRED (HONORABLE MENTIONS)

Aeschylus	*Prometheus Bound* (c. 456 B.C.)
George L. Aikens	*Uncle Tom's Cabin* (1852)
Edward Albee	*Zoo Story* (1958)
Anonymous	*Second Shepherd's Play* (c. 1385–1450)
Jean Anouilh	*The Waltz of the Toreadors* (1952)
John Arden	*Serjeant Musgrave's Dance* (1959)
Aristophanes	*The Birds* (414 B.C.)
	The Clouds (423 B.C.)
	Frogs (405 B.C.)
Alan Ayckbourn	*The Norman Conquest* (1973)
Amiri Baraka	*The Dutchman* (1964)
Samuel Beckett	*Krapp's Last Tape* (1958)
Edward Bond	*Lear* (1971)
Bertolt Brecht	*The Caucasian Chalk Circle* (1945)
	Galileo (1939)
Giordano Bruno	*The Candle-Maker* (1582)
Georg Büchner	*Danton's Death* (1835)
Karel Capek	*R.U.R.* (1921)
Anton Chekhov	*The Sea Gull* (1896)
	Uncle Vanya (1899)
Caryl Churchill	*Top Girls* (1982)
Jean Cocteau	*The Infernal Machine* (1934)
William Congreve	*Love for Love* (1695)

Nilo Cruz	*Anna in the Tropics* (2002)
Shelagh Delaney	*A Taste of Honey* (1958)
John Dryden	*All for Love* (1677)
Margaret Edson	*Wit* (1998)
T. S. Eliot	*The Cocktail Party* (1949)
George Etherege	*The Man of Mode* (1676)
Euripides	*Alcestis* (438 B.C.)
George Farquhar	*The Beaux' Stratagem* (1707)
John Ford	*'Tis Pity She's a Whore* (1633)
Michael Frayn	*Noises Off* (1982)
Max Frisch	*Biedermann and the Firebugs* (1958)
Federico García Lorca	*The House of Bernarda Alba* (1936)
	Yerma (1934)
Jean Giraudoux	*The Madwoman of Chaillot* (1945)
Susan Glaspell	*Trifles* (1916)
Carlo Goldoni	*The Servant of Two Masters* (1745)
Guan Hanqing	*The Injustice Done to Tou Ngo* (c. 13th century)
David Hare	*Plenty* (1978)
Hugo von Hofmannsthal	*Death and the Fool* (1893)
Hrosvitha	*Dulcitius* (c. 965)
David Henry Hwang	*M. Butterfly* (1988)
Henrik Ibsen	*Ghosts* (1882)
	Peer Gynt (1876)
	The Wild Duck (1885)
William Inge	*Picnic* (1953)
Eugène Ionesco	*The Chairs* (1952)
	Rhinoceros (1960)
Georg Kaiser	*From Morn to Midnight* (1912)
George Kaufman and Moss Hart	*You Can't Take It with You* (1936)
Thomas Kyd	*The Spanish Tragedy* (c. 1588)
George Lillo	*The London Merchant* (1731)
Niccolò Machiavelli	*Mandragola* (c. 1514–18)
Maurice Maerterlinck	*Pelléas and Mélisande* (1893)
David Mamet	*American Buffalo* (1977)

Christopher Marlowe	*The Jew of Malta* (c. 1588–92)
Molière	*The Miser* (1668)
Sean O'Casey	*Juno and the Paycock* (1924)
Clifford Odets	*Waiting for Lefty* (1935)
Joe Orton	*What the Butler Saw* (1969)
Suzan-Lori Parks	*Topdog/Underdog* (2001)
Harold Pinter	*The Caretaker* (1960)
Luigi Pirandello	*Enrico IV* (1922)
Plautus	*The Twin Menaechmi* (c. 205–184 B.C.)
Alexander Pushkin	*Boris Godunov* (1825)
Jean Racine	*Andromache* (1667)
Elmer Rice	*The Adding Machine* (1923)
Edmond Rostand	*Cyrano de Bergerac* (1897)
William Saroyan	*The Time of Your Life* (1939)
Friedrich von Schiller	*The Robbers* (1782)
Arthur Schnitzler	*La Ronde* (1903)
William Shakespeare	*As You Like It* (c. 1599–1600)
	Julius Caesar (1599)
	Measure for Measure (1604)
	The Merchant of Venice (c. 1596)
	Richard II (1595)
	Richard III (c. 1592–93)
	The Winter's Tale (1611)
George Bernard Shaw	*Heartbreak House* (1921)
Sam Shepard	*True West* (1980)
Richard Brinsley Sheridan	*The Rivals* (1775)
Neil Simon	*Lost in Yonkers* (1991)
Sophocles	*Electra* (c. 420–410 B.C.)
Wole Soyinka	*The Strong Breed* (1962)
Tom Stoppard	*Rosencrantz & Guildenstern Are Dead* (1967)
August Strindberg	*The Dream Play* (1907)
	The Father (1887)
Sudraka	*The Little Clay Cart* (c. 150)
John Millington Synge	*Riders to the Sea* (1904)
Takeda Izumo	*Chūshingura* (c. 1748)

Cyril Tourneur	*The Revenger's Tragedy* (1607)
Paula Vogel	*How I Learned to Drive* (1997)
John Webster	*The Duchess of Malfi* (c. 1614)
Frank Wedekind	*Spring's Awakening* (1891)
Thornton Wilder	*The Skin of Our Teeth* (1942)
Tennessee Williams	*Cat on a Hot Tin Roof* (1955)
Lanford Wilson	*Talley's Folly* (1979)
William Wycherley	*The Plain Dealer* (1677)

INDEX